Lecture Notes in Computer Science 582

Edited by G. Goos and J. Hartmanis

Advisory Board: W. Brauer   D. Gries   J. Stoer

W9-AHP-561

B. Krieg-Brückner (Ed.)

ESOP '92

4th European Symposium on Programming
Rennes, France, February 26–28, 1992
Proceedings

Springer-Verlag

Berlin Heidelberg New York
London Paris Tokyo
Hong Kong Barcelona
Budapest

Series Editors

Gerhard Goos
Universität Karlsruhe
Postfach 69 80
Vincenz-Priessnitz-Straße 1
W-7500 Karlsruhe, FRG

Juris Hartmanis
Department of Computer Science
Cornell University
5148 Upson Hall
Ithaca, NY 14853, USA

Volume Editor

Bernd Krieg-Brückner
FB 3 Mathematik und Informatik, Universität Bremen
Postfach 330440, W-2800 Bremen 33, FRG

CR Subject Classification (1991): D.3, F.3, D.2, F.4

ISBN 3-540-55253-7 Springer-Verlag Berlin Heidelberg New York
ISBN 0-387-55253-7 Springer-Verlag New York Berlin Heidelberg

Typesetting: Camera ready by author
Printing and binding: Druckhaus Beltz, Hemsbach/Bergstr.
45/3140-543210 - Printed on acid-free paper

Preface

This fourth European Symposium on Programming was held jointly with the seventeenth Colloquium on Trees in Algebra and Programming in Rennes, February 26-28, 1992. The previous symposia were held in France, Germany, and Denmark. Every even year, as in 1992, CAAP is held jointly with ESOP; every other year, it is part of TAPSOFT (Theory And Practice of SOFTware development). The proceedings of CAAP appear in an accompanying volume of Lecture Notes in Computer Science.

In the beginning, CAAP was devoted to algebraic and combinatorial properties of trees, and to their role in various fields of computer science. The scope of CAAP has been extended to other discrete structures, like graphs, equations and transformations of graphs, and their links with logical theories. The programme committee received 40 submissions (one being too late), from which 18 were selected.

ESOP addresses fundamental issues and important developments in the specification and implementation of programming languages and systems. It continues lines begun in France and Germany under the names "Colloque sur la Programmation" and the GI workshop on "Programmiersprachen und Programmentwicklung". The programme committee received 71 submissions, from which 26 were selected.

Programme Committees for

CAAP	ESOP
A. Arnold (Bordeaux)	E. Astesiano (Genova)
A. Bertoni (Milano)	G. Cousineau (Paris)
P. Darondeau (Rennes)	O.-J. Dahl (Oslo)
M. Dauchet (Lille)	H. Kirchner (Nancy)
R. De Nicola (Pisa)	B. Krieg-Brückner (Bremen)*
M. Dezani-Ciancaglini (Torino)	T. Maibaum (London)
J.W. Klop (Amsterdam)	P. Mosses (Aarhus)
M. Nivat (Paris)	B. Nordström (Göteborg)
A. Poigné (St. Augustin)	F. Orejas (Barcelona)
J.-C. Raoult (Rennes)*	D. Sannella (Edinburgh)
M. Steinby (Turku)	P. Wadler (Glasgow)
C. Stirling (Edinburgh)	R. Wilhelm (Saarbrücken)
W. Thomas (Kiel)	
J. Tiuryn (Warsaw)	(*chairmen)

Invited speakers for

CAAP	ESOP
B. Courcelle (Paris)	O.-J. Dahl (Oslo)
H. Ganzinger (Saarbrücken)	A. Tarlecki (Warsaw)

The conference was sponsored by INRIA, CNRS, and the University of Rennes, and supported by GI, the University of Bremen, and the township of Rennes.

I would like to thank all the members of the programme committees as well as the referees listed below for their care in reviewing and selecting the submitted papers. I also wish to express my gratitude to Jean-Claude Raoult and Elisabeth Lebret, who took care of the material organization.

Bremen, January 1992   Bernd Krieg-Brückner

List of Referees for ESOP 1992

Alt, F.	Guo, Y	Lang, B.	Qian, Z.
Amadio, R.	Gurr, D.	Langmaack, H	Raber, M.
Andrews, J.	Haberstrau, M.	Larsen, K.G.	Reggio, G.
Augustsson, L.	Hall, C.	Launchbury, J.	Rerny, D.
Baraki, G.	Hamilton, G.	Le Chenadec	Rety. P.
Berry, D.	Hammond, I	Len, D.	Rodriguez Artalejo, M.
Blenko, T.	Hammond, K.	Leroy, J.	Rothwell, N.
Boye, J.	Hankin, Ch.	Leroy, X.	Rouaix, F.
Bradfield, J.	Harland, J.	Liu, J.	Rusinowitch, M.
Breazu-Tannen, V.	Heckmann, R.	Lock, H.L.	Ryan, M.
Brown, D.F.	Heldal, R.	Longo, G.	Sahesen
Burn, G.L.	Henglein, F.	Loogen, R.	Salomaa, A.
Carlsson, M.	Hennicker, R.	Lugiez, D.	Salvesen, A.
Casas, R.	Hense, A.	Lysne, O.	Sander, G.
Castellani, I.	Hoffmann, B.	Maluszynski, J.	Sansom, P.
Cerioli, M	Holmström, S.	Martelli, M.	Schettini, A.M.
Chbong, H.	Holst, C.K.	Mathews, B.	Schmidt, D.
Clenaghan, K.	Hortala, T.	Mauri, F.	Schwartzbach, M.
Cousot, P.	Hughes, J.	Maus, A.	Seidl, H.
Cousot, R.	Hung Cheong, P.	Mayoh, B.	Seio, C.
Cregut, P.	Hunt	McCabe, F.	Stuckey, P.
Damm, W.	Jagadeesan, R.	Meldal, R.	Swart, E.
Davis, K.	Jensen, T.	Mery, D.	Tison, S.
Dybjer, P.	Johnson, T.	Mishra, P.	Tonnet, G.
Elvang-Goransson, M.	Jones, C.	Mitchell, J.	Traynor, O.
Engberg, U.	Jones, S.P.	Mitchell, K.	Trinder, P.
Farrés-Casals, J.	Jourdan, M.	Moggi, E.	v. Henke, F.W.
Fecht, Ch.	Kahrs, S.	Moura, H.	van Roy, P.
Field, T.	Kehler Holst, C.	Müller, F.	Veloso, P.
Fribourg, L.	Kelly, P.H.J.	Murthy, C.	Viry, P.
Frutos, D. de	Kent, S.	Nauny, M.	Vivarés, F.
Galmiche, D.	Kirchner, C.	Nielsen, M.	von Sydow, B.
Gehlot, V.	Kirchner, H.	Nielson, F.	Wang, A.
Gersdorf, B.	Kirkead, B.	Nielson, H.R.	Watt, D.A.
Giegerich, R.	Kirkerud, B.	Nieuwenhuis, R.	Weis, P.
Gilmore, S.	Knoop, J.	Owe, O.	Wilhelm, R.
Giovini, A.	Kramer, J.	Partain, W.	Wolff, B.
Gogolla, M.	Krogdahl, S.	Paterson, R.	Wright, A.K.
Goldsack, S.I.	Lafont, Y.	Phillips, I.	Zucca, E.

Contents

Model checking and Boolean graphs 1
H.R. Andersen

SIGNAL as a model for real-time and hybrid systems 20
A. Benveniste, M. Le Borgne, P. Le Guernic

Towards an adequate notion of observation 39
G. Bernot, M. Bidoit, T. Knapik

Proving safety of speculative load instructions at compile time 56
D. Bernstein, M. Rodeh, M. Sagiv

Typed norms 73
A. Bossi, N. Cocco, M. Fabris

Compositional refinements in multiple blackboard systems 93
X.J. Chen, C. Montangero

Fully persistent arrays for efficient incremental updates and voluminous reads . 110
T.-R. Chuang

Back to direct style 130
O. Danvy

Extraction of strong typing laws 151
K.-G. Doh, D.A. Schmidt

Detecting determinate computations by bottom-up abstract interpretation . . . 167
R. Giacobazzi, L. Ricci

ELIOS-OBJ - Theorem proving in a specification language 182
I. Gnaedig

Incremental garbage collection without tags 200
B. Goldberg

Approximate fixed points in abstract interpretation 219
C. Hankin, S. Hunt

Dynamic typing 233
F. Henglein

Automatic parallelization of lazy functional programs 254
G. Hogen, A. Kindler, R. Loogen

Reversing abstract interpretations 269
J. Hughes, J. Launchbury

A theory of qualified types 287
M.P. Jones

A semantics for multiprocessor systems 307
P. Krishnan

Interprocedural type propagation for object-oriented languages 321
J.-M. Larcheveque

Using the Centaur system to design SIMD parallel languages and programming
a case study 341
J.L. Levaire

The tensor product in Wadler's analysis of lists 351
F. Nielson, H.R. Nielson

Basic superposition is complete 371
R. Nieuwenhuis, A. Rubio

Observers for linear types 390
M. Odersky

Type inference for partial types is decidable 408
P. O'Keefe, M. Wand

A provably correct compiler generator. 418
J. Palsberg

An adequate operational semantics for sharing in lazy evaluation 435
S. Purushothaman, J. Seaman

Modules for an object-oriented specification language (Invited lecture) . . . 451
A. Tarlecki

Typing references by effect inference 473
A. K. Wright

Model Checking and Boolean Graphs*

Henrik Reif Andersen

Department of Computer Science, Aarhus University
Ny Munkegade 116, DK-8000 Aarhus C, Denmark
E-mail: henrikan@daimi.aau.dk

Abstract

This paper describes a method for translating a satisfaction problem of the modal μ-calculus into a problem of finding a certain marking of a boolean graph. By giving algorithms to solve the graph problem, we present a global model checking algorithm for the modal μ-calculus of alternation depth one, which has time-complexity $|A||T|$, where $|A|$ is the size of the assertion and $|T|$ is the size of the model (a labelled transition system). This algorithm extends to an algorithm for the full modal μ-calculus which runs in time $(|A||T|)^{ad}$, where ad is the alternation depth, improving on earlier presented algorithms. Moreover, a local algorithm is presented for alternation depth one, which runs in time $|A||T|\log(|A||T|)$, improving on the earlier published algorithms that are all at least exponential.

1 Introduction

Model checking is the problem of deciding whether a given structure constitutes a valid model for a logical assertion. Viewing the structure as describing a system of for example interacting processes and the logical assertion as a specification, model checking can be viewed as the process of verifying that a system meets its specification. We will use a generalisation of the modal μ-calculus presented by Kozen [Koz83] as the assertion language and as models we take labelled transition systems (essentially equivalent to labelled Kripke models). The modal μ-calculus is a very expressive modal logic (see e.g. [Koz83], [EL86], and [Dam90]) allowing a wide range of properties to be expressed, including what is often called liveness, safety, and fairness properties. Examples of such expressible properties are 'eventually an a-action will happen', 'it is always possible to do a b-action', and 'infinitely often a c-action can happen'. Labelled transition systems arise naturally in for example the operational semantics of process algebras as describing the behaviour of communicating concurrent systems.

This paper presents four results. Firstly, it shows that the problem of finding the sets of states in a finite labelled transition system satisfying a given formula with just one fixed-point operator, can be reduced to the problem of finding a fixed-point of a

---

*This work is supported by the ESPRIT Basic Research Action CEDISYS and by the Danish Natural Science Research Council.

monotone function on a boolean lattice consisting of a product of simple two-point lattices. Secondly, it is shown how this fixed-point can be found in linear time using a simple graph algorithm, thereby giving an $|A||T|$ model checking algorithm. Thirdly, this algorithm will be extended to the full calculus, giving an algorithm running in time $(|A||T|)^{ad}$, ad being the alternation depth – a measure of how intertwined minimal and maximal fixed-points are. Finally, a local algorithm, searching potentially only a part of the transition system, will be presented for the modal μ-calculus of alternation depth one. This algorithm will run in time $|A||T|\log(|A||T|)$.

Related work can be found in Emerson and Lei [EL86] which describes an $(|A||T|)^{ad+1}$ algorithm and defines the notion of alternation depth, in Arnold and Crubille [AC88] which describes an $|A|^2|T|$ algorithm for the case of one simultaneous fixed-point, in Cleaveland and Stirling [CS91] which describes an $|A||T|$ algorithm for alternation depth one, and finally in Larsen [Lar88], Stirling and Walker [SW89], Cleaveland [Cle90], and Winskel [Win89] which all describe local model checkers that are at least exponential – even for alternation depth one.

2 Logic and models

We will consider a version of the modal ν-calculus with simultaneous fixed-points. The expressive power will be equivalent to the modal ν-calculus with just unary fixed-points, in the sense that every assertion in our calculus has a logical equivalent containing only unary fixed-points. The simultaneous fixed-points will, however, be central to the development of efficient model checking algorithms as they allow to express *sharing* of subexpressions.

The version of the ν-calculus we will use is given by the following grammar:

$$A ::= T \mid F \mid A_0 \wedge A_1 \mid A_0 \vee A_1 \mid [\alpha]A \mid \langle\alpha\rangle A \mid X \mid (\nu\underline{X}.\underline{A})_i \mid (\mu\underline{X}.\underline{A})_i$$

The assertion variable X ranges over a set of variables *Var*. The usual notions of free variables and open and closed assertions will be used. The notation $\underline{X}$ is shorthand for $(X_1,\ldots,X_n)$, $\underline{A}$ for $(A_1,\ldots,A_n)$, where n should be clear from context. The assertion $(\nu\underline{X}.\underline{A})_i$ will denote the i'th component of the simultaneous maximal fixed-point $\nu\underline{X}.\underline{A}$. Dually $(\mu\underline{X}.\underline{A})_i$ denotes the i'th component of the minimal fixed-point $\mu\underline{X}.\underline{A}$. The usual unary fixed-point $\nu X.A$ corresponds to the case where $n = 1$, and for notational convenience we simply write $\nu X.A$ instead of $(\nu X.A)_1$.

As models we take *labelled transition systems* $T = (S, L, \rightarrow)$ where S is a set of states, L a set of labels, and $\rightarrow \subseteq S \times L \times S$ a transition relation. Given a transition system T, an assertion A will denote a subset of the states S of T. Recall that the set of subsets ordered by inclusion $(\mathcal{P}(S), \subseteq)$ forms a complete lattice which by taking pointwise ordering extends to a complete lattice $(\mathcal{P}(S)^n, \subseteq^n)$ on the n-ary product of $\mathcal{P}(S)$. Let $\pi_i : \mathcal{P}(S)^n \rightarrow \mathcal{P}(S)$ denote the projection onto the i'th component.

Due to the possibility of free variables the interpretation of assertions will be given relative to an environment ρ assigning a subset of S to each variable. We will use $\rho[U/X]$ to denote the environment which is like ρ except that X is mapped to U. The interpretation of A denoted $[\![A]\!]_T\, \rho$ is defined inductively on the structure of A as follows:

$$
\begin{aligned}
[\![T]\!]_T\, \rho &= S \\
[\![F]\!]_T\, \rho &= \emptyset \\
[\![A_0 \wedge A_1]\!]_T\, \rho &= [\![A_0]\!]_T\, \rho \cap [\![A_1]\!]_T\, \rho \\
[\![A_0 \vee A_1]\!]_T\, \rho &= [\![A_0]\!]_T\, \rho \cup [\![A_1]\!]_T\, \rho \\
[\![[\alpha]A]\!]_T &= \{s \in S \mid \forall s' \in S.\; s \xrightarrow{\alpha} s' \Rightarrow s' \in [\![A]\!]_T\, \rho\} \\
[\![\langle \alpha \rangle A]\!]_T &= \{s \in S \mid \exists s' \in S.\; s \xrightarrow{\alpha} s' \;\&\; s' \in [\![A]\!]_T\, \rho\} \\
[\![X]\!]_T\, \rho &= \rho(X) \\
[\![(\nu \underline{X}.\underline{A})_i]\!]_T\, \rho &= \pi_i(\nu \psi) \\
&\quad \text{where } \psi : (U_1, \ldots, U_n) \mapsto ([\![A_1]\!]_T\, \rho', \ldots, [\![A_n]\!]_T\, \rho'), \\
&\quad \text{and } \rho' = \rho[U_1/X_1, \ldots, U_n/X_n] \\
[\![(\mu \underline{X}.\underline{A})_i]\!]_T\, \rho &= \pi_i(\mu \psi) \\
&\quad \text{where } \psi \text{ is as above}
\end{aligned}
$$

For the fixed-points we notice that the map ψ on $\mathcal{P}(S)^n$ is monotonic in all variables. According to Tarski's theorem [Tar55] then ψ will have a maximal postfixed point given by

$$\bigcup \{ U \in \mathcal{P}(S)^n \mid U \subseteq^n \psi(U) \}, \tag{1}$$

which we denote $\nu \psi$. Similarly ψ will have a minimal prefixed point $\mu \psi$ given by

$$\bigcap \{ U \in \mathcal{P}(S)^n \mid \psi(U) \subseteq^n U \}. \tag{2}$$

Given a transition system $T = (S, L, \rightarrow)$ we will say that a state $s \in S$ satisfies the closed assertion A, if $s \in [\![A]\!]_T\, \rho$ for all environments ρ and write $s \models_T A$.

For the rest of this section we will concentrate on unnested fixed-points and describe how to transform the problem of satisfaction into a problem of finding a marking of a particular kind of graph. The transformation proceeds in three steps: First the unnested fixed-point is transformed into an equivalent simple fixed-point. Secondly this fixed-point is transformed into a modality free fixed-point from which we eventually construct a boolean graph.

We will say that $\nu \underline{X}.\underline{A}$ is an *unnested fixed-point* if no fixed-points appear in the body $\underline{A}$. Furthermore we will say that an unnested fixed-point $\nu \underline{X}.\underline{A}$ is *simple* if each of the components A_j of $\underline{A}$ contains at most one operator, i.e. A_j is on one of the forms

$$F, T, X_{j_0} \vee X_{j_1}, X_{j_0} \wedge X_{j_1}, [\alpha]X_{j'}, \langle \alpha \rangle X_{j'}, X_{j'}.$$

Any unary, unnested fixed-point assertion $\nu X.A$ can be translated into an equivalent simultaneous simple fixed-point assertion, where $n = |A|$ is the size of A, measured as the number of operators. The translation proceeds as follows: To each subexpression we associate a variable. This gives n variables $\{X_1, \ldots, X_n\}$. Define the n-ary fixed-point $\nu \underline{X}.\underline{A}$ by

$$A_i = \quad \begin{array}{l} \text{the expression associated with } X_i \text{ where all proper} \\ \text{subexpressions are replaced by their associated variables} \\ \text{and } X \text{ is replaced by } X_1, \end{array}$$

assuming that X_1 is associated with A. Using Bekić's theorem [Bek84] one can show the following proposition.

Proposition 1 *Let $\nu X.A$ be a closed unnested fixed-point and let $\nu \underline{X}.\underline{A}$ be the translated simple fixed-point. Then*

$$[\![(\nu \underline{X}.\underline{A})_1]\!]_T \, \rho \;\; = \;\; [\![\nu X.A]\!]_T \, \rho$$

for all environments ρ.

As an example $\nu X.[\alpha]X \wedge \langle \beta \rangle T$ will give raise to the 4-ary simple fixed-point

$$\nu \begin{pmatrix} X_1 \\ X_2 \\ X_3 \\ X_4 \end{pmatrix} . \begin{pmatrix} X_2 \wedge X_3 \\ [\alpha]X_1 \\ \langle \beta \rangle X_4 \\ T \end{pmatrix} .$$

The translation and proposition 1 generalises easily to unnested fixed-points of arbitrary arity. The number of variables of the resulting simple fixed-point will still be equal to the size of the original fixed-point assertion.

Given a transition system T and an assertion A, we will for each state s describe a method for finding an assertion B without modalities, which intuitively (when ignoring variables) has the property that $s \models_T A$ if and only if B denotes true.[1] In order to state this formally, we will interpret assertions without modalities – assertions built from the propositional fragment of our calculus – over the trivial one-state transition system $\bullet = (\{\bullet\}, \emptyset, \emptyset)$ with no transitions. Hence, every closed assertion A will either denote $\{\bullet\}$ or $\emptyset$ of the complete two-point lattice $\mathcal{P}(\{\bullet\})$. The lattice $\mathcal{P}(\{\bullet\})$ is nothing else than a distinct copy of the well-known Sierpinski space $\mathbf{O} = \{0,1\}$ with the partial ordering $0 \leq 0, 0 \leq 1, 1 \leq 1$, so we will often use 0 and 1 instead of $\emptyset$ and $\{\bullet\}$.

Assume that the set of states of T is numbered such that $S = \{s_1, \ldots, s_n\}$. Observe that the Sierpinski space $\mathbf{O}$ extends to a complete lattice $\mathbf{O}^n$ by extending the ordering pointwise, and note that there is an obvious isomorphism on lattices $in : \mathbf{O}^n \cong \mathcal{P}(S)$ defined by $in(x_1, \ldots, x_n) = \{s_i \in S \mid x_i = 1\}$.

Given a closed assertion A we will find modality free assertions $(A/s_1, \ldots, A/s_n)$ such that

$$[\![A]\!]_T \, \rho = in([\![A/s_1]\!]_\bullet \, \rho, \ldots, [\![A/s_n]\!]_\bullet \, \rho)$$

for all environments ρ. Having found such assertions we have by the definition of the in-map that $s_j \in [\![A]\!]_T \, \rho$ if and only if $[\![A/s_j]\!]_\bullet \, \rho = 1$, hence we have found modality free assertions with the wanted property.

We will define A/s_i by structural induction on A, so due to the fixed-points we will be confronted with open assertions. In order to handle these open assertions we will need a notion of *change of variables* which will relate the variables of A to the variables of the A/s_i's. Consider an assertion A with variables $\{X^1, \ldots, X^m\}$ and assume that to each variable X^i, σ assoicates a new set of variables $\sigma(X^i) = (X_1^i, \ldots, X_n^i)$ such that there are no name clashes between any of the new and any of the old variables. Say that a pair of environments (ρ, ρ') is *appropriate* for in and the change of variables σ if $\rho : Var \to \mathcal{P}(S)$ and $\rho' : Var \to \mathbf{O}$, and

$$\rho(X) = in(\rho'(X_1), \ldots, \rho'(X_n))$$

---

[1] Larsen and Xinxin [LX90] describes a similar translation.

for all variables X with $\sigma(X) = (X_1, \ldots, X_n)$. For two such appropriate environments assume inductively that we have found A/s_i's such that

$$\psi \circ in = in \circ \theta,$$

where $\psi(U) = [\![A]\!]_T\, \rho[U/X]$ and

$$\theta(U_1, \ldots, U_n) = ([\![A/s_1]\!]_{\scriptscriptstyle\bullet}\, \rho'[U_1/X_1, \ldots, U_n/X_n], \ldots, [\![A/s_n]\!]_{\scriptscriptstyle\bullet}\, \rho'[U_1/X_1, \ldots, U_n/X_n]).$$

We can then by the reduction lemma below conclude that $\mu\psi = in(\mu\theta)$, hence

$$[\![\mu X.A]\!]_T\, \rho \;\; = \;\; in([\![(\mu\underline{X}.\underline{A})_1]\!]_{\scriptscriptstyle\bullet}\, \rho', \ldots, [\![(\mu\underline{X}.\underline{A})_n]\!]_{\scriptscriptstyle\bullet}\, \rho'),$$

and we have found the modality free assertions corresponding to $\mu X.A$.

Lemma 2 *(Reduction lemma.)*
Suppose D and E are complete lattices of countable height, and $in : D \to E$ an ω-continuous function with $in(\bot_D) = \bot_E$. Suppose $\psi : E \to E$ and $\theta : D \to D$ are both monotonic and have the property

$$\psi \circ in = in \circ \theta.$$

We can then conclude that

$$\mu\psi = in(\mu\theta).$$

We are now able to state the full definition of A/s_i. Define for each state s_i the quotient A/s_i by structural induction on A as follows:

$$
\begin{aligned}
F/s_i &= F\\
T/s_i &= T\\
(A_0 \vee A_1)/s_i &= (A_0/s_i) \vee (A_1/s_i)\\
(A_0 \wedge A_1)/s_i &= (A_0/s_i) \wedge (A_1/s_i)\\
([\alpha]A)/s_i &= \textstyle\bigwedge_{\{j|s_i \overset{\alpha}{\to} s_j\}}(A/s_j)\\
(\langle\alpha\rangle A)/s_i &= \textstyle\bigvee_{\{j|s_i \overset{\alpha}{\to} s_j\}}(A/s_j)\\
X_j/s_i &= X_{ij}\\
&\quad \text{where } \sigma(X_j) = (X_{1j}, \ldots, X_{nj})
\end{aligned}
$$

For the k-ary fixed-point $\nu\underline{X}.\underline{A}$, assume that we have a change of variables σ with $\sigma(\underline{X}_j) = (\underline{X}_{1j}, \ldots, \underline{X}_{nj})$, and let the nk-ary fixed-point $\nu\underline{X}.\underline{A}$ be defined by

$$\underline{A}_{ij} = \underline{A}_j/s_i,$$

where $1 \le i \le n, 1 \le j \le k$. Take

$$(\mu\underline{X}.\underline{A})_j/s_i = (\mu\underline{X}.\underline{A})_{ji},$$

and similarly for the maximal fixed-point.[2] We have:

---

[2] We use double underlining as in $\underline{A}$ to indicate matrices of assertions, which of course in this context is just a convenient way of writing large vectors.

Theorem 3 *(Quotienting theorem)*
For an arbitrary assertion A, association of variables σ and appropriate pair of environments (ρ, ρ') we have

$$[\![A]\!]_T\, \rho = in([\![A/s_1]\!]_\bullet\, \rho', \ldots, [\![A/s_n]\!]_\bullet\, \rho').$$

The original problem of deciding whether a particular state s_j satisfies the closed assertion A can now be recast by applying the quotienting theorem:

$$
\begin{aligned}
s_j \models_T A \quad &\textit{iff} \quad s_j \in [\![A]\!]_T\, \rho \;\; \textit{for all } \rho \\
&\textit{iff} \quad s_j \in in([\![A/s_1]\!]_\bullet\, \rho', \ldots, [\![A/s_n]\!]_\bullet\, \rho') \\
&\textit{iff} \quad [\![A/s_j]\!]_\bullet\, \rho' = 1,
\end{aligned}
$$

where (ρ, ρ') is appropriate for σ and in. In other words, model checking can be reduced to deciding whether the assertion A/s_j denotes the top element of $\mathbf{O}$. An important point about the quotienting is that the resulting assertion consists entirely of disjunctions, conjunctions, variables, and fixed-point operators (viewing F and T as empty disjunctions and conjunctions). In particular, for an unnested k-ary fixed-point $\mu\underline{X}.\underline{A}$, we end up with an unnested fixed-point $\mu\underline{X}.\underline{A}$ in the lattice $\mathbf{O}^{k|S|}$. Moreover, if $\mu\underline{X}.\underline{A}$ is simple, the total size of $\mu\underline{X}.\underline{A}$ will be bounded by $|A||T|$, where $|T| = |S| + |L| + |\rightarrow|$, as simple calculations show:

$$
\begin{aligned}
|\mu\underline{X}.\underline{A}| \;&=\; \textstyle\sum_{j=1}^{|S|} \sum_{i=1}^{k} |\underline{A}_{ji}| \\
&=\; \textstyle\sum_{i=1}^{k} \sum_{j=1}^{|S|} |\underline{A}_i/s_j| \\
&\leq\; \textstyle\sum_{i=1}^{k} \sum_{j=1}^{|S|} max(1, |\{j' \mid \exists\alpha.\; s_j \xrightarrow{\alpha} s_{j'}\}|) \\
&\leq\; \textstyle\sum_{i=1}^{k} |T| \;=\; k|T| \;=\; |A||T|
\end{aligned}
$$

If $\mu\underline{X}.\underline{A}$ is *not* simple, this bound would not hold. As an example consider the assertion $\mu X.\langle\alpha\rangle[\alpha]\ldots\langle\alpha\rangle[\alpha]X$ (l diamond- and box-modalities), and assume that T is a transition system with n states, all connected to each other by α-transitions. Then the size of a single righthand-side of the resulting assertion will be:

$$|\langle\alpha\rangle[\alpha]\ldots\langle\alpha\rangle[\alpha]X/s_j| \;=\; |\bigvee_{i_1}\bigwedge_{i_2}\cdots\bigvee_{i_{l-1}}\bigwedge_{i_l} X_{i_l}| \;=\; n^l.$$

The significance of making the fixed-points simple is that values of subexpressions are shared across the disjunctions and conjunctions. In this example, we will get a resulting assertion of size $2ln^2$ – and not n^l – which is less than $|A||T|$.

In the analysis of time and space complexities we will make use of some general assumptions about the representations of assertions and transition systems. Firstly, variables will be assumed to be represented by natural numbers, which in turn will be assumed to be representable in a constant amount of memory.[3] Secondly, functions from an interval of the natural numbers to a set of 'simple' values, e.g. numbers, will be represented efficiently s.t. access to the value at one particular element in the domain can be performed in constant time (like 'arrays' in many programming languages). Thirdly, the transition

---

[3] As usual in complexity analysis we make the assumptions that integers can be stored in a constant amount of memory and that an arbitrary memory address can be accessed in constant timed, although it rather should be in time the logarithm of the size of the integer or memory address.

relations are represented as functions from the set of states (assumed to be an interval of natural numbers) into sets of pairs consisting of a label and a state. Labels are also assumed to be represented in a constant amount of memory.

Often we will use statements like 'this algorithm runs in time and space $K(n)$', where it actually should be 'in time and space asymptotically bounded by $K(n)$'. All these assumptions and slight abuses of language are standard in complexity analysis.

With these assumptions it is easy to see that the translations into simple fixed-points and boolean graphs can be performed in time and space $|A||T|$.

3   Boolean graphs

In the previous section we described how to transform an unnested fixed-point $\mu X.A$ (of arity 1 or higher) into first a simple k-ary fixed-point $\mu \underline{X}.\underline{A}$ and then, given a transition system with n states, into a nk-ary fixed-point $\mu \underline{X}.\underline{A}$ consisting of only conjunctions and disjunctions. By these transformations we have reduced the problem of finding a fixed-point over the lattice $\mathcal{P}(S)$ to a problem of finding a fixed-point of a boolean function over the lattice $\mathbf{O}^{nk}$. Viewing the variables as vertices of a graph and the dependencies between variables as directed edges, the body $\underline{A}$ defines a directed boolean graph, which essentially is nothing else than another representation of the function defined by $\underline{A}$.

Formally, a *boolean graph* G is a triple (V, E, L) where V is a set of vertices, $E \subseteq V \times V$ a set of directed edges, and $L : V \to \{\vee, \wedge\}$ is a total function labelling the vertices as disjunctive or conjunctive. The set $S(v)$ of *successors* and the set $P(v)$ of *predecessors* of a vertex v are defined by $S(v) = \{w | (v, w) \in E\}$ and $P(v) = \{w | (w, v) \in E\}$. Given a simple boolean k-ary fixed-point $\mu \underline{X}.\underline{A}$ we can define a graph $G_{\underline{A}} = (V, E, L)$ where

$$
\begin{aligned}
V &= \{i \mid 1 \le i \le k\} \\
E &= \{(i,j) \mid (A_i = \bigvee_{l \in I} X_l \text{ or } A_i = \bigwedge_{l \in I} X_l) \ \& \ j \in I\} \\
L(i) &= \begin{cases} \vee & \text{if } A_i = \bigvee_{l \in I} X_l \\ \wedge & \text{if } A_i = \bigwedge_{l \in I} X_l \end{cases}
\end{aligned}
$$

Note that there is an edge from i to j iff X_j is one of the disjuncts/conjuncts in A_i, expressing the fact that the value of X_i 'depends' on the value of X_j.

A *marking* of a boolean graph G is a function $m : V \to \{0, 1\}$ assigning values 0 and 1 to the vertices. The graph G induces a function g taking a marking m to a new marking $g(m)$ which is 'what can be computed from m', i.e. for a marking m define the marking $g(m)$ as

$$
g(m)(v) = \begin{cases} 1 & \text{if } L(v) = \wedge \ \& \ \forall w \in S(v).m(w) = 1 \\ & \text{or } L(v) = \vee \ \& \ \exists w \in S(v).m(w) = 1 \\ 0 & \text{otherwise} \end{cases}
$$

When G is constructed from a fixed-point $\mu \underline{X}.\underline{A}$ the function g is exactly the function defined by the body of the fixed-point $\mu \underline{X}.\underline{A}$, and m is nothing else than an element of $\mathbf{O}^n$, but thinking of m as a marking will be helpful in the development of the algorithms. As $\mathbf{O}^V$ is just an isomorphic copy of $\mathbf{O}^n$, $\mathbf{O}^V$ will be a complete lattice with the same ordering as $\mathbf{O}^n$, i.e. the pointwise extension of the Sierpinski ordering. The problem we have to solve is now: Given a boolean graph G defining the monotonic map $g : \mathbf{O}^V \to \mathbf{O}^V$, what is the minimal prefixed point $\mu g \in \mathbf{O}^V$?

4 Algorithms

In this section we will describe two algorithms for computing the minimal fixed-point of a boolean graph. The first will be global in the sense that it computes the complete fixed-point of the graph, and it will on a graph G have time and space complexity $|G|$. If G is constructed from an unnested fixed-point formula $\mu X.A$ and a transition system T as described in the previous section, the size of G will be $|A||T|$, hence we have a global model checking algorithm that in the worst-case is linear in the size of the assertion and linear in the size of the transition system.

The second will be local, in the sense that starting from a particular node x, it will only compute an approximation to the fixed-point, and in doing so only traverse a necessary subset of the graph. The approximation will be correct on x and on all nodes visited. This algorithm will on a graph G have worst-case space complexity $|G|$ and time complexity $|G| \log |G|$.

Both algorithms will be presented in the version for finding minimal fixed-points, the case of maximal fixed-points being completely dual.

4.1 A global algorithm

The global algorithm will start with the bottom element of the lattice $\mathbf{O}^V$ and gradually increase it until eventually the minimal fixed-point will be reached. Pictorially one can think of the algorithm as chasing ones around the graph; starting with nodes that are trivially forced to be one (conjunctive nodes with no successors), it will look for dependent nodes that are forced to be one, continuing until no further nodes can be forced to one – thereby having found the minimal fixed-point.

Figure 1 describes the algorithm. The function $st : V \to Z$, where Z is the set of integers, denotes the 'strength' of a node, i.e. the number of successors that must be one before this node will be forced to be one. The function g induced by G can be extended to a function on strengths by taking for all $v \in V$:

$$g(st)(v) = \begin{cases} |S(v) \cap st_{>0}| & \text{if } L(v) = \wedge \\ 1 - |S(v) \cap st_{\leq 0}| & \text{if } L(v) = \vee \end{cases}$$

where $st_{>0} = \{v | st(v) > 0\}$, i.e. the set of nodes which still needs some successors to become one, and $st_{\leq 0} = \{v | st(v) \leq 0\}$, i.e. the set of nodes which have enough successors that are one (the negative value indicates the 'excess' of ones). A strength defines a marking $\widehat{st}$ by

$$\widehat{st}(v) = \begin{cases} 1 & \text{if } st(v) \leq 0 \\ 0 & \text{if } st(v) > 0. \end{cases}$$

It is now easy to see that if $g(st) = st$ then $g(\widehat{st}) = \widehat{st}$, implying that $\widehat{st}$ is a fixed-point of g.

The set A denotes an 'active' set of nodes marked with ones, for which the consequences of becoming one has not yet been computed. Correctness can be shown from the invariant I:

$$I \equiv \begin{array}{l} A \subseteq st_{\le 0} \ \& \\ \widehat{st} \le \mu g \ \& \\ \forall v \in V. \ st(v) = \left\{ \begin{array}{ll} |S(v) \cap (st_{>0} \cup A)| & if \ L(v) = \wedge \\ 1 - |S(v) \cap (st_{\le 0} \setminus A)| & if \ L(v) = \vee \end{array} \right. \end{array}$$

Input: Boolean graph $G = (V, E, L)$, defining the function g.
Output: A marking $m : V \to \{0, 1\}$ equal to μg.

for all $v \in V$ **do** $st(v) := \left\{ \begin{array}{ll} |S(v)| & \text{if } L(v) = \wedge \\ 1 & \text{if } L(v) = \vee \end{array} \right.$

$A := st_{\le 0}$
while $A \ne \emptyset$ **do**
    choose some $v \in A$; $A := A \setminus \{v\}$
    for all $w \in P(v)$ **do**
        $st(w) := st(w) - 1$
        if $st(w) = 0$ **then** $A := A \cup \{w\}$
$m := \widehat{st}$

Figure 1: A global algorithm: Chasing 1's.

Theorem 4 *The algorithm of figure 1 correctly computes the minimal fixed-point μg and it can be implemented to run in time $O(|G|)$.*

Proof: It is a simple exercise to show that the invariant I holds immediately before the while-loop, and that it is preserved by the body. When the while-loop terminates we have $A = \emptyset$ which from the invariant implies that $st = g(st)$ and $\widehat{st}$ is a fixed-point, which by the second conjunct of the invariant is less than or equal to the minimal fixed-point, hence $\widehat{st} = \mu g$.

For the time complexity, first notice that whenever a node has been removed from the set A, it will never be inserted again as this only happens when its strength equals zero, and strengths always decrease. Hence the body of the outermost while-loop, will at most be executed once for each node v of the graph. Each execution of the innermost while-loop takes time proportional to the size of $P(v)$, i.e. the number of predecessors for the node v. In total the outermost while-loop takes time proportional to the sum of the number of predecessors, i.e. the total number of edges in G, and is thus bounded by $|G|$. The first loop and the last assignment are also bounded by $|G|$. $\square$

4.2 A local algorithm

Model checking is usually involved with deciding satisfaction for just one particular state, so it might seem overwhelming to have to compute the complete fixed-point in order to decide the value at just one particular state. This observation is central to the development of *local* model checkers with the idea being that starting from one particular state, only a 'necessary' part of the transition system will be investigated in order to determine satisfaction. Larsen [Lar88] describes such an algorithm for the case of one fixed-point, which in an improved version is used in the TAV system [LGZ89]. Stirling and Walker [SW89] and Cleaveland [Cle90] describes a similar method for the full modal μ-calculus based on tableaux, which has been used in the implementation of the Concurrency Workbench [CPS89]. Using a single key-property of maximal fixed-points Winskel, in [Win89] develops a very similar and quite simple model checker. Unfortunately, they all have very bad worst-case behaviours. Even for the fixed-point free subset of the modal μ-calculus they have worst-case time complexity which is at least exponential in the size of assertions, and for formulas with one fixed-point, worse than exponential in the number of transitions.

In this section we present a local algorithm for finding a fixed-point of a boolean graph, which will only visit a subset of the graph in the search for deciding the minimal fixed-point value for one particular node. This will be done in time proportional to the size of the subset being visited, hence in the worst-case it will be $|G|$. Unfortunately, in the initialisation phase the algorithm will need to visit each node in the graph once, and the running-time will then always be linear as for the global algorithm. Nevertheless the algorithm seems interesting as it works very differently from the global algorithm and still solves the same problem. Moreover after presenting the algorithm, we discuss a way of using the algorithm in a slightly revised version – avoiding the costly initialisation – as a basis for a local model checker, which will run in time $|B|\log|B|$ where B is the subset of the graph being traversed. Thus the worst-case behaviour will be $|A||T|\log(|A||T|)$, and we have a local model checker which in the worst-case is only a logarithmic factor worse than the global model checker.

Input: Boolean graph $G = (V, E, L)$, and a node $x \in V$.
Output: A marking $m : V \to \{0, 1\}$ and a set $B \subseteq V$ with $x \in B$
      such that m equals μg on B.

Initialisation:
      $B, A := \emptyset \quad m, p := \underline{0} \quad d := \underline{\emptyset}$
Method:
      $visit(x, \emptyset)$
      while $A \neq \emptyset$ **do**
            choose some $y \in A; A := A \setminus \{y\}$
            for all $w \in d(y)$ **do**
                  if $L(w) = \vee$ & $m(w) = 0$ **then**
                      $m(w) := 1 \quad A := A \cup \{w\}$
                ff $L(w) = \wedge$ **then**
                    $p(w) := p(w) + 1$
                    $fwtn(w, \emptyset)$
                fi

Figure 2: A local algorithm: Avoiding 1's.

```
    visit(x, P) =

if x ∉ B then
        B := B ∪ {x}
        if L(x) = ∨ then
            ok := false
            while p(x) < |S(x)| & ¬ok do
                w := S(x)_{p(x)}
                visit(w, P ∪ {x})
                if m(w) = 0 then d(w) := d(w) ∪ {x}  p(x) := p(x) + 1
                ff m(w) = 1 then ok := true
                fi
            if ok then m(x) := 1  A := A ∪ {x}
        ff L(x) = ∧ then
            fwtn(x, P)
    fi
```

Figure 3: Visit.

```
    fwtn(x, P) =

ok := false
while p(x) < |S(x)| & ¬ok do
    w := S(x)_{p(x)}
    visit(w, P ∪ {x})
    if m(w) = 0 then d(w) := d(w) ∪ {x}  ok := true
    ff m(w) = 1 then p(x) := p(x) + 1
    fi
if ¬ok then m(x) := 1  A := A ∪ {x}
```

Figure 4: Fwtn: 'find a witness'.

The local algorithm 'Avoiding 1's' is presented in figures 2, 3, and 4, and works as follows: Initially all nodes will be marked with a zero. We start with the node of interest, x say, and try to verify whether its minimal fixed-point marking is really a zero (the task of the *visit* procedure). This involves inspecting the successors each in turn, finding their minimal fixed-point markings, until, in the case of a conjunctive node, a zero is found, or in the case of a disjunctive node, a one is found, or all successors have been inspected. For this purpose we assume that the successors of each node v have been numbered from 0 to $(|S(v)| - 1)$, i.e. $S(v) = \{S(v)_0, \ldots, S(v)_{|S(v)|-1}\}$. The function $p : V \to \mathbb{N}$ is used in order to keep track of which successor $p(v)$ of v is being examined, or must be examined next.

Due to cycles in the graph, a node that at one point is found to be marked with zero, can later be changed into being marked with one, hence all nodes that were assigned a marking based on this particular node being zero might have to be changed as well. In order to be able to perform this updating efficiently, we keep for each node v a list of nodes $d(v)$ that should be informed in case the marking of v will change from zero to one. Thus $d : V \rightarrow \mathcal{P}(V)$ will for each node v denote a subset of its predecessors $P(v)$, and this set will grow as the algorithm proceeds.

The set $A \subseteq V$ contains nodes v that have changed marking from zero to one, and for which this information has not yet been spread to the nodes in $d(v)$. The set $B \subseteq V$ contains all nodes that have been visited. The procedure *fwtn* (short for 'find witness'), will for a conjunctive node v search the successors starting from number $p(v)$ for one with a zero marking, that 'witnesses' that v should have the marking zero. If no such exists, the node v will have to be marked with a one.

At any point in the execution of the algorithm, the situation will be as sketched in figure 5.

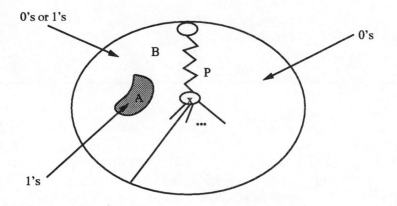

Figure 5: A typical situation of Avoiding 1's

Using a more involved invariant expressing essentially just the relationship between the variables explained above, and *amortised time analysis* (see f.ex. [CLR90]) it is possible to show the following theorem.

Theorem 5 *Given a boolean graph G with the induced function g. The algorithm described in figure 2 correctly computes an element m of $\mathbf{O}^V$ and a set $B \subseteq V$, such that*

$$m|_B = (\mu g)|_B,$$

and it can be implemented to run in time $O(|G|)$.

As an alternative to the linear time initialisation, we could just omit it. Instead we would have to somehow remember the nodes that had been visited and the check '$x \in B$' should be implemented by a search for x in the data structure representing B. Representing B as a balanced binary search tree this search could be done in logarithmic time. Moreover one could imagine the graph being constructed from the assertion and the transition system in a demand-driven fashion. Even the transition system could be build in a demand-driven manner from for instance a process algebraic term.

Assuming that each node x will be associated with a memory address a_x on which the values of d, p, d, and m at x will be stored, we have the following sketch of an algorithm. The initialisation is changed to:

$$B, A := \emptyset$$

The procedure *visit* is changed to:

$$visit(x, P) =$$

if $x \notin B$ **then**

    allocate a new memory cell with address a_x

    initialise d on x to $\emptyset$, p on x to 0, m on x to 0

    insert the pair (x, a_x) in B

    find $S(x)$ by performing the division

    if ...

        ... as before, where all accesses to m, d etc.

        are through the addresses stored in B ...

fi

The procedure *fwtn* will not be changed, except that all access to the variables m, p etc. will be through their addresses stored in B. The number of primitive steps performed by this algorithm will be as before, but we have to take into account the logarithmic factor coming from the searches in B. Hence the running time will be $|B| \log |B|$, which in the worst-case is $|G| \log |G|$.

5   Extensions to the full modal μ-calculus

In this section we will describe how the global algorithm Chasing 1's can be extended to yield a model checker for the full μ-calculus which has the running time $(|A||T|)^{ad}$, where ad is the alternation depth of the assertion A. For the precise definition of alternation depth, the reader is referred to [EL86].

Actually the algorithm will be slightly better than stated. Given an algorithm – like Chasing 1's – that can find a simultaneous unnested fixed-point in time $|A||T|$, we show that we can compute an arbitrary assertion of alternation depth k in time $|A|^k|S|^{k-1}|T|$. As $|T| = |S| + |L| + |\rightarrow|$ the resulting algorithm will be linear in the number of transitions, although, when the alternation depth is unbounded, exponential in the size of the assertion and the number of states. When the alternation depth is bounded, it will yield a polynomial time algorithm with a polynomial degree one less than the algorithm by Emerson and Lei [EL86].

Theorem 6 *Given an algorithm that can find a simultaneous unnested fixed-point ($\mu X.A$ and $\nu X.A$) on a transition system T in time $|A||T|$. There exists an algorithm that will compute an arbitrary assertion A of alternation depth k in time $|A|^k|S|^{k-1}|T|$ and space $|A||T|$.*

The proof can be found in appendix A.

This algorithm only assumes the presence of an efficient algorithm for handling the unnested case, and then by applying this at appropriate places handles the general case. Boolean graphs are not used, except in the base-case. Another attempt of extending the global algorithm to the full μ-calculus, could be through a generalisation of the boolean graphs. Assume that we are interested in computing the set denoted by the assertion A. First simplify all fixed-points appearing in A, then perform the division, and finally construct a boolean graph from the resulting modality-free assertion where the vertices are partitioned into disjoint sets $\{V_1, \ldots, V_n\}$ – one for each fixed-point. Now, a certain marking of this partitioned graph, reflecting the minimal and maximal fixed-points, would correspond to the element representing A. It is currently being investigated to what extent this approach can lead to new algorithms.

However, one application, which is described here, is in the generalisation of the local algorithm to alternation depth one.

The constructing of a *partitioned boolean graph* proceeds as follows: Given an assertion A. If the top-level operator is not a minimal or maximal fixed-point, change A into $\mu X.A$ for an arbitrary variable X (taking $\nu X.A$ would also do). Transform A into a normal form, where consecutive sequences of minimal (maximal) fixed-points are replaced by one minimal (maximal) fixed-point (as in the proof of theorem 6 in appendix A). Simplify all fixed-points. Assume that all variables appearing in different fixed-points of A are different, otherwise rename the variables so this is the case. Perform the division with respect to a change of variables σ and call the resulting assertion A'. Let A_i' be the right-handside corresponding to the variable X_i. Define the boolean graph $G_{A'} = (V, E, L)$ as follows:

$$
V \;=\; \text{the set of all variables appearing in } A'
$$
$$
E \;=\; \left\{ (X_i, X_j) \;\middle|\; \begin{array}{l} (A_i' = \bigvee M \text{ or } A_i' = \bigwedge M) \;\&\; X_j \in M \\ \text{or } A_i' = (\mu \underline{X}.\underline{A})_k \;\&\; X_j \text{ is the } k\text{'th variable in } \underline{X} \\ \text{or } A_i' = (\nu \underline{X}.\underline{A})_k \;\&\; X_j \text{ is the } k\text{'th variable in } \underline{X} \end{array} \right\}
$$
$$
L(i) \;=\; \begin{cases} \vee & \text{if } A_i' = \bigvee M \\ \wedge & \text{if } A_i' = \bigwedge M \text{ or } A_i' = (\mu \underline{X}.\underline{B})_k \text{ or } A_i' = (\nu \underline{X}.\underline{B})_k \end{cases}
$$

Note that there is an edge from X_i to X_j if X_j is one of the disjuncts/conjuncts in A_i', or if A_i' is a projection of a fixed-point, X_j is the variable of the fixed-point corresponding to that projection.

Assume that the fixed-points of A' are numbered from 1 to n and let V_i be the variables in the i'th fixed-point. Let $\mathcal{G}_{A'} = (G_{A'}, \mathcal{V}, \mathcal{L})$ be defined by:

$$
\mathcal{V} \;=\; \{V_1, \ldots, V_n\}
$$
$$
\mathcal{L}(V_i) \;=\; \begin{cases} \mu & \text{if the } i\text{'th fixed-point is a minimal one} \\ \nu & \text{if the } i\text{'th fixed-point is a maximal one} \end{cases}
$$

We will call such a $\mathcal{G}_{A'}$ a *partitioned boolean graph*.

Cycles in this partitioned boolean graph will be of a special kind if A has alternation depth one:

Proposition 7 *Let A be an assertion of alternation depth one. Then the partitioned boolean graph constructed from A as above will have the property that all cycles of the underlying boolean graph will consist of nodes that are all consistently labelled with only μ's or only ν's. Moreover, due to the transformation into normal form, they will all belong to the same component.*

Proof: (Sketch)

Assume that there exists a cycle with a node labelled μ and a node labelled ν. These nodes must belong to two different elements of the partitioning, V_i and V_j. Then either the i'th fixed-point contains the j'th fixed-point and the j'th fixed-point refers to a variable from the i'th fixed-point, or the other way around. In both cases these fixed-points could only come from an assertion of alternation depth at least two.

Assume that two nodes labelled μ belong to two different components of the partitioning. Then we would have a sequence of two minimal fixed-points, which contradicts the fact that A has been put into normal form. $\square$

Using this property, it is possible to give a local algorithm for alternation depth one:

Theorem 8 *There exists a local algorithm that for an assertion A of alternation depth one and a transition system T with a state s, determines whether s satisfies A in worst-case time-complexity $|A||T|\log(|A||T|)$.*

The proof can be found in appendix B.

6 Conclusion

The translation of a model checking problem into a problem of finding markings in boolean graphs shows the way to a rich world of algorithms. In this paper we have presented two graph algorithms to solve the problem, but considering the wealth of graph algorithms around, there should be plenty of possibilities for finding other interesting algorithms. Moreover the algorithms might have an interest on its own, as the graph problem – equivalent to the problem of finding fixed-points in the lattice $\mathbf{O}^n$ – is a very general problem. As an example of this, the global algorithm Chasing 1's has a very close resemblance with the pebbling algorithm in [DG84] for solving satisfiability of propositional Horn formulas in linear time, and Chasing 1's actually gives a linear time algorithm for solving that problem.

Another area of application is suggested by the Reduction lemma. Suppose you have a finite lattice D, a monotonic function f on D, and an ω-continuous function *in* from D into $\mathbf{O}^n$ for an appropriate n (we claim that such an n and function can always be found). If it is possible to find a function g on $\mathbf{O}^n$ which is related to f as required by the lemma, i.e. $in \circ f = g \circ in$, then the minimal fixed-point of f can be found efficiently, by computing μg and applying *in*. The time to compute μg will be bounded by the size of the description of μg as a simple fixed-point (in the sense of section 2), which might be much better than using the method of computing increasing approximants, as it was the case with the model checking problem.

The division idea, which is the key step in the translation from a fixed-point on a powerset into a fixed-point on the lattice $\mathbf{O}^n$, arose in work on trying to find compositional methods for reasoning about satisfaction. In [AW91] a general version of the division operator was presented ([AW91] also introduced the reduction lemma). Given a process term p and an assertion A, a method is described, which computes the assertion A/p with the property:

$$x \times p : A \;\; \text{iff} \;\; x : A/p,$$

where $\times$ is a parallel composition operator and $p : A$ is read as 'the process p satisfies the assertion A'. The assertion A/p was constructed such that it belongs to the modal μ-calculus with just unary fixed-points, and for the fixed-points an exponential blow-up could result from the application of Bekić's theorem. Currently we are investigating to what extent the ideas of sharing through n-ary fixed-points, as used in this paper, can be used in improving on these results.

Acknowledgements

I have had useful discussions with Glynn Winskel, Kim Skak Larsen, Gudmund Frandsen, and others at DAIMI.

References

[AC88] André Arnold and Paul Crubille. A linear algorithm to solve fixed-point equations on transitions systems. *Information Processing Letters*, 29:57–66, 1988.

[AW91] Henrik Reif Andersen and Glynn Winskel. Compositional checking of satisfaction. In Larsen and Skou [LS91]. To appear.

[Bek84] H. Bekić. Definable operations in general algebras, and the theory of automata and flow charts. *Lecture Notes in Computer Science*, 177, 1984.

[Cle90] Rance Cleaveland. Tableau-based model checking in the propositional mu-calculus. *Acta Informatica*, 27:725–747, 1990.

[CLR90] Thomas H. Cormen, Charles E. Leiserson, and Ronald L. Rivest. *Introduction to Algorithms*. McGraw-Hill, 1990.

[CPS89] Rance Cleaveland, Joachim Parrow, and Bernhard Steffen. The Concurrency Workbench: A semantics based tool for the verification of concurrent systems. Technical Report ECS-LFCS-89-83, Laboratory for Foundations of Computer Science, Uni. of Edinburgh, August 1989.

[CS91] Rance Cleaveland and Bernhard Steffen. A linear-time model-checking algorithm for the alternation-free modal mu-calculus. In Larsen and Skou [LS91]. To appear.

[Dam90] Mads Dam. Translating CTL* into the modal μ-calculus. Technical Report ECS-LFCS-90-123, Laboratory for Foundations of Computer Science, Uni. of Edinburgh, November 1990.

[DG84] William F. Dowling and Jean H. Gallier. Linear-time algorithms for testing the satisfiability of propositional Horn formulae. *Journal of Logic Programming*, 1(3):267–284, 1984.

[EL86] E. Allen Emerson and Chin-Luang Lei. Efficient model checking in fragments of the propositional mu-calculus. In *Symposium on Logic in Computer Science, Proceedings*, pages 267–278. IEEE, 1986.

[Koz83] Dexter Kozen. Results on the propositional mu-calculus. *Theoretical Computer Science*, 27, 1983.

[Lar88] Kim G. Larsen. Proof systems for Hennessy-Milner logic with recursion. In *Proceedings of CAAP*, 1988.

[LGZ89] Kim G. Larsen, J.C. Godskesen, and M. Zeeberg. TAV–Tools for Automatic Verification. Technical Report R 89-19, Aalborg Universitetscenter, 1989.

[LS91] Kim G. Larsen and Arne Skou, editors. *Proceedings of the 3rd Workshop on Computer Aided Verification, Aalborg*, LNCS. Springer-Verlag, July 1991. To appear.

[LX90] Kim G. Larsen and Liu Xinxin. Compositionality through an operational semantics of contexts. In M.S. Paterson, editor, *Proceedings of ICALP*, volume 443 of *LNCS*, pages 526–539. Springer-Verlag, 1990.

[SW89] Colin Stirling and David Walker. Local model checking in the modal mu-calculus. In *Proceedings of TAPSOFT*, 1989.

[Tar55] A. Tarski. A lattice-theoretical fixpoint theorem and its applications. *Pacific Journal of Mathematics*, 5, 1955.

[Win89] Glynn Winskel. A note on model checking the modal ν-calculus. In Ausiello, Dezani-Ciancaglini, and Rocca, editors, *Proceedings of ICALP*, volume 372 of *LNCS*, 1989.

Appendices

A   Proof of theorem 6

The algorithm will be given along with the analysis of its time-complexity and proof of correctness which is by induction on the size of the assertion A.
Proof: (Sketch)
Define the predicate P by

$$P(A) \quad \Leftrightarrow_{\text{def}} \quad \forall \rho. \; [\![A]\!]_T \, \rho \text{ can be computed in time } |A|^k |S|^{k-1}|T|,$$

where $k = ad(A)$. Assume inductively that for all $A', |A'| < |A| \Rightarrow P(A')$. We show by cases that $P(A)$ holds.

Case $\langle \alpha \rangle A$. Given a set $U \subseteq \mathcal{P}(S)$, the set $\{s \in S | \exists s' \in S. \; s \xrightarrow{\alpha} s' \ \& \ s' \in U\}$ can obviously be computed in time $|T|$. By the induction hypothesis, $[\![A]\!]_T \, \rho$ can be computed in time $|A|^k |S|^{k-1}|T|$, where $k = ad(A)$. Then $[\![\langle \alpha \rangle A]\!]_T \, \rho$ can be computed in time

$$|A|^k|S|^{k-1}|T| + |T| \;\leq\; (|A|+1)^k|S|^{k-1}|T|$$
$$= \; |\langle \alpha \rangle A|^k|S|^{k-1}|T|$$

where $k = ad(A) = ad(\langle \alpha \rangle A)$.

Case X. Computing $[\![X]\!]_T \, \rho = \rho(X)$ takes time $|S|$ by the assumptions on representations of sets. Trivially we have $|S| \leq |X|^1 |S|^0 |T|$.

Case $\mu X.A$. We just consider the case of a unary fixed-point, arbitrary arities being similar but more cluttered up with indices. If $\mu X.A$ contains closed proper subexpressions $A_1, \ldots, A_m$ then, by the induction hypothesis, compute $[\![A_1]\!]_T \, \rho, \ldots, [\![A_m]\!]_T \, \rho$ in time

$$\sum_{i=1}^{m} |A_i|^{ad(A_i)}|S|^{ad(A_i)-1}|T| \;\leq\; (\sum_{i=1}^{m} |A_i|)^k |S|^{k-1}|T|,$$

where $k = ad(A)$. Insert new constants $Q_1, \ldots, Q_m$ for $A_1, \ldots, A_m$ in A denoting $[\![A_1]\!]_T \, \rho, \ldots, [\![A_m]\!]_T \, \rho$ and call the new assertion B. Let $\{X_1, \ldots, X_n\}$ be the variables bound by the top-level μ-operators in B, and let $\{B_1, \ldots, B_n\}$ be the corresponding bodies.[4] Define

$$B' = \mu \begin{pmatrix} X_1 \\ \vdots \\ X_n \end{pmatrix} . \begin{pmatrix} B_1[X_2/\mu X_2.A_2, \ldots, X_n/\mu X_n.B_n] \\ \vdots \\ B_n[X_1/\mu X_1.B_1, \ldots, X_{n-1}/\mu X_{n-1}.B_{n-1}] \end{pmatrix}.$$

Using Bekić's theorem one can show that the first component of B' is equal to $\mu X.A$. Notice that $|B'| = |B| \leq |A|$.

---

[4]Here the variables should be thought of as identifying occurrences instead of just names.

If B' is now an unnested fixed-point, compute it in time $|B'||T|$ by the efficient algorithm for unnested fixed-points, hence $[\![B']\!]_T \rho$ has been computed in time

$$(\sum_{i=1}^m |A_i|)^k |S|^{k-1}|T| + |B'||T|$$
$$\leq |A|^k |S|^{k-1}|T|.$$

If B' is a nested fixed-point, let B'' denote the body of B'. Observe that B'' defines a monotonic function on $\mathcal{P}(S)^n$. We will use the method of increasing approximants to calculate B'. Define

$$U^0 = (\emptyset,\dots,\emptyset)$$
$$U^{p+1} = [\![B'']\!]_T \rho[U_1^p/X_1,\dots,U_n^p/X_n].$$

Compute by iteration U^p until $U^p = U^{p-1}$. The number of iterations is bounded by the height of the lattice $\mathcal{P}(S)^n$, which is $n|S|$. Each iterate can, by the induction hypothesis, be computed in time $|B''|^{k''}|S|^{k''-1}|T|$, where $k'' = ad(B'')$. Hence the total cost will be bounded by

$$(\sum_{i=1}^m |B_i|)^k |S|^{k-1}|T| + n|S||B''|^{k''}|S|^{k''-1}|T|$$
$$\leq (\sum_{i=1}^m |B_i|)^k |S|^{k-1}|T| + |B''|^{k''+1}|S|^{k''}|T|$$
$$\leq (|B''| + \sum_{i=1}^m |B_i|)^k |S|^{k-1}|T|,$$
as $k'' + 1 \leq k$ by the definition of alternation depth
$$= |B|^k |S|^{k-1}|T|.$$

The missing cases are very similar to the ones above. $\square$

B   Proof of theorem 8

Proof: (Sketch) Start with a node x in V_1. Run Avoiding 1's or Avoiding 0's (the dual of Avoiding 1's corresponding to a maximal fixed-point) depending on whether $\mathcal{L}(V_1) = \mu$ or $\mathcal{L}(V_1) = \nu$, until at some point the marking of a node y in another set V_j is needed. Suspend the evaluation and run Avoiding 1's or Avoiding 0's in V_j to find the value of this y. At some point a value in yet another set V_k might be needed, and so on. But due to the acyclic property of proposition 7 this process will stop at some point, when a node in some V_i can be determined without looking into other V_i's, and the suspended evaluations can then be resumed. Now, when the value of the node that started the search in a V_i has been determined, all the nodes visited in this search will have their correct markings, and need not be visited any more! Hence, when building the graph in a demand-driven fashion, the total execution time will be $|B|\log|B|$ where B is the subset of the graph being visited. $\square$

SIGNAL as a model for Real-Time and Hybrid Systems

Albert BENVENISTE, Michel LE BORGNE, Paul LE GUERNIC*

Abstract

Hybrid Systems are models of systems operating in real-time and handling events as well as "continuous" computations. The SIGNAL formalism for Hybrid Systems is presented in this extended abstract. Its expressive power is discussed, and a general method to associate various formal systems with it is presented and illustrated on deriving the present SIGNAL compiler.

1 Introduction: Real-Time and Hybrid Systems

It is commonly accepted to call *real-time* a program or system that receives external interrupts or reads sensors connected to physical world and outputs commands to it. As an example, let us discuss the case of an aircraft control system. Measurements are received from sensors and processed by the control loops to produces commands as outputs for the actuators: this involves various kinds of numerical computations. Switching from one operating mode to another one can be performed automatically or by the pilot: in both cases, events are received that control the various computations in some discrete event mode. For safety purposes, on-line failure detection and reconfiguration is performed by taking advantage of the redundancies in the aircraft system: actuators and sensor failure detection procedures are numerical computations that produce alarms and various detections which in turn result in reconfiguring the operating mode. From this follows that discrete events and computations are tightly coupled in a fairly symmetric way. Also, in aircraft systems, response times are often critical. They depend on the particular tasks being performed at the considered instant. On the other hand, timeouts due to timing constraints can influence the task being performed. To summarize, in real-time systems, both aspects of "what" should be implemented and "how fast" it should run must be considered. Similarly, aspects of "discrete control" and "continuous computations" deeply interact, and both interact also with response times via the mechanism of timeouts. The term of *Hybrid System (HS)* recently emerged

---

*A.B and P. L.G. are with INRIA-IRISA, M. L.B. is with IRISA-University, Campus Beaulieu, 35042 RENNES Cedex, FRANCE, name@irisa.fr. **Keywords:** real-time, semantics of programming languages, theory of parallel computation.

[3, 14] to refer to formalisms providing an attempt to cover the above mentioned issues in some unified way.

For instance, various kinds of transition systems are proposed in [10, 11] to combine qualitative and quantitative aspects of real-time. Similarly, [14] proposes to generalize a similar approach to Hybrid Systems. In both cases, the expressive power of the models is explicitly described in the axioms and inference rules of the semantics, so that expanding this expressive power is achieved by making the model more complicated. In this paper, we analyze an alternative formalism for HS that has beeen firstly proposed in [3, 2]. The main features of this formalism are:

1. it is both simple and "universal" as far as expressive power for specification is concerned: discrete events and computations are encompassed, and timing constraints can be specified; it does not rely on the notion of transition system, but handles "traces" or "behaviours", see [2];

2. it has various formal systems associated with it that can be used to verify or even synthesize some properties related to the above mentioned issues.

While "universal" expressive power is achieved realtively easily as we shall see later, only limited reasoning capability can be expected in turn, due to problems of undecidability. A major objective of this paper is to present a systematic approach to derive formal systems associated with our universal formalism, which concentrate on some particular property, e.g., discrete event features, timing constraints, etc...

2 Hybrid Systems and the SIGNAL language

A first major issue is that of the very nature of time for Hybrid Systems. Complex applications such as the one mentioned above are inherently distributed in nature. Hence every subsystem possesses its own time reference, namely the ordered collection of all the communications or actions this subsystem performs: in sensory based control systems, each sensor posses its own digital processing with proper sampling rate, actuators generally have a slower sampling rate than sensors, and moreover the software devoted to monitoring only reacts to various kinds of alarms that are triggered internally or externally. Hence the nature of time in Hybrid Systems is by no means universal, but rather local to each subsystem, and consequently multiform. This very fundamental remark justifies the kind of model for Hybrid System we use in this paper.

Our model handles infinite sequences of data with a certain kind of restricted asynchronism. Assume that each sequence, in addition to the normal values it takes in its range, can also take a special value representing the *absence* of data at that instant. The symbol used for absence is $\perp$. Therefore, an infinite time sequence of data (we shall refer to informally as a *signal* in this discussion) may look like

$$1, -4, \perp, \perp, 4, 2, \perp, ... \qquad (1)$$

which is interpreted as the signal being absent at the instants $n = 3, 4, 7, ...$ etc. *Systems specified via constraints on signals of the form (1) will be termed Hybrid Systems (HS).*

A typical way of specifying such constraints will be to write equations relating different signals. The following questions are immediate from this definition:

(1) If a single signal is observed, should we distinguish the following samples from each other?

$$\{1, -4, \perp, \perp, 4, 2, \perp, ...\} \ , \ \{\perp, 1, \perp, -4, \perp, 4, \perp, 2, \perp, ...\} \ , \ \{1, -4, 4, 2, ...\}$$

Consider an "observer"[1] who monitors this single signal and does nothing else. Since he is assumed to observe only *present* values, there is no reason to distinguish the samples above. In fact, the symbol $\perp$ is simply a tool to specify the *relative* presence or absence of a signal, given an *environment,* i.e. other signals that are also observed. Jointly observed signals taking the value $\perp$ simultaneously for any environment will be said to *possess the same clock,* and they will be said to possess different clocks otherwise. Hence clocks may be considered as equivalence classes of signals that are present simultaneously. This notion of time makes no reference to any "physical" universal clock: time is rather local to each particular subset of signals in consideration.

(2) How to interconnect two Hybrid Systems? Consider the following two Hybrid Systems specified via equations:

$$y_n = \text{ if } x_n > 0 \text{ then } x_n \text{ else } \perp \tag{2}$$

and the usual addition on sequences, namely

$$z_n = y_n + u_n \tag{3}$$

In combining these HS, it is certainly preferable to match the successive occurrences $y_1, y_2, ...$ in (3) with the corresponding *present* occurrences in (2) so that the usual meaning of addition be met. But this is in contradiction with the bruteforce conjunction of equations (2,3)

$$
\begin{aligned}
y_n &= \text{ if } x_n > 0 \text{ then } x_n \text{ else } \perp \\
z_n &= y_n + u_n
\end{aligned}
$$

which yields $z_n = \perp + u_n$ whenever $x_n \leq 0$. In appendix A a denotational model for HS firstly introduced in [3] and improved in [2] is reported as a complementary information, it provides an adequate answer to the question of how to properly interconnect equations (2,3). This model is then used to establish the semantics of the SIGNAL language we introduce informally in the following section. To summarize, our formalism will provide a *multiform* but *coherent* notion of time. Other formalisms using the same approach to handle time are the so-called *synchronous languages* [1, 8, 9].

---

[1]in the common sense, no mathematical definition is referred to here

2.1 SIGNAL-kernel

We shall introduce only the primitives of the SIGNAL language, and drop any reference to typing, modular structure, and various declarations; the interested reader is referred to [13]. SIGNAL handles (possibly infinite) sequences of data with time implicit: such sequences will be referred to as *signals*. At a given instant, signals may have the status *absent* (denoted by $\perp$) and *present*. If x is a signal, we denote by $\{x_n\}_{n\geq 1}$ the sequence of its values when it is present. Signals that are always present simultaneously are said to have the same *clock*, so that clocks are equivalence classes of simultaneously present signals. Instructions of SIGNAL are intended to relate clocks as well as values of the various signals involved in a given system. We term a system of such relations *program*; programs may be used as modules and further combined as indicated later.

A basic principle in SIGNAL is that a single name is assigned to every signal, so that in the sequel, identical names refer to identical signals. The kernel-language SIGNAL possesses 5 instructions, the first of them being a generic one.

  (i)   R(x1,...,xp)
  (ii)   y := x $1 init x0
  (iii) y := x when b
  (iv)   y := u default v
  (v)   P | Q
  (vi)   P !! x1,...,xp

(i) direct extension of instantaneous relations into relations acting on signals:

$$R(\mathrm{x}1, ..., \mathrm{x}p) \iff \forall n: \; R(\mathrm{x}1_n, ..., \mathrm{x}p_n) \text{ holds}$$

where $R(...)$ denotes a relation and the index n enumerates the instants at which the signals xi are present. Examples are functions such as z := x+y ($\forall n: z_n = x_n + y_n$). A byproduct of this instruction is that *all referred signals must be present simultaneously, i.e. they must have the same clock*. This is a generic instruction, i.e. we assume a family of relations is available. If R(...) is the universal relation, i.e., it contains all the p-tuples of the relevant domains, the resulting SIGNAL instruction only constrains the involved signals to have the same clock: the so obtained instruction will be written x ^= y and only forces the listed signals to have the same clock.

(ii) shift register.

$$\mathrm{y} := \mathrm{x} \; \$1 \; \mathrm{init} \; \mathrm{x}0 \iff \forall n > 1: \mathrm{y}_n = \mathrm{x}_{n-1}, \mathrm{y}_1 = \mathrm{x}0$$

Here the index n refers to the values of the signals when they are *present*. Again this instruction forces the input and output signals to have the same clock.

(iii) condition (b is boolean): y equals x when the signal x and the boolean b are available and b is true; otherwise, y is absent; the result is an event-based undersampling of signals. Here follows a diagram summarizing this instruction:

$$
\begin{array}{llllllllllllll}
\text{x}: & 1 & 2 & \bot & \bot & 3 & 4 & \bot & \bot & 5 & 6 & 9 & \cdots \\
\text{b}: & t & f & t & \bot & f & t & f & \bot & \bot & f & t & \cdots \\
\text{y}: & 1 & \bot & \bot & \bot & \bot & 4 & \bot & \bot & \bot & \bot & 9 & \cdots
\end{array}
$$

(iv) y merges u and v, with priority to u when both signals are simultaneously present; this instruction is the key to oversampling as we shall see later. Here follows a table summarizing this instruction:

$$
\begin{array}{llllllllllllll}
\text{u}: & 1 & 2 & \bot & \bot & 3 & 4 & \bot & \bot & 5 & \bot & 9 & \cdots \\
\text{v}: & \bot & \bot & \bot & 3 & 4 & 10 & \bot & 8 & 9 & 2 & \bot & \cdots \\
\text{y}: & 1 & 2 & \bot & 3 & 3 & 4 & \bot & 8 & 5 & 2 & 9 & \cdots
\end{array}
$$

Instructions (i-iv) specify the elementary programs.

(v) combination of already defined programs: signals with common names in P and Q are considered as identical. For example

```
(| y := zy + a
 | zy := y $1 x0 |)
```

denotes the system of recurrent equations:

$$
\begin{aligned}
y_n &= zy_n + a_n \\
zy_n &= y_{n-1}, \quad zy_1 = \text{x0}
\end{aligned}
\tag{4}
$$

On the other hand, the program

```
(| y := x when x>0
 | z := y+u |)
```

yields

$$
\text{if } x_n > 0 \text{ then } \begin{cases} y_n = x_n \\ z_n = y_n + u_n \end{cases}
$$
$$
\text{else} \quad y_n = u_n = z_n = \bot
\tag{5}
$$

where (x_n) denotes the sequence of present values of x. Hence the communication | causes $\bot$ to be inserted whenever needed in the second system z:=y+u. This is what we wanted for the example (2,3). Let us explain this mechanism more precisely. Denote by $u_1, u_2, u_3, u_4, \cdots$ the sequence of the present values of u (recall that y,z are present simultaneously with u). Then, according to point (1) of the discussion at the beginning of this section, $u_1, u_2, u_3, u_4, \cdots$ is equivalent to its following expanded version:

$$
\text{u}: \quad \bot, u_1, \bot, \bot, u_2, u_3, \bot, \bot, \bot, u_4, \bot, \cdots,
$$

for any finite amount of "$\bot$"s inserted between successive occurrences of u. Assuming all signals of integer type, suppose the following sequence of values is observed for x:

$$
\text{x}: \quad -2, +1, -6, -4, +3, +8, -21, -7, -2, +5, -9, \cdots
$$

Then the amount of inserted "⊥"s for the above expanded version of u turns out to fit exactly the negative occurrences of **x**: this flexibility in defining u allows us to match the present occurrences of **u** with the present occurrences of **y**, i.e., the positive occurrences of **x**. This mechanism is formalized in the model of the appendix.

(vi) restriction of program P to the mentioned list of signals: other signals involved in P are local and are not visible when communication is considered.

2.2 Some macros related to timing

An **event** type signal T (or "pure" signal) is an always *true* boolean signal. Hence "not T" denotes the boolean signal with clock T which always carries the value *false*. Given any signal X,

    T := event X

defines the **event** type signal T whose occurrences are simultaneous with those of X: it represents the clock of X. The variation

    T := when B

of the **when** operator defines the **event** type signal T which is present whenever the boolean signal B is present and has the value *true* and delivers nothing otherwise; it is equivalent to "T := B when B". Constraints may be defined on the clocks of signals; in this paper, the following notations are used:

X ^= Y   X and Y have the same clock;

X ^< Y   X is no more frequent than Y, which is equivalent to X ^= (X when event Y).

Finally, various kinds of *timers* will be useful, and some of them are listed below:

    Y := X in]S,T]   (i)
    N := #X in]S,T]   (ii)

The expression (i) delivers those present X's which occur within the left-open and right-closed interval]S,T], where S and T are both pure signals. Here follows a diagram showing the behaviour of this macro, we added the boolean signal "in]S,T]" which is delivered when X,S, or T is present, and is *true* within intervals]S,T] and *false* otherwise (this boolean is called BELONGS_TO_INTERVAL in the expansion of this macro we show below):

```
        X :  1  2  ⊥  ⊥  3  4  1  ⊥  5  6  9  ...
        S :  ⊥  ⊥  t  t  ⊥  ⊥  ⊥  ⊥  ⊥  t  ⊥  ...
        T :  t  ⊥  ⊥  ⊥  ⊥  t  ⊥  ⊥  ⊥  ⊥  t  ...
 in ]S,T] :  f  f  f  t  t  t  f  ⊥  f  f  t  ...
        Y :  ⊥  ⊥  ⊥  ⊥  3  4  ⊥  ⊥  ⊥  ⊥  9  ...
```

Expression (ii) counts the occurrences of X within the mentioned interval and is reset
to zero every S; this signal is delivered exactly when equation (i) delivers its output.
Expanding these macros and their variations on the shape of the considered intervals
([S,T[, [S,T], etc...) into the primitive SIGNAL statements is easily done. For instance,
(i) is defined via the following SIGNAL module:

```
(|(| IN_S_T ^= (S default T default (event X))
   |(| HITTING_S_T := (not T) default S default IN_S_T
     | IN_S_T := HITTING_S_T $1 init false |)|)
  | Y := X when IN_S_T |)
```

The hierarchy of submodules is depicted by the amount of |. This program is composed
of two blocks. The meaning of the second one (last equation) is immediate, thus we concentrate on the first one which purpose is to produce the boolean IN_S_T (corresponding
to "in]S,T]" discussed above). The first equation indicates when this signals has to
be delivered. The block composed of the equations 2 and 3 delivers the value of IN_S_T:
the boolean signal HITTING_S_T corresponds to "in [S,T[".

2.3   A few examples

The little programs implementing the formulae (4,5) illustrated how SIGNAL can be
used to specify flows of computations and the emission of events that can result. In this
subsection, we discuss other aspects of the language.

Specifying logical temporal properties: a single token buffer

Consider a memory with content M, which can be written (signal WRITE) and read (signal
READ):

```
(1)    (| M := WRITE default (M $1 init any)
(2)    | READ := M when (event READ) |)
```

The first instruction expresses that the memory M is refreshed when WRITE is received,
otherwise the previous value (M$1) is kept. Note that the clock of M is not entirely
determined, it only has to be more frequent than that of WRITE. The second equation
expresses that, when reading is wanted (event READ), it actually occurs and provides
us with a READ signal carrying the value of M. Consequently, the clock of M has to be
more frequent that that of READ. To proceed further on, let us encode the status (being
written or being read) of the memory as follows:

```
(3)   FULL := (event WRITE) default (not (event READ))
```

Now suppose that writing in the memory is allowed only when the previous value of the
memory has been read. This constraint is expressed by the following equation:

```
(4)   WRITE ^= when (not (FULL $1))
```

Conversely, if we want any written value to be read at most once, we have to write:

```
(5)   READ ^= when (FULL $1)
```

Finally, putting these three additional equations together specifies a single token buffer.

Specifying timing constraints

Assume now that the single token buffer is being used as a mailbox by some other module and it is desired that, when stored, a message must be read within some specified delay. A corresponding SIGNAL specification is as follows:

```
(| event READ ^< TICK
 | N := #TICK in ]WRITE,READ]
 | N < MAX_TIME |)
```

The first statement expresses that the mailbox can be checked at any TICK instant. The second equation counts the delay between writing and reading the message in terms of TICKs. Finally, the last statement expresses that the constraint (N < MAX_TIME) must be satisfied.

Basic problems

As the two above examples show, SIGNAL programs generally express *constraints* on the behaviors of their involved signals. This makes the composition of SIGNAL programs fairly obvious[2]. On the other hand, SIGNAL programs will generally attempt to specify real-time systems that are *transducers,* i.e., possess inputs that drive them and produce outputs. Hence implementing a SIGNAL specification consists in constructing a transducer producing all solutions to the considered system of SIGNAL equations. Getting a transducer form out of a SIGNAL specification written as constraints on signals requires a powerful compiler. This compiler must be able to "solve" the SIGNAL systems of equations in some way to transform them into some input/output map. So it has to be a sort of a "formal calculus system". One of the objectives of this paper is to explain informally how such formal calculi can be derived. By the way, other services are immediately provided such as proofs, since there is no distinction between properties to be checked (these are constraints) and programs on which properties must be checked (these are also constraints).

Discussion: expressive power and formal reasoning capability

As illustrated by the examples above, SIGNAL can be used to specify all key features we mentioned as being relevant to Hybrid Systems: computations, events and logic, timing constraints, and their mutual interaction. As far as the current SIGNAL compiler is concerned, the following should be noticed:

- the single token buffer specification involves only synchronization and logic and is thus fully handled by the SIGNAL compiler in the very same way as temporal logic does;

---

[2]this claim is also supported by the formal definition of the communication operator | in the appendix A which is very simple.

- in contrast, expressions such as "X := Y+Z" are handled via rewriting (each occurrence of the left hand-side can be replaced by the expression in the right hand-side), no formal property is handled about real signals, nor about their associated operations;

- finally, no formal calculus about quantitative time is performed by the current SIGNAL formal system, in particular it cannot be proved that performing two successive responses in less than $10\mu s$ results in an overall response time of less than $20\mu s$.

Hence the distinction between specifying and verifying must be emphasized: while the SIGNAL formalism has general expressive power [2], the SIGNAL formal system has limited (although quite powerful) capabilities. In [2, 3] we present a mathematical model for Hybrid Systems and use it to establish the semantics of SIGNAL. In particular it is shown in [2] that SIGNAL has maximum expressive power for Hybrid Systems description. In the next section we show ho to derive formal systems for reasoning about Hybrid Systems defined by SIGNAL.

3 Deriving formal calculi for Hybrid Systems

We first discuss the simple case of "pure" SIGNAL, i.e., of programs involving only synchronization and logic, i.e., event and logical data types. Then we discuss how this simple case can be generalized.

3.1 "Pure" SIGNAL: programs involving only synchronization and logic

Three labels are required to encode the status *absent, true, false*. The finite field $\mathcal{F}_3$ of integers modulo 3 is used for this purpose[3] via the coding:

$$\text{absent} \leftrightarrow 0, \text{ true} \leftrightarrow +1, \text{ false} \leftrightarrow -1$$

Using this coding, we define a mapping from syntactic SIGNAL expressions to equations in $\mathcal{F}_3$ (recall that all signals are of type event, logical). This mapping is shown in table 1. In this table, the first instruction is a sample of a SIGNAL instruction of type (i), other ones are encoded similarly. In the coding of the second instruction, α denotes the current value of the internal state of the delay. Here and in the sequel, the generic notation x' denotes the next value of x. In particular, the coding of the instruction B := A$1 involves two successive values of the state α; this equation expresses that, when a is received ($a^2 = 1$) it is fed into the next value α' of the state otherwise it is unchanged; then b receives the current state when a is received. Finally, clock(P) is the clock calculus of P and $\cup$ denotes conjunction.

---

[3]elements of $\mathcal{F}_3$ are written $\{0, +1, -1\}$

SIGNAL equation	$\mathcal{F}_3$ coding (or "clock calculus")
A or B = event A	$a^2 = b^2$, $ab(a-1)(b-1) = 0$
B := A\$1	$\alpha' = (1-a^2)\alpha + a$, $b = a^2\alpha$
y := x when b	$y = x(-b - b^2)$
y := u default v	$y = u + (1 - u^2)v$
P|Q	clock(P) $\cup$ clock(Q)

Table 1: Encoding "pure" SIGNAL programs

Let us apply this technique to the mailbox example. To simplify the notations, we denote the various signals by their first letter, e.g., w for WRITE, etc... Applying the rules of table 1 to each successive instruction yields

$$
\begin{array}{rlrl}
(1) & \mu' &=& (1 - m^2)\mu + m \ , \ zm = m^2\mu \\
(1) & m &=& w + (1 - w^2)zm \\
(2) & r &=& mr^2 \\
(3) & f &=& w^2 - (1 - w^2)r^2 \\
(\text{FULL \$1}) & \xi' &=& (1 - f^2)\xi + f \ , \ zf = f^2\xi \\
(4) & w^2 &=& zf - f^2 \\
(5) & r^2 &=& -zf - f^2
\end{array}
\qquad (6)
$$

A little algebra allows us to rewrite (6) as follows (comments are written for each equation):

$$
\begin{array}{rcl}
m^2 = f^2 &=& 1 \qquad\qquad \text{fastest clock, always present by convention} \\
f' &=& -f \qquad\qquad \text{FULL is a flip-flop} \\
zm' &=& m \\
w^2 &=& -f - 1 \qquad\quad \text{WRITE} \Leftrightarrow \text{ box full} \\
r^2 &=& f - 1 \qquad\quad\ \text{READ} \Leftrightarrow \text{ box empty} \\
r &=& mr^2 \\
m &=& w + (1 - w^2)zm \quad \text{M stores the written value}
\end{array}
\qquad (7)
$$

While (6) was given as a fixpoint equation, i.e., in an implicit form, (7) is in explicit form: reading the equations from top to down yields an execution mode. This explicit form reveals that the single-token is *not* a transducer: we cannot consider that WRITE acts as an input and READ is the output. Instead, FULL acting as a flip-flop drives the synchronization, and the additional input is the *value* carried by WRITE, not its clock. We say that (7) is a *solved form* of (6). Deriving (7) from (6) amounts to applying elimination techniques to polynomial functions over $\mathcal{F}_3$. When the specified system actually was equivalent to a transducer, calculating the solved form provides us with this equivalent transducer. A very efficient version of this technique has been developed for the SIGNAL compiler [13, 7].

3.2 Developing formal calculi for general Hybrid Systems

Consider the following SIGNAL program:

```
input   R:  3  ⊥  ⊥  4  ⊥  ⊥  ⊥  1  5  ⊥  ⊥  ⊥  ⊥   etc...
output  N:  3  2  1  4  3  2  1  1  5  4  3  2  1   etc...
```

Table 2: UPSAMPLING in SIGNAL

```
(| N := R default (ZN-1)
 | ZN := N$1
 | R ^= when (ZN=1) |)
```

In this program, R is assumed to be a strictly positive integer signal, and ZN has initial value 1. The behaviour of this program is depicted in table 2. This program serves as a basic mechanism for data dependent *upsampling* of the input signal R. It is a particular and powerful feature of the SIGNAL formalism that programs with upsampling can be specified, see [2] for an extensive discussion about this aspect. Two domains are encountered, namely the positive integers R, N, ZN, and the boolean (ZN=1).

Hence for general HS or SIGNAL programs the situation is drastically more difficult: infinite domains are involved such as integers, reals, etc... So the systems of equations corresponding to general SIGNAL programs will be *approximately* solved using a technique we shall describe now informally. We describe now how the above UPSAMPLING program is actually handled by the current SIGNAL compiler. While most of the formalisms for real-time or Hybrid Systems hide computations inside actions that are viewed as black-boxes [14, 10, 11], we refuse to do so, since such actions turn out to influence the real-time behaviour (comparing a real signal to a threshold can be a mechanism to produce interruptions). The following general procedure is proposed to overcome this difficulty:

1. Select the domains for which you want to provide a formal system; we already discussed this issue in the two preceding sections.

2. Equations involving other domains can be handled in the weakest way, namely via syntax-based rewriting; syntax-based rewriting algorithms amount to handling directed graphs; but these graphs vary dynamically according to the clock of the considered instant, we call them *dynamical graphs*.

The interested reader is referred to [3, 4] for details and formal definitions of dynamical graphs, we concentrate here on an informal discussion of the UPSAMPLING example. The coding of the three instructions of this program is given in table 3 (again we denote by B the boolean expression (ZN=1)). The notation $x \rightarrow y$ means that y depends on x when both are present, i.e., $x^2 y^2 = 1$. Similarly, the notation $x \xrightarrow{h^2} y$ means that y depends on x when $x^2 y^2 h^2 = 1$ holds; this latter notation is for instance used in the coding of the **default** instruction. Some comments follow. Capitals are used (e.g., N) to refer to values of present signals, while variables of the clock calculus are written in lower cases. Values of present signals depend on their clock (e.g., $n^2 \rightarrow$ N). The second line of the conditional dependency graph is the coding of the **default**: the double dependency $R \rightarrow N \xleftarrow{1-r^2} ZN$ is that between values, and the second one $n^2 r^2 \rightarrow N$ expresses that,

clock calculus	conditional dependency graph
$n^2 = r^2 + (1-r^2)zn^2$	$n^2 \rightarrow \text{N}, r^2 \rightarrow \text{R}, zn^2 \rightarrow \text{ZN},$
	$\text{R} \rightarrow \text{N} \xleftarrow{1-r^2} \text{ZN}, n^2r^2 \rightarrow \text{N}$
$zn^2 = n^2$	
$b^2 = zn^2$	$b^2 \rightarrow b, \text{ZN} \rightarrow b$
$r^2 = -b - b^2$	

Table 3: Encoding the UPSAMPLING program

to compute the output N it is needed to know the clock deciding which dependency will be in force at the considered instant.

This coding is hybrid in nature: two different algebras are involved, namely the algebra of polynomial expressions in $\mathcal{F}_3$ variables, and labelled directed graphs. These graphs specify evaluation schemes for run time. Based on the actual syntactic form of the clock calculus, it is also possible to associate a graph with the clock calculus. Performing this for the UPSAMPLING program yields

$$r^2 \rightarrow n^2 \xleftarrow{1-r^2} zn^2 \ (= n^2 = b^2)$$
$$b \rightarrow r^2$$

Combining this graph with the preceding one yields for instance the circuit $b \rightarrow r^2 \rightarrow n^2 = b^2 \rightarrow b$ which has a clock equal to $b^2r^2 = r^2 \neq 0$. Thus combining these two graphs does not provide a partial order, so no evaluation scheme is derived at this point.

To overcome this *we use the calculus of $\mathcal{F}_3$ to replace the present equations of the clock calculus by other ones that are equivalent, in such a way that the combined resulting graphs be gobally circuitfree.* For instance, we can replace the clock calculus of the UPSAMPLING program by its solved form

$$zn^2 = n^2 = b^2 \ , \ r^2 = -b - b^2$$

which yields the graph with a single branch $b \rightarrow r^2$. The resulting global graph is finally (arrows without input nodes denote inputs of the evaluation scheme):

$$\begin{aligned}
\text{(input clock)} \quad &\rightarrow b^2 = n^2 = zn^2 \rightarrow b \ , \ b^2 \rightarrow \text{ZN} \\
\text{(input: memory content)} \quad &\rightarrow \text{ZN} \rightarrow b \rightarrow r^2 \\
\text{(input: value of R)} \quad &r^2 \rightarrow \text{R} \ , \quad \rightarrow \text{R} \\
&\text{ZN} \xrightarrow{1-r^2} \text{N} \ , \ b^2 \rightarrow \text{N} \ , \ r^2 \rightarrow \text{N} \ , \ \text{R} \rightarrow \text{N}
\end{aligned}$$

No circuit is exhibited, so that a partial order can be associated with this graph. It is interesting to note that the input clock is that of the output N, and that only the value carried by R is an input: UPSAMPLING runs according to the demand driven mode.

Again, the method we presented here informally can be extended to other algebras. The current SIGNAL compiler is powered with a very fast implementation of the above procedure, see [13, 7]. Finally, the reader is referred to [4] for a formal presentation of the SIGNAL formal system in its present form.

3.3 Extension to other domains: quantitative real-time

We consider again the UPSAMPLING program, but we assume now that its input R is a positive *bounded* integer signal. Since all signals have now finite domains nothing really new happens compared to the elementary case of "pure" SIGNAL, for instance we may translate bounded integers into vectors of booleans. However we find it more convenient to use codings that are tightly tailored to each of these domains, since the resulting coding will generally be more compact, thus memory saving and efficient calculations should result; in particular, the very efficient formal calculi developed for $\mathcal{F}_3$ [13, 7] generalize to any $\mathcal{F}_p$.

Thus the boolean signal (ZN=1) is encoded using $\mathcal{F}_3$ as before. Similarly, the finite field $\mathcal{F}_p$ of integers modulo p can be used with p large enough to encode the integer signals R, N, ZN with the following mapping:

$$\text{absent} \leftrightarrow 0, \ 1 \leftrightarrow 1, \cdots, \ p-1 \leftrightarrow p-1$$

In this coding, clocks of integer signals are recovered as follows

$$\text{R absent} \leftrightarrow r^{p-1} = 0 \ , \ \text{R present} \leftrightarrow r^{p-1} = 1$$

From these remarks, the coding of the UPSAMPLING program follows (we denote by B the boolean signal (ZN=1):

$$n \ = \ r + (1 - r^{p-1})(zn - 1) \quad \text{(i)} \quad \text{first instruction}$$

$$
\begin{aligned}
\nu' &= (1 - n^{p-1})\nu + n \\
zn &= n^{p-1}\nu
\end{aligned}
\quad \text{(ii)} \quad \text{second instruction} \quad\quad (8)
$$

$$
\begin{aligned}
b &= zn^{p-1}\left(1 + (zn - 1)^{p-1}\right) \quad \text{(iii)} \quad \text{B as a function of ZN} \\
r^{p-1} &= -r - r^2 \quad\quad\quad\quad\quad\quad\quad \text{(iv)} \quad \text{last instruction}
\end{aligned}
$$

However in doing this, a new difficulty appears. Equations (i,ii) are polynomial equations within $\mathcal{F}_p$ and thus can be handled in a way similar to that of pure SIGNAL programs. Unfortunately, equation (iii) is a function mapping some $\mathcal{F}_p$-expression into $\mathcal{F}_3$; similarly, equation (iv) is a function mapping some $\mathcal{F}_3$-expression into $\mathcal{F}_p$. This is again a hybrid coding similar to that of the preceding subsection. We can handle it in two different ways.

1. Since B,ZN,R only are involved in the "hybrid" equations (iii,iv), we may first eliminate ν and N from equations (i,ii). This is equivalent to projecting the dynamical system (i,ii) onto the components (zn, r) only, and is generally performed using elimination techniques in $\mathcal{F}_p$ via efficient algorithms as mentioned before. In our case this yields the unique equation

$$zn' = r + (1 - r^{p-1})(zn - 1)$$

   which we handle in combination with (iii,iv) via exhaustive scanning. In this way of doing, efficient algorithms can be called for to project each homogeneous subsystem (here (i,ii)) onto its interfaces to other homogeneous ones (here B,ZN,R). Then the problem reduces to that of standard model checking techniques on the joint behaviour of the set of all such interfaces.

2. Perform first as before the reduction to the interfaces of the homogeneous subsystems. The remaining "hybrid" equations are then approximately solved using the graph method of the preceding subsection. This is a less powerful but likely faster method of compilation.

As sketched on this example, formal calculi can be developed for properties relevant to synchronization, logic, and quantitative timing. In particular, (qualitative and quantitative) *real-time specifications for discrete event systems can be synthesized.*

4 Conclusion

We have presented the SIGNAL formalism to specify Hybrid Systems. SIGNAL is currently used to specify and program real-time systems [13] according to the principles of synchrony [1].

SIGNAL is currently available under two different versions that were developed with different objectives. The INRIA H2 SIGNAL system provides the interface used in this article, and produces the intermediate level hierarchical code we have discussed. Sequential FORTRAN or C code is currently produced. Developments on distributed implementation are in progress based on this version. Tools for proving dynamical properties will be integrated in a short time. The CNET-TNI V3 version is commercially available from TNI Inc., Brest, France. SILDEX[4], a X-windows based graphical environment is provided for both program editing and on-line monitoring and supervision of the execution. C, FORTRAN, or ADA code is produced. Experiments have been performed based on this version to produce distributed OCCAM code for a multi-Transputer system. The SIGNAL environment has been experimented on significant applications in the area of signal processing and control: a speech recognition system, a radar system, a digital watch, a rail road crossing, an aircraft control system, were the major ones.

We have discussed the expressive power of SIGNAL and have illustrated its generality, formal studies are also available in [2] to support this claim.

We have presented an original and general method for deriving formal calculi for Hybrid Systems. The central notion of this method is that of *dynamical graph* and is used in the current SIGNAL compiler to handle synchronization, logic, and data dependencies.

Several directions for future research are currently pursued. Improving the efficiency and power of the formal system that handles $\mathcal{F}_3$–based dynamical graphs is a key issue to fast and efficient compilation [12]. Deriving efficient systems to handle bounded integers will open the route to quantitative real-time: a major issue is to handle the tradeoff efficiency/generality of such formal calculi. Finally, as lengthly discussed in [2], the SIGNAL formalism is already very close to models of stochastic processes: adding a *single* instruction to SIGNAL provided us with the SIGN*alea* extension [5]. SIGN*alea*

---

[4]SILDEX is a TradeMark of TNI.

is able to specify and handle various probabilistic real-time systems such as queuing networks or uncertain real-time information processing systems.

Appendix

A   A *trace* model for HS and a semantics of SIGNAL

In this appendix, a mathematical model for HS is presented, and used to formally define SIGNAL. The reader is referred to Section 2 for the motivation of the following definitions.

A.1   Histories, signals, clocks

Consider an alphabet (finite set) A of typed variables called *ports*. For each $a \in A$, $\mathcal{D}_a$ is the domain of values (integers, reals, booleans...) that may be carried by a at every instant. Introduce

$$\mathcal{D}_A = \bigcup_{a \in A} (\mathcal{D}_a \cup \{\bot\})$$

where the additional symbol $\bot$ denotes the absence of the value associated with a port at a given instant. For two sets A and B, the notation $A \to B$ will denote the set of all maps defined from A into B. Using this notation, we introduce the following objects.

Events.   Events specify the values carried by a set of ports at a considered instant. The set of the A-events (or "events" for short when no confusion is likely to occur) is defined as

$$\mathcal{E}_A = A \to \mathcal{D}_A$$

Events will be generally denoted by ϵ and their domain by $\mathcal{D}(\epsilon)$. We shall denote by $\bot$ the "silent" event ϵ such that $\epsilon(a) = \bot \ \forall a \in \mathcal{D}(\epsilon)$.

Traces.   Traces are infinite sequences of events. Let $\mathbf{N}_+ = \{1, 2, ...\}$ denote the set of integers, then the set of A-*traces* (or simply "traces") is defined as

$$\Theta_A = \mathbf{N}_+ \to \mathcal{E}_A$$

Compressions.   The *compression* of an A-trace T (deleting the silent events) is defined as the (unique) A-trace S such that:

$$S_n = T_{k_n}$$

where

$$k_0 = \min\{m \geq 0 : \ T_m \neq \bot\}, \ k_n = \min\{m > k_{n-1} : \ T_m \neq \bot\}$$

where $\min \emptyset = +\infty$ by convention. The compression of a trace T will be denoted by $T\!\downarrow$.

Histories and signals. The condition

$$T{\downarrow} \;=\; T'{\downarrow}$$

defines an equivalence relation on traces we shall denote by $T \sim T'$. The corresponding equivalence classes are called *histories*. The set of all possible histories on A will be denoted by Ω_A, so that we have[5]

$$\Omega_A = (\Theta_A)_{/\sim}$$

Elements of Ω_A will be generically denoted by ω_A or simply ω when no confusion can occur. While the notion of trace refers to a particular environment (since the $\perp$'s are explicitly listed), the notion of history does not. Since

$$\Omega_A = [\mathbf{N}_+ \to (A \to \mathcal{D}_A)]_{/\sim}$$

any $\omega_A \in \Omega_A$ may be written as

$$\omega_A = (\omega_a)_{a \in A} \tag{9}$$

and the ω_a's are termed *signals*. Hence a signal is a component of a history specified by selecting a particular port in the alphabet A. The notion of "signal" has been informally discussed in section 2-(1), where we motivated the definition of signals and histories as equivalence classes with respect to the relation $\sim$.

Clocks. Extend the domains $\mathcal{D}_a$ with another distinguished value $\top$, intended to encode the status "present" regardless of any particular value. Consider the map $chronos_{\mathcal{D}} \in \mathcal{D}_A \to \{\perp, \top\}$ defined by

$$chronos_{\mathcal{D}}(\perp) = \perp, \; chronos_{\mathcal{D}}(x) = \top \text{ for } x \neq \perp$$

For each event $\epsilon \in \mathcal{E}_A$, there is a unique map in $\mathcal{E}_A \to \mathcal{E}_A$ making the following diagram commutative, denote it by $chronos_{\mathcal{E}}$:

$$
\begin{array}{ccc}
 & A & \\
\epsilon \nearrow & & \searrow chronos_{\mathcal{E}}(\epsilon) \\
\mathcal{D}_A & \xrightarrow{chronos_{\mathcal{D}}} & \mathcal{D}_A
\end{array}
$$

Similarly, there is a unique map in $\Theta_A \to \Theta_A$, we denote by $chronos_\Theta$, making the following diagram commutative

$$
\begin{array}{ccc}
 & \mathbf{N}_+ & \\
T \nearrow & & \searrow chronos_\Theta(T) \\
\mathcal{E}_A & \xrightarrow{chronos_{\mathcal{E}}} & \mathcal{E}_A
\end{array}
$$

This map satisfies the condition $T_1 \sim T_2 \;\Rightarrow\; chronos_\Theta(T_1) \sim chronos_\Theta(T_2)$, so that it induces a map in $\Omega_A \to \Omega_A$ we shall now denote by *chronos*: the *chronos* of a history is another history which summarizes the status {present/absent} of each of its signals (i.e. components).

Now, given $\omega \in \Omega_A$ and $a \in A$, consider the signal of port a of the history $chronos(\omega)$: this signal summarizes the *relative* status present/absent of the signal ω_a given the other signals involved in the history ω. We shall call this signal the *clock* of ω_a, or the clock of a for short when no confusion is likely to occur, and denote it by $clock(\omega_a)$ or $clock(a)$.

---

[5] $_{/\sim}$ denotes here the quotient space by the relation $\sim$

A.2 HS

Definition of HS. A HS is simply a subset

$$\Omega \subset \Omega_A$$

of the set of all histories on A. In other words, we consider a SIGNAL program, as a way to specify "legal" histories.

Restricting HS. Consider a subset A' of the alphabet A. The inclusion $A' \subset A$ induces a projection from $\mathcal{E}_A$ onto $\mathcal{E}_{A'}$ we denote by $\epsilon \longrightarrow \epsilon_{!!A'}$. Following the same argument as for the definition of clocks, we derive the following family of *restrictions* we generically denote by $\cdot_{!!A'}$. First, the following commutative diagram

$$
\begin{array}{ccc}
 & \mathbf{N_+} & \\
T \nearrow & & \searrow T_{!!A'} \\
\mathcal{E}_A & \xrightarrow{\;!!A'\;} & \mathcal{E}_{A'}
\end{array}
$$

uniquely defines the restriction $T \longrightarrow T_{!!A'}$ on traces. Since $T_1 \sim T_2 \;\Rightarrow\; (T_1)_{!!A'} \sim (T_2)_{!!A'}$ holds, a restriction on histories $\omega \longrightarrow \omega_{!!A'}$ may be defined, which finally yields a restriction on HS we denote by

$$\Omega \longrightarrow \Omega_{!!A'}$$

This restriction maps the set of HS defined over the alphabet A onto the set of HS defined over the alphabet A'. The HS $\Omega_{!!A'}$ is called the *restriction* of Ω to (the subalphabet) A': only the signals with ports in A' are visible from outside and may be used for HS communication we shall define next.

HS communication. Consider two HS Ω_1, Ω_2 respectively defined over the alphabets A_1 and A_2. Set $A = A_1 \cup A_2$. Then $\Omega_1 | \Omega_2$ will denote the maximal[6] HS Ω defined over the alphabet A satisfying the following conditions:

$$\Omega_{!!A_1} \subseteq \Omega_1$$
$$\Omega_{!!A_2} \subseteq \Omega_2$$

In other words, the communication constrains the signals in Ω_1 and Ω_2 of shared port to be identical (i.e. to be present simultaneously and then carry the same value). This is exactly what we wanted while discussing the example of eqns (2,3).

A.3 The definition of SIGNAL

According to the preceding section, in order to specify an HS over a given alphabet, we have to describe a subset of all histories that can be built upon this alphabet. Since histories are defined as equivalence classes of traces with respect to the relation $\sim$, this may be done by *listing a family of constraints on the set of all traces* that can be built on this alphabet. The equivalence classes of the so specified traces are the specified histories. This is what we shall do next.

---

[6]with respect to the order by inclusion $\Omega' \subseteq \Omega$ defined on HS

Instruction (i):   R(x1,...xp)

$$\forall n \in \mathbf{N}_+, \forall i \ : \ \mathtt{xi}_n \neq \bot$$
$$\forall n \in \mathbf{N}_+ \ : \ R(\mathtt{x1}_n, ..., \mathtt{xp}_n) \text{ holds}$$

Here, the notation $\mathtt{xi}_n$ denotes the value carried by the port with name $\mathtt{xi}$ at the n-th instant of the considered trace. This notation will be further used in the sequel of this subsection.

Instruction (ii):   y := x $1 x0

$$\forall n \in \mathbf{N}_+ \ : \ \mathtt{x}_n \neq \bot$$
$$\forall n > 1 \ : \ \mathtt{y}_n = \mathtt{x}_{n-1}$$
$$\mathtt{y}_1 = \mathtt{x0}$$

Instruction (iii):   y := x when b

$$\forall n \in \mathbf{N}_+, \ \mathtt{y}_n = \begin{cases} \text{if } \mathtt{x}_n \neq \bot \text{ and } \mathtt{b}_n = true \ \text{ then } \mathtt{x}_n \\ \text{else } \bot \end{cases}$$

Instruction (iv):   y := u default v

$$\forall n \in \mathbf{N}_+, \ \mathtt{y}_n = \begin{cases} \text{if } \mathtt{u}_n \neq \bot \ \text{ then } \mathtt{u}_n \\ \text{else if } \mathtt{u}_n = \bot \text{ and } \mathtt{v}_n \neq \bot \ \text{ then } \mathtt{v}_n \\ \text{else } \bot \end{cases}$$

Instruction (v):   P | Q
We already defined the operator | on HS.

Instruction (vi):   P !!   x1,...,xp
We already defined the restriction on HS.

ACKNOWLEDGEMENT: the authors gratefully acknowledge Oded Maler and an anonymus reviewer for constructive criticism and fruitful remarks on preliminary versions of this paper.

References

[1] A. BENVENISTE, G. BERRY, "Real-Time systems design and programming", *Another look at real-time programming*, special section of *Proc. of the IEEE,* to appear Sept. 1991.

[2] A. BENVENISTE, P. LE GUERNIC, Y. SOREL, M. SORINE, "A denotational theory of synchronous communicating systems", INRIA Research Report 685, Rennes, France, 1987, to appear in *Information and Computation.*

[3] A. BENVENISTE, P. LE GUERNIC, "Hybrid Dynamical Systems Theory and the SIGNAL Language", *IEEE transactions on Automatic Control*, 35(5), May 1990, pp. 535–546.

[4] A. BENVENISTE, P. LE GUERNIC, C. JACQUEMOT, *Synchronous programming with events and relations: the* SIGNAL *language and its semantics*, IRISA Research Report 459, Rennes, France, 1989, to appear in *Science of Computer Programming*.

[5] A. BENVENISTE, "Constructive probability and the SIGNalea language", IRISA res. rep., 1991.

[6] B. BUCHBERGER, "Gröbner Bases: An Algorithmic Method in Polynomial Ideal Theory" N.K. Bose (ed.), Multidimensional Systems Theory, 184-232, D. Reidel Publishing Company.

[7] L. BESNARD, Thesis, IFSIC-IRISA, 1991.

[8] F. BOUSSINOT, R. DE SIMONE, "The ESTEREL language", *Another look at real-time programming*, special section of *Proc. of the IEEE*, to appear Sept. 1991.

[9] N. HALBWACHS, P. CASPI, D. PILAUD, "The synchronous dataflow programming language LUSTRE", *Another look at real-time programming*, special section of *Proc. of the IEEE*, to appear Sept. 1991.

[10] T.A. HENZINGER, Z. MANNA, A. PNUELI, "An Interleaving Model for Real-time", Jersalem Conf. on Information Technology 1990, IEEE Computer Society Press.

[11] T.A. HENZINGER, Z. MANNA, A. PNUELI, "Temporal proof methodologies for Real-time systems", POPL'91.

[12] M. LE BORGNE, A. BENVENISTE, P. LE GUERNIC, "Polynomial Ideal Theory Methods in Discrete Event, and Hybrid Dynamical Systems", in *Proceedings of the 28th IEEE Conference on Decision and Control*, IEEE Control Systems Society, Volume 3 of 3, 1989, pp. 2695–2700.

[13] P. LE GUERNIC, T. GAUTIER, M. LE BORGNE, C. LE MAIRE, "Programming real-time applications with SIGNAL", *Another look at real-time programming*, special section of *Proc. of the IEEE,* to appear Sept. 1991.

[14] X. NICOLLIN, J. SIFAKIS, S. YOVINE, "From ATP to Timed Graphs and Hybrid Systems", REX workshop "Real-Time, theory in practice", Mook, The Netherlands, June 3-7, 1991.

Towards an adequate notion of observation *

Gilles Bernot   **Michel Bidoit**   **Teodor Knapik**

LIENS C.N.R.S. U.R.A. 1327
Ecole Normale Supérieure
45 Rue d'Ulm
F − 75230 PARIS Cedex 05 France
e-mail: [bernot, bidoit, knapik] @dmi.ens.fr (Internet) or @frulm63.bitnet (Earn)

Abstract

One can attempt to solve the problem of establishing the correctness of some
software w.r.t. a formal specification at the semantical level. For this purpose, the
semantics of an algebraic specification should be the class of all algebras which correspond to the correct realizations of the specification. We approach this goal by
defining an **observational satisfaction relation** which is less restrictive than the
usual satisfaction relation. The idea is that the validity of an equational axiom
should depend on an **observational equality**, instead of the usual equality. We
show that it is not reasonable to expect an observational equality to be a congruence, hence we define an **observational algebra** as an algebra equipped with an
observational equality which is an equivalence relation but not necessarily a congruence. Since terms may represent computations, our notion of observation depends
on a set of observable terms. From a careful case study it follows that this requires
to take into account the **continuations** of suspended evaluations of observable terms.
The bridge between observations and observational equality is provided by an **indistinguishability relation** defined on the carriers of an algebra according to the
observations. In the general case, this relation is neither transitive nor a congruence.

1   Introduction

A fundamental aim of formal specifications is to provide a rigorous basis to establish
software correctness. Intuitively, a program P is a correct realization of a specification
SP if P satisfies all properties required by SP. On the other hand SP should be some
description of all its correct realizations. These notions can be, probably in the best

---

*This work is partially supported by ESPRIT Working Group COMPASS and C.N.R.S. GDR de
Programmation.

way, handled within an observational framework. Consequently, the aim of this paper is to provide an observational semantics of algebraic specifications so that the class of observational models of SP matches as well as possible the class of its correct realizations.

We may follow one of at least two directions in the development of an observational approach. The first of them was opened by Sannella and Tarlecki [16] (but also independently by Pepper [14]) and further generalized in [17]. The authors of these papers define the class of observational models (*behaviours* in their terminology) as an extension of the class of the usual models by an equivalence relation (called *observational equivalence*) between algebras, according to some observations Obs. This leads to a somewhat heterogeneous framework where the observational features are directly based on the usual ones. In particular the "observational consistency" always coincides with the usual one. These shortcomings can be avoided in an observational approach developed according to the second direction which mainly aims at defining a true observational satisfaction relation as in [8], [13] or [15]. Consequently, our paper follows this direction.

---

spec :	SWE	
	use : LIST, NAT	
sort :	Set	
generated by :		
	$\varnothing : \rightarrow$ Set	
	ins: Nat Set $\rightarrow$ Set	
operations :		
	$\_\in\_$: Nat Set $\rightarrow$ Bool	
	del : Nat Set $\rightarrow$ Set	
	enum : Set $\rightarrow$ List	
axioms :		
	ψ_1 :	ins(x,ins(x,s)) = ins(x,s)
	ψ_2 :	ins(x,ins(y,s)) = ins(y,ins(x,s))
	ψ_3 :	del(x, $\varnothing$) = $\varnothing$
	ψ_4 :	del(x, ins(x, s)) = del(x, s)
	ψ_5 :	x $\neq$ y $\Rightarrow$ del(x, ins(y, s)) = ins(y, del(x, s))
	ψ_6 :	x $\in \varnothing$ = false
	ψ_7 :	x $\in$ ins(x,s) = true
	ψ_8 :	x $\neq$ y $\Rightarrow$ x $\in$ ins(y,s) = x $\in$ s
	ψ_9 :	enum($\varnothing$) = nil
	ψ_{10} :	enum(ins(x,s)) = cons(x, enum(s))

Figure 1.1: Specification of sets with **enum**

In our approach, an equation $t = t'$ is observationally satisfied by an algebra if for any assignment ν of variables, the results of the evaluations of both $t\nu$ and $t'\nu$ are observationally equal. Unlike in similar approaches, we do not require an observational equality to be a congruence. This allows to better capture the correct realizations of specifications with some "loose" (underspecified) operations such as choose : Set $\rightarrow$ Nat: this operation, when applied to a nonempty set, should return an element of the set. For instance the realization of sets by lists such that choose returns the head of a list, should be considered as a correct realization of this specification. In this realization the lists $\langle n, m \rangle$ and $\langle m, n \rangle$ are observationally equal, since they are viewed as the same set. However $choose(\langle n, m \rangle)$ and $choose(\langle m, n \rangle)$ produces two Nat values which should not be observationally equal. The use of an observational equality being non necessarily a congruence allows to have an observational consistency which does not coincide with the usual one. For instance, the inconsistent specification SWE of sets with enum (see Figure 1.1) can be declared observationally consistent, provided that the inconsistencies are not observed. This is impossible within the approach of [17] since SWE has no behaviours whatever observations are. An observational model of this specification will be described in the following sections. This example points out that in our approach, some data types can be specified in a more straightforward way with less risk of introducing unexpected inconsistencies.

Our main contribution is to provide a suitable notion of observation. We claim that this notion should reflect at the specification level the following paradigm: a user observes the results of some specific computations. Since computations may be represented as evaluations of terms, the part of a specification devoted to observations should be some description of a set of (observable) terms. As soon as only some computations can be observed, it is impossible to distinguish some values from some others. For this reason our approach fully agrees with the following **Indistinguishability Assumption**:

Two values are indistinguishable with respect to some observations when it is impossible to establish they are different using these observations.

The bridge between observations and the observational equality is provided by an indistinguishability relation which is defined further according to the above assumption. From a careful case study it follows that this requires to take into account the **continuations** of suspended evaluations of observable terms. Even if very reasonable, we show that this assumption has some surprising consequences.

2 Basic Definitions

We assume that the reader is familiar with algebraic specifications (see e.g. [9] and [5]). A **signature** Σ consists of a finite set of **sort** symbols **Sorts**$[\Sigma]$ and a finite set of **operation names with arities** **Ops**$[\Sigma]$ (also denoted by Σ). We assume that each signature Σ is provided with an S-sorted set of variables X such that X_s is countable for each $s \in S$. We use the following conventions. Given a signature Σ (resp. Σ'), S (resp. S') denotes Sorts$[\Sigma]$ (resp. Sorts$[\Sigma']$) and X (resp. X') denotes the variables of Σ (resp. of Σ'). A **signature morphism** $\sigma : \Sigma \rightarrow \Sigma'$ maps each sort of S to a sort of S', each operation $(f : s_1 \ldots s_n \rightarrow s) \in \Sigma$ to an operation $\sigma(f)$ of Σ' with the arity $\sigma(s_1) \ldots \sigma(s_n) \rightarrow \sigma(s)$ and each variable of X_s to a variable of $X'_{\sigma(s)}$. Moreover, we assume that a signature morphism is always injective on variables[1]. The signatures with the signature morphisms form the usual category of signatures, written **Sig**.

The definition of **(total)** Σ-**algebras** and Σ-**morphisms** is the standard one. The **category of all** Σ-**algebras** is denoted by **Alg**$[\Sigma]$. Given an S-sorted set E, we denote by $\mathbf{T_{\Sigma(E)}}$ the free Σ-algebra over E. For instance $\mathbf{T_\Sigma}$ (resp. $\mathbf{T_{\Sigma(X)}}$) denotes the Σ-**algebra of ground terms** (resp. **terms with variables**), $\mathbf{T_{\Sigma(A)}}$ (resp. $\mathbf{T_{\Sigma(A \cup X)}}$) denotes the Σ-**algebra of ground terms** (resp. **terms with variables**) **over the carriers of a** Σ-**algebra**

---

[1]Without this assumption, which in a stronger form appears in [7] (page 36, Definition 55), it would be impossible to establish the satisfaction condition for most institutions.

A. Given a signature morphism $\sigma : \Sigma \to \Sigma'$ the σ-**reduct** of a Σ'-algebra A', written $A'|_{\sigma}$ is defined in the usual way and extending it on Σ'-morphisms we obtain the **forgetful functor** $-|_{\sigma} : \text{Alg}[\Sigma'] \to \text{Alg}[\Sigma]$. In the particular case of an inclusion $\Sigma \subseteq \Sigma'$, the corresponding forgetful functor is written $-|_{\Sigma}$.

From $T_{\Sigma(X)}$, the "=" symbol and connectives ($\neg$, $\vee$, $\wedge$, $\Rightarrow$, etc.) we construct the set **Wff**$[\Sigma]$ of **well formed Σ-formulae**. The satisfaction relation "$\models$" between Σ-algebras and Σ-formulae is the standard one.

A **valuation** is a morphism $\nu : X \to A$ which maps each $x \in X_s$ to a value $x\nu \in A_s$. The set of all valuations from X to A is written **Val**$[X,A]$. A **partial valuation** is a valuation preceded by an inclusion $X_0 \subseteq X$. From the freeness of $T_{\Sigma(X)}$ any valuation (resp. partial valuation) ν followed by the inclusion $A \subseteq T_{\Sigma(A)}$ (resp. $A \subseteq T_{\Sigma(A\cup X)}$) extends to a unique morphism (written ambiguously ν) from $T_{\Sigma(X)}$ to $T_{\Sigma(A)}$ (resp. $T_{\Sigma(A\cup X)}$) which maps each term $t \in (T_{\Sigma(X)})_s$ to a **valued term** $t\nu \in (T_{\Sigma(A)})_s$ (resp. **partially valued term** $t\nu \in (T_{\Sigma(A\cup X)})_s$). The **evaluation morphism** from $T_{\Sigma(A)}$ to A is defined as the unique Σ-morphism which maps each element of $(T_{\Sigma(A)})_s \cap A_s$ to itself. This morphism maps a valued term τ to its **evaluation result** written $\overline{\tau}$.

A **position** p in a term t is a sequence of integers which describe the path from the topmost position of t (denoted by the empty sequence) to the **subterm of t at position p** written $t|_p$. The set of all the positions of t is denoted by **Pos**(t). The replacement of $t|_p$ by a term r in t is written $t[r]_p$. The multiple replacement at parallel positions $p_1, \ldots, p_n$ is written $t[r_1 \ldots r_n]_{p_1 \ldots p_n}$.

Definition 2.1 *An (S-indexed)* **set of contextual variables** *is written* $\diamond$, *where each* $\diamond_s$ *is a singleton* $\{\diamond_s\}$. *A* **multicontext** *(resp.* **context***) over a Σ-algebra A is a partially valued term η with only one (resp. only one occurrence of a) contextual variable. Consequently, the set of all multicontexts over A, written* $MC_{\Sigma(A\cup\diamond)}$ *(the set of all contexts over A is written* $C_{\Sigma(A\cup\diamond)}$*) is defined as follows:*

$$MC_{\Sigma(A\cup\diamond)} = \bigcup_{s\in S} T_{\Sigma(A\cup\{\diamond_s\})}$$

Given $\eta \in MC_{\Sigma(A\cup\diamond)}$ (resp. $\eta \in C_{\Sigma(A\cup\diamond)}$) we can write $\eta : s \to s'$ instead of $\eta \in (T_{\Sigma(A\cup\{\diamond_s\})})_{s'}$. Application of η on $a \in A_s$ is written $\eta[a]$.

3   How to Observe and How to Compare

As mentioned in the introduction we need to define an indistinguishability relation on the carriers of an algebra in order to relax the satisfaction relation. Usually this is done using the concept of observable contexts. Since this concept was given only for sort ([8], [10], [13]) or signature[1] ([1], [4]) observation, we should start by defining it in the situation when we observe an arbitrary set of terms.

In the most usual framework one considers a set of observable sorts S_{Obs} which is a subset of the sorts of a specification. Then an observable context is any context $\eta : s \to s'$ with $s' \in S_{\text{Obs}}$. Given an element $a \in A_s$ we can observe it via η by evaluating $\eta[a]$. Hence we have the following trivial fact:

---

[1]In fact these approaches combine signature and sort observations.

Fact 3.1 *All the elements of a carrier of an algebra have the same observable contexts w.r.t. a set of observable sorts.*

Notice that it is unreasonable to hope that this fact could be extended to term observation. This affirmation is motivated by the specification THREE (c.f. Figure 3.1). Let A be a Sig[THREE]-algebra. It is clear that $g(a^A)$ does not produce an observable value, since $g(a)$ is not an observable term. Consequently, we should consider $g(\diamond)$ as an observable context of b^A and c^A only and, for a similar reason, $f(\diamond)$ as an observable context of a^A and b^A (but not of c^A). It follows from the above that observable contexts cannot be taken into account independently of the elements on which they apply. Therefore, we need to define the observable contexts of a given **element of an algebra**. Notice that such a definition is superfluous for observable sorts.

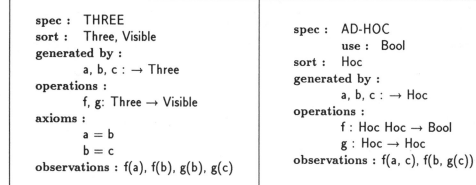

Figure 3.1: Two exotic specifications

Since Fact 3.1 cannot be extended to term observation we have a little trouble to declare some $a, b \in A_s$ indistinguishable. It seems reasonable to compare a and b with the same observable contexts. Thus in the previous example we compare a^A and b^A (resp. b^A and c^A) only via context $f(\diamond)$ (resp. $g(\diamond)$). We also notice that a^A and c^A have no common observable context. Consequently, these two values cannot be compared. However, according to our Indistinguishability Assumption, we do not consider that two elements can either be indistinguishable, distinguishable or incomparable. Our point of view is close to final semantics ([3], [11], [18]): we consider indistinguishable these pairs of elements, for which we do not observe the contrary. This is stated in the definition below (for a while assume already defined the notion of observable contexts):

Definition (comparator, version 1) *We call* **W-comparator** *(or shortly comparator) of elements a and b of a Σ-algebra, an observable context of a and b w.r.t. a set W of Σ-terms. We say that a W-comparator η* **distinguishes** *a and b iff $\overline{\eta[a]} \neq \overline{\eta[b]}$*

We can now state the following definition of indistinguishability:

Definition 3.2 *We say that two elements a and b of a given carrier of a Σ-algebra are* **indistinguishable** *w.r.t. a set of terms W $\in$ $T_{\Sigma(X)}$ (or* **W-indistinguishable***) written $a \sim_w b$, if there is no W-comparator which distinguishes them.*

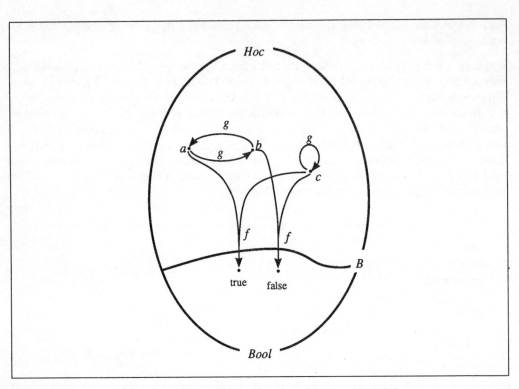

Figure 3.2: A model of the specification AD-HOC

Now, the crucial point is to define the observable contexts of an element of an algebra. Below we make a first attempt of such a definition. Next, this definition will be progressively refined. In this way we are going to introduce the concept of **continuations** which is one of the originalities of our approach.

Definition (observable contexts version 1) *Let* $W \subseteq T_{\Sigma(X)}$ *be a set of terms and* $a \in A$ *be an element of a Σ-algebra. We say that a context $\eta \in C_{\Sigma(A \cup \diamond)}$ is an* **observable context of a**, *if there is a term* $w \in W$, *with valuation* $\nu : X \to A$ *such that* $w\nu$ *has a leaf* l *verifying* $\eta[l] = w\nu$ *and such that l is either the constant of Σ interpreted in A as a or l is already a itself.*

The underlying intuition of this definition is that an instantiated observable term $w\nu$ denotes an "observable calculus" i.e. a calculus whose result can be directly observed. Consequently, an observable context η of a, instantiated by a represents an observable calculus with input a. Unfortunately, it is not adequate enough to only rely on input values. For instance consider the specification AD-HOC (c.f. Figure 3.1). According to the definition, the unique observable context of a^A (resp. b^A) is $f(\diamond, c)$ (resp. $f(\diamond, g(c))$) independently of the Sig[AD-HOC]-algebra A under consideration. Consequently, a^A and b^A are indistinguishable (no comparator) in any algebra A. Consider now the algebra B given in Figure 3.2 and try to partially evaluate in b the observable contexts of a^B and b^B. Since $g(c)$ evaluates to c^B, the evaluations of both $f(\diamond, c)$ and $f(\diamond, g(c))$ yield $f(\diamond, c^B)$. Then the question whether it is not preferable to consider $f(\diamond, c^B)$ as a comparator of a^B and b^B clearly arises. Notice that this comparator distinguishes these two values.

This first version of the definition of observable contexts has also another drawback: the entire carriers of some sorts can be, in an unreasonable way, devoid of observable context, as in the case of the specification PASS-BY (c.f. Figure 3.3). Here the elements of

spec : PASS-BY	
sort : Nat, Hidden, Visible	
generated by :	**spec :** SYM
0: → Nat	**use :** BOOL
succ: Nat → Nat	**sort :** Sym
operations :	**generated by :**
stage-one: Nat → Hidden	a, b : → Sym
stage-two: Hidden → Visible	**operations :**
axioms :	f : Sym Sym → Bool
$0 \neq succ(x)$	**observations :** f(a, a), f(b, b)
$x \neq succ(x) \Rightarrow succ(x) \neq succ(succ(x))$	
observations : stage-two(stage-one(x))	

Figure 3.3: Yet other exotic specifications

A_{Hidden} have no observable contexts in any algebra A. Thus they are all indistinguishable. Consequently, the algebras with the carrier of Hidden reduced to a singleton should be present among the observational models of PASS-BY. However, this could prevent from preserving the observable properties of Nat. In fact, the specification PASS-BY requires all reachable elements of Nat to be distinguishable i.e.

$$\text{stage-two(stage-one(succ}^i(0))) \neq \text{stage-two(stage-one(succ}^j(0)))\quad \text{for } i \neq j$$

should hold in **any** observational model. Of course, this is impossible when the carrier of Hidden is a singleton. We conclude that in the above example we should consider **stage-two($\diamond$)** as an observable context of any element which is reachable by the evaluation of **stage-one(x)** properly instantiated.

The examples PASS-BY and AD-HOC suggest that a better version of the definition of observable contexts should somehow take into account the super-terms of observable terms as well as their partial evaluations. Before to state this version, we need some reminders about partial evaluation.

Definition 3.3 *Let A be a Σ-algebra. We define the **partial evaluation relation**, written $\underset{\mathbf{pEv}}{\rightarrow}$, on $T_{\Sigma(A)}$ as follows. We say that a term $\tau_2 \in T_{\Sigma(A)}$ is the result of the partial evaluation of $\tau_1 \in T_{\Sigma(A)}$, written $\tau_1 \underset{\mathbf{pEv}}{\rightarrow} \tau_2$, if there is a position p in τ_1 such that $\tau_1[\overline{\tau_1|_p}]_p = \tau_2$.*

Fact 3.4 *The reflexive-transitive closure of $\underset{\mathbf{pEv}}{\rightarrow}$, written $\underset{\mathbf{pEv}}{\overset{*}{\rightarrow}}$ is an order.* □

Definition 3.5 *Let $W \subseteq T_{\Sigma(X)}$ be a set of terms and A be a Σ-algebra. The **closure by partial evaluations of W in A**, written $\widetilde{W}^A$, is defined as follows:*

$$\widetilde{W}^A = \{\tau \in T_{\Sigma(A)} \mid \exists\, w \in W\ \exists\, \nu : X \rightarrow A\ \ w\nu \underset{\mathbf{pEv}}{\overset{*}{\rightarrow}} \tau\}$$

The last notion can be used to state a better definition of observable contexts:

Definition (**observable contexts, version 2**) *Let* $W \in T_{\Sigma(X)}$ *be a set of observable terms and A be a Σ-algebra. We say that $\eta \in C_{\Sigma(A \cup \diamond)}$ is an* **observable context of** $a \in A_s$ *if $\eta[a] \in \widetilde{W}^A$.*

According to this definition an observable context η of $a \in A_s$ is obtained from some valued observable term $w\nu$ ($\nu : X \to A$), if a is an intermediate result of its evaluation. In fact, the above definition requires the term $\eta[a]$ to be obtained from $w\nu$ as a result of its partial evaluation. Thus the context η represents a calculus waiting for an input. If the value a is given as input, then the carrying out of this calculus corresponds exactly to a "continuation" of the evaluation of $w\nu$. However, the case of the specification SYM (c.f. Figure 3.3) shows that this approach is not yet satisfactory. For instance, let A be a Sig[SYM]-algebra such that $f^A(a^A, a^A) = true^A$ and $f^A(b^A, b^A) = false^A$. Applying the last definition we obtain:

$$\text{observable contexts of } a^A : \quad f(\diamond, a), f(a, \diamond)$$
$$\text{observable contexts of } b^A : \quad f(\diamond, b), f(b, \diamond)$$

Since the elements a^A and b^A have no comparator, they are declared indistinguishable. Nevertheless, the evaluation of the terms $f(a, a)$ and $f(b, b)$ allows to distinguish a^A and b^A. This motivates to consider $f(\diamond, \diamond)$ as a comparator of a^A and b^A. Consequently, **an adequate definition of continuation should be based on multicontexts instead of contexts.**

4 The Indistinguishability Relation

According to the previous discussion, we define continuations as follows:

Definition 4.1 *Let $W \subseteq T_{\Sigma(X)}$ be a set of observable terms and a be an element of a Σ-algebra A. We say that a multicontext $\eta \in MC_{\Sigma(A \cup \diamond)}$ is a* **W-continuation via** a *(a continuation via a, for short) if $\eta[a] \in \widetilde{W}^A$. The set of W-continuations via a is written* $\mathbf{cont_W}(a)$. *(If there is no ambiguity we omit the index W in this notation.)*

The definition of indistinguishability (c.f. 3.2) from the last section remains unchanged provided that we modify the definition of comparator which must be based on the notion of continuation.

Definition 4.2 *A* **W-comparator** *(comparator, for short) of elements a and b of a given carrier of a Σ-algebra, is any W-continuation via a and b. The set of all comparators of a and b is denoted by* $\mathbf{cmp_W}(a, b)$. *(If there is no ambiguity we omit the index W in this notation.) We say that a W-comparator η* **distinguishes** *a and b iff $\overline{\eta[a]} \neq \overline{\eta[b]}$.*

We illustrate these concepts by means of the specification SWE (see Figure 1.1).

Example 4.3 *We equip the specification SWE with the following set of observable terms*

$$\text{Obs}_{\text{SWE}} = \{x \in X\} \cup (T_{\text{Sig[LIST]}(X)})_{\text{Bool}} \cup (T_{\text{Sig[LIST]}(X)})_{\text{Nat}}$$

The algebra L which we would like to consider as a correct realization of SWE admits two copies of the carrier of the usual realization of lists: one for lists and the other for sets.

Consequently, enum^L is the bijection between these two copies preserving axioms ψ_9 and ψ_{10}. In other words $L|_{\text{Sig[LIST]}}$ and $L|_{\text{Sig[SET]}}$ are equal up to some appropriate renaming of operations. The continuations of $l \in L_{\text{List}}$ are the following ones:

$$\text{cont}(l) \quad = \quad \{\text{car}(\eta), \text{member}(n, \eta) \mid n \in L_{\text{Nat}}, \; \eta \in (\text{MC}_{\text{Sig[LIST]}}(L \cup \diamond))_{\text{List}}\}$$

Therefore, $\sim_{\text{Obs}_{\text{SWE}}}$ is the set theoretical equality on L_{List}. The continuations of $s \in L_{\text{Set}}$ are the following ones:

$$\text{cont}(s) \quad = \quad \{n \in \diamond_{\text{Set}} \mid n \in L_{\text{Nat}}\}$$

Thus $s, s' \in L_{\text{Set}}$ are indistinguishable if they contain the same elements.

We give below the first important theorem which will be useful in establishing some results about observational specifications w.r.t. the specification-building primitives.

Theorem 4.4 *Let $\sigma : \Sigma \to \Sigma'$ be a signature morphism, $W \subseteq T_{\Sigma(X)}$ and $W' \subseteq T_{\Sigma'(X')}$ be sets of terms such that $\sigma(W) \subseteq W'$ and A' be a Σ'-algebra. For all elements $a \in (A'|_\sigma)_s$ and any multicontext $\eta \in \text{MC}_{\Sigma(A'|_\sigma \cup \diamond)}$ we have:*

$$\eta \in \text{cont}_W(a) \quad \Rightarrow \quad \sigma(\eta) \in \text{cont}_{W'}(a)$$

The proof (omitted here) may be found in [12]. Notice that the converse of the above theorem does not hold even if $\sigma(W) = W'$.

The definition 3.2 express in which situation two elements of a Σ-algebra are indistinguishable. By the way, it defines an S-sorted relation $\sim_W = (\sim_W)_{s \in S}$ on an algebra, called **indistinguishability relation**. Since this relation is a step toward our observational semantics, we must study its properties w.r.t. at least the forgetful functor and the translation of observable terms in order to be able to cope with specification-building primitives.

Proposition 4.5 *Let $\sigma : \Sigma \to \Sigma'$ be a signature morphism, let $W \subseteq T_{\Sigma(X)}$ and $W' \subseteq T_{\Sigma'(X')}$ be sets of terms such that $\sigma(W) \subseteq W'$ and A' be a Σ'-algebra. For all $a, b \in (A'|_\sigma)_s$ we have that if a and b are W'-indistinguishable (in $A'_{\sigma(s)}$) then a and b are also W-indistinguishable (in $(A'|_\sigma)_s$).*

The proof (omitted here) may be found in [12]. Again, the converse result does not hold even if $\sigma(W) = W'$. The following fact is obvious from the definition of the indistinguishability relation.

Fact 4.6 *The indistinguishability relation is reflexive and symmetric.* □

The next fact fully agrees with our claims:

Fact 4.7 *The indistinguishability relation is not a congruence in general.*

Proof *It is enough to go back to Example 4.3. Recall that in the algebra L, sets are represented by lists. Let then $\langle n, m \rangle$ and $\langle m, n \rangle$ be two representations of the set $\{n, m\}$ in this algebra. On one hand we have $\langle n, m \rangle \sim_{\text{Obs}_{\text{SWE}}} \langle m, n \rangle$ but on the other hand enum$^L(\langle n, m \rangle) \not\sim_{\text{Obs}_{\text{SWE}}}$ enum$^L(\langle m, n \rangle)$ because of the comparator $\text{car}(\diamond)$ which distinguishes them.* □

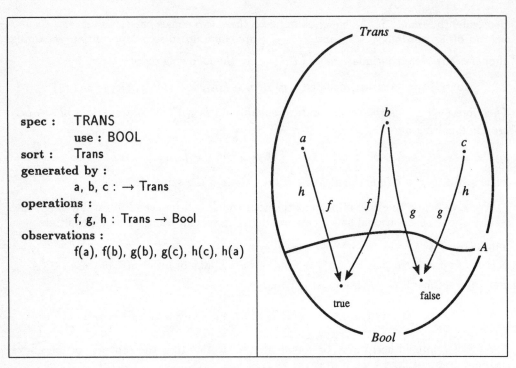

Figure 4.1: Specification TRANS and one of its models

We have also an unexpected negative result:

Fact 4.8 *The indistinguishability relation is not transitive in general.*

Consider the model A (see Figure 4.1) of the specification TRANS. In this algebra we have $a^A \sim_w b^A$ and $b^A \sim_w c^A$, but not $a^A \sim_w c^A$. The reason is that we did not impose any restriction on the set of observable terms. Consequently, nothing ensures that all the elements of a given data type can be observed in the same way. In the algebra A each of the elements a^A, b^A, c^A is observed differently, each pair among these elements is compared in some proper way, different from the others. This is the reason why the indistinguishability relation is not transitive. In fact, this surprising property results directly from our Indistinguishability Assumption according to which we have built definitions 3.2, 4.1 and 4.2 but in certain cases this could be explained by an "inconsistent" choice of observations and sometimes should be avoided. The next fact gives a sufficient condition to avoid this problem.

Fact 4.9 *Let A be a Σ-algebra and W be a set of Σ-terms. If $\text{cont}_W(a) = \text{cont}_W(b)$ for all $a, b \in A_s$ then the relation $\sim_w$ is transitive on A.*

Proof *Obvious.* □

Fact 4.10 *The relation $\sim_{\text{Obs}_{SWE}}$ from Example 4.3 is transitive.*

Proof *Follows directly from the above proposition, since in Example 4.3 we have shown that the elements of the same carrier set of L have the same continuations.* □

It is possible to have a definition of "$\sim_W$" which is always transitive. One may state that a and b are W-indistinguishable if they do in the sense of Definition 3.2 and if additionally $\text{cont}_W(a) = \text{cont}_W(b)$. In our opinion, such a definition will distinguish too much. For instance, if in a specification we observe only some **ground** terms then, according to Definition 3.2, a non reachable value will never be distinguished from any other value, whereas with the modified version of this definition, a non reachable value will always be distinguished from any reachable value. Consequently we are not enthusiastic about such a modification.

Since the problem of software correctness is the main motivation of our work, we want to provide a semantical framework which could be further extended with adequate theorem proving features. Incontestably, proving software correctness w.r.t. an algebraic specification requires at least equational reasoning. For this reason, an observational satisfaction relation cannot be directly based on the indistinguishability relation in contrast with the usual satisfaction relation based on the usual set-theoretic equality (of the elements of an algebra). Its non-transitive character would eliminate all possibility of equational reasoning. On the contrary, the non-congruence property does not disallow this possibility, subject to beware on some exotic operations such as **enum** (see Figure 1.1). For instance we can replace in some term t of SWE its subterm $t|_p = \text{ins}(s(0), \text{ins}(0, \emptyset))$ by $\text{ins}(0, \text{ins}(s(0), \emptyset))$ except when there is some occurrence of **enum** in t over the position p[1]. In addition we believe that there is no reason to expect an "observational equality" to be a congruence (as in [4]). This holds only in the particular case of sort observation (see [8], [13]).

5 Observational Algebras

At this moment we have a little trouble with the non-transitive character of the indistinguishability relation. Since this aspect seems to be crucial for establishing some proof methods, we introduce in this section a flexible concept of observational algebras.

Definition 5.1 *Given a signature Σ, an **observational Σ-algebra** is a pair $\langle A, \cong \rangle$ where A is a Σ-algebra and $\cong$ is an S-sorted equivalence relation on A, called **observational equality on A**. We note **OAlg[Σ]** the class of all observational Σ-algebras.*

Notice that any Σ-algebra A can be considered in a straightforward way as an observational Σ-algebra $\langle A, = \rangle$. The reader certainly realizes that our definition of observational algebras is similar to the one of structures in First Order Logic where each predicate symbol is interpreted by a relation. We consider the equality symbol "=" in the axioms as a particular predicate symbol. This symbol is explicitly interpreted in an algebra by a particular relation, namely an observational equality.

Example 5.2 *Consider L and Obs_{SWE} both defined in Example 4.3. Since $\sim_{\text{Obs}_{SWE}}$ is an equivalence relation (c.f. 4.10), the pair $\langle L, \sim_{\text{Obs}_{SWE}} \rangle$ is an observational Sig[SWE]-algebra.*

Definition 5.3 *An **observational Σ-morphism** $\mu : \langle A, \cong^A \rangle \to \langle B, \cong^B \rangle$ is any (usual) Σ-morphism from A to B which preserves observational equalities i.e:*

$$\forall a, b \in A_s \quad a \cong^A b \Rightarrow \mu(a) \cong^B \mu(b)$$

---

[1]More precisely, this replacement is impossible only if each node on the path from p to the closest enum over p (if there is one) is of sort Set.

Obviously OAlg[Σ] provided with the observational Σ-morphisms forms a category.

Definition 5.4 *Let* $\sigma : \Sigma \to \Sigma'$ *be a signature morphism. The* σ-**reduct** *of an observational* Σ'-*algebra* $\langle A', \cong' \rangle$ *is the observational* Σ-*algebra*

$$\langle A', \cong' \rangle|_\sigma = \langle A'|_\sigma, \ \cong'|_\sigma \rangle$$

where $A'|_\sigma$ *is the usual* σ-*reduct of the* Σ'-*algebra* A' *and* $(\cong'|_\sigma)_s = \cong'_{\sigma(s)}$ *for all* s ∈ S.

The mapping $\_|_\sigma$ extends on observational morphisms as in the usual framework. Consequently, it defines the corresponding **forgetful functor** from OAlg[Σ'] to OAlg[Σ].

Definition 5.5 *A* **solution** *of an equation* l = r *in an observational* Σ-*algebra* $\langle A, \cong \rangle$ *is a valuation* $\nu : X \to A$ *such that* $\overline{l\nu} \cong \overline{r\nu}$. *The set of all the solutions of an equation is written* $[l{=}r]_{\langle A, \cong \rangle}$. *The set of solutions of a formula* φ *is defined recursively w.r.t. the connectives* ¬ *and* ∧:

- *if* $\varphi = \neg\psi$ *then* $[\varphi]_{\langle A, \cong \rangle} = \text{Val}[X, A] \smallsetminus [\psi]_{\langle A, \cong \rangle}$
- *if* $\varphi = \psi \wedge \psi'$ *then* $[\varphi]_{\langle A, \cong \rangle} = [\psi]_{\langle A, \cong \rangle} \cap [\psi']_{\langle A, \cong \rangle}$

where ψ, ψ' *are* Σ-*formulae.*

Since all the connectives of the classical logic can be expressed by means of the connectives ¬ and ∧, the solutions of an arbitrary formula without quantifiers (i.e. implicitly universally quantified) are well defined by the above definition.

The following theorem relates solutions of a formula and its translation, on an observational algebra and on its σ-reduct:

Theorem 5.6 *Let* $\sigma : \Sigma \to \Sigma'$ *be a signature morphism,* $\langle A', \cong' \rangle$ *be an observational* Σ'-*algebra and* φ *be a* Σ-*formula. Let* $\nu : X \to A'|_\sigma$ *and* $\nu' : X' \to A'|_\sigma$ *be valuations such that* $x\nu = \sigma(x)\nu'$ *for all* x ∈ X. *Then*

$$\nu \in [\varphi]_{\langle A', \cong' \rangle|_\sigma} \quad \text{iff} \quad \nu' \in [\sigma(\varphi)]_{\langle A', \cong' \rangle}$$

A slightly different version of this theorem as well as its proof may be found in [12].

6   Observational Specifications

Definition 6.1 *An* **observational** Σ-**formula** *is a pair* $\langle \varphi, W \rangle$ *where* $\varphi \in \text{Wff}[\Sigma]$ *is a* Σ-*formula and* W ∈ $T_{\Sigma(X)}$ *is a set of terms. We note* **OWff[Σ]** *the set of all observational* Σ-*formulae.*

In a straightforward way we consider a set $\Phi = \{\varphi_1, \ldots, \varphi_n\}$ of formulae as a conjunction of formulae $\Phi = \varphi_1 \wedge \ldots \wedge \varphi_n$. Thus any pair $\langle \Phi, W \rangle$ can be viewed as a single observational formula and consequently, any observational specification can be viewed as composed by a single observational formula:

Definition 6.2 *An* **observational specification** *OSP is a triple* $\langle \Sigma, \Theta, W \rangle$, *where* Σ *is the signature of OSP and* $\langle \Theta, W \rangle \in \text{OWff}[\Sigma]$.

One may also define an observational specification as a pair $\langle \Sigma, \text{OAx} \rangle$ with OAx = $\{\langle \theta_1, W_1 \rangle, \ldots, \langle \theta_i, W_i \rangle, \ldots\}$. The possibility to associate observations separately to each axiom would increase the expressive power. (In particular, it allows an infinite set OAx.) However, in all examples it seems preferable to attach a unique set of observable terms to the whole specification.

We have now all the elements necessary to define an observational satisfaction relation:

Definition 6.3 *We say that an observational Σ-algebra $\langle A, \cong \rangle$* **satisfies** *an observational formula $\langle \psi, W \rangle$, written $\langle A, \cong \rangle \not\models \langle \psi, W \rangle$, iff:*

$$[\psi]_{\langle A, \cong \rangle} = \text{Val}[X, A] \tag{i}$$
$$\cong \; \subseteq \; \sim_W \tag{ii}$$

Models are defined as in the usual approach except that we use the observational satisfaction instead of the usual one:

Definition 6.4 *Let OSP = $\langle \Sigma, \Theta, W \rangle$ be an observational specification. We say that an observational Σ-algebra $\langle A, \cong \rangle$ is a* **model** *of OSP iff:*

$$\langle A, \cong \rangle \not\models \langle \Theta, W \rangle$$

We note **OAlg[OSP]** *the class of all observational models of OSP.*

Notice that OAlg[OSP] with observational Σ-morphisms is a full subcategory of OAlg[Σ].

Fact 6.5 *The observational algebra $\langle L, \sim_{\text{Obs}_{\text{SWE}}} \rangle$ described in Example 5.2, is a model of the observational specification* SWE.

Proof sketch *Since the observational equality on $\langle L, \sim_{\text{Obs}_{\text{SWE}}} \rangle$ is just the indistinguishability relation, we only need to prove that for any axiom θ of* SWE *we have*

$$[\theta]_{\langle L, \sim_{\text{Obs}_{\text{SWE}}} \rangle} = \text{Val}[X, L]$$

This is obvious for the axioms of LIST *since $L_{|\text{Sig}[\text{LIST}]}$ is the usual realization of lists and since from Example 4.3 we know that $\sim_{\text{Obs}_{\text{SWE}}}$ is the usual equality on $L_{|\text{Sig}[\text{LIST}]}$.*

Since the elements observationally equal on L_{Set} are different representations of the same set, it is clear that for the "standard" axioms $\psi_1, \psi_2, \ldots, \psi_8$ of sets (c.f. Figure 1.1), we have

$$[\psi_i]_{\langle L, \sim_{\text{Obs}_{\text{SWE}}} \rangle} = \text{Val}[X, L]$$

In matters of ψ_9 and ψ_{10}, it is not difficult to show that $[\psi_9]_{\langle L, = \rangle} = [\psi_{10}]_{\langle L, = \rangle} = \text{Val}[X, L]$ Then we can conclude that

$$[\psi_9]_{\langle L, \sim_{\text{Obs}_{\text{SWE}}} \rangle} = [\psi_{10}]_{\langle L, \sim_{\text{Obs}_{\text{SWE}}} \rangle} = \text{Val}[X, L]$$

This last step is justified by the fact that the axioms ψ_9 and ψ_{10} are equations and that $= \; \subseteq \; \sim_{\text{Obs}_{\text{SWE}}}$. Obviously, for any Σ-equation $t = t'$, any Σ algebra A and observational equalities $\cong^\alpha \; \subseteq \; \cong^\beta$ on A, we have $[t = t']_{\langle A, \cong^\alpha \rangle} \subseteq [t = t']_{\langle A, \cong^\beta \rangle}$ $\square$

In the above example we have considered a model of the form $\langle A, \sim_w \rangle$. Of course, this is possible only when $\sim_w$ is transitive. Moreover this model has a particular status: it is a terminal object in the category of all observational models formed with a given algebra A. This is quite analogous to the final data type of [11]. Notice that when $\sim_w$ is not transitive this category has often no terminal object. For instance, the category of observational models of TRANS based on the algebra A (see Figure 4.1) has no terminal object.

We examine now how our satisfaction relation behaves w.r.t. the variance of observational formulae (translation) and the covariance of algebras (σ-reduct). We start by the first requirement of Definition 6.3:

Proposition 6.6 *Let $\sigma : \Sigma \to \Sigma'$ be a signature morphism. For any set of terms* $W \subseteq T_{\Sigma(X)}$, *any observational Σ'-algebra $\langle A', \cong' \rangle$ and any Σ-formula φ we have:*

$$[\sigma(\varphi)]_{\langle A', \cong' \rangle} = Val[X', A'] \quad iff \quad [\varphi]_{\langle A', \cong' \rangle|_\sigma} = Val[X, A'|_\sigma]$$

The proof (omitted here) mainly uses Theorem 5.6 and may be found in [12]. The next step is to study the second condition of Definition 6.3 w.r.t. term translation and the forgetful functor. We examine first the if part of this condition.

Proposition 6.7 *Let $\sigma : \Sigma \to \Sigma'$ be a signature morphism. For all sets of terms* $W \subseteq T_{\Sigma(X)}$, $W' \subseteq T_{\Sigma'(X')}$ *such that $\sigma(W) \subseteq W'$ and for any observational Σ'-algebra $\langle A', \cong' \rangle$ we have:*

$$\cong' \subseteq \sim_{w'} \quad \Rightarrow \quad \cong'|_\sigma \subseteq \sim_w$$

where $\sim_{w'}$ and $\sim_w$ are the indistinguishability relations respectively on A' and $A'|_\sigma$.

The proof may be found in [12].

The next step should be to prove the converse of the above proposition restricted to $W' = \sigma(W)$. Unfortunately this does not hold in general[1]. Consequently the **satisfaction condition** (see [6] or [7]) does not hold in our approach without additional assumptions. Nevertheless an institution can be defined within this framework, under some restrictions on either signature morphisms or the set of observable terms (see [12]).

Up to now, we have not been studying modularity issues. We have only defined the semantics of "flat" specifications. In fact, as in [1], our observational semantics easily extends to a stratified loose observational semantics without additional assumptions. The next theorem shows that our observational semantics is compatible w.r.t. enrichment and renaming:

Theorem 6.8 *Let $\sigma : \Sigma \to \Sigma'$ be a signature morphism. For all observational specifications $OSP = \langle \Sigma, \Theta, W \rangle$ and $OSP' = \langle \Sigma', \Theta', W' \rangle$ such that $\sigma(\Theta) \subseteq \Theta'$ and $\sigma(W) \subseteq W'$ we have:*

$$OAlg[OSP']|_\sigma \subseteq OAlg[OSP]$$

Proof *From definitions 6.4 and 6.3 it is enough to prove:*

$$\forall \langle A', \cong' \rangle \in OAlg[\Sigma'] \quad [\Theta']_{\langle A', \cong' \rangle} = Val[X', A'] \; \Rightarrow \; [\Theta]_{\langle A', \cong' \rangle|_\sigma} = Val[X, A'|_\sigma] \quad (i)$$

$$\text{and} \; \forall \langle A', \cong' \rangle \in OAlg[\Sigma'] \qquad\qquad \cong' \subseteq \sim_{w'} \; \Rightarrow \; \cong'|_\sigma \subseteq \sim_w \qquad\qquad (ii)$$

---

[1] An example illustrating this fact may be found in [12].

- **Proof of (i)**

  Let $\langle A', \cong' \rangle \in \text{OAlg}[\Sigma']$ such that

  $$[\Theta']_{\langle A', \cong' \rangle} = \text{Val}[X', A']$$

  Since $\sigma(\Theta) \subseteq \Theta'$, by definition of solution of a conjunction of formulae (c.f. 5.5) we have $\sigma(\Theta)_{\langle A', \cong' \rangle} \supseteq \Theta'_{\langle A', \cong' \rangle}$. Hence $[\sigma(\Theta)]_{\langle A', \cong' \rangle} = \text{Val}[X', A']$ which according to Proposition 6.6 implies that

  $$[\Theta]_{\langle A', \cong' \rangle}\big|_{\sigma} = \text{Val}[X, A'\big|_{\sigma}]$$

- **Proof of (ii)** *follows directly from Proposition 6.7.*

□

This last result deserves some comments. Indeed, it is somehow surprising that we obtain such a strong result, without any further hypotheses w.r.t. the axioms of the specification, while similar results hold for other observational approaches only when axioms are restricted to equations. It is quite important to note that, in our approach, observational algebras are algebras equipped with some observational equality. To obtain a model of a given observational specification, this observational equality should be "compatible" with the given axioms and observations. The point is that this observational equality is preserved by forgetful functors. In other approaches, one could define as well an observational equality, but this equality is **deduced** from the specified observations. Hence, when we apply some forgetful functor, the set of observations is modified (and so is the corresponding observational equality), and the result of Theorem 6.8 cannot be obtained without very strong restrictions on the axioms and on the observations.

7 Concluding Remarks

We have provided a suitable notion of observation based on terms. First, we have investigated how the elements of a carrier of an algebra should be observed through terms. We have pointed out that an adequate notion of observation in this framework requires to take into account multicontexts and partial evaluations of observable terms. In this way, we have introduced the concept of continuations which underlies our definition of the indistinguishability relation. We have shown that this relation is neither a congruence nor an equivalence relation. These both results fully agree with our Indistinguishability Assumption. Notice that when we restrict to sort observation, our indistinguishability relation becomes a congruence similar to the Nerode congruence [8]. However, unlike in [13], in our approach, two observational algebras differing on non observable junk do not necessarily satisfy the same observational formulae. We do not privilege reachable elements, since this is most suitable for defining the observational semantics of parameterized specifications in a loose framework (which is the topic of our current research). Moreover, one could think that our indistinguishability relation coincide with Reichel's I-indistinguishability [15] when we restrict our approach to sort observation and Reichel's one to total algebras. This is not true, since we use multicontexts from $\text{MC}_{\Sigma(A \cup \diamond)}$ instead of $\text{MC}_{\Sigma(\diamond)}$. Consequently, in our approach non observable junk can influence the indistinguishability of two elements of a carrier of an algebra while it cannot in other works. Thus the roles of reachable and non reachable values are symmetric w.r.t. our indistinguishability relation.

Being convinced of the necessity of equational reasoning in proving abstract implementation correctness, we have introduced in our semantics an additional stage over the indistinguishability relation, namely the observational equality. Then we have defined observational algebras, observational formulae and the corresponding satisfaction relation. In this way we have developed an observational approach which has all properties required to define the semantics of an algebraic specification language, even if it does not provide an institution.

The main disadvantage of our approach is that the logical formulae we use are always implicitly universally quantified. Consequently, the first improvement is to redefine our satisfaction relation and to prove once again some results in order to take into account existential quantifiers. Finally, the most important area of further research is the development of proof methods on top of our approach.

References

[1] **Bernot G., Bidoit M.** Proving the correctness of algebraically specified software: Modularity and Observability issues *Proceedings of International Conference AMAST, Iowa City, 1991, 139-161*

[2] **Bernot G., Bidoit M., Knapik T.** Observational Approaches in Algebraic Specifications: a Comparative Study *Report LIENS-91-6, 1991*

[3] **Bergstra J.A., Tucker J.V.** Initial and Final Algebra Semantics for Data Type Specifications: Two Characterization Theorems. *SIAM Journal of Computing, vol 12 (1983), 366-387*

[4] **van Dieppen N.W.P.** Implementation of Modular Algebraic Specifications *(Ganzinger H. ed.) ESOP 88, Nancy, March 1988, LNCS 300, 64-78*

[5] **Ehrig H., Mahr B.** Fundamentals of Algebraic Specifications *ETACS Monographs on Theoretical Computer Science, Vol 6, Springer-Verlag, 1985*

[6] **Goguen J.A., Burstall R.** Introducing Institutions *(Clarke E., Kozen D. eds.) Proceedings of Logic of Programming Workshop, Carnegie Mellon, 1984, LNCS 164, 221-256*

[7] **Goguen J.A., Burstall R.** Institutions: abstract model theory for specification and programming *LFCS report ECS-LFCS-90-106 (1990)*

[8] **Goguen J.A., Meseguer J.** Universal Realization, Persistent Interconnection and Implementation of Abstract Modules *(Nielsen M., Schmidt E.M. eds.) ICALP, Aarhus, 1982, LNCS 140, 265-281*

[9] **Goguen J.A., Thatcher J.W., Wagner E.G.** An Initial Approach to the Specification, Correctness and Implementation of Abstract Data Types, *(Yeh R.T. ed.) Current Trends in Programming Methodology, Vol. 4: Data Structuring, Prentice Hall, 80-149 (1978)*

[10] **Hennicker R.** Context Induction: a Proof Principle for Behavioural Abstractions and Algebraic Implementations *Fakultät für Mathematik und Informatik Universität Passau, 1990 (Internal Report MIP-9001)*

[11] **Kamin S.** Final Data Types and Their Specification *ACM Transactions on Programming Languages and Systems, Vol 5, No 1, 97-123 (1983)*

[12] **Knapik T.** Sémantique Observationnelle des Spécifications Algébriques: application à la modularité et à l'implémentation *Ph. D. thesis in preparation, Université de Paris-Sud, Orsay 1992*

[13] **Nivela P., Orejas F.** Initial Behaviour Semantics for Algebraic Specification *(Sannella, Tarlecki eds.) Recent Trends in Data Type Specification, 5th Workshop on Specification of ADT, Gullane, September 1987, LNCS 332, 184-207*

[14] **Pepper P.** On the Correctness of Type Transformations *Talk at 2nd Workshop on Theory and Applications of Abstract Data Types, Passau, May 1983*

[15] **Reichel H.** Behavioural Validity of Conditional Equations in Abstract Data Types *Contributions to General Algebra 3, Proceedings of the Vienna Conference, June 1984*

[16] **Sannella D., Tarlecki A.** On Observational Equivalence and Algebraic Specification, *TapSoft, Berlin 1985, LNCS 185, 308-322*

[17] **Sannella D., Tarlecki A.** Toward Formal Development of Programs from Algebraic Specification Revisited, *Acta Informatica 25, 233-281 (1988)*

[18] **Wand M.** Final Algebra Semantics and Data Type Extension *Journal of Computer and System Sciences, Vol 19, 27-44 (1979)*

Proving Safety of Speculative Load Instructions at Compile-Time

David Bernstein
Michael Rodeh
Mooly Sagiv
IBM Israel Scientific Center
the Technion City, Haifa 32000, Israel
Email: bernstn@haifasc3.vnet.ibm.com

Abstract

Speculative execution of instructions is one of the primary means for enhancing program performance of superscalar and VLIW machines. One of the pitfalls of such compile-time speculative scheduling of instructions is that it may cause run-time exceptions that did not exist in the original version of the program.

As opposed to run-time hardware or software interception of such exceptions, we suggest that the compiler will analyze and prove the *safety* of those instructions that are candidates for speculative execution, rejecting the ones that have even a slight chance of causing an exception.

Load (moving a memory operand to a register) instructions are important candidates for speculative execution, since they precondition any follow-on computation on load-store architectures. To enable speculative loads, an algorithmic scheme for proving the safety of such instructions is presented and analyzed. Given a (novel) memory layout scheme which is specially tailored to support safe memory accesses, it has been observed that a significant part of load instructions can be proven safe and thus can be made eligible for speculative execution.

1 Introduction

The recent advent of superscalar and VLIW machines increases the need for aggressive instruction scheduling by optimizing compilers. If previously (for pipelined machines) it was sufficient to reorder instructions at the basic block level ([HG83], [War90]), it is evident now that for the newer machines, instructions have to be moved well beyond basic block boundaries. A few such efforts were described in [Ell85, EN89, GS90, BR91].

It turns out that very often, to further improve the utilization of machine resources, instructions have to be scheduled *speculatively*, i.e., moved ahead of a preceding branch to a place were it is not yet determined in the program that such instructions have to be executed at all. Previously, speculative execution was considered in the context of moving loop-invariants out of loops [ASU85], while recently, due to the evolution toward superscalar and VLIW machine designs, this type of transformations is being exploited in a much broader scope of code motions. In case the compiler guesses right the direction of the branch over which a speculative instruction is moved, such instruction computes useful results; otherwise the compiler must make sure that these results will not be used in the subsequent execution of the program.

One of the main problems of speculative execution of instructions, which is the focus of this paper, is that they may cause *program exceptions* which were not supposed to happen if these instructions were executed in their original (non-speculative) places. Kennedy first raises the problem of proving *safety* of such instructions [Ken72], with the motivating example of moving a division loop invariant instruction out of a loop (which is a special case of speculative code motion). The reasons for program exceptions are diverse: arithmetic operations may result in an overflow, memory access instructions (loads and stores) may reference an invalid memory address, etc. In most of the previous work it was suggested that prevention of such exceptions must be supported by hardware or software in run-time, some of them even proposed to disable the exceptions of speculative instructions all together (for more details, see Section 8).

Our proposal is different than all previous work on speculative scheduling and it extends Kennedy's technique of [Ken72]. We suggest to determine, at compile-time, which instructions are *safe*, i.e., which instructions will never cause exceptions that would not have occurred in the original version of P. Then, only safe instructions will be candidates for speculative execution. Using this approach, in the optimized version of the program we have no problem to allow the exceptions to occur, in a way similar to the original (non-optimized) program. Thus, the advantage of our approach is that it both preserves the *debuggability* of the program (meaning - exceptions do not have to be masked) and does not require any hardware support for speculative execution. In this paper we concentrate on proving safety of load instructions (which is one of the most important classes of speculative instructions), even though our techniques can be applied to additional types of instructions as well. In particular, this paper does not address the issue of profitability of speculative scheduling which may be affected by the underlying architecture (e.g., an increased number of cache misses, page faults, and register pressure), neither it deals with guaranteeing correct results for speculative code motions. These problems were partially covered in [Ell85, BR91].

The crucial question is: What fraction of speculative load instructions can be proven safe at compile time? Our experience is that, for a set of benchmarks we considered, provided a certain model of memory layout is assumed, a significant part of load instructions can be proven safe at compile-time. These results are summarized in Section 7.

In our set-up, the address of a load instruction is defined by (the contents of) a machine register plus a displacement. Our first result is a linear-time algorithm for determining the safety of a load instruction whose address is defined by register r, using the information about the existence of different memory-access instructions (loads or stores) in different points of the program whose addresses are defined by the same register r. This algorithm does not take into account the contents of the registers, i.e., the assumption is that the value of r is unchanged during the portion of the program under inspection. In his original paper [Ken72], Kennedy also describes an iterative backward algorithm for proving safety. His algorithm is less accurate than ours, since we also use forward information and safety of certain register assignment statements (for a technical comparison see Section 8).

The second result is an efficient algorithm for proving safety in case the value of r may change during the execution of the program by statements like $r = r + c$, where c is a constant. Here we take advantage of the observation that, if accessing location (r) is valid $((r)$ is the contents of $r)$, then the access to location $(r) + k$, where k is the size of the page in the memory system, is valid as well. In Section 5, we describe the requirements on the memory layout that are needed to make this assumption legitimate.

The accuracy of our algorithms depends on two assumptions. The first assumption is that every execution path of the program can be taken. The second assumption is that there are no program statements, like $r_1 = r_2 + c$, or $r_1 = r_2 + r_3$. In fact, we show that the problem of proving safety in the simple case when only register transfer statements (i.e., statements of the form $r_1 = r_2$) are allowed is CO-NP-hard. For this case we do provide an iterative conservative approximation algorithm (see [Kil73, KU76]).

The paper is organized as follows. In the next section we start with the definition of the problem. Then, in Section 3, the first algorithm is presented. Register transfer statements are discussed in Section 4 (including CO-NP-hardness result). In Section 5 we define our novel memory layout scheme. Then, in Section 6, the second algorithmic result is presented. Some experimental results are described in Section 7. Section 8 contains a discussion on related work.

2 Definition of the Problem

Here we formally state the problem of proving safety, so as to lay a basis for discussion. In the rest of this paper, P is a terminating low level program that uses a set of registers R. We assume that references to memory locations are done by load instructions of the form $load\ r', (r)$. By convention, we say that such instruction includes a memory reference to a location whose address is the contents of r (denoted by $ref(r)$).

Let i be an instruction that includes $ref(r)$ and pt a point in P. We say that the insertion of i before pt is *safe* if it does not cause an exception that would not have occurred in the original version of P. The speculative code motion that was presented in the introduction can be viewed as consisting of two separate actions, namely, an instruction is deleted from one point in P and inserted into another point. In the rest of the paper we will deal only with proving the safety of insertions of instructions into new places of the program (as it is reflected in the above definition of safety). Notice that deletions of instructions from P cannot create new exceptions, so it is not related to the problem of safety. The discussion of the data dependency correctness of deletions and insertions is out of the scope of this paper. However, the combination of insertion and deletion, while taking into account data dependency, enables instruction motions, an essential element of instruction scheduling.

The above definition of safety is implicit since the notion of exception was not defined. Let π be an execution sequence of P and let pt be a point in P along π. Let h be the value of r at at point pt of π. Then, the insertion of $ref(r)$ before pt is *safe* along π if one of the following is true:

1. there is an instruction in π which refers to h as address.

2. h is a valid address.

This definition implies that if h is referred as address, the insertion of $ref(r)$ cannot create new exceptions; otherwise, it is safe only when h is known to be a valid address. The notion of a valid address is defined by the programming language and/or the operating system[1].

We say that the insertion of $ref(r)$ before pt is *strongly safe* if it is safe at pt along every execution sequence of P in which pt appears. In Sections 3 and 4, we consider the algorithmic problem of

---

[1]In languages like C, the storage allocation of heap objects is only defined as part of the operating system support.

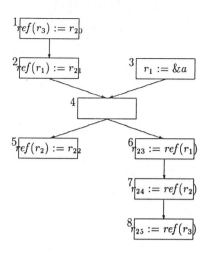

Figure 1: A program control flow graph for a conditional construct

finding strongly safe references. In Section 5, we extend the class of valid addresses by providing a new memory layout scheme, and refine the algorithms accordingly.

3 A Path Analysis Algorithm

In the rest of this paper, $G = (V, E)$ is the program control flow graph of the given program fragment P; each vertex $v \in V$ represents a single instruction in the program, and there is an edge $(v, u) \in E$ if the program control can flow directly from vertex v to vertex u (e.g., see [WZ85]). Thus, every point in P corresponds to a vertex in G. A vertex v can use the contents of register $r \in R$, and can assign a new value to r, as the last operation in v, denoted by $def(r)$. For example, Figure 1 contains the program control flow graph for a program fragment which corresponds to a conditional construct. Instruction 7 contains $def(r_{24})$.

A path π in G which starts at a vertex $v \in V$ is r-$definition$ $free$ for $r \in R$ if every vertex u on π other than v does not include $def(r)$. Such a path is $maximal$ if every successor of the last vertex in π contains $def(r)$. In the program control flow graph of Figure 1, the paths $(1, 2, 4, 5)$ and $(3, 4, 6, 7, 8)$ are r_1 maximal definition free and the path $(1, 2, 4, 6, 7)$ is not. Since the only definition of r_1 appears in a source vertex 3, all the paths in G are r_1-definition free. Figure 2 contains another program control flow graph for a loop construct. This loop is a simplified version of a traversal on a linked list. Assuming that the next pointer is located in the first field of the list records, instruction 4 increments r_1 to the next list element. Instruction 6 contains $r_3 := ref(r_2)$ but should have contained $r_3 := ref(r_2 + k)$ where k the relative place of the data within the record. The path $(2, 4, 5)$ in this program control flow graph is not r_1-definition free.

In the rest of this section, we present a simplified algorithm for proving safety by only considering definition free paths. An r-definition free path π starting at v is $ref(r)$ $safe$ if one of the following conditions holds:

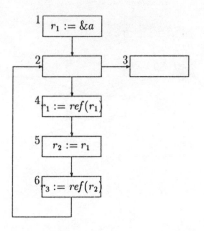

Figure 2: A control flow graph of a loop construct

1. v does not include $def(r)$ and one of the vertices in π includes $ref(r)$.

2. v contains an instruction which assigns a valid address to r or a vertex in π other than v includes $ref(r)$.

If a path from v is $ref(r)$ safe then the insertion of $ref(r)$ is safe before every vertex in π other than v along every execution path of P which contains π. The path $(1,2,4,6,7,8)$ in the program control flow graph of Figure 1 is $ref(r_3)$ safe but $(3,4,5)$ is not.

Lemma 3.1 *Let $v \in V$ and $r \in R$. Then, the insertion of $ref(r)$ before v is strongly safe if the following conditions are met:*

1. *For every source vertex v_0 of G and for every maximal r-definition free path π from v_0 which goes through v, π is $ref(r)$ safe.*

2. *If $u \in V$ contains a definition of r then every maximal r-definition free path π from u which goes through v, π is $ref(r)$ safe.*

□

The r_3-definition free path $(3,4,5)$ in the program control flow graph of Figure 1 is not $ref(r_3)$ safe. This indicates that the insertion of $ref(r_3)$ is not strongly safe before any vertex in this path. In particular, it is not strongly safe before vertex 4 which is a candidate place for speculative execution of the instruction $r_{25} := ref(r_3)$.

We now construct an algorithm which checks the conditions of Lemma 3.1 for $r \in R$ and every vertex $v \in V$. Thus, the algorithm can be applied separately for every $r \in R$.

First, let us define $G_1[r]$ to be the graph which includes the definition free paths for r in G. Technically, let s and t be new vertices. Let $V_d[r] \subseteq V$ be the vertices which include $def(r)$. Since a vertex $v \in V_d$ can contain both $ref(r)$ and $def(r)$, v is duplicated in $G_1[r]$; this is done by adding

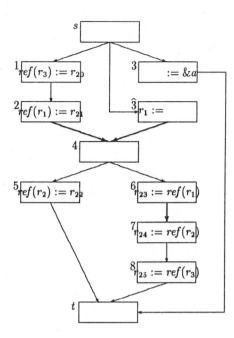

Figure 3: The graph $G_1[r_1]$ for the example of Figure 1

a second copy of v denoted $\hat{v}$. Thus, $G_1[r] = (V_1[r], E_1[r])$, where $V_1[r] = V \cup \{\hat{v} | v \in V_d[r]\} \cup \{s, t\}$ and $(u, v) \in E_1[r]$ if one of the following conditions holds:

1. $u = s$ and v is a source in G.

2. $u = s$ and $v = \hat{w}$ where $w \in V_d[r]$.

3. $(u, v) \in E$ where $u \notin V_d[r]$.

4. $u = \hat{w}$, $w \in V_d[r]$ and $(w, v) \in E$.

5. $u \in V_d[r]$ and $v = t$.

6. u is a target in G and $v = t$.

Thus, any path from s to t in $G_1[r]$ corresponds to a path which may start with a definition of r and is subsequently r-definition free. Figure 3 contains $G_1[r_1]$ for the program control flow graph of Figure 1. Since only r_1 is assigned in this program, $G_1[r_2] = G_1[r_3] = G_1[r_4]$ is the graph which consists of connecting s to 1 and 3, and connecting 5 and 8 to t. Figure 4 contains $G_1[r_1]$ for the program control flow graph of Figure 2.

Now, let $G_2[r]$ be the graph obtained from $G_1[r]$ by deleting edges which emanate from vertices with an evidence of safety, i.e., $G_2[r] = (V_1[r], E_2[r])$ where $E_2[r] \subseteq E_1[r]$ and $(u, v) \in E_1[r] - E_2[r]$ if and only if $u \in V$ and u contains an instruction which assigns a valid address to r or $v \in V$ and v contains $ref(r)$. The graph $G_2[r]$ may be used to check the safety of $ref(r)$ based on the following lemma.

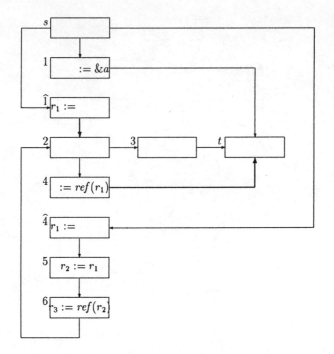

Figure 4: The graph $G_1[r_1]$ for the example of Figure 2

Lemma 3.2 *For a vertex $v \in V$, there does not exist a path in $G_2[r]$ from s to t which goes through v if and only if the conditions of Lemma 3.1 for v and r are met.* □

Thick lines in Figure 3 and Figure 4 denote edges in $G_1[r_1]$ which do not appear in $G_2[r_1]$. Figure 3 shows that the insertion of $ref(r_1)$ in strongly safe before every vertex but 3, since the only path from s to t in $G_2[r_1]$ is $(s, 3, t)$. On the other hand, in Figure 4, the insertion of $ref(r_1)$ is not detected as strongly safe before any vertex but 4, since there exist paths from s to t either by $(s, 1, t)$, or by $(s, \hat{4}, 5, 6, 2, 3, t)$.

Lemma 3.2 suggests that an ordered depth first search (DFS) algorithm may be applied to $G_2[r]$ starting at s so as to detect safety. Initially, all the vertices are marked as allowed to have insertions of $ref(r)$ which are (strongly) safe. When the algorithm backtracks from t, it marks its predecessors vertices as being unsafe for the insertion of $ref(r)$.

The correctness of the path analysis algorithm stems from Lemmas 3.1 and 3.2.

The complexity of the path analysis algorithm for $r \in R$ is $O(|E_2[r]|) = O(|V| + |E|)$ and thus linear in the size of the program.

The conditions in Lemma 3.1 are sufficient, but not necessary to prove that the insertion of $ref(r)$ is strongly safe. Therefore, the path analysis algorithm yields conservative, but not necessarily accurate results. For example, as mentioned above, the insertion of $ref(r_1)$ is not detected as strongly safe before vertex 2 in Figure 2 although it is. This insertion is safe due to the instruction in vertex 6 and the fact that $r_1 = r_2$ there. Indeed, the conditions of Lemma 3.1 are syntactical in the sense that values are not taken into account. Only for a class of programs in which for every instruction i that includes $def(r)$, the validity of the address that is assigned to r is known from the properties of i (i.e., there is no case in which, looking on i, we are not sure if the assigned address is valid), the path analysis algorithm is exact, i.e., the conditions of Lemma 3.1 are necessary.

4   Tracking Values

4.1   The Negative Result

Theorem 4.1 *The problem of detecting that a reference to a register is safe is CO-NP hard even under the following assumptions on the analyzed program P:*

1. *all the control flow paths in P are executable;*

2. *the control flow graph does not contain loops;*

3. *the only instructions in P are load instructions and register transfer instructions of the form $r_1 := r_2$.*

Proof: By reduction from the satisfiability problem. For example, Figure 5 contains a program for the satisfiability of an example formula.   □

The reader may notice the similarity between Theorem 4.1 and negative results of solving data flow problems in presence of aliasing (e.g., [Mye81, Lar89, SFRW90]). In fact, the essence of all these results is that to track alias effects accurately one needs to keep track of all the possible sets of address variables which are equal.

```
if · · ·
        then x₁ := f
        else x'₁ := f
if · · ·
        then x₂ := f
        else x'₂ := f
if · · ·
        then x₃ := f
        else x'₃ := f
if · · · { code for x₁ ∨ x₂ }
        then r := ref(x₁)
        else r := ref(x₂)
if · · · { code for x'₁ ∨ x'₂ ∨ x₃ }
        then r := ref(x'₁)
        else if · · ·
                    then r := ref(x'₂)
                    else r := ref(x₃)
```

Figure 5: $ref(f)$ is safe at the program entry if and only if $(x_1 \vee x_2) \wedge (x'_1 \vee x'_2 \vee x_3)$ is not satisfiable

4.2   Conservative Approximations

We now develop an iterative algorithm which is more accurate than the path analysis algorithm of Section 3. The problem of detecting that the insertion of $ref(r)$ before v is safe along an execution path π can be divided into two problems. In the *forward* problem the path segment from the beginning of π to v is analyzed, while in the *backward* problem the path segment of π from v to the end of π is analyzed. We say that the insertion of $ref(r)$ before $v \in V$ is *forward safe* along an execution sequence π of P if the value of r at v on π is either referred to as an address or is known to be a valid address. Such insertion before v is *backward safe* along π if the value of r at v on π is referred as address. Notice that in this case the value of r may be assigned prior to v on π. Thus, to determine that the insertion is backward safe along π, the path segment of π from the beginning of the program to v also need to be considered.

The insertion of $ref(r)$ before $v \in V$ is *forward* (respectively *backward*) *strongly safe* if it is forward (respectively backward) safe along every execution path which goes through v. We have the following simple lemma.

Lemma 4.2 *An insertion of $ref(r)$ before $v \in V$ is strongly safe if and only if it is either forward strongly safe or it is backward strongly safe.* □

In the rest of this section we present a forward iterative algorithm to detect that an insertion is forward strongly safe. A backward iterative algorithm for detecting that an insertion is backward safe can be specified, in a similar fashion. The combination of both algorithms provides an approximation

vertex	val_b						val_a					
	r_1	r_2	r_3	$ref(r_1)$	$ref(r_2)$	$\&a$	r_1	r_2	r_3	$ref(r_1)$	$ref(r_2)$	$\&a$
1	1	2	3	4	5	6	1	2	3	4	5	1
2	1	2	3	4	5	6	1	2	3	4	5	6
3	1	2	3	4	5	6	1	2	3	4	5	6
4	1	2	3	4	5	6	1	2	3	4	5	6
5	1	2	3	4	5	6	1	1	3	4	5	6
6	1	1	3	4	5	6	1	1	3	4	3	6

Table 1: Value numbers for the example of Figure 2

scheme for proving safety which is more accurate than the path analysis algorithm presented in Section 3.

Two expressions in the program e_1 and e_2 are *equivalent* before $v \in V$ if their values are equal before v at every execution path of P which goes through v. If two expressions e_1 and e_2 are equivalent, then any evidence for the safety of e_1 is also an evidence for the safety of e_2. Thus, an algorithm which finds a conservative approximation of equalities may be useful in proving safety. In the sequel, we shall use the information on equivalences which is represented by global value numbers, i.e. an association of hash values with symbolic expressions. Thus, e_1 and e_2 are equivalent before v if $val_b[v](e_1) = val_b[v](e_2)$ where $val_b[v](e)$ is the value number of e before v. The notion of equivalence after v (denoted by $val_a[v](e)$) is similarly defined. Efficient algorithms for computing global values numbers are known (e.g., [RL77, AWZ88, RWZ88]). Table 1 contains possible value numbers for the example of Figure 2.

Given value numbers of every $v \in V$, we now sketch an iterative algorithm for computing forward strong safety. The algorithm maintains at every $v \in V$ and for every value val before v a boolean value $s_b[v](val)$ which describes the strong safety of this number before v. For convenience, the algorithm also maintains as auxiliary information $s_a[v](val)$ which describes the strong safety of this number after v. Initially, for every source vertex v of G, $s_a[v](val) = true$ and $s_b[v](val)) = true$ if and only if there exists an expression e such that e always holds a valid address and $val = val_b[v](e)$. For any other $v \in V$, the initialization is $s_b[v](val) = s_a[b](val) = true$. The algorithm iterates on G using a DFS order and stops when no new information is derived. Let v be an assignment statement of the form $r := e$. Let $r_1, r_2, \ldots, r_n$ be the registers referred as addresses in e. Then, $s_b[v](val)$ is computed in the iteration using the equation:

$$s_b[v](val) = \begin{cases} true & \exists i : 1 \le i \le n, val = val_b[v](r_i) \\ \wedge\{s_a[u](val_a[u](e))|(u,v) \in E, \exists e, val_b[v](e) = val\} & \text{otherwise} \end{cases} \quad (1)$$

Also, $s_a[v](val)$ is computed by:

$$s_a[v](val) = \begin{cases} s_b[v](val_b[v](e)) & val = val_a[v](r) \\ s_b[v](val) & \text{otherwise} \end{cases} \quad (2)$$

The treatment of other type of instructions is similar. Table 2 exemplifies the application of the iterative algorithm to the program of Figure 2, with the value numbers of Table 1. Undefined value numbers are denoted by ϕ. We see that two iterations are sufficient in this case and that the insertion of $ref(r_1)$ is detected as strongly safe before vertex 2 of Figure 2.

iteration	vertex	s_b						s_a					
		1	2	3	4	5	6	1	2	3	4	5	6
0	1	f	f	f	f	f	t	t	t	t	t	t	t
0	2,3,4,5,6	t	t	t	t	t	t	t	t	t	t	t	t
1	1	f	f	f	f	f	t	t	f	f	f	f	φ
1	2	t	f	f	f	f	t	t	f	f	f	f	t
1	3	t	f	f	f	f	t	t	f	f	f	f	t
1	4	t	f	f	f	f	t	f	f	f	f	f	t
1	5	f	f	f	f	f	t	f	φ	f	f	f	t
1	6	t	φ	f	f	f	t	f	φ	f	f	φ	t

Table 2: The safety vectors for the example of Figure 2

```
if ···
     then r₁ := r₂
     else r₁ := r₃
load r', (r₂)
load r', (r₃)
```

Figure 6: A program which demonstrates the inaccuracy of the conservative algorithm

Lemma 4.3 *When the forward iterative algorithm terminates, for every $r \in R$ and $v \in V$ s.t. $s_b[v](val_b[v](r))$ holds, the insertion of $ref(r)$ before v is forward strongly safe.* □

The opposite direction of Lemma 4.3 does not hold. The first reason is that value numbers are not always exact, i.e., it is possible that two expressions are equivalent and yet they get two different value numbers. Moreover, even when the value numbers are accurate, the algorithm may fail to detect safety. For example, in the program fragment of Figure 6, the insertion of $ref(r_1)$ as the last statement in the program is forward strongly safe and yet will not be detected as such by our algorithm. The reason is that the algorithm does not use the fact that r_1 is either r_2 or r_3, and thus since both of these registers are referred, $ref(r_1)$ becomes safe.

5 Memory Organization

In this section, the domain of valid addresses is extended by suggesting a new memory layout organization. In Section 6, by taking advantage of this extended memory layout support, we improve the algorithms of Sections 3 and 4, so as to allow more instructions to be scheduled speculatively without causing memory exceptions.

The first simple but very important type of memory layout support is to assume that address 0 is allowed for access by load instructions. This appears to be extremely useful, since the usual interpretation of **nil** pointers is 0. Thus, a memory access through a **nil** pointer references memory at address 0. For example, consider the following piece of code:

$$if\ (c \neq 0)\ then\ a = *c; \qquad\qquad (3)$$

The insertion of $a = *c$ before the comparison $c \neq 0$ is strongly safe under the assumption that zero is a valid address. This assumption may have negative impact on the debuggability of programs, since memory accesses through **nil** pointer will be allowed. The main motivation for this extension to our approach is that all the Unix implementations that we have checked allow this kind of read access to 0 address.

It is evident that in practice, many of the memory references are within small distances of other memory references. To take advantage of this property in a general context, we suggest to use page padding, i.e., to allocate dummy pages on both sides of the data segment(s), as well as on both sides of address 0, and allow these pages to be accessed by load instructions. This type of extended memory layout support has a minor negative impact on debuggability: only in some rare cases of dangling references that happen to access variables that are mapped closed to the end of the data segment, exceptions may be lost.

Intuitively, the above assumption on page padding implies that if we find in a program a memory reference to address a, then the accesses to all the addresses in the range $[a - k, a + k]$, for some fixed k (e.g., k is the size of the page in the memory system), will not cause exceptions. Also, by the same padding property, the memory accesses in the range of $[-k, k]$ are allowed as well. (Notice that to support memory accesses to negative virtual addresses, a special type of operating system support is required.)

To put this extended memory layout support in a formal way, we modify the definition of safety on an execution path from Section 2. Let π be an execution sequence of P, and let pt be a point in P along π. Let h be the value of r at π in pt. Then, the insertion of $ref(r)$ before pt is *safe* along π if there exists l such that $|l - h| \leq k$, and one of the following conditions is true:

1. there is an instruction in π which refers to l as address.

2. l is a valid address.

6 Exploiting the Improved Memory Layout

The notion of valid addresses has served as a parameter of both the path analysis algorithm presented in Section 3 and the conservative algorithms of Section 4.2. Thus, these algorithms can easily handle the refinements to valid addresses as those that were presented in Section 5.

Limited form of condition statement can also be handled. For example, the conditional statement in (3) (see Section 5) may be handled by inserting a dummy $ref(c)$ in the empty else clause of this statement. This dummy assignment uses the fact that is legal to refer to c when $c = 0$. After this assignment has been inserted, the path analysis algorithm will find that the insertion of $ref(c)$ is strongly safe before the whole conditional statement.

Supporting page padding is somewhat more complicated than that. A simple conservative approximation is obtained by allowing displacements as part of the specification of an address for a memory reference. Here, instructions of the form: $ref(r + \Delta)$, where $-k \leq \Delta \leq k$, are allowed. The path analysis algorithm will interpret such instruction as a reference to address r, and will use this information to prove safety. By the extended definition of safety in Section 5, Lemma 3.1 remains true.

The main problem with this approach is that the assignment instructions of the form $r_1 := r_2 + \Delta$ are always interpreted as unsafe. For example, if r_2 is referred prior to such an instruction v, then, for every l such that $-k - \Delta \leq l \leq k - \Delta$, the insertion of $ref(r_1 + l)$ is strongly safe after v. In the rest of this section, the algorithm of Section 4.2 is refined to handle such instructions.

Since Lemma 4.2 remains true for the extended definition of safety, we now refine the conservative forward and backward algorithms of Section 4, so as to handle instructions of the form $r_1 := r_2 + \Delta$ where Δ is an integer literal constant.

Recall that the data structure in the algorithm of Section 4.2 is the safety boolean vectors $s_b[v](val)$ and $s_a[v](val)$. To handle page padding, these boolean vectors are replaced by sets of integers denoted by capital letters $S_b[v](val)$ where $z \in S_b[v](val_b[v](e))$ if the insertion of $ref(r + z)$ before v is strongly safe. The sets $S_a[v](val)$ after v are similarly defined.

For a set of integers S and an integer z, we define $S + z$ as follows:
$$S + z \stackrel{\text{def}}{=} \{z' + z | z' \in S\}.$$
Also, let $S_k = \{z : -k \leq z \leq k\}$ and $\top$ be an element which denotes the universe set of integers.

For every source vertex v of G, the new initialization is $S_a[v](val) = \top$ and $S_b[v](val)) = S_k$ if there exists an expression e such that e always holds valid addresses and $val = val_b[v](e)$, and otherwise $S_b[v](val) = \phi$. For any other $v \in V$, the initialization is $S_b[v](val) = S_a[b](val) = \top$.

Let v be an assignment statement of the form $r := e_0 + z$ where z is an integer literal. Let $r_1, r_2, \ldots, r_n$ be the registers referred as addresses in e. Then, $S_b[v](val)$ is computed in the iteration using the equation:
$$S_b[v](val) = \begin{cases} \cap\{S_a[u](val_a[u](e))|(u, v) \in E, \exists e, val_b[v](e) = val\} \cup S_k & \exists i : 1 \leq i \leq n, val = val_b[v](r_i) \\ \cap\{S_a[u](val_a[u](e))|(u, v) \in E, \exists e, val_b[v](e) = val\} & \text{otherwise} \end{cases}$$
Also, $S_a[v](val)$ is computed by:
$$S_a[v](val) = \begin{cases} S_b[v](val_b[v](e_0)) - z & val = val_a[v](r) \\ S_b[v](val) & \text{otherwise} \end{cases}$$
The treatment of other types of instructions is similar.

Lemma 6.1 *When the forward iterative algorithms terminates, for every $r \in R$, $v \in V$ and $z \in S_b[v](val_b[v](r))$, the insertion of $ref(r + z)$ before v is strongly safe.* $\Box$

Similarly to the forward algorithm, a backward iterative algorithm can be suggested.

7 Experimental results

Here we present experimental results for proving safety of speculative loads in the context of a prototype for *global scheduling* for the IBM RS/6000 machine [BR91]. The implemented algorithm yields results which are less accurate than the path analysis algorithm of Section 3, but they are comparable. Also, for efficiency, the analysis in the implemented algorithm was done locally. For example, for proving safety of a load instruction in a loop, only program statements in this loop were considered. The implemented algorithm assumes the memory layout organization that was described in Section 5.

We have evaluated this algorithm on a set of benchmarks (written in C) as follows:

program	total	safe	p-unsafe	p-safe
LI	1286	81%	1%	18%
EQNTOTT	640	43%	6%	51%
ESPRESSO	2759	41%	2%	57%
GCC	6865	55%	2%	43%

Table 3: Experimental results for safety of speculative loads

1. LI: LISP interpreter,

2. EQNTOTT: translation of Boolean equations into truth tables,

3. ESPRESSO: logic minimization,

4. GCC: the GNU C compiler,

The results are presented in Table 3 which provides the following information:

1. **total**: the total number of load instructions considered for proving their safety. Notice that not all of these instructions will be subsequently scheduled for speculative execution.

2. **safe**: a fraction of load instructions that were proved safe.

3. **p-unsafe** (probably unsafe): a fraction of load instructions which refer to addresses loaded from unknown memory places. It is in general hard, if not impossible, to prove safety of these instructions.

4. **p-safe** (potentially safe): a fraction of load instructions that were not proved safe, but are not **p-unsafe**. These instructions are natural candidates for improving the accuracy of the algorithms for proving safety.

It is worthwhile to notice that there is a considerable fraction of load instructions that were not proved safe, but usually they do not cause exceptions when scheduled speculatively (**p-safe** column). This means that, by extending the current algorithm in a way similar to the suggestions in Section 4.2 and using more global information, we should be able to prove safety of even a larger fraction of speculative loads than was shown in Table 3.

8   Related work

Kennedy's safety algorithm in [Ken72] determines that the insertion of a general expression e is safe before a vertex v, i.e., the computation of e before v will not raise new exceptions. This is done by scanning the program iteratively in a backward direction. An expression e is detected as safe before a vertex v only if all the paths after v contain a computation of e. Since Kennedy's algorithm does not take into account values, it is comparable to the path analysis algorithm of Section 3. In the sequel, we explain why our path analysis algorithm is more accurate than Kennedy's.

The path analysis algorithm can be also extended to find the safety of a general expression e. The graph $G_1[e]$ for an expression e is defined by connecting every definition of an argument in e into the vertex t. The edges in $G_1[e] - G_2[e]$ are ones which either contain the usage of e, or a safe definition (like an assignment of a valid address). Of course, one needs to reformulate the set of safe definitions, according to the particular expression and exception. For example, if one wishes to determine that x/y does not raise a divide by zero exception, then any assignment to y of the form $y := c$ where $c \neq 0$ may be considered as safe. The path analysis algorithm identifies more safe expressions (and in particular expressions of the form $ref(r)$) since:

1. The path analysis algorithm also takes into account forward information. For example, if $ref(r)$ appears in all the paths to a certain vertex, then the path analysis algorithm will determine that $ref(r)$ is strongly safe, whereas Kennedy's algorithm will not.

2. The path analysis algorithm handles safe definitions which are considered unsafe by Kennedy. Kennedy's algorithm may be also modified to handle safe definitions.

Proposing a different direction for handling exceptions, Hennessy [Hen81] suggests to annotate the program, telling where exceptions may happen, so as to disable optimization on those parts of the program.

Considering the safety problem of speculative execution, in [CMC$^+$91] it was suggested to have special non-interruptible machine opcodes for speculative instructions which will smooth all the exceptions resultant by them. The disadvantage of this approach is that we lose the debuggability of the program. For example, it may happen that in its original place an instruction was causing an exception (say, because of a program bug); then after it was moved speculatively, no exception is raised.

Alternatively, the interrupt handling routine of the operating system can be modified, so as to intercept the exceptions at run-time. The compiler is supposed to record the addresses of speculative instructions in a place that is accessible from the interrupt routine. Then, this routine can determine if the exception was caused by a speculative instruction and handle it respectively. The advantage of this approach is that it does not require special opcodes for speculative instructions, but it suffers of the same problem of missed exceptions.

Yet another approach is advocated in [Ebc88]. There, in addition to having non-interruptible opcodes for speculative instructions, there is a special bit for every machine register which is set when the contents of the register is invalid. When a speculative instruction causes an exception, it is not raised, but the result register of the instruction is marked as invalid. This architecture allows to proceed with computing arithmetic instructions whose operands are invalid (if one of the operands is invalid, the result is also invalid). Only when an instruction that has side-effects (like store to memory, branch, etc.) uses an invalid operand, an exception is raised. This approach improves on the previous two, since it does not miss program exceptions. However, it does require significant hardware support and run-time handling of speculative instructions.

Finally, in [SLH90] a massive hardware support for speculative instructions was suggested. It was proposed there that the hardware will not commit on the results of the speculative instructions and will not raise exceptions resultant by them until the direction of the branch over which these instructions were moved is known. This approach allows to determine the exact reason and place of the exceptions caused by speculative execution. Being powerful by its nature, this approach is expensive in both the real-estate on the chip required to implement the hardware support as well as the run-time required to maintain the results of the speculative instructions.

9 Conclusions

Safe loads using the extended memory layout approach point to a very interesting research direction, in which the domain of legal memory accesses is extended beyond the domain which is needed for correct execution of the program. By supporting the extended memory layout, new opportunities for more efficient code are created. It is not clear whether other elements of a given computing model may exhibit the same property, e.g., can their domain be extended so as to allow new optimization techniques.

Acknowledgments

We would like to thank Reinhard Wilhelm for pointing out the work of Kennedy. We would also like to thank Marty Hopkins for numerous useful suggestions, and Doron Cohen and Yuval Lavon for the help in the implementation of the algorithms.

References

[ASU85] A.V. Aho, R. Sethi, and J.D. Ullman. *Compilers: Principles, Techniques and Tools.* Addison-Wesley, 1985.

[AWZ88] B. Alpern, M.N. Wegman, and F.K. Zadeck. Detecting equality of variables in programs. In *ACM Symposium on Principles of Programming Languages*, pages 1–11, 1988.

[BR91] D. Bernstein and M. Rodeh. Global instruction scheduling for superscalar machines. In *SIGPLAN Conference on Programming Languages Design and Implementation*, pages 241–255, 1991.

[CMC+91] P.P. Chang, S.A. Mahlke, W.Y. Chen, N.J. Warter, and W.W. Hwu. IMPACT: An architectural framework for multiple-issue processors. In *IEEE Conference on Computer Architecture*, pages 266–275, 1991.

[Ebc88] K. Ebcioglu. Some design ideas for a VLIW architecture for sequential-natured software. In *IFIP Conference on Parallel Processing*, 1988.

[Ell85] J.R. Ellis. *Bulldog: A Compiler for VLIW Architectures.* PhD thesis, Yale University, February 1985.

[EN89] K. Ebcioglu and T. Nakanati. A new compilation technique for parallelizing regions with unpredictable branches on a VLIW architecture. In *Workshop on Languages and Compilers for Parallel Computing*, 1989.

72

[GS90]   R. Gupta and M.L. Soffa. Region scheduling: An approach for detecting and redistribut-
          ing parallelism. *IEEE Transactions on Software Engineering*, 16(4):421–431, 1990.

[Hen81]   J.L. Hennessy. Program optimization and exception handling. In *ACM Symposium on
          Principles of Programming Languages*, pages 200–206, 1981.

[HG83]   J.L. Hennessy and T. Gross. Postpass code optimization of pipeline constraints. *ACM
          Transactions on Programming Languages and Systems*, 5:422–448, 1983.

[Ken72]   K. Kennedy. Safety of code motion. *Intern. J. Computer Math.*, 3:117–130, 1972.

[Ken81]   K. Kennedy. A survey of data flow analysis techniques. In S.S. Muchnick and N.D.
          Jones, editors, *Program Flow Analysis: Theory and Applications*, chapter 1, pages 5–54.
          Prentice-Hall, 1981.

[Kil73]   G.A. Kildall. A unified approach to global program optimization. In *ACM Symposium
          on Principles of Programming Languages*, pages 194–206, 1973.

[KU76]   J.B. Kam and J.D. Ullman. Global data flow analysis and iterative algorithms. *Journal
          of the ACM*, 23(1):158–171, 1976.

[Lar89]   J.R. Larus. *Restructuring Symbolic Programs for Concurrent Execution on Multiproces-
          sors*. PhD thesis, University of California, 1989.

[Mye81]   E.W. Myers. A precise inter-procedural data flow algorithm. In *ACM Symposium on
          Principles of Programming Languages*, pages 219–230, 1981.

[RL77]   J.H. Reif and H.R. Lewis. Symbolic evaluations and the global value graph. In *ACM
          Symposium on Principles of Programming Languages*, pages 104–118, 1977.

[RWZ88]   B.K. Rosen, M.N. Wegman, and F.K. Zadeck. Global value numbers and redundant
          computations. In *ACM Symposium on Principles of Programming Languages*, pages 12–
          27, 1988.

[SFRW90] S. Sagiv, N. Francez, M. Rodeh, and R. Wilhelm. A logic-based approach to data
          flow analysis problems. In P. Deransart and J. Małuszynkski, editors, *LNCS 456, 2nd
          Workshop on Programming Language Implementation and Logic Programming*. Springer-
          Verlag, 1990.

[SLH90]   M.D. Smith, M.S. Lam, and M.A. Horowitz. Boosting beyond static scheduling in a
          superscalar processor. In *IEEE Conference on Computer Architecture*, pages 344–354,
          1990.

[War90]   H. Warren. Instruction scheduling for the IBM RISC System/6000. *IBM Journal on
          Research and Development*, pages 85–92, 1990.

[WZ85]   M.N. Wegman and F.K. Zadeck. Constant propagation with conditional branches. In
          ACM Symposium on Principles of Programming Languages, 1985.

Typed Norms *

A. Bossi, N. Cocco, M. Fabris
Dip. di Matematica Pura e Applicata
Università di Padova
via Belzoni, 7 - 35131 - PADOVA - ITALY
e.mail: Bossi, Cocco@pdmat1.unipd.it

Abstract

In this paper *typed norms*, a class of functions to evaluate terms which have a specified structure, are defined and studied. The required structure is described by means of a *type schema* which has to be *well formed*, that is well defined and unambiguous. By interpreting the type schema in a semantic domain, we associate a set of typed norms to it. Such norms can distinguish among: (1) terms which have the required structure and hence are evaluated in the semantic domain, (2) terms which do not have it and hence are evaluated to "false", (3) terms which could have instances with the required structure and hence are evaluated to "may be". In the first two cases the term cannot change its "main" structure by applying a substitution to it, and hence its value is fixed. This is an interesting property allowing us to describe terms properties which cannot be affected by further computation, once they have been reached. The applications of typed norms can be determined by choosing the language of the type schema and the semantic domain. In the examples we show how a simple proof method for universal termination of pure Prolog programs, we proposed in [BCF91a, BCF91b], is extended to deal with a larger class of programs.

1. Introduction

In [BCF91a, BCF91b] we have studied a rather simple and general technique for proving universal termination of a pure Prolog program (without extra-logical features) with respect to a class of goals. Universal termination is a strong property requiring that all the derivations of a query in the class are finite and hence that all its solutions are reached. The basic idea in our approach was to keep the verification technique as simple as possible and to single out the parts of the proof which can be automatized while retaining the maximum of generality. The

---

* This work has been partially supported by "Progetto Finalizzato Sistemi Informatici e Calcolo Parallelo" of CNR under Grant n. 89.00026.69

generality of the method is due to the fact that it is just an adaptation of the technique which is used in traditional procedural programming: a computation is proved to terminate by associating a partial function to each cycle in it. This function maps the computation states into a well-founded set, and its value has to decrease at each iteration. The simplicity of our proposal is related to an important observation: *when we reason informally about termination of a given query in a program, we consider terms with a structure which is fixed at least in the part traversed by the program.* In this way we get convinced that the traversal is actually finite. We never simulate the actual computation by considering the composition of unifiers in the derivation! We reason only at a syntactic level. This observation leads us to the definition of *rigid terms*, namely terms with the property of having an associated measure which is fixed, independent from substitutions and hence from the computation. We define also *a class of norms, semi-linear ones*, which have the nice property of allowing a syntactic characterization of rigid terms. Our termination proofs make use of predicates annotations in order to express useful information such as rigidity of terms or relations among terms in the same atom. Such annotations, in the form of *pre/post specifications*, must be *well-behaved with respect to substitutions*, which means that, if they hold at a certain point, then they hold through the following computation since they cannot be falsified by unification. Also the *ordering functions* we associate to cycles, are *not increasing with respect to substitutions*. In this way it is possible to reason at a syntactic level, on the program text, thus simplifying the termination proof. Moreover it is possible to automatize to a certain extent rigidity analysis which is basic to the methodology.

Semi-linear norms are characterized by a simple recursive schema which is at the same time their strength and their weakness. The strength lays obviously on the simplicity of use and clarity of definition. A semi-linear norm associates a weight to every term and for every term it can be decided if it is rigid or not with respect to such a norm. A term which is not rigid can become rigid by substitution. However in the definition of semi-linear norms there are some restrictions. The recursive schema of a semi-linear norm gets into the term structure by only one level. Moreover so far it is not defined how different semi-linear norms can be linked to work together. The definition of a semi-linear norm is recursively based only onto itself and it is easy to understand that this is a severe restriction. Then semi-linear norms can be considered as an interesting, but limited, tool for analyzing terms. Furthermore, while evaluating the weight of a term, since we traverse the term into depth, we could also at the same time check or collect other useful information, such as the type of the term. For all these reasons we extended the definition of semi-linear norms thus allowing the application of our verification technique for universal termination to a larger class of programs.

In this paper *typed norms*, a class of functions assigning a value in a semantic domain to terms which have a specified structure, are defined and studied. The required structure is described by means of a *type schema* which has to be *well formed*. The interpretation of a well formed type schema produces a set of *typed norms*. Such norms are still simple but more powerful than semi-linear ones, while retaining all the properties which make semi-linear norms useful for termination proofs. Typed norms assign a value to a term if and only if it has a precise structure, the one described by the type schema. If the term has such a structure, then this structure and the associated value cannot be modified by further instantiating the term. If the term has not such a structure, it is possible to distinguish between the possibility and the impossibility of gaining it. Both having a fixed structure and the impossibility of gaining it, are well-behaved properties for a term, namely properties which cannot be falsified by applying further substitutions. Type schemata and typed norms give the possibility of performing also some type checking. This may be very interesting if we want to deal with properties like unifiability, which seems fundamental for verifying more complex properties such as existential termination, finite failure or universal termination without finite failure.

The paper is structured in the following way. In section 2 the notation for terms and the language for analyzing them are introduced. In section 3 type schemata are defined in order to describe and verify structural properties of terms. In section 4 type schemata are interpreted, thus associating to them a set of typed norms. Such norms can be used to evaluate the terms satisfying the structural properties defined by the corresponding schema. A few examples of using such typed norms for universal termination proofs are shown in section 5. It is not possible to deal with these examples with semi-linear norms as defined in [BCF91a, BCF91b]. In section 6 the conclusions follow. An example of a different application of typed norms, namely verifying correct typing in a program, is also given.

2.   A language for analyzing terms

We use the standard notation and terminology of [Llo87] or [Apt90] for logic programs. Term(F, V) denotes the set of terms built up in the standard way on a set F of n-ary function symbols and on a set V of variables. Var(t) denotes the set of variables of a term t. If $\rho = \{X_1/t_1, ..., X_n/t_n\}$ is a substitution, then we indicate respectively with $Dom(\rho) = \{X_1, ..., X_n\}$ and $Cod(\rho) = \{t_1, ..., t_n\}$ its domain and codomain.

We distinguish between the language of the program, that is the object language, and a language for analyzing it.

2.1 Definition.   Let L = <VAR, FUN> be our <u>object language</u>, where VAR ={X, Y, Z, ...} is the set of variables and FUN = $\{f_1, ..., f_m\}$ is the set of n-ary, n≥0, function symbols. <u>A term analyzer language, L*, on L</u> is given by:

L* = <VAR, FUN, MVAR, TYPE, EVAL>

where MVAR = {x, y, z, ...} is a set of new <u>metavariables</u> such that VAR ∩ MVAR = ∅;

TYPE = {A_1, ..., A_n} and EVAL = {g_1, ..., g_m} are two sets of function symbols, the type function symbols and the evaluable function symbols respectively, such that FUN, TYPE and EVAL are disjoint sets (TYPE ∩ FUN = ∅, EVAL ∩ FUN = ∅ and TYPE ∩ EVAL = ∅).

The type functions, TYPE, are used for checking the membership of a term into a specific set of terms. If the checked term is in the set, the type functions rewrite it into a ground term with only evaluable function symbols. This new term can be evaluated in a semantic domain.

Example.   Let us consider L* such that FUN = {o, succ(_), nil, list(_, _)}, TYPE = {Nat, Loa}, EVAL = {0, 1, +(_, _)}.

Nat can be defined so that it selects some terms, representing natural numbers such as succ(succ(o)), and it maps them into other ground terms evaluable in a semantic domain, in our example +(1, +(1, 0)) which can be evaluated to 2.

Similarly Loa (list of anything) could select well formed lists, such as list(X, list(o, nil)), and map them into a rewriting, +(1, +(1, 0)) in our case, which can be interpreted as the length of the list.

2.2 Definition.   Let L* = <VAR, FUN, MVAR, TYPE, EVAL> be a term analyzer language.

T*   = Term(FUN, MVAR ∪ VAR).

T   = Term(FUN, VAR) is the set of terms in the object language.

The set of tests on L* is the set of all the terms built up on FUN and MVAR which are not metavariables: $TEST_{L^*}$ = (Term(FUN, MVAR) - MVAR).

Let t' be a term in T*. The closure of t' in T is the set of all the terms in T that are obtained from t' by substituting its variables with terms in T: Close(t') = {t | t ∈ T, ∃ρ. (t = t'ρ)}.

Note that tests cannot be metavariables since they are meant to represent a particular term structure.

2.3 Definition.   Let t be a term in T and test in $TEST_{L^*}$

t satisfies test iff t ∈ Close(test).

t could satisfy test if t does not satisfy test but some of the proper instances of t do.

t cannot satisfy test iff neither t nor any instance of t satisfies test.

ρ is a clean mgu of t and test if t = testρ and then Dom(ρ) = Var(test) and T ⊃ Cod(ρ).

Unification among t and test can be used to determine when t satisfies test. We can state the following propositions:

1)   t satisfies test iff t and test have a clean mgu, such a clean mgu is unique;

2)   t could satisfy test iff t and test are unifiable but they have no clean unifier;

3)   t cannot satisfy test iff t and test are not unifiable.

These three cases are mutually exclusive and decidable [BCF91c].

An mgu as in (2) is called <u>a dirty mgu of t and test</u>. It is dirty in the sense that it changes t. Note that tρ might not be in $\mathbb{T}$.

Examples.

- list(succ(X), nil) satisfies the test list(x, y) and a clean mgu for them is ρ={x/succ(X), y/nil}.

- list(Y, Y) satisfies list(x, x) too and a clean mgu for them is ρ={x/ Y}. Also σ = {Y/ x} is an mgu for them, but it is not clean.

- list(succ(X), Y) could satisfy list(x, x). A dirty mgu for them is ρ={x/succ(X), Y/succ(X)}.

- list(X, X) could satisfy list(x, succ(y)). A dirty mgu for them is ρ={x/succ(y), X/succ(y)}.

- list(o, X) cannot satisfy the test list(succ(o), x) since they are not unifiable.

The following proposition states some trivial consequences of definition 2.3.

2.5 Proposition.   Let test ∈ $TEST_{L*}$ and t ∈ $\mathbb{T}$.

1)   t satisfies test iff Close(test) ⊇ Close(t).

2)   t could satisfy test iff

    i)   Close(test) ∩ Close(t) ≠ ∅;   ii)   Close(test) ⊉ Close(t).

3)   t cannot satisfy test iff Close(test) ∩ Close(t) = ∅.

2.6   Definition.   Two tests, <u>test₁</u>, <u>test₂</u> ∈ $TEST_{L*}$, <u>are independent</u> iff Close(test₁) and Close(test₂) are disjoint sets: Close(test₁) ∩ Close(test₂) = ∅.

<u>A is a set of independent tests</u> if any two tests in A are independent.

Let A, B be sets of tests. <u>A and B are independent</u> if whenever test$_a$ ∈ A and test$_b$ ∈ B, then test$_a$ and test$_b$ are independent.

2.7   Proposition.

1)   test₁, test₂ ∈ $TEST_{L*}$ are independent iff they cannot be unified in $\mathbb{T}*$ even after renaming variables.

2)   Let A be a set of independent tests and t be in $\mathbb{T}$. Three mutually exclusive cases are possible:

    i)   t cannot satisfy any test in A;

    ii)   t satisfies one test in A and it cannot satisfy the others;

    iii)   t could satisfy one or more tests in A and it cannot satisfy the others.

Examples.

- The set A = {nil, o, list(x, succ(y)), list(o, nil)} is a set of independent tests.

- B = {succ(x), succ(succ(x))} is not a set of independent tests since the two tests can be unified in T^* after renaming one of them.

- succ(o) cannot satisfy any test in A.

- list(X, nil) satisfies list(o, nil) in A and it cannot satisfy the remaining tests in A.

- list(X, Y) could satisfy the last two tests in A, but it cannot satisfy nil or o.

3. Type schemata

In this section schemata describing structural properties of terms are introduced. They are expressed in the language defined in the previous section. The schemata have been restricted in order to insure simple definitions and at the same time maintaining the maximum of generality. Such schemata can be applied to terms of the object language in order to verify if they have the described structural properties. The verification is a rewriting process: each schema defines a way of traversing the terms and then it allows one to collect information during the traversal. When we apply a schema to a term three cases are possible:

a)   the rewriting ends, in this case the term has the structure specified by the type schema and some useful information has been computed while traversing it;

b)   the rewriting is not possible, in this case the term cannot have the specified structure;

c)   the rewriting is suspended which means that the term could be instantiated so that the specified property might hold for the instance.

We distinguish two kinds of expressions on L^*: type expressions and analysis expressions.

3.1 Definition.   Let L^* = <FUN, VAR, MVAR, TYPE, EVAL> be a term analyzer language and T = Term(FUN, VAR) the terms in the object language.

A type expression is defined inductively as follows:

i)   if g is an evaluable function of arity 0 in EVAL, then g is a type expression;

ii)   if A is a type function in TYPE and x is a metavariable in MVAR, then A(x) is a type expression;

iii)   if g is an evaluable function of arity h in EVAL and $t_1, ..., t_h$ are type expressions, then $g(t_1, ..., t_h)$ is a type expression.

$T\_EXP_{L^*}$ is the set of type expressions on L^*.

An analysis expression can be obtained from a type expression by substituting each metavariable x in MVAR with a term t in T.

A_EXP$_{L*}$ is the set of analysis expressions on L*.

An evaluable expression is an analysis expression containing no type symbol.

E_EXP$_{L*}$ is the set of evaluable expressions on L*.

Note that in type expressions type function symbols are applied to metavariables only and this is the only place where metavariables can occur. As a consequence, in analysis expressions the variables of the object language can appear only inside arguments of type function symbols and evaluable expressions are necessarily ground expressions.

3.2 Definition. Let L* be a term analyzer language.

A type schema, TS$_{L*}$, on L* is a finite set of equalities in the following form:

A(test) = typexp

where A is in TYPE, test is in TEST$_{L*}$, typexp is in T_EXP$_{L*}$ and each metavariable in typexp occurs only once and it occurs also in test.

Def(A) is the set of equalities associated to the type function symbol A in TS$_{L*}$:

A(test$_1$) = typexp$_1$, ..., A(test$_k$) = typexp$_k$,

the set of tests associated to A in TS$_{L*}$ is Test(A) = {test$_1$, ..., test$_k$} and

the type expression associated to test$_i$ is typexp$_i$.

In the following we assume that L* is fixed and so we simply write TEST, T_EXP, A_EXP, ... Moreover, in order to improve readability, we write type expressions and analysis expressions using infix notation for the functions in EVAL and assume properties (commutativity, associativity, ...) of the intended interpretation of these functors when this interpretation is clear.

Examples.   Let FUN = {o, nil, empty, succ(_), list(_, _), tree(_, _, _)}.

1)   TYPE$_1$= {Nat, Lon}.   EVAL$_1$ = {ntrue, ltrue, ∧(_, _)}.

TS$_1$: {Nat = natural number, Lon = list of naturals}

Nat(o) = ntrue   Lon(nil) = ltrue

Nat(succ(x)) = Nat(x)   Lon(list(x, y)) = Nat(x) ∧ Lon(y).

2)   TYPE = {Nat, Lon, Nln, Stree}.   EVAL$_2$ = {0, 1, +(_, _)}.

TS$_2$: {Nat = natural number, Lon = list of naturals, Nln = nested list of naturals, Stree = symmetric tree}

Nat(o) = 0   Lon(nil) = 0

Nat(succ(x)) = 1 + Nat(x)   Lon(list(x, y)) = 1 + Nat(x) + Lon(y).

Nln(nil) = 0

Nln(list(x, y)) = 1+ Nat(x) + Nln(y)   Stree(empty) = 0

Nln(list(x, y)) = 1+ Nln(x) + Nln(y)   Stree(tree(x, y, y)) = 1+ Stree(y).

3.3 Definition. Let TS be a type schema.

The set of not empty types in TS, NEMPTY(TS), is recursively defined as the closure

NEMPTY(TS) = {A | A ∈ TYPE and there exists an equality A(test) = typexp in TS

such that for all B in typexp, B ∈ NEMPTY(TS)}.

It is reasonable to require from a type schema to have a correct recursive definition, namely it must actually define something and it must give a unique definition. In order to express the second property, we need to define the concept of "separate" types. The intuition is the following: if two types are separate, a term cannot belong to both of them.

3.4 Definition. Let A, B, C, D be type function symbols in a type schema TS. Let x ∈ MVAR.

A and B are separate in TS iff every pair of equalities in Def(A) × Def(B) is separable.

A pair of equalities, A(test$_1$) = typexp$_1$ and B(test$_2$) = typexp$_2$, in TS is separable iff

i)   either test$_1$ and test$_2$ are independent or

ii)   test$_1$ and test$_2$ are equal and for some variable x there exist a subexpression C(x) of typexp$_1$ and a subexpression D(x) of typexp$_2$, such that C and D are separate in TS.

Examples.   In TS$_2$, Test(Nat) and Test(Nln) are independent, hence Nat and Nln are separate. On the contrary, Lon and Nln are not separate since Test(Lon) and Test(Nln) are not independent and Lon(nil) = 0 and Nln(nil) = 0, thus condition (ii) is not satisfied.

3.5   Definition.   A type schema TS is well formed iff

1)   TYPE = NEMPTY(TS);

2)   for every A ∈ TYPE, every pair of (distinct) equalities in Def(A) are separable.

The first condition is meant to ensure a basis for each recursive type definition. The second condition is meant to guarantee a unique result when applying the type schema to a term.

Examples.   TS$_1$ and TS$_2$ are well formed schemata. Regarding condition (2), the only not trivial case is given by the two recursive definitions of Nln in TS$_2$. list(x, y) is a common test while Nat and Nln are separate.

A well formed type schema represents sets of terms in the object language which have the structures specified by the schema itself. Such sets correspond to the closures of the equations associated to the type functions with respect to instantiation in T.

3.6 Definition. Let A be a type function symbol in a well formed type schema TS and let t be a term in T.

1) <u>t belongs to A in TS</u> if

    i)   in TS there exists $A(\text{test}(x_1, ..., x_m)) = \text{typexp}$, such that t satisfies test: $t = \text{testρ}$, with $ρ = \{x_1/ s_1, ..., x_m/ s_m\}$, and

    ii)   for all subexpressions $B(s_j)$ of typexpρ s_j belongs to B.

2) <u>t cannot belong to A in TS</u> if

    either for all test $\in$ Test(A), t cannot satisfy test,

    or   there exists $\text{test}(x_1, ..., x_m) \in$ Test(A) such that

        t satisfies test: $t = \text{testρ}$, $ρ = \{x_1/ s_1, ..., x_m/ s_m\}$, and

        for every equation $A(\text{test}(x_1, ..., x_m)) = \text{typexp}$ in Def(A),

        there exists a subexpressions $B(s_j)$ of typexpρ such that s_j cannot belong to B.

3) <u>t could belong to A in TS</u> if neither (1) nor (2) holds.

From definitions 3.4, 3.5 and 3.6 we have the following proposition.

3.7 Proposition. Let TS be a well formed type schema.

1) For any type function A in TYPE, at least one term belongs to A.

2) For any term t in T, one and only one of the three cases of definition 3.6 holds.

3) Let A and B be two separate type function symbols, then

    if t belongs to A, then t cannot belong to B.

The rewriting process described by a well formed type schema can be represented by a derivation tree. Building such a tree for a type function applied to a term corresponds to verifying if the term belongs to the type.

3.8 Definition. Let TS be a well formed type schema, let exp be an analysis expression. <u>The derivation tree of exp in TS, TREE(exp)</u>, is a tree whose nodes are labelled either by an analysis expression or by **fail**. TREE(exp) is built up in the following way:

    label the root with exp;

    repeat

      choose and mark a not marked leaf node, exp';

      if exp' has a subexpression B(s) such that s does not unify with any test in Test(B)

          then   add a single marked leaf: **fail**

          else   **if**   exp' has at least one subexpression B(s) such that s satisfies $\text{test}_1 = ... = \text{test}_n$ in Test(B) with the clean mgu ρ,

                    then choose the leftmost B(s);

                        add n leaves to exp': exp'$σ_j$,

                        where $σ_j = [B(s)/\text{typexp}_j\, ρ]$, with $1 \le j \le n$,

    until all the leaves have been marked.

Examples.

1) Let us consider the type schema TS_2 and let us build the derivation tree of Nln(list(list(succ(o), nil), nil)).

$$\underline{\text{Nln(list(list(succ(o), nil), nil))}}$$

/ \

1+ $\underline{\text{Nat(list(succ(o), nil))}}$ + Nln(nil)   1+ $\underline{\text{Nln(list(succ(o), nil))}}$ + Nln(nil)

/ / \

fail   1+ 1+ $\underline{\text{Nat(succ(o))}}$+ Nln(nil) + Nln(nil)   1+ 1+ $\underline{\text{Nln(succ(o))}}$+ Nln(nil)+ Nln(nil)

| |

1+ 1+ 1+ $\underline{\text{Nat(o)}}$+ Nln(nil) + Nln(nil)   **fail**

|

1+ 1+ 1+ 0 + $\underline{\text{Nln(nil)}}$ + Nln(nil)

|

1+ 1+ 1+ 0 + 0 + $\underline{\text{Nln(nil)}}$

|

1+ 1+ 1+ 0 + 0 + 0

2) Let us consider again the type schema TS_2 and the derivation tree of Nln(list(list(succ(X), nil), nil)).

$$\underline{\text{Nln(list(list(succ(X), nil), nil))}}$$

/ \

1+ $\underline{\text{Nat(list(succ(X), nil))}}$ + Nln(nil)   1+ $\underline{\text{Nln(list(succ(X), nil))}}$ + Nln(nil)

/ / \

fail   1+ 1 + $\underline{\text{Nat(succ(X))}}$+ Nln(nil) + Nln(nil)   1 + 1+ $\underline{\text{Nln(succ(X))}}$+ Nln(nil) + Nln(nil)

| |

1+ 1 +1+ Nat(X)+ $\underline{\text{Nln(nil)}}$ + Nln(nil)   **fail**

|

1+ 1 +1+ Nat(X)+ 0 + $\underline{\text{Nln(nil)}}$

|

1+ 1 + 1 + Nat(X) + 0 + 0

3.9 Lemma. Let TS be a well formed type schema. For every exp in A_EXP, TREE(exp) is finite.

The lemma is a consequence of the fact that in the left side of the equations in TS a type can never be applied to a metavariable; therefore each equation corresponds to term decomposition. A complete proof is given in [BCF91c].

3.10 Lemma. Let TS be a well formed type schema and let exp be in A_EXP.

If exp contains at least one type function symbol, then one of the following three exclusive cases holds:

1) (failed tree) all the leaves in TREE(exp) are labelled by **fail** and there exists at least one subexpression of exp, B(s), such that s cannot belong to B;

2) (success tree) all the leaves in TREE(exp) are labelled by **fail** except one which is labelled by an evaluable expression (ground and containing no type function symbols) and for any subexpression of exp, B(s), s belongs to B;

3) (expansible tree) the leaves in TREE(exp) are partitioned into two sets:

    i)   a possibly empty set of leaves labelled by **fail**;

    ii)   a not empty set of leaves labelled by expressions which contain only subexpressions B(s) such that s could belong to B.

The proof is by induction on the depth of TREE(exp) and it is given in [BCF91c].

3.11 Corollary. Let TS be a well formed type schema, A be in TYPE and t in T.

1)   TREE(A(t)) is failed iff t cannot belong to A;

2)   TREE(A(t)) is successful iff t belongs to A;

3)   TREE(A(t)) is expansible iff t could belong to A.

3.12 Proposition. Let TS be a well formed type schema, A be in TYPE and t in T.

1)   If t belongs to A, then for every substitution σ such that $T \supset Cod(\sigma)$, tσ belongs to A and TREE(A(tσ)) has the same evaluable leaf as TREE(A(t)).

2)   If t cannot belong to A, then for every substitution σ such that $T \supset Cod(\sigma)$, tσ cannot belong to A.

The proof is given in [BCF91c] by induction on the complexity of the term t.

Both belonging to a type and the impossibility to belong to it are properties which are invariant wrt substitution. Moreover, by Lemma 3.10 and its Corollary, it is possible to transfer information about the structure from a term to its subterms and viceversa. These are exactly the properties we need for verifying universal termination of logic programs with our method, as we will see in the next section.

4. Typed Norms

The evaluable expressions we defined in section 3 can be interpreted. Their interpretation depends on the analysis we want to perform on terms. A particular interpretation is determined by giving a semantic domain in order to associate a meaning to the evaluable function symbols already introduced. We need to distinguish three cases: when a term has the required structural property and hence it can be rewritten and interpreted, when it cannot have the required structural property and when it could have it, if properly instantiated. In order to represent the last two cases we introduce two special semantic values: **false** and **maybe**.

4.1 Definition. Let I be a not empty set and EVAL be a set of evaluable function symbols. <u>An interpretation of EVAL in I, [ ]</u>, is defined in this way:
1) $[f] = c \in I$, if f has arity 0;
2) $[f] = f_I : I^n \to I$, if f has arity n>0.
I is <u>a semantic domain</u>.

The interpretation can be naturally extended to all evaluable expressions:
$$[f(t_1, ..., t_h)] = f_I ([t_1], ..., [t_h]).$$

4.2 Definition. Let TS be a type schema, I a not empty set and [ ] an interpretation of EVAL in I. Let T be the set of terms in the object language and A be in TYPE.
<u>The typed norm $| \; |_{I,A}$ associated to A by TS and [ ]</u>, is the function
$$| \; |_{I,A} : T \to I \cup \{\textbf{maybe, false}\}$$
defined in the following way:
1) $|t|_{I,A} = \textbf{false}$ iff   t cannot belong to A;
2) $|t|_{I,A} = \textbf{maybe}$ iff   t could belong to A;
3) $|t|_{I,A} = [exp] \in I$ iff   t belongs to A and exp is the label of the only evaluable leaf in TREE(A(t)).

Example. Let us consider TS_1 with the interpretation
1) $I = \{\textbf{true}\}$ and [ntrue] = **true**, [ltrue] = **true**, $[\wedge] = \wedge$ (the usual logical "and"). It induces the typed norms $| \; |_{I,Nat}$ and $| \; |_{I,Lon}$ such that
$|list(succ(o), nil)|_{I,Lon} = \textbf{true}$. In fact TREE(Lon(list(succ(o), nil))) is successful and its only evaluable leaf is (ntrue $\wedge$ ltrue);
$|list(succ(o), X)|_{I,Lon} = \textbf{maybe}$. In fact TREE(Lon(list(succ(o), X))) is expansible. Its only suspended leaf is (ntrue $\wedge$ Lon(X));
Such norms determine if a term is either a natural number or a list containing only natural numbers.

2) $I = N$ and $[ltrue] = 0$, $[ntrue] = 1$, $[\wedge] = +$, where + is the usual sum of natural numbers. It induces the typed norms $| \cdot |_{I,Nat}$ and $| \cdot |_{I,Lon}$ such that

$|list(o, list(succ(o), list(succ(succ(o)), nil)))|_{I,Nat} = 3$. In fact $TREE(Lon(list(o, list(succ(o)), list(succ(succ(o)), nil))))$ is successful. Its only evaluable leaf is $(1+1+1+0)$.

$|list(o, X)|_{I,Nat} = $ **maybe**. In fact $TREE(Lon(list(o, X)))$ is expansible. Its only suspended leaf is $(1+Lon(X))$.

Such norms determine the length of a list of natural numbers.

Let A be a type function in a well formed type schema TS and I a not empty set. Let t be in T and $| \cdot |_{I,A}$ be a typed norm. From 4.2 and the properties of $TREE(A(t))$ stated in section 3, we have that:

1)   for every substitution σ such that $T \supset Cod(\sigma)$,
    i)   if $|t|_{I,A} \in I$, then $|t\sigma|_{I,A} = |t|_{I,A}$;
    ii)   if $|t|_{I,A} = $ **false**, then $|t\sigma|_{I,A} = $ **false**;

2) $|t|_{I,A} \in I$ iff
    there is one and only one equation in TS, $A(test) = typexp(B_1(x_1), ..., B_n(x_n))$, such that
    i)   t satisfies test, $t=test\rho$;
    ii) $|t|_{I,A} = typexp(|x_1\rho|_{I,B1}, ..., |x_n\rho|_{I,Bn})$;

3) $| \cdot |_{I,A}$ is a total function;

4)   there exists $t \in T$ such that $|t|_{I,A} \in I$.

Typed norms include semi-linear norms [BCF91a, BCF91b]. Let $|...|$ be a semi-linear norm on T defined as follow:

    for all functions f in FUN,
    $|f(t_1, ..., t_n)| = c_f + |t_{i1}| + ... + |t_{im}|$,   where $c_f \in N$, and $\{1, ..., n\} \supseteq \{i_1, ..., i_m\}$.

Let TYPE = {Semil} and EVAL = {c_f | f in FUN} $\cup$ {+(_, _)}. The type schema, TS, corresponding to $|...|$ is defined as follows:

1)   for all functions f in FUN the schema contains an equality
    $Semilin(f(x_1, ..., x_n)) = c_f + Semilin(x_{i1}) + ... + Semilin(x_{im})$,
    where $x_1, ..., x_n$, are distinct variables;

2)   there are not other equalities.

It is clear that, for all t in T, $TREE(Semilin(t))$ has no branching.

4.3 Proposition.   Let $|...|$ be a semi-linear norm on T, TS the corresponding type schema and [] an interpretation in N given by $[c_f] = c_f$ and $[+(_, _)] = +$. Let $| \cdot |_{N,Semilin}$ be the typed norm induced by TS.

For every t in T:

1) $|t| = n$ and rigid(t) $\Leftrightarrow$ $|t|_{N,Semilin} = n$.

2) $|t| = n$ and not-rigid(t) $\Leftrightarrow$ $|t|_{N,Semilin} = $ **maybe**.

$VREL_{||}(t)$ are the variables in the label of the only leaf node in TREE(Semilin(t)).

5.   Applications

In this section we give a few examples of universal termination proofs for logic programs, which are not feasible by using semi-linear norms and which are feasible by using typed norms. The verification methodology is the one we defined in [BCF91a, BCF91b], hence the proof is still reasonably simple. The only novelty is the possibility of using typed norms to analyze also programs which traverse the terms in a complex way. The class of goals for which universal termination is ensured does still include not ground goals, only the part of the terms which is traversed by the program need to be fixed. We briefly recall our verification technique in the first example, the other verification examples are only sketched for brevity. From now on we adopt the notation for lists which is usual in logic programming and we use underlined symbols, such as $\underline{x}$ or $\underline{t}$, to denote tuples. Moreover, for simplicity's sake, we shall often write A(t) instead of "t belongs to A" and $\neg$A(t) instead of "t cannot belong to A".

1)   Let us consider the following program.
P_1:   1:   check([X| Xs]) :- check(Xs).
        2:    check([X]) :- nat(X).
        3:    nat(s(X)) :- nat(X).
        4:    nat(o).

check(t) holds if t is a not empty list with a natural number as its last element.

If t is a list with a variable as tail or if it is a list of fixed length whose last element is a variable X or $s^n(X)$, then the program loops. We would like to prove that the class of goals described by $\{:- p(t).\}$, where t is a non-empty list whose last element belongs to **N**, universally terminates in P_1. A semi-linear norm cannot be used since it cannot distinguish the last element of a list from the other ones. But we can very naturally define a typed norm for this purpose. In P_1, FUN = $\{o, s(\_), [], [\_|\_]\}$ is the set of program language functors.

Let TYPE = {Length, Nat, Empty} and EVAL = $\{0, 1, +(\_, \_)\}$ and consider the following type schema:

TS: Lastn([x| y]) = 1 + Lastn(y)   Nat(s(x)) = 1 + Nat(x)
      Lastn([x| y]) = Nat(x) + Empty(y)   Nat(o) = 0
      Empty([]) = 0

The type schema is well formed. Consider the interpretation $\{|\ |_{N,Lastn}, |\ |_{N,Nat}, |\ |_{N,Empty}\}$ of TS determined by the usual interpretation of EVAL in **N**.

I t I$_{N,Lastn}$ ∈ N means that that t belongs to Lastn. The description of the class of goals we are considering becomes: {:- check(t).; Lastn(t)}.

Our termination proof technique [BCF91a, BCF91b] is similar to the one used in procedural programming. When considering a program without mutual recursion, the general method can be simplified and it consists in

(a)   associating to each predicate symbol p in the program *a pre/post specification* {Pre($\underline{x}$)} p($\underline{x}$) {Post($\underline{x}$)}, *well-behaved with respect to substitutions*, in order to state terms properties which can be useful for proving termination. Well-behaved with respect to substitutions means that if an instance p($\underline{t}$) of p satisfies its precondition (postcondition) then every further instantiation p($\underline{t\sigma}$) also satisfies it;

(b)   proving the correctness of such a specification. Following the criterion proposed in [BC89, BCF91b] this can be done by proving, for each clause $a_0(\underline{t_0})$:- $a_1(\underline{t_1})$, ..., $a_n(\underline{t_n})$. in the program, that the following two conditions are satisfied:

    1) $\forall \underline{x}. (\text{Pre}_0(\underline{t_0}) \wedge (\wedge_{i=1}^{k-1} \text{Post}_i(\underline{t_i}))) \rightarrow \text{Pre}_k(\underline{t_k})$, for all k in 1, ..., n;

    2) $\forall \underline{x}. (\text{Pre}_0(\underline{t_0}) \wedge (\wedge_{i=1}^{n} \text{Post}_i(\underline{t_i}))) \rightarrow \text{Post}_0(\underline{t_0})$;

(c)   finding *an ordering function f, not increasing with respect to substitutions*, which maps the calling instances of each recursive predicate into N. A calling instance of a predicate p is an invocation of p in the computation. Not increasing with respect to substitutions means that if p($\underline{t}$) is a calling instance of p, then for every substitution σ: $f(p(\underline{t\sigma})) \leq f(p(\underline{t}))$.

(d)   proving, for every recursive clause $a_0(\underline{t_0})$:- $a_1(\underline{t_1})$, ..., $a_m(\underline{t_m})$. and every $a_k(\underline{t_k})$, which is a recursive call of $a_0(\underline{t_0})$, that the following condition holds:

    $\forall \underline{x}. (\text{Pre}_0(\underline{t_0}) \wedge (\wedge_{j=1}^{k-1} \text{Post}_j(\underline{t_j})) \rightarrow (f(a_k(\underline{t_k})) < f(a_0(\underline{t_0})))$,

    namely the information given in the specification ensures that the value of the ordering function on the head is greater than the value on the recursive call.

Steps (b) and (d) of the method can be handled in a simple way since the pre/post specifications and the ordering functions "well-behave" with respect to substitutions and this allows us to ignore the actual computation (that is real unification) and to reason at a syntactic level. For further details see [BCF91a, BCF91b].

We now apply the technique to our example. Due to space limitations, we describe only points (a) and (c). The proofs required in points (b) and (d) are rather simple.

a)   The pre/post specification we associate to each predicate is

    {Lastn(t) ∨ Empty(t)} check(t) {true}

    {Nat(t)} nat(t) {true}.

The specification is rather trivial since the clauses have no local variables and moreover each predicate has arity one. Hence no relation among terms need to be known for proving termination. The meaning of the specification is the following: the predicate check is called with an argument in Lastn and nat is called with an argument in Nat. Such a specification is clearly well-behaved wrt substitutions since it deals only with the structure of input terms.

c) The ordering function is intended to measure the part of the term which is traversed by the program. As an ordering function we can associate the weight of the input terms defined by the typed norm induced by TS:

$$f: \quad check(t) \quad \rightarrow \quad | t |_{N,Lastn} \qquad\qquad \text{if } Lastn(t)$$
$$| t |_{N,Empty} \qquad\qquad \text{if } Empty(t)$$
$$0 \qquad\qquad\qquad\qquad \text{otherwise}$$
$$nat(t) \quad \rightarrow \quad | t |_{N,Nat} \qquad\qquad \text{if } Nat(t)$$
$$0 \qquad\qquad\qquad\qquad \text{otherwise}$$

The ordering function is not increasing wrt substitutions. In fact t belongs to the type at every invocation of the predicate and then the weight of the input term t does not change by instantiating it as shown in section 4.

2) Let us now consider the following program.

P₂: 1: change([], []).
2: change([X, Y| Xs], [Z, Y| Zs]) :- q(X, Z), p(Y), change(Xs, Zs).
3: q([], []).
4: q([X| Xs], [a| Zs]) :- q(Xs, Zs).
5: p([]).
6: p([X| Xs]) :- nat(X), p(Xs).
7: nat(0).
8: nat(s(X)) :- nat(X).

The predicate change(t_1, t_2) holds when

i) t_1 is a list of lists whose length is even and its elements in even positions are lists of natural numbers;

ii) t_2 is equal to t_1 but with the elements in odd positions substituted by lists of "a" of the same length of the original elements.

Let us consider for example the class of goals {:- change(t_1, t_2).}, where t_1 is a finite list whose length is even (no variables in tail position) and whose elements in even positions are lists of natural numbers while the elements in odd positions are finite lists. We want to prove that all the goals in the class universally terminate in **P₂**. Semi-linear norms cannot be used in this example too. Since we need to associate different measures to the same functor list. Element lists in odd positions should have a weight corresponding to their length and elements lists in even positions should be weighted by the sum of the natural numbers which are their elements. Moreover the list of lists, given in input to the predicate change, should have a weight given by the sum of the weights of its elements. This corresponds to consider the following type schema with the standard interpretation on N.

TYPE = {N, Length, Sum, Nat}   EVAL = {0, 1, +}

TS: $N([]) = 0$ $Length([]) = 0$

$N([x, y| z]) = Length(x) + Sum(y) + N(z)$ $Length([x| y]) = 1 + Length(y)$

$Sum([]) = 0$ $Nat(o) = 0$

$Sum([x| y]) = Nat(x) + Sum(y)$ $Nat(s(x)) = 1 + Nat(x)$

The description of the class of goals we are interested in becomes: $\{:- change(t_1, t_2).; N(t_1)\}$. The termination proof then follows the usual path.

3)   As a last example, let us consider the following program:

split([b| Xs], [b| Ys], Zs) :- split(Xs, Ys, Zs).

split([a| Xs], Ys, [a| Zs]) :- split(Xs, Ys, Zs).

split([], [], []).

split(t_1, t_2, t_3) is true if t_1 is a list of b's and a's, t_2 a list of b's, t_3 a list of a's and the number of a's in t_1 is equal to the length of t_3, while the number of b's is equal to the length of t_2.

Let us consider the following type schema (with its obvious interpretation):

Finitel([]) = 0

Finitel([x| y]) = 1 + Finitel(y)

and the specification

$\{Finitel(t_1)\}$ split(t_1, t_2, t_3) $\{| t_1 |_{N,Finitel} = | t_2 |_{N,Finitel} + | t_3 |_{N,Finitel}\}$.

With this specification, we can easily prove that all the goals in the class $\{:- split(t_1, t_2, t_3).;$ Finitel(t_1)$\}$ universally terminate. But in this termination proof we do not distinguish between termination due to a finite failure of the computation, for example when the first list does not contain only a's and b's, and successful termination. This distinction can be sometimes very useful or even necessary. To this purpose we can further specialize both the specification and the typed norms in this way:

Alist([]) = 0   Blist([]) = 0

Alist([a| y]) = 1 + Alist(y)   Blist([b| y]) = 1 + Blist(y)

ABlist([]) = 0

ABlist([b| y]) = 1 + ABlist(y)

ABlist([a| y]) = 1 + ABlist(y)

and

$\{ABlist(t_1)\}$ split(t_1, t_2, t_3) $\{| t_1 |_{N,ABlist} = | t_2 |_{N,Blist} + | t_3 |_{N,Alist}\}$.

The information in the postcondition can help us to detect some goals which terminate by finite failure. For example the goals:

1)   split([a, b, a, a], [a, b], [a, a])   2)   split([a, c, a, a], X, Y).

3)   split([X, Y, Z], [X], [Z, c])   4)   split([a, a, b], [b, b], [a, a])

all terminate by finite failure. They are in the class we are interested in, but they all have a property, invariant wrt substitutions, which falsifies the postcondition. We can prove that the program is correct wrt the specification and then, when split is invoked in a way that satisfies the precondition and it terminates successfully, its postcondition must hold. Hence all the previous goals must fail. In our examples:

1) $\mid t_2 \mid_{N,Blist}$ = **false**;   2) $\mid t_1 \mid_{N,ABlist}$ = **false**;

3) $\mid t_3 \mid_{N,Alist}$ = **false**;   4) $\mid t_1 \mid_{N,ABlist} \neq \mid t_2 \mid_{N,Blist} + \mid t_3 \mid_{N,Alist}$.

In this way we can identify a class of finite failing goals: the ones which satisfy the preconditions and falsify (in a three valued logic {**true, maybe, false**}) the postcondition. Note that we cannot say anything about failure or success of other goals such as:

split([a, b, a, b], [b, b], [a, a]); split([a, b, a, a], X, Y); split([X, Y, Z], [X, a], [Z]); split([X, Y, Z], [X, Y], [Z]); split([X, X, X, Z], [b, b], [a, a]).

6.   Conclusions

In this paper we defined a language for describing *type schemata* and studied a class of functions, the *typed norms*, which can be associated to such schemata by means of an interpretation in a semantic domain. Typed norms can check if a term has the structure described by the schema. There are three possibilities: the term has the required structure, the term cannot have the required structure and the term could be instantiated in a way to have such a structure. In the first case, when there is a positive answer, the typed norm can associate a value in the semantic domain to the term. Both having the required structure and the impossibility to gain it, are *well behaved properties* for a term, that is properties which cannot be falsified by applying further substitutions to the term. Typed norms still have all the interesting characteristics of *semi-linear norms*, we studied in [BCF91a, BCF91b] for verifying universal termination of pure Prolog programs. With typed norms we can then apply our simple verification method to a much larger class of programs. A few examples of such verifications, which were not possible by using only semi-linear norms, are also given.

We are also considering different fields of application for typed norms and pre/post specifications. One could be a simple (when compared with less abstract ones, such as in [CM91]) characterization of unifiability. This seems to be fundamental for analyzing more complex properties of logic programs such as existential termination (the existence of one finite successful derivation), finite failure and for distinguishing successful and failing computations in universal termination. Also some type checking could be feasible by using these norms. For example let us consider the type schema TS_1 defined in the examples, the usual interpretation on N and let us take the simple program:

     sum(o, X, X).

sum(s(X), Y, s(Z)) :- sum(X, Y, Z).

This program correctly defines the sum over natural numbers if we know that its domain of application is restricted to triples of natural numbers. In fact only the first term in $sum(t_1, t_2, t_3)$ is strictly typed by the program. By using preconditions, we can express the application domain and then verify that the typing is correct with respect to such a domain and to the meaning we intend for the program. In this example we can use the well-behaved specification

$$\{Nat(t_1), Nat(t_2))\} \; sum(t_1, t_2, t_3) \; \{Nat(t_3)\},$$

and our simple inductive method [BC89, BCF91b] and verify that the program is correct with respect to the specification. This corresponds to a type checking.

Our work is strongly related to many other works dealing with the verification or the synthesis of program properties. On one hand there are the works on logic program termination such as [VP86, Bez89, AP90, AP91] which characterize classes of programs with interesting termination properties, or [UG88, Plü90a, Plü90b, VS91] where automatic termination proofs are based on systems of inequalities among term sizes, or [FG85, Bau88, WS89, WS91, AP90, AP91, Dev90, BCF91a, BCF91b, CM91] where more general techniques for verifying termination are proposed. On the other hand there are the works on Abstract Interpretation for moding and for groundness analysis and for type checking and type inference [BJCD87, Deb89, JB90, MS90, FS90, CFW91]. The invariance of typed norms with respect to substitutions corresponds to the requirement of closure under instantiation in Abstract Interpretation, this allows us to hope for a partial automatization of the verification process.

References

[AP90]   Apt K.R., Pedreschi D., Studies in Pure Prolog: Termination, in *Proceedings Symposium on Computational Logic*, J. W. Lloyd Ed., Basic Research Series 1, Springer-Verlag (1990), 150-176.

[Apt90]   Apt K.R., Introduction to Logic Programming, in *Handbook of Theoretical Computer Science*, J. van Leeuwen Ed., Elsevier Science Publishers 1990.

[AP91]   Apt K.R., Pedreschi D., Proving Termination of General Prolog Programs. Technical Report, CWI, Amsterdam, 1991.

[Bau88]   M. Baudinet. Proving termination properties of PROLOG Programs. In *Proceedings of the 3rd Annual Symposium on Logic in Computer Science (LICS)*, Edinburgh, Scotland (1988), 336-347.

[Bez89]   Bezem M., Characterizing Termination of Logic Programs, in *Proceedings NACLP'89*, E. L. Lusk, R. A. Overbeek, Eds., The MIT Press (1989), 69-80.

[BC89]   Bossi A., Cocco N., Verifying Correctness of Logic Programs, in *Proceedings TAPSOFT'89*, Vol. 2, J. Diaz, F. Orejas, Eds., LNCS 352, Springer-Verlag, (1989), 96-110.

[BCF91a] Bossi A., Cocco N., Fabris M., Proving Termination of Logic Programs by Exploiting Term Properties, in *Proceedings CCPSD-TAPSOFT '91*, S. Abramsky, T.S.E. Maibaum, Eds., LNCS 494, Springer-Verlag, (1991), 153-180.

[BCF91b] Bossi A., Cocco N., Fabris M., Norms on terms and their use in proving universal termination of a logic program, CNR Technical Report "Progetto Finalizzato Sistemi Informatici e Calcolo Parallelo", n. 4/29 (March 1991).

[BCF91c] Bossi A., Cocco N., Fabris M., Typed Norms for Logic Programs. Technical Report Dip. Matematica Pura e Applicata, Università di Padova, Italy, (December 1991).

[BJCD87] Bruynooghe M., Janssens G., Callebaut A., Demoen B., Abstract Interpretation: towards the global optimization of Prolog programs, In *Proceedings Symp. on Logic Programmming*, IEEE Society Press, (1987), 192-204.

[CFW91] Cortesi A., Filè G. Winsborough W., Prop Revisited: Propositional Formula as Abstract Domain for Groundness Analysis. In *Proceedings of LICS 91*. Amsterdam, The Netherlands (July 1991), IEEE Computer Society Press, 322-327.

[CM91] Colussi L., Marchiori E, Proving Correctness of Logic Programs Using Axiomatic Semantics, in *Proceedings ICLP'91*, K. Furukawa, Ed., The MIT Press (1991) 629-642.

[Deb89] Debray S., Static Inference of Modes and data Dependencies in Logic Programs, *ACM Trans. on Programming Languages and Systems 11*, No. 3, (1989), 418-450.

[Dev90] Deville Y., *Logic Programming Systematic Program Development*, Addison-Wesley 1990.

[FGKP85] Francez N., Grumberg O., Katz S., Pnueli A., Proving Termination of Prolog Programs. In *Logics of Programs* LNCS 193, Springer-Verlag, 1985, 89-105.

[FS91] Filè G. and Sottero P., Abstract Interpretation for Type Checking. In *Procceding of PLILP 91*, J. Maluszynski and M. Wirsing (eds), LNCS 528, Springer-Verlag, (1991), 311-322.

[JB90] Janssens G., Bruynooghe M., Deriving Descriptions of Possible Values of Program Variables by means of Abstract Interpretation, Technical Report CW 107, Dept. of Computer Science, K.U. Leuven, (March 1990), to appear in Journal of Logic Programming.

[[Llo87] Lloyd J. W., *Foundations of Logic Programming*, second edition, Springer-Verlag, 1987.

[MS90] Marriott K., Søndergaard H., Abstract Interpretation of Logic Programs: the Denotational Approach. In *Proceedings GULP '90*, A. Bossi (ed.), Padova (June 1990), 399-425.

[Plü90a] Plümer L., Termination Proofs for Logic Programs based on Predicate Inequalities, in *Proceedings ICLP'90*, (1990), 634-648.

[Plü90b] Plümer L., *Termination Proofs for Logic Programs*, Lecture Notes in Artificial Intelligence 446, Springer-Verlag, 1990.

[UG88] Ullman J.D., Van Gelder A., Efficient Tests for Top-Down Termination of Logical Rules, *JACM 35*, No. 2, (1988), 345-373.

[VP86] Vasak T., Potter J., Characterisation of Terminating Logic Programs, in *Proceedings Int. Symposium on Logic Programming '86*, IEEE, (1986) 140-147.

[VS91] Verschaetse K., De Schreye D., Deriving Termination Proofs for Logic Programs Using Abstract Procedures. In *Proceedings ICLP'91*, Paris, June 1991. The MIT Press, 301-315.

[WS89] Wang B., Shryamasunder R.K., Proving Termination of Logic Programs, In *Perspective in Theoretical Computer Science*, Commemorative Volume, Ed. R. Narasimhan, World Scientific Publishers, Singapore, 380-397 (1989).

[WS91] Wang B., Shryamasunder R.K., Methodology for Proving the Termination of Logic Programs, In *Proceedings STACS'91*. Hamburg, Germany, February 1991.

Compositional Refinements In Multiple Blackboard Systems[1]

X. J. Chen

Scuola Normale Superiore
Piazza dei Cavalieri 7, 56100 Pisa, Italy

C. Montangero
Dipart. di Informatica, Univ. di Pisa
Corso Italia 40, 56100 Pisa, Italy

Abstract

In this paper we introduce CONESP, a concurrent system built according to the SMoLCS methodology to provide an abstract model of the coordination language Extended Shared Prolog (ESP). ESP is based on the integration of the blackboard paradigm with Logic Programming. CONESP is a hierarchy of entities, each consisting of a passive blackboard tree and a collection of active components including parallel agents and dynamic (sub) entities. An implementation relation between two hierarchies is defined, which is shown to be compositional.

ESP is being used in the Oikos environment for software process modeling. The results of this paper are the base for the formal verification of the correctness of the software process models built by stepwise-refinements in Oikos.

1 Introduction

This paper presents the first results towards an algebraic treatment of software process specifications in Oikos [1], and of the related refinement method.

Software process modeling deals with the problem of describing the entire life cycle of software production. Among the current approaches, Darwin [11] has a declarative approach, introducing Law Ruled environments; Marvel [9] models tool activation with a rule based language, emphasizing automatic planning; Arcadia [14] is a very comprehensive approach to software process enactment, resting on the extension of Ada with a relational calculus; Melmac [8] introduces an intermediate level representation of software processes by high-level Petri Nets.

Oikos is an environment for software process modeling which integrates the blackboard paradigm with Logic Programming in a hierarchical system. In fact, the blackboard paradigm is suitable to deal with the problems related to the cooperation and coordination among people and machines, and Logic Programming allows to specify software processes declaratively. An essential feature of Oikos is that process specifications are developed by step-wise refinements: the hierarchy is well suited to such an approach. In Oikos, all the software process modeling entities, like processes, environments, roles, services, etc. are represented by a blackboard system which is dynamically organized into a hierarchy.

---

[1]This work has been partially founded by Progetto Finalizzatto Sistemi Informatici e Calcolo Parallelo, Sotto Progetto 6 under contract 91.00920.PF69.

Oikos exploits the logic distributed language Extended Shared Prolog [1,6] to enact, i.e. execute, software processes. As the name shows, ESP extends Shared Prolog [4]: this paper gives a formal specification of ESP extending the one given for Shared Prolog. In doing so, we are taking into account the need of proving the correctness of the refinements that are essential in the Oikos approach. Therefore, our formal description accomodates smoothly a notion of refinement, i.e. how an ESP system can implement another one (in general, with more details and with a higher degree of parallelism).

To cover the characteristics of ESP we introduce CONESP, a concurrent system constructed using labelled transition system according to the Structured Monitored Linear Concurrent Systems (SMoLCS) methodology [2,13]. SMoLCS is a methodology for the formal specification of concurrent systems and languages, especially useful in the formal description of large complex systems with multilevel architecture and interference among the sequential part and the concurrent part.

The paper is organized in this way: section 2 and 3 review ESP and SMoLCS; section 4 describes CONESP and section 5 defines the implementation relation in ESP, with the proof that it is compositional.

2 Shared Prolog and ESP

Shared Prolog and ESP are based on the blackboard model of problem solving. According to this model, the knowledge on a particular problem is partitioned into distinct subsets, in order to keep domain knowledge separated from control knowledge and to organize communications via a centralized data structure, named blackboard.

2.1 Shared Prolog

A Shared Prolog system is composed of a unique blackboard and of a collection of agents working in parallel and communicating via the blackboard. Neither a global state nor a global clock must be assumed.

The behavior of an agent is defined by a theory, which is a Prolog program extended by a guard mechanism coordinating communication and synchronization via the blackboard. More precisely, a theory is a Prolog program augmented with a set of activation patterns, each having form:

{In_Guard} Read_Guard | Body {Out_Set}

which specifies: (i) a set of atoms to be consumed before the theory can be activated (In_Guard); (ii) some conditions to be verified on the blackboard before the theory can be activated (Read_Guard); (iii) the initial goal of the logic program of the theory (Body); (iv) a set of atoms that will be written on the blackboard at the end of the activation (Out_Set).

A blackboard holds a multiset of facts which are Prolog atoms. Getting/putting facts exploits unification. Input and output on the blackboard are mutually exclusive.

2.2 ESP

An ESP system has a tree of blackboards. Each node on this hierarchy is a blackboard containing agents, facts, and subsystems. Each agent belongs to a blackboard, i.e. its source of facts, and has a list of targets to put its facts.

ESP patterns extend Shared Prolog patterns in three ways: First, there are several Out_Sets, each followed by a target (denoted by symbol "@", the target of the agent's own blackboard may be omitted); second, the failure of execution of Prolog program may also cause output. So, the output is divided in two: a success Out_Set and a failure Out_Set, separated by ";". The failure Out_Set is optional, and if there's no failure Out_Set when the Prolog execution fails, nothing will be written on the blackboards. Finally, there may be several *read guards* and *in guards* in a pattern. Generally, an ESP pattern has the following form:

$$read_1 \; \{in_1\} \; \ldots \; read_n \; \{in_n\} \qquad\qquad n > 0$$

$$| \; body$$

$$\{succ_1\}[@target_1] \ldots \{succ_m\}[@target_m] \qquad\qquad m > 0$$

$$[; \; \{fail_1\}[@target_1] \ldots \{fail_p\}[@target_p] \;] \qquad\qquad p > 0$$

Example   *SeqImp* in figure 1 gives the initial state of the ESP program in table 1, which models a Sequential Machine:

theory $coord(Target2, Target3) : -$
   $\{input(X), state(Y)\}$
   $|$
   $\{input1(X), input2(Y)\}@Target3$
\#
   $\{out(X)\}$
   $|$
   $\{state(X)\}$
   $\{output(X)\}@Target2$

theory $pcomb(Target) : -$
   $\{input1(X), input2(Y)\}$
   $|$
   $f(X, Y, Z).$
   $\{out(Z)\}@Target$
  with
    $f(X, Y, Z)$:- computes Z from X, Y.

Table 1. The theories of *SeqImp*

There are two blackboards (represented by boxes with their names on up-left corners) named *Seq* and *Comb* respectively.

Blackboard *Comb* and the agent on it (working on theory *pcomb* in Table 1) model the combinational network of the Sequential Machine, while blackboard *Seq* and the agent on it (working on theory *coord*) model the rest of the machine: inputs are sent to *Seq*, and the agent on *Seq* feeds them to *Comb* together with the current state, receives the output, updates the state and produces the output of the Sequential Machine.

Blackboard *Seq* contains a fact *state(initial)*, and an agent (denoted by a circle) with three targets (denoted by arrows from circles to blackboards) for its output: its own blackboard *Seq* (denoted by number 1), the outer system (2) and blackboard *Comb* (3). This agent works on theory *coord* which uses parameter $Target2/Target3$ as its second/third target. In this example, they are instantiated as $UP/Comb$ (Note: UP

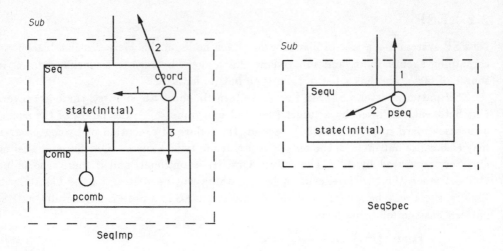

Figure 1: Two specifications of the Sequential Machine

is a special blackboard name for all outside targets). $Target1$ is omitted since it is the agent's own blackboard. Theory $coord$ has two patterns (separated by #). In the first pattern, it consumes facts that match $input(X)$ and $state(Y)$ respectively, and then gives facts $input1(X)$ and $input2(Y)$ to its third target $Target3$. In the second pattern, it consumes facts that match $out(X)$ and then gives facts like $state(X)$ to its own blackboard and facts like $output(X)$ to its second target $Target2$. In both these patterns, the $Body$ is empty.

Initially, blackboard $Comb$ contains no facts but only an agent working on theory $pcomb$, which has only one pattern and one target which is instantiated to blackboard Seq. This pattern consumes facts of form $input1(X)$ and $input2(Y)$, executes goal $f(X, Y, Z)$ by the Prolog program (beginning from keyword $with$ in the theory), and then gives output $out(Z)$ to its target.   □

The blackboard hierarchy is dynamic, i.e. new subtrees of blackboards may be created at run-time. At the same time, the targets of the agents are also dynamically defined. So the total dynamicity of the system means: the agents, the sources from where to absorb information and the targets to where to send information may change. Due to the lack of space, we no longer deal with the dynamic facets of ESP.

2.3   Refinements in ESP

A software process model may be very large. To deal with it, one may construct, at first, a small system with a simple structure only to describe the main properties (the tasks to fulfill), then substitute it with another one with more implementation details. For example, consider $SeqSpec$ in figure 1, where theory $pseq$ is

> **theory** $pseq(Target)$: −
> $\qquad \{input(X), state(Y)\}$
> $\qquad |$

$$f(X,Y,Z).$$
$$\{output(Z)\}@Target$$
$$\{state(Z)\}$$

with

$f(X,Y,Z)$:- the same as that in theory *pcomb*.

It can be seen as the initial specification of the Sequential Machine corresponding to *SeqImp* in figure 1. So one may use *SeqSpec* at the beginning and then substitute it by *SeqImp*.

The problem rises: is this substitution correct? I.e., is *SeqImp* a correct implementation of *SeqSpec*, which means: can *SeqImp* generate all I/O streams that can be generated by *SeqSpec*, and will it not generate spurious streams in the context of the substitution? The way to solve the problem is to forget intermediate derivations, which is done by the monitoring step in CONESP that gives the support to define the implementation relation in CONESP.

3 A Brief Overview of SMoLCS

To build CONESP, which is the formal system that defines ESP semantics, we adopt the SMoLCS methodology [2,3,13] which is based on labelled transition system. A set of processes is described by a labelled transition system, in which *states* represent the states of processes, and *transitions* represent the capability of the processes to evolve from one state to another while the interaction with the outside world is represented by the label. In other words, the label contains the information for the condition of the external environment so that the capability of the processes to evolve becomes effective. This interpretation of labelled transition system has turned to be classical since it was inspired by CCS [10] and SOS [12]. In the simplest case, when the transition is purely internal to the system and there is no relationship with the environment, the label can be dropped or better represented by a special label.

Based on labelled transition system, SMoLCS is a methodology intended to add abstraction and modularity to the specification of concurrent systems and languages, especially considered for the formal description of large systems.

Def. A labelled transition system is a triple $(STATE, LABEL, \Longrightarrow)$ where

$STATE/LABEL$ is a set of *states/labels* of the system, and

$\Longrightarrow \subseteq STATE \times LABEL \times STATE$ is the transition relation.

Note Usually, we simply write $s \overset{l}{\Longrightarrow} s'$ if $(s,l,s') \in \Longrightarrow$.

Example If agent $Agent_1$ can put facts F onto blackboard B, and then changes into $Agent_1'$, this can be represented by

$$Agent_1 \xoverset{Send(B,F)}{\Longrightarrow} Agent_1'$$

□

Given transition systems for the simple components, the dynamic activity of a compound system is defined in SMoLCS in a canonical way, following three steps: syncronization, parallelism and monitoring, which are specified by giving appropriate abstract data types. In this way, one can easily modify part of a specification, which is badly needed in practice for large projects. To fix notations, in the following we review these steps, which are applied in the next section to define CONESP.

The syncronization step defines those transitions that represent syncronized actions of a group of process components and their effects on global information: given a transition system CTS (with transition relation $\Longrightarrow$) that represents the process components, the syncronization step defines a new algebraic transition system STS where the transition relation $\longrightarrow$ corresponds to the syncronized actions of a group of process components.

The state of STS is a couple whose elements are a multiset of states in CTS and some values (called global information of the process components) representing the status of the passive components. Here, passive means that it has no transitions of its own, but may be changed as a consequence of the transitions of processes. Thus, the states in STS have form

$$< g, pr_1 \mid \ldots \mid pr_n >$$

where g is the global (passive) part, pr_i are states of CTS, and $pr_1 \mid \ldots \mid pr_n$ is a multiset of (parallely composed) process states in CTS.

The transitions of STS are deduced from the transitions of CTS by STS axioms that have the following form:

$$\bigwedge_{1 \leq j \leq n} pr_j \overset{l_j}{\Longrightarrow} pr_j' \wedge Cond \supset < g, pr_1 \mid \ldots \mid pr_n > \overset{sl}{\longrightarrow} < g', pr_1' \mid \ldots \mid pr_n' >$$

where sl is a new label denoting the interaction of $pr_1, \ldots, pr_n$ with the outside, and $Cond$ expresses that the actions of process components pr_i $(i = 1, ..., n)$ can be syncronized. The intuitive meaning of such an axiom is that, if each pr_i can evolve into the new process state pr_i' by performing the action l_i, and $Cond$ holds, then the whole system can evolve into the new state $< g', pr_1' \mid \ldots \mid pr_n' >$ by some label sl, while the global information g is relatively changed into a new one w.r.t. the actions $l_1, \ldots, l_n$.

The parallelism step defines those transitions that represent the admissible parallel executions of a group of syncronized actions and their complex transformation of global information. For example, the problem of mutual exclusion is faced on this step.

The actions on this step are defined by using a composition function $\parallel$ (binary, commutative and associative) on actions of a group of process components. Intuitively, it defines that two actions can be executed in parallel (without syncronization). The actions that need to be considered for the composition are the syncronized actions defined in the syncronization step and those already obtained by composition.

The following axiom expresses the capability of two actions to be executed in parallel:

$$< g, ms_1 > \overset{sl_1}{\longrightarrow} < g_1, ms_1' > \wedge < g, ms_2 > \overset{sl_2}{\longrightarrow} < g_2, ms_2' > \wedge Cond \supset$$

$$< g, ms_1 \mid ms_2 > \overset{sl_1 \parallel sl_2}{\longrightarrow} < g', ms_1' \mid ms_2' >$$

where $Cond$ defines the transformation of the global information (from g to g' as a function of g and g') caused by action $sl_1 \parallel sl_2$.

The Monitoring step may define some global restrictions on the transitions of the entire system, like restricting the labels which can be observed from the outside.

Analogously to the previous steps, the monitoring step is also defined by giving a new (modular) concurrent system starting from the concurrent system obtained in parallelism step. The axioms on this step offer some conditions under which the action in parallelism step

$$< g, mp > \overset{pl}{\longrightarrow} < g', mp' >$$

is allowed by the monitor and it will become an action of this step represented by transition

$$< g, mp \mid mp_1 > \overset{l}{\longrightarrow} < g', mp' \mid mp_1 >$$

where mp_1 represents the multiset of the states of the active components in previous step, and l represents the interaction of the resulting action with the external environment.

4 CONESP, a concurrent system for ESP

In this section, we describe an ESP-entity as an abstract data type and then introduce the derivations that define its behaviors.

4.1 CONESP Entities

CONESP is constructed as a hierarchy of ESP-entities, where each ESP-entity corresponds to a blackboard system in ESP. An ESP-entity named $NAME$ can be expressed as:

$$NAME :< TR, AC >$$

where $< TR, AC >$ represents the state of the entity: a passive blackboard tree TR and a collection AC of parallel active components (separated by "$\mid$").

4.1.1 TR: the blackboard tree

The passive part TR represents the blackboard tree of ESP and is a dynamic structure describing the evolving state of the dynamic system. Its nodes are multisets of facts. Each blackboard in the tree has a unique name. This passive part is specified as an abstract data type TREE using partial algebra [7]. We give here only a simple example.

Example 4.1.1 The passive part of the ESP-entity representing the blackboard tree of $SeqImp$ in figure 1 can be specified as

$$(R(Seq, \{state(initial)\}), Seq, Comb, \phi) \hspace{3cm} (Trimp)$$

where ϕ is the empty multiset of facts. In general, (TR, B_1, B_2, F) is a tree generated from tree TR by adding a new blackboard B_2 under blackboard B_1, with the initial set of facts F. Also, $R(B, F)$ denotes a tree with only a root B containing facts F.

4.1.2 AC: a collection of active components

There are two kinds of active components: the agents and (sub) ESP-entities.

Each agent in an entity has a coordinate blackboard, denoting the source to get facts. In order to meet the characteristics in ESP that each agent has a list of targets to give its output, we also explicitly express, for each agent, this dynamic binding as a list of targets. Besides, each agent has a predefined theory, the task it executes. In this sense, we explicitly specify an agent in CONESP together with these three elements as prefixes. Generally, we express an agent as

$$(B, Th, Tar) : Astate$$

where B is the blackboard of the agent, Th is its theory, Tar is its target list, $Astate$ is a state holding execution information and is discussed in section 4.2.1.

Note The target list of an agent includes parameters and may be changed dynamically.

Example 4.1.2.1 The agents in $SeqImp$ (figure 1) are expressed as

$$(Seq, coord, [Seq, UP, Comb]) : nil \qquad\qquad (Agimp1)$$

$$(Comb, pcomb, [Seq]) : nil \qquad\qquad (Agimp2)$$

Note: Here, nil is the state, in which an agent is ready to activate the patterns in its theory. □

The detailed structure of an ESP-entity is shown in figure 2.

Example 4.1.2.2 The initial entity $SeqImp$ in figure 1 (named Sub) can be described as

$$Sub :< Trimp, Agimp1 \mid Agimp2 >. \qquad\qquad (SeqImp)$$

Example 4.1.2.3 The entity named $UpName$ (figure 3, right) contains entity $SeqImp$ and some other active components $UpAc$, and is expressed as

$$UpName :< UpTr, UpAc \mid SeqImp >$$

where $UpTr$ is its passive part.

4.2 CONESP Specifications

The structure of CONESP specifications is as follows: (i) Agent Transition describes how the agents work on their theories. (ii) Syncronization Step describes the syncronized transitions of entities including the syncronization among agents, blackboards, and subentities. (iii) Parallelism Step describes the entity transitions on all agents and subentities. On this step, conditions w.r.t. ESP, e.g. mutual exclusion on blackboard,

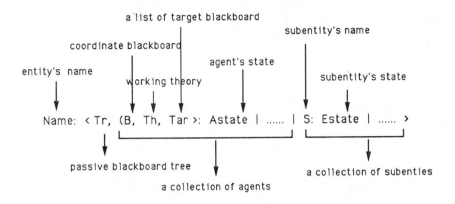

Figure 2: structure of entities in CONESP

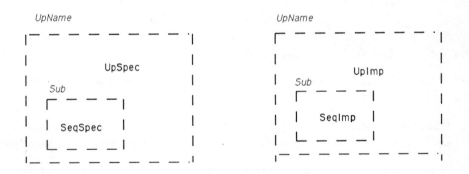

Figure 3: ESP-entity examples

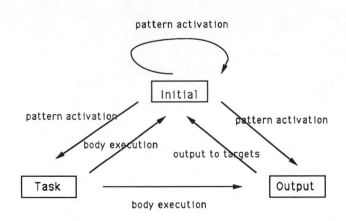

Figure 4: execution states of theories in CONESP

will be given. (iv) Observational Step describes the observable actions and related transitions.

We use the following sorts for the axiom quantifiers: *bid* for blackboard identifier and subentity's names, *facts* for multiset of Prolog atoms (sort *fact*) in a blackboard, *th* for theory's names, *name* for entity's names, *sub* for substitutions, *tree* for passive blackboard trees, *tar* for lists of agent's targets, *ag/ent* for agents/entities and *ac* for active components (whenever it is convenient we will distinguish between agents and entities).

4.2.1 Agent Transition (theory execution)

Like in Shared Prolog, each agent works recursively on its theory, having three execution states as shown in figure 4:

1. It may stay in state *Initial*. In this state, the agent is ready for pattern activation, i.e. to choose, among those in its theory, a pattern whose guards are satisfiable.

2. It may stay in state *Task*, ready to do the task of this activated pattern, e.g. $Prolog(Body\theta)$, which indicates that the agent is going to execute Prolog program for goal $Body\theta$. Here $Body$ is the body part of the pattern chosen in the previous step, and θ is the substitution got from the previous step. Such *Tasks* are described as internal derivations, i.e. we do not go into the details of Prolog execution. Other tasks include creating subentities, deleting subentities, instantiating targets, deleting targets and are not dealt with here, due to the lack of space.

3. After finishing a task, the agent is in state *Output*, and is going to give output to its targets. This output comes from the Out_Set of the pattern together with

the substitution from pattern activation in the first step and, if it has successfully terminated the body, the resetting substitution.

Generally, we use *nil* for state *Initial*; *A.nil* for state *Output* where A is the output set denoted by ε if it is empty; $A.(B; C).nil$ for the state *Task* where A is the task to fulfill and B/C is the success/failure output set.

Note Since the body part and postactivation part in ESP theory may be empty, we may also go from state *Initial* to state *Output* or to itself, from *Task* to *Initial*. □

The change from one state to another should satisfy the corresponding rules on agent transitions including pattern activation, body execution, output to targets. Generally, we have the following schema for pattern activation:

$\forall \, B : bid, \; T : tar, \; \theta : sub$

$$(B, Th, T) : nil \xrightarrow{\; Activate(B, I_{Th, Pa}, R_{Th, Pa}, \theta) \;}$$

$$(B, Th, T) : Prolog(Goal_{Th, Pa}\theta).(Succ_{Th, Pa}\theta; Fail_{Th, Pa}\theta).nil$$

for each pattern Pa in theory Th such that its body is a Prolog goal $Goal_{Th, Pa}$.

Note

1. CONESP specification is parameterized and this is only a schema: for any theory Th in the program, it may be applied to any of its pattern Pa provided that its body part is a Prolog goal.

2. $Prolog(F)$ calls for Prolog program using F (including variables) as a goal. $I_{Th, Pa}/R_{Th, Pa}$ is the In_Guard/Read_Guard of pattern Pa in theory Th.

3. $Succ_{Th, Pa}/Fail_{Th, Pa}$ has form $AddF(target_1, out_1) \parallel \ldots \parallel AddF(target_m, out_m)$ corresponding to the success/failure Out_Set (cfr. section 2.2) of pattern Pa in theory Th. $AddF(target_i, F)$ adds a set of facts F to the i-th target of the agent.

4. Blackboard B and target T are parameters for the coordinate blackboard in which this theory is executed, and the instantiation for the targets of this theory. Substitution θ appears also as a parameter. Its value will come from the communication with its blackboard by matching $I_{Th, Pa}$ and $R_{Th, Pa}$ in blackboard B (See next step for the communication between agents and their blackboards).

As a special case when the Body part of a pattern is empty, the agent goes directly to give the success Out_Set after activating the pattern.

Example 4.2.1 Theory *coord*'s first pattern (section 2.2) has an empty body part. For agent *Agimp*1 (Example 4.1.2.1) in entity *SeqImp* (figure 1), the agent's blackboard and targets being instantiated by *Seq*, *Seq*, *UP* and *Comb* respectively, we have

$\forall \, \theta : sub$

$$Agimp1 \xrightarrow{\; Activate(Seq, \{state(X), input(Y)\}, \varepsilon, \theta) \;}$$

$$(Seq, coord, [Seq, UP, Comb]) : AddF(3, \{input1(X), input2(Y)\}\theta).nil \qquad (Agimp1')$$

4.2.2 Syncronization Step

An agent's action includes creating/deleting subentities, pattern activation (getting facts), internal derivation (those that have no effects on other part of the entity, e.g. instantiating/deleting targets, executing Prolog program), sending facts to targets (blackboards or subentities).

An entity may receive facts from an agent from outside. As we hide all the details of an entity to outside, the agent knows neither the structure of the entity nor any blackboard name in it. For the moment, we adopt the principle that the agent from outside sends facts to an entity by calling its name, and the facts are put into the root of the entity. We use $Send(S, F)$ to describe the agent's action of sending facts F to entity S, and we use $In(S, F)$ to describe that the entity receives facts from outside. On the other hand, an entity may send facts F into a blackboard B in super entity, which is described as $Out(B, F)$. Thus, as an active component, an entity acts in two ways: $In(S, F)$ and $Out(B, F)$. These two actions are distinct from the others.

On this step, we define entity transitions of syncronized actions and their effects to the blackboard tree. The rules for syncronizations considering these actions have the canonical form in the same step in SMoLCS (cfr. section 3). Notice that in blackboard systems, no two agents can communicate directly, but via the blackboard. So the syncronization happens only between agent and blackboard, between subentity and blackboard, and between agent and subentity. Here we only show how the agent's pattern activation effects its blackboard and causes the transition of its entity.

When an agent is in *Initial* state, it may activate a pattern in its theory provided that In_Guard and Read_Guard of this pattern can be satisfied by the current state. This test is done by

$$eval(In\_Guard, Read\_Guard, Blackboard1) = < Blackboard2, \theta >$$

where function *eval* takes the In_Guard, the Read_Guard, the blackboard of the system ($Blackboard1$), and returns, if the evaluation succeeds, the set of atoms ($Blackboard2$) to be retracted from blackboard ($Blackboard1$) and the computed substitution (θ) to be passed to the rest of the pattern. Otherwise, the special symbol $FAILURE$ is returned (cfr. [4]).

From section 4.2.1, we know that in $Agent \xrightarrow{Activate(B,I,R,\theta)} Agent'$, the agent has coordinate blackboard B, the activated pattern has In_Guard I, Read_Guard R, and the matching between the guards and facts in blackboard B should be θ. So we have

$$\forall\, Tr : tree,\ Pr, Pr' : ac,\ B : bid,\ I, R, F : facts,\ Ename : name, \theta : sub$$

$$Pr \xrightarrow{Activate(B,I,R,\theta)} Pr' \wedge eval(I, R, getb(Tr, B)) = < F, \theta > \wedge D(< Tr, Pr >)\ \supset$$

$$Ename :< Tr, Pr > \xrightarrow{Rec(B,F)} Ename :< delf(Tr, B, F), Pr' >$$

for the entity transition of theory activation, where the matched facts F are deleted ($delf(Tr, B, F)$) from the blackboard B in the tree Tr.

Note Partial algebras [5] are used. Here $D(< Tr, Pr >)$ denotes the definedness of entity $Ename :< Tr, Pr >$. Condition $eval(I, R, getb(Tr, B)) = < F, \theta >$ guarantees the definedness of $< delf(Tr, B, F), Pr' >$ since we have that $D(< Tr, Pr >)$. $getb$ is a function that, given a tree and a blackboard name in the tree, returns the multiset of facts on the named blackboard in the tree.

Example 4.2.2   Once entity $SeqImp$ (Example 4.1.2.2) receives a fact $input(a)$ from outside into its blackboard Seq, it transforms into $SeqImp_1$, i.e.

$$Sub :< Trimp_1, Agimp1 \mid Agimp2 >.$$

where $Trimp_1 = addf(Trimp, Seq, \{input(a)\})$. The transition in which $Agimp1$ activates the first pattern of theory $coord$ (Example 4.2.1), can be used in entity $SeqImp_1$, because both $state(X)$ and $input(Y)$ can be matched on blackboard Seq in the tree $Trimp_1$. In other words,

$$eval(\{state(X), input(Y)\}, \varepsilon, getb(Trimp_1, Seq)) =< F, \theta_0 >$$

is true with

$$F = \{state(initial),\ input(a)\} \qquad \theta_0 = \{X \leftarrow initial,\ Y \leftarrow a\}$$

So we have

$$Sub :< Trimp_1, Agimp1 > \xrightarrow{Rec(Seq, \{state(initial),\ input(a)\})} Sub :< Trimp_2, Agimp1' >$$

where $Trimp_2 = delf(Trimp_1, Seq, \{state(initial), input(a)\})$

4.2.3   Parallelism Step

According to SMoLCS, we describe here how the transitions introduced in the previous step may happen in parallel, on all active components. The essence of this step is to give conditions under which if entity $Entity_1$ may transit into $Entity_2$ by $Act_1 \parallel \ldots \parallel Act_n$, and may transit into $Entity_3$ by Act_{n+1}, then it may transit into $Entity_4$ by $Act_1 \parallel \ldots \parallel Act_n \parallel Act_{n+1}$.

From ESP, we know that no two accesses to the same blackboard are allowed at a time. This also satisfies the condition in Shared Prolog that among several patterns of a theory, only one can succeed at a time. So, if we want to put an action $Sact$ on syncronization step into an action $Pact$ on parallelism step, we must test if $Sact$ is going to access any blackboard already used in $Pact$.

Example 4.2.3   It is always possible to put the internal action τ into any transition on parallelism step, without any condition. For example, suppose the τ action is executed by a collection of active components Prs_1

$$Ename :< Tr, Prs_1 > \xrightarrow{\tau} Ename :< Tr, Prs_1' >$$

and suppose a collection of active components Prs_2 may change into Prs_2' by action $Rec(B, F)$ which changes the blackboard tree Tr into Tr':

$$Ename :< Tr, Prs_2 > \xrightarrow{Rec(B,F)} Ename :< Tr', Prs_2' >$$

then without any condition, we have

$$Ename :< Tr, Prs_1 \mid Prs_2 > \xrightarrow{Rec(B,F)} Ename :< Tr', Prs_1' \mid Prs_2' >$$

4.2.4   Monitoring Step

In section 4.2.3, we have seen that an entity has two kinds of actions for the communication with the outside. On this step, function $Visible$ is introduced to select out these actions from those in parallelism step, leaving all the others denoted by τ, e.g.

$$Visible(Out(B_1, F_1) \parallel Rec(B_2, F_2)) = Out(B_1, F_1)$$

Besides, we add a restriction on this step that no two output actions of an entity can succeed at a time, i.e.

$$A \xrightarrow{\quad Out(B,F)\parallel Other \quad} A'$$

on the parallelism step, implies

$$A \xrightarrow{\quad Out(B,F) \quad} A'$$

on this monitoring step, provided that there's no other action $Out(B', F')$ appearing in $Other$.

From the previous two steps, we know that action

$$In(S_1, F_1) \parallel \ldots \parallel In(S_n, F_n) \text{ for } n > 1$$

is not allowed because this means, according to our principle of the communications between entity and subentity (section 4.2.2), to access the root of the blackboard tree at the same time, which is not allowed according to the mutual exclusion on blackboard.

As a consequence, we have only four kinds of actions on this step ($F, F' : facts$, $B : bid$, $S : name$):

$$\tau,\ In(S, F),\ Out(B, F),\ In(S, F) \parallel Out(B, F')$$

5   Implementation Relation

Based on the monitoring step, we turn to the sequences of the actions defined on monitoring step in order to give a suitable notion of implementation relation in ESP, as announced in section 2.3.

We want to consider action sequences (of sort seq) that start from a given state, but not all of them. For the initial state $SeqImp$, for example, we expect that the inputs are unifiable to $input(X)$ or $state(X)$ (which are all that make sense for $SeqSpec$), but not to $out(X)$.

Def.   Action sequence $l_1 \ldots l_n$ *is covered by* X, denoted by $l_1 \ldots l_n \sqsubset X$, if

l_i is $In(S, F)$ or $In(S, F) \parallel Out(B, F')$ implies $F \subseteq X$.   □

Notice that F' can be any set of facts, i.e. only the input set is concerned.

Function IIF is thus introduced to get from a given entity the interesting input facts under our consideration. For instance, $IIF(SeqSpec)$ contains all the facts unifiable to $input(X)$ or $state(X)$, while $IIF(SeqImp)$ contains all the facts unifiable to $input(X)$ or $state(X)$ or $out(X)$. So the sequences used to compare $SeqSpec$ and $SeqImp$ should be covered by $IIF(SeqSpec)$.

Observing predicate $Perform(\sigma, A, X)$ is used to characterize our observations — the action sequence σ starting from the initial state A and covered by set of facts X. By definition,

$$Perform(l_1 \ldots l_n, A, X) \equiv \bigwedge_{i=1}^{n} A_i \xrightarrow{l_i} A_{i+1} \wedge l_1 \ldots l_n \sqsubseteq X$$

Now we introduce our implementation relation, denoted by $\rightsquigarrow$. $A \rightsquigarrow B$ means that B is an implementation of A:

Def. $A \rightsquigarrow B$ iff $IIF(A) \subseteq IIF(B)$ and

$\forall \sigma : seq.\ Perform(\sigma, A, IIF(A))$ iff $Perform(\sigma, B, IIF(A))$.

Example Now our problem on Sequential Machine can be stated as

$\forall \sigma : seq.$

$Perform(\sigma, SeqSpec, IIF(SeqSpec)) \equiv Perform(\sigma, SeqImp, IIF(SeqSpec))$? $\square$

It is easy to see that if $X_1 \subseteq X_2$ then

$Perform(\sigma, A, X_2)$ implies $Perform(\sigma, A, X_1)$.

So we have the following

Fact $\rightsquigarrow$ is transitive.

Lemma If A_1 and B_1 have the same name S, $A_1 \rightsquigarrow B_1$ and agents in R only send facts in $IIF(A_1)$ to S (i.e. in their actions $Send(S, F)$, F always belong to $IIF(A_1)$), then

$$EA_1 = N :< Tr_1, A_1 \mid R > \rightsquigarrow EB_1 = N :< Tr_1, B_1 \mid R >$$

Proof We prove for the universe U of facts,

$Perform(\sigma, EA_1, U)$ implies $Perform(\sigma, EB_1, U)$

The proof of the other direction is analogous.

Consider any $l_1 \ldots l_n : seq$, s.t. for $1 \leq i \leq n$, we have $EA_i \xrightarrow{l_i} EA_{i+1}$

where $EA_{i+1} = N :< Tr_{i+1}, A_{i+1} \mid R_{i+1} >$ and $A_i \xrightarrow{l_i^A} A_{i+1}$.

Now, since the environment behaves correctly, i.e. agents in R_i only send facts in $IIF(A_1)$ to S, we have $l_1^A \ldots l_n^A \sqsubseteq IIF(A_1)$, and since $A_1 \rightsquigarrow B_1$, we can find B_i s.t. $B_i \xrightarrow{l_i^A} B_{i+1}$. Given now

$EB_i = N :< Tr_i, B_i \mid R_i >$ and $EB_{i+1} = N :< Tr_{i+1}, B_{i+1} \mid R_{i+1} >$,

we have

$$EB_i \xrightarrow{l_i} EB_{i+1}$$

because we only need to consider syncronization between S and the environment and, according to CONESP specifications, the conditions for syncronization do not include information in the entities (e.g. A_i, B_i), but the information in the syncronized actions (e.g. l_i^A). $\square$

The composibility of $\rightsquigarrow$ may be stated as

Theorem If $A_i \rightsquigarrow B_i$ (i=1,2,...,n), where A_i, B_i have name S_i, agents in R only use facts in $IIF(A_i)$ in their actions $Send(S_i, F)$, and

$$E = N :< Tr, A_1 \mid \ldots \mid A_n \mid R > \rightsquigarrow N :< Tr', A_1 \mid \ldots \mid A_n \mid R' >$$

then $E \rightsquigarrow N :< Tr', B_1 \mid \ldots \mid B_n \mid R' >$

Proof immediate by Lemma and transitivity. □

This composition theorem protects the implementation relation when subentities are substituted by their implementation. So we may solve, for instance, the problem shown in figure 3. That is: if we substitute a subentity ($SeqSpec$) by its implementation ($SeqImp$) which has more implementation details, the total entity ($UpSpec$) is also changed into its implementation ($UpImp$).

6 Future Work

We are now working on proof techniques. In the basic cases, the proof that $A \rightsquigarrow B$ must be done by the definition and it envolves considerations of too many action sequences. We expect to reduce their number, by considering only those that are necessary for the proof. We call these sequences **relevant action sequences**, and we are considering two methods to construct them: (i) choosing most general facts for input; (ii) finding necessary combinations of facts as input, in order to give output. Other proof techniques are also under development, especially to deal with recursion in the execution trees of CONESP.

Acknoledgements

The authors gratefully acknowledge G. Reggio for her comments on earlier drafts.

References

[1] V. Ambriola, P. Ciancarini, and C. Montangero. Software process enactment in Oikos. In R. N. Taylor, editor, *Proc. of ACM SIGSOFT '90, ACM Soft. Eng. Notes 15(6)*, Dec. 1990.

[2] E. Astesiano and G. Reggio. Direct semantics of concurrent languages in the SMoLCS approach. *IBM Journal of Research and Development*, 31(5), Sep 1987.

[3] E. Astesiano and G. Reggio. SMoLCS-Driven concurrent calculi. In G. Goos and J. Hartmanis, editors, *Lecture Notes in Computer Science (249): Proc. of TAPSOFT'87*, Springer-Verlag, 1987.

[4] A. Brogi and P. Ciancarini. The concurrent language Shared Prolog. *ACM Transactions on Programming Languages and Systems*, 13(1):99 – 123, Jan. 1991.

[5] M. Broy and M. Wirsing. Partial abstract types. *Acta Informatica*, 18, 1982.

[6] A. Bucci, P. Ciancarini, and C. Montangero. A distributed logic language based on multiple tuple spaces. In *Proc. of Logic Programming Conference*, Tokyo, July 1991 (to appear in LNCS).

[7] X. J. Chen. *A Formalism Towards Software Process Modelling*. PhD thesis, Scuola Normale Superiore, Pisa, Italy (in preparation).

[8] W. Deiters and V. Gruhn. Managing software processes in the environment Melmac. In R. N. Taylor, editor, *Proc. of ACM SIGSOFT '90, ACM Soft. Eng. Notes 15(6)*, Dec. 1990.

[9] G. E. Kaiser, P. H. Feller, and S. S. Popovich. Intelligent assistence for software development and maintenance. In *IEEE Software*, 1988.

[10] R. Milner. A calculus for communicating systems. In G. Goos and J. Hartmanis, editors, *Lecture Notes in Computer Science (92)*, Springer-Verlag, 1980.

[11] N. H. Minsky and D. Rozenshtein. Configuration management by consensus: an application of Law-Governed systems. In R. N. Taylor, editor, *Proc. of ACM SIGSOFT '90, ACM Soft. Eng. Notes 15(6)*, Dec. 1990.

[12] G. Plotkin. *A Structural Approach to Operational Semantics*. Technical Report, Computer Science Deot. Aarhus Univ. Denmark, 1981. DAIMI-FN-19.

[13] G. Reggio. *Una Metodologia per la Specifica di Sistemi e Linguaggi Concurrenti*. PhD thesis, Dept. of Maths, Univ. of Genova, Italy, 1986.

[14] R. N. Taylor. Arcadia: a software development environment research project. In P. Henderson, editor, *Proc. of ACM SIGSOFT '88, ACM Soft. Eng. Notes 13(5)*, Nov. 1988.

Fully Persistent Arrays for Efficient Incremental Updates and Voluminous Reads

Tyng–Ruey Chuang
Department of Computer Science
Courant Institute of Mathematical Sciences
New York University*

Abstract

The array update problem in a purely functional language is the following: once an array is updated, both the original array and the newly updated one must be preserved to maintain referential transparency. We devise a very simple, fully persistent data structure to tackle this problem such that

- each incremental update costs $O(1)$ worst–case time,

- a *voluminous* sequence of r reads cost in total $O(r)$ amortized time, and

- the data structure use $O(n + u)$ space,

where n is the size of the array and u is the total number of updates. A sequence of r reads is voluminous if r is $\Omega(n)$ and the sequence of arrays being read forms a path of length $O(r)$ in the version tree. A voluminous sequence of reads may be mixed with updates without affecting either the performance of reads or updates.

An immediate consequence of the above result is that if a functional program is single–threaded, then the data structure provides a simple and efficient implementation of functional arrays. This result is not new. What is new is that many multi–threaded functional array applications also exhibit the incremental updates/voluminous reads execution pattern. Those applications can also be efficiently implemented by the proposed data structure.

A comparison of our method to previous approaches to the array update problem is briefly discussed. Empirical results have been collected to measure the effectiveness of the proposed data structure.

1 Survey and Motivation

The array update problem in the implementation of a purely functional programming language is the following: once an array is updated, both the original array and the newly updated one must be preserved, preferably at a small cost, to maintain the referential transparency of functional programs. Copying the whole array is usually regarded as being too inefficient. Depending on different perspectives of this problem, there have

---

*Author's address: 251 Mercer Street, New York, NY 10012, U.S.A. E–mail: chuang@cs.nyu.edu. This research has been supported, in part, by the National Science Foundation (#CCR–8909634) and DARPA (DARPA/ONR #N00014–91–J1472).

been various approaches to solve it. We classify three popular approaches to the array update problem. They are the compile–time analysis approach, the language restriction approach, and the run–time data structure approach. We briefly state the advantage and disadvantage of the three approaches, as well as our motivation to design yet another run–time structure to tackle this problem.

1.1 Compile–Time Analysis

Let us use the term *access* to include both read and update operations to a data structure. Schmidt [21] defines a program to be *single–threaded* if all accesses to the variables in the program only refer to the most recent versions. A program is called *multi–threaded* if it is not single–threaded. A non–standard semantics can be devised to detect, at compile time, single–threaded accesses to arrays in a functional program and, in those cases, to generate code to update arrays destructively. This approach is taken, for example, in the works of Schwartz [22,23], Hudak & Bloss [16], Bloss [9,10], and Odersky [19].

The advantage of this approach is that it is possible to generate very efficient code because no overhead is spent in maintaining multiple versions of arrays. The disadvantage is that the analyses usually assume some particular evaluation order of a functional program, which is unspecified in the standard semantics. Also, they are incomplete, as are all interesting semantics analyses, in the sense that there remains programs which are single–threaded but not detected by the analyses. In addition, such analyses are expensive (they may have exponential time complexity with respect to program size) and not universal (they currently apply to first–order languages only).

1.2 Language Restriction

Instead of using compile–time analysis to detect single–threaded programs, a functional programming language can be restricted so that only single–threaded programs can be expressed. These restrictions are usually expressed in terms of type rules. Therefore, for well–typed programs, no compile–time analysis for detecting destructible updates is ever needed and all array updates can be done destructively and efficiently. This approach has been explored by Guzmán & Hudak [14] and Wadler [25,26]. The remaining task is to check, at compile time, whether or not a program is well–typed with respect to the single–threading type scheme. The type checking algorithms are usually complicated.

A common drawback of the compile–time analysis approach and the language restriction approach is that they cannot deal with programs which mostly use arrays in a multi–threaded manner. In those programs, old versions of an array must be kept around for possible future accesses, and few destructive updates may be performed.

1.3 Run–Time Data Structure

There also has been much effort to make various data structures persistent such that, during a series of modifications, the old versions, as well as the newest version, of a data structure can still be accessed. Following the terminology of Driscoll, Sarnak, Sleator & Tarjan [13], a data structure is *partially persistent* if all versions can be read but only the newest version can be updated. A data structure is *fully persistent* if every version can be both read and updated.

An array can be easily made fully persistent if it is represented as a balanced search tree. But then we lose much of an array's constant–time accessibility because a read or update operation will take $O(\log n)$ time for an array of size n. Dietz [12] proposes a sophisticated method to achieve $O(\log \log n)$ amortized access time when the arrays are large (say, $n = 2^{10}$) and the total number of operations to be performed is n.

Some techniques, which are called *reversible difference list* or *trailer*, have been used to implement fully persistent arrays. They can be found, for examples, in the works of Holmstrom [15], Hughes [18], Aasa, Holmstrom & Nilsson [6] and Bloss [9,10]. These techniques seem to be variations of the shallow binding scheme devised by Baker [7,8]. Under these techniques, an access to the newest version will take $O(1)$ time; but an access to an old version will take time linear to the number of differences between the old version and the current version. These techniques are good for single–threaded programs because those programs always access the newest version of an array. However, they are bad for multi–threaded programs because accesses to old versions are costly.

A common drawback of the run–time data structure approach is the overhead for maintaining multiple versions of a data structure, even when only the newest version is needed. The storage occupied by inaccessible versions of a data structure may have to be reclaimed.

1.4 Motivation and Outline

Previous attempts to make arrays fully persistent do not work well in multi–threaded cases because they use too little random access memory (RAM) to represent multiple versions of an arrays. Instead, they depend mostly on indirect reference by pointers. In fact, previous data structures use only one set of RAM for multiple versions of an array. An array's random accessibility is then lost once there have been many updates being performed to the array.

We propose here a variation of Baker's shallow binding scheme which holds multiple sets of RAM. We call this method the *fragmented shallow binding scheme*. This scheme employs multiple sets of RAM, which we will later call *caches*, to improve the efficiency of those programs which access arrays in a multi–threaded way. Although there is still a restriction — reads have to be voluminous — it seems that a major portion of multi–threaded applications do fit the incremental updates/voluminous reads restriction.

The outline of this paper is the following. After a short introduction to the shallow binding scheme in section 2, we describe in section 3 how to implement fully persistent arrays by the fragmented shallow binding scheme. Section 4 contains detailed complexity analysis of the proposed scheme. Empirical results are presented in section 5. Section 6 is a short discussion of related issues.

2 Deep Binding and Shallow Binding

In a higher–order functional language, where functions can be passed as arguments and returned as results, there may be more than one accessible environment during a program's execution. In an implementation of a higher–order functional language, it is essentially important to design an efficient data structure to support the following two operations: variable lookup in the current environment and context switch between environments.

In the *deep binding* scheme, the environments are represented as a *context tree* where each node in the tree introduces a new binding of a value to a variable. An environment is represented as a path from its most recent binding to the initial binding in the context tree. The lookup for a variable v in an environment E is performed by searching the path of E, looking for the most recent value bound to v. Under the deep binding scheme, a context switch between environments costs constant time but a variable lookup in an environment may cost time linear to the length of its binding path.

In order to improve the performance of variable lookup, Baker [7] develops the *shallow binding* scheme where a *cache* is introduced to record the bindings of variables in the *current environment*. Variable lookup in the current environment is performed by a constant–time reference to the cache. The current environment is also made the root of the context tree. However, only one environment, the current environment, possesses the cache. Other non–current environments are still represented as binding paths leading to the current environment.

A context switch between environments in the shallow binding scheme will involve a sequence of *rotations* in the context tree. The entire process for a sequence of rotations is called *rerooting*. A rotation is performed between the current environment (*i.e.*, the root node in the context tree) and one of its children. Suppose that the current environment E binds variable v to value a in its cache, and its child node n binds v to b. Then a rotation between node E and node n will make n the current environment and E n's child. Node n will inherit node E's cache and will change variable v's value to b. Node E will only record the binding of variable v to value a; it will not possess the cache anymore. A rerooting is a sequence of rotations to make the desired environment current.

Figure 1 pictures how rotation and rerooting work under the shallow binding scheme. We will show how to use, and to modify, the shallow binding scheme to implement functional arrays in the next section.

3 Functional Arrays and Their Implementations

A data structure for functional arrays must support the following operations.

- *Create n*: Return an array of size n. Each entry of the array is not initialized.

- *Update A_j i v*: Return an array $A_{j'}$ which is functionally identical to array A_j except $A_{j'}(i) = v$. Array A_j is not destroyed and can be accessed further.

- *Read A_j i*: Return $A_j(i)$.

We can use the shallow binding scheme to implement *Create*, *Update*, and *Read* as the following.

- *Create n*:
  Allocate a cache of size n. Allocate a node of one field and have this field point to the cache. This node is the *root node*. Return the address of the root node.

- *Update A_j i v*:
  Allocate a node of three fields and have it store i, v, and A_j (note that A_j is an address). Return the address of this newly allocated node.

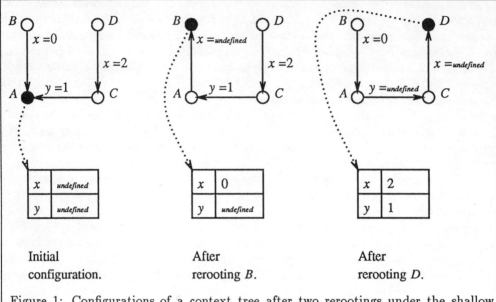

Figure 1: Configurations of a context tree after two rerootings under the shallow binding scheme. The first rerooting consists of a single rotation, and the second rerooting consists of three rotations. A, B, C, and D are environments, and black nodes denote the current environments. Note that only the current environment points to the cache.

- *Read A_j i*:
  Do a rerooting starting from the node pointed to by A_j. After the rerooting, A_j points to the root node which again points to a cache. Return the ith entry in the cache.

For example, the three configurations in figure 1 can be thought as being resulted from the following three successive sequences of operations,

- $A = Create\ 2;\ B = Update\ A\ i_x\ 0;\ C = Update\ A\ i_y\ 1;\ D = Update\ C\ i_x\ 2;$

- *Read B i*; and

- *Read D j*.

We now use the term *version tree* to refer to the context tree in the shallow binding implementation of functional arrays. It is easy to verify that a *Create n* operation takes $O(n)$ time and uses $O(n)$ space. Each *Update* takes $O(1)$ time and additional $O(1)$ space. A *Read* uses no space but takes time proportional to the distance between the new root node and the old root node, which can be as large as the total number of updates being performed. However, after a *Read A_j i* operation, each additional read to either array A_j, or one of A_j's children in the version tree, will cost only additional $O(1)$ time. This is because, after the *Read A_j i* operation, A_j points to the root node and, in case the read is directed to one of A_j's children, the rotation between A_j and one of its children only costs $O(1)$ time.

It is not difficult to see why we insist on voluminous reads now. Because, after the initial read of a voluminous sequence, each read of the sequence will cost only additional $O(1)$ time. However, there is still one problem. The distance between the new root node and the old root node may be far greater than the volume of the reads, which makes rerooting expensive. The trick is to allocate caches during a long rerooting and, at the same time, keep the total numbers of entries in all caches proportional to the total numbers of updates being performed. By performing this trick, we make sure that the large cost of a long rerooting can be paid off by the small cost of future shorter rerooting. By keeping the total number of entries in caches proportional to the total number of updates, we make sure that only linear space (with respect to the total number of updates) is used.

Before describing the details of the new implementation scheme for efficient increment updates and voluminous reads, let us first define *VRead*, the voluminous read operation.

- *VRead* $[A_{j_0}, A_{j_1}, \ldots, A_{j_{l-1}}]$ $[i_0, i_1, \ldots, i_{l-1}]$: Return a list of l elements, where the list's kth element has value $A_{j_k}(i_k)$. It is required that l be $\Omega(n)$ and the path consisting of $A_{j_0}, A_{j_1}, \ldots, A_{j_{l-1}}$ in the version tree be of length $O(l)$. n is the array size. [1]

Notice that *Read* will also be supported by the new data structure. However, as we will see, an individual *Read* will cost $O(n)$ amortized time in the worst cases.

We now describe the *fragmented shallow binding scheme*, which supports *Create*, *Update*, *Read*, and *VRead*. The implementation of *Create* and *Update* are the same as before. *Read* and *VRead* are implemented in the following way.

- *Read* A_j i:
  Let d be the distance between the node p pointed to by A_j and the root node of the tree in which p resides.

  - If $d \leq 2n$, do a rerooting starting from node p and then return the ith entry in the cache pointed to by p. Note that node p is the root node after the rerooting.

  - If $d > 2n$, then cut the link between node p and the root node equally into $k = \lceil \frac{d}{n} \rceil$ segments such that each segment has at least $\lfloor \frac{d}{k} \rfloor$ nodes. Call these segments $s_0, s_1, \ldots, s_{k-1}$. Let H_i and T_i respectively be the first node and last node of segment $s_i, 0 \leq i \leq k - 1$. Note that H_0 is the root node and T_{k-1} is node p.
    Do a rerooting starting from node T_0, duplicate the cache pointed to by T_0, allocate a new root node and have it point to the new cache. Make H_1 point to this newly allocated root node. Repeat the above procedure for T_1 and H_2, T_2 and $H_3, \ldots, T_{k-2}$ and H_{k-1}, and T_{k-1}. When all rerooting is done, we have cut the tree in which node p originally resides into k disjoint trees such that each tree has its own root node (which points to its own cache).
    After the cutting and rerooting, A_j points to root node T_{k-1} which again points to a cache. Return the ith entry in the cache.

---

[1] $O(f(x))$ is defined as the set of all functions $g(x)$ such that there exist positive constants C and x_0 with $|g(x)| \leq C\ f(x)$ for all $x \geq x_0$. $\Omega(f(x))$ is the set of all functions $g(x)$ such that there exist positive constants C and x_0 with $g(x) \geq C\ f(x)$ for all $x \geq x_0$ (see [20], for example). In the definition of *VRead*, it simply says that the volume of the read sequence is at least the magnitude of the size of the array, and the length of the path is at most the magnitude of the volume of the read sequence.

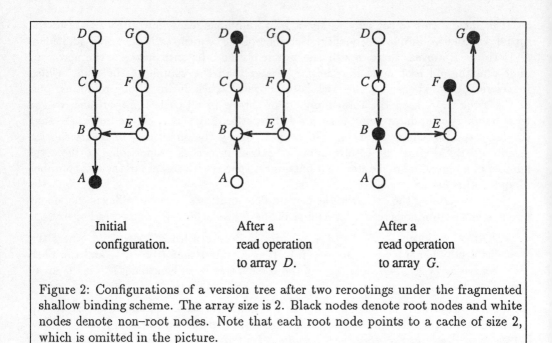

Initial configuration.	After a read operation to array D.	After a read operation to array G.

Figure 2: Configurations of a version tree after two rerootings under the fragmented shallow binding scheme. The array size is 2. Black nodes denote root nodes and white nodes denote non–root nodes. Note that each root node points to a cache of size 2, which is omitted in the picture.

- VRead $[A_{j_0}, A_{j_1}, \ldots, A_{j_{l-1}}]$ $[i_0, i_1, \ldots, i_{l-1}]$:
  Perform (in their specified ordering) the following operations: $v_0 = Read \ A_{j_0} \ i_0$; $v_1 = Read \ A_{j_1} \ i_1$; ...; and $v_{l-1} = Read \ A_{j_{l-1}} \ i_{l-1}$. Return $[v_0, v_1, \ldots, v_{l-1}]$.

Figure 2 illustrates what a version tree of an array of size 2 will look like after two rerootings under the fragmented shallow binding scheme. The three configurations in figure 2 can be thought as resulting from the following three successive sequences of operations,

- $A = Create \ 2$; $B = Update \ A \ i_b \ b$; $C = Update \ B \ i_c \ c$; $D = Update \ C \ i_d \ d$; $E = Update \ B \ i_e \ e$; $F = Update \ E \ i_f \ f$; $G = Update \ F \ i_g \ g$;

- Read $D \ i$; and

- Read $G \ j$.

In order to analyze the time and space complexity of the above implementation, let us first introduce some terminology. Since a rerooting may cut a tree into a set of disjoint trees, the resulting data structure is more likely to be a forest rather than a tree. Among the many nodes in a particular tree of the forest, we will use the term *backward gate* (*b–gate* for short) for the node whose link between itself and its parent has been cut. Similarly, a *forward gate* (*f–gates* for short) is a node whose link to one of its children has been cut.

Suppose that each tree in the forest is viewed as a *region* and an imaginary bridge is used to connect those regions that were connected previously. Then it is not difficult to see that the resulting region graph is also a tree. Let us call it a *region tree*. Note that the root region in the region tree has no b–gate and the leaf regions have no f–gates. To simplify the analysis, let us assign the b–gate of the root region to the root node of the version tree (as if no rerooting had ever occurred). Also note that the locations of b–gates and f–gates in a region will not change once they are created, regardless of further operations being performed on the data structure. For example, in the final configuration in figure 2, the region including nodes A, B, C, and D has A as b–gate and B as f–gate. The region including nodes E and F has E as b–gate and F as f–gate. The region including node G has G as b–gate but has no f–gate.

It can be easily shown that once cutting has occurred in the data structure, then each region contains at least $\lfloor \frac{2n+1}{3} \rfloor$ non–root nodes, where n is the array size.

4 Time and Space Complexity of the Fragmented Shallow Binding Scheme

We will use the potential method described by Tarjan [24] to analyze the amortized time complexity of a sequence of *Update* and *VRead* operations, starting from a single *Create* operation. A potential function Φ maps any configuration D of a data structure into its potential $\Phi(D)$, which can be viewed as the amount of energy stored in the configuration. The *amortized time* of an operation is defined to be $t+\Phi(D')-\Phi(D)$, where t is the actual time needed by the operation, and D and D' are the configurations of the data structure before and after the operation, respectively. We can regard amortized time as a fixed amount of cost. If this fixed amount is larger than the actual need, then the remaining amount is stored in the data structure for future use. If the fixed amount is less than the actual need, then the energy released from the data structure will compensate the difference.

With this definition, the total actual time for a sequence of m operations can be written as

$$\sum_{i=1}^{m} t_i = \sum_{i=1}^{m}(a_i - (\Phi_i - \Phi_{i-1})) = \sum_{i=1}^{m} a_i - (\Phi_m - \Phi_0),$$

where t_i and a_i are the actual time and amortized time of the ith operation, respectively. Φ_i is a shorthand for $\Phi(D_i)$. Φ_0 is the initial configuration of the data structure and Φ_m is the final one. If the difference between Φ_m and Φ_0 remains positive, then the total amortized time is an upper bound of the total actual time.

We define the potential of a configuration D in the fragmented shallow binding scheme as

$$\Phi(D) = 3(NR(D) - n \cdot R(D)) + \sum_{S \in D} W(S)$$

where $NR(D)$ is the total number of non–root nodes in D, $R(D)$ is the total number of root nodes in D, n is the size of array, and $W(S)$ is the weight of a region S. The weight of a region is defined as the distance between the root node and the b–gate in the region. It is clear that the minimal weight of a region is 0 and the maximal weight can be as large as the total number of non–root nodes in the region. Also note that a region's weight stores the exact amount of energy to move the root node of the region to the region's b–gate.

The intuition behind the definition of the potential function is that the more root nodes (*i.e.*, the more regions, hence, the more caches) a configuration has, the less potential it keeps; and, for each region, the more distant its cache is from its b–gate, the more potential it has. The constant 3 in the potential function Φ may vary if we change the way cutting is performed during a long rerooting. The constant 3 is chosen here because a link is cut only when its length is roughly 3 times larger than the size of the array. It also makes the following lemma true.

Lemma 4.1 If a reroot operation involves cutting the data structure, then the amortized time of the rerooting is less than or equal to 0. □

PROOF. If cutting occurs during a rerooting, then the distance d between the old root node and new root node in the original region must be greater then $2n$, where n is the array size. Let $d = (k+3)n - r$, where $0 \leq k$ and $0 \leq r \leq n-1$. After the rerooting, the original region is cut into $k+3$ regions, and the difference between the total weight of the $k+3$ regions and the weight of the original region is less than or equal to d. That is, $\sum_{S \in D'} W(S) - \sum_{S \in D} W(S) \leq d$, where D and D' are, respectively, the configurations of the data structure before and after the rerooting.

Let a be the amortized time of the rerooting and t be the actual time. We have $\Phi(D') - \Phi(D) \leq -3(k+2)n + d$. It is clear that d units of actual time suffices to perform the rerooting. We then have the amortized time

$$a = t + (\Phi(D') - \Phi(D)) \leq d + (-3(k+2)n + d) = -kn - 2r \leq 0.$$

◇

Before establishing the amortized time complexity for other operations, we state without proof two simple observations. First, we define a *walk* in a region tree as a sequence of either rotation between adjacent nodes in a region or, if the walk crosses several regions, the crossing of bridges between the regions (where each bridge consists of a b–gate/f–gate pair of nodes). We also define the *depth* of a region in the region tree as the number of bridges between itself and the root region. For example, in the final configuration in figure 2, the region including A, B, C, and D has depth 0, while the region including E and F has depth 1 and the region including G has depth 2. We then have the following two observations.

Proposition 4.2

1. If a walk leaves a region s via a b–gate/f–gate g, then the same walk will enter region s only via gate g during its first return to s (if the walk does return to s).

2. During a walk, if the current position is in a region of depth k, then the walk cannot lead to another different region also of depth k without first going to a region of depth $k-1$.

□

We can draw the course of a walk on a plane with the time step as the X–axis and the depth of the current visited region as the Y–axis, as in figure 3. According to the above proposition, then, in the specific walk illustrated in figure 3, regions S, T, and W are the same region, but they may differ from region U. Furthermore, the f–gates s and

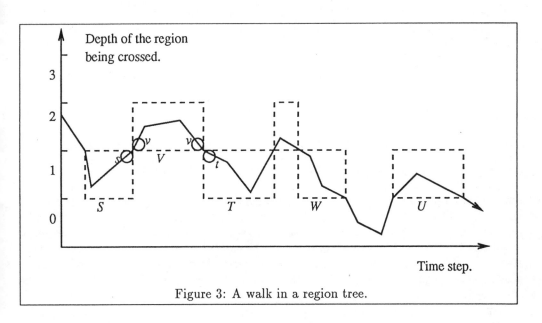

Figure 3: A walk in a region tree.

t are the same node because region V has only one b–gate, v, and v is bridged to both s and t.

Let us give an example. Suppose that the following *VRead* operation,

$$VRead\ [G, E, G, F, G, F, F, A, B, C, D]\ [i_0, i_1, i_2, i_3, i_4, i_5, i_6, i_7, i_8, i_9, i_{10}],$$

where $0 \leq i_k \leq 1$ for each index i_k, is issued to the final configuration in figure 2. The length of path formed by the above *VRead* is 13. (2 for G to E, 2 for E to G, 1 for G to F, 1 for F to G, 1 for G to F, 0 for F to F, 3 for F to A, 1 for A to B, 1 for B to C, and 1 for C to D.) Therefore, the *VRead* can be accomplished as a walk of 13 steps in the region tree. Each step of the walk first makes the current visited node the root node, then performs a *Read* operation if required. For example, the following 13–step walk accomplishes the above *VRead* operation.

> G (0 rotation, 1 read), F (0 rotation, 0 read), E (1 rotation, 1 read), F (1 rotation, 0 read), G (0 rotation, 1 read), F (0 rotation, 1 read), G (0 rotation, 1 read), F (0 rotation, 2 read), E (1 rotation, 0 read), B (0 rotation, 0 read), A (1 rotation, 1 read), B (1 rotation, 1 read), C (1 rotation, 1 read), D (1 rotation, 1 read).

Each of the above steps performs the operations in the parenthesis on the currently visited node. The rotations are used to make the current node the root node, and the reads fetch the required data. The course of the above walk is roughly pictured by figure 3.

However, the implementation of *VRead* as described in section 3 does not use a walk to accomplish a *VRead* operation. It does not move the root node of a region to the entrance gate whenever the next read operation enters the region from another region. Neither does it move the root node of a region to the exit gate whenever the next read operation leaves the region to another region. As a result, it will use less rotations than the walk sequence described above does. This is because the distance between two nodes A and B in a region is always less than the sum of the distance from A to an f–gate/b–gate g and the distance from g to B. This matters when the read operations to A and B are interrupted by a read operation to a node outside the current region. For example, the implementation described in section 3 only uses the following operations to accomplish the same *VRead* operation.

> G (0 rotation, 1 read), E (1 rotation, 1 read), G (0 rotation, 1 read), F (1 rotation, 1 read), G (0 rotation, 1 read), F (0 rotation, 1 read), F (0 rotation, 1 read), A (1 rotation, 1 read), B (1 rotation, 1 read), C (1 rotation, 1 read), D (1 rotation, 1 read).

The concept of a walk is introduced to prove the following crucial lemma.

Lemma 4.3 A *VRead* operation of volume l costs $O(l)$ amortized time. ☐

PROOF. By the definition of *VRead*, the sequence of arrays being read forms a path of length $d = O(l)$ in the region tree. In the worst cases, the *VRead* operation must be accomplished by a walk of d steps in the region tree. For each step during the walk, two tasks are performed: a rotation between the current root node and the next node in the path (plus bridge–crossing if the two nodes reside in different regions), and possibly several reads in the new root node. In the following, we will count the read cost and the rotation cost in a *VRead* operation separately.

However, there is one complication: at the beginning of a *VRead*, a rerooting may be needed to make the first node in the walk the root node, and, if the walk crosses several regions, a rerooting may be needed every time the walk crosses a bridge between two regions (which is to make the walk's first node in the destined region the root node).

It is clear that a read to a root node costs one unit of time and the operation changes no potential of the data structure. Therefore, without counting the rotation cost, the total read cost for a *VRead* of volume l is l. It remains to count the cost for rotations.

Assume that the walk goes through, in order, regions $s_0, s_1, \ldots, s_{k-1}$. Also assume that d_i rotations are needed by the walk to cross region $s_j, 0 \le j \le k - 1$. We have $\sum_{j=0}^{k-1} d_i = d$. For region $s_j, 1 \le j \le k - 2$, there are four possible ways for a walk may cross the region. They are shown in figure 4. The amortized cost for each case will be analyzed. Let us assume that a region s_j has weight $W(s_j)$ and potential Φ_j before the crossing, and weight $W(s_j')$ and potential Φ_j' afterward.

The actual cost for crossing a region s_j includes two parts: the cost for rerooting, which makes the entrance gate of the region the root node, and the cost for d_j rotations. Recall that we have shown in lemma 4.1 that if a rerooting involves cutting then its amortized cost is less than or equal to 0. Therefore, it suffices to analyze the situation where the rerooting does not involve any cutting.

The amortized costs for crossing each of the four cases in figure 4 are the following.

- Case 1. The actual cost t_j equals $W(s_j) + d_j$ because the crossing needs $W(s_j)$ time, exactly the weight of region s_j, to move the root node to the b–gate, and needs additional d_j time to rotate the root from the b–gate to the f–gate. We then have amortized cost

$$a_j = t_j + (\Phi_j' - \Phi_j) = (W(s_j) + d_j) + (W(s_j') - W(s_j)) = d_j + W(s_j') \le 2d_j.$$

Note that $W(s_j') \le d_j$ because the weight of region s_j is 0 when the crossing starts at its b–gate and each rotation only increases the weight of s_j at most by one.

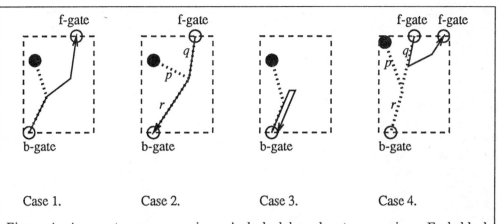

Figure 4: 4 ways to cross a region. A dashed box denotes a region. Each black node represents the root node before the crossing. The direction of each crossing is depicted by the solid line with an arrow head. The dotted line is used to illustrate the changing weight of the region.

- Case 2. Assume that, as pictured, the rerooting first reduces the weight of s_j from $p+r$ to r, then increases it to $q+r$. The actual cost for the rerooting is then $p+q$. For the rotations, the actual cost is d_j. It can be shown that $0 \le p, 0 \le q, 0 \le r$, and $r+q \le d_j$. Then, we have amortized cost

$$a_j = t_j + (\Phi_j' - \Phi_j) = (p+q+d_j) + (0 - (p+r)) = d_j + (q-r) \le 2d_j.$$

- Case 3. Similar to case 1, except that the weight of s_j after the crossing is 0. We then have

$$a_j = t_j + (\Phi_j' - \Phi_j) = (W(s_j) + d_j) + (0 - W(s_j)) = d_j.$$

- Case 4. Similar to case 2, except that the weight of s_j after the crossing may be as large as $q + r + d_j$. We then have

$$a_j = t_j + (\Phi_j' - \Phi_j) \le (p+q+d_j) + ((q+r+d_j) - (p+r)) = 2d_j + 2q.$$

Except for case 4, the amortized cost for crossing region s_j is bounded by $2d_j$.

Let w denote the region which has the least depth among the crossed regions. By proposition 4.2, such a region is unique. Suppose that a region s of depth greater than w is crossed as in case 4. Let s be s_j for some $1 \le j \le k-2$. Then either region s was crossed as $s_{j'}, j' < j$, by case 1 in order to exit from region w, or s will be crossed as $s_{j'}, j' > j$, by case 2 in order to enter region w. Furthermore, by proposition 4.2, the two crossings s_j and $s_{j'}$ will use a same f–gate as the exit/entrance gate. Therefore, no rerooting is necessary between the transition from $s_{j'}$ to s_j (or from s_j to $s_{j'}$).

We can then combine s_j and $s_{j'}$ as they are a single crossing in region s. The combined crossing will be of case 1 or 2 depending of what case $s_{j'}$ is. The combined amortized cost is then less than $2(d_j + d_{j'})$. It is possible that between s_j and $s_{j'}$, there are other case 4 crossings at the same region. If so, we can combine those case 4 crossings and make them as they are a single case 4 crossing. For example, in figure 3, the crossings at regions S, T, and W can be combined as a single case 2 crossing. (Note that regions S, T, and W are the same region.)

In the above, we assume that region s is of depth greater than w, the deepest region ever crossed. Suppose that $s = w$ is crossed as in case 4. Then the above analysis still holds except that all the crossing to w may be of case 4. In such a case, we can combine them into a single case 4 crossing. The combined amortized cost is $2\sum_{j \in J} d_j + 2q$, for some subset $J \subseteq \{1..(k-2)\}$. Furthermore, since the rerooting does not involve any cutting, we have $q \leq 2n$

Summarizing the total amortized cost for $s_j, 1 \leq j \leq k - 2$, we have

$$\sum_{j=1}^{k-2} a_j = 2q + 2\sum_{j=1}^{k-2} d_j \leq 4n + 2\sum_{j=1}^{k-2} d_j.$$

It is not difficult to see that s_0 and s_{k-1} each costs at most $4n + 2d_0$ and $4n + 2d_{k-1}$ amortized time, respectively. Therefore, we have the total amortized time

$$\sum_{j=0}^{k-1} a_j = (a_0 + a_{k-1}) + \sum_{j=1}^{k-2} a_j \leq 12n + 2d.$$

Adding both the cost for read (which is l) and rotation (which is at most $12n + 2d$), the total amortized time for a *VRead* of volume l is at most $l + 12n + 2d$, which is $O(l)$ because l is $\Omega(n)$ and d is $O(l)$. $\diamond$

We then can show the following main result.

Theorem 4.4 Let a *VRead* operation of volume l be counted as l individual operations, a *Create n* operation be counted as n individual operations, and an *Update* operation be counted as 1 individual operation. Then a sequence of *Create, Update,* and *VRead* operations can be implemented in $O(m)$ time and $O(n + u)$ space by the fragmented shallow binding scheme if the sequence has m individual operations, starts from a single *Create n* operation, and has u *Update* operations. $\square$

PROOF. Let a_i and t_i denote respectively the amortized and actual time for the ith *individual* operation in the sequence, and Φ_{i-1} and Φ_i respectively be the potential of the data structure before and after the ith individual operation. Also recall that the potential of a configuration D of the data structure is defined as

$$\Phi(D) = 3(NR(D) - n \cdot R(D)) + \sum_{S \in D} W(S).$$

The first operation in the sequence is a *Create n* operation. It needs $n + 1$ units of actual time, and space, to allocate and initialize both a cache of size n and a root node. Therefore, the total amortized time for the first n individual operations is described by

$$\sum_{i=1}^{n} a_i = \sum_{i=1}^{n} t_i + (\Phi_n - \Phi_0) = (n+1) + 3(-n) = -2n + 1.$$

Suppose that the ith individual operation, $n < i \leq m$, is an *Update* operation. It will need 1 unit of actual time and 1 unit of space to complete the operation. The amortized time a_i is then

$$a_i = t_i + (\Phi_i - \Phi_{i-1}) = 1 + 3 = 4.$$

Suppose that the ith to $(i+l-1)$th individual operations constitute a *VRead* operation of volume l. By lemma 4.3, the total amortized time for the *VRead* is $O(l)$. That is, it is less than $C_i \cdot l$ for some constant $C_i \geq 0$.

The total amortized cost for the m individual operations is then

$$\sum_{i=1}^{m} a_i = \sum_{i=1}^{n} a_i + \sum_{i=n+1}^{m} a_i \leq (-2n + 1) + C(m - n),$$

for some constant $C = max\{4, C_{i_1}, C_{i_2}, \ldots, C_{i_j}\}$. Constants $C_{i_1}, C_{i_2}, \ldots, C_{i_j}$ are derived from the j *VRead* operations in the whole sequence.

If the final configuration of the data structure has $k > 1$ regions, then it can be shown that each region has at least $\lfloor \frac{2n+1}{3} \rfloor$ nodes. Therefore, we have its potential as

$$\Phi_m \geq 3(k \left\lfloor \frac{2n + 1}{3} \right\rfloor - n \cdot k) + 0 \geq 0,$$

when the array size $n \geq 1$. If the final configuration has only one region, then its potential is

$$\Phi_m \geq 3(0 - n \cdot 1) + 0 = -3n.$$

Therefore, the total actual time for the entire m individual operations is

$$\sum_{i=1}^{m} t_i = \sum_{i=1}^{m} a_i - (\Phi_m - \Phi_0) \leq (-2n + 1 + C(m - n)) + 3n.$$

The total actual time is $O(m)$ because $m \geq n$. It is clear that the data structure use only $O(n + u)$ space, where u is the total number of *Update* operations in the sequence. $\diamond$

Corollary 4.5 A sequence of m *Read* and *Update* operations, which starts from a single *Create* n operation and includes u *Update* operations, can be implemented in $O(n + m)$ time and $O(n + u)$ space by the fragmented shallow binding scheme if all the *Read* operations in the sequence can be partitioned into disjoint voluminous subsequences. It does not matter if *Update* operations are mixed in the voluminous sequences of *Read*. $\square$

PROOF. Since an *Update* operation does not change the weight of the region to which it is applied, *Update* will not change the amortized cost analysis for *VRead* in the proof of Lemma 4.3. Except that the amortized cost of the *Update* operation is now incorporated in the summarization of the amortized cost for the voluminous *Read* operations. But this does not change the total amortized cost of the entire m operations either. The proof then follows immediately from theorem 4.4. $\diamond$

Note that disjoint voluminous sequences of reads arise naturally in many functional array applications due to the dense locality of their accesses to arrays. Compile–time partition of *Read* operations into voluminous sequences may not be necessary in most cases to achieve good running time. Also the fragmented data structure resulted from the fragmented shallow binding scheme is likely to make voluminous sequences of reads disjoint. The empirical results in section 5 will show that the above observations are valid.

5   Examples and Empirical Results

Is it practical to use the fragmented shallow binding scheme to implement functional arrays? Before answering this question, we have to argue first that functional arrays are often used in an incremental updates/voluminous reads style. In single–threaded accesses to functional arrays, the entire read sequence is voluminous because each read is applied to the newly updated array and the total number of rotations needed in all the read operations is bounded by the the total number of updates being performed. For multi–threaded applications of functional arrays, we observe that many of them will read every entry of an array if there is ever a need to read the array. If a long sequence of reads is not directed to a single array, it is usually directed to a sequence of closely related arrays. Both of these multi–threaded read patterns are voluminous.

We can take the full histogram problem as an example in the multi–threaded case. The full histogram problem is to classify a sequence of incoming events into a fixed set of categories, and to query either the distribution of events among the categories in a certain past time step, or to query the evolution of the events of a particular category in a certain sequence of past time steps. The queries can occur while events are still coming in. It is common to represent the fixed set of categories as an array and have each entry of the array store the number of events which have happened so far in the given category. To answer the query of distribution of events, all entries of the array have to be read. Also, the evolution of events of a category can be accessed by straight–line sequence of reads to the arrays in the version tree. Both the distribution query and the evolution query are implemented by voluminous reads.

We give empirical results collected from the execution of four sample programs to support our argument. The programs are for the multiplication of two matrices (each of size 100×100), all the safe positions for 8 queens, the transitive closures of a graph of 100 nodes, and the simulation of a histogram involving 10,000 events in 100 categories. The Warshall [27] algorithm is used in the transitive closures program, and all intermediate closures (which are those considering only paths through node 0 to node $i, 0 \leq i \leq 99$) are preserved.

Except for the matrix multiplication program, all programs are multi–threaded. After the results are computed, each program also reads every entry of the resulting arrays. We do this because otherwise the fragmented shallow binding scheme will have a clear advantage over other implementation schemes. This is because much of the work in the fragmented shallow binding scheme only occurs when reads are performed to the resulted arrays. Also, no effort is spent in partitioning the *Read* operations into voluminous sequences in the fragmented shallow binding implementation; the ordering of *Read* operations is left as it is (specified by the program).

Table 1 shows the total number of *Create*, *Update*, and *Read* operations being performed; the total number of root nodes and non–root nodes in the resulted data structure;

	create	update	read	root node (cache size)	non–root node	rerooting	rotation
matrix	202	40200	2070102	202 (100)	40200	20202	40200
queens	1	2056	41018	1 (8)	2056	2056	5020
closures	1	9803	5328354	49 (100)	9803	14851	27415
histogram	2	20101	37625	60 (100)	20001	25070	37713

Table 1: Operation counts of the four programs.

	destructive	fragmented shallow	shallow	copying
matrix	43.08 (1.47)	50.38 (5.91)	50.32 (5.09)	84.73 (10.34)
queens	not applicable	1.12 (0.07)	1.10 (0.05)	1.10 (0.05)
closures	not applicable	58.99 (2.19)	59.07 (2.22)	66.00 (5.54)
histogram	not applicable	4.23 (1.95)	19.26 (12.06)	1455.45 (603.03)

Table 2: Execution times of the four programs.

and the total number of rerootings and rotations being performed. We can see that

(the number of non–root nodes) + (the cache size) · (the number of root nodes),

which is the total space used, is about the magnitude of the number of updates. The number of rotations, which is the total time spent in rerooting nodes, is about the magnitude of the number of read operations too. Also note that the total number of reads being performed is far greater than the total number of updates being performed in each of the four programs. These statistics are very likely the result of incremental updates/voluminous reads execution patterns, which make the fragmented shallow binding scheme very much applicable. Figure 5 and figure 6 show the traces of the four programs' read sequences. The traces show that most of the entire read sequence in each of the four programs is voluminous.

Table 2 shows the execution times of the four programs. The programs are implemented in Standard ML of New Jersey, version 0.66, and run on a Sparc workstation (Sun 4/290, with 32 MB of physical memory) Each entry in the table is of the format total time (garbage collection time), as provided by the System.Timer module of SML of New Jersey. Each datum in the table is the average of the data from three runs.

Four sets of timing are shown. In the cases where array updating is done destructively all the time, where the fragmented shallow binding scheme is used, where the shallow binding scheme is used, and where the whole array is copied when being updated. The same program is used in all four sets of experiments; it just calls different implementation of the array module in each case. Also note that the destructive updating implementation of functional arrays is not applicable to the 8–queens, transitive closures, and histogram programs because those programs are multi–threaded.

According to the results in table 2, the fragmented shallow binding scheme performs well. It is as fast as the shallow binding scheme when arrays are mostly used in single–threaded ways; and is far better in case when a program uses arrays mostly in a multi–threaded way, as demonstrated in the histogram example. But it is clear from the 8–queens example that for the fragmented shallow binding scheme to be effective, the array size had better be large.

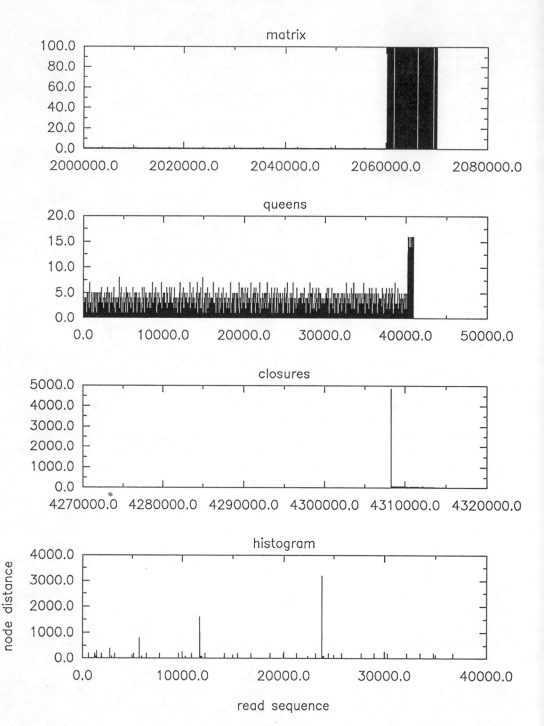

Figure 5: Trace graphs for the read sequences of the four programs. The X–axis is for the read sequence, and the Y–axis is for the distance between the current root node and the node to be read. Due to the large number of reads in the matrix and the histogram programs, only parts of their traces are shown. Note that each graph has its own scale.

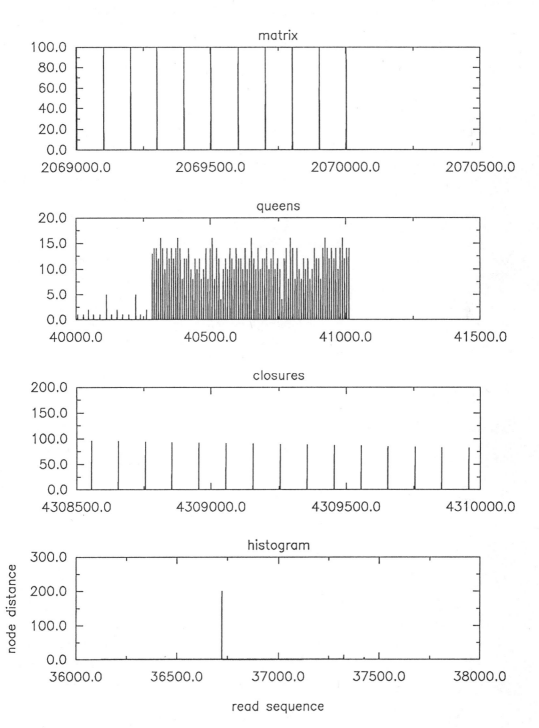

Figure 6: Magnified versions of the trace graphs. Only some interesting portions are shown.

6 Future Work

There remains several performance issues to be addressed. For example, does the fragmented shallow binding scheme perform well in a lazy functional language? How about in a parallel system where the voluminous read sequences are not coordinated and may intervene with one another?

We believe the fragmented shallow binding scheme will perform well in a lazy evaluation setting because the an update operation is in fact carried out lazily. In our scheme, the result of an *Update* operation is computed only if there is a need to read the resulting array afterward. That is, the rerooting operation, which makes the desired version of an array current, is performed (if necessary) only during a *Read* operation, not during an *Update* operation. On the other hand, however, it remains to be seen if read operations will typically lead to voluminous sequences in a lazy evaluation setting.

Regarding uncoordinated voluminous *Read* sequences in a parallel system, it has been observed that performance will suffer if the sequences intervene with one another. This is because the cost spent in rerooting may not be paid off by voluminous reads. In the worst case, each read in a voluminous sequence may have to do a long rerooting. But we view this as a common problem faced by sharing aggregate data structures in a parallel system, not a problem caused by the fragmented shallow binding scheme *per se*. On the other hand, the fragmented shallow binding scheme also has its advantage because its data structure is more likely to be fragmented and to be distributed well.

7 Acknowledgment

I am very grateful to Malcolm Harrison for introducing the idea of shallow binding to me, to Atul Sibal for suggesting that having multiple caches is better than a single caches, and to Chia–Hsiang Chang for helping me with the proof of lemma 4.3. I am also very grateful to Benjamin Goldberg, my advisor, for his encourage and support, and for the time he spent with me to improve the presentation of this paper, to Henry G. Baker for making several detailed comments on a draft of this paper and sending me related literature, to Annika Aasa for providing literature, and to the referees for their helpful comments.

References

[1] *12th Annual ACM Symposium on Principles of Programming Languages*. A.C.M., January 1985. New Orleans, Louisiana, U.S.A.

[2] *Functional Programming Languages and Computer Architecture*. A.C.M./Addison–Wesley, September 1989. Imperial College, London, U.K.

[3] *Proceedings of the 1990 ACM Conference on Lisp and Functional Programming*. A.C.M., June 1990. Nice, France.

[4] *18th Annual ACM Symposium on Principles of Programming Languages*. A.C.M., January 1991. Orlando, Florida, U.S.A.

[5] *Proceedings of the Symposium on Partial Evaluation and and Semantics–Based Program Manipulation*. A.C.M., June 1991. New Haven, Connecticut, U.S.A. Also appears as *SIGPLAN Notices*, 26(9), September 1991.

[6] Annika Aasa, Sören Holmström, and Christina Nilsson. An efficiency comparison of some representations of purely functional arrays. *BIT*, 28(3):490–503, 1988.

[7] Henry G. Baker, Jr. Shallow binding in Lisp 1.5. *Communications of the ACM*, 21(7):565–569, July 1978.

[8] Henry G. Baker. Shallow binding makes functional arrays fast. *SIGPLAN Notices*, 26(8):145–147, August 1991.

[9] Adrienne Gael Bloss. *Path Analysis and the Optimization of Non–Strict Functional Languages*. PhD thesis, Department of Computer Science, Yale University, May 1989. Also appears as report YALEU/DCS/RR–704.

[10] Adrienne Bloss. Update analysis and the efficient implementation of functional aggregates. pages 26–38. In [2].

[11] Frank Dehne, Jörg–Rüdiger Sack, and Nicola Santoro, editors. *Algorithms and Data Structures*. Ottawa, Canada, August 1989. Lecture Notes in Computer Science, Volume 382, Springer–Verlag.

[12] Paul F. Dietz. Fully persistent arrays. pages 67–74. In [11].

[13] James R. Driscoll, Neil Sarnak, Daniel D. Sleator, and Robert E. Tarjan. Making data structures persistent. *Journal of Computer and System Sciences*, 38(1):86–124, February 1989.

[14] Juan C. Guzmán and Paul Hudak. Single–threaded polymorphic lambda calculus. In *Proceedings of 5th Annual IEEE Symposium on Logic in Computer Science*, pages 333–343. I.E.E.E., June 1990.

[15] Sören Holmström. How to handle large data structures in functional languages. In *Proceedings of the SERC Chalmers Workshop on Declarative Programming Languages*. University College London, 1983.

[16] Paul Hudak and Adrienne Bloss. The aggregate update problem in functional programming systems. pages 300–314. In [1].

[17] Paul Hudak, Simon Peyton Jones, and Philip Wadler, editors. *Report on the Programming Language Haskell — A Non–Strict, Purely Functional Language, Version 1.1*. August 1991. Available from Yale University and University of Glasgow.

[18] John Hughes. An efficient implementation of purely functional arrays. Technical report, Department of Computer Sciences, Chalmers University of Technology, 1985.

[19] Martin Odersky. How to make destructive updates less destructive. pages 25–36. In [4].

[20] Paul Walton Purdom, Jr. and Cynthia A. Brown. *The Analysis of Algorithms*. Holt, Rinehart and Winston, 1985.

[21] David A. Schmidt. Detecting global variables in denotational specifications. *ACM Transactions on Programming Languages and Systems*, 7(2):299–310, April 1985.

[22] J. T. Schwartz. Optimization of very high level languages — i. value transmission and its corollaries. *Computer Languages*, 1(2):161–194, June 1975.

[23] J. T. Schwartz. Optimization of very high level languages — ii. deducing relationships of inclusion and membership. *Computer Languages*, 1(3):197–218, September 1975.

[24] Robert Endre Tarjan. Amortized computational complexity. *SIAM Journal on Algebraic and Discrete Methods*, 6(2):306–318, April 1985.

[25] Philip Wadler. Comprehending monads. pages 61–78. In [3].

[26] Philip Wadler. Is there a use for linear logic? pages 255–273. In [5].

[27] Stephen Warshall. A theorem on boolean matrices. *Journal of the Association for Computing Machinery*, 9(1):11–12, January 1962.

Back to Direct Style

Olivier Danvy
Department of Computing and Information Sciences
Kansas State University *
danvy@cis.ksu.edu

Abstract

While a great deal of attention has been devoted to transforming direct-style (DS) functional programs into continuation-passing style (CPS), to the best of our knowledge, the transformation of CPS programs into direct style has not been investigated. This paper describes the mapping of continuation-passing λ-terms to their applicative-order direct style counterpart. We set up foundations and outline applications of the direct style transformation.

We derive the direct style transformer from a non-standard denotational semantics of the untyped λ_v-calculus, that we prove congruent to the standard one.

Under precise conditions (linear occurrences of continuation parameters and no first-class use of continuations due to control operators such as call/cc), we show the DS and the CPS transformations to be inverse.

The direct style transformation can be used in partial evaluation, based on the fact that semantics-based program manipulation performs better when source programs are first transformed into CPS. As a result, specialized programs are expressed in CPS as well. The DS transformation maps them back to direct style.

Keywords

Direct style transformation, continuation-passing style transformation,
λ_v-calculus, Scheme.

---

*Manhattan, Kansas 66506, USA. Part of this work was supported by NSF under grant CCR-9102625. Another part was carried out while visiting Xerox PARC in summer 1991.

1 Introduction

A considerable amount of work is dedicated to the continuation-passing style (CPS) transformation: van Wijngaarden transforms ALGOL 60 programs to eliminate labels [34]. Mazurkiewicz proves algorithms [24]. Fischer compares the generalities of implementations based on retention and deletion strategies [13]. Strachey and Wadsworth formalize control flow in the denotational semantics of programming languages with jumps [33]. Reynolds and Plotkin identify the evaluation order independence of CPS terms [30, 29]. Felleisen bases several syntactic theories of sequential control on continuations [10, 11]. Steele reveals CPS to be a well-suited intermediate representation for compiling strict functional languages [32] and Appel builds his implementation of SML on a preliminary transformation into CPS [1]. The CPS representation is at the core of Wand's combinator-based compilers [36] and is also used for compiling programs by program transformation [21, 14]. Together with first-class continuations as a programming paradigm [15], continuations are generally agreed to be an essential item in programming languages [16]. They also are ubiquitous in many areas of Computer Science: Moggi formalizes them using monads [25]. Filinski discovers values and continuations to be dual in a category theoretical sense [12]. Griffin and Murthy point out that the CPS transformation corresponds to the double negation translation in proof theory [17, 26].

Yet to the best of our knowledge, the inverse transformation, *i.e.*, transforming CPS terms into direct style (DS), has not been investigated despite its obvious value, *e.g.*, to disassemble CPS programs into something readable. Yet there is a need for the DS transformation, for example in the area of partial evaluation (*cf.* Section 5). Moreover, like the CPS transformation [8], the DS transformation can be derived formally.

1.1 Towards a direct style transformer

In a CPS term, continuations are produced by function composition and consumed by function application. In an empty context, the continuation is initialized with the identity function, *i.e.*, the identity element for function composition.

For example, if *dfac* and *cfac* respectively denote the DS and the CPS definitions of the factorial function, they are related by the traditional congruence relation

$$\forall n \in Nat, \forall k \in [Nat \rightarrow Ans], \; cfac(n,k) = k(dfac(n))$$

where *dfac*: $Nat \rightarrow Nat$ and *cfac*: $Nat \times [Nat \rightarrow Ans] \rightarrow Ans$ for some domain of final answers. An answer is the result of the expression that introduced the initial continuation and whose computation involved calling *cfac*.

$$cfac \stackrel{rec}{=} \lambda(n,k).n = 0 \rightarrow k(1), cfac(n-1, \lambda v. k(n \times v))$$

Intuitively, we want to transform a CPS term into a DS term by symbolically applying the continuation of an expression such as the recursive call

$$cfac(n-1, \lambda v. k(n \times v))$$

to this expression, letting the continuation of this expression be the identity function. For example, using this intuition on the factorial function yields the following definition.

$$fac \stackrel{rec}{=} \lambda(n,k).n = 0 \rightarrow k(1), (\lambda v. k(n \times v))(fac(n-1, \lambda v. v))$$

This definition can be simplified into

$$fac \stackrel{rec}{=} \lambda(n,k).n = 0 \rightarrow k(1), k(n \times (fac(n-1, \lambda v. v)))$$

If we carry out this transformation for all expressions, k will always denote the identity function and therefore we only need to apply the functions extending the continuation to all the expressions where continuations are extended (in practice: applications and conditional expressions), letting their continuation be identity. As a final step, we can get rid of all the continuation arguments (since they only denote identity). Going back to the example, this treatment yields the usual (direct style) definition of the factorial function.

$$dfac \stackrel{rec}{=} \lambda(n).n = 0 \rightarrow 1, n \times (dfac(n-1))$$

1.2 Overview

This paper is organized as follows. Section 2 reviews the CPS transformation and specifies the BNF of CPS terms. The derivation of the DS transformer for λ_v-terms (*i.e.*, call-by-value λ-terms) is described in Section 3. The CPS transformer and the DS transformer are inverses of each other. This point is addressed in Section 4. The need for going back to direct style is illustrated with semantics-based program manipulation in Section 5. Section 5 also illustrates the use of shifting back and forth between direct and continuation-passing styles. Section 6 situates our approach among related work. Finally Section 7 puts this investigation into perspective.

2 Transformation into Direct vs. into Continuation-Passing Style

The CPS transformation is generally perceived to be a complicated affair. Similarly, CPS terms (such as in a continuation semantics) are perceived as unfriendly to read and to understand, unless one develops a particular skill for it. CPS terms do not appear amenable to an inverse transformation into direct style,[1] otherwise this transformation would already be part of the debugging package of a compiler. These observations motivated us to investigate the direct style transformation. In particular, we wanted to derive it soundly rather than coming up with just another algorithm. Since the CPS transformation can be derived from a continuation semantics of the λ_v-calculus [2, 8, 35], we chose to derive the DS transformer from a direct semantics of the λ_v-calculus dedicated to CPS λ-terms.

2.1 The CPS transformation

Here is the abstract syntax for λ-terms (where the symbol @ denotes an application)

$$
\begin{array}{ll}
e \in \text{Exp} & \text{— domain of expressions} \\
l \in \text{Lam} & \text{— domain of } \lambda\text{-abstractions} \\
op \in \text{Opr} & \text{— domain of primitive operators} \\
c \in \text{Cst} & \text{— domain of first-order constant values} \\
i \in \text{Ide} & \text{— domain of identifiers}
\end{array}
$$

$$
\begin{aligned}
e ::=\ & c \mid x \mid l \mid @\, e_0\,(e_1, ..., e_n) \mid e_0 \rightarrow e_1, e_2 \mid op\,(e_1, ..., e_m) \\
& \mid \text{let } (i_1, ..., i_n) = (e_1, ..., e_n) \text{ in } e_0 \mid \text{letrec } (i_1, ..., i_n) = (l_1, ..., l_n) \text{ in } e_0 \\
l ::=\ & \lambda\,(i_1, ..., i_n).e
\end{aligned}
$$

Let us present a one-pass CPS transformer for applicative order (call-by-value) λ-terms as we derived it in an earlier work [8]. This transformer is an optimized version of Fischer & Plotkin's CPS transformer [13, 29].

---

[1] For example, one could try to specify a relation between DS and CPS terms, express it in Prolog, and try to give Prolog a CPS term in the hope of producing the corresponding DS term. Unfortunately, our experience shows that this process is prone to looping.

$$[\![c]\!] \;=\; \overline{\lambda}\kappa.\overline{@}\kappa\,c$$

$$[\![x]\!] \;=\; \overline{\lambda}\kappa.\overline{@}\kappa\,x$$

$$[\![\lambda\,(x_1, ..., x_n)\,.\,e]\!] \;=\; \overline{\lambda}\kappa.\overline{@}\kappa\,(\underline{\lambda}(x_1, ..., x_n, k).\overline{@}[\![e]\!]\,(\overline{\lambda}v.\underline{@}k\,v))$$

$$[\![@\,e_0\,(e_1, ..., e_n)]\!] \;=\; \overline{\lambda}\kappa.\overline{@}\,[\![e_0]\!]$$
$$\overline{\lambda}v_0.\overline{@}\,[\![e_1]\!]$$
$$\overline{\lambda}v_1.\,...\,\overline{@}\,[\![e_n]\!]$$
$$\overline{\lambda}v_n.\underline{@}v_0\,(v_1, ..., v_n, \underline{\lambda}v.\overline{@}\kappa\,v)$$

$$[\![e_0\;\rightarrow\;e_1, e_2]\!] \;=\; \overline{\lambda}\kappa.\underline{\text{let}}\;k = \underline{\lambda}a.\overline{@}\kappa\,a$$
$$\underline{\text{in}}\;\overline{@}[\![e_0]\!]\,(\overline{\lambda}p.p\xrightarrow{\;}\overline{@}[\![e_1]\!]\,(\overline{\lambda}m.\underline{@}k\,m)\,,$$
$$\overline{@}[\![e_2]\!]\,(\overline{\lambda}n.\underline{@}k\,n))$$

$$[\![op\,(e_1, ..., e_m)]\!] \;=\; \overline{\lambda}\kappa.\overline{@}\,[\![e_1]\!]$$
$$\overline{\lambda}v_1.\,...\,\overline{@}\,[\![e_m]\!]$$
$$\overline{\lambda}v_m.\overline{@}\kappa\,(\underline{op}\,(v_1, ..., v_m))$$

$$[\![\text{let}\,(i_1, ..., i_n) = (e_1, ..., e_n)\,\text{in}\,e_0]\!] \;=\; \overline{\lambda}\kappa.\overline{@}\,[\![e_1]\!]$$
$$\overline{\lambda}v_1.\,...\,\overline{@}\,[\![e_n]\!]$$
$$\overline{\lambda}v_n.\overline{@}\kappa\,(\underline{\text{let}}\,(i_1, ..., i_n) = (v_1, ..., v_n)$$
$$\underline{\text{in}}\;\overline{@}[\![e_0]\!]\,\kappa)$$

$$[\![\text{letrec}\,(i_1, ..., i_n) = (l_1, ..., l_n)\,\text{in}\,e_0]\!] \;=\; \overline{\lambda}\kappa.\underline{\text{letrec}}\,(i_1, ..., i_n) = (\overline{@}[\![l_1]\!]\,(\overline{\lambda}f_1.f_1),$$
$$...,$$
$$\overline{@}[\![l_n]\!]\,(\overline{\lambda}f_n.f_n))$$
$$\underline{\text{in}}\;\overline{@}[\![e_0]\!]\,\kappa$$

where k is a fresh variable.

Figure 1: The CPS transformation

These equations can be read as a two-level specification à la Nielson and Nielson [28]. Operationally, the overlined λ's and @'s correspond to functional abstractions and applications in the translation program, while only the underlined occurrences represent abstract-syntax constructors.

The result of transforming a term e into CPS in any context (represented with a unary function: the continuation) is given by

$$\underline{\lambda}k.\overline{@}[\![e]\!]\,(\overline{\lambda}v.\underline{@}k\,v)$$

By construction, if the CPS transformer produces the term $\lambda\,k\,.\,e$, then the term $@\,(\lambda\,k\,.\,e)(\lambda\,v\,.\,v)$ has the same meaning as the original DS term.

2.2 Simplified CPS terms

In the transformation above as in the present work, we disregard the simplifications due to tail-calls, η-reductions, or identity let expressions. For example, the direct style conditional expression

$$\lambda\,(x)\,.\,x\;\rightarrow\;y,\;@\,f\,(z)$$

is transformed into

$$\lambda\,k\,.\,@\,k\,(\lambda\,(x, k')\,.\,\text{let}\,k'' = \lambda\,v\,.\,@\,k'\,v\,\text{in}\,x\;\rightarrow\;@\,k''\,y,\;@\,f\,(z, \lambda\,v\,.\,@\,k''\,v))$$

Of course, in practice, we reduce this to

$$\lambda\,k\,.\,@\,k\,(\lambda\,(x,\,k')\,.\,x\ \to\ @\,k'\,y,\ @\,f\,(z,\,k'))$$

instead,[2] but these simplifications actually complicate the development of this section — hence the purity. In practice, our CPS transformer produces such simplified terms [8] and our DS transformer handles them as well, using a refinement of the following BNF.[3]

2.3 Abstract syntax of CPS terms

Let us give the BNF of CPS terms as they are produced by the CPS transformer of last section. Since a fresh variable k is introduced for each abstraction and each conditional expression, let us index each non-terminal with this k as an inherited attribute. Much as Reynolds [30], we distinguish between "serious" and "trivial" expressions. Serious expressions e^k inherit a continuation k and trivial expressions t^k denote values that are passed to a continuation k.

A CPS term is of the form $\lambda\,k\,.\,e^k$, where e^k is defined by the following attribute grammar.

$e \in \mathrm{Exp}$	— domain of expressions
$l \in \mathrm{Lam}$	— domain of λ-abstractions
$op \in \mathrm{Opr}$	— domain of primitive operators
$c \in \mathrm{Cst}$	— domain of first-order constant values
$i, v, k \in \mathrm{Ide}$	— domain of identifiers

$$
\begin{aligned}
e^k ::=\ & @\,k\,t^k \\
 &\mid @\,t_0^k\,(t_1^k,\,...,\,t_n^k,\,\lambda\,v\,.\,e^k) &&\text{where } v \neq k \\
 &\mid \mathrm{let}\ k' = \lambda\,v\,.\,e_1^k \text{ in } t^{k'}\ \to\ e_2^{k'},\,e_3^{k'} &&\text{where } v \neq k \text{ and } k \notin FV(t^{k'}\ \to\ e_2^{k'},\,e_3^{k'}) \\
 &\mid \mathrm{let}\ (i_1,\,...,\,i_n) = (t_1^k,\,...,\,t_n^k) \text{ in } e^k &&\text{where } \forall j \in \{1,...,n\},\,i_j \neq k \\
 &\mid \mathrm{letrec}\ (i_1,\,...,\,i_n) = (l_1^k,\,...,\,l_n^k) \text{ in } e^k &&\text{where } \forall j \in \{1,...,n\},\,i_j \neq k \\
t^k ::=\ & c \\
 &\mid i &&\text{where } i \neq k \\
 &\mid l^k \\
 &\mid op\,(t_1^k,\,...,\,t_m^k) \\
l^k ::=\ & \lambda\,(i_1,\,...,\,i_n,\,k')\,.\,e^{k'} &&\text{where } k \notin FV(\lambda\,(i_1,\,...,\,i_n,\,k')\,.\,e^{k'})
\end{aligned}
$$

Each non-terminal is indexed with an identifier k denoting the current continuation. This attribute k allows us to restrict the BNF to CPS terms that correspond to purely functional terms. For example, a λ-term such as $\lambda\,(x,\,k)\,.\,@\,k'\,x$ is not produced by this BNF. We refer to this constraint as the *passing constraint*. The passing constraint is embodied in the first production $e^k ::= @\,k\,t^k$, in that *only the current continuation can be applied*.

2.4 Syntactic properties of CPS terms

The distinction between serious expressions e and trivial expressions t (and l) is captured in the following property. This property can be checked with the attribute grammar.

Proposition 1 $k \notin FV(t^k)$ □

---

[2] Sometimes, the form $\lambda\,x k'\,.\,x\ \to\ k'y,\ f z k'$ is preferred if the term occurs in an empty context, since the continuation corresponding to an empty context is the identity function — the point here is only the dropping of $\lambda\,k\,.\,@\,k\,...$

[3] For a simpler fix: the various η-redexes can be restored at syntax analysis time.

Corollary 1 $k \notin FV(l^k)$ □

The following syntactic property of CPS λ-terms is motivated by the passing constraint — at any stage in an evaluation, there is only one "current" continuation.

Proposition 2 *A CPS term resulting from the CPS transformation of a pure λ-term (i.e., a λ-term without* call/cc*) needs only one variable k to denote the current continuation.*

Proof: By structural induction over the attribute grammar above.

Here are the two productions where a new continuation is introduced.

$$e^k ::= \ldots \mid \text{let } k' = \lambda v . e_1^k \text{ in } t^{k'} \;\rightarrow\; e_2^{k'}, e_3^{k'} \quad \text{where } v \neq k$$
$$\text{and } k \notin FV(t^{k'} \;\rightarrow\; e_2^{k'}, e_3^{k'})$$
$$\mid \ldots$$
$$l^k ::= \lambda(i_1, \ldots, i_n, k') . e^{k'} \qquad\qquad \text{where } k \notin FV(\lambda(i_1, \ldots, i_n, k') . e^{k'})$$

These two productions come with the condition that k does not occur free in the body of the let expression and in the λ-abstraction. If we replace k' by k as a formal parameter of the let and of the λ, then all occurrences of k in the bodies will refer to this k, by virtue of lexical scope. *A fortiori*, they will not occur free in the let expression nor in the λ-abstraction.   □

In practice, a fresh identifier k (*i.e.*, an identifier that does not occur free in the DS term to be CPS-transformed) is provided by the CPS transformer. We use this fresh identifier as a BNF attribute to ensure that only the current continuation is applied and also to distinguish the identifier representing the current continuation from the other identifiers. Its unicity (*cf.* Proposition 2) motivates the following revision.

2.5   Revised abstract syntax of CPS terms

Let us state the BNF of CPS λ-terms where continuations are denoted with a unique and fresh identifier k. The whole BNF is parameterized with this identifier k. Since the k-attribute is now unnecessary, we have stripped it off.

A CPS term is of the form $\lambda k . e$, where e is defined by the following grammar.

$e \in \text{Exp}_k$	— domain of expressions
$l \in \text{Lam}_k$	— domain of λ-abstractions
$op \in \text{Opr}$	— domain of primitive operators
$c \in \text{Cst}$	— domain of first-order constant values
$i, v \in \text{Ide}$	— domain of identifiers s.t. $k \notin \text{Ide}$
$k \in \{k\}$	— singleton domain of continuation identifiers

$$e ::= @\, k\, t$$
$$\mid @\, t_0\, (t_1, \ldots, t_n, \lambda v . e)$$
$$\mid \text{let } k = \lambda v . e_1 \text{ in } t \;\rightarrow\; e_2, e_3$$
$$\mid \text{let } (i_1, \ldots, i_n) = (t_1, \ldots, t_n) \text{ in } e$$
$$\mid \text{letrec } (i_1, \ldots, i_n) = (l_1, \ldots, l_n) \text{ in } e$$
$$t ::= c$$
$$\mid i$$
$$\mid l$$
$$\mid op\, (t_1, \ldots, t_m)$$
$$l ::= \lambda(i_1, \ldots, i_n, k) . e$$

2.6 A linearity property

CPS terms also satisfy the following linearity property.

Proposition 3 *In a CPS term, a continuation parameter occurs linearly.* □

This property can be proven by structural induction over the CPS transformation of Section 2.1. The linearity can be characterized with the following inference rules (where "$\otimes$" stands for "exclusive or"). A continuation $\lambda v . e$ is linear in its parameter v when the following judgement

$$v \vdash e$$

is satisfied. The linearity property will be used last in the derivation of the DS transformer.

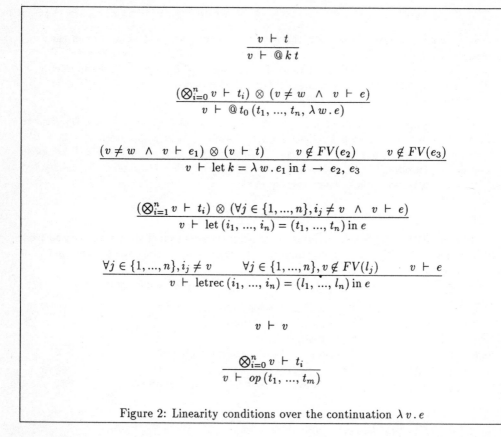

$$\frac{v \vdash t}{v \vdash @\, k\, t}$$

$$\frac{(\bigotimes_{i=0}^{n} v \vdash t_i) \otimes (v \neq w \ \wedge \ v \vdash e)}{v \vdash @\, t_0\, (t_1, ..., t_n, \lambda w . e)}$$

$$\frac{(v \neq w \ \wedge \ v \vdash e_1) \otimes (v \vdash t) \qquad v \notin FV(e_2) \qquad v \notin FV(e_3)}{v \vdash \mathrm{let}\, k = \lambda w . e_1 \,\mathrm{in}\, t \ \rightarrow \ e_2, e_3}$$

$$\frac{(\bigotimes_{i=1}^{n} v \vdash t_i) \otimes (\forall j \in \{1, ..., n\}, i_j \neq v \ \wedge \ v \vdash e)}{v \vdash \mathrm{let}\, (i_1, ..., i_n) = (t_1, ..., t_n) \,\mathrm{in}\, e}$$

$$\frac{\forall j \in \{1, ..., n\}, i_j \neq v \qquad \forall j \in \{1, ..., n\}, v \notin FV(l_j) \qquad v \vdash e}{v \vdash \mathrm{letrec}\, (i_1, ..., i_n) = (l_1, ..., l_n) \,\mathrm{in}\, e}$$

$$v \vdash v$$

$$\frac{\bigotimes_{i=0}^{n} v \vdash t_i}{v \vdash op\, (t_1, ..., t_m)}$$

Figure 2: Linearity conditions over the continuation $\lambda v . e$

3 Derivation of the Direct Style Transformer

This section is organized as follows. First we define the denotational semantics of CPS terms from the usual denotational semantics of the λ_v-calculus (reproduced in Appendix A). We express it as a core semantics and a standard interpretation. We prove a property of this specification. Then we successively present non-standard interpretations (together with their congruence proofs) that are increasingly better suited to the derivation of a direct style transformer. Finally, we view the last non-standard semantics as a mapping from syntax to syntax (since denotations are also expressed using λ-expressions). Improving its binding times yields the direct style transformer.

3.1 Core semantics and its standard interpretation

Based on the usual denotational semantics of λ_v-calculus (*cf.* Appendix A), let us derive the meaning of CPS terms in an empty context. The meaning of the term

$$[\![@\,(\lambda\,k\,.\,e)\,(\lambda\,v\,.\,v)]\!]$$

is given by the standard interpretation of e

$$\mathcal{E}_k[\![e]\!]\,\rho_{init}[k\,\mapsto\,Id]$$

where Id denotes the identity function and is the continuation representing an empty context.

This way we can give a denotation for each of the terms defined by the BNF. We stick to the distinction between serious and trivial terms by mapping them to their meaning using two valuation functions $\mathcal{E}_k$ and $\mathcal{T}_k$. These valuation functions can be derived from the usual valuation function $\mathcal{E}$ shown in Appendix A.

$$
\begin{array}{rcl}
Ide_k & = & Ide \cup \{k\} \\
Var_k & = & Var \cup \{k\} \\
Val & = & (Cst + Fun)_\bot \\
Env_k & = & Var_k \rightarrow Val \\
Fun & = & Val^+ \rightarrow Val
\end{array}
\qquad
\begin{array}{rcl}
\mathcal{E}_k & : & Exp_k \rightarrow Env_k \rightarrow Val \\
\mathcal{T}_k & : & Triv_k \rightarrow Env_k \rightarrow Val \\
\mathcal{L}_k & : & Lam_k \rightarrow Env_k \rightarrow Fun \\
\mathcal{C} & : & Cst \rightarrow Val \\
\mathcal{I}_k & : & Ide_k \rightarrow Var_k \\
\mathcal{O} & : & Opr \rightarrow Val^* \rightarrow Val
\end{array}
$$

where $Id = \lambda(v)\,.\,v \in Fun$

For simplicity, and as in appendix A, we will identify the syntactic domain of identifiers Ide_k and the semantic domain of variables Var_k. Therefore, a syntactic identifier i is mapped to a semantic variable i.

There is only one point to be noted in the following equations. We have parameterized them with four combinators Send, App, Close, and Cond:

Send: $Val \rightarrow Fun \rightarrow Val$
App: $Fun \rightarrow Val^+ \rightarrow Val$
Close: $Var_k^+ \rightarrow [Env_k \rightarrow Val] \rightarrow Env_k \rightarrow Fun$
Cond: $[Env_k \rightarrow Val] \rightarrow [Env_k \rightarrow Val] \rightarrow [Env_k \rightarrow Val] \rightarrow Env_k \rightarrow \{k\} \rightarrow Fun \rightarrow Val$

This technique of defining a core semantics and a standard interpretation can be found in Nielson's work on data flow analysis by abstract interpretation [27] and in Jones and Mycroft's work on Minimal Function Graphs [18]. Today Jones and Nielson are developing this technique as a convenient format for specifying abstract interpretations [19].

$$
\begin{array}{rcl}
\mathcal{E}_k[\![@\,k\,t]\!]\,\rho & = & \textbf{let } v = \mathcal{T}_k[\![t]\!]\,\rho \textbf{ in Send } v\,(\rho\,k) \\[1mm]
\mathcal{E}_k[\![@\,t_0\,(t_1,\,...,\,t_n,\,\lambda\,v\,.\,e)]\!]\,\rho & = & \textbf{let } v_0 = \mathcal{T}_k[\![t_0]\!]\,\rho,\ v_1 = \mathcal{T}_k[\![t_1]\!]\,\rho,\ ...,\ v_n = \mathcal{T}_k[\![t_n]\!]\,\rho \\
& & \textbf{in App } v_0\,(v_1,\,...,\,v_n,\,\lambda(a).\mathcal{E}_k[\![e]\!]\,\rho[v \mapsto a]) \\[1mm]
\mathcal{E}_k[\![\textbf{let } k = \lambda\,v\,.\,e_1 \textbf{ in } t \rightarrow e_2,\,e_3]\!]\,\rho & = & \textbf{let } \kappa = \lambda(a).\mathcal{E}_k[\![e_1]\!]\,\rho[v \mapsto a] \\
& & \textbf{in Cond }(\mathcal{T}_k[\![t]\!])\,(\mathcal{E}_k[\![e_2]\!])\,(\mathcal{E}_k[\![e_3]\!])\,\rho\,k\,\kappa
\end{array}
$$

$$\mathcal{E}_k[\![\text{let } (i_1, ..., i_n) = (t_1, ..., t_n) \text{ in } e]\!] \rho \;=\; \textbf{let } v_1 = \mathcal{T}_k[\![t_1]\!] \rho, ..., v_n = \mathcal{T}_k[\![t_n]\!] \rho$$
$$\textbf{in } \mathcal{E}_k[\![e]\!] \rho[i_1 \mapsto v_1, ..., i_n \mapsto v_n]$$

$$\mathcal{E}_k[\![\text{letrec } (i_1, ..., i_n) = (l_1, ..., l_n) \text{ in } e]\!] \rho \;=\; \textbf{letrec } (f_1, ..., f_n) = (\mathcal{L}_k[\![l_1]\!] \rho[i_1 \mapsto f_1, ..., i_n \mapsto f_n],$$
$$...,$$
$$\mathcal{L}_k[\![l_n]\!] \rho[i_1 \mapsto f_1, ..., i_n \mapsto f_n])$$
$$\textbf{in } \mathcal{E}_k[\![e]\!] \rho[i_1 \mapsto f_1, ..., i_n \mapsto f_n]$$

$$\mathcal{T}_k[\![c]\!] \rho \;=\; \mathcal{C}[\![c]\!]$$
$$\mathcal{T}_k[\![i]\!] \rho \;=\; \rho\, i$$
$$\mathcal{T}_k[\![l]\!] \rho \;=\; \mathcal{L}_k[\![l]\!] \rho$$
$$\mathcal{T}_k[\![op\,(t_1, ..., t_m)]\!] \rho \;=\; \textbf{let } v_1 = \mathcal{T}_k[\![t_1]\!] \rho, ..., v_m = \mathcal{T}_k[\![t_m]\!] \rho$$
$$\textbf{in } \mathcal{O}[\![op]\!]\,(v_1, ..., v_m)$$

$$\mathcal{L}_k[\![\lambda\,(i_1, ..., i_n, k)\,.\,e]\!] \rho \;=\; \text{Close}\,(i_1, ..., i_n, k)\,(\mathcal{E}_k[\![e]\!])\,\rho$$

The following four combinators specify the standard interpretation of this core semantics.

Send: $Val \rightarrow Fun \rightarrow Val$
Send $v\,\kappa \;=\; \kappa(v)$

App: $Fun \rightarrow Val^+ \rightarrow Val$
App $f\,(v_1, ..., v_n, \kappa) \;=\; f(v_1, ..., v_n, \kappa)$

Close: $Var_k^+ \rightarrow [Env_k \rightarrow Val] \rightarrow Env_k \rightarrow Fun$
Close $(i_1, ..., i_n, k)\,\theta\,\rho \;=\; \lambda(v_1, ..., v_n, \kappa).\theta\,\rho[i_1 \mapsto v_1, ..., i_n \mapsto v_n, k \mapsto \kappa]$

Cond: $[Env_k \rightarrow Val] \rightarrow [Env_k \rightarrow Val] \rightarrow [Env_k \rightarrow Val] \rightarrow Env_k \rightarrow \{k\} \rightarrow Fun \rightarrow Val$
Cond $\theta\,\theta_2\,\theta_3\,\rho\,k\,\kappa \;=\; \theta\,\rho[k \mapsto \kappa] \rightarrow \theta_2\,\rho[k \mapsto \kappa], \theta_3\,\rho[k \mapsto \kappa]$

Actually, this last combinator can be refined, as captured in the following property.

Proposition 4 *For all expressions t and legal environments $\rho[k \mapsto \kappa]$,*

$$\mathcal{T}_k[\![t]\!]\,\rho[k \mapsto \kappa] \;=\; \mathcal{T}_k[\![t]\!]\,\rho$$

Proof: By construction of any trivial term t, k does not occur free in t (*cf.* Proposition 1). Hence, evaluating t in an environment is insensitive as to whether this environment binds k or not. □

Therefore we can rewrite the definition of Cond as follows.

Cond: $[Env_k \rightarrow Val] \rightarrow [Env_k \rightarrow Val] \rightarrow [Env_k \rightarrow Val] \rightarrow Env_k \rightarrow \{k\} \rightarrow Fun \rightarrow Val$
Cond $\theta\,\theta_2\,\theta_3\,\rho\,k\,\kappa \;=\; \theta\,\rho \rightarrow \theta_2\,\rho[k \mapsto \kappa], \theta_3\,\rho[k \mapsto \kappa]$

3.2 Towards a direct style transformer (revisited)

Intuitively, if a procedure terminates, its continuation is guaranteed to be sent the "result" of this procedure (this passing constraint over continuations was captured in the k attribute). This intuition can be extended to arbitrary expressions: if evaluating an expression terminates, its continuation is guaranteed to be sent the corresponding value.

Suppose that, instead of the denotation of the current continuation, we pass the denotation of the identity procedure (*i.e.*, the identity function) when we call a procedure. This function would then be applied to the "result" of this procedure and would return it. If we send this result to the current continuation, the computation would proceed as before.

This intuition can be extended to arbitrary expressions: if we evaluate a terminating expression in an environment where the continuation identifier is bound to the identity function, this function will be applied to an intermediate value and will return it. Should we send this value to the current continuation, the computation would continue as before.

Regarding non-termination, this intuition still holds: if a procedure does not terminate, its continuation will never be applied to any "result." Therefore substituting the identity function for its continuation does not change the (absence of) result of the whole computation. Ditto for expressions whose evaluation does not terminate — substituting the identity function for their continuation in the environment will make the evaluation diverge as well.

The following section formalizes these intuitions as properties of the denotational semantics above.

3.3 Semantic properties of CPS λ-terms

Definition 1 *A value $f \in Val$ is* well-behaved *if*

$$f = \lambda(v_1, ..., v_n, \kappa) . \text{let } v = f(v_1, ..., v_n, Id)$$
$$\text{in } \kappa(v)$$

*whenever $f \in Fun$, $f \in Val^{n+1} \rightarrow Val$, and $n > 0$. (NB: as in Appendix A, the **let** construct is strict.)*

Definition 2 *An environment $\rho \in Env$ is* well-behaved *if $\forall i \in Var$, $\rho\, i$ is well-behaved.*

Based on these two definitions, let us prove the three following properties.

Proposition 5 ($\mathcal{E}$-property) *For all expressions $e \in \text{Exp}_k$ and well-behaved environments $\rho[k \mapsto \kappa]$ binding k to some $\kappa \in Val \rightarrow Val$,*

$$\mathcal{E}_k[\![e]\!]\, \rho[k \mapsto \kappa] = \text{let } v = \mathcal{E}_k[\![e]\!]\, \rho[k \mapsto Id]$$
$$\text{in } \kappa(v)$$

Proposition 6 ($\mathcal{L}$-property) *For all expressions $\lambda(i_1, ..., i_n, k).e \in \text{Lam}_k$ and well-behaved environments ρ,*

$$\mathcal{L}_k[\![\lambda(i_1, ..., i_n, k).e]\!]\, \rho = \lambda(v_1, ..., v_n, \kappa) . \text{let } v = \mathcal{E}_k[\![e]\!]\, \rho[i_1 \mapsto v_1, ..., i_n \mapsto v_n, k \mapsto Id]$$
$$\text{in } \kappa(v)$$

Proposition 7 ($\mathcal{T}$-property) *For all expressions $t \in \text{Triv}_k$ and well-behaved environments ρ, $\mathcal{T}_k[\![t]\!]\, \rho$ is well-behaved.*

Proof: By mutual structural induction over the syntactic categories e, t, and l [31, Section 1.2]. In particular, the equality

$$\mathcal{E}_k[\![\text{letrec } (i_1, ..., i_n) = (l_1, ..., l_n) \text{ in } e]\!]\, \rho[k \mapsto \kappa]$$
$$= \text{let } v = \mathcal{E}_k[\![\text{letrec } (i_1, ..., i_n) = (l_1, ..., l_n) \text{ in } e]\!]\, \rho[k \mapsto Id]$$
$$\text{in } \kappa(v)$$

is proved by fixpoint induction. This requires proving the two following lemmas [31, Section 6.7].

Lemma 1 *The predicate "is well-behaved" is inclusive over the domain $Val^{n+1} \rightarrow Val$.*

Lemma 2 $\perp_{Fun}$ *is well-behaved.*

$\square$

3.4 Non-standard interpretation and its congruence proof

The continuation gets extended with another function only for applications and for conditional expressions, whose meanings are defined by the combinators App and Cond. The properties above suggest the following non-standard combinators.

$$\text{App}': Fun \rightarrow Val^+ \rightarrow Val$$
$$\text{App}'\, f\, (v_1, ..., v_n, \kappa)\; =\; \textbf{let }v = f(v_1, ..., v_n, Id)\textbf{ in }\kappa(v)$$

$$\text{Cond}': [Env_k \rightarrow Val] \rightarrow [Env_k \rightarrow Val] \rightarrow [Env_k \rightarrow Val] \rightarrow Env_k \rightarrow \{k\} \rightarrow Fun \rightarrow Va$$
$$\text{Cond}'\, \theta\, \theta_2\, \theta_3\, \rho\, k\, \kappa\; =\; \theta\, \rho\; \rightarrow\; \textbf{let }v_2 = \theta_2\, \rho[k \mapsto Id]\textbf{ in }\kappa(v_2),$$
$$\textbf{let }v_3 = \theta_3\, \rho[k \mapsto Id]\textbf{ in }\kappa(v_3)$$

Together with Send' and Close' (which do not change)

$$\text{Send}' = \text{Send}$$
$$\text{Close}' = \text{Close}$$

App' and Cond' define a non-standard interpretation of the core semantics.

Proposition 8 *The standard and the non-standard interpretations define the same language.*

Proof: by structural induction, using the $\mathcal{E}$, $\mathcal{L}$, and $\mathcal{T}$-properties. Here are the only interesting cases.
Let f be well-behaved.

$$
\begin{aligned}
&\text{App}\, f\, (v_1, ..., v_n, \kappa) \\
=\; &f(v_1, ..., v_n, \kappa) &&\text{— definition of App} \\
=\; &(\lambda(v_1, ..., v_n, \kappa)\,.\,\textbf{let }v = f(v_1, ..., v_n, Id)\textbf{ in }\kappa(v))(v_1, ..., v_n, \kappa) &&\text{— }f\text{ is well-behaved} \\
=\; &\textbf{let }v = f(v_1, ..., v_n, Id)\textbf{ in }\kappa(v) &&\text{— }\beta\text{-reduction} \\
=\; &\text{App}'\, f\, (v_1, ..., v_n, \kappa) &&\text{— definition of App}'
\end{aligned}
$$

$$
\begin{aligned}
&\text{Cond}\, (\mathcal{T}_k[\![t]\!])\, (\mathcal{E}_k[\![e_2]\!])\, (\mathcal{E}_k[\![e_3]\!])\, \rho\, k\, \kappa \\
=\; &\mathcal{T}_k[\![t]\!]\, \rho\; \rightarrow\; \mathcal{E}_k[\![e_2]\!]\, \rho[k \mapsto \kappa], &&\text{— definition of Cond} \\
&\qquad\qquad\quad \mathcal{E}_k[\![e_3]\!]\, \rho[k \mapsto \kappa] \\
=\; &\mathcal{T}_k[\![t]\!]\, \rho\; \rightarrow\; \textbf{let }v_2 = \mathcal{E}_k[\![e_2]\!]\, \rho[k \mapsto Id]\textbf{ in }\kappa(v_2), &&\text{— }\mathcal{E}\text{-property} \\
&\qquad\qquad\quad \textbf{let }v_3 = \mathcal{E}_k[\![e_3]\!]\, \rho[k \mapsto Id]\textbf{ in }\kappa(v_3) \\
=\; &\text{Cond}'\, (\mathcal{T}_k[\![t]\!])\, (\mathcal{E}_k[\![e_2]\!])\, (\mathcal{E}_k[\![e_3]\!])\, \rho\, k\, \kappa &&\text{— definition of Cond}'
\end{aligned}
$$

□

Under the present interpretation, and intuitively, k denotes Id at every point. The following section captures this intuition in another interpretation of the core semantics that we prove congruent to the present one.

3.5 One step further

Let $Env'_k = \langle\{\rho \in Env_k \mid \rho\, k = Id\}, \sqsubseteq_{Env_k}\rangle$. Env'_k is a cpo.
Let us define three new valuation functions.

$$\mathcal{E}'_k : \text{Exp}_k \rightarrow Env'_k \rightarrow Val$$
$$\mathcal{T}'_k : \text{Triv}_k \rightarrow Env'_k \rightarrow Val$$
$$\mathcal{L}'_k : \text{Lam}_k \rightarrow Env'_k \rightarrow Fun$$

as a $\mathcal{E}_k$, $\mathcal{T}_k$, and $\mathcal{L}_k$ interpretation with Env'_k domain and App' and Cond' as combinators.

Proposition 9 $\mathcal{E}'_k$, $\mathcal{T}'_k$, and $\mathcal{L}'_k$ are well defined and

$$\begin{cases} \mathcal{E}'_k[\![e]\!]\,\rho &= \mathcal{E}_k[\![e]\!]\,\rho & \text{whenever } e \in \mathrm{Exp}_k \\ \mathcal{T}'_k[\![t]\!]\,\rho &= \mathcal{T}_k[\![t]\!]\,\rho & \text{whenever } t \in \mathrm{Triv}_k \\ \mathcal{L}'_k[\![l]\!]\,\rho &= \mathcal{L}_k[\![l]\!]\,\rho & \text{whenever } l \in \mathrm{Lam}_k \end{cases}$$

and whenever $\rho \in Env'_k$.

Proof: By structural induction on the syntax of Exp_k, Triv_k, and Lam_k. We must verify that all environments built within the right-hand sides of semantic equations are in Env'_k.

Here is the main step. There are only two cases where a new k is introduced: in λ-abstractions and in conditional expressions. The $\mathcal{L}$-property tells us that the environment is extended with the continuation parameter denoting Id. In the case of conditional expressions, Cond' tells us that the consequent and alternative expressions are evaluated in an environment where the new continuation parameter denotes Id.

Equality immediately follows from well definedness since $\mathcal{E}'_k$ uses the same semantic equations as $\mathcal{E}_k$.

Finally let us notice that the meaning of the term

$$[\![@ \, (\lambda\, k \,.\, e) \, (\lambda\, v \,.\, v)]\!]$$

is given by the standard interpretation of e

$$\mathcal{E}_k[\![e]\!]\,\rho_{init}[k \mapsto Id]$$

where k denotes Id. This establishes the "initial environment" for an expression. $\qquad\square$

Let us use Env'_k from now on. This suggests going one step further with a new interpretation where the identity function is *not* passed at call sites but is introduced at definition sites instead. This intuition is captured in the following domain and combinators.

$Fun'' = Val^* \to Val$

$App''\colon Fun'' \to Val^+ \to Val$
$App''\, f\,(v_1, ..., v_n, \kappa) \;=\; \mathbf{let}\; v = f(v_1, ..., v_n)\; \mathbf{in}\; \kappa(v)$

$Close''\colon Var^+ \to [Env'_k \to Val] \to Env'_k \to Fun''$
$Close''\,(i_1, ..., i_n, k)\, b\, \rho \;=\; \lambda(v_1, ..., v_n)\,.\,b\,\rho[i_1 \mapsto v_1, ..., i_n \mapsto v_n, k \mapsto Id]$

$Send'' = Send'$
$Cond'' = Cond'$

Proposition 10 $\mathcal{E}'_k$, $\mathcal{T}'_k$, and $\mathcal{L}'_k$ with Fun'', App'', and $Close''$ are well-defined and equal $\mathcal{E}'_k$, $\mathcal{T}'_k$, and $\mathcal{L}'_k$ with Fun, App', and $Close'$.

Proof: By structural induction on the syntax of Exp_k, Triv_k, and Lam_k. Here is the essential step.

App$'$ (Close$'$ $(i_1, ..., i_n, k) \, b \, \rho) \, (v_1, ..., v_n, \kappa)$

$= $ **let** $v = (\lambda(v_1, ..., v_n, \kappa) . b \, \rho[i_1 \mapsto v_1, ..., i_n \mapsto v_n, k \mapsto \kappa])(v_1, ..., v_n, Id)$

　　in $\kappa \, (v)$　　　　　　　　　　　　　　　　　— definition of App$'$ and Close$'$

$= $ **let** $v = b \, \rho[i_1 \mapsto v_1, ..., i_n \mapsto v_n, k \mapsto Id]$

　　in $\kappa \, (v)$　　　　　　　　　　　　　　　　　— β-reduction

$= $ **let** $v = (\lambda(v_1, ..., v_n) . b \, \rho[i_1 \mapsto v_1, ..., i_n \mapsto v_n, k \mapsto Id])(v_1, ..., v_n)$

　　in $\kappa \, (v)$　　　　　　　　　　　　　　　　　— abstraction

$= $ App$''$ (Close$''$ $(i_1, ..., i_n, k) \, b \, \rho) \, (v_1, ..., v_n)$　　— definition of App$''$ and Close$''$

$\square$

Let us go back to the denotation of $[\![@ \, k \, t]\!]$.

$$\mathcal{E}'_k[\![@ \, k \, t]\!] \, \rho \; = \; \textbf{let } v = \mathcal{T}'_k[\![t]\!] \, \rho \textbf{ in } \text{Send}' \, v \, (\rho \, k)$$

By definition of Env'_k, the second argument of Send$'$ is always Id. Let us capture this property in a new definition of this combinator:

　　Send$''$: $Val \; \to \; Fun \; \to \; Val$

　　Send$''$ $v \, (\rho \, k) \; = \; (\rho \, k)(v)$

　　　　　　　　　　$= \; Id(v)$

　　　　　　　　　　$= \; v$

Proposition 11 $\mathcal{E}'_k$ with Send$''$ is well-defined and equals $\mathcal{E}'_k$ with Send$'$.　　　　$\square$

This leads us to the following equivalent denotation of $[\![@ \, k \, t]\!]$

$$\mathcal{E}'_k[\![@ \, k \, t]\!] \, \rho \; = \; \textbf{let } v = \mathcal{T}'_k[\![t]\!] \, \rho \textbf{ in } \text{Send}'' \, v \, (\rho \, k)$$
$$\; = \; \textbf{let } v = \mathcal{T}'_k[\![t]\!] \, \rho \textbf{ in } v$$
$$\; = \; \mathcal{T}'_k[\![t]\!] \, \rho$$

The syntactic continuation k is only looked up in the environment in the denotation of $[\![@ \, k \, t]\!]$, which, we just saw, can be simplified into an expression where k is *not* looked up in the environment. Therefore at this point, k is completely useless.

Now we are equipped enough to actually derive the direct style transformer.

3.6　From the non-standard denotational specification to a definitional interpreter, and from the interpreter to a compiler based on binding time analysis

It is possible to take the denotational specification of the last section literally as a functional program, following Reynolds's definitional interpreter insight [30]; and then to analyze its binding times, as customary in partial evaluation, to compile and to generate the corresponding compiler [20, 5].

Although straightforward, the derivation is a bit lengthy, so for conciseness, let us instead consider the denotational specification above as a rewriting system from syntax to semantics. Still with an eye on binding times, we will alter this rewrite system in a meaning-preserving way, yielding the final direct style transformer. This is done in the following section.

3.7 Viewing the denotational specification as a rewriting system

Let us take the homomorphic metaphor of denotational semantics (*i.e.*, from syntax to semantics) literally, based on the fact that both the syntax and the semantics are expressed as λ-terms. Taking the equations above as specifying a syntactic rewrite system and letting variables denote themselves (which makes the environment useless) leads to the direct style transformer. We decide that our target language is to be the λ_v-calculus, so there is no need for the strict **let** expressions anymore; we unfold them.

The term $@(\lambda k . e)(\lambda v . v)$ is rewritten as $[\![e]\!]$, where the rewrite function $[\![\ ]\!]$ is defined inductively as follows (for concision, we have unfolded the Send, App, Close, and Cond combinators of the last non-standard interpretation).

$$
\begin{aligned}
[\![@ \, k \, t]\!] &= [\![t]\!] \\
[\![@ \, t_0 \, (t_1, ..., t_n, \lambda v . e)]\!] &= @(\lambda v.[\![e]\!])(@[\![t_0]\!]([\![t_1]\!], ..., [\![t_n]\!])) \\
[\![\text{let } k = \lambda v . e_1 \text{ in } t \rightarrow e_2, e_3]\!] &= @(\lambda v.[\![e_1]\!])([\![t]\!] \rightarrow [\![e_2]\!], [\![e_3]\!]) \\
[\![\text{let } (i_1, ..., i_n) = (t_1, ..., t_n) \text{ in } e]\!] &= \text{let } (i_1, ..., i_n) = ([\![t_1]\!], ..., [\![t_n]\!]) \text{ in } [\![e]\!] \\
[\![\text{letrec } (i_1, ..., i_n) = (l_1, ..., l_n) \text{ in } e]\!] &= \text{letrec } (i_1, ..., i_n) = ([\![l_1]\!], ..., , [\![l_n]\!]) \text{ in } [\![e]\!] \\
[\![c]\!] &= c \\
[\![i]\!] &= i \\
[\![op \, (t_1, ..., t_m)]\!] &= op([\![t_1]\!], ..., [\![t_m]\!]) \\
[\![\lambda \, (i_1, ..., i_n, k) . e]\!] &= \lambda \, (i_1, ..., i_n) . [\![e]\!]
\end{aligned}
$$

Figure 3: Syntax-directed transformation into direct style

Alternatively, this rewriting can be seen as going from an environment model to a Church-style encoding of binding relations. Wand has proven that these two encodings are equivalent [37].

3.8 The actual direct style transformer

The rewriting system of Section 3.7 can be subjected to an important binding time improvement based on the linearity property of continuation parameters. Since the body of a continuation is linear in its argument (*cf.* Proposition 3), and due to the call-by-value nature of our setting, the outer redex produced by the translation of applications can actually be reduced *at translation time*. Based on this improvement, it is possible to map a term such as

$$\lambda k.k(\lambda xk.gx(\lambda v.fv(\lambda a.ka)))$$

into

$$\lambda x.f(gx)$$

instead of mapping it to

$$\lambda x.((\lambda v.(\lambda a.a)(fv))(gx))$$

only. By the same token, the β-redex produced by the translation of conditional expressions should be reduced at translation time as well.

Using the same two-level notation as in Section 2, let us reexpress the DS transformation, distinguishing between translation time and run time constructs.

$$
\begin{aligned}
[\![@\, k\, t]\!] &= [\![t]\!] \\
[\![@\, t_0\, (t_1,\, ...,\, t_n,\, \lambda\, v\,.\, e)]\!] &= \overline{@}(\overline{\lambda}v.[\![e]\!])\,(\overline{@}[\![t_0]\!]\,([\![t_1]\!],\, ...,\, [\![t_n]\!])) \\
[\![\text{let } k = \lambda\, v\,.\, e_1 \text{ in } t\ \to\ e_2,\, e_3]\!] &= \overline{@}(\overline{\lambda}v.[\![e_1]\!])\,([\![t]\!] \underset{\rightharpoonup}{}\, [\![e_2]\!]\,,\,[\![e_3]\!]) \\
[\![\text{let } (i_1,\, ...,\, i_n) = (t_1,\, ...,\, t_n) \text{ in } e]\!] &= \underline{\text{let}}\, (i_1,\, ...,\, i_n) = ([\![t_1]\!],\, ...,\, [\![t_n]\!])\, \underline{\text{in}}\, [\![e]\!] \\
[\![\text{letrec } (i_1,\, ...,\, i_n) = (l_1,\, ...,\, l_n) \text{ in } e]\!] &= \underline{\text{letrec}}\, (i_1,\, ...,\, i_n) = ([\![l_1]\!],\, ...,\, ,[\![l_n]\!])\, \underline{\text{in}}\, [\![e]\!] \\
[\![c]\!] &= c \\
[\![i]\!] &= i \\
[\![op\, (t_1,\, ...,\, t_m)]\!] &= \underline{op}\, ([\![t_1]\!],\, ...,\, [\![t_m]\!]) \\
[\![\lambda\, (i_1,\, ...,\, i_n,\, k)\,.\, e]\!] &= \underline{\lambda}(i_1,\, ...,\, i_n).[\![e]\!]
\end{aligned}
$$

Figure 4: The DS transformation

4 Are the CPS and DS Transformations Inverse?

Proposition 12 *The DS and the CPS transformations are inverses of each other, up to α-conversion.*

Proof: This proof is not immediate because of the translation-time simplifications (specified by the overlined @ and λ in Sections 1 and 4). Therefore we cannot line up producers and consumers together and simplify the composition of these two transformations. Instead, let us stage these two transformations.

Let $\mathcal{D}$ denote the DS transformation. We stage $\mathcal{D}$ as follows.

$$\mathcal{D} = \mathcal{D}_2 \circ \mathcal{D}_1$$

$\mathcal{D}_1$ is specified in Section 3.7. It maps a CPS term into a non-simplified DS term (*i.e.*, a λ-term with $\overline{@}$ and $\overline{\lambda}$). $\mathcal{D}_2$ carries the β-reductions involving $\overline{@}$ and $\overline{\lambda}$.

Correspondingly, let $\mathcal{C}$ denote the CPS transformation. We stage $\mathcal{C}$ as follows.

$$\mathcal{C} = \mathcal{C}_2 \circ \mathcal{C}_1$$

$\mathcal{C}_1$ maps a DS term into a term specified by the following BNF.

$$
\begin{aligned}
e &::=\ s\ |\ t \\
s &::=\ \overline{@}(\overline{\lambda}v.e)\,(@\, t_0\, (t_1,\, ...,\, t_n)) \\
&\quad |\ \overline{@}(\overline{\lambda}v.e_1)\,(t\ \to\ e_2,\, e_3) \\
&\quad |\ \text{let}\, (i_1,\, ...,\, i_n) = (t_1,\, ...,\, t_n)\, \text{in}\, e \\
&\quad |\ \text{letrec}\, (i_1,\, ...,\, i_n) = (t_1,\, ...,\, t_n)\, \text{in}\, e \\
t &::=\ c \\
&\quad |\ i \\
&\quad |\ op\, (t_1,\, ...,\, t_m) \\
&\quad |\ \lambda\, (i_1,\, ...,\, i_n)\,.\, e
\end{aligned}
$$

Intuitively, $\mathcal{C}_1$ transforms a λ-term into a head form by introducing a bunch of β-redexes and then sequentializing them [6]. $\mathcal{C}_1$ and $\mathcal{D}_2$ are inverses of each other.

Using a unique identifier k, $\mathcal{C}_2$ introduces continuations. It is the inverse of $\mathcal{D}_1$. $\qquad\square$

5   Semantics-Based Program Manipulation

CPS matters when one manipulates programs based on their semantics because it makes flow analyses yield more precise results [27]. As a program specialization technique, partial evaluation benefits from pre-transforming source programs into CPS [4]. Since residual programs are expressed in CPS, they are good candidates for the DS transformation, if partial evaluation is to be seen as a source-to-source transformation.

6   Comparison with Related Work

Properly speaking, there are no related works since (again to the author's best knowledge) transforming continuation-passing terms into direct style has not been explored so far. There appears to be two main classes of applications for the CPS transformation: for program analysis and transformation, and for functional reasoning about control operators. Our DS transformation covers the first class but not the second. It can be extended by relaxing the passing constraint over CPS terms, as investigated in "Back to Direct Style II" [9]. Further, relaxing the linearity property on continuation parameters is handled by inserting a let or a sequence expression. Finally, relaxing the CPS texture amounts to introducing control operators such as shift and reset [7].

7   Conclusions and Issues

Work in semantics-based program manipulation revealed the need for a transformation into direct style. We have shown that such transformations exist and we have derived one for call-by-value soundly. In the area of partial evaluation, we have applied the CPS transformation to source programs and the DS transformation to specialized programs, obtaining substantial improvements.

A number of issues remain to be explored. Here are a few of them.

- Currently the DS transformer assumes continuations to occur as the last parameter. However nothing in a general-purpose partial evaluator ensures that residual continuations occur last. How could the DS transformer cope with continuations occurring anywhere?

- Can the DS transformer be extended to produce DS terms including control operators such as call/cc? (NB: in collaboration with Lawall, we have extended the DS transformer to handle first-class continuations [9].)

- Does there exist a DS transformer towards λ_n-terms? (NB: we have derived one at this time.)

- The DS and the CPS transformations are too strong in that they are global. Often we know that parts of our programs are "trivial" in Reynolds's sense [30] and therefore they do not need to be transformed. Can we minimize the extent of the DS and CPS transformations? We understand that Wadler's use of monads corresponds to this, together with instrumenting the continuation to receive not only a value but also a single-threaded resource, e.g., for monitoring [35, 22].

- CPS programs are single-threaded in their continuation and therefore their control is inherently sequential. Could the DS transformer be used as a tool for parallelization? We are thinking of a programming style where DS sub-terms would be evaluated in parallel and CPS terms would be evaluated sequentially.

- The CPS transformation corresponds to other transformations in constructive mathematics [17, 26]. Can the DS transformation have a similar equivalent?

- Finally the DS transformer can contribute to derive program analyzers for CPS code that are at least as good as program analyzers for DS code. Here is the idea.

  Let $\mathcal{C}$ and $\mathcal{D}$ be inverse CPS and DS transformers, respectively; and let $\mathcal{A}_d$ and $\mathcal{A}_c$ be program analyzers for DS and for CPS programs, respectively, such that

  $$\mathcal{A}_c \circ \mathcal{C} \sqsupseteq \mathcal{A}_d$$

  In other terms, analyzing a DS program should yield a result which is at least as good as analyzing the CPS counterpart of this program (*cf.* Section 5). We can isolate $\mathcal{A}_c$ by composing $\mathcal{C}$ on the right

  $$\mathcal{A}_c \circ \mathcal{C} \circ \mathcal{D} \sqsupseteq \mathcal{A}_d \circ \mathcal{C}$$

  and by simplifying (composition is associative, and $\mathcal{C}$ and $\mathcal{D}$ are inverses of each other)

  $$\mathcal{A}_c \sqsupseteq \mathcal{A}_d \circ \mathcal{C}$$

  There are two ways to read this equation.

  1. Trivial way: "To analyze a CPS program, first map it back to DS and then analyze it by conventional means. The result is guaranteed not to get worse."
  2. Insightful way: "To derive an analyzer of CPS terms, symbolically compose (and simplify!) an analyzer of DS terms and the DS transformer."

  The latter way offers a practical insight to build program analyzers for CPS programs that are at least as good as existing program analyzers for DS programs. Such a class of new program analyzers appears to be needed in modern compilers for strict functional languages (Scheme, ML). Tarditi is working on this class of new program analyzers at Carnegie-Mellon University.

Acknowledgements

This work benefited from Karoline Malmkjær's patient and sharp-witted comments and from David Schmidt's interest and rigor. Thanks are also due to Andrzej Filinski, Charles Consel, Jim des Rivières, Peter Sestoft, and Julia Lawall.

A   Denotational Semantics of the λ_v-Calculus

This appendix addresses the λ_v-calculus applied to the usual first-order constants (boolean, numbers, *etc.*) and extended with conditional expressions, recursive definitions, and primitive operations. Primitive operators either map first-order arguments to first-order results or are data structure constructors and destructors such as in list operations.

Abstract Syntax

$e \in \mathrm{Exp}$	— domain of expressions
$l \in \mathrm{Lam}$	— domain of λ-abstractions
$op \in \mathrm{Opr}$	— domain of primitive operators
$c \in \mathrm{Cst}$	— domain of first-order constant values

$i \in \text{Ide}$ — domain of identifiers

$$e ::= c \mid i \mid l \mid @\, e_0\,(e_1,\, ...,\, e_n) \mid op\,(e_1,\, ...,\, e_m) \mid$$
$$e_1 \rightarrow e_2,\, e_3 \mid \text{let } (i_1,\, ...,\, i_n) = (e_1,\, ...,\, e_n) \text{ in } e_0 \mid \text{letrec } (i_1,\, ...,\, i_n) = (l_1,\, ...,\, l_n) \text{ in } e_0$$
$$l ::= \lambda\,(i_1,\, ...,\, i_n)\,.\,e$$

NB: The symbol @ denotes an application.

Semantic Domains

$$
\begin{array}{ll}
Val = (Cst + Fun)_\perp & \mathcal{E} : \text{Exp} \rightarrow \text{Env} \rightarrow \text{Val} \\
Env = Var \rightarrow Val & \mathcal{L} : \text{Lam} \rightarrow \text{Env} \rightarrow \text{Fun} \\
Fun = Val^* \rightarrow Val & \mathcal{C} : \text{Cst} \rightarrow \text{Val} \\
 & \mathcal{I} : \text{Ide} \rightarrow \text{Var} \\
 & \mathcal{O} : \text{Opr} \rightarrow \text{Fun}
\end{array}
$$

For simplicity, we identify the syntactic domain of identifiers Ide and the semantic domain of variables Var. Literally speaking, a syntactic identifier i is mapped into a semantic variable $\mathcal{I}[\![i]\!]$, but we will refer to this variable as i. Identifying identifiers and variables allows to refer to them uniformly. This makes it easier to read the following equations.

Valuation functions

We assume the semantic **let** construct to be strict. This ensures the call-by-value nature of the defined language. We also leave out the injection and projection of summands, for simplicity.

$$
\begin{aligned}
\mathcal{E}[\![c]\!]\,\rho &= \mathcal{C}[\![c]\!] \\
\mathcal{E}[\![i]\!]\,\rho &= \rho\,i \\
\mathcal{E}[\![l]\!]\,\rho &= \mathcal{L}[\![l]\!]\,\rho \\
\mathcal{E}[\![@\, e_0\,(e_1,\, ...,\, e_n)]\!]\,\rho &= \text{let } v_0 = \mathcal{E}[\![e_0]\!]\,\rho,\ v_1 = \mathcal{E}[\![e_1]\!]\,\rho,\ ...,\ v_n = \mathcal{E}[\![e_n]\!]\,\rho \\
 &\quad \text{in } v_0(v_1,\, ...,\, v_n) \\
\mathcal{E}[\![op\,(e_1,\, ...,\, e_m)]\!]\,\rho &= \text{let } v_1 = \mathcal{E}[\![e_1]\!]\,\rho,\ ...,\ v_m = \mathcal{E}[\![e_m]\!]\,\rho \\
 &\quad \text{in } \mathcal{O}[\![op]\!]\,(v_1,\, ...,\, v_m) \\
\mathcal{E}[\![e_1 \rightarrow e_2,\, e_3]\!]\,\rho &= \text{let } b = \mathcal{E}[\![e_0]\!]\,\rho \text{ in } b \rightarrow \mathcal{E}[\![e_1]\!]\,\rho,\ \mathcal{E}[\![e_2]\!]\,\rho \\
\mathcal{E}[\![\text{let } (i_1,\, ...,\, i_n) = (e_1,\, ...,\, e_n) \text{ in } e_0]\!]\,\rho &= \text{let } v_1 = \mathcal{E}[\![e_1]\!]\,\rho,\ ...,\ v_n = \mathcal{E}[\![e_n]\!]\,\rho \\
 &\quad \text{in } \mathcal{E}[\![e_0]\!]\,\rho[i_1 \mapsto v_1,\, ...,\, i_n \mapsto v_n] \\
\mathcal{E}[\![\text{letrec } (i_1,\, ...,\, i_n) = (l_1,\, ...,\, l_n) \text{ in } e_0]\!]\,\rho &= \text{letrec } (f_1,\, ...,\, f_n) = (\mathcal{L}[\![l_1]\!]\,\rho[i_1 \mapsto f_1,\, ...,\, i_n \mapsto f_n], \\
 &\quad\quad\quad\quad ..., \\
 &\quad\quad\quad\quad \mathcal{L}[\![l_n]\!]\,\rho[i_1 \mapsto f_1,\, ...,\, i_n \mapsto f_n]) \\
 &\quad \text{in } \mathcal{E}[\![e_0]\!]\,\rho[i_1 \mapsto v_1,\, ...,\, i_n \mapsto v_n] \\
\mathcal{L}[\![\lambda\,(i_1,\, ...,\, i_n)\,.\,e]\!]\,\rho &= \lambda(v_1,\, ...,\, v_n).\mathcal{E}[\![e]\!]\,\rho[i_1 \mapsto v_1,\, ...,\, i_n \mapsto v_n]
\end{aligned}
$$

The meaning of a term $[\![e]\!]$ is given by $\mathcal{E}[\![e]\!]\,\rho_{init}$ where ρ_{init} denotes the initial environment.

References

[1] Andrew W. Appel. *Compiling with Continuations*. Cambridge University Press, 1992.

[2] Anders Bondorf. Automatic autoprojection of higher-order recursive equations. *Science of Computer Programming*, 1991. To appear.

[3] William Clinger and Jonathan Rees, eds. Revised[4] report on the algorithmic language Scheme. *LISP Pointers*, IV(3):1–55, July-September 1991.

[4] Charles Consel and Olivier Danvy. For a better support of static data flow. In *Proceedings of the 1991 Conference on Functional Programming and Computer Architecture*, number 523 in Lecture Notes in Computer Science, pages 496–519, Cambridge, Massachusetts, August 1991. Springer-Verlag.

[5] Charles Consel and Olivier Danvy. Static and dynamic semantics processing. In *Proceedings of the Eighteenth Annual ACM Symposium on Principles of Programming Languages*, pages 14–24, Orlando, Florida, January 1991. ACM Press.

[6] Olivier Danvy. Three steps for the CPS transformation. Technical Report CIS-92-2, Kansas State University, Manhattan, Kansas, 1992.

[7] Olivier Danvy and Andrzej Filinski. Abstracting control. In LFP'90 [23], pages 151–160.

[8] Olivier Danvy and Andrzej Filinski. Representing control, a study of the CPS transformation. Technical Report CIS-91-2, Kansas State University, Manhattan, Kansas, 1991.

[9] Olivier Danvy and Julia L. Lawall. Back to direct style II: First-class continuations. Technical Report CIS-92-1, Kansas State University, Manhattan, Kansas, 1992.

[10] Matthias Felleisen, Daniel P. Friedman, Eugene Kohlbecker, and Bruce Duba. A syntactic theory of sequential control. *Theoretical Computer Science*, 52(3):205–237, 1987.

[11] Matthias Felleisen and Robert Hieb. The revised report on the syntactic theories of sequential control and state. Technical Report Rice COMP TR89-100, Department of Computer Science, Rice University, Houston, Texas, June 1989. To appear in Theoretical Computer Science.

[12] Andrzej Filinski. Declarative continuations: An investigation of duality in programming language semantics. In D.H. Pitt et al., editors, *Category Theory and Computer Science*, number 389 in Lecture Notes in Computer Science, pages 224–249, Manchester, UK, September 1989.

[13] Michael J. Fischer. Lambda calculus schemata. In *Proceedings of the ACM Conference on Proving Assertions about Programs*, pages 104–109. SIGPLAN Notices, Vol. 7, No 1 and SIGACT News, No 14, January 1972.

[14] Pascal Fradet and Daniel Le Métayer. Compilation of functional languages by program transformation. *ACM Transactions on Programming Languages and Systems*, 13:21–51, 1991.

[15] Daniel P. Friedman. Applications of continuations. Report 237, Computer Science Department, Indiana University, Bloomington, Indiana, January 1988. Tutorial of the Fifteenth Annual ACM Symposium on Principles of Programming Languages, San Diego, California.

[16] Daniel P. Friedman, Mitchell Wand, and Christopher T. Haynes. *Essentials of Programming Languages*. MIT Press and McGraw-Hill, 1991.

[17] Timothy G. Griffin. A formulae-as-types notion of control. In *Proceedings of the Seventeenth Annual ACM Symposium on Principles of Programming Languages*, pages 47–58, San Francisco, California, January 1990. ACM Press.

[18] Neil D. Jones and Alan Mycroft. Data flow analysis of applicative programs using minimal function graphs. In *Proceedings of the Thirteenth Annual ACM Symposium on Principles of Programming Languages*, pages 296–306, January 1986.

[19] Neil D. Jones and Flemming Nielson. Abstract interpretation: a semantics-based tool for program analysis (chapter in preparation). In *The Handbook of Logic in Computer Science*. North-Holland, 1991.

[20] Neil D. Jones, Peter Sestoft, and Harald Søndergaard. MIX: A self-applicable partial evaluator for experiments in compiler generation. *LISP and Symbolic Computation*, 2(1):9–50, 1989.

[21] Richard Kelsey and Paul Hudak. Realistic compilation by program transformation. In *Proceedings of the Sixteenth Annual ACM Symposium on Principles of Programming Languages*, pages 281–292, Austin, Texas, January 1989.

[22] Amir Kishon, Paul Hudak, and Charles Consel. Monitoring semantics: A formal framework for specifying, implementing, and reasoning about execution monitors. In *Proceedings of the ACM SIGPLAN'91 Conference on Programming Languages Design and Implementation*, pages 338–352, Toronto, Ontario, June 1991.

[23] *Proceedings of the 1990 ACM Conference on Lisp and Functional Programming*, Nice, France, June 1990.

[24] Antoni W. Mazurkiewicz. Proving algorithms by tail functions. *Information and Control*, 18:220–226, 1971.

[25] Eugenio Moggi. Computational lambda-calculus and monads. In *Proceedings of the Fourth Annual Symposium on Logic in Computer Science*, pages 14–23, Pacific Grove, California, June 1989. IEEE.

[26] Chetan R. Murthy. An evaluation semantics for classical proofs. In *Proceedings of the Sixth Symposium on Logic in Computer Science*, Amsterdam, The Netherlands, July 1991. IEEE.

[27] Flemming Nielson. A denotational framework for data flow analysis. *Acta Informatica*, 18:265–287, 1982.

[28] Flemming Nielson and Hanne Riis Nielson. Two-level semantics and code generation. *Theoretical Computer Science*, 56(1):59–133, January 1988.

[29] Gordon D. Plotkin. Call-by-name, call-by-value and the λ-calculus. *Theoretical Computer Science*, 1:125–159, 1975.

[30] John C. Reynolds. Definitional interpreters for higher-order programming languages. In *Proceedings of 25th ACM National Conference*, pages 717–740, Boston, 1972.

[31] David A. Schmidt. *Denotational Semantics: A Methodology for Language Development*. Allyn and Bacon, Inc., 1986.

[32] Guy L. Steele Jr. Rabbit: A compiler for Scheme. Technical Report AI-TR-474, Artificial Intelligence Laboratory, Massachusetts Institute of Technology, Cambridge, Massachusetts, May 1978.

[33] Christopher Strachey and Christopher P. Wadsworth. Continuations: A mathematical semantics for handling full jumps. Technical Monograph PRG-11, Oxford University Computing Laboratory, Programming Research Group, Oxford, England, 1974.

[34] Adriaan van Wijngaarden. Recursive definition of syntax and semantics. In T. B. Steel, Jr., editor, *Formal Language Description Languages for Computer Programming*, pages 13–24. North-Holland, 1966.

[35] Philip Wadler. Comprehending monads. In LFP'90 [23], pages 61–78.

[36] Mitchell Wand. Semantics-directed machine architecture. In *Proceedings of the Ninth Annual ACM Symposium on Principles of Programming Languages*, pages 234–241, January 1982.

[37] Mitchell Wand. A short proof of the lexical addressing algorithm. *Information Processing Letters*, 35:1–5, 1990.

```
    (lambda (f l)      ; [A -> B] * List(A) -> List(B)
      (letrec ([loop (lambda (l)
                      (if (null? l)
                         '()
                         (cons (f (car l)) (loop (cdr l)))))])
        (loop l)))

(lambda (k)
  (k (lambda (f l k)    ; [A * [B -> Ans] -> Ans] * List(B) * [List(B) -> Ans] -> Ans
      (letrec ([loop (lambda (l k)
                      (if (null? l)
                         (k '())
                         (f (car l) (lambda (v)
                                      (loop (cdr l) (lambda (vs)
                                                      (k (cons v vs))))))))])
        (loop l k)))))
```

Figure 5: Interconvertible DS and CPS definitions of the map procedure in Scheme
As can be noticed, the CPS transformation commits the order of evaluation of sub-expressions in an application, which is not in the true spirit of Scheme [3].

```
(lambda (x) x)                      (lambda (k) (k (lambda (x k) (k x))))
```

Figure 6: Interconvertible DS and CPS definitions of the identity procedure in Scheme

Extraction of Strong Typing Laws
from Action Semantics Definitions

Kyung-Goo Doh* and David A. Schmidt*

Department of Computing and Information Sciences

Kansas State University, Manhattan, Kansas 66506, U.S.A.

{doh,schmidt}@cis.ksu.edu

Abstract: We describe a method that automatically extracts a type checking semantics, encoded as a set of type inference rules, from an action semantics definition of a programming language. The type inference rules are guaranteed to enforce strong typing, since they are based on an underlying metasemantics for action semantics, which uses typing functions and natural transformations to give meaning. Next, we use the type checking semantics to extract a dynamic semantics definition from the original action semantics definition. We present an example.

1   Introduction

The key component of a compiler-based programming language is its typing system. A compiler-based language should have a static semantics (hereafter, called a *typing semantics*) that matches the structure of the data types and operations that underlie the language. A typing semantics is accompanied by a dynamic semantics, which gives meaning to the well typed programs in the language.

A language is *statically typed* if the typing annotations of the phrases in a program can be calculated without running the program. The language is *strongly typed* if every program that is completely annotated with typings (such a program is *well typed*) will not produce an operator-operand incompatibility error (a *typing error*) when it is run. A statically typed language should be implemented by a compiler that annotates programs with typings, and the typing annotations make the language strongly typed. (Algol60 is an example of a statically typed language that is not strongly typed, due to imprecise typing of procedure parameters [27].)

These goals place upon the language designer the burden of designing a typing semantics that enforces strong typing. Since the design of a strongly typed language is nontrivial, a language designer would do best to follow a methodology based on a formal semantics; the methodology should support a method for deriving the typing semantics and showing that it is a strong typing. But this is surprisingly difficult to do with existing semantics methods. Consider a definition in denotational semantics [33]; here is a sample clause of a definition:

---

*Partially supported by NSF Grants CCR-8822378 and CCR-9102625.

$$\mathcal{E}[\![\text{is\_zero E}]\!] = \lambda e.\lambda s. \ cases \ (\mathcal{E}[\![\text{E}]\!]e \ s) \ of$$
$$isInteger(i) \rightarrow (i =_{int} 0)$$
$$[\![\ isReal(r) \rightarrow (r =_{real} 0.0)$$
$$[\![\ isBoolean(b) \rightarrow error$$
$$\cdots end$$

The clause suggests the typing rule:

$$\frac{typings\_in(e) \vdash \text{E} : \tau}{typings\_in(e) \vdash \text{is\_zero E} : Boolean} \qquad \tau \in \{Integer, Real\}$$

but the formal derivation of the rule from the clause is intricate. Noteworthy attempts are by Barbuti and Martelli [1] and Montenyohl and Wand [19], where a separate typing semantics is handwritten and proved to enforce strong typing with respect to the original semantics. Then, hand transformations are performed on the original semantics to derive a dynamic semantics.

An approach that is often relevant is the application of a partial evaluator to the semantics definition [11, 14, 15, 35]. When supplied with a semantics definition, a partial evaluator produces a compiler. The generated compiler takes a source program as input, translates the program into an expression in the semantic metalanguage, and evaluates the static parts of the expression. The result is a compiled program that contains only dynamic operations. If a typing semantics is encoded within a semantics definition, and it is static, then the compiler performs type checking. This occurs in Montenyohl and Wand's example [19], as demonstrated by Consel and Danvy [6]. Of course, there is no guarantee that the semantics definition contains a static typing semantics. Also, a partial evaluator does not extract the typing semantics and present it separately, which is our goal here.

Finally, a language designer might apply operational or axiomatic semantics techniques and hand code the typing and dynamic semantics. Then, hand proofs must be done for static and strong typing properties [3, 10, 34]. This task is daunting.

None of the above approaches are completely satisfactory, so we report another approach, based on Mosses and Watt's *action semantics* [20, 21, 25, 24, 26, 36], which surmounts the problems noted above. From an action semantics definition of a programming language, we can mechanically extract a typing semantics that is a static and a strong typing. The proofs of static and strong typing are immediate, from general results about the model for action semantics notation [12]. Further, we show how to calculate the dynamic semantics of a language from its typing semantics and the original action semantics definition. The result is a strong typing semantics and a dynamic semantics, which can be used along the lines suggested by Lee and Pleban [16, 17] and Nielson and Nielson [28, 29] to define a compiler for the language. Since the typing semantics can be represented in inference rule format, it also serves as documentation of the typing structure for the language designer and users.

The remainder of the paper goes as follows. We first introduce action semantics notation; next, we describe the approach for extracting the typing semantics and dynamic semantics; and finally, we apply the algorithms to an example language definition.

Functional facet: Its types are *Proper-functional-type* $\cup$ { *ns* }, where:

$t \in$ *Proper-functional-type*

$t ::= int \mid real \mid bool \mid t_1 \times t_2 \mid t_1 \rightarrow t_2$

The ordering is the smallest reflexive, transitive ordering such that:

$int \leq real$

$t \leq ns$ for all t

$t_1 \times t_2 \leq t'_1 \times t'_2$ iff $t_1 \leq t'_1$ and $t_2 \leq t'_2$

$t_1 \rightarrow t_2 \leq t'_1 \rightarrow t'_2$ iff $t'_1 \leq t_1$ and $t_2 \leq t'_2$

Declarative facet: Its types are *Proper-declarative-type* $\cup$ { *ns* }, where:

$d \in$ *Proper-declarative-type*

$d ::= \{i : t_i\}_{i \in I}$ where I is a finite set of identifiers.

The ordering is the smallest reflexive, transitive ordering such that:

$d \leq ns$ for all d

$\{i : t_i\}_{i \in I} \leq \{i : t'_i\}_{i \in I}$ iff for all $i \in I$, $t_i \leq t'_i$

Figure 1: Facets

2 Action Semantics

Action semantics is a high level notation for writing modular programming language definitions [21, 25, 24, 26, 36]. The notation consists of combinator-like entities, called *actions*, that operate upon *facets*. A facet is a collection of types, and a type is a collection of values. The *functional facet* contains those data types that can be used as temporary values ("transient information" [21]) in a computation. Types like *int*, *bool*, *real*, *int* $\times$ *bool*, and so on, belong to the functional facet. Actions that take arguments and produce answers in the functional facet include arithmetic and logical operations. A second facet is the *declarative facet*, which contains types of identifier, value binding ("scoped information"). The types in the declarative facet are record types [5, 13, 31]; an example type is {A:*int*, B:*bool*}, which describes those binding sets ("records") that map A to an integer value and B to a boolean value. Actions that take arguments and produce answers in the declarative facet include operations for making and finding bindings (in a symbol table). A third facet is the *imperative facet*, which contains types of storage structures. Actions include operations for accessing and updating primary storage. Yet another is the *communicative facet*, which describes structures for communication and has actions for file and message input/output. Due to lack of space, we will not explore the last two facets.

The set of types for each facet also includes an error type, which we call *ns* (for "nonsense"). An output of *ns* type occurs when an action receives an argument whose type is incompatible with the action, that is, when a typing error arises. For example, an *ns*-typed output occurs when a boolean value is given to an addition action.

The types in a facet can be ordered to express subtyping relationships. For example, we might have *int* $\leq$ *real* in the functional facet, that is, *int* is a subtype of *real* [13, 31], or {A:*int*} $\leq$ {A:*real*} in the declarative facet. Figure 1 shows the internal structure

Action	Kind	Typing function	Meaning
copy	F→F	$\lambda t:F.t$	$\lambda t:F.\lambda v:t.v$
give(n:t_0)	1→F	$\lambda t:1.t_0$	$\lambda t:1.\lambda v:t.n$
eqzero	F→F	$\lambda t:F.$ *if* $t \leq real$ *then bool*	$\lambda t:F.$ *cases* t *of* $\quad int : \lambda v:int.(v =_{int} 0)$ $\quad real : \lambda v:real.(v =_{real} 0.0)$ $\quad else : \lambda v.error$ $\quad end$
add	F→F	$\lambda t:F.$ *if* $fst(t) \leq real$ *and* $snd(t) \leq real$ *then* $fst(t) \sqcup snd(t)$	$\lambda t:F.$ *cases* t *of* $\quad int\times int : \lambda(v_1,v_2):int\times int. v_1 +_{int} v_2$ $\quad int\times real : \lambda(v_1,v_2):int\times real. coerce\text{-}real(v_1)+_{real}v_2$ $\quad real\times int : \lambda(v_1,v_2):real\times int. v_1 +_{real} coerce\text{-}real(v_2)$ $\quad real\times real : \lambda(v_1,v_2):real\times real. v_1 +_{real} v_2$ $\quad else : \lambda(v_1,v_2). error$ $\quad end$
bind I	F→D	$\lambda t:F.\{I:t\}$	$\lambda t:F.\lambda v:t.\{I=v\}$
find I	D→F	$\lambda d:D.$ *if* $\{I:t\}\in d$ *then* t	$\lambda d:D.\lambda r:d.r.I$

Note: *"if C then T"* abbreviates *"if C then T else ns"*
$\quad fst(t_1 \times t_2) \doteq t_1,\ snd(t_1 \times t_2) = t_2$
$\quad fst(int) = fst(real) = fst(bool) = ns = snd(bool) = snd(real) = snd(int)$
$\quad$*"r.I"* is record indexing

Figure 2: Actions

of the two facets we use in this paper. (Note that the type sets of the two facets form sup-semilattices. Also, the typing ordering for the declarative facet is simpler than the version that is normally used; see [13].)

An action is a mapping whose domain and codomain are facets. For example, the action copy : $F \rightarrow F$ is the identity mapping on the functional facet. ("F" stands for the functional facet, and "D" stands for the declarative facet.) Since the functional facet contains many types, copy is in fact a family of identity functions: an identity function for integer inputs, an identity for boolean inputs, an identity for real inputs, and so on. Thus, copy $= \{\lambda v:t.v\}_{t\in F}$, which we also write as $\lambda t:F.\lambda v:t.v$. We can summarize copy's behavior with the *typing function* $T_{copy} = \lambda t:F.t$, which states that, whenever copy receives an input of type t, its output is of type t.

Each action, a, has a typing function, T_a, that characterizes its behavior. In analogy with the typing system in Automath [8], a typing function $\lambda t:F.f(t)$ encodes the second order type $\forall t:F.f(t)$. Further, the typings are "shallow," in the sense of ML types [18]. This makes actions into polymorphic functions, where the polymorphism can be parametric, inclusive, or ad-hoc. A mathematical view is that an action, a, is a natural transformation in $\mathcal{I} \overset{\cdot}{\rightarrow} \mathcal{I} \circ T_a$, where $\mathcal{I}$ is the interpretation functor that maps the type names in the facets to the value sets they represent and where T_a is treated as an endofunctor on the facet. Details are found in [12].[1]

---

[1]A related model, which is based on *unified algebra* rather than category theory, is described in

Action	Kind	Typing function	Meaning
a_1 then a_2	$K_1 \rightarrow K_3$	$\lambda k : K_1.\ \mathbf{T}_{a_2}(\mathbf{T}_{a_1}(k))$	$\lambda k : K_1.\ \lambda v : k.a_2(\mathbf{T}_{a_1}(k))(a_1(k)(v))$
	where $a_1 : K_1 \rightarrow K_2$ and $a_2 : K_2 \rightarrow K_3$		
a_1 and a_2	$K_1 \rightarrow K_2$	$\lambda k : K_1.\mathbf{T}\mathrm{merge}_{K_2}(\mathbf{T}_{a_1}(k), \mathbf{T}_{a_2}(k))$	$\lambda k : K_1.\lambda v : k.\mathrm{merge}_{K_2}(\mathbf{T}_{a_1}(k), \mathbf{T}_{a_2}(k))$ $(a_1(k)(v), a_2(k)(v))$
	where $a_1 : K_1 \rightarrow K_2$ and $a_2 : K_1 \rightarrow K_2$		
a_1 andthen a_2	$D \rightarrow F$	$\lambda d : D.\mathbf{T}_{a_2}(\mathbf{T}_{a_1}(d), d)$	$\lambda d : D.\lambda r : d.a_2(\mathbf{T}_{a_1}(d), d)(a_1(d)(r), r)$
	where $a_1 : D \rightarrow F$ and $a_2 : F \times D \rightarrow F$		
a_1 else a_2	$F \times D \rightarrow F$	$\lambda(t, d) : F \times D.$ $\quad if\ t \leq bool$ $\quad then\ \mathbf{T}_{a_1}(d) \sqcup \mathbf{T}_{a_2}(d)$	$\lambda(t, d) : F \times D.$ $\quad if\ t \leq bool$ $\quad then\ \lambda(v, r) : t \times d.\ if\ v\ then\ a_1(d)(r)$ $\qquad\qquad\qquad\qquad else\ a_2(d)(r))$ $\quad else\ \lambda(v, r) : t \times d.error$
	where $a_1 : D \rightarrow F$ and $a_2 : D \rightarrow F$		
furthermore a	$D \rightarrow D$	$\lambda d : D.\mathbf{T}_a(d)@d$	$\lambda d : D.\lambda r : d.a(d)(r)\ cat\ r$
	where $a : D \rightarrow D$		
	$F \times D \rightarrow D$	$\lambda(t, d) : F \times D.\mathbf{T}_a(t)@d$	$\lambda(t, d) : F \times D.\lambda(v, r) : t \times d.a(t)(v)\ cat\ r$
	where $a : F \rightarrow D$		

where $\mathbf{T}\mathrm{merge}_F(t_1, t_2) = t_1 \times t_2$
$\quad \mathrm{merge}_F(t_1, t_2)(v_1, v_2) = (v_1, v_2)$
$\quad \mathbf{T}\mathrm{merge}_D(d_1, d_2) = \ if\ have\text{-}disjoint\text{-}fields(d_1, d_2)\ then\ d_1@d_2$
$\quad \mathrm{merge}_D(d_1, d_2) = \ if\ have\text{-}disjoint\text{-}fields(d_1, d_2)\ then\ \lambda(r_1, r_2).r_1\ cat\ r_2\ else\ \lambda(r_1, r_2).error$
$\quad$"@" represents record type concatenation
$\qquad$(e.g., $\{A : int, B : bool\}@\{B : int, C : real\} = \{A : int, B : bool, C : real\}$)
$\quad$"cat" represents record concatenation
$\qquad$(e.g., $\{A = 0, B = false\}\ cat\ \{B = 1, C = 2.2\} = \{A = 0, B = false, C = 2.2\}$)

Figure 3: Action Combinators

The relationship between the typing function and the action it describes is exact: if $\mathbf{T}_a(t) = t'$, then for all arguments v of type t, $a(t)(v)$ has type t'. In particular, if $\mathbf{T}_a(t) = ns$, then $a(t)(v)$ is an error.[2] This exact relationship is no accident. It is demanded by the mathematical model we use, for the typing functions and facets constitute the operator names and sort names, respectively, of a signature of a category-sorted algebra [30, 32]. The actions and value sets form the operations and carriers, respectively, of the category-sorted algebra. This relationship lets us extract the strong typing laws from a language definition. The formalities of category sorted algebra and action semantics are described in [12].

Actions exist for all the fundamental operations of programming languages: value passing, arithmetic, binding creation and lookup, storage allocation and updating, and so on [20, 24, 26, 36]. Our version of action notation is combinator-based, for technical and historical reasons, but it is interconvertible with the notation in Mosses' book [25].

Figure 2 presents the actions we use in this paper. We have already seen action copy. give($n : t_0$) emits n as its output. Since give requires no input, we use a degenerate facet,

---

[21, 22, 23].
[2]Also, typing functions are "ns-strict": $\mathbf{T}_a(ns) = ns$, for all actions a.

Abstract Syntax
  D $\in$ Declaration
  E $\in$ Expression
  N $\in$ Int-numeral
  R $\in$ Real-numeral

  D ::= val I = E | D_1, D_2
  E ::= N | R | $E_1 + E_2$ | if E_1 then E_2 else E_3 | is-zero E | I | let D in E end

Action Semantics
  declare : Declaration $\rightarrow$ Action$_{D \rightarrow D}$
    declare[[val I = E]] = evaluate[[E]] then bind I
    declare[[D_1, D_2]] = declare[[D_1]] and declare[[D_2]]
  evaluate : Expression $\rightarrow$ Action$_{D \rightarrow F}$
    evaluate[[N]] = give([[N]] : int)
    evaluate[[R]] = give([[R]] : real)
    evaluate[[$E_1 + E_2$]] = (evaluate[[E_1]] and evaluate[[E_2]]) then add
    evaluate[[if E_1 then E_2 else E_3]] = evaluate[[E_1]] andthen (evaluate[[E_2]] else evaluate[[E_3]])
    evaluate[[is_zero E]] = evaluate[[E]] then eqzero
    evaluate[[I]] = find I
    evaluate[[let D in E end]] = (furthermore declare[[D]]) then evaluate[[E]]

Figure 4: An Example Expression Language

called 1, for its domain. **eqzero** checks if a number is zero; **add** adds a pair of numbers; **bind** I maps a value into a binding set with a single binding for I to the value; and **find** I maps a binding set to the value bound to I in the set.[3]

Actions are composed into compound actions with combinators. For example, actions $a_1 : K_1 \rightarrow K_2$ and $a_2 : K_2 \rightarrow K_3$ can be sequentially composed into a_1 **then** $a_2 : K_1 \rightarrow K_3$ by the **then** combinator. (The codomain facet of a_1 must match the domain facet of a_2.) Combinators possess typing functionals that map the typing functions of the component actions into a typing function for the compound action. Figure 3 gives the definitions and typing functions for the combinators we use.

In addition to sequential composition, we have the parallel composition a_1 **and** a_2, which gives its input to both a_1 and a_2 and allows them to evaluate in parallel; the results are "merged." The compound action a_1 **andthen** a_2 is a combination of **then** and **and**. The action a_1 **else** a_2 models choice: the input, a Boolean, selects a_1 or a_2 for evaluation. Finally, **furthermore a** concatenates the binding set produced by a to the input binding set.

Figure 4 gives a language definition in action semantics.

---

[3]A reader familiar with Montenyohl and Wand's work [19] will notice that the structure of the meanings of the actions in Figure 2 match the structure of denotations in [19] following factorization and static replacement. This is not surprising, since the structure is a natural one for a language with static and dynamic stages. What is significant is that the meanings in Figure 2 *must* have proper structure because they are natural transformations – the category theory model makes the representations correct.

3   Derivation of the Typing Semantics

We derive the typing semantics for a language definition by deriving a typing rule for each semantic equation in the definition. This is done in two steps: (i) calculate the typing function for the semantic equation; (ii) translate the equation into an inference rule. For example, the semantic equation:

$$\textsf{evaluate } [\![\textsf{is\_zero } E]\!] = \textsf{evaluate } [\![E]\!] \textsf{ then eqzero}$$

has as its typing function:

$$\textsf{typing } [\![\textsf{is\_zero } E]\!] = \lambda d{:}\textsf{D}.\ \textit{if } \textsf{typing } [\![E]\!](d) \le \textit{real then bool}$$

This typing function is translated into the rule:

$$\frac{d \ \vdash\ E\ :\ t{\le}real}{d\ \vdash\ \textit{is\_zero } E\ :\ bool}$$

We now present the details.

3.1   Calculation of Typing Functions

Typing functions have the syntax:

$F \in$ Typing-function-expression $C \in$ Constraint
$T \in$ Type-expression $I \in$ Type-identifier
$A \in$ Atomic-expression $O \in$ Primitive-operator

$\quad F ::= \lambda I.T$
$\quad T ::= A \mid FT \mid if\ C\ then\ T \mid O(T_1,\ldots,T_n), n \ge 0$
$\quad A ::= I \mid O(A_1,\ldots,A_n), n \ge 0$
$\quad C ::= A_1 \le A_2 \mid C_1\ and\ C_2 \mid O(A_1,\ldots,A_n), n \ge 0$

(Recall that "$if\ C\ then\ T$" abbreviates "$if\ C\ then\ T\ else\ ns$.") Primitive operators, O, include constants like int and operators like fst from the third column of Figure 2.

A typing function expression is normalized by these rules:

(1) $(\lambda I.T)A \Rightarrow [A/I]T$
(2) $F(if\ C\ then\ T) \Rightarrow if\ C\ then\ FT$
(3) $O(T_1,\ldots,(if\ C\ then\ T_i),\ldots,T_n) \Rightarrow if\ C\ then\ O(T_1,\ldots,T_i,\ldots,T_n)$
(4) $if\ C_1\ then\ if\ C_2\ then\ T \Rightarrow if\ C_1\ and\ C_2\ then\ T$
(5) $fst(T_1 \times T_2) \Rightarrow T_1$
(6) $fst(int) \Rightarrow ns$

Rules similar to (5) and (6) are used for the other primitive operators.

The rules are confluent and strongly normalizing [9]; they remove nested lambda abstractions and "flatten" a typing function expression with nested occurrences of "$if\ C\ then\ T$" into an expression with at most one occurrence. Importantly, normal forms must have the format "$\lambda I.\ if\ C\ then\ A$", which proves crucial for building the inference rules.

Here is an example rewriting:

$$\mathbf{T}_{\text{eqzero then copy}} = \lambda t.\mathbf{T}_{\text{copy}}(\mathbf{T}_{\text{eqzero}}(t))$$

$$= \lambda t.(\lambda t'.t')((\lambda t'.if\ t' \leq real\ then\ bool)(t))$$

$$\Rightarrow \lambda t.(\lambda t'.t')(if\ t \leq real\ then\ bool) \qquad\qquad \text{by (1)}$$

$$\Rightarrow \lambda t.if\ t \leq real\ then\ (\lambda t'.t')bool \qquad\qquad \text{by (2)}$$

$$\Rightarrow \lambda t.if\ t \leq real\ then\ bool \qquad\qquad\qquad \text{by (1)}$$

A semantic equation's typing function is derived in a similar fashion. Given a semantic equation: valuate $[\![op\ E_1 \ldots E_n]\!] = \cdots$ valuate $[\![E_1]\!] \cdots$ valuate $[\![E_n]\!] \cdots$
we wish to calculate $\mathbf{T}_{\text{valuate}}\ [\![op\ E_1 \ldots E_n]\!]$, which we also call typing $[\![op\ E_1 \ldots E_n]\!]$. We replace each action, a, by $\mathbf{T}_a$; occurrences of valuate $[\![E_i]\!]$ are replaced by "primitive operators" $\mathbf{T}_{\text{valuate}}[\![E_i]\!]$. We then apply the rewriting rules to normalize.

Here is an example. For the equation:

$$\text{evaluate}[\![E_1 + E_2]\!] = (\text{evaluate}[\![E_1]\!]\ \text{and evaluate}[\![E_2]\!])\ \text{then add}$$

The derivation goes:

$\mathbf{T}_{\text{evaluate}\ [\![E_1+E_2]\!]}$
$= \text{typing}[\![E_1 + E_2]\!]$
$= \mathbf{T}_{(\text{evaluate}\ [\![E_1]\!]\ \text{and evaluate}\ [\![E_2]\!])\ \text{then add}}$
$= \lambda d.\mathbf{T}_{\text{add}}(\mathbf{T}_{\text{evaluate}\ [\![E_1]\!]\ \text{and evaluate}\ [\![E_2]\!]}(d))$
$= \lambda d.\mathbf{T}_{\text{add}}(\mathbf{T}_{\text{evaluate}\ [\![E_1]\!]}(d) \times \mathbf{T}_{\text{evaluate}\ [\![E_2]\!]}(d))$
$= \lambda d.\mathbf{T}_{\text{add}}(\text{typing}[\![E_1]\!](d) \times \text{typing}[\![E_2]\!](d))$
$= \lambda d.(\lambda t.\ if\ fst(t) \leq real\ and\ snd(t) \leq real\ then\ fst(t) \sqcup snd(t))$
$\qquad\qquad\qquad (\text{typing}[\![E_1]\!](d) \times \text{typing}[\![E_2]\!](d))$
$\Rightarrow \lambda d.\ if\ fst(\text{typing}[\![E_1]\!](d) \times \text{typing}[\![E_2]\!](d)) \leq real\ and$
$\qquad snd(\text{typing}[\![E_1]\!](d) \times \text{typing}[\![E_2]\!](d)) \leq real$
$\qquad then\ fst(\text{typing}[\![E_1]\!](d) \times \text{typing}[\![E_2]\!](d)) \sqcup snd(\text{typing}[\![E_1]\!](d) \times \text{typing}[\![E_2]\!](d))$
$\Rightarrow^* \lambda d.\ if\ \text{typing}[\![E_1]\!](d) \leq real\ and\ \text{typing}[\![E_2]\!](d) \leq real$
$\qquad then\ \text{typing}[\![E_1]\!](d) \sqcup \text{typing}[\![E_2]\!](d)$

3.2 Translation into Inference Rules

We can simply translate a semantic equation's typing function into an inference rule. A first step is to rewrite the typing function so that occurrences of phrases typing $[\![E_i]\!](T)$ have explicit names. This is done by the rewriting rule:

$$\lambda I.\mathcal{C}[\text{typing}\ [\![E_i]\!](A)] \Rightarrow \lambda I.\ let\ I' = \text{typing}\ [\![E_i]\!](A)\ in\ \mathcal{C}[I']$$

where $\mathcal{C}[\ ]$ is a context,
A contains no occurrences of any typing $[\![E_j]\!]$-phrases, and
I' is a fresh identifier

Here is the derivation of the new form of typing function for the example from the previous section:

$$
\begin{aligned}
\textsf{typing } [\![E_1 + E_2]\!] = {} & \lambda d.\textit{if } \textsf{typing } [\![E_1]\!](d) \leq \textit{real and } \textsf{typing } [\![E_2]\!](d) \leq \textit{real} \\
& \textit{then } \textsf{typing } [\![E_1]\!](d) \sqcup \textsf{typing } [\![E_2]\!](d) \\
\Rightarrow {} & \lambda d.\textit{let } t_1 = \textsf{typing } [\![E_1]\!](d) \\
& \textit{in if } t_1 \leq \textit{real and } \textsf{typing } [\![E_2]\!](d) \leq \textit{real} \\
& \textit{then } t_1 \sqcup \textsf{typing}[\![E_2]\!](d) \\
\Rightarrow {} & \lambda d.\textit{let } t_1 = \textsf{typing } [\![E_1]\!](d) \textit{ and} \\
& \quad t_2 = \textsf{typing } [\![E_2]\!](d) \\
& \textit{in if } t_1 \leq \textit{real and } t_2 \leq \textit{real then } t_1 \sqcup t_2
\end{aligned}
$$

The general form of typing function is now:

$$
\begin{aligned}
\textsf{typing } [\![\textrm{op } E_1 \ \ldots \ E_n]\!] = {} & \lambda t. \textit{ let } t_1 = \textsf{typing } [\![E_1]\!](t_1') \textit{ and} \\
& \qquad \vdots \qquad\quad \vdots \\
& \quad t_n = \textsf{typing } [\![E_n]\!](t_n') \\
& \textit{in if } C \textit{ then } A
\end{aligned}
$$

where C and A contain no occurrences of any $\textsf{typing}[\![E_i]\!]$. This format can always be obtained, since the normalization of the original typing function removed all nested λ-abstractions, hence there is no danger in violating binding scopes by moving a $\textsf{typing}[\![E_i]\!](A)$ to the front of a typing function.

Now, the typing function is simply reformatted into the rule:

$$
\frac{t_1' \vdash E_1 \ : \ t_1 \ \cdots \ t_n' \vdash E_n \ : \ t_n}{t \vdash \textrm{op } E_1 \ldots E_n \ : \ A} \qquad \textit{if } C
$$

which is the typing rule for "op $E_1 \ldots E_n$".

In the case of the above example, we find that the typing rule for addition is:

$$
\frac{d \vdash E_1 \ : \ t_1 \qquad d \vdash E_2 \ : \ t_2}{d \vdash E_1 + E_2 \ : \ t_1 \sqcup t_2} \qquad \textit{if } t_1 \leq \textit{real and } t_2 \leq \textit{real}
$$

We can reformat the rule more attractively by moving the constraints on t_1 and t_2 to the antecedents:

$$
\frac{d \vdash E_1 \ : \ t_1 {\leq} \textit{real} \qquad d \vdash E_2 \ : \ t_2 {\leq} \textit{real}}{d \vdash E_1 + E_2 \ : \ t_1 \sqcup t_2}
$$

Since the transformation steps in this and the previous section are purely syntactic in nature, the characterization property of the typing functions is preserved in the inference rules. Thus, not only have we derived static typing rules, we have derived strong typing rules, and indeed, the rules are the "strongest" that they can be, in the sense that they state *exactly* the conditions under which a program phrase will not produce a typing error.

4 Dynamic Semantics

The typing semantics defines a sublanguage of the original language. We should "specialize" the semantics definition to the sublanguage defined by the typing semantics. The result is the dynamic semantics.

In action semantics, each action is a polymorphic function, that is, a collection of monomorphic functions that behave consistently (cf. the definitions in Figure 2). But when actions are composed, not all of the monomorphic functions in an action are needed. For example, the action copy, as it appears in the action expression eqzero then copy, can be narrowed to a single monomorphic function – the identity map on booleans – since eqzero emits only boolean values. A similar phenomenon arises in a language definition: the composition of the actions in a semantics equation limits the domains of the arguments to the actions. For example, the typing rule:

$$\frac{d \vdash \mathrm{E} : t{\leq}real}{d \vdash \mathsf{is\_zero}\ \mathrm{E} : bool}$$

allows us to specialize the semantic equation for is_zero E to:

$$\mathsf{evaluate}\ [\![d \vdash \mathsf{is\_zero}\ \mathrm{E} : bool]\!] = \mathsf{evaluate}\ [\![d \vdash \mathrm{E} : t \leq real]\!]\ \mathsf{then}\ \mathsf{eqzero}_{\{int,real\}}$$

that is, the semantic equation is specialized to operate on bool-typed phrases, and the action eqzero is restricted to a set of just two functions: one that checks integers for zero and one that checks reals for zero. The other functions in the action are discarded.

Specialization proves to be important for compiler construction. In [16, 17], Lee and Pleban propose that actions like eqzero and copy should be implemented as code generation routines, and a program is compiled by mapping it through the semantics definition to an action expression. Then, the actions in the action expression translate to target code. Since the meaning of an action is a family of monomorphic functions, the implementation of an action is a table of code generation routines, one for each monomorphic function. For example, the table of code generation routines for the eqzero action would be:

$$integer \Rightarrow \text{``code to check if fixed point number is zero''}$$
$$real \quad \Rightarrow \text{``code to check if floating point number is zero''}$$
$$bool \quad \Rightarrow \text{``code to generate exception''}$$
$$\vdots$$

The specialization of eqzero in the above semantic equation means that its code generation table need only contain the first two entries.

The specialization step goes as follows: given the typing rule:

$$\frac{t_1 \vdash \mathrm{E}_1 : t'_1 \quad \cdots \quad t_n \vdash \mathrm{E}_n : t'_n}{t \vdash \mathsf{op}\ \mathrm{E}_1 \ldots \mathrm{E}_n : t'}$$

for the semantics equation:

$$\mathsf{valuate}\ [\![\mathsf{op}\ \mathrm{E}_1\ \ldots\ \mathrm{E}_n]\!] = \cdots\ \mathsf{valuate}\ [\![\mathrm{E}_1]\!]\ \cdots\ \mathsf{valuate}\ [\![\mathrm{E}_n]\!]\ \cdots$$

we label the occurrences of **valuate** $[\![E_i]\!]$ with t_i, t'_i, giving: **valuate** $[\![t_i \vdash E_i : t'_i]\!]$. Next, we propagate the t_i, t'_i information throughout the right-hand side of the equation. As a result, every action in the right-hand side is labeled by input-output typing information, which allows us to specialize the actions.

An example shows how this is done. Once again, here is the typing rule for $E_1 + E_2$:

$$\frac{d \vdash E_1 : t_1{\leq}real \quad d \vdash E_2 : t_2{\leq}real}{d \vdash E_1{+}E_2 : t_1{\sqcup}t_2}$$

and its semantic equation:

$$\text{evaluate } [\![E_1 + E_2]\!] = (\text{evaluate } [\![E_1]\!] \text{ and evaluate } [\![E_2]\!]) \text{ then add}$$

If we draw the semantic equation as a tree, then the propagation of typing information can be viewed as a post-order tree traversal algorithm with synthesized and inherited attributes. An action, **a**, that appears as a node in the tree, is of course associated with its typing function, $\mathbf{T_a}$. The input type, i, to the node is an inherited attribute, and $\mathbf{T_a}(i)$ is the synthesized attribute for the node. If we write the inherited attributes and subscripts and the synthesized attributes as superscripts on the tree, we obtain:

$\text{evaluate}[\![d \vdash E_1 + E_2 : t_1 \sqcup t_2]\!] =$

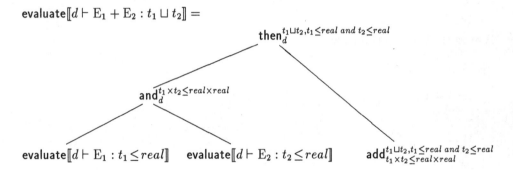

When an inherited attribute, d_i, is passed to a leaf, $\text{evaluate}[\![d_i \vdash E_i : t_i]\!]$, we claim that the synthesized attribute for the leaf is t_i. This allows the analysis to proceed throughout the entire tree, even though the value of E_i is unknown.

The linearized version of the above tree is:

$$\text{evaluate}[\![d \vdash E_1 + E_2 : t_1 \sqcup t_2]\!] =$$
$$(\text{evaluate}[\![d \vdash E_1 : t_1 \leq real]\!] \text{ and}_d \text{ evaluate}[\![d \vdash E_2 : t_2 \leq real]\!])$$
$$\text{then}_d \text{ add}_{t_1 \times t_2 \leq real \times real}$$

where we display the inherited attributes only. As a result of the analysis, we note that the **add** action can be specialized to four entries in its code generation table.

5 An Example Expression Language

We now derive the typing and dynamics semantics for the language in Figure 4.

Typing Functions

$\textbf{typing} : \text{Declaration} \rightarrow \text{Typing-Function}_{D \rightarrow D}$

$\textbf{typing}[\![\text{val } I = E]\!] = \lambda d.\ \{I : \textbf{typing}[\![E]\!](d)\}$

$\textbf{typing}[\![D_1, D_2]\!] = \lambda d.\ \textit{if have-disjoint-fields}(\textbf{typing}[\![D_1]\!](d), \textbf{typing}[\![D_2]\!](d))$
$\qquad\qquad\qquad \textit{then } \textbf{typing}[\![D_1]\!](d)@\textbf{typing}[\![D_2]\!](d)$

$\textbf{typing} : \text{Expression} \rightarrow \text{Typing-Function}_{D \rightarrow F}$

$\textbf{typing}[\![N]\!] = \lambda d.\ \textit{int}$

$\textbf{typing}[\![R]\!] = \lambda d.\ \textit{real}$

$\textbf{typing}[\![E_1 + E_2]\!] = \lambda d.\ \textit{if } \textbf{typing}[\![E_1]\!](d) \leq \textit{real and } \textbf{typing}[\![E_2]\!](d) \leq \textit{real}$
$\qquad\qquad\qquad \textit{then } \textbf{typing}[\![E_1]\!](d) \sqcup \textbf{typing}[\![E_2]\!](d)$

$\textbf{typing}[\![\text{if } E_1 \text{ then } E_2 \text{ else } E_3]\!] = \lambda d.\ \textit{if } \textbf{typing}[\![E_1]\!](d) \leq \textit{bool}$
$\qquad\qquad\qquad\qquad \textit{then } \textbf{typing}[\![E_2]\!](d) \sqcup \textbf{typing}[\![E_3]\!](d)$

$\textbf{typing}[\![\text{is\_zero } E]\!] = \lambda d.\ \textit{if } \textbf{typing}[\![E]\!](d) \leq \textit{real then bool}$

$\textbf{typing}[\![I]\!] = \lambda d.\ \textit{if } \{I : t\} \in d\ \textit{ then } t$

$\textbf{typing}[\![\text{let } D \text{ in } E \text{ end}]\!] = \lambda d.\ \textbf{typing}[\![E]\!](\textbf{typing}[\![D]\!](d)@d)$

Typing (Static) Semantics

Declaration

val I = E $\qquad\qquad : \qquad \dfrac{d \vdash E : t}{d \vdash \text{val } I = E : \{I{:}t\}}$

$D_1, D_2 \qquad\qquad : \qquad \dfrac{d \vdash D_1 : d_1 \quad d \vdash D_2 : d_2}{d \vdash D_1, D_2 : d_1@d_2} \quad \textit{if have-disjoint-fields}(d_1, d_2)$

Expression

N $\qquad\qquad\qquad : \qquad \dfrac{}{d \vdash N : \textit{int}}$

R $\qquad\qquad\qquad : \qquad \dfrac{}{d \vdash R : \textit{real}}$

$E_1 + E_2 \qquad\qquad : \qquad \dfrac{d \vdash E_1 : t_1 \leq real \quad d \vdash E_2 : t_2 \leq real}{d \vdash E_1 + E_2 : t_1 \sqcup t_2}$

if E_1 then E_2 else E_3 $\quad : \quad \dfrac{d \vdash E_1 : bool \quad d \vdash E_2 : t_2 \quad d \vdash E_3 : t_3}{d \vdash \text{if } E_1 \text{ then } E_2 \text{ else } E_3 : t_2 \sqcup t_3}$

is_zero E $\qquad\qquad : \qquad \dfrac{d \vdash E : t \leq real}{d \vdash \text{is\_zero } E : bool}$

I $\qquad\qquad\qquad : \qquad \dfrac{}{d \vdash I : t} \quad \textit{if } \{I : t\} \in d$

let D in E end $\qquad : \qquad \dfrac{d \vdash D : d' \quad d'@d \vdash E : t}{d \vdash \text{let } D \text{ in } E \text{ end} : t}$

Specialized (Dynamic) Semantics

declare: Decorated-Declaration $\rightarrow$ Mono-Action$_{D \rightarrow D}$
  declare$[\![d \vdash \text{val } I = E : \{I : t\}]\!] = $ evaluate$[\![d \vdash E : t]\!]$ then$_d$ bind I_t
  declare$[\![d \vdash D_1, D_2 : d_1 @ d_2 \text{ if } have\text{-}dispoint\text{-}fields(d_1, d_2)]\!] = $
    declare$[\![d \vdash D_1 : d_1]\!]$ and$_d$ declare$[\![d \vdash D_2 : d_2]\!]$

evaluate: Decorated-Expression $\rightarrow$ Mono-Action$_{D \rightarrow F}$
  evaluate$[\![d \vdash N : int]\!] = $ give$([\![N]\!] : int)_d$
  evaluate$[\![d \vdash R : real]\!] = $ give$([\![R]\!] : real)_d$
  evaluate$[\![d \vdash E_1 + E_2 : t_1 \sqcup t_2]\!] = $
    (evaluate$[\![d \vdash E_1 : t_1 \leq real]\!]$ and$_d$ evaluate$[\![d \vdash E_2 : t_2 \leq real]\!]$)
    then$_d$ add$_{t_1 \times t_2 \leq real \times real}$
  evaluate$[\![d \vdash \text{if } E_1 \text{ then } E_2 \text{ else } E_3 : t_2 \sqcup t_3]\!] = $
    evaluate$[\![d \vdash E_1 : bool]\!]$ andthen$_d$ (evaluate$[\![d \vdash E_2 : t_2]\!]$ else$_d$ evaluate$[\![d \vdash E_3 : t_3]\!]$)
  evaluate$[\![d \vdash \text{is_zero } E : bool]\!] = $ evaluate$[\![d \vdash E : t \leq real)]\!]$ then$_d$ eqzero$_{t \leq real}$
  evaluate$[\![d \vdash I : t \text{ if } \{I : t\} \in d]\!] = $ find I_d
  evaluate$[\![d \vdash \text{let } D \text{ in } E \text{ end} : t]\!] = $
    (furthermore$_d$ declare$[\![d \vdash D : d']\!]$) hence$_d$ evaluate$[\![d' @ d \vdash E : t]\!]$

6 Extensions and Future Work

The result of previous sections can be extended to deal with more complex language features: abstraction and recursive bindings. Higher order constructs can be analyzed:

$$\text{evaluate } [\![\text{lam } I . E]\!] = \text{abstract } ((\text{furthermore } (\text{bind } I)) \text{ then evaluate } [\![E]\!])$$

where abstract a converts an action a into a functional facet value. Given $\mathbf{T}_{\text{abstract a}} = \lambda d.\, t \rightarrow \mathbf{T}_a(t, d)$, the typing function is:

$$\text{typing } [\![\text{lam } I . E]\!] = \lambda d.\, t \rightarrow \text{typing } [\![E]\!](\{I : t\} @ d)$$

which gives the rule:

$$\frac{\{I : t\} @ d \vdash E : t'}{d \vdash \text{lam } I . E : t \rightarrow t'}$$

This is the typing rule for lambda abstraction in ML [7]. But the typing rule for ML's polymorphic "let" cannot be derived here, since it requires a subphrase to have the quantified type $\forall t.F[t]$, and such types are not included in Figure 1. A facet might include quantified types, cf. page 7 of [2], but we leave this for further exploration.

Recursive definitions can also be handled. Action semantics uses a recursively$_I$ a to define scope of recursive binding of I in action a. Thus:

$$\text{evaluate } [\![\text{fix } I . E]\!] = \text{recursively}_I \text{ evaluate } [\![E]\!]$$

where $\mathbf{T}_{\text{recursively}_I\ a} = \text{fix}\ (\lambda f.\lambda d.\mathbf{T}_a(\{I\!:\!f(d)\}@d))$. The typing function for the action semantics equation is: $\text{fix}\ F$, where $F = \lambda f.\lambda d.\textsf{typing}\ [\![E]\!]\ (\{I\!:\!f(d)\}@d)$, provided that we make the facets into pointed cpos. We use the fixed point property to derive the typing rule:

$$t' = (\text{fix}\ F)d = \text{let}\ t = \textsf{typing}\ [\![E]\!]\ (\{I : t'\}@d)\ \text{in}\ t$$

But $t = t'$, and we obtain the expected rule:

$$\frac{\{I:t\}@d \vdash E\ :\ t}{d \vdash \text{fix}\ I\ .\ E\ :\ t}$$

We are currently implementing the results in this paper as part of an action semantics-directed prototyping system. The system utilizes tools developed by Brown, Moura, and Watt [4], and future integration of their results with ours is likely.

Acknowledgements

Deryck Brown, Olivier Danvy, Erik Meijer, Peter Mosses and the referees made helpful comments on earlier drafts of this paper.

References

[1] R. Barbuti and A. Martelli. A structured approach to static semantics correctness. *Science of Computer Programming*, 3:279–311, 1983.

[2] Heuk Barendregt and Kees Hermerik. Types in lambda calculi and programming languages. In Neil D. Jones, editor, *ESOP90, Proceedings of European Symposium on Programming*, pages 1–35. Lecture Notes in Computer Science 432, Springer-Verlag, 1990.

[3] D. Bjørner and O.N. Oest, editors. *Towards a formal description of ADA*. Lecture Notes in Computer Science 98. Springer, Berlin, 1980.

[4] Deryck Brown, Hermano Moura, and David Watt. Towards a realistic semantics-directed compiler generator. In *Proceedings of Glasgow Functional Programming Workshop, Isle of Skye, Scotland*, 1991.

[5] Luca Cardelli and Peter Wegner. On understanding types, data abstraction, and polymorphism. *Computing Surveys*, 17(4):471–522, 1985.

[6] Charles Consel and Olivier Danvy. Static and dynamic semantics processing. In *Proceedings of the 18th Annual ACM Symposium on Principles of Programming Languages*, pages 14–24, 1991.

[7] Luis Damas and Robin Milner. Principal type-schemes for functional programs. In *Proceedings of the 9th Annual ACM Symposium on Principles of Programming Languages*, pages 207–212, 1982.

[8] N.G. de Bruijn. *The Mathematical Language AUTOMATH, its usage, and some of its extensions*, pages 29–61. Lecture Notes in Mathematics 125. Springer, Berlin, 1970.

[9] Kyung-Goo Doh. *Action semantics-directed prototyping*. PhD thesis, Kansas State University, Manhattan, Kansas, USA, forthcoming.

[10] J. Donahue. *Complementary Definitions of Programming Language Semantics.* Lecture Notes in Computer Science 42. Springer-Verlag, 1976.

[11] A.P. Ershov. On the essence of compilation. In *Formal Description of Programming Concepts*, pages 391–420. IFIP, North-Holland, Amsterdam, 1978.

[12] Susan Even and David A. Schmidt. Category-sorted algebra-based action semantics. *Theoretical Computer Science*, 77:71–95, 1990.

[13] Susan Even and David A. Schmidt. Type inference for action semantics. In Neil D. Jones, editor, *ESOP90, Proceedings of European Symposium on Programming*, pages 118–133. Lecture Notes in Computer Science 432, Springer-Verlag, 1990.

[14] Y. Futamura. Partial evaluation of computation process – an approach to a compiler-compiler. *Systems, Computers, Controls*, 2(5):45–50, 1971.

[15] Neil D. Jones, Peter Sestoft, and Harald Sondergaard. Mix: a self-applicable partial evaluator for experiments in compiler generation. *Journal of LISP and Symbolic Computation*, 2(1):9–50, 1989.

[16] Peter Lee. *Realistic Compiler Generation.* The MIT Press, Cambridge, Massachusetts, 1989.

[17] Peter Lee and Uwe F. Pleban. A realistic compiler generator based on high-level semantics. In *Proceedings of the 14th Annual ACM Symposium on Principles of Programming Languages*, pages 284–295, 1987.

[18] John C. Mitchell and Robert Harper. The essence of ML. In *POPL88, Proceedings of the 15th Annual ACM Symposium on Principles of Programming Languages*, pages 28–46. ACM, 1988.

[19] Margaret Montenyohl and Mitchell Wand. Correct flow analysis in continuation semantics. In *Conference Record of the 15th Annual ACM Symposium on Principles of Programming Languages*, pages 204–218, 1988.

[20] Peter D. Mosses. Abstract semantic algebras! In *Formal Description of Programming Concepts II, Proceedings of the IFIP TC2 Working Conference, Garmisch-Partenkirchen, 1982*, pages 45–72. IFIP, North-Holland, Amsterdam, 1983.

[21] Peter D. Mosses. Unified algebras and action semantics. In *STACS89, Proceedings of Symposium on Theoretical Aspects Computer Science, Paderborn*. No. 349, Lecture Notes in Computer Science, Springer-Verlag, 1989.

[22] Peter D. Mosses. Unified algebras and institutions. In *LICS89, Proceedings of the 4th Annual Symposium on Logic in Computer Science*, pages 304–312. IEEE, 1989.

[23] Peter D. Mosses. Unified algebras and modules. In *POPL89, Proceedings of the 16th Annual ACM Symposium on Principles of Programming Languages*, pages 329–343. ACM, 1989.

[24] Peter D. Mosses. An introduction to action semantics. In *Lecture Notes for the Marktoberdorf Summer School*, 1991.

[25] Peter D. Mosses. *Action Semantics.* Tracts in Theoretical Computer Science. Cambridge University Press, Newton, Massachusetts, 1992.

[26] Peter D. Mosses and David A. Watt. The use of action semantics. In *Formal Description of Programming Concepts III*. IFIP, North-Holland, Amsterdam, 1987.

[27] P. Naur. Revised report on the algorithmic language Algol 60. *Communications of the ACM*, 6(1):1–17, 1963.

[28] Flemming Nielson and Hanne Riis Nielson. Code generation from two level denotational meta-languages. In Neil D. Jones, editor, *Programs as Data Objects*, pages 192–205. Lecture Notes in Computer Science 217, Springer-Verlag, 1986.

[29] Flemming Nielson and Hanne Riis Nielson. Pragmatic aspects of two-level denotational metalanguages. In Neil D. Jones, editor, *ESOP86, Proceedings of European Symposium on Programming*, pages 133–143. Lecture Notes in Computer Science 213, Springer-Verlag, 1986.

[30] John Reynolds. Using category theory to design implicit conversions and generic operators. In Neil D. Jones, editor, *Semantics-Directed Compiler Generation*, pages 211–258. Lecture Notes in Computer Science 94, Springer-Verlag, 1980.

[31] John Reynolds. The essence of Algol. In J. deBakker and J.C. vanVliet, editors, *Algorithmic Languages*, pages 345–372. North-Holland, Amsterdam, 1981.

[32] John Reynolds. *Semantics as a design tool*. Course lecture notes, Computer Science Dept., Carnegie-Mellon University, Pittsburgh, PA, 1988.

[33] David A. Schmidt. *Denotational Semantics – A Methodology for Language Development*. Allyn and Bacon, Newton, Massachusetts, 1986.

[34] Robert D. Tennent. *Principles of Programming Languages*. Prentice-Hall International, Englewood Cliffs, New Jersey, 1981.

[35] V.F. Turchin. The concept of a supercompiler. *ACM Transactions on Programming Languages and Systems*, 8(3):292–325, 1986.

[36] David A. Watt. *Programming Language Syntax and Semantics*. Prentice-Hall International, Englewood Cliffs, New Jersey, 1991.

Detecting Determinate Computations by Bottom-up Abstract Interpretation

Roberto Giacobazzi , Laura Ricci
Dipartimento di Informatica
Università di Pisa
Corso Italia 40, 56125 Pisa
{giaco,ricci}@di.unipi.it

Abstract

One of the most interesting characteristics of logic programs is the ability of expressing nondeterminism in an elegant and concise way. On the other hand, implementation of nondeterminism poses serious problems both in the sequential and in the concurrent case. If determinate computations are detected through a static analysis, a noticeable reduction of the execution time may be obtained. This work describes a static analysis to detect determinate computations. The analysis does not require the knowledge of the activating modes of the predicate and it derives determinacies which may be inferred from the success set of the program.

1 Introduction

One of the main features of logic programming is the ability to compute a set of output bindings for each variable of a query. While this characteristic supports an elegant and concise definition of non-deterministic behaviours, it poses serious problems both in a sequential and in a concurrent implementation of the language. In several cases, the ability of logic programs to compute multiple bindings is not exploited: in this case a logic program has a determinate behaviour, i.e. it produces a single output value for a given query, or for a class of queries satisfying some properties. Recently, some analyses [6,4,11,10,12] have been proposed to statically detect when a computation is determinate. The knowledge of determinate computations, i.e. determinacies, supports optimization of the program execution time [5] end of bottom-up evaluators [10].

Even if the analysis to detect determinancies is related to the control features of the language implementation, we show that determinancies may be inferred by a bottom up analysis that does not require any knowledge of the type and activating modes of a predicate. The analysis derives those determinacies that may be inferred from the success set of the program. The definition of the analysis requires the investigation of the relation between the input values of a predicate and those returned by the refutation of the predicate itself. Some recent proposals [1,6,8,12] characterize such a relation through the notion of dependence. This notion has been exploited, for instance, to describe the relation between the groundness of a set of arguments of a predicate upon invocation and the groundness of another set of arguments, after the refutation of the predicate. We refine such notion through that of *deterministic ground dependence*. A ground dependence from a set of input arguments to a set of output ones is deterministic if, whenever the input arguments are ground, the refutation binds any output argument to a single ground term. The definition of deterministic ground dependences supports a refined notion of functionality, i.e. functionality is inferred with respect to subsets of arguments rather than to whole predicates. The analysis has been defined and validated through a bottom-up abstract interpretation technique. It integrates the theory of hypergraphs with the semantics of logic programs in order to obtain a powerful program analysis tool. The information useful to characterize deterministic computations is produced by applying an abstract interpretation which returns an abstract model of the program. This approximation is obtained by the finite computation of the least fixpoint of an abstraction of the immediate consequence operator T_P. In order to have such an abstraction, a suitable set of abstract domains and operators, supporting the definition of T_P, is given.

Section 2 introduces some basic notions on hypergraph theory and semantics of logic programs, Section 3 formally defines the abstract domains and abstract operators for the analysis and abstract fixpoint semantics for deterministic dependences analysis, Section 4 shows some significant examples, while Section 5 deals with some concluding remark.

2 Preliminaries

We assume the reader familiar with the notions of lattice theory, hypergraph theory [2], semantics of logic programs [7] and the basic concepts of logic programming [9].

In the following we will denote by $S/\{s\}$ the set S where the element $\{s\}$ has been removed.

A *hypergraph* $\mathcal{G}$ is a pair $(\mathcal{N}, \mathcal{E})$ where $\mathcal{N} = \{v_1, ..., v_n\}$ is a (finite) set of *nodes* and $\mathcal{E} = \{e_1, ..., e_m\}$ is a set of *hyperarcs*, where for each $i = 1, ..., m$, $e_i = \langle T, H \rangle$ such that $T \subseteq \mathcal{N}$ (the tail) and $H \in \mathcal{N}$ (the head). In the following we denote by $Tail(e)$ and $Head(e)$ the tail and the head of any hyperarc e. The "tail" and "head" notions are extended to deal with sets of hyperarcs. A hyperarc e is *satisfied* by a set of nodes $\mathcal{N}'$ iff $Tail(e) \subseteq \mathcal{N}'$. A *graph* Ψ is a hypergraph $(\mathcal{N}_\Psi, \mathcal{E}_\Psi)$ where $\forall e \in \mathcal{E}_\Psi$, $|Tail(e)| = 1$ (we denote by $|T|$ the number of elements is T). Given a graph Ψ, the nodes n and n' are *connected* in Ψ iff there exists a path $\pi \subseteq \mathcal{E}_\Psi$ where $\pi = \{e_1, ..., e_k\}$ such that $n = Tail(e_1)$, $n' = Head(e_k)$ and $\forall j = 1, ..., k-1$, $Head(e_j) = Tail(e_{j+1})$. The connection between the nodes n and n' (by means of a path π) in a graph Ψ will be denoted by: $n \mapsto_\Psi^\pi n'$. The graph, denoted by $\Psi_\mathcal{G}$, associated with the hypergraph $\mathcal{G} = (\mathcal{N}, \mathcal{E})$ is obtained by reducing each hyperarc: $\langle \{s_1, ..., s_m\}, h \rangle \in \mathcal{E}$, in a set of arcs $\{\langle s_1, h \rangle ... \langle s_m, h \rangle\}$. In the following we will denote by $\Im_\mathcal{G}(n', n) = \{\pi \mid n' \mapsto_{\Psi_\mathcal{G}}^\pi n\}$ the set of paths π defining a connection from n' to n in the graph $\Psi_\mathcal{G}$ associated with the hypergraph $\mathcal{G}$.

Given a hypergraph $\mathcal{G} = (\mathcal{N}, \mathcal{E})$, let $\mathcal{E}' \subseteq \mathcal{E}$. The sets of nodes $\mathcal{N}'$ and the node n are *connected* in $\mathcal{G}$, by means of the hyperarcs in $\mathcal{E}'$, denoted by $\mathcal{N}' \rightarrow_\mathcal{G}^{\mathcal{E}'} n$, iff all the hyperarcs in $\mathcal{E}'$ are satisfied by $\mathcal{N}' \cup Head(\mathcal{E}')$, $\forall i \in \mathcal{N}'$: $\Im_{(\mathcal{N},\mathcal{E}')}(i,n) \neq \emptyset$ and $\forall e \in \mathcal{E}'$, $\forall i \in Tail(e)$: $i \notin \mathcal{N}'$, $\exists \bar{n} \in \mathcal{N}'$ such that $\Im_{(\mathcal{N},\mathcal{E}'/\{e\})}(\bar{n},i) \neq \emptyset$. We call $\mathcal{E}'$ a *connection* from $\mathcal{N}'$ to n in $\mathcal{G}$. A connection $\mathcal{E}'$ from $\mathcal{N}'$ to n in a hypergraph $\mathcal{G}$ is *minimal* iff for each $e \in \mathcal{E}$, $\mathcal{N}' \not\to_{\mathcal{G}}^{\mathcal{E}'/\{e\}} n$.

Example 2.1 *Let us consider the following hypergraph and some connections with v_5*

$$\mathcal{G} = \quad \begin{array}{c} \overset{a}{\longrightarrow} \\ v_1 \ v_2 \ v_3 \ v_4 \ v_5 \\ \underset{c}{} \ \underset{e}{} \ \underset{d}{} \\ _b \end{array} \qquad \{v_4\} \to_{\mathcal{G}}^{\{d,c,e,a\}} v_5, \ \{v_3\} \to_{\mathcal{G}}^{\{c,e,a\}} v_5, \ \{v_1,v_2\} \to_{\mathcal{G}}^{\{a\}} v_5, \ \ldots$$

while $\forall \mathcal{E}' \subseteq \{a,b,c,d,e\}$: $\{v_1\} \not\to_{\mathcal{G}}^{\mathcal{E}'} v_5$, $\{v_5\} \not\to_{\mathcal{G}}^{\mathcal{E}'} v_5$.

Notice that the definition of connection requires that any node in the tail of an hyperarc which is not in the set of starting nodes $\mathcal{N}'$ can be reached from some starting node, without using the hyperarc itself. This condition avoids considering, in a connection, a hyperarc (e.g. a), such that each non-starting node (v_2) in the tail can only be reached from some starting node (v_1) by means of a path using the hyperarc itself (the hyperarc becomes auto-satisfied). As a consequence $\not\exists \mathcal{E}' \subseteq \{a,b,c,d,e\}$: $\{v_1\} \to_{\mathcal{G}}^{\mathcal{E}'} v_5$.

The declarative semantics of logic programs in [7] is based on an *extended Herbrand Universe* containing also non-ground terms. It allows to declaratively characterize the ability of logic programs to compute answer substitutions (which are non-ground in general). Let us consider the set $Cons$ of term constructors, and a denumerable set Var of variables. The free $Cons$-algebra on Var is denoted as $T_{Cons}(Var)$. A substitution ϑ is a mapping from Var into $T_{Cons}(Var)$, such that $\{x \in Var \mid \vartheta(x) \neq x\}$ is finite. ε denotes the empty substitution. $\vartheta_{|G}$ denotes the restriction of the substitution ϑ to the variables occurring in G, which is extended as an identity, for any $x \in Var(G)$ such that $\vartheta(x)$ is undefined. We denote by mgu a total function which maps a pair of syntactic objects (e.g. atoms, terms,...) to an idempotent most general unifier of the objects, if such exists; $fail$ otherwise. The *extended Herbrand Universe* U_P is defined as $T_{Cons_P}(Var)/\approx$, where $t_1 \approx t_2$ iff $\exists \vartheta_1, \vartheta_2 \mid t_1\vartheta_1 = t_2 \wedge t_2\vartheta_2 = t_1$. Let $Pred$ be a finite set of predicate symbols. An *atom* is an object of the form $p(t_1,...,t_n)$ where $t_1,...,t_n \in T_{Cons_P}(Var)$ and p is an n-ary predicate symbol (i.e. $p \in Pred^n$). The set of atoms is denoted $Atoms$. We denote by $Var(a)$ the set of variables in any syntactic object a. The *Base of interpretations* B_P is $Atoms/\approx$ where $\approx$ extends to atoms in the obvious way. An *interpretation* I is any subset of B_P. Standard results on model-theoretic and fixpoint semantics apply to the extended domains as well as in the ground case [7]. In particular, the fixpoint semantics for a logic program P (denoted as $\mathcal{F}(P)$) is defined by means of an immediate consequences operator T_P [7]. It derives possibly non-ground atoms by means of a bottom-up inference rule which is based on unification, as in the top-down SLD resolution.

We assume the reader familiar with the basic notions of *abstract interpretation* as defined in [3]. In the following an abstract interpretation supporting our analysis for definite logic programs is developed according to a bottom-up technique [1] based on an abstraction of the declarative and fixpoint semantics in [7].

3 Abstract Domains

This section introduces an analysis for ground and ground-deterministic dependences. Informally, a ground dependence does exist between a set of arguments T of an atom A and another argument h, iff whenever the arguments in T are ground, the refutation of A produces a set of ground bindings for h. A ground dependence is determinate, i.e. deterministic ground dependence, iff the refutation produces at most one binding for h. Consider the logic program

$append([], X, X) : -.$

$append([X|Xs], Y, [X|Ys]) : -append(Xs, Y, Ys).$

the refutation of the goal $append([a|[]], [b|[]], Z)$ in the program produces only one binding for Z ($\{Z = [a|b|[]]\}$), while the goal $append(X, Y, [a|b|[]])$ produces multiple bindings for X and Y ($\{X = [a|[]], Y = [b|[]]\}$, $\{X = [a|b|[]], Y = []\}$, etc.). In the first case the groundness of the first two arguments uniquely determines the groundness of the third one, while, in the second case, a non-deterministic dependence does exist between the third argument and the first one and between the third and the second one.

Let P be a definite logic program, we denote by $U_P^\sharp = \{g, ng\}$ the *abstract universe of terms* where g represents the ground term set, and ng the possibly non-ground one. Two terms are ground-equivalent ($\approx_{ground}$) iff both are ground or non-ground terms. As a consequence, $U_P^\sharp$ can be considered as a set of abstract objects representing equivalence classes of terms, modulo ground equivalency. It is trivial to prove that $U_P^\sharp$ is a finite lattice since for each ground term there exists a non-ground term which is greater than it (i.e. $g \leq_g ng$). The elements in $U_P^\sharp$ will be denoted as $t^\sharp$.

Definition 3.1 *A dependence representation $\mathcal{D}$ is a triple $(\mathcal{N}, \mathcal{V}, \mathcal{E})$, where*

- $(\mathcal{N}, \mathcal{E})$ *is a hypergraph such that*

    $\mathcal{N}$ *is a finite set of symbols called the* domain *of the representation $(Dom(\mathcal{D}))$,*

    $\mathcal{E}$ *is a set of labelled hyperarcs of the form $\langle T, h \rangle_l$, where $l \in \{d, ?, \perp\}$,*

- $\mathcal{V} \subseteq \mathcal{N} \times U_P^\sharp$ *such that $|\mathcal{V}| = |\mathcal{N}| \wedge \forall (s, t^\sharp), (s', t'^\sharp) \in \mathcal{V}, s \neq s'$.*

A *dependence* is a hyperarc in a dependence representation. An *autodependence* is a dependence $\langle T, h \rangle_l$ such that $h \in T$. Dependence representations which are defined over the same domain $\mathcal{N}$ are called *homogeneous*.

The hypergraph notation is useful to represent dependence information in a concise way. Dependence representations are hypergraphs enhanced with a suitable set of labels (for nodes and hyperarcs). Since both the elements of $\mathcal{V}$ and the elements of $\mathcal{E}$ are defined on the same set of nodes $\mathcal{N}$, we will often omit the reference to the underlying set of nodes when this can be deduced by the context. Labels associated with nodes will correspond to the *mode information* (a mode analysis is considered in our framework), while the labels associated with the dependence notion represent the type of the corresponding dependence (d and ? mean *deterministic* and *don't know* respectively, while $\perp$ means *undefined*). Hyperarc labels can be structured as a lattice, $(\{d, ?, \perp\}, \leq_d)$, where

$d \leq_d$? and $\perp \leq_d d$. Let Ψ be a graph with labelled arcs and π_v^h be a path from the node v to h in Ψ. We denote by $\Lambda(\pi_v^h)$ the set of labels in the path π_v^h. This notation naturally extends to sets of hyperarcs.

Definition 3.2 *Given a dependence representation $\mathcal{D} = (\mathcal{N}, \mathcal{V}, \mathcal{E})$, a hyperarc $e \in \mathcal{E}$ is redundant in $\mathcal{D}$ iff $e = \langle T, h \rangle$? and $h \in T$, or $e = \langle T, h \rangle_l$ and $\exists T' \subseteq T$, $T \neq \emptyset$, $\exists \mathcal{E}' \subseteq \mathcal{E}$, $e \notin \mathcal{E}'$ such that $T' \rightarrow_{(\mathcal{N}, \mathcal{E})}^{\mathcal{E}'} h$ and $lub_{\leq_d}(\Lambda(\mathcal{E}')) \leq_d l$.*

A hyperarc is redundant in a dependence representation iff it does not add any information to the representation itself (i.e. either it is an autodependence labelled by ?, or there exists a connection with the same target which is more concise ($T' \subseteq T$) and captures a stronger dependence relation). Notice that a connection is deterministic iff all its labels are d. In the following we will use a suitable graphical notation for dependence representations.

Example 3.1 *Let us consider the non-redundant dependence representation*

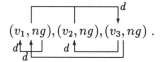

$$(v_1, ng), (v_2, ng), (v_3, ng) .$$

Note that the hyperarcs $\langle \{v_2, v_3\}, v_1 \rangle_d$, $\langle \{v_1, v_3\}, v_2 \rangle_d$ and the autodependences $\langle \{v_3\}, v_3 \rangle_d$, $\langle \{v_1, v_2\}, v_2 \rangle_d$, $\langle \{v_1, v_2, v_3\}, v_1 \rangle_d$, $\langle \{v_1, v_2, v_3\}, v_2 \rangle_d$, $\langle \{v_1, v_2, v_3\}, v_3 \rangle_d$, $\langle \{v_1, v_2\}, v_1 \rangle_d$, $\langle \{v_2, v_3\}, v_2 \rangle_d$, $\langle \{v_2, v_3\}, v_3 \rangle_d$, $\langle \{v_2\}, v_2 \rangle$? are redundant if added to the previous dependence representation. As an example, $\langle \{v_3\}, v_3 \rangle_d$ is redundant since v_3 can be reached by the node itself without considering that autodependence. Of course, all the previous dependences are redundant even if they are labelled with ?.

3.1 Abstract Atoms

Definition 3.3 *An* abstract atom *is a pair of the form $(p, \mathcal{D}_p)$ (usually denoted as $p(\mathcal{D}_p)$) where p is an n-ary predicate symbol in Pred and $\mathcal{D}_p$ is a non-redundant dependence representation such that $Dom(\mathcal{D}_p) = \{1, ..., n\}$ (the nodes represent the argument positions in the atom).*

Definition 3.4 *The* abstract base, *denoted as $B_P^\sharp$, is the set of non-redundant abstract atoms $p(\mathcal{D}_p)$, for each $p \in Pred$.*

Definition 3.5 *An* α-interpretation *is any subset of the abstract base having at most one occurrence for each predicate symbol. We will denote such a set as $\Xi^\sharp$ ($\Xi^\sharp \subseteq 2^{B_P^\sharp}$).*

To make the analysis more concise we will return non-redundant dependences and we will approximate success patterns with their least upper bound, allowing in each α-interpretation at most one abstract atom per predicate symbol [1,8].

Definition 3.6 *Let $p(\mathcal{D}_p)$, $p(\mathcal{D}'_p)$ be two abstract atoms, where $\mathcal{D}_p = (\{1..n\}, \mathcal{V}_p, \mathcal{E}_p)$, $\mathcal{D}'_p = (\{1..n\}, \mathcal{V}'_p, \mathcal{E}'_p)$, $\mathcal{V}_p = \{(1, t_1^\sharp), ..., (n, t_n^\sharp)\}$ and $\mathcal{V}'_p = \{(1, t_1'^\sharp), ..., (n, t_n'^\sharp)\}$.*

$$p(\mathcal{D}_p) \sqsubseteq p(\mathcal{D}'_p) \;\; \textit{iff}$$

- $\forall i = 1, ..., n:\;\; t_i^\sharp \leq_g t_i'^\sharp$

- $\forall \langle T', h \rangle_{l'} \in \mathcal{E}'_p$ either $t_h'^\sharp = ng,\; t_h^\sharp = g$ and $\forall e \in \mathcal{E}_p:\;\; Head(e) \neq h$ or $\langle T', h \rangle_{l'}$ is redundant in $(\{1..n\}, \mathcal{V}_p, \mathcal{E}_p \cup \{\langle T', h \rangle_{l'}\})$.

Proposition 3.1 $\sqsubseteq$ *is a partial ordering.*

Let $I_1^\sharp, I_2^\sharp \in \Xi^\sharp$, $I_1^\sharp \leq_\alpha I_2^\sharp$ iff $\forall p(\mathcal{D}_p) \in I_1^\sharp$, $\exists p(\mathcal{D}'_p) \in I_2^\sharp$: $p(\mathcal{D}_p) \sqsubseteq p(\mathcal{D}'_p)$.

Example 3.2

$$\{\ q(ng,ng,ng)\} \leq_\alpha \{q(ng,ng,ng)\},\ \{\ p(ng,g,ng,ng)\} \leq_\alpha \{\ p(ng,ng,ng,ng)\},$$

$$\{\ p(ng,ng,ng,ng)\} \leq_\alpha \{\ p(ng,ng,ng,ng)\}.$$

Since each α-interpretation includes at most one atom for each predicate symbol, it is easy to prove that $\leq_\alpha$ is a partial ordering and whenever $I_1^\sharp \subseteq I_2^\sharp$, then $I_1^\sharp \leq_\alpha I_2^\sharp$. Moreover, since *Pred* is finite and for each n-ary predicate symbol $p \in Pred$ there always exists a finite set of abstract atoms in $B_P^\sharp$ defined on p, it is easy to prove that $(\Xi^\sharp, \leq_\alpha)$ is a finite lattice [1].

3.2 Abstract Substitutions

To develop an abstract interpretation based upon a declarative semantics, we also have to reconsider the substitution notion within the abstract framework [1].

Given a finite set of variables V, we denote by $Subst_V$ the set of substitutions ϑ defined on $\bar{V}$ for each $\bar{V} \subseteq V$. Let $\Phi_1, \Phi_2 \in 2^{Subst_V}$, $\Phi_1 \leq_S \Phi_2$ iff
$$(\forall \vartheta \in \Phi_1, \exists \vartheta' \in \Phi_2 \mid \vartheta \leq \vartheta') \wedge (\forall \vartheta \in \Phi_2, \exists \vartheta' \in \Phi_1 \mid \vartheta \leq \vartheta' \;\Rightarrow\; \Phi_1 \subseteq \Phi_2).$$

Definition 3.7 *An* abstract substitution $\vartheta^\sharp$ *is a non-redundant dependence representation such that* $Dom(\vartheta^\sharp) = V$ *(the nodes are the symbols of variables in V).*

Thus, an abstract substitution $\vartheta^\sharp$ can be represented as a hypergraph of bindings of the form $(X/t^\sharp)$ where $X \in V$ and $t^\sharp \in U_P^\sharp$.

Given a finite set V_n of variable symbols $\{x_1, ..., x_n\}$ such that $x_i \neq x_j$ for each $i \neq j$: $Subst_{V_n}^\sharp$ denotes the set of abstract substitutions defined on the set of variables V_k, for each $V_k \subseteq V_n$. We can deal with a finite set of variables because of the bottom-up approach. In fact, in this kind of analysis the meaningful substitutions are only those referring the finite amount of variables occurring in program clauses. Let $\Sigma_{V_n}^\sharp \subseteq 2^{Subst_{V_n}^\sharp}$ such that $\forall \Phi^\sharp \in \Sigma_{V_n}$, $\Phi^\sharp$ contains at most one abstract substitution $\vartheta^\sharp$ such that $Dom(\vartheta^\sharp) = V_k$, for each $V_k \subseteq V_n$. Note that any element in $\Sigma_V^\sharp$ can be handled as an α-interpretation. As a matter of fact, abstract substitutions can be considered as abstract atoms having a different predicate symbol of arity k for each $V_k \subseteq V_n$. Thus, since the preorder $\sqsubseteq$ can be defined between any homogeneous dependence representations, independently from the domain, an ordering relation $\leq_\Sigma$ can be defined by extending the $\leq_\alpha$ on the domain of sets of abstract substitutions. It is easy to prove that [1] given a finite set of variables V_n, $(\Sigma_{V_n}^\sharp, \leq_\Sigma)$ is a finite lattice.

3.3 Galois Connections

Let $I \in 2^{B_P}$ and $p \in Pred$. In the following we denote by $I \downarrow p$ the set of atoms in I having the same predicate symbol p.

Let $I \downarrow p = \{p(t_{1_1}, ..., t_{1_n}), ..., p(t_{m_1}, ..., t_{m_n})\}$. We define an abstraction map $abs : 2^{B_P} \to \Xi^{\sharp}$ such that $abs(I) = \bigcup\limits_{p \in Pred} abs(I \downarrow p)$ where $abs(I \downarrow p) = \emptyset$ if $I \downarrow p = \emptyset$ and $abs(I \downarrow p) = p(\mathcal{D}_p)$ such that $\mathcal{D}_p = (\{1..n\}, \mathcal{V}_p, \mathcal{E}_p)$ otherwise; where

- $\mathcal{V}_p = \{(i, t_i^{\sharp}) \mid i = 1, ..., n\}$ where $t_i^{\sharp} = \begin{cases} g & \text{iff } \forall j = 1, ..., m, \ Var(t_{j_i}) = \emptyset, \\ ng & \text{otherwise,} \end{cases}$

- Let $T = \{i_1, ..., i_k\}$; $\langle T, h \rangle_l \in \mathcal{E}_p$ iff $\langle T, h \rangle_l$ is non-redundant in $\mathcal{D}_p$ and

  $- \ \forall j = 1, ..., m, \ Var(t_{j_h}) \subseteq \bigcup\limits_{i \in T} Var(t_{j_i}),$

  $- \ l = \begin{cases} d & \text{iff } \forall \ r, f \in \{1, ..., m\}, \ r \neq f, \ mgu(t_{r_{i_1}}, ..., t_{r_{i_k}}, t_{f_{i_1}}, ..., t_{f_{i_k}}) = fail, \\ ? & \text{otherwise.} \end{cases}$

Example 3.3 Let $I = \{q(a, b), q(b, b), q(c, d)\}$, then $abs(I) = \{\ q(\ g\ ,\ g\ )\}$.

In this case, the groundness of the first argument of q uniquely determines the groundness of itself, moreover it uniquely determines the groundness of the second one. Since both the abstract arguments are ground, this information is relevant only because of the deterministic label (d) associated with the hyperarc. The (non-redundant) dependence from the second to the first argument is irrelevant and can be discarded by the analysis.

Autodependences allow to detect the source of determinism in an atom. As a matter of fact, a deterministic autodependence represents a set of arguments containing at least a deterministic term (i.e. a single choice term). The framework is designed in order to handle general (possibly auto) dependences. However, in order to let the paper more readable, in the following we will often omit any (possibly non-redundant) auto dependence in abstract objects, thus showing only the inter-argument dependences, which are more relevant for the analysis point of view.

Example 3.4 Let $I = \{p(X, X, d), p(a, b, c)\}$, $abs(I) = \{\ p(ng, ng, g)\ \}$.

The non-redundant autodependences $\langle\{3\}, 3\rangle_d$, $\langle\{1, 2\}, 1\rangle_d$ and $\langle\{1, 2\}, 2\rangle_d$ (which are not shown) show that the first two arguments and the third one deterministically determines their own groundness (the sets of argument positions $\{1, 2\}$ and $\{3\}$ are the two sources of the determinism for the predicate p in I). As a matter of fact, for any concrete atom $p(t_1, t_2, t_3)$ having either the first two arguments or the third one ground, there exists at most one possiblity of unifying it with atoms in I.

Let $I = \{p(f(X, Y), Z, g(X, Y, Z)), p(a, b, c)\}$, the dependence representation associated with $abs(I)$ is shown in example 3.1, where $v_1 = 1$, $v_2 = 2$ and $v_3 = 3$.

Analogously we can define a monotonic abstraction map $abs_{\Sigma} : 2^{Subst_V} \to \Sigma_V^{\sharp}$. There are no concretization maps *conc* such that $(abs, conc)$ is a Galois connection between interpretations and α-interpretations. Thus, in order to define a Galois connection between the concrete and the abstract domain of computation, we have to consider sets of interpretations as single objects. Let us consider the following partial ordering relations defined on sets of interpretations and α-interpretations respectively:

- $\forall D_1, D_2 \in 2^{(2^{B_P})}$, $D_1 \preceq D_2$ iff $(\forall I_1 \in D_1 \; \exists I_2 \in D_2 \mid I_1 \subseteq I_2) \wedge$
  $(\forall I_2 \in D_2 \; \exists I_1 \in D_1 \mid abs(I_2) \leq_\alpha abs(I_1) \Rightarrow D_1 \subseteq D_2)$,

- $\forall D_1^\sharp, D_2^\sharp \in 2^{\Xi^\sharp}$, $D_1^\sharp \preceq_\alpha D_2^\sharp$ iff
  $(\forall I_1^\sharp \in D_1^\sharp, \; \exists I_2^\sharp \in D_2^\sharp \mid I_1^\sharp \leq_\alpha I_2^\sharp) \wedge (\forall I_2^\sharp \in D_2^\sharp, \; \exists I_1^\sharp \in D_1^\sharp \mid I_2^\sharp \leq_\alpha I_1^\sharp \Rightarrow D_1^\sharp \subseteq D_2^\sharp)$.

It is easy to prove that $(2^{(2^{B_P})}, \preceq)$ and $(2^{\Xi^\sharp}, \preceq_\alpha)$ are complete lattices.

Proposition 3.2 *The pair of functions (α, γ) such that*

- $\alpha : 2^{(2^{B_P})} \to 2^{\Xi^\sharp}$ *where* $\alpha(D) = \{abs(I) \mid I \in D\}$,

- $\gamma : 2^{\Xi^\sharp} \to 2^{(2^{B_P})}$ *where* $\gamma(D^\sharp) = \{I \mid \exists I^\sharp \in D^\sharp \wedge abs(I) = I^\sharp\}$,

holds the conditions on the Galois insertion [3] between $(2^{(2^{B_P})}, \preceq)$ and $(2^{\Xi^\sharp}, \preceq_\alpha)$.

3.4 Abstract Unification (α-mgu)

The *abstract most general unifier* $\alpha\text{-}mgu : B_P^n \times B_P^{\sharp n} \to Subst_V^\sharp \cup \{fail\}$, takes two n-tuples of concrete and abstract atoms respectively and returns an abstract substitution which is defined on the set of variables of the concrete atoms. It spreads ground information on the variables of the concrete atoms and it generates a dependence between a set of variables T and a variable x iff there exists a connection, in the abstract atom, between the nodes corresponding with the variables in T and the node corresponding with a term having x as variable. The resulting dependence is deterministic if such a connection contains only deterministic labels. Furthermore, it is enough to have a deterministic connection to return a deterministic dependence.

Definition 3.8 *Let $\mathcal{E}'$ be a connection between a set of nodes $\mathcal{N}'$ and a node $n \in \mathcal{N}$ in a dependence representation $\mathcal{D} = (\mathcal{N}, \mathcal{V}, \mathcal{E})$. $\mathcal{E}'$ is relevant iff $lub_{\leq_d}(\Lambda(\mathcal{E}')) \neq \bot$.*

The notion of minimality naturally extends to relevant connections (i.e. a *minimal relevant connection* is any connection $\mathcal{E}'$ such that $\forall e \in \mathcal{E}'$, $\mathcal{E}'/\{e\}$ is not a relevant connection). Let us consider the concrete and the abstract atoms, $p(t_1, ..., t_n)$ and $p(\mathcal{D}_p)$ respectively, where $\mathcal{D}_p = (\{1..n\}, \mathcal{V}_p, \mathcal{E}_p)$ and let $R \subseteq \{1, ..., n\}$ be the set of indexes such that $\forall i \in R$, $Var(t_i) = \emptyset$. We define a dependence representation associated with the unification process: $\mathcal{D}_{\alpha-mgu} = (\mathcal{N}_{\alpha-mgu}, \mathcal{V}_{\alpha-mgu}, \mathcal{E}_{\alpha-mgu})$ where

- $\mathcal{N}_{\alpha-mgu} = \{1, ..., n\} \cup Var(p(t_1, ..., t_n)) \cup \{\otimes_i \mid i \in R\}$,

- $\mathcal{V}_{\alpha-mgu} = \mathcal{V}_p \cup \{(\otimes_i, g) \mid \exists i \in \{1..n\} : Var(t_i) = \emptyset\} \cup \{(x, ng) \mid \exists x \in Var(t_1..t_n)\}$;

- $\mathcal{E}_{\alpha-mgu} = \mathcal{E}_p \cup \{\langle\{\otimes_i\}, i\rangle_\bot, \langle\{i\}, \otimes_i\rangle_\bot \mid \exists i \in \{1..n\} : Var(t_i) = \emptyset\} \cup$
  $\{\langle\{x_1, ..., x_k\}, i\rangle_\bot, \langle\{i\}, x_1\rangle_\bot, ..., \langle\{i\}, x_k\rangle_\bot \mid \exists i \in \{1..n\} : Var(t_i) = \{x_1, ..., x_k\}\}$.

The abstract unification process works on this dependence representation and consists of the following two steps:

1. *Ground information propagation*
   It is an iterative process on the hypergraph $\mathcal{G}_{\alpha-mgu} = (\mathcal{N}_{\alpha-mgu}, \mathcal{E}_{\alpha-mgu})$ which changes the labels in $\mathcal{V}_{\alpha-mgu}$. The process replaces any labelled node $(v, ng) \in \mathcal{V}_{\alpha-mgu}$ with (v, g) iff there exists a hyperarc $e \in \mathcal{E}_{\alpha-mgu}$ such that $Head(e) = v$ and $\forall v_i \in Tail(e): (v_i, g) \in \mathcal{V}_{\alpha-mgu}$ [1]. The process halts when no more labels can be changed.

2. *α-substitution definition*
   This process considers the transformed hypergraph and returns an abstract substitution $\vartheta^{\sharp} = (Var(t_1, ..., t_n), \mathcal{V}_{\vartheta}, \mathcal{E}_{\vartheta})$ such that
   $\mathcal{V}_{\vartheta} = \{(x, t^{\sharp}) \in \mathcal{V}_{\alpha-mgu} \mid x \in Var(t_1, ..., t_n)\}$,
   $\forall x_k \in Var(t_1, ..., t_n)$, $\langle T, x_k \rangle_l \in \mathcal{E}_{\vartheta}$ iff $\langle T, x_k \rangle_l$ is non-redundant in $\vartheta^{\sharp}$ and if $\bar{\mathcal{E}}$ is the set of minimal relevant connections from T to x_k, then $\bar{\mathcal{E}} \neq \emptyset$ and $l = glb_{\leq_d}\left\{ lub_{\leq_d}(\Lambda(\mathcal{E}')) \mid \mathcal{E}' \in \bar{\mathcal{E}} \right\}$.

The condition $lub_{\leq_d}(\Lambda(\pi)) \neq \perp$ avoids the introduction of irrelevant hyperarcs, labelled by $\perp$. As a matter of fact, we are only interested in those connections $\mathcal{E}'$ containing at least a hyperarc in $\mathcal{E}_p$. Notice that $\mathcal{D}_{\alpha-mgu}$ can be redundant.

(X, ng)
$\uparrow\perp$
Example 3.5 Let $\mathcal{D}_{\alpha-mgu} = (1, ng)$, and $\mathcal{E}_1' = \{\langle\{X\}, 1\rangle_{\perp}, \langle\{1\}, X\rangle_{\perp}, \langle\{1\}, 1\rangle_{?}\}$, $\mathcal{E}_2' = \{\langle\{X\}, 1\rangle_{\perp}, \langle\{1\}, X\rangle_{\perp}\}$. $\sqcup\uparrow_?$
Note that $\forall i = 1, 2: \{X\} \to_{\mathcal{D}_{\alpha-mgu}}^{\mathcal{E}_i'} X$, *but since* $\mathcal{E}_2'$ *contains only undefined* $(\perp)$ *hyperarcs, only* $\mathcal{E}_1'$ *is "relevant" in the unification process.*

Example 3.6 *The ground information propagation applied to the dependence representation associated with the abstract unification of* $p(f(X, Y), a)$ *and* $p(ng, ng)$ *is* $(\perp$ *labels are omitted):* $\sqcup\_\sqcup_?$

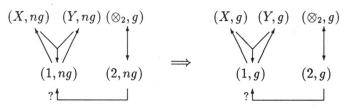

It is easy to extend the previous abstract unification algorithm to any n-tuple $(n \geq 1)$ of atoms, as shown in the following example.

Example 3.7 *Let us consider the abstract unification of the concrete and abstract atoms*

$$p(X, Y), q(Y, Z, W), r(Z, X) \text{ and } p(ng, ng), q(ng, ng, ng), r(ng, ng).$$

Since there exist shared variables between the concrete atoms $p(X,Y)$, $q(Y,Z,W)$, $r(Z,X)$, the unification hypergraph contains multiple connections between the corresponding variables and the abstract terms (the predicate symbol is subscripted in any corresponding argument position). The corresponding dependence representation is

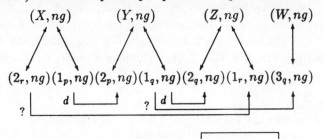

The resulting abstract substitution is: $(Z/ng, Y/ng, X/ng, W/ng)$.

Proposition 3.3 (α-*mgu monotonicity*)

Let A be an atom. Given a pair of abstract atoms $A^\natural$, $A'^\natural$ such that $\{A^\natural\} \leq_\alpha \{A'^\natural\}$, $\alpha\text{-}mgu(A, A^\natural) \leq_\Sigma \alpha\text{-}mgu(A, A'^\natural)$.

3.5 Substitution Application (α-apply)

In order to develop a deterministic ground dependence analysis we have to define the application of abstract substitutions (returned by the abstract unification process) to concrete atoms, i.e. $\alpha\text{-}apply : 2^{(B_P \times Subst^!_V)} \to \Xi^\natural$. Given a set of pairs of concrete atoms (having the same predicate symbol) and abstract substitutions, it returns an abstract atom which collects the deterministic ground information belonging to this set.

Let $S \in 2^{(B_P \times Subst^!_V)}$ such that $S \downarrow p = \{(p(t_{1_1}, ..., t_{1_n}), \vartheta^\natural_1), ..., (p(t_{m_1}, ..., t_{m_n}), \vartheta^\natural_m)\}$, and let $\mathcal{N}_{i_j} = \{x(j) \mid x \in Var(t_{i_j})\}$ be the set of variables in t_{i_j}, indexed according to the corresponding argument position.

For each pair $(p(t_{i_1}, ..., t_{i_n}), \vartheta^\natural_i)$ where $\vartheta^\natural_i = (\mathcal{N}_{\vartheta_i}, \mathcal{V}_{\vartheta_i}, \mathcal{E}_{\vartheta_i})$, we generate a dependence representation $\mathcal{D}_{\alpha-apply_i} = (\mathcal{N}_{\alpha-apply_i}, \mathcal{V}_{\alpha-apply_i}, \mathcal{E}_{\alpha-apply_i})$ such that:

- $\mathcal{N}_{\alpha-apply_i} = \mathcal{N}_{\vartheta_i} \cup (\bigcup_{j=1}^{n} \mathcal{N}_{i_j})$;

- $\mathcal{V}_{\alpha-apply_i} = \mathcal{V}_{\vartheta_i} \cup \{(x(j), ng) \mid \exists j = 1..n : x(j) \in \mathcal{N}_{i_j}\}$;

- $\mathcal{E}_{\alpha-apply_i} = \mathcal{E}_{\vartheta_i} \cup \{\langle\{x(j)\}, x\rangle_\perp, \langle\{x\}, x(j)\rangle_\perp \mid \exists(x, t^\natural) \in \mathcal{V}_{\vartheta_i}, \exists j = 1..n : x(j) \in \mathcal{N}_{i_j}\}$
  (if $\exists(x, t^\natural) \in \mathcal{V}_{\vartheta_i}$, $\exists j = 1..n : x(j) \in \mathcal{N}_{i_j}$, $x(j)$ is a *linked variable*).

Example 3.8 *The dependence representation associated with the pair*

$$(p(f(X,Y), Z, f(X,U)), (Z/ng, U/ng, Y/g))\ is:$$

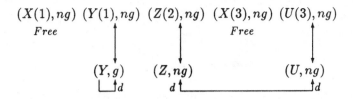

Let us consider a ground information propagation on $\mathcal{G}_{\alpha-apply_i} = (\mathcal{N}_{\alpha-apply_i}, \mathcal{E}_{\alpha-apply_i})$, $i = 1, ..., m$, which is analogous to the α-mgu case. We define

$$\alpha\text{-}apply(S) = \bigcup_{p \in Pred} \alpha\text{-}apply(S \downarrow p)$$

where $\alpha\text{-}apply(S \downarrow p) = \begin{cases} \emptyset & \text{if } S \downarrow p = \emptyset \\ p(\mathcal{D}_p) & \text{otherwise} \end{cases}$, such that $\mathcal{D}_p = (\{1..n\}, \mathcal{V}_p, \mathcal{E}_p)$ and

- $\forall (j, t_j^\sharp) \in \mathcal{V}_p : t_j^\sharp = \begin{cases} g & \text{iff} & \forall i = 1, ..., m : \mathcal{N}_{i_j} = \emptyset \\ & & \text{(the term was already ground)} \\ & & \text{or the nodes in } \mathcal{N}_{i_j} \text{ are labelled } g, \\ ng & \text{otherwise,} \end{cases}$

- $e = \langle \{r_1, ..., r_k\}, h \rangle_l \in \mathcal{E}_p$ iff e is non-redundant in $\mathcal{D}_p$ and for each $i = 1, ..., m$:

  - $Free(\mathcal{N}_{i_h}) \subseteq \bigcup_{u=r_1}^{r_k} Free(\mathcal{N}_{i_u})$, where $Free(\mathcal{N}_{i_j})$ is the set of variables x such that $x(j)$ is not linked with any node in the hypergraph $\mathcal{G}_{\alpha-apply_i}$;

  - for each linked node $y(h) \in \mathcal{N}_{i_h}$, there exists $T \subseteq \bigcup_{u=r_1}^{r_k} \mathcal{N}_{i_u}$ such that, if $\bar{\mathcal{E}}_{i_{y(h)}}^T$ is the set of minimal relevant connections from T to $y(h)$ in $\mathcal{G}_{\alpha-apply_i}$, then $\bar{\mathcal{E}}_{i_{y(h)}}^T \neq \emptyset$;

  - $l = \begin{cases} d & \text{iff } \forall z, f \in \{1, ..., m\}, z \neq f : mgu(t_{z_{r_1}}, ..., t_{z_{r_k}}, t_{f_{r_1}}, ..., t_{f_{r_k}}) = fail, \\ & \exists y(h) \in \mathcal{N}_{i_h}, \exists T \subseteq \bigcup_{u=r_1}^{r_k} \mathcal{N}_{i_u} : \bar{\mathcal{E}}_{i_{y(h)}}^T \neq \emptyset \wedge \\ & d = glb_{\leq_d} \left\{ lub_{\leq_d}(\Lambda(\mathcal{E}')) \mid \mathcal{E}' \in \bar{\mathcal{E}}_{i_{y(h)}}^T \right\}, \\ ? & \text{otherwise.} \end{cases}$

Example 3.9 *The following examples show the results of the application of the α-apply operator in some interesting cases:*

$S_1 = \{(p(X, Z), (\overset{d\lceil\quad\rceil}{X/ng, Z/ng})), (p(f(X), K), (\overset{d\lceil\quad\rceil}{X/ng, K/ng}))\}$, $\alpha\text{-}apply(S_1) =$

$\{ p(\overset{?\lceil\quad\rceil}{ng, ng}) \}$;

$S_2 = \{(p(f(X, Y), Z, f(X, U)), (\overset{\lceil\quad\rceil d\;\lceil\rceil d}{Z/ng, U/ng, Y/g})), (p(0, X, X), \emptyset)\}$, $\alpha\text{-}apply(S_2) =$

$\{ p(ng, ng, ng) \}$ *(see example 3.8).*

Let I be a finite set of atoms, and $S = I \times \{\emptyset\}$. By α-apply definition we have α-apply$(S) = abs(I)$.

Proposition 3.4 (α-apply monotonicity)
 Given two sets of pairs of concrete atoms (having the same predicate symbol) and abstract substitutions $\{(A_1, \vartheta_1^\sharp), ..., (A_k, \vartheta_k^\sharp)\}$ and $\{(A_1, \vartheta_1'^\sharp), ..., (A_k, \vartheta_k'^\sharp)\}$, such that $\forall i = 1, ..., k : \vartheta_i^\sharp \leq_\Sigma \vartheta_i'^\sharp$, it follows that

$$\alpha\text{-}apply(\{(A_i, \vartheta_i^\sharp) \mid i = 1, ..., k\}) \leq_\alpha \alpha\text{-}apply(\{(A_i, \vartheta_i'^\sharp) \mid i = 1, ..., k\}).$$

3.6 Abstract Interpretation

The approximation of the concrete fixpoint semantics is given in terms of the fixpoint of a finitely converging monotonic operator defined in terms of α-mgu and α-apply.

Definition 3.9 *Given a logic program P, let $I^\sharp$ be an interpretation. The abstract immediate consequence operator associated with the program P, $T_P^\sharp : \Xi^\sharp \to \Xi^\sharp$, is defined as follows*

$$T_P^\sharp(I^\sharp) = \alpha\text{-}apply(\left\{ (p(\bar{t}), \vartheta^\sharp) \,\middle|\, \begin{array}{l} \exists p(\bar{t}) : -B_1, ..., B_n \in P, \; \exists B_1'^\sharp, ..., B_n'^\sharp \in I^\sharp, \\ \vartheta^\sharp = \alpha - mgu(B_1, ..., B_n, B_1'^\sharp, ..., B_n'^\sharp), \\ \vartheta^\sharp \neq fail \end{array} \right\}).$$

The correctness of $T_P^\sharp$ $(abs(T_P(I)) \leq_\alpha T_P^\sharp(abs(I)))$ follows by the correctness of α-mgu and α-apply. Let $lfp(f)$ denote the least fixpoint of a given function f. Since the lattice $(\Xi^\sharp, \leq_\alpha)$ is finite, there exists a finite positive number k such that $\mathcal{F}^\sharp(P) = lfp(T_P^\sharp) = T_P^\sharp \uparrow k$.

Let us consider the concrete and the abstract operators

- $\mathcal{T}_P : 2^{(2^{B_P})} \to 2^{(2^{B_P})}$, such that $\mathcal{T}_P(D) = \{T_P(I) \mid I \in D\}$,

- $\mathcal{T}_P^\sharp : 2^{\Xi^\sharp} \to 2^{\Xi^\sharp}$ such that $\mathcal{T}_P^\sharp(D^\sharp) = \{T_P^\sharp(I^\sharp) \mid I^\sharp \in D^\sharp\}$.

It is easy to prove that for each logic program P, $\{\mathcal{F}(P)\}$ and $\{\mathcal{F}^\sharp(P)\}$ are fixpoints of $\mathcal{T}_P$ and $\mathcal{T}_P^\sharp$ respectively ($\mathcal{T}_P \uparrow \omega = \{\mathcal{F}(P)\}$ and $\mathcal{T}_P^\sharp \uparrow k = \{\mathcal{F}^\sharp(P)\}$). Thus, by $T_P^\sharp$ correctness: $\alpha(\mathcal{T}_P \uparrow \omega) \preceq_\alpha \mathcal{T}_P^\sharp \uparrow k$ (or equivalently [3] $\mathcal{T}_P \uparrow \omega \preceq \gamma(\mathcal{T}_P^\sharp \uparrow k)$).

4 Applications

In the following example [14] we show the overall analysis by describing the composition of the operators defined in Section 3. Consider the predicate r defined as follows

$$r(g(X), g(X)) : - .$$

$$r(f(X), g(Y)) : -r(Y, X).$$

Let us examine the behaviour of our analysis:

$$T_r^{\#^1}(\emptyset) = \alpha\text{-}apply(\{(r(g(X),g(X)),\emptyset)\}) = \{\; r(\overset{d}{ng},ng)\}.$$

In the first step, the abstract unification returns the pair $(r(g(X),g(X)),\emptyset)$ only. A ground dependence is detected between the first and the second argument and on the other way round by $\alpha\text{-}apply$. Since the argument of $\alpha\text{-}apply$ is a set of pairs including only one element, the resulting dependences are labelled as deterministic.

$$T_r^{\#^2}(\emptyset) = \alpha\text{-}apply(\{(r(g(X),g(X)),\emptyset),(r(f(X),g(Y)),(X/ng,Y/ng))\}) = \{\; r(\overset{d}{ng},ng)\}.$$

In the second step, $\alpha\text{-}apply$ considers two pairs: the one returned by the previous step and the one produced by the abstract unification of the abstract atom returned by the previous step with the concrete atom in the body of the non-unit clause of r. Since the second arguments of the concrete atoms in the pairs unify, this step returns a single deterministic dependence from the first argument to the second one.

$$T_r^{\#^3}(\emptyset) = \alpha\text{-}apply(\{(r(g(X),g(X)),\emptyset),(r(f(X),g(Y)),(X/ng,Y/ng))\}) = \{\; r(\overset{?}{ng},ng)\}.$$

The third step (fixpoint) detects that the dependence between the first and the second argument is a non-deterministic one. As in the previous steps, the first two arguments do not unify, but, since no deterministic dependence exists between the abstract terms associated with the variables X and Y, no deterministic dependence is returned. Let us consider the program

$sumlist([],0) : -.$

$sumlist([X|Xs],S) : -sumlist(Xs,Ss),plus(X,Ss,S).$

$select(X,[X|Xs],Xs) : -.$

$select(X,[Y|Ys],[Y|Zs]) : -select(X,Ys,Zs).$

$check(X,Y) : -select(Y,X,R),sumlist(X,Y).$

The predicate $sumlist(X,Y)$ is such that Y is the sum of the elements of the list X. The predicate $plus$ is assumed to be a predefined one. The dependences of $plus$ relevant for the analysis are a deterministic one from the first and the second argument to the third one and a non-deterministic one from the third argument to the first and the second, respectively. The list X includes relative numbers. The predicate $select(X,L_1,L_2)$ is such that L_2 is the list L_1 where exactly one occurrence of X has been removed. The predicate $check(X,Y)$ is such that Y is an element E of the list X and E is equal to the sum of the elements of X. The dependences detected by the analysis of $sumlist$ and of $select$ may be easily deduced from the declarative meaning of the predicates (only some dependences of $sumlist$ and $select$ are shown):

$$sumlist(ng,ng) \qquad select(ng,ng,ng).$$

The dependences of *sumlist* and *select* are propagated, through abstract unification, to the body of *check*. In the hypergraph built by abstract unification, the variable Y is the target of two paths. Both of them have the variable X as source node, but only one is labelled by d. In this case, a deterministic dependence between the variables X and Y is returned. Therefore, there exists a deterministic dependence between the first and the second argument of *check*. As a matter of fact, since the sum of the elements in the list is uniquely determined, all the elements selected from the list are equivalent, hence the dependence may be considered as a deterministic one. The analysis infers deterministic dependences among arguments rather than determinacy of whole predicates. Let us consider the following modified version of predicate check:

$$check(X, Y, R) : -select(Y, X, R), sumlist(X, Y).$$

In this case also a non-deterministic dependence is detected between the first argument and the third one. As a matter of fact, if a list includes several elements equal to its sum, distinct lists are returned even by removing the same element.

$$check(ng, ng), \quad check(ng, ng, ng).$$

The two former examples show that our analysis can return deterministic dependences not detected by previous analyses. In particular, the last example shows the importance of defining deterministic dependences among arguments rather than for the whole predicate.

Let us finally consider the classical example:

$$append([], X, X) : -.$$

$$append([X|Xs], Y, [X|Ys]) : -append(Xs, Y, Ys).$$

The analysis detects the following dependences: $append(ng, ng, ng)$ (see Example 3.8 and 3.9).

5 Conclusions

Our analysis of determinate computations extends previous proposals in several directions. The ground dependence notion, introduced in the database framework [11], has been extended in order to handle recursive clauses. Hence, the analysis returns significative results not only in the case of database programming, but also in other cases, such as programs manipulating recursive data structures. We recall that determinacy is inferred with respect to arguments rather than to whole predicates. This means that a ground instance of a set of arguments may uniquely determine another set of arguments of a predicate, while producing multiple bindings for other arguments. With respect to [14], our proposal can detect both ground and ground deterministic dependences in a single step, and requires no knowledge of the types of the predicates nor of the activating modes of a predicate. Our abstract interpretation can be easily integrated with further analyses, such as depth-k [13], type and general functional ones. By pairing our analysis with a term structure one (e.g. depth-k), dependences among subterms may be detected. Furthermore, it is possible to relax the ground dependences condition in order to obtain a more general analysis of functional dependences.

References

[1] R. Barbuti, R. Giacobazzi, and G. Levi. A General Framework for Semantics-based Bottom-up Abstract Interpretation of Logic Programs. Technical Report TR 12/91, Dipartimento di Informatica, Università di Pisa, 1991. To appear in *ACM Transactions on Programming Languages and Systems.*

[2] C. Berge. *Graphs and Hypergraphs.* North-Holland, 1973.

[3] P. Cousot and R. Cousot. Abstract Interpretation: A Unified Lattice Model for Static Analysis of Programs by Construction or Approximation of Fixpoints. In *Proc. Fourth ACM Symp. Principles of Programming Languages*, pages 238–252, 1977.

[4] S. Debray and D.S. Warren. Functional Computations in Logic Programs. *ACM Transactions on Programming Languages and Systems*, 11-3:451–481, 1989.

[5] B. Demoen, P. VanRoy, and Y.D. Willems. Improving the Execution Speed of Compiled Prolog with Modes, Clause Selection and Determinism. In H. Ehrig, R. Kowalski, G. Levi, and U. Montanari, editors, *Proc. TAPSOFT 1987*, volume 250 of *Lecture Notes in Computer Science*, pages 111–125. Springer-Verlag, Berlin, 1987.

[6] P. Deransart and J. Maluszynski. Relating Logic Programs and Attribute Grammars. *Journal of Logic Programming*, 2:119–156, 1985.

[7] M. Falaschi, G. Levi, M. Martelli, and C. Palamidessi. Declarative Modeling of the Operational Behavior of Logic Languages. *Theoretical Computer Science*, 69(3):289–318, 1989.

[8] R. Giacobazzi and L. Ricci. Pipeline Optimizations in AND-Parallelism by Abstract Interpretation. In D. H. D. Warren and P. Szeredi, editors, *Proc. Seventh Int'l Conf. on Logic Programming*, pages 291–305. The MIT Press, Cambridge, Mass., 1990.

[9] J. W. Lloyd. *Foundations of Logic Programming.* Springer-Verlag, Berlin, 1987. Second edition.

[10] M.J. Maher and R. Ramakrishnan. Dèjà Vu in Fixpoints of Logic Programs. In E. Lusk and R. Overbeck, editors, *Proc. North American Conf. on Logic Programming'89*, pages 963–980. The MIT Press, Cambridge, Mass., 1989.

[11] A.O. Mendelzon. Functional Dependencies in Logic Programs. In *Proc. of the Eleventh International Conference on Very Large Data Bases*, pages 324–330, 1985.

[12] L. Ricci. *Compilation of Logic Programs for Massively Parallel Systems.* PhD thesis, Universitá di Pisa, Feb. 1990. T.D. 3-90.

[13] T. Sato and H. Tamaki. Enumeration of Success Patterns in Logic Programs. *Theoretical Computer Science*, 34:227–240, 1984.

[14] J. Zobel and P. Dart. On Logic Programs, Functional Dependencies, and Types. Technical report, University of Melbourne, 1990.

ELIOS-OBJ
Theorem proving
in a specification language

I. Gnaedig
INRIA Lorraine - CRIN
Technopôle de Nancy-Brabois - BP 101
54600 Villers-lès-Nancy
France
E-mail: gnaedig@loria.fr

Abstract

In the context of the executable specification language *OBJ3*, an order-sorted completion procedure is implemented, providing automatically convergent specifications from user-given ones. This feature is of first importance to ensure unambiguity and termination of the rewriting execution process. We describe here how we specified a modular completion design in terms of inference rules and control language, using *OBJ3* itself. On another hand, the specific problems encountered to integrate a completion process in an already reduction-oriented environment are pointed out.

1 Introduction

OBJ3 is a programming language based on equational logic: programs are given in terms of abstract data types and their semantics relies on order sorted algebras, which enables inclusion of types. The problem approached here is the correctness of axiom sets, in the following sense. The operational semantics of *OBJ3* is rewriting, which means that when a program is executed on a given value, the set of axioms is interpreted and used as a set of rewrite rules that reduces the value to its normal form. We have to establish whether computations are correct with respect to validity in initial models, whether results are unique and - last but not least - whether computation always terminates.

The completion process of a rewrite rule set is able to ensure the previous requirements. Starting from any axiom set, it provides, when it succeeds (this is a semi-decidable problem), an equivalent set of rules with the same deduction power, confluent (the result of rewriting an expression does not depend of the way the rules are applied: it is unambiguous), and terminating (there is no infinite rewrite chain). Hence, it can be seen as an automatic prover of program correctness. We intend here to design and implement an integrated programming environment, named *ELIOS-OBJ*, allowing programming and proving in the same context.

Our goal here has three aspects: to provide the user with a tool for proving correctness of specifications in the context of *OBJ3*, namely with an order-sorted semantics; to propose an implementation of order-sorted completion described and proved in [6]; and to point out some problems arising in integrating theorem proving aspects (completion here) with programming aspects (the *OBJ3* language).

We describe completion in a high-level formalism allowing modularity and general expressiveness, using inference rules. This approach, first presented for completion in [1], has also be implemented in [13]. A control language is proposed, to combine these inference rules in any kind of strategy. In this formalism, completion can be considered as a particular instance of general deduction mechanisms, described by inference rules and control, as equational proofs, inductive proofs, equation solving by unification, disunification... The specification of our implementation is given in *OBJ3* itself.

The main definitions and the algebraic context are given in Section 2. Section 3 recalls results on order sorted completion established in [5, 6], expressed in terms of inference rules and control. Section 4 describes the control language for expressing and implementing different completion strategies. Section 5 presents the features of the orientation engine, transforming axioms into rules. Section 6 presents an investigation towards the integration of a theorem prover into a programming context. It points out the technical problems encountered in implementing completion in *OBJ3*. They are mainly due to the fact that features for an efficient rewrite engine (as integrated in *OBJ3*) are not necessarily compatible with completion mechanisms. Some examples of completion in *ELIOS-OBJ* are given and illustrated in Section 7.

2 Order-Sorted Algebra

In this section the basic notions about order-sorted algebras are shortly summarized [7].

Given an index set S, an S-sorted set A is just a family of sets, one for each $s \in S$; we will write $\{A_s | s \in S\}$. Similarly, given two S-sorted sets A and B, an S-sorted function $\alpha : A \to B$ is an S-indexed family $\alpha = \{\alpha_s : A_s \to B_s | s \in S\}$. Assume a fixed partially ordered set $(S, \leq)$, called the **sort set**.

An **order-sorted signature** is a triple $(S, \leq, \Sigma)$ where S is a sort set, Σ is an $S^* \times S$ -indexed family $\{\Sigma_{w,s} | w \in S^*, s \in S\}$, and $(S, \leq)$ is a partially ordered set. Elements of Σ are called operators. When the sort set S is clear, we write Σ for (S, Σ). Similarly, when the partially ordered set $(S, \leq)$ is clear, we write Σ for $(S, \leq, \Sigma)$. For operators, we write $f : w \to s$ for $f \in \Sigma_{w,s}$. We say that the rank of f is $w \to s$. An important special case is when w is λ, the empty string; then $f \in \Sigma_{\lambda,s}$ denotes a constant of sort s. Note that the ordering $\leq$ on S extends to strings of the same length in S^* by $s_1...s_n \leq s'_1...s'_n$ iff $s_i \leq s'_i$ for $i = 1, ..., n$; similarly, $\leq$ extends to pairs $(w, s) \in S^* \times S$ by $(w, s) \leq (w', s')$ iff $w \leq w'$ and $s \leq s'$.

Let $(S, \leq, \Sigma)$ be an order-sorted signature. A $(S, \leq, \Sigma)$-**algebra** A consists of a family $\{A_s | s \in S\}$ of subsets of A, called the **carriers** of A, and a function $f_A : A_w \to A_s$ for each $f \in \Sigma_{w,s}$ where $A_w = A_{s_1} \times ... \times A_{s_n}$ when $w = s_1...s_n$ and A_w is a one point set when $w = \lambda$, such that:

1. $s \leq s'$ in S implies $A_s \subseteq A_{s'}$ and

2. $f \in \Sigma_{w,s} \cap \Sigma_{w',s'}$ with $s' \leq s$ and $w' \leq w$ implies $f_A : A_w \to A_s$ equals $f_A : A_{w'} \to A_{s'}$ on $A_{w'}$.

Following [7], we define the order-sorted Σ-term algebra $\mathcal{T}_\Sigma$ as the least family $\{\mathcal{T}_{\Sigma,s} | s \in S\}$ of sets satisfying the following conditions:

- $\Sigma_{\lambda,s} \subseteq \mathcal{T}_{\Sigma,s}$ for $s \in S$;

- $\mathcal{T}_{\Sigma,s'} \subseteq \mathcal{T}_{\Sigma,s}$ if $s' \leq s$;

- if $f \in \Sigma_{w,s}$ with $w = s_1...s_n \neq \lambda$ and if $t_i \in \mathcal{T}_{\Sigma,s_i}$ then (the string) $f(t_1...t_n) \in \mathcal{T}_{\Sigma,s}$.

- for $f \in \Sigma_{w,s}$, let $T_f : T_w \to T_s$ map $t_1, ..., t_n$ to (the string) $f(t_1...t_n)$.

Following [9], we denote by $\mathcal{D}(t)$ the set of occurrences of t i.e. the domain of the term t viewed as a partial function from $\mathcal{N}^*$ to Σ. We denote by $t_{|\omega}$ the subterm of t at occurrence ω and by $t[\omega \leftarrow t']$ the result of the replacement by t' of $t_{|\omega}$ for $\omega \in \mathcal{D}(t)$. Clearly T_Σ is an order-sorted Σ-algebra.

We restrict to the class of regular signatures. Essentially, regularity asserts that overloaded operations are consistent under restriction to subsorts, so that each well-formed expression on the function symbols has a least sort. An order-sorted signature Σ is **regular** iff for any $w_0 \in S^*$ such that there is a $f \in \Sigma_{w,s}$ with $w_0 \leq w$, then there is a least $(w', s') \in S^* \times S$ such that $f \in \Sigma_{w',s'}$ and $w_0 \leq w'$. Under that condition, T_Σ is an initial order-sorted Σ-algebra [7]. In this case, for any $t \in T_\Sigma$, there is a least $s \in S$, called **lowest sort** of t and denoted $LS(t)$.

2.1 Equations and rewrite rules

An S-**sorted variable set** is an S-indexed family $X = \{X_s | s \in S\}$ of disjoint sets. A variable x of sort s is also denoted $(x : s)$. Given an order-sorted signature $(S, \leq, \Sigma)$ and a variable set X that is disjoint from Σ, $(S, \leq, \Sigma(X))$ is defined by $\Sigma(X)_{\lambda,s} = \Sigma_{\lambda,s} \cup X_s$ and $\Sigma(X)_{w,s} = \Sigma_{w,s}$ for $w \neq \lambda$.

Note that if Σ is regular, so is $\Sigma(X)$. We can now form $T_{\Sigma(X)}$ and then view it as a Σ-algebra; let us denote this Σ-algebra by $T_\Sigma(X)$. It is the **free** Σ-algebra generated by X. $\mathcal{V}(t)$ denotes the set of variables of the term t.

To get an adequate notion of satisfaction (see [11]), an additional hypothesis on the set of sorts S must be satisfied: An order-sorted signature $(S, \leq, \Sigma)$ is **coherent** iff each of the connected components of S for $\leq$ (i.e. each equivalence class under the transitive symmetric closure of $\leq$) has a maximum, and Σ is regular. We will only consider here order-sorted signatures that are coherent.

A Σ-**equation** is a triple (X, t, t') where X is a variable set and $t, t' \in T_\Sigma(X)$ with $LS(t)$ and $LS(t')$ in the same connected component of $(S, \leq)$. We will use the notation $((\forall X)t = t')$.

2.2 Order-sorted rewriting

For $(S, \leq, \Sigma)$ a coherent order-sorted signature and X, Y two S-sorted variable sets, a **substitution** is an S-sorted function $\sigma : X \to T_\Sigma(Y)$, extended in a unique way to $\sigma : T_\Sigma(X) \to T_\Sigma(Y)$.

Operationally, order-sorted equations are used as rewrite rules. An order-sorted **rewrite rule** is an order-sorted equation $((\forall X)l = r)$ satisfying $\mathcal{V}(r) \subseteq \mathcal{V}(l)$ and denoted $((\forall X)l \to r)$. A **match** from a term $t \in T_\Sigma(X)$ to a term $t' \in T_\Sigma(Y)$ is a substitution σ such that $\sigma(t) = t'$.

Let R be a set of rewrite rules. A term $t \in T_\Sigma(Y)$ rewrites to t' with a rewrite rule $((\forall X)l \to r)$ in R at occurrence ω, which is denoted $t \to_Y^R t' = t[\omega \leftarrow \sigma(r)]$ whenever

1. there is a match $\sigma : X \to T_\Sigma(Y)$ from l to t at occurrence ω $(\sigma(l) = t_{|\omega})$

2. there is a sort s such that, for x a variable of sort s, $t[\omega \leftarrow x]$ is a well-formed term and $\sigma(l), \sigma(r) \in T_{\Sigma,s}(Y)$.

The difficulty is that $\sigma(l)$ and $\sigma(r)$ may have different sorts, and the second condition in the previous definition is needed to avoid that replacements produce ill-formed terms.

We define $\xrightarrow{*}_Y^R$ to be the reflexive transitive closure of $\to_Y^R$ and $\longleftrightarrow *_Y^R$ to be its symmetric, reflexive and transitive closure. This last equivalence relation is called **order-sorted replacement of equals by equals**. For the notion of *order-sorted* replacement of equals by equals to be correct and complete with respect to order-sorted deduction, the rewriting relation has to be confluent and sort-decreasing [11].

An order-sorted term rewriting system R is **sort-decreasing** iff $\forall t, t' \in T_\Sigma(Y)$, $t \to_Y^R t'$ implies $LS(t) \geq LS(t')$.

In order to give decidable criteria for this property to hold, we need the notion of specialization. A sorted set of variables X can be viewed as a pair $(\bar{X}, \mu)$ where $\bar{X}$ is a set of variable names (i.e. unsorted variables) and μ, the sort assignment, maps the variable names to the set of sorts $\mu : \bar{X} \to S$. The ordering $\leq$ on S is extended to sort assignments by

$$\mu \leq \mu' \Leftrightarrow \forall x \in \bar{X}, \mu(x) \leq \mu'(x)$$

We then say that μ' **specializes** to μ via the substitution $\rho : (x : \mu'(x)) \to (x : \mu(x))$ called a **specialization** of $X = (\bar{X}, \mu')$ into $\rho(X) = (\bar{X}, \mu)$.

The notion is then extended to equations and rewrite rules. A specialization of an equation $(\forall X)(l = r)$ is another equation $(\forall \rho(X))(\rho(l) = \rho(r))$ where ρ is a specialization of X. A specialization of a rule $(\forall X)(l \to r)$ is the rule $(\forall \rho(X))(\rho(l) \to \rho(r))$ where ρ is a specialization of X.

If the set of sorts is finite, or if each sort has only a finite number of sorts below it, a finite sorted set of variables has a finite number of specializations. This allows deciding the sort-decreasing property. A set of rules R is **sort-decreasing** iff any rule of R is **sort-decreasing**, that is iff for any rule $((\forall X)l \to r)$ of R, for any specialization ρ of X, the lowest sort of $\rho(l)$ is greater or equal than the lowest sort of $\rho(r)$. An order-sorted term rewriting system R is sort-decreasing if R is a sort-decreasing set of rules.

The definitions R being **confluent** are similar to the unsorted case. Let R be an order-sorted term rewriting system. R is **confluent** iff for any terms $t, t', t'' \in T_\Sigma(Y)$, $t \overset{R}{\longrightarrow}_Y t'$ and $t \overset{R}{\longrightarrow}_Y t''$ implies there exists t_0 such that $t' \overset{*}{\underset{R}{\longrightarrow}}_Y t_0$ and $t'' \overset{*}{\underset{R}{\longrightarrow}}_Y t_0$. R is **Church-Rosser** iff for any terms $t, t' \in T_\Sigma(Y)$, $t \leftrightarrow \overset{*}{\underset{R}{}}_Y t'$ implies there exists t_0 such that $t \overset{*}{\underset{R}{\longrightarrow}}_Y t_0$ and $t' \overset{*}{\underset{R}{\longrightarrow}}_Y t_0$.

When the variable set Y can be deduced from the context, we allow it to be omitted and we write $t \longrightarrow^R t'$ for $t \longrightarrow_Y^R t'$.

2.3 Critical pairs

Two reductions applied to a same term can sometimes overlap, yielding critical pairs. Let $\mathcal{G}(t)$ be the set of occurrences ω in t such that the subterm of t at occurrence ω is not a variable. A unifier of two terms t and t' is a substitution σ such that $\sigma t = \sigma t'$.

A non-variable term t' and a term t **overlap** at occurrence ω in $\mathcal{G}(t)$ with a substitution σ iff σ is a unifier of $t_{|\omega}$ and t'.

Given two rules $g \to d$ and $l \to r$ such that $\mathcal{V}(g) \cap \mathcal{V}(l) = \emptyset$ and l and g overlap at occurrence ω of $\mathcal{G}(g)$ with the substitution σ, then the pair $(p = \sigma(g[\omega \leftarrow r]), q = \sigma(d))$ is called a **critical pair** of the rule $l \to r$ on the rule $g \to d$ at occurrence ω (a trivial one if $\omega = \epsilon, l = g, r = d$).

3 Completion in order sorted algebras

In [6] we describe the completion process in order-sorted algebras by a set of inference rules. Although [6] presents results on equational completion, we implement here completion in the empty theory. This more simple process enables us to focus on interaction and interface between the completion and the language, instead of problems specific to completion.

Recall that an ordering on terms is compatible (with the term structure) if $s \succ t$ implies $f(...s...) \succ f(...t...)$, for all terms s, t and all contexts $f(......)$ such that $f(...s...)$ and $f(...t...)$

are well-formed. A reduction ordering is a well-founded and compatible ordering. A reduction ordering warrants termination of a rewriting system R, if $\sigma l \succ \sigma r$ for each rule $l \to r$ of R, and every substitution σ [2].

Let P be a set of equations and $\succ$ a reduction ordering. As pointed out previously, the signature of the algebra, P is defined on, has to be coherent. The *completion procedure* transforms, if possible, P into a confluent and terminating set of rules R, having the same deduction power. This transformation can be described by a derivation chain of the form $(P^0, R^0) \vdash (P^1, R^1)... \vdash (P^n, R^n)... \vdash (P^\infty, R^\infty)$ (that may be constant from a given rank n). The completion transformation is based on the well known basic mechanisms: orienting an axiom of P into a terminating and sort-decreasing rule, adding equational consequences named critical pairs, and reducing the left-hand-side and the right-hand-side of axioms and rules. Order-sorted completion can be expressed by the following inference rules:

1. Orienting an equation
$$\frac{P \cup \{s = t\}, R}{P, R \cup \{s \to t\}} \quad \text{if } s \succ t \ \& \ s \to t \text{ sort} - \text{decreasing}$$

2. Adding a critical pair
$$\frac{P, R}{P \cup \{s = t\}, R} \quad \text{if } u \to^R s \ \& \ u \to^R t$$

3. Simplifying an equation
$$\frac{P \cup \{s = t\}, R}{P \cup \{u = t\}, R} \quad \text{if } s \to^R u$$

4. Deleting an equation
$$\frac{P \cup \{s = s\}, R}{P, R}$$

5. Simplifying the right-hand side of a rule
$$\frac{P, R \cup \{s \to t\}}{P, R \cup \{s \to u\}} \quad \text{if } t \to^R u$$

6. Simplifying the left-hand side of a rule
$$\frac{P, R \cup \{s \to t\}}{P \cup \{u = t\}, R} \quad \text{if } s \to^R_{l \to r} u \ \& \ s \rhd l$$

where $\rhd$ is the proper specialization ordering , defined by $s \rhd l$ iff $\exists \sigma, \sigma(l) = s_{|\omega}$ with $\omega \neq \epsilon$, or $\sigma(l) = s$ and σ is not a renaming.

With respect to the completion procedure for unsorted rewriting described in [1], the modifications for the order-sorted completion are localized in the conditions of the first inference rule, where the sort-decreasing test for a new rule must be performed. Remark that the sort-decreasing test in the rule 5 is not needed since $s \to t$ and $t \to u$ sort-decreasing implies $s \to u$ sort-decreasing (by definition of a sort-decreasing rule and by transitivity of the ordering $\leq$ on sorts).

Furthermore, except for the sort-decreasing test, it appears that the specific sort problems are hidden in the definition of rewriting and critical pairs: order-sorted matching, order-sorted unification.

4 Specifying control for completion

The concept of inference rules previously chosen for describing the theoretical aspects of completion, will be completed by a control mechanism on these inference rules, to give particular completion procedures. Control specifies the order in which inference rules are applied. As required in [6], the control has to be fair, which means that all critical pairs of the resulting set of rules R^∞ have to be computed, and the resulting set of pairs P^∞ has to be empty. If the completion is fair and does not fail, then R^∞ is Church-Rosser and sort-decreasing.

Here is developed a simple control language, aimed at expressing any "combination" of inference rules and at providing effective completion procedures. Note that this control language is general enough to be applied on any activity described with inference rules (and on any working universe named UNIVERSE); it is not specific to completion since it doesn't depend on the inference rules themselves.

The language used for describing control is *OBJ3* itself. So, we attempt in the same time to test expressiveness of *OBJ3* for describing an already complex problem. The effective implementation is made in Kyoto Common Lisp, like *OBJ3*.

Let us start from the definition of the specific completion universe. The working domain COMP-UNIVERSE is a pair of sets: the set P of axioms to be oriented and the set R of current rules generated by completion.

Note that the subsort mechanism of *OBJ3* allows an elegant "error-handling" feature used here when completion fails on a given universe: we just have to define a sort *Comp-universe-with-failure* including the sort *Comp-universe*. Hence, when finishing with success, the completion procedure gives a pair (E, R) of sort *Comp-universe*. When instead failing, it returns an error result of sort *Comp-universe-with-failure*. The modules BOOL, PAIR, PAIRS and RULES used in the following specify respectively the booleans, a pair, a set of pairs and a set of rules. They are not detailed here.

```
obj COMP-UNIVERSE is

protecting  PAIRS, RULES .
sorts Comp-universe Comp-universe-with-failure .
subsorts Comp-universe < Comp-universe-with-failure .
op <_,_> : Pairs Rules -> Comp-universe .
op P : Comp-universe -> Pairs .
op R : Comp-universe -> Rules .
var p : Pairs .
var r : Rules .

eq P(<p,r>) = p .
eq R(<p,r>) = r .

jbo
```

The *protecting* feature is a mechanism for importing modules in *OBJ3* (to become familiar with the *OBJ3* syntax, read [8]).

Let us now define strategies by a control on inference rules. The completion can then be seen as the application of a chosen strategy (available for instance in a strategy library) on a completion universe. This is a simple way to describe concisely a completion strategy, looking it as independent of the data structures (axioms and rules), it is working on. In other words, the strategy (specified in STRAT-COMP) is a constant with respect to the completion universe U, as specified below:

```
obj COMPLETION is

protecting STRAT-COMP .
protecting COMP-UNIVERSE .
op completion : Comp-universe Strat-comp -> Comp-universe .
var U : Comp-universe .
var s : Strat-comp .

eq : completion(U,s) = apply(s,U) .

jbo
```

We now have to define how the *apply* operation works on a strategy and a universe, introducing here our control language on inference rules. It is expressed in the module STRAT by the classical basic instructions of imperative programming languages: a test *if-then-else*, a loop *while-do*, a sequence operator *concat*, an iterator *iter*. This module is parametrized by the modules TE, expressing the notion of test, IT, expressing the notion of iterator, and INF, defining inference rules written $< U, U', C >$.

```
obj STRAT[TE : TEST, IT : ITERATOR, INF : INFERENCE-RULE] is

protecting UNIVERSE BOOL .
sort Strategy .
op empty-strategy : -> Strategy .
op while_do_ : Test Strategy -> Strategy .
op if-then-else : Bool Strategy Strategy -> Strategy .
op apply : Strategy Universe -> Universe .
op _concat_ : Strategy Strategy -> Strategy .
op iter : Strategy Iterator -> Strategy .
vars C : Bool .
vars S S' : Strategy .
vars U U' : Universe .
var I : Iterator .
var B : Test .

eq apply(empty-strategy, U) = U .

eq apply(<U,U',C>) = if C then U' else U .

eq apply(while B do S,U) = if test-apply(B, U)
                              then apply(while B do S,
                                         apply(S,U))
                              else U .

eq apply((if-then-else(B,S,S'),U) = if test-apply(B, U)
                                       then apply(S,U)
                                       else apply(S',U) .
```

```
eq apply((S concat S'),U) = apply(S',apply(S,U)) .

eq apply(iter(S, I), U) = if iter-apply(I, U) diff error
                          then apply(iter(S, I),
                                       iter-apply(I, apply(S, U)))
                          else U .
jbo .
```

The operation *apply* is itself defined through more specific operations: *test-apply* and *iter-apply*, working respectively on tests and iterators defined in the following two specifications, for the completion case.

```
obj COMP-TEST is

Protecting COMP-UNIVERSE, BOOL, PAIRS, PAIR, RULES .
Sort Comp-Test .
op non-empty-set-of-pairs : -> Comp-Test .
op is-trivial-pair : -> Comp-Test .
op orientable-pair : -> Comp-Test .
op non-empty-critical-pairs : -> Comp-Test .
op test-apply : Comp-Test Comp-Universe -> Bool .
var U : Comp-universe .

eq test-apply(non-empty-set-of-pairs, U) = non-empty(P(U)) .
eq test-apply(is-trivial-pair, U) = is-trivial(current(P(U))) .
eq test-apply(orientable-pair, U) = is-orientable(current(P(U)))
eq test-apply(non-empty-critical-pairs, U) = non-empty(critical-pairs(R(U))) .

jbo .

obj COMP-ITERATOR is

Protecting COMP-UNIVERSE PAIRS RULES .
Sort Comp-Iterator .
op for-each-pair : -> Comp-Iterator .
op for-each-rule : -> Comp-Iterator .
op iter-apply : Comp-Iterator Comp-Universe -> Comp-Universe .
var U : Comp-universe .

eq iter-apply(for-each-pair, U) = <increment-on-set((P(U)), R(U)> .
eq iter-apply(for-each-rule, U) = <P(U), increment-on-set(R(U))> .

jbo .
```

Note that the operations used to define *test-apply* and *iter-apply* are working at lower level than the previous ones, and on data structures, that we will not specify here: *non-empty* is a test of non-emptyness of a set, *current* gives the current element of a set, *is-trivial* and *is-orientable* are working on a pair of terms, *increment-on-set* manages the access to elements of a set, and *critical-pairs* gives the critical pairs of a set of rules.

Then the specification of a strategy for completion can be designed, using the the module STRAT instantiated by the parameters COMP-TEST, COMP-ITERATOR and COMP-INFERENCE-RULE.

The last parameter COMP-INFERENCE-RULE defines inference rules for completion, adapted from those of Section 3: *normalize-lhs-pair, normalize-rhs-pair, delete-pair, orient-pair-l-to-r, orient-pair-r-to-l, normalize-rhs-rule, simplify-lhs-rule, failure-inf-rule, add-critical-pairs.*

Remark that, in order to be used in an operational way, the first inference rule *orienting an equation* has been splitted in *orient-pair-l-to-r* and *orient-pair-r-to-l*, the third rule *simplifying an equation* has been splitted in *normalize-lhs-pair* and *normalize-rhs-pair*. Note also that the orientation failure case is handled by a new inference rule: *failure-inf-rule*.

```
obj STRAT-COMP

Protecting STRAT[COMP-TEST, COMP-ITERATOR, COMP-INFERENCE-RULE] .
Sort Strat-comp .
op strat-simple : -> Strat-comp .

eq strat-simple = while non-empty-critical-pairs do

                while non-empty-set-of-pairs do
                 normalize-lhs-pair concat
                 normalize-rhs-pair concat
                if is-trivial-pair
                then   delete-pair
                else if orientable-pair
                        then   orient-pair-l-to-r concat
                               orient-pair-r-to-l concat
                               iter( normalize-rhs-rule concat
                                       simplify-lhs-rule,
                                   for-each-rule)
                        else   failure-inf-rule
                        endif
                endif
                end while concat
                add-critical-pairs

                end while .

jbo .
```

5 The orientation engine

The test *orientable-pair* includes the complete mechanism for orienting an axiom in order sorted completion, depending on two criteria. First, the axiom has to be oriented in a sort-decreasing way. Second, it has to be oriented according to some reduction ordering, to ensure termination of the computed rewrite system.

A decidable criterion for sort-decreasingness is given through the notion of specialization (see Section 2). For implementing the sort-decreasing test, the rule specialization computing algorithm, already existing in *OBJ3* for defining the rewrite engine [8], is used.

To handle the termination problem, an usual simplification ordering is chosen: the left-to-right lexicographical path ordering (*LPO* in short) [10]. This ordering is based on a basic ordering on the set F of symbols of the signature: the precedence (denoted by $>_F$). In our system, like in *REVE* [12, 3], the precedence is empty when the completion starts, and incrementally enriched by interaction of the user, as new rules are oriented.

Termination of rewriting in an order sorted algebra can be proved without considering the sort information of operators and terms in the algebra. If a rewriting relation terminates in the homogeneous algebra, then it terminates in the corresponding order sorted algebra. Therefore, the *LPO* is used, where the precedence, namely the ordering on operators, does not take into account the sort information on operators, i.e. their rank. Let us give an example.

```
obj  PRECEDENCE is
sorts Nat Int .
subsorts Nat < Int .
op _+_ : Nat Nat -> Nat .
op _+_ : Int Int -> Int .
op - : Int -> Int .
vars x y : Nat .
eq -(x + y) = (-x) + (-y) .
eq -(-(x + y)) = x + y .
jbo
```

Let us try to orient both axioms into rewrite rules. For ensuring termination, we have to prove $-(x + y) >_{LPO} (-x) + (-y)$. Let us note, the top symbol of the right hand side is "$+ : Int\ Int \to Int$". The unequality is true if we assume $- >_F +$. We do not precise in the precedence, what "+" of the signature, we are handling with. That means that "$-$" is greater than any "+" of the signature. For the second axiom to be oriented, the previous precedence hypothesis can then be used, although the "+" operator is "$+ : Nat\ Nat \to Nat$" in both sides of the axiom.

The choice made in our orientation engine is to treat sort-decreasingness, before termination. If an axiom is not sort-decreasing, the user can reverse it or orient it by hand (in this last case, correction of rewriting is not warranted, see Section 2). If however a given axiom is not orientable for the current *LPO*, he can backtrack for chosing another precedence, before trying to reverse it. The structure of our orientation engine, hidden in the test *orientable-pair* (already presented in the STRAT-COMP module) looks like:

```
obj ORIENTATION-ENGINE is

Protecting PAIR .
op orientable-pair : Pair -> Bool .
op orientable-pair-l-to-r : Pair -> Bool .
op orientable-pair-r-to-l : Pair -> Bool .
Var p : Pair .

eq orientable-pair (p) = if orientable-pair-l-to-r (p)
                         then true
                         else if orientable-pair-r-to-l (p)
                              then true
                              else false .
```

```
eq orientable-pair-l-to-r (p) = if sort-decreasing (p)
                                 then if is-LPO-oriented (p)
                                      then true
                                      else false
                                 else false .

eq orientable-pair-r-to-l (p) = orientable-pair-l-to-r (reverse(p)) .

jbo
```

where the *reverse* operation transforms an equality $g = d$ into its symmetrical equality $d = g$, and *is-LPO-oriented* is the orientation test using the *LPO*.

This algorithm is used interactively, each time a pair can be oriented into a rule. But the orientation can also be "forced" "by hand", or the pair can be postponed in the current set of axioms, or simply completion can be interrupted and the original set of axioms restored.

6 The technical problems of integrating completion in OBJ3

The goal of our work was to develop an order-sorted completion algorithm interfaced with *OBJ*3. In order to rewrite a minimum amount of code and to have an integrated design of completion in the language, we wanted to reuse already existing tools like the matching algorithm, the rewrite engine, the specialization algorithm. For a given *OBJ* specification, we have also chosen to perform completion on the internal *OBJ*3 form of the axiom set obtained after compilation of the given specification. Completion works directly on the same structures as the rewrite engine; it modifies them to give directly the compiled *OBJ* module, corresponding to the completed set of axioms.

Recall that one goal of this work was to discover and solve the problems of integrating a theorem prover in a programming language interpreter. As known, execution of programs and theorem proving have very different requirements and the design of the first is not easily compatible with the requirements of the second.

For instance, an operation like reduction of terms is used in two different ways, first in the reduction process of the *OBJ* language, where it requires efficiency for applying the rules, second in the simplification mechanism of the completion procedure, where instead it requires efficiency for updating the set of rules. The problems encountered during the integration of a completion procedure in *OBJ3* are now enumerated, and the proposed choices and compromises are explained.

6.1 Adapting *OBJ3* specifications to completion context

OBJ3 provides a mechanism of *order-sorted conditional rewriting*. Until now, however, order-sorted completion only works on unconditional rules. A filter has been implemented, for transforming conditional specifications into unconditional ones, by discarding conditional axioms, before a completion is started on an *OBJ* module.

OBJ3 allows *manipulating booleans*, in any user-defined module, adding implicitly an importation of an *OBJ* predefined module for booleans containing associative-commutative operators like and, or, xor (exclusive or) [8]. Since our completion doesn't handle associative-commutative axioms, and since this predefined module is already complete, we suppress this systematic importation. Instead, booleans are explicitly imported by the user, only if desired.

Let us also take into account the general *importation mechanism*. For the evaluation of a term in an *OBJ3* module, all axioms of all recursively imported modules are used for rewriting. Let us give an *OBJ3* example.

```
obj NAT_S is
sort Nat_s .
op 0 : -> Nat_s .
op s : Nat_s -> Nat_s .
var x, y : Nat_s .
eq  0 + x = x .                          (1)
eq  s(x) + y = s(x + y) .                (2)
jbo


obj FIBO_S is
protecting NAT_S .
op _+_ : Nat_s Nat_s -> Nat_s .
op fib : Nat_s -> Nat_s .
var x, y : Nat_s .
eq  fib(0) = 0 .                         (3)
eq  fib(s(0)) = s(0) .                   (4)
eq  fib(s(s(x))) = (fib(x) + fib(s(x))) . (5)
jbo
```

In the previous specification, the definition of the Fibonacci function is built on the integers defined in NAT_S. So the rewrite mechanism of *OBJ3* uses the axioms of NAT_S (interpreted as rules) in addition to those of FIBO_S, to reduce terms of FIBO_S. For example, the term $fib(0 + 0)$ defined in FIBO_S is reduced in $fib(0)$ using (1), before $fib(0)$ is reduced in 0 using (3).

The first possible alternative for completion would be to collect recursively all imported axioms, adding them to those of the current module, and completing the resulting set. This process causes problems with respect to the design of *OBJ3*. Any rule is attached to the module, in which the top operator of left hand side has been declared. Provided new rules may appear during completion, the question is to which module they must be attached. Theorem proving would be involved to prove that the definitions of modules are not changed. Moreover, this mechanism of putting together all the imported axioms for completion would be a contradiction to the modularity of *OBJ3*. Our completion procedure thus applies on axioms of a module in a modular way, without considering the eventually imported rules.

This fact emphasizes the difficulties for integrating a proof mechanism in a modular programming language, and suggests to investigate a theory of modular proofs in the completion context, related to the problem of preserving properties of rewrite systems when considering their union. Results have already been given for confluence and termination of the direct sum of two rewrite systems, that is the union of two rewrite systems having disjoint sets of function symbols. In particular, it is shown in [15] that two term rewriting systems are left-linear, confluent and terminating if and only if the direct sum of these systems is so. Let us also cite a work concerning termination [14], and a work concerning confluence and termination in the case of sorted rewrite systems [4].

6.2   Completion and the static *OBJ3* rewrite engine

The first problem was *to dynamically update the set of rules in the rewrite engine of* OBJ3 during the completion. Two solutions were possible: to write a new rewriting procedure independent of *OBJ*, for ensuring reduction in completion, or to use the already existing engine of *OBJ*. The second way was chosen for reusability and integration reasons. But the *OBJ* rewrite engine is very close to the set of reducing rules itself. Let us present its mechanism. For efficiency reasons, rules are specialized [11], and then installed in different data structures: for any operator f appearing as top in a left-hand-side of rule is attached:

- a rule-ring for the rules which top of right-hand-side is also f (the "top-respecting" rules)

- a rule set for other rules whose top of left-hand-side is f.

Then the procedures for rewriting or normalizing a term strongly interact with this structure. Installing such a reduction engine is quite expensive. But note that in *OBJ*, since axioms of a module are interpreted as rewrite rules, the rewrite engine is installed once for all, at compiling time. The problem is different with completion since the set of rules changes dynamically. The rewrite engine has then to be redefined each time the set of rules has to be used (by applying inference rules for rewriting), after it has changed. This is the part of the "rule generation" process, inserted between inference rules in the completion strategy, as follows:

```
eq strat-simple = while non-empty-critical-pairs do

                while non-empty-set-of-pairs do
                normalize-lhs-pair concat
                normalize-rhs-pair concat
                if is-trivial-pair
                then delete-pair
                else if orientable-pair
                    then orient-pair-l-to-r concat
                        orient-pair-r-to-l concat
                        rule-generation
                        iter(normalize-rhs-rule concat
                            simplify-lhs-rule concat
                            rule-generation,
                            for-each-rule)
                    else failure-inf-rule
                    endif
                endif
                end while concat
                add-critical-pairs

                end while .
```

The second problem is also related to the rewriting process. Several *features for improving the reduction* of a term to its normal form were integrated in *OBJ3*. The first one is concerned with the *rewriting strategy assigned to operators*. For example, a strategy *[2 1 0]* given to the operator f means that any term whose top is f will be normalized successively at the occurrences 2, 1 and 0. This strategy is given by the user, in defining the operators. By default, an algorithm computes a strategy for operators during the compilation of modules. It is clear that a term with f as top operator is not reducible at the top f if f is not the top of a left hand side of rule. *OBJ3* then assigns to such operators a rewriting strategy where the occurrence 0 never appears.

Then the matching test for rewriting terms at an f occurrence is avoided. Provided completion can orient axioms in the right hand side direction, terms with f on top can become reducible, and the previous $OBJ3$ feature leads the rewriting strategy to be incomplete. The completeness of computations was restored by adding the *[0]* occurrence to any operator strategy.

The second optimizing feature of rewriting in $OBJ3$ consists in *marking the terms in normal form*, for avoiding to try to reduce them in further computations. Again, since completion dynamically changes the set of rules R, a normal form at a given step of completion can become reducible further. The solution chosen here is to update the "normal form mark" of terms, by deleting it each time R is modified.

All the previous features for improving efficiency of rewriting in *OBJ3* lie on the fact that the set of rules is not considered as evolving. The solution for a further prototype of such an integrated programming environment could be the design of two different rewrite engines: one flexible and dynamic with respect to the rewrite rules (for completion), the other one designed for efficiency of rewriting and used only when executing programs (installed after completion for example).

7 Examples of completion in ELIOS-OBJ

We now give examples of completion in *ELIOS-OBJ*. An $OBJ3$ program specifying the predicate *is-even* on integers is given. Then a completion is performed on this program to give an equivalent one, warranted to be terminating and unambiguous for any data. We also illustrate on this example that an interreduced set of rules can lead to a more efficient execution. For obtaining the same result, the program is executed on the data $is - even(p(p(0)))$ in 5 steps before completion, instead of 1 after.

```
tarsky.loria.fr% cat even.obj

obj EVEN is

  sorts Zero NzNeg Neg NzPos Pos Int Boolean .
  subsorts Zero < Neg < Int .
  subsorts Zero < Pos < Int .
  subsorts NzNeg < Neg .
  subsorts NzPos < Pos .

  op 0 : -> Zero .
  op s : Pos -> NzPos .
  op p : Neg -> NzNeg .
  op true : -> Boolean .
  op false : -> Boolean .
  op is-even : Int -> Boolean .
  op opposite : NzNeg -> NzPos .

  var x : Pos .
  var y : NzNeg .

  eq is-even (0) = true .
  eq is-even (s(0)) = false .
```

```
 eq is-even (s(s(x))) = is-even (x) .
 eq is-even (y) = is-even (opposite(y)) .
 eq opposite (p(0)) = s(0) .
 eq opposite (p(y)) = s (opposite(y)) .

jbo


tarsky.loria.fr% elios-obj

        ********************************************************
        Welcome to ELIOS-OBJ, a sympathetic OBJ with completion
        ********************************************************
        ***********************************
                ******************

                Copyright 1988 SRI International
                Copyright 1991 I. Gnaedig - INRIA Lorraine & CRIN

        To have the list of available commands, do: 'help', 'h' or '?'


ELIOS-OBJ> in ex/even
==========================================
obj EVEN


ELIOS-OBJ> reduce is-even(p(p(0))) .
reduce in EVEN : is-even(p(p(0)))
rewrites: 5
result Boolean: true

ELIOS-OBJ> complete EVEN .

        The starting equations for completion are those
        of the current module:
"EVEN"

Only UNCONDITIONAL equations are retained. They are:

is-even(0) = true
is-even(s(0)) = false
is-even(s(s(x:Pos))) = is-even(x:Pos)
is-even(y:NzNeg) = is-even(opposite(y:NzNeg))
opposite(p(0)) = s(0)
opposite(p(y:NzNeg)) = s(opposite(y:NzNeg))


.../...
```

The complete set of rules is:

```
is-even(0) -> true
is-even(s(0)) -> false
is-even(s(s(v1:Pos))) -> is-even(v1:Pos)
is-even(opposite(v2:NzNeg)) -> is-even(v2:NzNeg)
opposite(p(0)) -> s(0)
opposite(p(v3:NzNeg)) -> s(opposite(v3:NzNeg))
is-even(p(0)) -> false
is-even(s(opposite(v7:NzNeg))) -> is-even(p(v7:NzNeg))
is-even(p(p(0))) -> true
is-even(p(p(v9:NzNeg))) -> is-even(v9:NzNeg)
```

```
ELIOS-OBJ> reduce is-even(p(p(0))) .
reduce in EVEN : is-even(p(p(0)))
rewrites: 1
result Boolean: true
ELIOS-OBJ>
```

A second example is given below. It specifies an addition on integers, themselves described in terms of successors of zero and opposites of successors of zero.

```
tarsky.loria.fr% cat addition.obj

obj ADDITION is

  sorts Zero NzNat Nat Int .
  subsorts Zero < Nat .
  subsorts NzNat < Nat .
  subsorts Nat < Int .

  op 0 : -> Zero .
  op s : Nat -> NzNat .
  op _+_ : Nat Nat -> Nat .
  op _+_ : Int Int -> Int .
  op - _ : Int -> Int .

  vars x y : Nat .

  eq 0 + x = x .
  eq x + 0 = x .
  eq x + s(y) = s(x + y) .
  eq s(x) + y = s(x + y) .
  eq - - x = x .
  eq - 0 = 0 .
  eq (- x) + (- y) = - (x + y) .
  eq s(x) + (- s(y)) = x + (- y) .
  eq - s(x) + s(y) = - x + y .

jbo
```

```
ELIOS-OBJ> in ex/addition
=============================================
obj ADDITION


ELIOS-OBJ> complete ADDITION .

...\...

The complete set of rules is:

0 + v1:Nat -> v1:Nat
v2:Nat + 0 -> v2:Nat
v3:Nat + s(v4:Nat) -> s(v3:Nat + v4:Nat)
s(v5:Nat) + v6:Nat -> s(v5:Nat + v6:Nat)
- (- v7:Nat) -> v7:Nat
- 0 -> 0
- v8:Nat + - v9:Nat -> - (v8:Nat + v9:Nat)
s(v10:Nat) + - s(v11:Nat) -> v10:Nat + - v11:Nat
- s(v12:Nat) + s(v13:Nat) -> - v12:Nat + v13:Nat
0 + - v27:Nat -> - v27:Nat
- v28:Nat + 0 -> - v28:Nat
```

Acknowledgments

We would like to thank Claude and Hélène Kirchner for fruitful discussions concerning the design of completion in $OBJ3$, and Pierre Lescanne for carefully reading previous versions of this paper.

References

[1] L. Bachmair and N. Dershowitz. Completion for rewriting modulo a congruence. In *Proceedings 2nd Conference on Rewriting Techniques and Applications, Bordeaux (France)*, volume 256 of *Lecture Notes in Computer Science*, pages 192–203, Bordeaux (France), May 1987. Springer-Verlag.

[2] N. Dershowitz. Termination of rewriting. *Journal of Symbolic Computation*, 3(1 & 2):69–116, 1987.

[3] R. Forgaard and J. Guttag. Reve: A term rewriting system generator with failure-resistant Knuth-Bendix. Technical report, MIT-LCS, 1984.

[4] H. Ganzinger and R. Giegerich. A note on termination in combinations of heterogeneous term rewriting systems. *Bulletin of European Association for Theoretical Computer Science*, 31, February 1987.

[5] I. Gnaedig, C. Kirchner, and H. Kirchner. Equational completion in order-sorted algebras. In M. Dauchet and M. Nivat, editors, *Proceedings of the 13th Colloquium on Trees in Algebra and Programming*, volume 299 of *Lecture Notes in Computer Science*, pages 165–184. Springer-Verlag, 1988.

[6] I. Gnaedig, C. Kirchner, and H. Kirchner. Equational completion in order-sorted algebras. *Theoretical Computer Science*, 72:169–202, 1990.

[7] J.A. Goguen and J. Meseguer. Order-sorted algebra I: Partial and overloaded operations, errors and inheritance. Technical report, SRI International, Computer Science Lab, 1988. Given as lecture at a Seminar on Types, Carnegie-Mellon University, June 1983.

[8] J.A. Goguen and T. Winkler. Introducing OBJ3. Technical Report SRI-CSL-88-9, SRI International, 333, Ravenswood Ave., Menlo Park, CA 94025, August 1988.

[9] G. Huet and D. Oppen. Equations and rewrite rules: A survey. In R.V. Book, editor, *Formal Language Theory: Perspectives and Open Problems*, pages 349–405. Academic Press, New York, 1980.

[10] S. Kamin and J.-J. Lévy. Attempts for generalizing the recursive path ordering. *Inria, Rocquencourt*, 1982.

[11] C. Kirchner, H. Kirchner, and J. Meseguer. Operational semantics of OBJ-3. In *Proceedings of 15th International Colloquium on Automata, Languages and Programming*, volume 317 of *Lecture Notes in Computer Science*, pages 287–301. Springer-Verlag, 1988.

[12] P. Lescanne. Computer experiments with the REVE term rewriting systems generator. In *Proceedings of 10th ACM Symposium on Principles of Programming Languages*, pages 99–108. Association for Computing Machinery, 1983.

[13] P. Lescanne. Implementation of completion by transition rules + control: ORME. In H. Kirchner and W. Wechler, editors, *Proceedings 2nd International Workshop on Algebraic and Logic Programming, Nancy (France)*, volume 463 of *Lecture Notes in Computer Science*, pages 262–269. Springer-Verlag, 1990.

[14] M. Rusinowitch. On termination of the direct sum of term rewriting systems. *Information Processing Letters*, 26(2):65–70, 1987.

[15] Y. Toyama, J.W. Klop, and H.P. Barendregt. Termination for the direct sum of left-linear term rewriting systems. In N. Dershowitz, editor, *Proceedings 3rd Conference on Rewriting Techniques and Applications, Chapel Hill (North Carolina, USA)*, volume 355 of *Lecture Notes in Computer Science*, pages 477–491. Springer-Verlag, April 1989.

Incremental Garbage Collection Without Tags

Benjamin Goldberg

Department of Computer Science
Courant Institute of Mathematical Sciences
New York University[1]

Abstract

Garbage collection algorithms that do not require tagging of data have been around since the early days of LISP. With the emergence of strongly-typed languages that require heap allocation, interest in tag-free garbage collection has increased. Several papers published recently describe methods for performing tag-free copying garbage collection by retaining compile-time type information at run time. However, all of these algorithms have the "stop and collect" property, in which program execution is suspended for a significant amount of time during garbage collection. For many programs an incremental garbage collection method, in which the garbage collection overhead is spread evenly throughout the computation, is desirable.

Methods for incremental copying garbage collection have been around since the 1970's. However, these algorithms (the most notable of which is Baker's algorithm) rely on tagged data. In this paper, we present a method for performing incremental copying garbage collection without tags. We then extend this method to work for polymorphically typed languages, and to provide breadth-first copying for improved performance and data locality.

1. Introduction

Copying garbage collectors have been around for a long time, and have traditionally been used for LISP systems. These algorithms typically rely on tagged data to determine the correct handling of each heap allocated structure. In dynamically typed languages like LISP, type tags are required by the run-time type checker and can also be used by the garbage collector.

With the advent of a number of strongly typed languages, such as ML [MLH90], that utilize heap storage, run-time type tags are used solely for the purpose of garbage collection. The overhead required to maintain tagged data can be significant for the following reasons:

- Extra space is often necessary to store the type tag for a datum.
- If a few bits of an integer or pointer are used for the tag, this reduces the size of number that can be represented (leading to more bignums, if supported), reduces the accessible address space, or forces word-alignment on byte-addressable machines.
- Before arithmetic operations or pointer dereferences can occur, the type tags must be stripped from the operands and reinstated in the result.

Recently, several papers [Appel89][Goldberg91] described copying garbage collectors that do

---

1. Author's address: 251 Mercer Street, New York, NY 10012, USA. Email: goldberg@cs.nyu.edu. This research has been supported, in part, by the National Science Foundation (#CCR-8909634) and DARPA (DARPA/ONR #N00014-91-J1472).

not require tagged data. However, these methods, like most copying collectors, have the stop-and-collect property in which the execution of the user program may be suspended for a long period of time during garbage collection. This is usually unacceptable for real-time programs.

A copying collector for LISP that does not exhibit the stop-and-copy behavior was described in [Baker78]. The algorithm is *incremental*, that is, the garbage collection process occurs frequently throughout execution, but only copies a few structures at a time. Thus, the user-program is suspended for very short periods of time. However, the incremental garbage collector relies heavily on the use of LISP's run-time type tags.

In this paper, we describe a garbage collection method for strongly typed languages that is both incremental and tag-free. We then extend the algorithm so that it copies in a breadth-first manner, similar to LISP copying collectors, for improved performance and locality. Finally, we describe an incremental, tag-free garbage collection algorithm for polymorphically typed languages like Standard ML.

1.1. Related Work

There are two areas of work related to this paper. The first is the area of incremental copying garbage collection, which is itself based on the more general topic of copying garbage collection. The second area is tag-free garbage collection. Both of these topics have been studied for many years, but, up until now, there have been no incremental tag-free garbage collectors.

1.1.1 Copying Garbage Collection

Algorithms for copying garbage collection are well known and we will spend little time discussing them. The basic idea is that there are two heaps, typically called TO space and FROM space. At any time during execution of the user program only FROM space is in use. When FROM space is exhausted, all the structures (e.g. cons cells in LISP) that can be accessed by the user program are copied into TO space. Exactly which cells are accessible by the user program is determined by a search (either depth-first, breadth-first, or a combination of the two) starting from all locations that correspond to variable names in the program. During the copying phase, the user program is suspended. When the user program resumes executing, the heaps will have been flipped – TO space has become FROM space and vice-versa.

One of the advantages of a copying collector over the simple mark-and-sweep collector is that free storage is compacted. This makes storage allocation very inexpensive, and is accomplished by simply incrementing a pointer (called the heap pointer) that points to the beginning of free space. The disadvantage is, of course, that two heaps are required. There are many varieties of copying collectors, and they are surveyed in [Cohen81] and [Rudalics88].

1.1.2 Incremental Copying Garbage Collection

In 1978, Baker [Baker78] described a method (generally referred to as "Baker's Algorithm") for performing incremental copying garbage collection in LISP implementations. Like the basic copying collector, there are two heaps. However, at any given time both spaces may contain live data structures. New cells are allocated in TO space, and each time a cell is allocated by the **cons** operation a few cells are copied from FROM space to TO space as well. Since only a few cells are copied at a time, program execution is never suspended for very long. Eventually, all reachable (i.e. user-accessible) cells in FROM space will have been copied into TO space. At that point the heaps can be flipped.

It will be helpful for our discussion to think of incremental garbage collection as a process that suspends and resumes many times during execution, and can run only for short periods. Of course, the cost of suspension and resumption must be very low.

To understand Baker's algorithm, three questions need to be answered:

Q1. How can one guarantee that the meaning of the program is not changed by the incremental movement of cells?

Q2. How are the appropriate cells in FROM space found in order to be copied each time?

Q3. How can one guarantee that when TO space is exhausted, all the reachable cells in FROM space have been copied to TO space and the heaps can be flipped?

The details can be found in [Baker78]. We will describe as much of Baker's algorithm as is necessary to provide a basis for understanding our method.

Two facets of Baker's algorithm (and the serial and concurrent collection algorithms that Baker based his work on, such as [Steele75], [DLMSS75], [Lamport75], [FY69], [Minsky63] and [Cheney70]) answer question Q1:

- As the contents of each cons cell is copied into TO space, the old cell is overwritten with the new address of the cell in TO space. In other words, when a cell is copied, a forwarding address is left behind.

- When a cons cell in FROM space is referenced, a check is made to determine if the cell has been copied to TO space. If so, its forwarding address is followed to find the correct cell. A forwarding address is always recognizable, because its type tag indicates that it is a pointer and no ordinary pointer in FROM space can point to TO space. In addition, whenever a cell is accessed via a `car` or `cdr` operation, it is also copied into TO space.

Thus, any access to a cons cell will return the same result whether or not the cell has been copied. For this reason, the use of this incremental garbage collection method will not change the meaning of a program.

To answer question Q2, let us assume a stack-based implementation, in which variables in an activation record may point into the heap. The garbage collector must be sure to copy all the cons cells reachable from variables in the stack. Thus by the time the heaps are ready to be flipped, the following cells must have been copied into TO space:

- All cells in FROM space pointed to by variables in the stack, and
- All cells in FROM space pointed to by cells in TO space.

So, each time the garbage collector is invoked (i.e. at every call to `cons`) it copies a few cells in FROM space referenced from the stack, and a few cells in FROM space referenced by cells in TO space.

The method, illustrated in figure 1, is as follows:

- There is an extra pointer, called SS, into the stack. It points to the topmost activation record which could possibly contain pointers into FROM space. Each time the heaps are flipped, SS is reset to point to the top of the stack. At that time all pointers in the stack point to FROM space. When garbage collection occurs, the activation record that SS points to is traversed and the cells that its variables point to are copied into TO space. The variables in that activation record are updated with the new addresses in TO space. When all the variables in the activation record have been updated, SS is decremented to point to the activation record below. In addition, if the activation record that SS points to is popped off the stack, then SS is decremented.

- When SS reaches the bottom of the stack, all the variables in the stack point to TO space. In order to guarantee this, whenever a new activation record is created (and it must be above SS), all variables in the activation record must point into TO space. Therefore, any cell passed as a parameter to the activation record must first be moved to TO space.

- An extra pointer into TO space, called S, is used. It points to the oldest cell in TO space that could possibly contain a pointer into FROM space. That is, it must point to the oldest cell that was copied from FROM space but whose children have not been copied. Only those cells in TO space between S and the heap pointer (where new cells are allocated) could possibly point into FROM space.

- Each time the garbage collector is invoked, the `car` and `cdr` fields of the cell that S points to are examined to see if they contain pointers into FROM space. In order to do this, their type tags must be checked (to distinguish pointers from integers). If they do point into FROM space, then the cells that they point to are copied into TO space (if they haven't been already) and the pointers are updated. S is then incremented to point to the next cell in TO space. When S reaches the heap pointer, none of the cells in TO space can point into FROM space.

- When SS reaches the bottom of the stack and S has reached the heap pointer, then all reachable cells have been copied into TO space and all reachable pointers point into TO space. At any time after this, the heaps can safely be flipped.

Figure 1 shows how the stack and TO space are logically partitioned by SS and S. It illustrates a simplified version of Baker's algorithm since, in the actual method, new cells are allocated in a different portion of TO space than copied cells.

Baker's algorithm copies list structures in a *breadth-first* manner. The first cell of the list is copied into TO space. When S points to that cell, it's children are copied into TO space, and so on. This has implications for data locality, which can affect cache and paging performance, since adjacent cells in a list occupy adjacent locations in the heap.

If TO space is exhausted before SS reaches the bottom of the stack or before S reaches the heap pointer, then execution cannot continue. This may have happened for one of two reasons: Either the data accessible by the user program is greater than the size of each heap, or the incre-

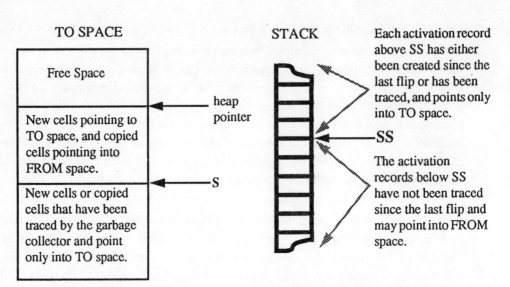

Figure 1. Stack and TO space organization in Baker's algorithm (simplified).

mental collection algorithm did not copy enough cells from FROM space to TO space. The first problem, of course, cannot be solved by the system. The second problem, though, corresponds to question Q3 listed previously.

The solution is to be sure that each time the garbage collector is invoked, a sufficient number of cells are copied to guarantee that they will all be copied by the time TO space is exhausted. However, if too many cells are copied each time, there will be too long a delay for real-time programs. In Baker's method, the garbage collector is invoked at each call to **cons** and copies k cells into TO space. Baker's analysis (based partly on [Wadler76] and [Muller76]) is as follows: Assume that when the spaces are flipped, there are N accessible cells in FROM space. In order to guarantee that all N cells can be copied into TO space before TO space is exhausted, it must be the case that

$$k \geq \frac{N}{H - N}$$

where H is the size of each heap. Put another way, if it is required that the program be interrupted for no longer than the time to copy k cells, for some k, then the size H of each heap must satisfy:

$$H \geq N (1 + \frac{1}{k})$$

This assumes that the number N of accessible cells stays relatively constant during execution. This situation is called an equilibrium condition, because old cells are discarded at the rate that new cells are created.

Since the garbage collector must also traverse the stack, each time the collector is invoked during a **cons** operation it must also trace k′ locations in the stack, where the ratio k′/k is the same as the ratio of the number of variables in the stack to the number of cells in use. The value of k′ can be recomputed at each flip. See [Baker78] for details.

1.2. Garbage Collection without Tags

The fundamental idea behind tag-free garbage collection is that compile-time type information is retained at run-time, but is not retained in the form of type tags. When the garbage collector traverses a data structure, it must be able to find the type information for that structure. How that type information is found, and how it is represented, differs in previously published algorithms.

In 1970, Branquart and Lewi [BL70] described two tag-free garbage collection algorithms for Algol68. The first, called the *interpretive method*, associates a template with each type that describes the structure of variables of that type. As the garbage collector traverses a data structure, it also traverses the corresponding template to determine the appropriate actions. The second method, called the *compiled method*, associates a garbage collection routine (which we shall refer to as a gc_routine) with each type in the user program. The gc_routine is executed when the garbage collector encounters a variable of the corresponding type. These garbage collection routines are produced by the compiler based on the types defined in the user's program.

Both methods described by Branquart and Lewi rely on a run-time table mapping stack locations representing local variables to type templates (interpretive method) or garbage collection routines (compiled method). This table must be updated whenever a new local variable is created. As the garbage collector traverses the stack, it looks in the table to find the type template or garbage collection routine for each variable. Because Algol68 discourages heap allocation of structures bound to local variables, the table seldom needs to be updated. Type templates or garbage collection routines can be associated directly with global variables, since their location is fixed during the computation.

In 1975, Diane Britton [Britton75] extended both the interpretive and compiled methods for Pascal. Instead of a table mapping locations to type templates or garbage collection routines, each activation record in the stack contains an extra pointer to a template or garbage collection routine corresponding to all the variables in the activation record.

In 1989 Peyton Jones and Salkid [PJS89] described a garbage collection scheme for their tagless graph reduction abstract machine. Because they implement a lazy language, each data structure is contained in a closure (that may represent an unevaluated value). The closure contains a pointer to a table of appropriate routines for the closure, including the garbage collection routines. It is not clear how this method would be adapted for strict languages like Standard ML.

Also in1989, Andrew Appel [Appel89] outlined an interpretive method in which the template describing the variables in each activation record is accessed via the return pointer stored in the activation record. The beauty of this method is that no run-time overhead is incurred during normal execution. The only overhead occurs during the garbage collection process itself. Appel also suggested how tag-free garbage collection could be extended for polymorphically typed languages.

In 1991, we [Goldberg91] described a compiled method that, like Appel's method, used the return pointer of an activation record to find the garbage collection routine to trace the variables in the activation record. We then described how common program analyses, like live variable analysis, can optimize the garbage collection process by not copying reachable structures that will not subsequently be referenced.

Details of a tag-free garbage collection algorithm using the compiled method for a monomorphically typed language can be found in [Goldberg91]. For our purposes here, it is sufficient to describe it as follows:

- For each function f in the program, the compiler generates a garbage collection routine, or *gc_routine* for short, for tracing the variables in an activation record for f. Actually, since the number and types of variables in the activation record may differ at different points of execution of the body of f, several gc_routines are generated – one for each function call in f during which garbage collection could occur. Garbage collection can only occur during a function call, since the only way to allocate heap space is by calling a primitive function such as **cons**.

- In the code for f, the address of a gc_routine is associated with each call instruction (at some offset within the code segment). Thus the appropriate gc_routine for an activation record for f can be found by examining the return address of the next activation record on the stack.

- If a variable in f's activation record is bound to a closure representing some function g, the type of g will not necessarily reflect the types of the variables stored in the closure. Therefore, associated with the code for g (pointed to by the closure's code pointer) is a gc_routine for tracing the variables in the closure. This gc_routine is found at some offset from the start of g's code.

- When the garbage collector encounters an activation record for f, it simply calls the gc_routine associated with the current call instruction in f's code.

In a copying collector, whenever a cell is copied a forwarding address must be left behind. Since pointers are not tagged, how can a forwarding address be distinguished from an integer with the same value? The answer relies on knowing the type of the cell. If it is a cons cell, then in a strongly typed language the **cdr** field of the cell must contain a pointer. Thus, the forwarding address is placed in the **cdr** field, and if the **cdr** of a cons cell contains a pointer into TO space, then it must be a forwarding address.

In all of the tag-free collection algorithms, the garbage collector is invoked when the current space is exhausted, and runs until it has finished copying all reachable heap-allocated structures into the other space. To be incremental, Baker's algorithm relies on tracing the fields of cells already copied into TO space. Since the tag-free collection algorithms trace only from the stack, it is not obvious how they can be made incremental. This is the problem that we have solved.

2. Making Tag-Free Garbage Collection Incremental

In order to make our tag-free garbage collection incremental, the following conditions must be satisfied:

- The type information for a heap allocated structure must be available to the garbage collector when the structure is being traced.
- After an incremental collection, memory must be in a consistent state. That is, the value of all reachable structures must remain the same. Furthermore, it must be apparent whether a cell in FROM space has been copied into TO space and, if so, what the address of the new cell in TO space is.
- When TO space is full, all reachable structures in the FROM space must have been copied to the TO space. Thus, the spaces can safely be flipped.

Baker's algorithm satisfies the last two conditions, and the correctness of our method rests on the correctness of Baker's algorithm. However, Baker's algorithm relies on the ability to trace the children (`car` and `cdr` in the LISP case) of the cells that have already been copied into the TO space. The tags of the cells in TO space and the tags of their children are examined to determine how to copy the children. This is not possible in a tag-free garbage collector.

We now describe the incremental version of our tag-free garbage collector. Like Baker, we use a pointer, SS, that, at all times, points to the topmost activation record in the stack that could possibly contain pointers into FROM space (see the description of its use in section 1.1.2). Whenever a new activation record is created (above SS), all cells passed as parameters are first copied to TO space. Thus, the new activation record cannot contain pointers into FROM space. When the spaces are flipped, the SS register is modified to point to the top of the stack. After the flip, all the variables that had previously pointed to the TO space now point to the FROM space.

Instead of tracing from the cells that have just been copied to TO space as in Baker's algorithm, our method must always trace from the variables in activation records on the stack, since the type information is only associated with each activation record. However, the number k of cells to be copied by the collector each time may be less than the number of cells comprising the variables of the activation record that SS points to. Thus, it might be necessary for a gc_routine to suspend after k cells have been copied. This routine will have to resume during the next collection.

Of primary concern is how a suspended gc_routine for an activation record is represented. A gc_routine for an activation record simply calls the appropriate gc_routine for each variable in the activation record. Since an activation record's gc_routine is non-recursive, its state can simply be represented by a closure containing the address of the next instruction to execute and its local variables. The only gc_routine for an activation record that could possibly be suspended is the one for the activation record that SS points to. Thus, a single closure is sufficient to represent the suspended state of the garbage collection process and can be stored in some special area of memory (i.e. not in the heap). The maximum storage needed to represent a suspended gc_routine is known at compile-time and can be allocated in advance.

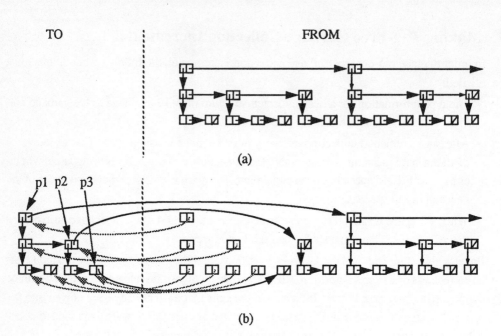

Figure 2. A partially copied list

We must consider the gc_routines that correspond to the types of the variables in each activation record. Since k may be less than the number of cells in a single structure, the gc_routine for a given structure may itself have to be suspended. Since the strongly typed languages that we are interested in, like Standard ML, support lists and user-defined recursive data types, we must be certain that a suspended gc_routine can be represented in a small amount of space, independent of the size of the structure.

For the moment, we will use a monomorphically typed version of Standard ML as the target language. The primary predefined data structure is the list. If the gc_routine for a list is suspended, information must be saved describing where in the list the tracing should resume. This information consists of m pointers, where m is the depth of the list (i.e. number of hd operations that can be applied to the list before returning a non-list value). The depth of each list is defined by its type and is fixed throughout the computation. The ith pointer points into TO space to the last cell at depth i in the list that was copied before the gc_routine was suspended. Figure 2 shows a list of depth three that has been partially copied to TO space and the three pointers, labeled p1, p2, and p3, representing the state of the list. The grey arrows represent the forwarding address pointers. When the gc_routine tracing the list resumes, it simply starts tracing at the cells referenced by p1, p2, and p3.

Standard ML (and most other strongly typed languages) allow recursive user-defined types. A common example of this is the definition of a tree in Standard ML:

```
datatype tree = leaf of int | node of tree * tree
```

When encountering a variable of type tree, a tagged collection algorithm (such as Baker's) would simply copy the root node of the tree from FROM space into TO space. While tracing from the newly copied cells in TO space, the rest of the tree would eventually be copied. No stack of visited nodes and no recursion is required.

In tag-free collection, it is certainly also desirable to avoid recursion and the explicit use of a stack to trace the elements of a tree. Not only do we want to avoid using heap space during copying, but also we do not want to save a large data structure representing the suspended tree.

The use of recursion or an explicit stack is avoided through the use of the (well-known) pointer reversal technique (surveyed in [Knuth73]) on the cells of the tree in FROM space. In this depth-first traversal method, as each node n is encountered during the traversal, it is modified to point to its parent. Thus, when the subtree rooted at n has been traversed, the parent of n can be found to continue the traversal. This clearly changes the structure of the tree during the traversal. Most importantly, since garbage collection may suspend in the middle of the tree traversal, it appears that the tree could be left in an inconsistent state.

Luckily, this is not the case. As each node is encountered, it is copied into TO space. Thus, as long as a forwarding address is written into the old node, the rest of the node can be overwritten. For example, in the Standard ML of New Jersey implementation [AM87] a full word is allocated for the value constructor field (`leaf` or `node` in this case). This field can be overwritten with the forwarding address and one of the remaining fields can contain the pointer to the node's parent. Thus, whenever the gc_routine suspends, the state of the tree remains consistent, being comprised of those nodes that have been copied into TO space and those nodes that have yet to be encountered by the garbage collector. Figure 3 shows the node-at-a-time copying of the graph representing a tree structure. Garbage collection can suspend at any time, and the only information that must be saved is the address in FROM space of the last cell copied into TO space. In each step in figure 3, a cell is annotated by a ● to show which address would have to be saved if garbage collection suspended at that point.

The overhead of this tree copying method is admittedly greater than that of Baker's algorithm. In our method, certain steps in the tree traversal involve following a number of pointers back to an ancestor in the tree (for example, between steps (e) and (f) in figure 3). This is due to our tree traversal being depth first. In the next section we describe a breadth-first copying collector for recursive data structures.

Our algorithm is still incomplete for the following reason: If garbage collection suspends during the tracing of variables in some activation record R, there is no guarantee that R will still be on the stack when garbage collection resumes. The function call represented by R may have returned and, if so, R will have been popped off of the stack. Thus the SS register will have been decremented. Another possibility is that R is still on the stack, but the gc_routine that suspended is no longer appropriate for resumption. This would be the case if the function represented by R has continued executing and the structure (number and types of variables) R has changed since the last garbage collection.

Therefore, in order for the suspended gc_routine to resume, the following conditions must be satisfied:

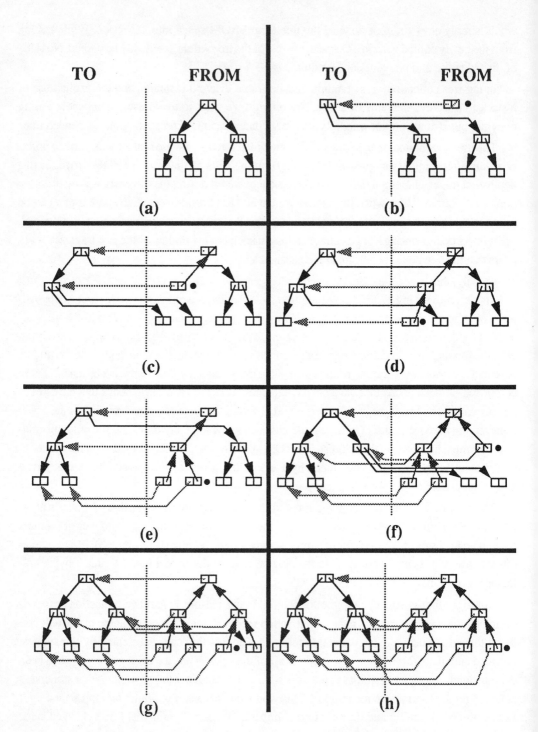

Figure 3. Incremental copying garbage collection using pointer reversal

- The value of SS must be the same as when the gc_routine suspended.

- The suspended gc_routine is the same as the one for the activation record that SS currently points to.

The first condition means that the activation record R being traced previously is still on the stack. The second condition does not mean that the function corresponding to R has not executed since the last garbage collection, but only that garbage collection has resumed at the same call instruction within the function. For example, the call instruction may be inside a loop and get executed many times. It is still safe, however, to resume the suspended gc_routine if the conditions are met. The number, stack locations, and types of the variables in the activation record will be the same as during the previous garbage collection. The only possible change could be in the value of those variables. If the value of a variable has changed, this may have two effects:

1. The variable may contain new cells created since the last garbage collection. If so, these cells must already be in TO space and therefore need not be traversed by the garbage collector.

2. Cells in FROM space that will be traversed by the suspended gc_routine may no longer be reachable from the variables in the activation record. At worst, this means that unreachable cells will be copied into TO space (this property certainly exists in Baker's algorithm as well).

In both cases, the garbage collection process remains safe.

3. Breadth-first Incremental Tag-Free GC

Our incremental tag-free method differs from Baker's algorithm in an important way. Recursive structures, such as the nested lists and trees discussed in section 2, are copied in a depth first manner using our method and in a breadth manner using Baker's method. This has two effects:

- During garbage collection the time required to find the next cell to copy into TO space is not constant. In our tree example, this time can be proportional to the depth of the tree. This can be a severe disadvantage in real-time systems, which were the motivation for developing incremental methods in the first place!

- Depending on access patterns to a data structure, a breadth-first copying collector may have desirable data locality properties. If the structures are accessed in a breadth-first manner, then it is beneficial to copy them in a breath first manner to achieve better cache and paging performance.

The problem of breadth-first tag-free garbage collection was left as an open problem in [Appel89]. We now describe an breadth-first copying collection that is both tag-free and incremental.

We first consider homogeneous, but arbitrarily nested, lists. Three aspects of the algorithm must be specified, namely:

1. The transformation of the cells of the list in FROM space after they have been copied into TO space.

TO   FROM

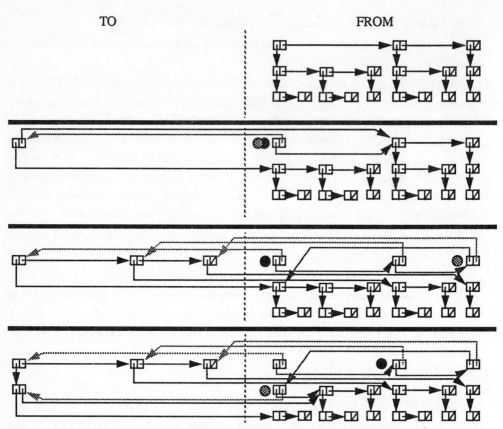

Figure 4. Breadth-first copying of a list with depth=3

2. How the state of a partially copied list is captured efficiently (in time and space).

3. How type information is retained. That is, how does the algorithm keep track of the depth of the cell (which determines the type of the cell) that is currently being copied?

Various stages of a breadth-first copy of a list of depth three are illustrated[1] in figures 4 and 5. There are two pointers, which we call **grey** and **black** corresponding to the grey and black circles in the illustration, that both traverse the list in a breadth-first fashion. The **grey** pointer always points to the cell in FROM space that was most recently copied. The **black** pointer always points to the parent cell of the next sublist that **grey** should encounter. Thus, when **grey** gets to the end of a sublist, the next sublist is found using the **black** pointer.

The three issues above are resolved as follows:

1. After each cell is copied into new space, the **cdr** field of the old cell contains the forwarding address, as usual. The **car** of the cell, however, is modified to point to the next cell in the list to be visited. If the next cell was part of the same sublist, then it is found

---

1. We have chosen to illustrate the algorithms using figures rather than code (and space limitations precluded doing both). We hope the reader finds the figures enlightening!

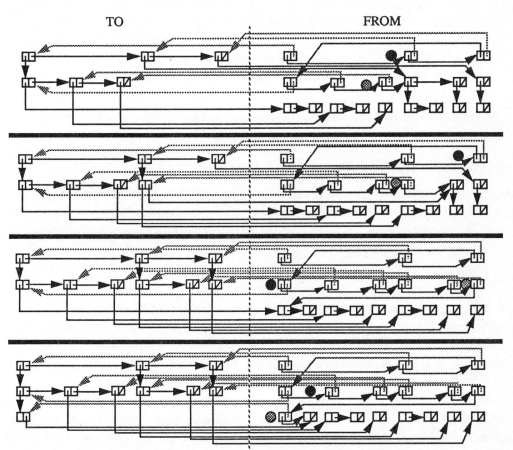

TO   FROM

Figure 5. Breadth-first copying of a list with depth=3 (continued)

by following the **cdr** of the last copied cell. If the next cell is actually part of a different sublist, then it can be found using the **black** pointer (actually **car(cdr black)** - see the illustrations). Since **grey** will traverse the list in a breadth-first manner, modifying the old nested lists into one long list, the **black** pointer traverses the modified list (always behind **grey**) by following the pointers in the **car** fields of the cells.

2. The state of the partially copied list is completely captured by the **grey** and **black** pointers.

3. An extra global counter, called **depth**, is used to keep track of the depth of the cell currently being copied. This counter is incremented each time all the cells at the same level have been copied. This is easily determined: There are two other counters, called **greycount** and **blackcount** that count the number of cells traversed by **grey** and by **black**, respectively, at their current level. The number of cells copied at one level of the list is the number of parents of the sublists at the next level. Each time **grey** starts to traverse a new level, **blackcount** is set to **greycount** (i.e. the number of elements of the level above) and **greycount** is set to zero. Whenever a new cell is copied,

greycount is incremented. Whenever **black** is advanced, **blackcount** is decremented. Thus, when **grey** points to the last element of a sublist (i.e. its **cdr** is nil), and **blackcount** is zero, then all the cells of the current level have been copied. At that point, **depth** is incremented, and **greycount** and **blackcount** are reset as described above.

The breadth-first method described for lists is easily extended to trees and other user-defined recursive types. Figure 6 illustrates the method for trees.

4. Incremental Tag-Free GC for Polymorphic Languages

In a polymorphically typed language, different calls to a function may be passed arguments of different types. The same variable in different activation records of the same function may have different types. Thus, the gc_routines for the function (which all activation records for the function share) cannot know the precise types of its variables. This would seem to preclude tag-free garbage collection.

However, Appel [Appel89] suggested a solution to this problem. The types of the arguments to a polymorphic function determine the types of its parameters and local variables. Thus, if the garbage collector cannot determine the type of a variable in a polymorphic function's activation record, then the calling procedure (found by the return address and dynamic link) is examined to determine the type of the arguments. If the calling procedure is itself polymorphic, then its caller may have to be examined, and so on. This continues (that is, traversing down the dynamic chain) until the precise type of each variable in the current activation record can be determined. The types of the variables in the outermost function in the program, corresponding to the bottom activation record in the stack, are known. Therefore, each traversal of the stack will terminate successfully.

Since Appel's solution may require many traversals of the stack, [Goldberg91] described a method requiring a single traversal of the stack. The garbage collector starts at the bottom of the stack by calling the gc_routine of the outermost function. As each successive activation record is encountered, its gc_routine is passed encoded type information from the previous (i.e. caller's) activation record's gc_routine. This encoded type information describes the types of the arguments that were passed in the call that created the activation record. Each gc_routine reconstructs the types of the local variables from the encoded type information that was passed to it. It then passes encoded type information to the next activation record's gc_routine.

Because the incremental tag-free garbage collection method described in section 2 starts from the top of the stack after the heaps are flipped, and proceeds down the stack (as SS is decremented), there is no way for the type information to be propagated from the gc_routines of activation records further down the stack. Even if we simply reversed the order of the traversal of the stack, the practicality of the method would suffer. Every garbage collection would require the traversal of the stack from the bottom activation record to the activation record currently being collected in order to propagate the necessary type_gc_routines.

To solve this problem, we modify our method in the following way:

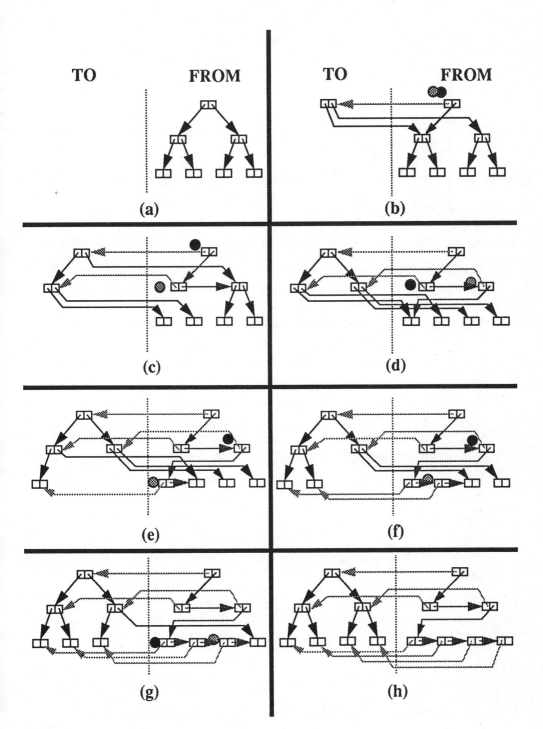

Figure 6. Breadth-first incremental copying garbage collection of trees

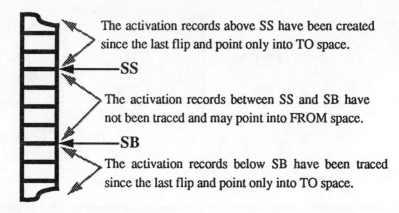

The activation records above SS have been created since the last flip and point only into TO space.

—SS

The activation records between SS and SB have not been traced and may point into FROM space.

—SB

The activation records below SB have been traced since the last flip and point only into TO space.

Figure 7. Stack organization for incremental collection for polymorphic languages

- In addition to SS, another pointer, SB, into the stack is used. When the spaces are flipped, SB is set to point to the bottom activation record in the stack. When garbage collection resumes, the gc_routine for the activation record pointed to by SB (not SS) is executed. When that gc_routine is finished, SB is incremented to point to the next activation record. As before, when the spaces are flipped, SS is set to point to the top activation record in the stack. When the activation record that SS points to is popped off the stack, SS is decremented to point to the activation record below.

- At any time, all activation records below SB have already been traced. The activation records above SS have been created since the last flip and can only point into TO space. Thus, the only activation records that need to be traced by the garbage collector are those between SB and SS. Figure 7 shows how the stack is logically partitioned by SS and SB.

- When garbage collection suspends, the type information that has propagated to the most recently traced activation record (i.e. the one that SB points to) is saved. When garbage collection resumes, this type information is available. There is no need to traverse the stack from the bottom each time the garbage collector resumes.

- When SB = SS, all activation records have been traced and no more copying is required until TO space is exhausted and the flip occurs.

[Goldberg91] describes in detail how type information is propagated up the stack during stop-and-copy garbage collection. The method described in that paper needs only be adapted in the ways described here in order to be used in an incremental collector.

References

[AM87]

Appel, A.W. and MacQueen, D.B. A Standard ML Compiler. In *Proceedings of the Conference on Functional Programming and Computer Architecture*. Springer-Verlag LNCS 274, pp 301-324, 1987.

[Appel89]

Appel, A.W. Runtime Tags Aren't Necessary. In *Lisp and Symbolic Computation*, 2, 153-162, 1989.

[Baker78]

Baker, H.G. List Processing in Real Time on a Serial Computer. In *Comm. ACM*, 21,4 (April 1978), 280-294.

[BL70]

Branquart, P. and Lewi, J. A Scheme of Storage Allocation and Garbage Collection for Algol-68. In *Algol-68 Implementation*, North-Holland Publishing Company, 1970.

[Britton75]

Britton, D.E. *Heap Storage Management for the Programming Language Pascal*. Master's Thesis, University of Arizona, 1975.

[Cheney70]

Cheney, C.J. A nonrecursive list compacting algorithm. *Comm. ACM*, 13,11 (Nov 1970), 677-678.

[Cohen81]

Cohen, J. Garbage Collection of Linked Data Structures. In *ACM Computing Surveys, 13(3)*, 341-367. September 1981.

[DLMSS75]

Dijkstra, E.W., Lamport, L., Martin, A.J., Scholten, C.S., Steffens, E.F.M. On-the-fly garbage collection: An exercise in cooperation. E.W. Dijkstra note EWD496, June 1975.

[FY69]

Fenichel, R.R, and Yochelson, J.C. A LISP garbage-collector for virtual-memory computer systems. *Comm. ACM*, 12,11 (Nov. 1969), 611-612.

[Goldberg91]

Goldberg, B. Tag-free garbage collection for strongly typed programming languages. *Proceedings of the ACM SIGPLAN'91 Symposium on Programming Language Design and Implementation*, June 1991.

[Knuth73]

Knuth, D.E. *The Art of Computer Programming. Volume 2: Fundamental Algorithms*, 2nd Ed. Addison-Wesley, 1973.

[Lamport75]

Lamport, L. On-the-fly garbage collection: Once more with rigor. CA-7508-1611, Mass. Computer Associates, Wakefield, Mass., Aug. 1975.

[Minsky63]

Minsky, M.L. A LISP garbage collector algorithm using serial secondary storage. Memo 58, M.I.T. A.I Lab., M.I.T, Cambridge, Mass., Oct. 1963.

[MLH90]

Milner, R., Tofte, M., and Harper, R. *The Definition of Standard ML*. MIT Press. 1990.

[Muller76]

Muller, K.G. On the feasibility of concurrent garbage collection. Ph.D. thesis, Tech. Hogeschool Delft, The Netherlands, March 1976.

[PJS89]

Peyton Jones, S. L and Salkid, J. The spineless tagless G-machine. *Proceedings of the 1989 Conference on Functional Programming Languages and Computer Architecture*, London, Sept. 1989.

[Rudalics88]

Rudalics, M. *Multiprocessor List Memory Management*. Ph.D. Thesis, Johannes Kepler University, Austria. RISC-LINZ report 88-87.0, December 1988.

[Steele75]

Steele, G.S. Jr. Multiprocessing compactifying garbage collection. In *Comm. ACM*, 18,9 (Sept. 1975), 495-508.

[Wadler76]

Wadler, P.J., Analysis of an algorithm for real-time garbage collection. *Comm. ACM*, 19,9 (Sept. 1976), 491-500.

Approximate Fixed Points in Abstract Interpretation

Chris Hankin and Sebastian Hunt

Department of Computing

Imperial College of Science, Technology and Medicine

180 Queen's Gate, London SW7 2BZ

Abstract

Much of the earlier development of abstract interpretation, and its application to imperative programming languages, has concerned techniques for finding fixed points in large (often infinite) lattices. The standard approach in the abstract interpretation of functional languages has been to work with small, finite lattices and this supposedly circumvents the need for such techniques. However, practical experience has shown that, in the presence of higher order functions, the lattices soon become too large (although still finite) for the fixed-point finding problem to be tractable. This paper develops some approximation techniques which were first proposed by Hunt and shows how these techniques relate to the earlier use of widening and narrowing operations by the Cousots.

1. Introduction

Any account of abstract interpretation of functional languages must address the problem of defining a suitable abstraction of functional values. There are a number of alternatives, ranging from the relational approach espoused in the Cousot's work and instantiated in the minimal function graph approach of [Jon85] to the approach of [BHA86] where functions are abstracted by functions. In the following we will adopt the latter approach. In such a setting it is well-known that the problem of finding fixed points, the central operation in abstract interpretation, is of n-iterated exponential complexity [Mey85]. There was a naive expectation that the development of clever algorithms such as the frontiers algorithm [CPJ85], [MH87], [HH91] would ameliorate this situation but practical experience has shown that this was misplaced optimism.

In [Hun89] and [HH91], we developed a formal approach to allow the evaluation of approximate fixed points, in fact generating upper and lower bounds for the true fixed point. In the classical approach to abstract interpretation pioneered by Patrick and Radhia Cousot it is common to work with lattices that do not satisfy the ascending chain condition and, in this context, it is essential to work with approximate fixed points; they have developed a general theory of widening and narrowing operations to support this work. It is possible to relate our approach to the widening/narrowing approach of the Cousots and this is our programme in this paper; indeed our work constitutes the only published example of higher-order widening/narrowing.

In the next section, we review the main results from [HH91]. Section 3 develops the theory somewhat further and presents a scheme for using the approach in fixed point computation. Section 4 defines widening and narrowing operations and demonstrates the correspondence between the two approaches. We conclude with Section 5.

2. The Abstraction Ordering

We work with a family of finite lattices L:

$$2 \in L \text{ where } 2 \equiv (\{0,1\}, 0 \leq 1)$$
$$D_\perp \in L \text{ if } D \in L$$
$$D^\top \in L \text{ if } D \in L$$
$$D_1 \times D_2 \in L \text{ if } D_i \in L, i = 1,2$$
$$[D \rightarrow D'] \in L \text{ if } D, D' \in L$$

where $[D \rightarrow D']$ is the lattice of monotonic functions from D to D'. Such a family of finite lattices has proved to be useful in a wide range of analyses including strictness analysis, parallel sharing analysis, and binding time analysis.

We define an abstraction ordering on L:

$$2 \leq D \text{ for all } D \in L$$
$$D_\perp \leq D'_\perp \text{ if } D \leq D'$$
$$D^\top \leq D'^\top \text{ if } D \leq D'$$
$$D_1 \times D_2 \leq D'_1 \times D'_2 \text{ if } D_1 \leq D'_1 \text{ and } D_2 \leq D'_2$$
$$[A \rightarrow B] \leq [A' \rightarrow B'] \text{ if } A \leq A' \text{ and } B \leq B'^1$$

Notice that $\leq$ is a partial order.

---

[1] Note that $\leq$ does not capture the usual notion of approximation which has $\rightarrow$ contravariant in its first argument. We will see that $\leq$ means that there is a Galois connection between the two lattices - this amounts to the standard domain theoretic practice of using embedding/projection pairs to avoid the contravariance of $\rightarrow$.

We introduce the categories **FL**, **FL**[ec] and **FL**[ep].

FL	finite lattices, monotone maps
FL[ec]	finite lattices, embedding-closure pairs
FL[ep]	finite lattices, embedding-projection pairs[2]

We write the left and right components of an embedding-closure (embedding-projection) pair ϕ as ϕ^e and ϕ^c (ϕ^e and ϕ^p). Given an embedding-closure pair ϕ, ϕ^e and ϕ^c determine each other uniquely. Similarly for embedding-projection pairs. Thus **FL**[ec] and **FL**[ep] may both be viewed as sub-categories of **FL**.

We introduce the functors $\_\bot$, $\_^\top$, $\_\times\_$ and $\_\to\_$ on **FL**[ec] and **FL**[ep]. These functors have the same (formal) definitions for both categories. The definitions of these functors are the expected ones, in particular:

$$A \to B = [A \to B]$$

for $\phi : A_1 \to A_2$ and $\psi : B_1 \to B_2$,
$\phi \to \psi : [A_1 \to B_1] \to [A_2 \to B_2]$ is defined by
$$(\phi \to \psi)^e f = \psi^e \circ f \circ \phi^c$$
$$(\phi \to \psi)^c g = \psi^c \circ g \circ \phi^e$$

It is straightforward to verify that these are indeed functors on the appropriate category (**FL**[ep] and **FL**[ec]). We next define two pairs of maps between pairs of lattices related by the abstraction ordering. The safe maps give overestimates of values and the live maps give underestimates.

Definition 2.1

For each $A \leq B \in L$, we define an **FL**[ec]-morphism $Safe_{A,B} : A \to B$. We write $UpS_{A,B}$ for $Safe_{A,B}{}^e$ and $DownS_{B,A}$ for $Safe_{A,B}{}^c$:

$$UpS_{2,B}\, a \quad = \quad \bot_B \text{ if } a = 0$$
$$\top_B \text{ if } a = 1$$

$$DownS_{B,2}\, b \quad = \quad 0 \text{ if } b = \bot_B$$
$$1 \text{ otherwise}$$

$$Safe_{A_\bot, B_\bot} \quad = \quad (Safe_{A,B})_\bot$$
$$Safe_{A^\top, B^\top} \quad = \quad (Safe_{A,B})^\top$$
$$Safe_{A1 \times B1, A2 \times B2} = Safe_{A1,A2} \times Safe_{B1,B2}$$

---

[2] An embedding-closure pair is a pair of continuous functions $(e{:}A \to B, c{:}B \to A)$ such that:
$$e \circ c \geq id \quad \text{and} \quad c \circ e = id$$
and an embedding-projection pair is a pair of continuous functions $(e{:}A \to B, p{:}B \to A)$ such that:
$$e \circ p \leq id \quad \text{and} \quad p \circ e = id.$$

$$\text{Safe}_{[A1 \to B1],[A2 \to B2]} = \text{Safe}_{A1,A2} \to \text{Safe}_{B1,B2}$$

[]

We must verify that:

i) $\text{UpS}_{2,B} \circ \text{DownS}_{B,2} \geq \text{id}_B$

ii) $\text{DownS}_{B,2} \circ \text{UpS}_{2,B} = \text{id}_2$

These verifications are routine.

Definition 2.2

For each $A \leq B \in L$, we define an $\textbf{FL}^{cp}$-morphism $\text{Live}_{A,B} : A \to B$. We write $\text{UpL}_{A,B}$ for $\text{Live}_{A,B}^e$ and $\text{DownL}_{B,A}$ for $\text{Live}_{A,B}^p$. The definitions of the Live maps are (formally) identical to those of the Safe maps except for $\text{DownL}_{B,2}$ which is:

$$\text{DownL}_{B,2}\, b \quad = \quad \begin{array}{l} 1 \text{ if } b = T_B \\ 0 \text{ otherwise} \end{array}$$

[]

It is tempting to say that the Live maps are dual to the Safe maps, i.e.:

$$\text{Live}_{A,B} \quad = \quad \text{Safe}_{A^{OP},B^{OP}}$$

We cannot actually say this since the family L is not closed under the operation of forming opposites. However, we can establish an order ($\leq$) isomorphism $O : L \to L$ such that for each $A \in L$ we have:

$$O(A) \cong A^{OP}$$

Thus:

$$
\begin{array}{lcl}
O(2) & = & 2 \\
O(A_\perp) & = & (O(A))^T \\
O(A^T) & = & (O(A))_\perp \\
O(A \times B) & = & O(A) \times O(B) \\
O([A \to B]) & = & [O(A) \to O(B)]
\end{array}
$$

Note that $O(O(A)) = A$. For each $A \in L$, the isomorphism of A^{OP} and $O(A)$ is established via the (contravariant) map $R_A : A \to O(A)$:

$$
\begin{array}{lcl \quad lcl}
R_2\, 0 & = & 1 & R_2\, 1 & = & 0 \\
R_{A\perp}\, \perp & = & T & R_{A\perp}\,(\text{lift } a) & = & \text{colift}(R_A\, a) \\
R_A T\, T & = & \perp & R_A T\,(\text{colift } a) & = & \text{lift}(R_A\, a) \\
R_{A \times B}\,(a,b) & = & (R_A\, a,\, R_B\, b) & & & \\
R_{[A \to B]}\, f & = & R_B \circ f \circ R_{O(A)} & & &
\end{array}
$$

Note that:

$$R_{O(A)} \circ R_A \quad = \quad id_A$$

A key property of the R maps is the following:

Lemma 2.3

For all $A, B \in L$:

$$R_B(\, f\, a\,) \quad = \quad (R_{[A \to B]}\, f)\, (R_A\, a) \qquad\qquad []$$

Fact 2.4

For all $A \le B \in L$:

i) $\quad UpL_{O(A),O(B)} \quad = \quad R_{[A \to B]}(UpS_{A,B})$

ii) $\quad DownL_{O(B),O(A)} = \quad R_{[B \to A]}(DownS_{B,A}) \qquad\qquad []$

The following properties of the Safe and Live maps are standard for embedding-closure pairs and embedding-projection pairs [GHK*80]:

- UpS and UpL are injective
- DownS and DownL are onto and strict
- UpS is T-preserving and UpL is strict .

In addition we have the following:

Lemma 2.5

For all $A \le B \in L$, $UpS_{A,B}$ is strict.

Proof

induction on the height of the proof that $A \in L$ $\qquad\qquad []$

Corollary 2.6

For all $A \le B \in L$, $UpL_{A,B}$ is T-preserving.

Proof

Let $A \le B \in L$. Since $O : L \to L$ is an order isomorphism, we can write A as $O(A')$ and B as $O(B')$. Then

$$UpL_{O(A'),O(B')}\, T_{O(A')}$$

$=$	$(R(UpS_{A',B'}))\, T_{O(A')}$	by Fact 2.4
$=$	$(R(UpS_{A',B'}))\, (R \perp_{A'})$	since R an isomorphism of A'^{OP} onto $O(A')$
$=$	$R(\, UpS_{A',B'} \perp_{A'})$	by Lemma 2.3
$=$	$R(\, \perp_{B'})$	by the Lemma 2.5
$=$	$T_{O(B')}$	since R an isomorphism of B'^{OP} onto $O(B')$ []

In what follows we will assume "dual" results such as this corollary to be clear and will not spell out the details of their proof.

Lemma 2.7

For all $A \leq B \leq C \in L$:

    i) $\text{Safe}_{A,C} \quad = \quad \text{Safe}_{B,C} \circ \text{Safe}_{A,B}$

    ii) $\text{Safe}_{A,A} \quad = \quad \text{id}_A$

Proof

(i) proof by induction over the type of A:

$A \equiv 2$:

$$UpS_{B,C}(UpS_{2,B}\, 0) \quad = \quad UpS_{B,C}\, \bot_B, \text{ by definition}$$
$$= \quad \bot_C, \text{ by Lemma 2.5}$$
$$UpS_{B,C}(UpS_{2,B}\, 1) \quad = \quad UpS_{B,C}\, T_B, \text{ by definition}$$
$$= \quad T_D \text{ since } UpS \text{ is top-preserving}$$
$$DownS_{B,2}(DownS_{C,B}\, x) = 0 \Rightarrow DownS_{C,B}\, x = \bot_B$$
$$\Rightarrow \quad x = \bot_C{}^3$$

in this case $DownS_{C,2}\, x = 0$ as well.

$$DownS_{B,2}(DownS_{C,B}\, x) = 1 \Rightarrow DownS_{C,B}\, x \neq \bot_B, \text{ by definition}$$
$$\Rightarrow \quad x \neq \bot_C, \text{ since } DownS \text{ is strict.}$$

and thus $DownS_{C,2}\, x = 1$.

The result follows by extensionality.

The inductive cases are all the same and follow from the functorial properties of the constructors that we use; we illustrate two cases - the unary functor $\_\bot$ and the binary functor $\_\times\_$:

$A \equiv A'_\bot$:

Then $B \equiv B'_\bot$ and $C \equiv C'_\bot$ and then:

$$Safe_{A'_\bot, C'_\bot} \quad = \quad (Safe_{A',C'})_\bot$$
$$= \quad (Safe_{B',C'} \circ Safe_{A',B'})_\bot \text{ by IH}$$
$$= \quad (Safe_{B',C'})_\bot \circ (Safe_{A',B'})_\bot \text{ since } \_\bot \text{ is a functor}$$
$$= \quad Safe_{B,C} \circ Safe_{A,B}$$

$A \equiv A1 \times A2$:

Then $B \equiv B1 \times B2$ and $C \equiv C1 \times C2$ and:

---

[3]Both implications hold because DownS is bottom-reflecting which follows by a simple argument using the properties of embedding-projection pairs.

$$Safe_{A,C} = Safe_{A1,C1} \times Safe_{A2,C2}$$
$$= (Safe_{B1,C1} \circ Safe_{A1,B1}) \times (Safe_{B2,C2} \circ Safe_{A2,B2})$$
$$\text{by IH}$$
$$= (Safe_{B1,C1} \times Safe_{B2,C2}) \circ (Safe_{A1,B1} \times Safe_{A2,B2})$$
$$= Safe_{B,C} \circ Safe_{A,B}$$

(ii) follows from $Safe_{2,2} = id_2$ since functors ($\_\times\_$, $\_\to\_$, etc...) preserve identities.

[]

Thus we may view Safe as being a functor from the (poset) category L to $\mathbf{FL}^{cc}$. By the "dual" of the Lemma, Live is a functor from L to $\mathbf{FL}^{cp}$.

The main result concerning these maps and their interaction with the least fixed point operator, **fix**, in [HH91] is the following:

Fact 2.8

For all lattices D, D' $\in$ L such that D' $\leq$ D:

(i) $fix_{D'} = DownS\ fix_D$

        $fix_{D'} = DownL\ fix_D$

(ii) $UpS\ fix_{D'} \geq fix_D$

        $UpL\ fix_{D'} \leq fix_D$ []

2.8(ii) gives a formal basis for the method of finding upper and lower bounds for a true fixed point by iterating in a smaller lattice using safe and live approximations, respectively. In this paper we develop this technique and relate it to Cousot's widening and narrowing operations.

3. Further Properties of the Abstraction Ordering

We start by noting that x is a *pre-fixed point* of f if:

$$x \leq f(x)$$

and a *post-fixed point* of f if:

$$f(x) \leq x$$

We can now state and prove one of the main results of the paper.

Proposition 3.1

Let A' $\leq$ A $\in$ L, and let:

$$D \quad \equiv \quad [A \to A]$$
$$D' \quad \equiv \quad [A' \to A']$$

Then for all $f \in D$ and for all $x \in A'$:

$$(DownS_{D,D'}\, f)\, x = x \quad \Rightarrow \quad f\,(UpS_{A',A}\, x) \le UpS_{A',A}\, x$$

Proof

$$
\begin{aligned}
UpS_{A',A}\, x \quad &= \quad UpS_{A',A}((DownS_{D,D'}\, f)x) & \text{by assumption}\\
&= \quad (UpS_{A',A} \circ DownS_{A,A'} \circ f \circ UpS_{A',A})x & \text{by definition}\\
&\ge \quad f\,(UpS_{A',A}\, x)
\end{aligned}
$$

$$[]$$

Corollary 3.2

For any $[A \to A]$, $[A' \to A']$, $[A'' \to A''] \in L$, with $A'' \le A' \le A$ then for all $g \in [A \to A]$ and any fixed point x of $(DownS_{[A \to A],[A'' \to A'']}\, g)$, we have:

$$(DownS_{[A \to A],[A' \to A']}\, g)\, (UpS_{A'',A'}\, x) \le UpS_{A'',A'}\, x$$

Proof

Use Proposition 3.1 with $f = DownS_{[A \to A],[A' \to A']}\, g$ and use Lemma 2.7 $\qquad []$

This result says that when any fixed point of the approximation of g in a smaller lattice is embedded into any larger lattice it becomes a post-fixed point of the approximation of g in that larger lattice. The dual result for the live maps is that any fixed point becomes a pre-fixed point in the larger lattice.

Proposition 3.3

For any $D, D', D'' \in L$, such that:

$$D \quad \equiv \quad [A \to A]$$
$$D' \quad \equiv \quad [A' \to A']$$
$$D'' \quad \equiv \quad [A'' \to A'']$$

with $A'' \le A' \le A$ and for any $f \in D$:

(i) $\quad UpS_{A'',A'}(fix_{A''}(DownS_{D,D''}\, f)) \ge fix_{A'}(DownS_{D,D'}\, f)$

(ii) $\quad UpL_{A'',A'}(fix_{A''}(DownL_{D,D''}\, f)) \le fix_{A'}(DownL_{D,D'}\, f)$

Proof

These follow immediately from Fact 2.8 (ii) and Lemma 2.7(i).

$$[]$$

Finally, we restate some obvious properties of pre- and post-fixed points.

Fact 3.4

For all $f \in [A \to A]$ and $x \in A$:

(i) if x is a pre-fixed point of f and x is less than $\mathbf{fix}_A f$ then $\{f^n(x) \mid n \geq 0\}$ is an ascending chain and for all n:
$$f^n(x) \leq \mathbf{fix}_A f$$
Moreover, since we are working with finite lattices, the chain will eventually stabilise and the limit will be $\mathbf{fix}_A f$.

(ii) if x is a post-fixed point of f and x is greater than $\mathbf{fix}_A f$ then $\{f^n(x) \mid n \geq 0\}$ is a descending chain and for all n:
$$f^n(x) \geq \mathbf{fix}_A f$$
However, notice that the limit of such a descending chain may not be $\mathbf{fix}_A f$ but some other fixed point. (Thus the need for the generality of Corollary 3.2)   []

We can now present the scheme for finding approximate fixed points (to any desired accuracy):

Step 1: Choose some small lattice in which the problem of finding fixed points is tractable and iterate from bottom to find the least fixed point of both the safe and live abstractions of the function.

Step 2: The previous step gives upper and lower bounds for the true fixed point. If these agree on the interesting arguments, or if a safe answer is sufficient, use the upper bound; otherwise

Step 3: Apply UpS to the safe approximation and UpL to the live approximation to move to a larger, intermediate lattice and iterate down from the resultant post-fixed point and up from the resultant pre-fixed point. Repeat Step 2.

One word of caution: if the post-(pre-)fixed point of the safe (live) image of the function in some intermediate lattice happens to be a fixed point then no further improvement of the upper(lower) bound is possible. On the other hand, when the pre-fixed point is a fixed point, it must be the least fixed point.

4. Widening and Narrowing Operations

We start by recalling some definitions and results from [Cou81].

Definition 4.1

For any complete lattice L, an operation $\nabla \in \mathbb{N} \to ((L \times L) \to L)$ is a *widening operation* iff it satisfies the following conditions:

(i) $\forall j > 0, \forall x,y \in L, x \vee y \leq x \, \nabla(j) \, y$

(ii)   For all ascending chains $x_0 \leq x_1 \leq \ldots \leq x_n \leq \ldots$ in L, the chain $y_0 = x_0$, $y_1 = y_0 \, \nabla(1) \, x_1, \ldots y_n = y_{n-1} \, \nabla(n) \, x_n$ is eventually stable; i.e. there exists a $k \geq 0$ such for all $i \geq k$, $y_i = y_k$.

[]

A widening operator may be used to generate an "accelerated" fixed point iteration (which in general will overshoot the least fixed point) as shown by the following proposition.

Proposition 4.2

Let f be a monotone operator on L and ∇ a widening operator. The limit u of the sequence:

$$x_0 = \bot$$
$$x_{n+1} = x_n, \text{ if } f(x_n) \leq x_n$$
$$x_{n+1} = x_n \, \nabla(n+1) \, f(x_n), \text{ otherwise}$$

can be computed in a finite number of steps. Moreover $\mathbf{fix}(f) \leq u$ and $f(u) \leq$ []

The iteration process described by the proposition and its relationship to the Ascending Kleene Chain is illustrated in the following figure:

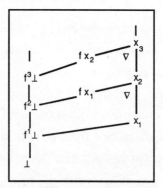

Let $f : B \to B$ with $A \leq B \in L$ and consider the sequence $(\text{DownS } f)^n \bot$. For the purposes of comparison with widening, we embed this sequence into B using UpS. It is easily shown that the resulting sequence $UpS((DownS\ f)^n\ \bot)$ is just $(UpS \circ DownS \circ f)^n\ \bot$, giving the modified diagram:

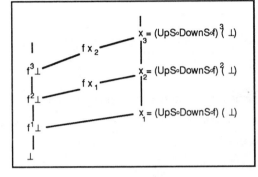

and consequently we have:

Lemma 4.3

For any lattices $D, D' \in L$, such that $D' \leq D$:

$$\lambda j.\lambda(x,y).x \vee UpS_{D'D}(DownS_{D,D'}\ y))$$

is a widening operation.

Proof

Observe that $UpS_{D'D}(DownS_{D,D'}\ y)) \geq y$ by the definition of embedding-closure pairs and thus:

$$x \vee UpS_{D'D}(DownS_{D,D'}\ y)) \geq x \vee y$$

Any ascending chain must be eventually stable since the lattices are all finite.

$$[]$$

In our earlier discussion, we presented three steps for computing approximate fixed points. We have now shown the equivalence of step 1 of that process and the Cousot's notion of widening. However, it may be preferable to use the approach of the last section for efficiency reasons since the explicit use of the widening operator requires us to work in a larger lattice.

Still considering the safe maps, we now turn to the process of refining the approximation and start by defining the concept of narrowing.

Definition 4.4

For any complete lattice L, an operation $\Delta \in \mathbb{N} \to ((L \times L) \to L)$ is a *narrowing operation* iff it satisfies the following conditions:

(i) $\forall j > 0, (\forall x,y \in L: y \le x),\ \ y \le x\,\Delta(j)\,y \le x$

(ii)   For all descending chains $x_0 \ge x_1 \ge \dots \ge x_n \ge \dots$ in L, the chain y_0
       $= x_0,\ y_1 = y_0\,\Delta(1)\,x_1,\ \dots\ y_n = y_{n-1}\,\Delta(n)\,x_n$ is eventually stable; i.e.
       there exists a $k \ge 0$ such for all $i \ge k,\ y_i = y_k$.

$[]$

Proposition 4.5

Let f be a monotone operator on L and Δ a narrowing operator. Let $u \in L$ be such that $\mathbf{fix}\,f \le u$
and $f(u) \le u$. The decreasing chain:

$$x_0 = u$$
$$x_{n+1} = x_n\,\Delta(n+1)\,f(x_n)$$

is eventually stable. Moreover $\forall k \ge 0,\ \mathbf{fix}(f) \le x_k$.

$[]$

Step 3 of the procedure outlined in the last section proposed the use of a decreasing iteration
which we might reasonably expect to correspond to a narrowing. We now present a very
general process, which corresponds to Step 3, in which each iterate may be from a different
intermediate lattice. We consider a sequence of lattices $A_1,\dots A_n$ such that $A_i \le A_{i+1}$ and $A_n \equiv$
A, then we have $D_i \equiv [A_i \to A_i]$. We construct the sequence:

$$z_0,\ z_1,\ \dots$$

where

$$z_0 \quad = \quad \text{The fixed point found in Step 1}$$
$$z_{i+1} \quad = \quad (\text{DownS}_{D,Di+1}\ f)\,(\text{UpS}_{Ai,Ai+1}\ z_i)$$

The embedding of $\{z_n\}$ into A via the maps $\text{UpS}_{Ai,A}$ results in the decreasing sequence
associated with the narrowing operation defined in the following Lemma.

Lemma 4.6

For any sequence of lattices $A_0, A_1, \dots, A_n = A \in L$, such that $A_i \le A_{i+1}$ (the A_i need not be
distinct), $D_i \equiv [A_i \to A_i]$, $D \equiv D_n$, $f \in D$:

$$\Delta \equiv \lambda j.\lambda(x,y).x \wedge \text{UpS}_{Aj,A}(\text{DownS}_{A,Aj}\ y)$$

is a narrowing operation.

Proof

$$x\,\Delta(j)(u)\,y \quad = \quad x \wedge \text{UpS}_{Aj,A}(\text{DownS}_{A,Aj}\ y)$$

$$\leq \quad x \quad \text{by definition of } \wedge$$

Since $\text{UpS}_{Aj,A}(\text{DownS}_{A,Aj}\, y) \geq y$ (by the defining property of embedding-closure pairs), we also have for $y \leq x$ that:

$$x\, \Delta(j)(u)\, y \quad \geq \quad y$$

Eventual stability of the sequence follows from finiteness of the lattices.

[]

To summarise: the upwards iteration in the smaller lattice using a safe approximation of the function corresponds to widening and the refinement of the upper bound by iterating downwards in intermediate lattices corresponds to narrowing.

The situation with live maps is somewhat less straightforward. The live approximations approach the true fixed point from below; this is true both of the initial approximation and the successive refinements. This runs counter to the development of [Cou81] and later work. In [Cou78] alternative definitions of widening and narrowing operators are introduced but these do not correspond very closely to our application. This merits further investigation.

As a closing remark notice that the exact correspondence proved in Lemma 4.3 gives the basis for an alternative proof of the post-fixed point property proved in Proposition 3.1 since any widening operation has this property [Cou78].

5. Conclusions

We have developed the work on approximate fixed points first reported in [Hun89] and shown how it connects with the widening/narrowing approach used in traditional abstract interpretation. We have presented a scheme which computes arbitrarily precise upper and lower approximations of the true least fixed point of a function.

An alternative approach is based on the observation that often only a small part of the function graph is actually required. If a suitable superset of the subgraph (which avoids the plateaux problems described in [CPJ85]) can be identified then an accurate fixed point in the superset can be used. Since the needed elements of the graph may be many orders of magnitude smaller than the cardinality of the graph, this accurate fixed point can be computed very efficiently. These ideas, which are related to Jones and Mycroft's minimal function graphs [Jon85] are currently being developed.

Acknowledgements

We are indebted to our colleagues on the Semantique project for their willingness to discuss this work and for their constructive criticism; specifically, the categorical approach used in Section 2 was suggested by John Hughes and has led to a considerbale simplification of our work. The first author was partially funded by ESPRIT BRA 3124 - Semantique and both authors were partially funded by ESPRIT BRA 3074 - SemaGraph.

References

[BHA86]   G. L. Burn, C. L. Hankin and S. Abramsky, *Strictness Analysis for Higher-order functions*, Science of Computer Programming 7 (1986), pp 249-278, North-Holland.

[Cou78]   P. Cousot, *Méthodes Itératives de Construction et d'Approximation de Points Fixes d'Opérateurs Monotones sur un Treilli, Analyse Sémantique des Programmes*, Thèse d'Etat, Université de Grenoble, 1978.

[Cou81]   P. Cousot, *Semantic foundations of program analysis*, in Muchnick S. S. and Jones N. D. (eds) *Program Flow Analysis*, pp 303-342, Prentice-Hall, 1981.

[CPJ85]   C. Clack and S. L. Peyton Jones, *Strictness Analysis - a practical approach*, in J. -P. Jouannaud (ed), *Functional Programming Languages and Computer Architecture, LNCS* 201, pp 35-49, Springer Verlag.

[GHK*80]   G. K. Gierz, K. H. Hoffmann, K. Keimel, J. D. Lawson, M. Mislove, and D. S. Scott, *A Compendium of Continuous Lattices*, Springer Verlag.

[Hun89]   S. Hunt, *Frontiers and open sets in abstract interpretation*, in D. MacQueen (ed), *Functional Programming Languages and Computer Architecture,* pp 1-11, ACM Press.

[HH91]   S. Hunt and C. L. Hankin, *Fixed Points and Frontiers: a new perspective*, Journal of Functional Programming **1**(1), pp 91-120, Cambridge University Press.

[Jon85]   Jones N. D. and Mycroft A. *Dataflow Analysis of Applicative Programs using Minimal Function Graphs*, privately circulated manuscript, October 1985.

[Mey85]   A. R. Meyer, *Complexity of Program Flow Analysis for Strictness: Application of a Fundamental Theorem of Denotational Semantics*, private communication.

[MH87]   C. C. Martin and C. L. Hankin, *Finding Fixed Points in Finite Lattices*, in G. Kahn (ed), *Functional Programming Languages and Computer Architecture, LNCS* 274, pp 426-445, Springer Verlag.

Dynamic Typing*

Fritz Henglein
University of Copenhagen
Universitetsparken 1
2100 Copenhagen Ø
Denmark
Internet: henglein@diku.dk

Abstract

We present an extension of a statically typed language with a special type *dyn* and explicit type tagging and checking operations (coercions). Programs in run-time typed languages are viewed as incomplete programs that are to be *completed* to well-typed programs by explicitly inserting coercions into them.

Such completions are generally not unique. If the meaning of an incomplete program is to be the meaning of *any* of its completions and if it is too be unambiguous it is necessary that all its completions are *coherent* (semantically equivalent). We characterize with an equational theory the properties a semantics must satisfy to be coherent.

Since "naive" coercion evaluation does not satisfy all of the coherence equations we exclude certain "unsafe" completions from consideration that can cause avoidable type errors at run-time.

Various *classes* of completions may be used, parameterized by whether or not coercions may only occur at data creation and data use points in a program and whether only primitive coercions or also induced coercions. For each of these classes any term has a *minimal completion* that is optimal in the sense that it contains no coercions that could be avoided by a another coercion in the same class. In particular, minimal completions contain no coercions at all whenever the program is statically typable.

If only primitive type operations are admitted we show that minimal completions can be computed in almost-linear time. If induced coercions are also allowed the minimal completion can be computed in time $O(nm)$ where n is the size of the program and m is the size of the value flow graph of the program, which may be of size $O(n^2)$, but is typically rather sparse.

Finally, we sketch how this explicit dynamic typing discipline can be extended to let-polymorphism by parameterization with respect to coercions.

The resulting language framework leads to a seamless integration of statically typed and dynamically typed languages by relying on type inference for programs that have no type information and no explicit coercions whatsoever.

---

*This research has been supported by Esprit BRA 3124, Semantique.

1 Introduction

We present an extension of the (statically) typed λ-calculus with a special type *dyn* and *explicit coercions* representing run-time tagged values and associated tagging and checking operations as they are found in run-time typed (dynamically typed with implicit coercions) languages. A program in a run-time typed language can be embedded into this language without relying on a fixed translation, but instead permitting all possible *completions* of the program with inserted explicit coercions such that the typing rules are satisfied.

Since there are generally many different completions for the same run-time typed program we characterize *coherence* of completions by an equational theory that includes the equality $c^{-1}; c = \iota$ where c is a tagging operation, c^{-1} its corresponding checking operation, ι denotes the identity ("no-op") coercion, and ";" denotes left-to-right sequential composition. This equality does not hold for "naive" coercion evaluation as the left-hand side may produce a type error (in some context) where the right-hand side does not. Thus we define and restrict ourselves to a class of *safe* completions, all of which are equivalent under naive coercion evaluation.

Making coercions explicit makes enables reasoning about them in an implementation-independent fashion and bringing efficiency concerns to bear. We prove that certain classes of completions have *minimal* completions that avoid as many coercions as possible within the type system. In particular, a minimal completion of a statically typable program contains guaranteed no coercions, unlike the *canonical completion* used by (unoptimized) implementations of run-time typed languages.

We give efficient algorithms for computing minimal completions. For completions that use only primitive coercions we present an algorithm that computes a minimal completion in almost-linear time, $O(n\alpha(n,n))$, where α is an inverse of Ackermann's function. For completions that may also use induced coercions there is an algorithm that executes in time $O(nm)$ using the fastest known dynamic transitive closure algorithm under edge additions. Here n is the size of the input program and m is the size of its value flow graph; in the worst case the value flow graph is dense, i.e. m is $O(n^2)$, but for well-designed programs it is typically sparse.[1]

Finally, we discuss an extension to a let-polymorphic type discipline, in which let-bound variables can be parameterized by coercions.

The resulting language framework, which we refer to simply as *dynamic typing*, leads to a seamless integration of statically typed and run-time typed languages by connecting implicitly and explicitly dynamically typed programs by automatic type inference (completion). Both static and dynamic language programmers profit from such integration. The static language programmer has a universal interface type for communicating with the environment and may choose to use operations that require run-time checking. The dynamic language programmer has a way of expressing type properties that can be checked *statically* instead of dynamically; i.e., once instead of repeatedly. More importantly, abstract data types can be integrated into a dynamically typed language in a modular and representation-

---

[1] This algorithm is not presented for space reasons.

independent fashion. In principle they do not even have to be implemented in the same language. The type system together with the coercions make sure that no undetected representation-dependent effects slip through.

An immediate application of the minimal completion algorithms is in tag optimization of run-time typed languages such as Scheme, Common LISP or SETL. The completion algorithms extended to let-polymorphism may also be applicable in ML-like languages for improved type error identification and recovery since they keep track of the creation and use points of values.

2 Dynamically typed lambda calculus

In this section we introduce the *dynamically typed λ-calculus (dynamic λ-calculus)*. It is an extension of the (statically) typed λ-calculus with a distinguished type constant *dyn* and special embedding and projection functions we call *coercions*.

We can think of elements of type *dyn* as "(type) tagged" values; that is, as tag-value pairs where the tag indicates the type of the value component. Coercions represent a special class of functions that embed values into the "universal" type *dyn* and project them back from *dyn*. In general, for every type constructor TC of arity k there is an *embedding* that maps elements of type $TC(dyn, \ldots, dyn)$ to *dyn* by pairing them with their type. For example, the coercion *func* maps a function f of type $dyn \to dyn$ to *dyn*. Note that since f is required to have domain and codomain type *dyn* it is sufficient to tag f with the type *constructor*, $\to$, alone as all the arguments to $\to$ are required to be *dyn*. This is in contrast to the dynamic typing disciplines described in [Myc84,ACPP91,LM91] where values of *any* type may be tagged with their type *expression*.

For every embedding c for type constructor TC there is a corresponding *projection*, denoted by c^{-1}, that maps elements of type *dyn* to $TC(dyn, \ldots, dyn)$: it checks whether its argument has the tag TC; if so, it strips the tag and returns the untagged value; if not, it generates a (run-time) type error. It is possible to include a general typecase form (see [ACPP91]) in the language; this way projections can be *defined* instead of added as language primitives; e.g.,

$$\begin{aligned}
&\textbf{typecase } e \textbf{ of}\\
&\quad ([func]f)\ f\\
&\quad\quad \textbf{else } \epsilon_{dyn \to dyn}\\
&\textbf{end}
\end{aligned}$$

is the definition of $func^{-1}$, where $\epsilon_{dyn \to dyn}$ represents a run-time type error. Indeed, general type dispatching can be described, which is not "directly" possible with projections alone; e.g.,

$$\begin{aligned}
&\textbf{typecase } e \textbf{ of}\\
&\quad ([func]f)\ \textbf{typecase } (f([bool]true))\ \textbf{of}\\
&\quad\quad\quad ([bool]b)\ b\\
&\quad\quad\quad\quad \textbf{else } \epsilon_{bool}\\
&\quad\quad \textbf{end}\\
&\quad ([bool]b)\ b\\
&\textbf{end.}
\end{aligned}$$

In this paper we are primarily interested in automatically *inferring* embeddings and projections in programs that use them implicitly, as is the case in run-time typed languages where they correspond to tagging and check-and-untag operations (see Section 3). Consequently we omit the general typecase form for the present purposes.

Coercion type signatures are expressions of the form $\tau \rightsquigarrow \tau'$, where τ, τ' are type expressions (see below). Taking embeddings and projections and the identity function, ι, as *primitive coercions* we can build a calculus of coercions as follows:

- coercions can be (functionally) composed to form new coercions as long as their types match up;

- for every type constructor TC of $k > 0$ arguments there is a *coercion constructor* that takes k coercions, one for each argument position, as inputs and combines them to a new coercion.

For example, if $c_1 : \tau_1 \rightsquigarrow \tau'_1, c_2 : \tau_2 \rightsquigarrow \tau'_2$ are coercions then $c_1 \rightarrow c_2 : (\tau'_1 \rightarrow \tau_2) \rightsquigarrow (\tau_1 \rightarrow \tau'_2)$ is an *induced* coercion that operates on functions f of type $\tau'_1 \rightarrow \tau_2$. It returns a function of type $\tau_1 \rightarrow \tau'_2$, which is the composition of (in diagrammatical order) coercion c_1, function f and finally coercion c_2. Using β- and η-equality it is possible to *define* the coercion constructor $\rightarrow$ by $c \rightarrow c' = \lambda y.\lambda x.[c'](y([c]x)).$[2]

Coercions defined only from embeddings and the identity (no projections) are *positive coercions*; those defined only from projections and the identity (no embeddings) are *negative coercions*. A language with *only* positive coercions corresponds to a "coercion formulation" of a subtyping discipline; c.f. [Tha88,BCGS89,CG90]. If negative coercions are added to a subtyping theory without explicit coercions (e.g.,[FM88]) in a naive fashion this leads to a complete collapse of the type hierarchy — every type is equal to *dyn*. In this sense the presence of negative coercions makes dynamic typing fundamentally different from subtyping.

The pure dynamically typed λ-calculus with only the type constructor $\rightarrow$ is operationally uninteresting since no type errors can occur. In this case the coercions have no operational significance and may be ignored during execution. For this purpose we use as a vehicle for our investigations the dynamically typed λ-calculus with an additional primitive type, the Booleans. The type expressions in this language are generated by the production

$$\tau ::= \alpha \mid bool \mid \tau' \rightarrow \tau'' \mid dyn$$

The typing rules for the dynamic λ-calculus with Booleans are given in Figure 1 in natural deduction style. Throughout this paper we use the following notational conventions: $e, e', \ldots$ denote (dynamically typed or untyped) λ-terms; $c, c', d, d', \ldots$ denote coercions; $\tau, \tau', \ldots$ denote type expressions; and $\alpha, \beta, \ldots$ are type variables. Introduction of a typing assumption for a variable x hides all other assumptions for x until it is discharged. If $e : \tau$ is derivable from a set of typing assumptions A we write $A \vdash e : \tau$. We say e is a *dynamically typed λ-term* if $A \vdash e : \tau$ for some typing assumptions A and type expression τ.

The rule (COERCE) is the only rule with which additional typings beyond those of the simply typed λ-calculus can be inferred. Note that on the one hand

---

[2]We treat $c \rightarrow c'$ separately since we do not rely on β- and/or *eta*-equality. See Section 4.

(ABSTR) $[x : \tau']$

$$\frac{e : \tau}{\lambda x.e : \tau' \to \tau}$$

(APPL) $\quad e : \tau' \to \tau$

$$\frac{e' : \tau'}{ee' : \tau}$$

(CONST) $\quad true, false : bool$

(IF) $\quad e : bool$

$\quad\quad e' : \tau$

$\quad\quad e'' : \tau$

$$\frac{}{\textbf{if } e \textbf{ then } e' \textbf{ else } e'' : \tau}$$

($\to$-EMBED) $\quad func : (dyn \to dyn) \leadsto dyn$

($\to$-PROJ) $\quad func^{-1} : dyn \leadsto (dyn \to dyn)$

($\to$-CONSTR) $\quad c_1 : \tau_1 \leadsto \tau_1'$

$\quad\quad\quad c_2 : \tau_2 \leadsto \tau_2'$

$$\frac{}{c_1 \to c_2 : (\tau_1' \to \tau_2) \leadsto (\tau_1 \to \tau_2')}$$

(BOOL-EMBED) $\quad bool : bool \leadsto dyn$

(BOOL-PROJ) $\quad bool^{-1} : dyn \leadsto bool$

(NOP) $\quad \iota : \tau \leadsto \tau$

(COMP) $\quad c_1 : \tau \leadsto \tau'$

$\quad\quad\quad c_2 : \tau' \leadsto \tau''$

$$\frac{}{c_1 ; c_2 : \tau \leadsto \tau''}$$

(COERCE) $\quad e : \tau$

$\quad\quad\quad c : \tau \leadsto \tau'$

$$\frac{}{\lceil c \rceil e : \tau'}$$

Figure 1: Typing rules for the dynamically typed λ-calculus with Booleans

coercions cannot *directly* be passed as arguments to or returned from functions. On the other hand, every coercion $c : \tau \leadsto \tau'$ can be represented by the function and "first-class" value $\lambda x.[c]x : \tau \to \tau'$. Since not *all* ($\lambda$-definable) functions are coercions, however, we keep coercions strictly separately from arbitrary functions.

Induced coercions give us the effect of tagging with full type expressions since for every type τ there is a coercion $c : \tau \leadsto dyn$; e.g., $[bool^{-1} \to bool; func](\lambda x : bool.\text{if } x \text{ then } false \text{ else } true$ has type dyn. Yet a general typecase form with matching on full type expressions is counter to our desire to treat this dynamically typed λ-term as equivalent to $[func](\lambda x : dyn.\text{if } [bool^{-1}]x \text{ then } [bool]false \text{ else } [bool]true$ (see [Tha90] and Section 4 of this paper).

We shall not give a semantics of the dynamically typed λ-calculus, but leave this question deliberately open at this point. In Section 3 we will treat an *untyped* λ-term as an *incomplete* program into which explicit coercions must be *inserted* to form a dynamically typed λ-term. In Section 4 (resp. 5) we *characterize* the semantic properties that a semantics of the dynamically typed λ-calculus must satisfy if all possible (resp. safe) *completions* of an untyped λ-term are to be *coherent*, i.e., denote the same value.

3 Completions

In the implementation of programming languages with implicit dynamic type checking, type handling operations are in effect "inserted" into the source code in a canonical fashion: Every variable is assigned type *dyn*; at every program point where a value is *created* (e.g., by a constant or a λ-abstraction) the corresponding tagging operation (embedding) is inserted; and at every program point where a value is *used* (e.g., by the test in a conditional or by a function application), the appropriate check-and-untag operation (projection) is inserted. In this fashion the resulting "completed" program satisfies the typing rules of Section 2.

The main disadvantage of this scheme is that dynamic type operations are *always* used, even in cases where they could be omitted; in particular, statically well-typed programs are also annotated with type operations, which typically results in slower execution compared to execution without any type operations.[3]

We view a program with implicit run-time checking as an *incompletely typed* program; that is, a program from which coercions (and type declarations of variables) have been omitted. It is the task of the type inferencer to *complete* this program by inserting explicit coercions such that the typing rules are satisfied. This extends the role of conventional type inferencers in that not only type information but also identity and placement of coercions in the source program are inferred.

Formally, the *untyped λ-terms (with Booleans)* are generated by the production

$$e ::= x \mid \lambda x.e' \mid e'e'' \mid true \mid false \mid \text{if } e' \text{ then } e'' \text{ else } e'''.$$

The *erasure* of a dynamically typed λ-term e is the untyped λ-term that arises from "erasing" all coercions from e (including the square brackets, of course).

---

[3] We use as a fundamental assumption that operations on untagged data are generally more efficient than the corresponding operations on tagged data, which also have to perform tagging and checking.

Conversely, a *completion* of an untyped λ-term e is a dynamically typed λ-term whose erasure is e. Since there is generally more than one completion for the same incomplete program we treat the resulting ambiguity as a problem of *coherence* [BCGS89,CG90] (see Section 4) or *safety* (c.f. [Tha90]; see Section 5) of the semantics of the completions.

A completion models the process of making coercions explicit that are implicit, but nonetheless present, in run-time typed languages. The process of making them explicit opens the opportunity for source-level compile-time optimization.

Note that the "local" translation of untyped λ-terms to dynamically typed λ-terms described at the beginning of this section is a completion in this sense; we shall call it the *canonical completion* of an untyped λ-term. Intuitively, it *maximizes* the use of embeddings and projections.

We illustrate this translation for the familiar fixpoint combinator Y of Church. The Y-combinator is defined by

$$Y = \lambda f.(\lambda x.f(xx))(\lambda y.f(yy)).$$

Its canonical translation into the dynamically typed λ-calculus is

$$
\begin{aligned}
Y_c \;=\; & [func]\lambda f : dyn. \\
& [func^{-1}][func](\lambda x : dyn.[func^{-1}]f([func^{-1}]xx)) \\
& [func](\lambda y : dyn.[func^{-1}]f([func^{-1}]yy)).
\end{aligned}
$$

The canonical translation generates a dynamically typed λ-term for *every* untyped λ-term. Thus we have the following proposition.

Proposition 1 *Every untyped λ-term has at least one completion.*

Another possible completion for the Y-combinator that actually minimizes the use of coercions is

$$
\begin{aligned}
Y_m \;=\; & \lambda f : dyn \rightarrow dyn. \\
& (\lambda x : dyn \rightarrow dyn.f(x[func]x)) \\
& (\lambda y : dyn.f([func^{-1}]yy)),
\end{aligned}
$$

which is of type $(dyn \rightarrow dyn) \rightarrow dyn$. Y_m looks, in an intuitive sense, more "efficient" than Y_c because fewer type operations have to be executed during its evaluation.

4 Coherence

Completions induce a congruence relation on dynamically typed λ-terms and coercions: $e' \cong e''$ if $A \vdash e' : \tau$ and $A \vdash e'' : \tau$ for some set of typing assumptions A and type expression τ, and e', e'' have the same erasure; $c' \cong c''$ if $x : \tau \vdash [c']x : \tau'$ and $x : \tau \vdash [c'']x : \tau'$ for some τ, τ'. If any two such congruent λ-terms, respectively coercions, are semantically equivalent, we can define the meaning of an untyped λ-term as the meaning of *any arbitrary one* of its completions. This opens the

$$(c; c'); c'' = c; (c'; c'') \tag{1}$$
$$c; \iota = c \tag{2}$$
$$\iota; c = c \tag{3}$$
$$c; c^{-1} = \iota \tag{4}$$

$$\iota \to \iota = \iota \tag{5}$$
$$(c \to c'); (d \to d') = (d; c) \to (c'; d') \tag{6}$$
$$[\iota]e = e \tag{7}$$
$$[c'][c]e = [c; c']e \tag{8}$$
$$[c \to d]\lambda x.e = \lambda x.[d](e\{x \mapsto [c]x\}) \tag{9}$$
$$([c \to d]e)e' = [d](e([c]e')) \tag{10}$$

$$[c]\text{if } e \text{ then } e' \text{ else } e'' = \text{if } e \text{ then } [c]e' \text{ else } [c]e'' \tag{11}$$

Figure 2: Conversions for dynamically typed λ-terms with Boolean truth values

door to *intensional* considerations: finding operationally efficient completions by taking the *global* program structure into account. This is addressed in Section 6. In this section we characterize the properties a semantics of the dynamically typed λ-calculus must satisfy to be coherent (yield the same meaning) for *all* completions of any untyped λ-term.

Consider the equational theory given in Figure 2 over dynamically typed λ-terms and (well-formed) coercions.

Theorem 1 *(Coherence of completions)*
The equational axioms and rules of Figure 2 together with the additional *rule* $c^{-1}; c = \iota$ *(for every embedding c) is an axiomatization of completion congruence; that is, for all dynamically typed λ-terms e', e'' we have $e' \cong e''$ if and only if $e' = e''$ is derivable with the standard equational axioms and inference rules (reflexivity, symmetry, transitivity, congruence under arbitrary contexts). Furthermore, the axiom system is irredundant; i.e., no rule or axiom can be derived from the others.*

We need a lemma for the proof that guarantees that coercions are congruent exactly when they have the same type signature. The *coercion equalities* are the axioms and rules in Figure 2 in which no λ-terms occur, together with the additional equation $c^{-1}; c$.

Lemma 2 *(Equality of coercions)*
Let $c : \tau \rightsquigarrow \sigma, c' : \tau' \rightsquigarrow \sigma'$ be arbitrary coercions. Then $c = c'$ is derivable from the coercion equalities if and only if $\tau = \tau'$ and $\sigma = \sigma'$.

It is easy to see that for every coercion $c : \tau \rightsquigarrow \tau'$, primitive or induced, there is an "inverse" coercion $c' : \tau' \rightsquigarrow \tau$ such that $c; c' = \iota$ and $c'; c = \iota$. We reserve the notation c^{-1} for projections corresponding to (primitive) embeddings, however, as we have no need for a general inverse operation on coercions.

Proof: (Proof of theorem) Let $e' = e''$ be derivable. By inspection of the axioms and rules it can be verified that e' and e'' have the same erasure. Similarly it can be checked that $A \vdash e' : \tau$ if and only if $A \vdash e'' : \tau$. It follows that they are congruent completions; i.e., $e' \cong e''$.

For the converse, we call a dynamically typed λ-term *head coercion free* (c.f. [CG90]) if it is *not* of the form $[c]e'$. W.l.o.g. we may assume that coercions are only applied to head coercion free λ-terms and every head coercion free subterm has exactly one coercion applied to it. This follows from $[c_k] \ldots [c_1]e = [c_1; \ldots; c_k]e$ for $k \geq 2$ and $e = [\iota]e$. We prove $e' \cong e'' \Rightarrow e' = e''$ by induction on the erasure e of e' and e''.

(Basis, I) If $e = x$ then $e' = [c']x, e'' = [c'']x$. This implies $c, c' : A(x) \rightsquigarrow \tau$ and thus $c = c'$ by Lemma 2.

(Basis, II) If $e = true$ or $e = false$ then similar as above.

(Inductive step, I) If $e = \lambda x.f$ then $e' = [c']\lambda x : \tau'.f'$ and $e'' = [c'']\lambda x : \tau''.f''$. Since there is a coercion from any type to any other type there are coercions $d : \tau'' \leq \tau', d' : \upsilon' \leq \upsilon''$ such that $[d \rightarrow d']\lambda x : \tau'.f' = \lambda x : \tau''.[d']f'\{x \mapsto [d]x\}$. That is, we have for $A\{x : \tau''\}$ the completions $[d']f'\{x \mapsto [d]x\}$ and f'' of type υ'', and by inductive hypothesis, $[d']f'\{x \mapsto [d]x\} = f''$. Consequently we have $[c''][d \rightarrow d']\lambda x : \tau'.f' = [c'']\lambda x : \tau''.f''$. Since $(d \rightarrow d'; c''), c' : \tau' \leq \tau''$ we know $(d \rightarrow d'; c'') = c'$ and the result follows.

(Inductive step, II) If $e = fg$, then $e' = [c'](f'g')$ and $e'' = [c''](f''g'')$ where $f' : \sigma' \rightarrow \upsilon', f'' : \sigma'' \rightarrow \upsilon''$. There are coercions $d : \sigma'' \rightarrow \sigma', d^{-1} : \sigma' \leq \sigma'', d' : \upsilon' \rightarrow \upsilon''$. We have $[d \rightarrow d']f' = f''$ and $[d^{-1}]g' = g''$ by induction hypothesis, and thus $[c'']([d \rightarrow d']f'[d^{-1}]g') = [c''](f''g'')$. We get $[c''][d'](f'g') = [c''](f''g'')$. Because of uniqueness of coercions it follows that $(d'; c'') = c'$ and the result follows.

It is easy to construct for every axiom and rule a pair of congruent completions such that they cannot be proved congruent without it. (End of proof) ∎

This shows that, *independent of $\beta-$ and η-equality, all* congruent completions of an untyped λ-term have the same behavior if and only if their meanings satisfy the equations in Figure 2.

5 Safety

In the characterization of coherence of completions (Theorem 1) we have used the equality $c^{-1}; c = \iota$. Accordingly, we have the equality $[bool; func^{-1}; func; bool^{-1}]true = true$ since $bool; func^{-1}; func; bool^{-1} = bool; \iota; bool^{-1} = bool; bool^{-1} = \iota$ and $[\iota]true = true$. With naive evaluation of coercions, however, this equality does *not* hold: $[bool; func^{-1}; func; bool^{-1}]true$ is evaluated by first applying the tagging operation $bool$ to $true$, then the check-and-untag operation $func^{-1}$ and finally $func$ and $bool^{-1}$. Since the tag of the value after applying $bool$ is "*bool*", however, the second operation, $func^{-1}$ generates a type error. In contrast, evaluating $true$ by itself yields no type error. So $c^{-1}; c = \iota$ does *not* hold with naive evaluation of coercions.

In view of Theorem 1 we have three possibilities to address this problem:

1. Allow arbitrary completions, retain naive evaluation of coercions, but give up on coherence of completions.

2. Allow arbitrary completions and devise a different evaluation strategy for coercions to retain coherence.

3. Retain naive evaluation of coercions, but restrict the class of admissible completions to retain coherence.

Since we envisage the process of completing an untyped program to be automatic, Option 1 is least attractive since it puts the task of deciding the *meaning* of a program into the hands of the completion process, over which a programmer has no control.[4]

We can accomplish Option 2 if coercions are not evaluated until a value is used (as a function in an application or in the test of a conditional). In this way every type operation just adds itself as a tag (even check-and-untag operations!) to a value and at the point of use the resulting sequence of tags is *simplified* by rewriting until an untagged value of the correct type is reached or a type error is generated (see [Tha90]). This form of "simplificational" coercion evaluation has two disadvantages: it is inefficient since it requires complex, long-living tagging and symbolic rewriting, and it gives delayed error messages.

Since naive coercion evaluation is more conventional, generally more efficient, and reports type errors earlier we adopt Option 3. Notice that with naive coercion evaluation $C[c^{-1}; c]$ generates a type error or yields the same value as $C[\iota]$ for *any* context C; never a different (proper) value. We replace the equalities of the form $c^{-1}; c = \iota$ by *inequalities* $\iota \sqsubseteq c^{-1}; c$ for all embeddings c and extend them to other coercions, $d \sqsubseteq d'$, and dynamically typed λ-terms, $e' \sqsubseteq e''$, by combining them with the equalities of Figure 2 and closing them under reflexivity, transitivity and arbitrary context. Here an equality $e' = e''$ is interpreted as the inequalities $e' \sqsubseteq e''$ and $e'' \sqsubseteq e'$. An inequality $e' \sqsubseteq e''$ expresses that, in any context, if e' generates a type error then so does e'' in the same context. These inequalities are a syntactic analogue to Thatte's semantic "wrongness" relation in a fixed denotational interpretation [Tha90].

We say that a completion e' of e is *safe* if for every congruent completion e'' we have $e' \sqsubseteq e''$. Intuitively, this guarantees that e' generates as few type errors as possible at run-time; i.e., it does not generate *avoidable* type errors. More importantly, it can be shown that for safe completions naive and simplificational coercion evaluation behave equivalently. So by restricting ourselves to safe completions we can reap the benefits of combining the efficiency and simplicity of naive coercion evaluation with unambiguous semantics and still retain a great degree of freedom of choosing amongst different *safe* completions.

Analogous to the proof of Theorem 1 we can show that every untyped λ-term has a safe completion. In fact, the canonical completion is safe.

Proposition 3 *(Safety of canonical completions)*
Every untyped λ-term has at least one safe completion.

---

[4]This is a fundamental difference from the dynamic typing disciplines of [ACPP89] and [LM91] since in those type systems the programmer is expected to control coercions completely.

Note that for two congruent safe completions e', e'' of an untyped λ-term e we can derive $e' = e''$ from the equational axiom system in Figure 2 alone, *without* the equation $c^{-1}; c = \iota$.

6 Minimal completions

As we have seen, the canonical completion of an untyped λ-term is safe. But it is also inefficient. In this section we define a general syntactic criterion for discussing which completion is operationally "better" than another. This criterion is robust in the sense that no particular concrete operational semantics, implementation technology, *etc.*, is assumed, but only that execution of a tagging operation (embedding) and then its corresponding check-and-untag operation (projection) is less efficient than executing nothing at all. For various classes of safe completions we report efficient algorithms for computing *minimal* (optimal) completions w.r.t. to that syntactic criterion. In particular, we describe a theoretically and practically very efficient algorithm for a class of completions that has possible applications in the optimization of run-time typed languages such as Scheme, Common LISP, SETL and others.

Consider the coercion equality $(c; c^{-1}) = \iota$ (Figure 2). With naive coercion evaluation the left-hand side and the right-hand side are equivalent since first tagging a value and then untagging it again has the same effect as doing nothing at all to the value. Clearly, however, literally *executing* the left-hand side is wasteful and unnecessary. Based on this observation we define a preorder on *safe* completions by replacing the equality $c; c^{-1} = \iota$ with the inequality

$$\iota \leq c; c^{-1}.$$

We extend $\leq$ to arbitrary coercions and dynamically typed λ-terms by adding the *remaining* equalities of Figure 2 (*without* the equality $(c; c^{-1}) = \iota$, of course) and closing it under reflexivity, transitivity and arbitrary contexts ($e = e'$ is interpreted as $e \leq e'$ and $e' \leq e$).

Intuitively, if we have $e \leq e'$ then e and e' are observably equivalent (i.e., $e = e'$ can be proved from the equational theory of Figure 2), but e has no more coercions than e'. This expresses itself by e' having *syntactically* fewer coercions than e, but it also executes fewer coercions at run-time for any reasonable operational semantics.

A completion e' is *minimal* in a class of safe congruent completions C if it is in C and for every e'' in C we have $e' \leq e''$. In this sense a minimal completion is an operationally optimal completion in a class w.r.t. to ordering $\leq$. Note, however, that minimal completions need not be unique as there may be distinct safe congruent completions e', e'' such that both $e' \leq e''$ and $e'' \leq e'$. For any untyped λ-term e, type assumptions A and type expression τ we define four different classes of safe completions e' of e such that $A \vdash e' : \tau$: completions that use only primitive coercions (embeddings and projections) and place them at data creation and data use points only; completions that use only primitive coercions (and place them anywhere); completions that use arbitrary coercions, but place them at data creation and data use points only; and arbitrary completions (using arbitrary coercions placed anywhere). We denote these four completion classes by $C_{pf}^{A,\tau}(e), C_{p*}^{A,\tau}(e), C_{*f}^{A,\tau}, C_{**}^{A,\tau}(e)$, respectively.

Henceforth let A, e, τ be fixed, but arbitrary. We shall simply write C_{pf}, C_{p*}, C_{*f} and C_{**}, respectively, for the four classes above. Let C be any one of these.

Theorem 2 *C has a minimal completion.*

Let e be of size n. We denote by m the size of the *value flow graph* of e. This is essentially the higher-order extension of the call graph of a program; its construction is also called closure analysis [Ses89]. In the worst case m is $O(n^2)$, but for well-designed programs the value flow graph is typically sparse, i.e., $m = O(n)$.

Theorem 3 *A minimal completion of C can be computed in the complexity given in the following chart.*[5]

completions	only primitive coercions	arbitrary coercions
only at fixed places	$O(n\alpha(n,n))$	$O(nm)$
at arbitrary places	$O(n\alpha(n,n))$	$O(nm)$

These results follow from the constraint system characterization and normalization that is the heart of our (minimal) completion algorithms. The algorithms are variants on two basic algorithms, one for completions with only primitive coercions, the other for completions with arbitrary coercions. The first of these two can be viewed as an instrumented unification closure algorithm with some additional postprocessing and has been used for efficient binding-time analysis [Hen91]. At the core of the second algorithm is an efficient dynamic transitive closure algorithm (e.g., La Poutré and van Leeuwen [LPvL87] and Yellin [Yel88]) for computing value flow graphs (closure analysis); it has been used for the efficient solution of a specialized semi-unification problem [Hen90]. We only describe the minimal completion algorithm for C_{pf}; that is, for completions that use only primitive coercions, which are placed at creation and use points only. We restrict ourselves to closed λ-terms. We shall not present algorithms or proofs for the other cases as this would substantially lengthen this paper.

Our type inference algorithm for C_{pf} consists of the following steps

1. For given λ-term e construct a type constraint system C;

2. normalize C to C' with respect to a set of constraint transformation rules;

3. construct a "minimal" solution from C';

4. translate the minimal solution into a (minimal) completion of e.

The advantage of "distilling" the essence of type inference into constraint systems is that it frees the type inference problem from the syntactic structure of programs and permits solution strategies that are *not* strictly syntax-directed.

---

[5] α is an inverse of Ackermann's function, which may be considered a small constant for all practical purposes [Tar83].

For a λ-term e associate a type variable α_x with every λ-bound and free variable x (w.l.o.g. we assume they are distinct) and with every subterm occurrence e' of e associate a type variable $\alpha_{e'}$ with e'. Define $C(e)$ as follows.

1. If $e = \lambda x.e'$ then $C(e) = \{\alpha_x \to \alpha_{e'} \overset{?}{\le} \alpha_e\} \cup C(e')$;

2. if $e = e'@e''$ then $C(e) = \{\alpha_{e''} \to \alpha_e \overset{?}{\le} \alpha_{e'}\} \cup C(e') \cup C(e'')$;

3. if $e = \textbf{if } e' \textbf{ then } e'' \textbf{ else } e'''$ then $C(e) = \{bool \overset{?}{\le} \alpha_{e'}, \alpha_{e''} = \alpha_{e'''}, \alpha_e = \alpha_e''\} \cup C(e') \cup C(e'') \cup C(e''')$;

4. if $e = c$ then $C(e) = \{bool \overset{?}{\le} \alpha_e\}$ where $c = true$ or $c = false$;

5. if $e = x$ (x variable) then $C(e) = \{\alpha_e \overset{?}{=} \alpha_x\}$.

Figure 3: Extracting typing constraints

6.1 Basic constraint system extraction

A type constraint system is a multiset of constraints of the following forms.

$$\alpha \to \alpha' \overset{?}{\le} \beta$$
$$bool \overset{?}{\le} \beta$$
$$\alpha \overset{?}{=} \alpha'$$

where α, α', β denote type variables or the type constant dyn. A *solution* of a constraint system C is a substitution S of type expressions for type variables such that

- for $\alpha \to \alpha' \overset{?}{\le} \beta$ in C there exists a primitive coercion[6] c such that $c : S(\alpha) \to S(\alpha') \le S(\beta)$;

- for $bool \overset{?}{\le} \beta$ in C there exists a primitive coercion c such that $c : bool \le S(\beta)$;

- for $\alpha \overset{?}{=} \alpha'$ we have $S(\alpha) = S(\alpha')$; and

- $S(\alpha) = \alpha$ for all α *not* occurring in C.

Note that in general we can develop our treatment of constraints over an arbitrary term algebra representing type expressions. This is useful in a realistic setting where we have a multitude of predefined basic types and type constructors (and possibly also user-defined types and type constructors).

---

[6] Recall that ι is a primitive coercion.

First we define the constraint "extraction" function C. It is given in Figure 3. The solutions of $C(e)$ and the completions of e are in a very close relation, as expressed in the following theorem.

Theorem 4 *(Soundness and completeness of constraint characterization)*
The completions of e and the solutions of $C(e)$ are in a one-to-one correspondence.

Proof: Analogous to Theorem 1 in [Hen91]. (End of proof) ■
Let us write $e_1 = \lambda x.f(xx)$ and $e_2 = \lambda y.f(yy)$. Church's fixed point combinator is $Y = \lambda f.e_1 e_2$. Then the constraints $C(Y)$ for Y are:

$$\alpha_x \to \alpha_{xx} \overset{?}{\le} \alpha_x$$
$$\alpha_{xx} \to \alpha_{f(xx)} \overset{?}{\le} \alpha_f$$
$$\alpha_x \to \alpha_{f(xx)} \overset{?}{\le} \alpha_{e_1}$$
$$\alpha_y \to \alpha_{yy} \overset{?}{\le} \alpha_y$$
$$\alpha_{yy} \to \alpha_{f(yy)} \overset{?}{\le} \alpha_f$$
$$\alpha_y \to \alpha_{f(yy)} \overset{?}{\le} \alpha_{e_2}$$
$$\alpha_{e_2} \to \alpha_{e_1 e_2} \overset{?}{\le} \alpha_{e_1}$$
$$\alpha_f \to \alpha_{e_1 e_2} \overset{?}{\le} \alpha_Y.$$

6.2 Constraint system normalization

Constraint system normalization transforms $C(e)$ into an equivalent constraint system $C'(e)$ over the same class of constraints. It preserves the set of solutions, but it generates normal forms that make it easy to construct concrete solutions since it eliminates *all* constraints that *cannot* be solved equationally.

Let $G(C)$ be the graph defined on type variables occurring in C such that there is a directed edge from α to β whenever there is a constraint $\alpha \to \alpha' \overset{?}{\le} \beta$ or $\alpha' \to \alpha \overset{?}{\le} \beta$ in C. We say C is *cyclic* if $G(C)$ is; and *acyclic* otherwise. The transformation rules for normalizing $C(e)$ are given in Figure 4.

The normalization of $C(e)$ results in a substitution S and a normal form constraint system $C'(e)$ with the following properties:

1. For all inequality constraints $\ldots \overset{?}{\le} \alpha$ in $C'(e)$ the right-hand side, α, is a (type) variable.

2. There is at most one constraint of the form $\ldots \overset{?}{\le} \alpha$ in $C'(e)$ for every α.

3. C is acyclic.

4. No constraints of the form $\alpha \overset{?}{=} \alpha'$ are in $C'(e)$.

Let C be a constraint system with constraints of the form

- $\alpha \to \alpha' \stackrel{?}{\leq} \alpha''$,

- $bool \stackrel{?}{\leq} \alpha$, and

- $\alpha \stackrel{?}{=} \alpha'$

where $\alpha, \alpha', \alpha'' \in V \cup \{dyn\}$. The transformation rules are:

1. (inequality constraint rules)

   (a) $C \cup \{\alpha \to \alpha' \stackrel{?}{\leq} \gamma, \beta \to \beta' \stackrel{?}{\leq} \gamma\} \Rightarrow C \cup \{\alpha \to \alpha' \stackrel{?}{\leq} \gamma, \alpha \stackrel{?}{=} \beta, \alpha' \stackrel{?}{=} \beta'\}$;

   (b) $C \cup \{\alpha \to \alpha' \stackrel{?}{\leq} \gamma, bool \stackrel{?}{\leq} \gamma\} \Rightarrow C \cup \{\alpha \to \alpha' \stackrel{?}{\leq} \gamma, bool \stackrel{?}{\leq} \gamma, \gamma \stackrel{?}{=} dyn\}$;

   (c) $C \cup \{\alpha \to \alpha' \stackrel{?}{\leq} dyn\} \Rightarrow C \cup \{\alpha \stackrel{?}{=} dyn, \alpha' \stackrel{?}{=} dyn\}$;

   (d) $C \cup \{bool \stackrel{?}{\leq} dyn\} \Rightarrow C$;

2. (equational constraint rules)

   (a) $C \cup \{dyn \stackrel{?}{=} \alpha\} \Rightarrow C \cup \{\alpha \stackrel{?}{=} dyn\}$ if α is a type variable;

   (b) $C \cup \{dyn \stackrel{?}{=} dyn\} \Rightarrow C$;

   (c) $C \cup \{\alpha \stackrel{?}{=} \alpha'\} \stackrel{S}{\Rightarrow} S(C)$ if α is a type variable and $S = \{\alpha \mapsto \alpha'\}$;

3. (occurs check rule)

   (a) $C \Rightarrow C \cup \{\alpha \stackrel{?}{=} dyn\}$ if C is cyclic and α is on a cycle in $G(C)$.

Figure 4: Normalizing constraints

Theorem 5 *(Correctness of constraint normalization)*

If $C \overset{S}{\Rightarrow} C'$ and $\mathcal{U}$ is the set of solutions of C' then $\{U \circ S | U \in \mathcal{U}\}$ is the set of solutions of C.

Normalization of $C(Y)$ results in the substitution

$$S_Y = \{\alpha_x, \alpha_{xx}, \alpha_{f(xx)}, \alpha_y, \alpha_{yy}, \alpha_{f(yy)}, \alpha_{e_2}, \alpha_{e_1 e_2} \mapsto dyn\}$$

and the normalized constraint system $C'(Y)$ containing

$$dyn \to dyn \overset{?}{\leq} \alpha_f$$

$$dyn \to dyn \overset{?}{\leq} \alpha_{e_1}$$

$$\alpha_f \to dyn \overset{?}{\leq} \alpha_Y$$

6.3 Solution construction

We can construct a "canonical" solution from normal form constraint system $C'(e)$ by simply unifying all inequalities. The properties of a normal form constraint system guarantee that all the constraints in $C'(e)$ can be satisfied *equationally*. We shall call this solution the *minimal solution* of $C'(e)$ and, by extension, of $C(e)$. Because of Theorem 4 this solution corresponds to a unique completion e' of e that has some type τ. It can be shown by induction on e that for any other completion e'' in C_{pf} of type τ there exists a coercion $c : \tau \leadsto \tau$ such that $e'' = [c]e'$ is derivable in the equational system of Figure 2 *without* using equality $c; c^{-1} = \iota$. Since $\iota \leq c$ this implies $e' \leq e''$, which shows that e' is minimal in C_{pf}.

Theorem 6 *(Complexity of computing minimal completions)*

The minimal completion of an untyped λ-term of size n can be computed in time $O(n\alpha(n, n))$ and space $O(n)$ where α is an inverse of Ackermann's function [Tar83].

Proof: (Sketch) It is easily seen that constraint extraction and minimal solution construction construction can be implemented in linear time.[7] In [Hen91] an amortization argument is given that shows that constraint normalization is implementable in time $O(n\alpha(n, n))$ (and space $O(n)$) using the union/find data structure with ranked union and path compression [GI91]. (End of proof) ∎

The minimal solution of $C'(Y)$ is the substitution

$$U_Y = \{\alpha_f, \alpha_{e_1} \mapsto dyn \to dyn, \alpha_Y \mapsto (dyn \to dyn) \to dyn\}$$

The resulting minimal completion in $C_{pf}(Y)$ is

$$\begin{aligned}
Y_{mf} &= \lambda f : dyn \to dyn. \\
&\quad (\lambda x : dyn. f([func^{-1}]xx)) \\
&\quad [func](\lambda y : dyn. f([func^{-1}]yy)).
\end{aligned}$$

---

[7]We assume type expressions may be represented with sharing to avoid the well-known exponential blow-up of string representations of the solutions of unification problems.

Comparing it to the completion Y_m in Section 3 note that $Y_m < Y_{mf}$; i.e., $Y_m \leq Y_{mf}$, but not $Y_{mf} \leq Y_m$. So Y_m is "better" than Y_{mf}, but Y_m is *not* in $C_{pf}(Y)$, but Y_m is the minimal completion in $C_{p*}(Y)$.

7 Polymorphism

In this section we sketch an extension of dynamic typing to a type discipline with let-polymorphism [Mil78]. A thorough and satisfactory treatment of polymorphic dynamic typing will have to be deferred to future work.

A minimal completion of e for one context C cannot generally be extended to a safe completion for $C'[e]$ where C' is another context for e. Consider the following example from [Tha90], in which we assume we have also lists and integers in our language: $e = \lambda x.cons\ 1\ x$. Its minimal completion in the context $C[] = car([](cons\ 1\ nil)) + 1$ is $\lambda x.cons\ 1\ x : list(integer) \rightarrow list(integer)$. However, in the context $C'[] = [](cons\ true\ nil)$ its minimal completion is $\lambda x.cons\ ([integer]1)\ x : list(dyn) \rightarrow list(dyn)$. Note that the first completion of e in the context C cannot be extended to a *safe* completion for $C'[e]$[8], and that there is *no* completion of e with the apparent polymorphic generalization $\forall \alpha.list\ (\alpha) \rightarrow list\ (\alpha)$ of these two completions. This has the implication, as observed by Thatte [Tha88], that instantiating an "unknown" coercion in a completion of e must be delayed and instantiated separately in every context in which e is used. In a polymorphic type discipline this necessitates that the language provide for passing coercions as arguments to let-bound variables. Through such formal coercion parameters the different contexts of the applied occurrences of a let-bound variable x can pass the concrete coercions to x that are necessary to safely evaluate the body bound to x.

These considerations motivate an extension of the dynamically typed λ-calculus to let-polymorphic programs where let-bindings may be *parameterized* by formal coercion parameters. In this way we can give a completion of $\lambda x.cons\ 1\ x$ that fits both contexts $C[]$ and $C'[]$ above:

$$\text{let } f[c] = \lambda x.cons\ ([c]1)\ x \text{ in}$$
$$car((f[\iota])(cons\ 1\ nil)) + 1$$
$$\ldots$$
$$(f[integer])(cons\ true\ nil)$$

Unfortunately formal coercion parameters are easily used where they are not even necessary. Consider for example **let** $f = \lambda y.y$ **in** $f\ true$. One completion of type *bool* is **let** $f[c] = [c]\lambda y.y$ **in** $(f[\iota])true$. Clearly an operationally preferable completion is simply **let** $f = \lambda y.y$ **in** $f\ true$, also of type *bool*.

It remains to extend the notions of minimality to dynamically typed λ-terms with let-expressions in such a fashion that minimal principal completions coincide with static principal typings for statically polymorphically typable λ-terms.

We do not anticipate any problems with integrating other language features into dynamic typing with polymorphism such as exceptions, side-effects, continua-

---

[8] If simplificational coercion evaluation is used then $(c^{-1}; c = \iota$ is valid and minimal completions may be used as principal completions.

tions and pointers beyond those already observed for statically typed polymorphic languages.

8 Related work

Dynamic typing in a static language can be found in several programming languages. For a survey and historical perspective we refer the reader to [ACPP91].

The main motivation behind the work of Abadi, Cardelli, Pierce and Plotkin [ACPP89,ACPP91] and Leroy and Mauny [LM91] is in using type Dynamic as a universal interface to a changing environment that may contain persistent objects, concurrently executing programs or generally elements not under complete control of a single program. As a consequence these languages have very powerful explicit constructs for tagging and checking values that are both conceptually complex and expensive to implement. This is not an attractive model in a language in which tagging and checking values may be *inferred* since different completions may have very different and unexpected behavior (c.f. remarks by Thatte [Tha90]). By relying on a fixed number of tags — one for each type constructor — dynamic typing is conceptually easier and less expressive than full type tagging; the corresponding typecase form needs to match only type constructors, not complete type expressions and can thus be implemented efficiently using switches (indirect jumps).

In the absence of negative coercions dynamic typing turns into a subtyping discipline with *dyn* functioning as the "top" type. Thatte [Tha88] has investigated such a language with induced coercions where coercions are inserted at fixed places (function applications). He characterized the typability problem as a problem of solving subtyping constraints, but left its decidability open.[9] This problem has recently been shown to be decidable by O'Keefe and Wand [OW91]. The notion of coherence arises in coercion interpretations of subtyping. Breazu-Tannen, Cardelli, Coquand, Gunter and Scedrov [BCGS91] use coherent translations from a language with subtyping into one without, to provide models for a language integrating subtyping (inheritance), parametric polymorphism and recursive types. Similarly, Curien and Ghelli [CG90] give an axiomatization of coherence in $F_\le$ using explicit coercions and use it to show typable $F_\le$ programs have minimal types.[10] Our equational characterization of coherence extends the first-order subset of $F_\le$ with negative coercions and a rule relating λ-terms to each other that have different types bound to the same variable.

Thatte introduced negative coercions in [Tha90]. In his type system the distinction between positive and negative coercions is carried over to induced coercions. Positive coercions may be placed anywhere, but negative coercions can only be placed at use points. Programs are required to have explicit type declarations for every variable; they are completed with explicit coercions such that the resulting program is a convergent completion with explicit coercions. (Thatte's semantically defined notion of convergence has motivated the syntactic notion of safety

---

[9]Note that λ-bound variables have no type declarations in this type inference problem, which sets it apart from the (easier) type checking problem for the first-order fragment of $F_\le$.

[10]An error was later discovered in their proof of decidability of typability in $F_\le$; recently Pierce [Pie91] has announced that type checking $F_\le$ is undecidable.

in this paper.) The denotational semantics is similar to Abadi et al.'s [ACPP91], and the operational semantics uses a form of simplificational evaluation of coercions in which values are tagged with sequences of full type expressions. Note that our completion problem is more general in that programs do not require type declarations for variables and that may insert arbitrary coercions any place.

Gomard [Gom90] inspired our approach to dynamic typing by type inference. He describes type inference for implicitly typed programs with no required type information at all. In dynamic typing terms his algorithm produces a completion with primitive coercions in which positive coercions may only occur at creation points (λ-abstractions, constants). Negative coercions for checking functions may occur at application points, but no negative coercions for base types are permitted; instead tagged versions of base operations are used. As a consequence tagging may "spread" to every point reachable from a single tagging operation. His type inference algorithm is a backtracking adaptation of Algorithm W [Mil78] that executes $\Theta(n^2)$ calls to a unification procedure and thus runs in time $\Theta(n^3)$ with an optimal unification algorithm. Our completion algorithm improves this bound to almost-linear time and "isolates" tagging operations better.

Cartwright and Fagan [CF91] present a very ambitious extension of ML's type inference system with regular recursive types, union types and implicit subtyping based on extension of unions. Dynamic type checking operations are not included in the type system, but they are added during type inference as a consequence of unification failure. All (non-type-variable) types are represented as union types, which are encoded using a type representation scheme pioneered by Remy [Rem89] for record-based inheritance. There are several problems, however, both with the type system and with the "Remy encoding".[11] A typing rule for induced containments of union types is missing (e.g., $\tau_1 \subseteq \tau_3, \tau_2 \subseteq \tau_4 \vdash \tau_1 + \tau_2 \subseteq \tau_3 + \tau_4$) and the subtyping rule for recursive types in the stated form $t \subseteq u \Rightarrow T \subseteq U \vdash \mu t.T \subseteq \mu u.U$ is unsound. The Remy encoding results in restricting subtyping steps to language primitives; yet, on the other hand, it permits encoding of polymorphic types that are not expressible in the original type system. As a consequence the encoding has typing power incomparable to the original type system. For example, for primitive types $bool, integer$ and $f0 : (bool + integer) \rightarrow bool$ the expression

$$\text{let } twice = \lambda f.\lambda x.f(fx) \text{ in}$$
$$\text{let } f1 = twice\, f0 \text{ in}$$
$$\text{if } (f1(\text{if } false \text{ then } true \text{ else } 6)) \text{ then } 0 \text{ else } 1$$

is typable in the original type system without negative coercions, but not in the Remy encoded system. On the other hand,

$$\text{let } cons1 = \lambda x.cons\, 1\, x \text{ in}$$
$$car(cons1(cons\, 1\, nil)) + 1$$
$$\cdots$$
$$cons1(cons\, true\, nil)$$

(adapted from [Tha88]) is not typable in the original type system, but it is in the Remy encoded system. Furthermore, counter to a claim in their paper cur-

---

[11]A revision of this paper, in which these problems are addressed and rectified, is currently underway.

rently there appears to be no known linear-time algorithm for circular unification (unification closure) [KR90].

9 Conclusion

Dynamic typing promises to integrate the advantages of compile-time and run-time type checked programming languages without inheriting their disadvantages. In particular, inferring minimal completions of implicitly dynamically typed programs makes it possible to "only pay for the amount of dynamic typing that is unavoidable" in the underlying static type system.

To estimate the practicality of the minimal completion algorithms we have presented we plan on implementing them for Scheme. Since we do not believe that completions with induced coercions lead to better results in most cases than with only primitive coercions we expect the almost-linear time minimal completion algorithms to be of particular practical value, both to programmers and to optimizers. For a practical adaptation of dynamic typing to a polymorphic type discipline the problem of minimizing the number of coercion parameters to let-bound variables needs to be addressed. It is an intriguing prospect that a polymorphic minimal completion algorithm may lead to novel implementation techniques and optimizations for conventional run-time typed languages.

Acknowledgements

This paper would not have reached the form it has without Satish Thatte's insights, comments and corrections. I am especially greatful for his inquisitive questions that led to the definition of safety. I am also grateful for helpful discussions with members of the TOPPS group at DIKU. Finally, I would like to thank one anonymous referee for some corrections and helpful suggestions for improved exposition. Needless to say, any remaining mistakes and expository deficiencies are entirely my own fault.

References

[ACPP89] M. Abadi, L. Cardelli, B. Pierce, and G. Plotkin. Dynamic typing in a statically-typed language. In *Proc. 16th Annual ACM Symp. on Principles of Programming Languages*, pages 213–227, ACM, Jan. 1989.

[ACPP91] M. Abadi, L. Cardelli, B. Pierce, and G. Plotkin. Dynamic typing in a statically typed language. *ACM Transactions on Programming Languages and Systems (TOPLAS)*, 13(2):237–268, April 1991. Presented at POPL '89.

[BCGS89] V. Breazu-Tannen, T. Coquand, C. Gunter, and A. Scedrov. Inheritance and explicit coercion. In *Proc. Logic in Computer Science (LICS)*, pages 112–129, 1989.

[BCGS91] V. Breazu-Tannen, T. Coquand, C. Gunter, and A. Scedrov. Inheritance as implicit coercion. *Information and Computation*, 93(1):172–221, July 1991. Presented at LICS '89.

[CF91] R. Cartwright and M. Fagan. Soft typing. In *Proc. ACM SIGPLAN '91 Conf. on Programming Language Design and Implementation, Toronto, Ontario*, pages 278–292, ACM, ACM Press, June 1991.

[CG90]   P. Curien and G. Ghelli. Coherence of subsumption. In A. Arnold, editor, *Proc. 15th Coll. on Trees in Algebra and Programming, Copenhagen, Denmark*, pages 132–146, Springer, May 1990.

[FM88]   Y. Fuh and P. Mishra. Type inference with subtypes. In *Proc. 2nd European Symp. on Programming*, pages 94–114, Springer-Verlag, 1988. Lecture Notes in Computer Science 300.

[GI91]   Z. Galil and G. Italiano. Data structures and algorithms for disjoint set union problems. *ACM Computing Surveys*, 23(3):319–344, Sept. 1991.

[Gom90]   C. Gomard. Partial type inference for untyped functional programs (extended abstract). In *Proc. LISP and Functional Programming (LFP), Nice, France*, July 1990.

[Hen90]   F. Henglein. Fast left-linear semi-unification. In *Proc. Int'l. Conf. on Computing and Information*, Springer, May 1990. Lecture Notes of Computer Science, Vol. 468.

[Hen91]   F. Henglein. Efficient type inference for higher-order binding-time analysis. In *Proc. Conf. on Functional Programming Languages and Computer Architecture (FPCA), Cambridge, Massachusetts*, pages 448–472, Springer, Aug. 1991. Lecture Notes in Computer Science, Vol. 523.

[KR90]   P. Kanellakis and P. Revesz. *On the Relationship of Congruence Closure and Unification*, chapter 2, pages 23–41. *Frontier Series*, Addison-Wesley, ACM Press, 1990.

[LM91]   X. Leroy and M. Mauny. Dynamics in ML. In *Proc. Conf. on Functional Programming Languages and Computer Architecture (FPCA), Cambridge, Massachusetts*, pages 406–426, Springer, Aug. 1991. Lecture Notes in Computer Science, Vol. 523.

[LPvL87]   J. La Poutré and J. van Leeuwen. Maintenance of transitive closures and transitive reductions of graphs. In *Proc. Int'l Workshop on Graph-Theoretic Concepts in Computer Science*, pages 106–120, Springer-Verlag, June 1987. Lecture Notes in Computer Science, Vol. 314.

[Mil78]   R. Milner. A theory of type polymorphism in programming. *J. Computer and System Sciences*, 17:348–375, 1978.

[Myc84]   A. Mycroft. Dynamic types in statically typed languages. Aug. 1984. Unpublished manuscript, 2nd draft version.

[OW91]   P. O'Keefe and M. Wand. Type inference for partial types is decidable. Sept. 1991. Submitted to ESOP '92.

[Pie91]   B. Pierce. *Bounded Quantification is Undecidable*. Technical Report CMU-CS-91-161, Carnegie Mellon University, July 1991. To be presented at POPL '92.

[Rem89]   D. Remy. Typechecking records and variants in a natural extension of ML. In *Proc. 16th Annual ACM Symp. on Principles of Programming Languages*, pages 77–88, ACM, Jan. 1989.

[Ses89]   P. Sestoft. Replacing function parameters by global variables. In *Proc. Functional Programming Languages and Computer Architecture (FPCA), London, England*, pages 39–53, ACM Press, Sept. 1989.

[Tar83]   R. Tarjan. *Data Structures and Network Flow Algorithms*. Volume CMBS 44 of *Regional Conference Series in Applied Mathematics*, SIAM, 1983.

[Tha88]   S. Thatte. Type inference with partial types. In *Proc. Int'l Coll. on Automata, Languages and Programming (ICALP)*, pages 615–629, 1988.

[Tha90]   S. Thatte. Quasi-static typing. In *Proc. ACM Symp. on Principles of Programming Languages*, pages 367–381, ACM, Jan. 1990.

[Yel88]   D. Yellin. *A Dynamic Transitive Closure Algorithm*. Technical Report RC 13535, IBM T.J. Watson Research Ctr., June 1988.

Automatic Parallelization of Lazy Functional Programs

*Guido Hogen, Andrea Kindler and Rita Loogen**

RWTH Aachen, Lehrstuhl für Informatik II
Ahornstraße 55, W-5100 Aachen, Germany

Abstract

We present a parallelizing compiler for lazy functional programs that uses strictness analysis to detect the implicit parallelism within programs. It generates an intermediate functional program, where a special syntactic construct 'letpar', which is semantically equivalent to the well-known *let*-construct, is used to indicate subexpressions for which a parallel execution is allowed. Only for sufficiently complex expressions a parallelization will be worthwhile. For small expressions the communication overhead may outweigh the benefits of the parallel execution. Therefore, the parallelizing compiler uses some heuristics to estimate the complexity of expressions.

The distributed implementation of parallelized functional programs described in [Loogen et al. 89] enabled us to investigate the impact of various parallelization strategies on the runtimes and speedups. The strategy, which only allows the parallel execution of non-predefined function calls in strict positions, shows the best runtimes and reasonable speedup results.

1 Introduction

Due to their side effect free nature, functional programs contain implicit parallelism, which consists of independent subexpressions that can be evaluated in parallel. In lazy functional languages, one has to take into account that only subexpressions, whose result is necessary for the overall computation, may be evaluated. So, one has to use some analysis to determine the demanded subexpressions of a program. In general, strictness analysis is proposed for that purpose, because demanded subexpressions are always strict arguments of their context.

During the last decade, a lot of foundational work has been done on strictness analysis methods, see e.g. [Mycroft 81], [Maurer 85], [Burn et al. 86], [Burn 87a,b], [Hudak, Young 86], [Wadler 87], [Wadler, Hughes 87]. The implementation of strictness analysers has been considered in [Clack, Peyton-Jones 85] — with a generalization in [Martin, Hankin 87] — and in [Young, Hudak 86] and [Nöcker 90].

The aim of our work has been to implement a strictness analyser and use it as the kernel of a parallelizing compiler for lazy functional programs. The compiler generates an intermediate functional program, where a special syntactic construct '*letpar*' is used to indicate subexpressions for which a parallel execution is allowed. Although the theoretical foundations of the parallelization process are well-understood, there is a lack of practical experience. Especially the question of how to decompose a program with strictness annotations into sufficiently complex parallel processes has not yet been investigated.

Recently, it has been questioned whether an automatic parallelization of functional programs is at all possible [Vrancken 90]. Of course, one cannot expect that a parallelizing compiler automatically transforms a sequential algorithm into a parallel one. It will always remain the task of the programmer to design the parallel algorithm. The advantage of using a functional programming language instead of a 'parallel' conventional language like OCCAM or Parallel C is that the programmer needs not to think about distribution, communication and synchronization of parallel processes. He "only" has to *specify* the process system, the *management* of the dynamic processes is done by the runtime system. The automatic parallelization — as we understand it — simplifies the portability of programs. The *same* functional program can be executed on either a sequential or, after parallelization, on a parallel system.

---

*email: {ghogen,kindler,rita}@zeus.informatik.rwth-aachen.de

Most projects on the implementation of functional programming languages on parallel architectures directly use a functional language with explicit parallelism, given by special annotations or syntactic constructs, as source language, where it is either claimed that the programmer is responsible for the specification of parallelism and its correctness with respect to the semantics of programs, or that some parallelizing compiler should transform functional programs into their 'parallel' source language, see e.g. [Hudak 86], [Raber et al. 88], [van Eekelen et al. 88], [Hammond, Peyton Jones 90], [McBurney, Sleep 90]. These and several other projects concentrate on the efficient implementation of functional languages plus explicit parallelism on parallel distributed or shared memory architectures rather than on the detection and exposition of parallelism in conventional functional programs.

The work on strictness analysis has often been motivated by the detection of implicit parallelism in functional programs, but up to now only few approaches exist on the use of strictness analysers for that purpose. The first papers that describe a parallelizing compiler, whose structure is similar to ours, are [Hudak, Goldberg 85a,b]. They use some first order strictness analysis over flat domains to detect parallelizable subexpressions and then also use some, not further specified, heuristics to decide which subexpressions should really be executed in parallel.

Our approach can be seen as a continuation of Hudak's and Goldberg's work. We use an advanced strictness analyser that is based on the evaluation transformer approach of [Burn 87a,b], which takes into account context information to handle data structures in an appropriate way. Higher order functions are also supported. It is implemented by the frontier's algorithm, that was introduced in [Clack, Peyton-Jones 85] and extended to include higher-order functions and general lattices in [Martin, Hankin 87].

The main new aspects of our work lie in the discussion and comparison of strategies for the decomposition of analysed programs into parallel processes. Experimental results show that these strategies may have a great impact on the runtimes of parallelized programs and the achievable speedup values.

In this paper we concentrate on three natural decomposition strategies which are compared with respect to runtime experiments using the distributed implementation of [Loogen et al. 89]. It turns out that the strategy, which only allows the parallel execution of non-predefined function applications, gives the best results for our example programs.

The treatment of functions with functional parameters reveals an important property of our parallel implementation, namely the facility to perform a *dynamic parallelization*, which exploits parallelism that cannot be detected by our parallelizing compiler. As it is only possible to parallelize applications where the function is definitely strict in some arguments and as functional parameters may be instantiated by non strict functions, the parallelization of applications of functional parameters is not at all possible. For this reason, a *static parallelization* of higher order functions is not feasible, in general. This is the situation where the dynamic parallelization applies. It allows the parallel evaluation of "complex" arguments of dynamically created applications, i.e. applications of functional parameters that are instantiated by some strict function at runtime, or applications, whose evaluation has been delayed. Consequently, it might be the case that a functional program is evaluated in parallel, although it does not contain any *letpar*-construct, i.e. explicit (static) parallelism.

[Burn 88] and [Lester, Burn 89] also present a realization of the evaluation transformer model of parallel evaluation of functional programs. The main difference to our approach lies in the fact that they allow parallel evaluation wherever possible. This may lead to the generation of too small processes, for which the overhead of the parallel execution is higher than the benefits.

The paper is organized as follows. Section 2 describes the parallelizing compiler. In Section 3 we review our implementation of parallelized functional programs on a distributed memory system (transputers). A comparison of different parallelization strategies with runtime results is contained in Section 4. The dynamic parallelization of higher order functions is discussed in Section 5. Section 6 finally contains some conclusions and hints at future work.

2 Structure of the Parallelizing Compiler

The parallelizing compiler translates a lazy functional program into a system of *parallelized combinators*, i.e. a set of global function definitions, in which the places, where a parallel evaluation of subexpressions may take place, are indicated by a special syntactic construct. This transformation needs three phases as

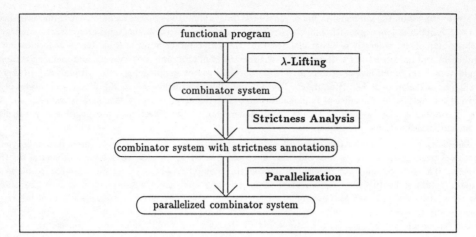

Figure 1: Structure of the Parallelizing Compiler

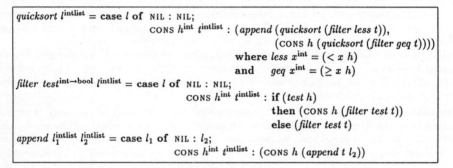

Figure 2: Example Program

indicated in Figure 1. We explain the main ideas of these phases using the quicksort program given in Figure 2.

2.1 λ-Lifting

The translation of functional programs with nested function definitions into a system of global function definitions (combinators) is called λ-lifting and was introduced in [Johnsson 85]. λ-lifting has several advantages, especially with respect to the parallel execution of functional programs. For the evaluation of functional programs with nested function definitions, one has to use a central environment structure which contains the bindings of global variables during the evaluation of local function applications. Such a central structure is of course an obstacle for a parallel implementation, especially when the target architecture is a distributed memory system. λ-lifting lifts local function definitions to the upper level by extending the parameter list of such functions by the global variables that occur in their body. By explicitly passing the values of global variables to the function, a central environment structure becomes superfluous. The value of a combinator application only depends on the arguments. Thus, it causes no problems to pass combinator applications to other processors for evaluation.

λ-lifting of the example program in Figure 2 simply lifts the local non-recursive functions *less* and *geq*, by extending their parameter list by the global variable h. Each occurrence of the local functions is replaced by an application of the new global function to the global variable. Thus the function *quicksort* is replaced by

$$quicksort\ l^{intlist} = \textbf{case}\ l\ \textbf{of}\ \text{NIL} : \text{NIL};$$
$$\text{CONS}\ h^{int}\ t^{intlist} : (append\ (quicksort\ (filter\ (global\_less\ h)\ t)),$$
$$(\text{CONS}\ h\ (quicksort\ (filter\ (global\_geq\ h)\ t))))$$

$$global\_less\ h^{int}\ x^{int} = (< x\ h)$$
$$global\_geq\ h^{int}\ x^{int} = (\geq x\ h)$$

Figure 3: λ-Lifted Example Program

the system given in Figure 3. The functions *filter* and *append* are omitted, because they are not changed.

In general, λ-lifting is more involved, especially for mutually recursive local function definitions. A complete algorithm is described in [Johnsson 85].

2.2 Strictness Analysis

Strictness analysis is used to detect the maximal source of parallelism within a program. Here, we use the technique of abstract interpretation to determine the strictness properties of combinator systems [Abramsky, Hankin 87]. The analysis applies only to monomorphic programs, but in [Abramsky 85] it has been shown that the result of the analysis of any monomorphic instance of a polymorphic function is valid for all instances.

Monomorphic programs are interpreted over the abstract base domains $\{0,1\}$ and $\{0,1,2,3\}$ following the approach of [Mycroft 81, Burn et al. 86, Wadler 87]. The abstract domains have the following intuitive meaning:

- $\{0,1\}$ with $0 < 1$ is the abstraction of non-structured base domains.

    0   represents   the bottom value $\perp$.
    1   represents   all values.

- $\{0,1,2,3\}$ with $0 < 1 < 2 < 3$ is the abstraction of the domains of algebraic data structures.

    0   represents   the bottom value $\perp$, i.e. the non-defined structure.
    1   represents   in addition, partial and infinite structures.
    2   represents   in addition, finite structures (with possibly undefined entries).
    3   represents   all structures, i.e. in addition, finite structures with defined entries.

The abstract interpretation is defined in such a way that:

> The standard interpretation of a function definition is strict in an argument i, if its abstract interpretation is strict in this argument.

Thus, strictness in the abstract interpretation is a decidable approximation of strictness in the standard interpretation.

Example: The abstract interpretation of the combinators of our small example program is as follows. $F^{\natural}$ denotes the abstract interpretation of a combinator F.

$quicksort^{\natural}$	
$l^{\natural}$	
0	0
1	0
2	2
3	3

$filter^{\natural}$				
$test^{\natural} \backslash l^{\natural}$	0	1	2	3
$b^{\natural} \to 0$	0	0	0	3
$b^{\natural} \to b^{\natural}$	0	1	1	3
$b^{\natural} \to 1$	0	1	3	3

$append^{\natural}$				
$l_1^{\natural} \backslash l_2^{\natural}$	0	1	2	3
0	0	0	0	0
1	1	1	1	1
2	1	1	2	2
3	1	1	2	3

$global^{less}_{geq}$		
$h^{\natural} \backslash x^{\natural}$	0	1
0	0	0
1	0	1

The boxed entries show the strictness properties of the combinators. We can determine the strictness property by applying $F^{\natural}$ to $\perp$ in the tested argument position and to the top values of the abstract domain in all other positions. E.g., *append* is strict in its first argument, because $append^{\natural}(0,3) = 0$, but not in its second argument, since $append^{\natural}(3,0) = 1 > 0$. The combinators *global_less/geq* are strict in both arguments.

To compute the abstract interpretation of combinator systems, we apply the *frontier method* of [Clack, Peyton-Jones 85], which has been extended in [Martin, Hankin 87] to handle higher order functions and data structures.

In order to handle data structures in an appropriate way, we use the *evaluation transformer model of computation*, which has been introduced in [Burn 87a]. In this model, expressions are annotated by *evaluators*, which indicate the amount of evaluation that can be done on these expressions. The following evaluators are distinguished:

ξ_0 — means no evaluation,

ξ_1 — evaluates expressions to weak head normal form,

ξ_2 — evaluates the structure of data types, i.e. all constructor nodes, but no entries. For example, the structure of a list is its spine.

ξ_3 — evaluates the structure of data types and each element of the data type to weak head normal form.

The first two evaluators are common for the lazy evaluation of functional programs. Evaluation to *weak head normal form* means that data structures are evaluated up to their top level constructor and functional values are evaluated, until a partial application[1] of a base function, constructor or combinator is reached. Expressions of a base type are completely evaluated. The additional evaluators allow a more accurate treatment of data structures, because they enable an earlier and more extensive evaluation of components and thus may reveal more implicit parallelism.

The evaluators are ordered by $\xi_0 < \xi_1 < \xi_2 < \xi_3$. There is a close correspondence of evaluators and abstract domain values:

> The evaluation of an expression with evaluator ξ_i terminates if and only if the abstract value of the expression is greater than or equal to i.

An *evaluation transformer* is a function that maps evaluators of a function application to suitable evaluators for the argument expressions. So it can be used to determine for each application, which amount of evaluation can be done on the arguments, when the evaluator for the whole application is known.

Thus, the *evaluation transformer* of an n-ary function F consists of n functions, $ET_i(F)$, $1 \le i \le n$, which map the evaluator of an application of F to the evaluator for the ith argument. It can simply be determined using the abstract interpretation of F (for details see [Burn 87a]).

Example: The evaluation transformers of the combinators in our example program are as follows:

ξ	$ET(quicksort)$ $ET_1(\xi)$			ξ	$ET(filter)$ $ET_1(\xi)$	$ET_2(\xi)$	ξ	$ET(append)$ $ET_1(\xi)$	$ET_2(\xi)$	ξ	$ET(global \ldots)$ $ET_1(\xi)$	$ET_2(\xi)$
ξ_0	ξ_0			ξ_0	ξ_0	ξ_0	ξ_0	ξ_0	ξ_0	ξ_0	ξ_0	ξ_0
ξ_1	ξ_2			ξ_1	ξ_0	ξ_1	ξ_1	ξ_1	ξ_0	ξ_1	ξ_1	ξ_1
ξ_2	ξ_2			ξ_2	ξ_0	ξ_2	ξ_2	ξ_2	ξ_2			
ξ_3	ξ_3			ξ_3	ξ_0	ξ_2	ξ_3	ξ_3	ξ_3			

If an application of *quicksort* is evaluated with evaluator ξ_1, it is e.g. safe to evaluate the argument list with ξ_2. Intuitively this is true, because it is only possible to determine the top level constructor of the result list, if it is empty, contains only one element or if the minimum element has been determined. As sorting of the list (CONS $\perp$ NIL) yields the list itself, without that the non defined entry is accessed, the maximal possible evaluator for the argument list is ξ_2.

Evaluation transformers can also be introduced for arbitrary expressions. One simply views the expression as a function of its direct subexpressions. In this case, one even gets more specific information, because it is possible to use the abstract interpretation of the other subexpressions instead of assuming the top value of the abstract domains for these, when determining the strictness properties of argument subexpressions. In general, this approach is called *context sensitive* strictness analysis. We therefore call the evaluation transformer of an arbitrary expression e *context sensitive* and denote it by $ET^{cs}(e)$.

---

[1]Partial applications correspond to λ-abstractions.

2.3 Parallelized Combinator Systems

In the parallelized combinator systems, explicit parallelism is indicated by the following *letpar*-construct:

$$\begin{array}{llll}
\textbf{letpar} & y_1 & = & F_1(e_{11}, \ldots, e_{1n_1}) \quad \textbf{if } ev_1 \\
\textbf{and} & & \cdots & \\
\textbf{and} & y_p & = & F_p(e_{p1}, \ldots, e_{pn_p}) \quad \textbf{if } ev_p \\
\textbf{in } e
\end{array}$$

where the subexpressions of an expression e, for which it is decided that a parallel execution may be worthwhile, are abstracted out of the expression and represented by combinator applications. Thereby, new combinators are introduced, if a subexpression is not yet a combinator application. Thus, in the *letpar*-construct,

- y_i are local variables, which replace the abstracted subexpressions in e,

- F_i denote (possibly new) combinators with n_i parameters in the defining equations,

- e and e_{ij} are applicative expressions built from variables, predefined constants and functions, constructors and combinators by application, *if_then_else*, *case*, *let* and *letpar*-constructs,

- ev_i are evaluators.

The meaning of a *letpar*-expression is, that the combinator applications $F_i(e_{i1}, \ldots, e_{in_i})$ *may be* evaluated in parallel with the main stream of evaluation, e, if the evaluator of the whole expression is stronger, i.e. greater, than or equal to ev_i. Whether a parallel evaluation really takes place at runtime, depends on the workload of the distributed system. Evaluation of a *letpar*-expression first leads to the parallel activation of the combinator applications, for which the evaluator allows a parallel execution. Then the evaluation of the body e proceeds until the result of a parallel subexpression, represented by y_j, is needed and not yet available. In this case, the evaluation of e is suspended until the parallel subprocess yields its result. In the meantime, the processor is free to evaluate some other process.

The resulting process system is hierarchical. The execution of a parallelized combinator system starts with the evaluation of the main expression. *letpar*-expressions generate parallel subprocesses, that can be executed on other processor elements. By the execution of parallel processes, further processes may be generated. When a process terminates, its result is communicated to the father process, i.e. the process that generated the subprocess.

2.4 Parallelization

Principally, each expression of a program, for which an evaluator different from ξ_0 can be determined, can be evaluated in parallel. Such a maximal parallelization may however not be optimal, because a parallel evaluation always causes an overhead that might be greater than its gain. The expression, that is to be evaluated in parallel, must be encoded in a message that is passed to another processor element and there must be decoded. In the same way, the result[2] of the parallel evaluation must be transferred back to the original processor element. In order to guarantee that the parallel execution of an expression is profitable, one has to ensure that the expression has enough evaluation complexity (whatever this means). In general, it will not be possible to determine the complexity of expressions exactly, even if one focusses on a special implementation technique and target architecture. So, one has to use some heuristics.

In order to translate combinator systems into parallelized combinator systems, we use, in addition to the evaluator information given by the evaluation transformers of the combinators, constructors and base functions, an oracle function

$$oracle : Expressions \rightarrow \{ \text{ true, false } \}$$

that determines whether a parallelization is allowed or not. The oracle functions, that we used in our experiments, are presented in Section 4. In the remainder of this section, we describe the parallelization algorithm and finish with a possible parallelization of our example program.

The parallelization algorithm transforms expressions into expressions, hopefully containing the *letpar*-construct. On the top level it is applied to the bodies of the combinator definitions. The most important

---

[2]in the case of data structures at least the top-level constructor

case is the treatment of general applications $(e_0\ e_1\ldots e_m)$. First, one has to determine the sets of parameters, for which a parallelization is allowed,

- $O := \{i \mid 0 \le i \le m, oracle(e_i) = \text{true}\}$,

and the set of parameters, for which an evaluator stronger than ξ_0 can be expected,

- $P := \{i \mid 0 \le i \le m, \exists \xi : ET_i^{cs}((e_0\ e_1\ldots e_m))(\xi) > \xi_0\}$.

The subexpressions, whose indices are in $O \cap P$, can be evaluated in parallel. For the subexpressions in $O \setminus P$, the oracle allows a parallel execution, but the non-strict context forbids an evaluation. As it is possible that such expressions are dynamically passed to a strict context, we providently replace these expressions, if necessary, by a combinator application in order to enable a parallel evaluation. Our implementation does not only support the explicit parallelism introduced by the *letpar*-construct, but also the parallel execution of strict, not yet evaluated, arguments, which themselves are combinator applications, as only combinator applications can be distributed in the system. This is an additional source of parallelism, which may lead to the generation of parallel processes where a static parallelization during compile time is not possible. Consequently, our approach ensures that a delayed activation of the subexpressions, whose indices are in $O \setminus P$, may nevertheless lead to a parallel evaluation. The effect of this *dynamic parallelization* in the case of higher order functions is shown in Section 5.

In order to avoid unnecessary process switches, the parallelization should ensure that enough work is kept on the processor element that evaluates the *letpar*-expression and does the parallel activation of the subprocesses. Thus, two cases are distinguished in the parallelization algorithm. If the oracle says that the whole expression can be evaluated in parallel, all parallelizable subexpressions are abstracted out. Otherwise, the leftmost parallelizable subexpression is kept for execution on the same processor element.

In order to keep as much locality as possible and to avoid flooding the system with parallel processes whose results are not yet needed, we abstract expressions only one level out. Thus, we parallelize e.g. an expression $(F \ldots (G \ldots (H \ldots) \ldots) \ldots)$,
where we assume that the shown subexpressions are in strict parameter positions and allowed to be parallelized by the oracle, in the following way

$$\text{letpar } y = (F_{p1} \ldots) \text{ if} \ldots \qquad \text{where the subsequent combinator is introduced:}$$
$$\text{in } (F \ldots y \ldots) \qquad\qquad F_{p1} \ldots = \text{ letpar } y = (H \ldots) \text{ if} \ldots$$
$$\text{in } (G \ldots y \ldots)$$

Another possibility would be to generate the expression

$$\text{letpar } y_1 = (H \ldots) \text{ if} \ldots$$
$$\text{in letpar } y_2 = (G \ldots y_1 \ldots) \text{ if} \ldots \ ,$$
$$\text{in } (F \ldots y_2 \ldots)$$

which may however lead to unfavourable situations, because the result of the subprocess H of G will not be directly communicated to the place where G is executed, but via the processor element, where H has been activated. Thus, locality is lost. Furthermore, it may be disadvantageous to start subprocesses before the processes that consume their result, especially when the subprocesses need a lot of resources and produce a lot of output. The advantage of the second approach is a broader and faster parallelization with an early activation of subprocesses. Note that there is always a trade-off between parallelism and locality.

Let us come back to the problem of parallelizing an application $(e_0\ e_1\ldots e_m)$. Let $O \cap P = \{i_1, \ldots, i_p\}$ and $vars(e_j) = \{v_{j1}, \ldots, v_{jh_j}\}$ be the set of all (free) variables in e_j $(j \in O)$.

- If $oracle((e_0\ e_1\ldots e_m)) = \text{true}$, the parallelization algorithm produces the expression

$$\begin{aligned}
\text{letpar} \quad y_1 &= (F_{i_1}^{new} v_{i_1 1} \ldots v_{i_1 h_{i_1}}) \text{ if } ev_{i_1}\\
\text{and} & \quad \ldots\\
\text{and} \quad y_p &= (F_{i_p}^{new} v_{i_p 1} \ldots v_{i_p h_{i_p}}) \text{ if } ev_{i_p}\\
\text{in } & (exp_0\ exp_1 \ldots exp_m),
\end{aligned}$$

where

- new combinators F_j^{new} $(j \in O)$ with defining equations "$F_j^{\text{new}} v_{j1} \ldots v_{jh_j} = \text{parallelize}(e_j)$" are introduced,

- $ev_{i_j} = \min\{\xi \mid ET_{i_j}^{cs}((e_0\ e_1 \ldots e_m))(\xi) > \xi_0\}$ and

- $exp_k = \begin{cases} y_j & \text{if } k = i_j \in O \cap P \\ (F_k^{\text{new}} v_{k1} \ldots v_{kh_k}) & \text{if } k \in (O \setminus P) \quad (0 \leq k \leq m). \\ \text{parallelize}(e_k) & \text{otherwise} \end{cases}$

- If $oracle((e_0\ e_1 \ldots e_m)) = false$, a similar parallelization takes place, except that the expression, whose index is the minimal element of $O \cap P$, is not abstracted out for parallel activation, but kept in the body of the *letpar*-expression for local execution.

The parallelization of *if-then-else* and *case* expressions consists of an independent parallelization of their subexpressions. The treatment of *let*-expressions can be reduced to the parallelization of applications, because a *let*-expression can be viewed as a special application.

The parallelization of our *quicksort* example, assuming an oracle that only returns true for (complete) combinator applications, leads to the parallelized combinators given in Figure 4. The other combinators of the example remain unchanged.

$$
\begin{aligned}
&quicksort\ l^{\text{intlist}} = \textbf{case } l \textbf{ of } \text{NIL} : \text{NIL}; \\
&\qquad\qquad\qquad\qquad\quad \text{CONS } h^{\text{int}}\ t^{\text{intlist}} : \\
&\qquad\qquad\qquad\qquad\quad \textbf{letpar } y_1 = (F^{\text{new}}\ h\ t) \textbf{ if } \xi_1 \\
&\qquad\qquad\qquad\qquad\quad \textbf{in } (append\ y_1\ (\text{CONS } h\ \textbf{letpar } y_2 = (filter\ (global\_geq\ h)\ t) \textbf{ if } \xi_1 \\
&\qquad\qquad\qquad\qquad\qquad\qquad\qquad\qquad\qquad\qquad\qquad\quad \textbf{in } (quicksort\ y_2))\ ) \\
&F^{\text{new}}\ h^{\text{int}}\ t^{\text{intlist}} = \textbf{letpar } y = (filter\ (global\_less\ h)\ t) \textbf{ if } \xi_1 \\
&\qquad\qquad\qquad\qquad\quad \textbf{in } (quicksort\ y)
\end{aligned}
$$

Figure 4: Parallelized Example Program

When the expression, that is abstracted out for parallel execution, is already a combinator application, we avoid the introduction of new combinators during the parallelization process. In our example in Figure 4, we have not introduced new combinators for the 'parallel' call of *filter*. In fact, our current implementation always avoids the generation of new combinators when the subexpression, for which a parallel execution is decided, is already a combinator application. This implies that the parallel execution of arguments of the combinator application is not enabled.

3 The Underlying Parallel Implementation

The parallel implementation of the combinator systems is based on a parallel abstract machine (PAM) [Loogen et al. 89], that consists of a finite number of identical processor elements with local storage. The processor elements communicate by exchanging messages via an interconnection network.

PAM has a modular structure. Each processor element consists of two independent processing units (see Figure 5):

- a *communication unit* that is responsible for the organizational aspects of the parallelization of the reduction process, and

- a *reduction unit* that executes the parallelized functional program by code-directed graph reduction.

The two processing units communicate by exchanging messages in a local shared memory.

The modularization permits a decentralization of the parallel program execution by separating the overhead of parallelism — message handling, work distribution, workload balancing — from the reduction process. This leads to a better exploitation of parallelism.

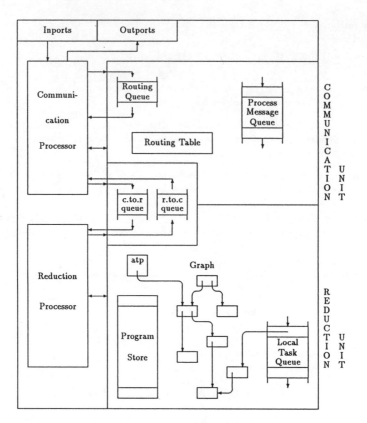

Figure 5: Structure of a Processing Unit

3.1 Program Execution

In the parallel abstract machine, program execution is done within the reduction units by *distributed code-directed graph reduction*.

The parallelized combinator program is translated into abstract machine code, that is copied into the program store of each reduction unit. For each potential (combinator, evaluator)-pair, a machine code sequence is generated that controls the execution of combinator calls with this evaluator. The evaluation transformer information is integrated into this code sequence. So, the (first) evaluator of each subexpression can be determined at compile time. In particular, it is fixed which *letpar*-expressions yield parallel processes. At run time, one only has to choose the appropriate code sequence for a combinator and its evaluator.

Each code sequence for a combinator has two different entry points which correspond to the two different activation modes for applications. The first entry point leads to the potentially parallel activation of the arguments of the combinator using the evaluator given by its evaluation transformer, before the second entry point is passed which immediately leads to the evaluation of the combinator body. The second entry point can be used when it is known that the evaluation of the arguments of the combinator has already been initiated. This is the case for combinator applications within the program, which are *directly activated*. The evaluation of the arguments is initiated just before the combinator call, using the evaluator given by the context sensitive evaluation transformer of the application. The first entry point is used for *indirectly activated* applications, where we distinguish two cases. On the one hand, combinator applications can be dynamically created by some "higher order" applications. On the other hand, the evaluation of a combinator application may be delayed, because it appears in a non-strict context. When such applications are activated, one cannot assume that the arguments have already been evaluated.

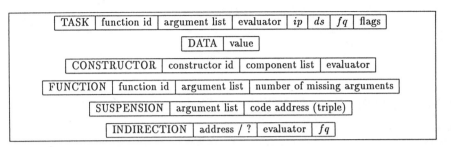

Figure 6: Graph Nodes

The main runtime structure is a *graph* which contains the following types of nodes (see also Figure 6):

- the activation blocks for the combinator calls, called *task nodes*, which are not, as usual, allocated on a stack, but, in order to support the parallelism, in the decentral graph structure,

  — Each task node contains the whole status information of the combinator call evaluation, i.e. a local instruction pointer (ip), a local data stack[3] (ds), a list of tasks waiting for the result (fq, father queue), the evaluator etc. This decentral organisation makes task switches very simple and cheap. —

- *terminal nodes*, where we distinguish data, constructor and function nodes, which represent expressions in weak head normal form,

- *suspension nodes*, which represent expressions whose evaluation is not yet demanded, due to the lazy evaluation strategy, and finally

- *indirection nodes*, which reserve place for the result of parallel processes, which are executed on other processor elements, or for terminal nodes, which have to be transferred from other processor elements.

At each time, a reduction unit executes at most one task, whose task node is indicated by the so called *active task pointer* (atp). A task is executed until it is finished or suspended. A suspension occurs, when a task has to wait for some information that is locally not yet available.

During a task execution, new local tasks or even parallel processes may be generated. The local tasks are kept in a *local task queue*, while the parallel processes are encoded into a process message and passed to the communication processor.

A task switch, triggered by a task termination or suspension, means that the reduction unit inspects the local task queue for a new task. If this queue is empty, the communication processor is asked to pass a new parallel process to the reduction unit. When a parallel process is passed to the reduction unit, it will be executed in this unit until it finishes.

3.2 Message Handling

Each reduction unit can be seen as a sequential reduction machine that has been extended for multitasking and message handling. Four types of messages are necessary for the parallelization of the reduction process:

- *process messages* to distribute the parallel processes among the processor elements,

- *answer messages* to communicate the result of distributed parallel processes and the contents of shared subgraphs,

- *request messages* to ask for graph nodes that are allocated on other processor elements and

- *activation messages* to activate the evaluation of subgraphs on other processor elements.

---

[3]The maximum storage requirements can be computed at compile time.

A parallel process always corresponds to a combinator application. Thus, it is completely specified by the combinatorname, the list of arguments, the evaluator with which the parallel process has to be evaluated, and finally the return-address (the address where the result of the task has to be sent to). These are exactly the contents of a process message. When a parallel process is initiated, an indirection node for the result of the process is generated and an appropriate process message is passed to the communication processor.

Access to an indirection or task node leads to the suspension of a task, i.e. its execution is stopped and its address is written into the accessed indirection or task node. For that purpose, indirection nodes and task nodes incorporate lists fq containing addresses of task nodes, which are waiting for the result of these nodes, i.e. for the indirection node to be overwritten by the result of a parallel process or the contents of a graph node, that lies on another processor element (both communicated by an answer message), and for the task to finish, respectively.

If a task needs access to a global node, a new indirection node is generated, a request message containing the address of this indirection node is sent to the global address and the address of the task is written into the new indirection node. When a task finishes or an indirection node is overwritten by the contents of an answer message, the tasks whose addresses are noted in the task or indirection node are reactivated.

Each communication processor maintains in its local store a process queue, that contains process messages that have been passed from other processor elements or from the reduction unit. When a process message from the reduction unit is passed to the communication processor, it will decide whether to keep it in the own process queue or to distribute it to a neighbour processor[4] depending on the load balancing strategy.

3.3 The Concrete Implementation

The abstract machine has been implemented on an OCCAM/Transputersystem [Loogen et al. 89, Hogen 91], where one processor element of the abstract machine runs on one transputer. Asynchronous message passing is simulated by buffering messages to ensure that no processor is ever blocked because it has to wait for a communication.

As the interconnection network does not provide a full interconnection of all transputers, messages must be routed through the network. The current implementation realizes a simple *static routing scheme*, where a routing table determines for each processor element, via which neighbour a message to that processor must be passed.

Experiments with our implementation showed that a very simple *passive load balancing strategy* is in general sufficient [Kuchen, Wagener 90]: Processors, which have no work and run idle, send *workrequest messages* to locally connected processor elements. These messages may then be answered by process messages, if the addressed processor has enough work and decides to distribute some processes. Otherwise, they are answered by *nowork messages*.

4 Investigation of Parallelization Strategies

In Section 2, we described the parallelizing compiler, up to the function *oracle* : *Expressions* → {true, false} used in the final phase to decide whether a parallelization is allowed or not. As the resulting parallelized combinator program strongly depends on the choice of this oracle function, we investigated four different oracle functions, which realize different levels of parallelization, with our implementation.

1. $seq : e \mapsto$ false does not allow any parallelization.

2. $comb : e \mapsto \begin{cases} \text{true} & \textit{if } e \text{ is a complete combinator application} \\ \text{false} & \textit{otherwise} \end{cases}$

   only allows the parallel execution of combinator applications. This strategy, in general, realizes a very natural parallelization, that very often resembles the parallelization that one would intuitively produce by hand.

   Assuming that an atomic expression is a variable, base function, constructor or combinator, we define

3. $nested : e \mapsto \begin{cases} \text{true} & \textit{if } e \text{ is not an atomic expression and has not only atomic subexpressions} \\ \text{false} & \textit{otherwise} \end{cases}$

---

[4]A neighbour processor is a physically connected processor.

nested allows more parallelism than *comb*, but parallelizes still less than

4. $max : e \mapsto \left\{ \begin{array}{ll} \text{true} & \textit{if } e \text{ is not an atomic expression} \\ \text{false} & \textit{otherwise} \end{array} \right\}$ which produces the *maximal parallelization*.

Note that these oracle functions are completely independent from the underlying implementation. They consider only the structure of expressions.

The parallelizing compiler has been implemented in Turbo-Pascal[5] under MS-DOS[6] [Kindler 91]. It translates lazy functional programs into parallelized combinator systems, which are translated into abstract machine code for the PAM by an additional compiler, also written in Turbo-Pascal [Hogen 91]. The abstract machine code must finally be transferred to the transputer system, where it is, up to now, interpreted by an implementation of the PAM on one, four and twelve transputers, respectively [Hogen 91].

Problem	Oracle	Runtime (sec)			Speedup				
					1 PE	4 PE's		12 PE's	
		1 PE	*4 PE's*	*12 PE's*	*abs.*	*rel.*	*abs.*	*rel.*	*abs.*
genfib(21)	seq	44.269	—	—	—	—	—	—	—
	comb	60.390	15.254	5.581	0.73	3.96	*2.90*	11.18	*7.93*
	nested	71.538	17.921	6.093	0.62	3.99	2.47	11.74	7.27
	max	71.564	17.921	6.087	0.62	3.99	2.47	11.76	7.27
genfib(22)	seq	71.618	—	—	—	—	—	—	—
	comb	97.707	24.569	8.739	0.73	3.98	*2.91*	11.57	*8.20*
	nested	115.748	28.950	9.749	0.62	4.00	2.47	11.87	7.35
	max	115.775	28.931	9.760	0.62	4.00	2.48	11.86	7.34
hanoi(12)	seq	7.938	—	—	—	—	—	—	—
	comb	8.460	2.151	0.795	0.94	3.93	*3.69*	10.64	*9.98*
	nested	13.788	3.475	1.224	0.58	3.97	2.28	11.27	6.49
	max	18.307	4.628	1.611	0.43	3.96	1.72	11.36	4.93
hanoi(13)	seq	15.876	—	—	—	—	—	—	—
	comb	16.920	4.266	1.496	0.94	3.97	*3.72*	11.31	*10.61*
	nested	27.578	6.917	2.369	0.58	3.99	2.30	11.64	6.70
	max	36.617	9.197	3.140	0.43	3.98	1.73	11.66	5.06
queens(6)	seq	31.169	—	—	—	—	—	—	—
	comb	33.373	8.775	3.299	0.93	3.80	*3.55*	10.12	*9.45*
	nested	49.940	13.062	4.834	0.62	3.82	2.39	10.33	6.45
	max	56.804	14.824	5.459	0.55	3.83	2.10	10.41	5.71
queens(7)	seq	147.219	—	—	—	—	—	—	—
	comb	157.518	40.833	14.520	0.93	3.86	*3.61*	10.85	*10.14*
	nested	238.108	61.298	21.713	0.62	3.88	2.40	10.97	6.78
	max	271.721	69.750	24.573	0.54	3.90	2.11	11.04	5.99

Table 1: Measurements on 1, 4 and 12 Transputers

In Table 1 the runtimes and speedups, that have been measured for the different parallelizations of three example programs on 1, 4 and 12 transputers, are reported. The example programs are the following:

- *genfib* computes for a given number i a list containing the first i fibonacci numbers, where each number is computed by a separate call of the fibonacci function.

- *hanoi* solves for a given number n the 'Towers of Hanoi' problem starting with n slices.

- *queens* computes for a given number n all solutions of the queens problem on an $n \times n$ chessboard.

---

[5]Turbo Pascal is a trademark of Borland International.
[6]MS-DOS is a trademark of Microsoft Corporation.

We distinguish two speedup values. The *relative speedup* is the ratio of the runtime of a parallelized program on one processor element (PE) to the runtime of the same program on 4 or 12 processors, respectively. The *absolute speedup* is the ratio of the runtime of the sequential version of the program on 1 processor to the runtime of the parallelized version on 4 or 12 processors, respectively.

The runtimes for the different parallelized versions on 1 processor element show that already the introduction of the *letpar*-construct causes a non-neglectable overhead, which is due to the additional combinator calls and the abstraction of the parallel expression in the *letpar*-expressions. The maximal parallelization of the *hanoi* program runs more than twice as long on one transputer as the sequential version.

Although the nested and maximal parallelizations show the best relative speedups, their performance with respect to the sequential programs, indicated by the absolute speedup, is very poor. The relative speedups can only be used to get an impression of the quality of the parallel implementation and the distributed process management. To rate the quality of the parallelization, one has to consider the absolute speedups. It turns out that the parallelization using the oracle *comb* shows the best absolute speedups and accordingly the best runtimes on 4 and 12 processors.

This is a consequence of the fact, that the strategy *comb* is especially suited to our implementation, because of the presupposition that parallel processes correspond to combinator applications. The other strategies have to introduce new combinators to meet this requirement, but additional combinator calls cause additional overhead. It becomes clear that the overhead of the additional parallelization is not compensated by the profits of the parallel execution. This might, however, be different for more complex problems.

5 Dynamic Parallelization of Higher Order Functions

An important advantage of functional programming languages is the modularity and abstraction that can be achieved by using higher order functions, which allow to define general recursion schemes that can then be adapted to special situations. Consider the higher order function *foldint*, given in Figure 7, that can e.g. be used to compute the factorial function: "*fac* n^{int} = (*foldint* 1 *n id* ∗)", where "*id n* = *n*" is the identity combinator, or the list of the first *n* square numbers: "*squares* n^{int} = (*foldint* 1 *n sqr append*)", where "*sqr i* = (CONS (∗ *i i*) NIL)".

$$foldint\ i^{int}\ j^{int}\ f^{int \to *}\ g^{* \times * \to *} = \textbf{if}\ (=\ i\ j)\ \textbf{then}\ (f\ i)\ \textbf{else let}\ med = (/\ (+\ i\ j)\ 2)$$
$$\textbf{in}\ (g\ (foldint\ i\ med\ f\ g)\ (foldint\ (+\ med\ 1)\ j\ f\ g))$$

∗ is a type variable that can be instantiated by an arbitrary type.

Figure 7: Example of a Higher Order Function

These examples show that the higher order function *foldint* will often be called with strict functional parameters, so that it would be possible and advantageous to evaluate the recursive calls in the body of this function in parallel. Our parallelizing compiler is, however, not able to detect this implicit parallelism, because the parallelization is done independently from the actual parameters of the function in the program. As the parallel evaluation of the recursive calls is not correct with respect to the underlying non-strict semantics (laziness) if the higher order function is called with non-strict functional parameters, a parallelization is not possible.

Consequently, programs may contain implicit parallelism that cannot be expressed explicitly using the *letpar*-construct of the intermediate language. To exploit this kind of parallelism, our implementation allows the parallel activation of arguments of indirectly activated combinator or base function applications. In order to avoid the generation of too small processes, a parallel activation takes only place if the argument expression is a combinator application. Note that the parallelizing compiler always transforms expressions, for which the *oracle* function allows a parallel execution, into combinator applications, no matter in which context (strict or non-strict) they occur.

In Table 2 it is shown, that the dynamic parallelization applies to the *foldint*-function when its functional argument *g* is instantiated by the strict base function +. Although no static parallelization takes place, reasonable speedups are obtained, because the indirect activation of the dynamically created application of

Problem	Runtime (sec)			Speedup	
	1 PE	4 PE's	12 PE's	4 PE's	12 PE's
(foldint 1 1000 id +)	9.124	2.659	1.053	3.43	8.66
(foldint 1 2000 id +)	18.252	5.244	1.951	3.48	9.36
(foldint 1 5000 id +)	45.638	13.032	4.719	3.50	9.67
(foldint 1 10000 id +)	91.273	25.990	9.321	3.51	9.79

Table 2: Measurements of Dynamic Parallelism

the base function + leads to the generation of parallel processes for the recursive calls of *foldint*. Note that the relative and absolute speedup values collapse, because the parallelized version of *foldint* is identical to the sequential version.

6 Conclusions and Future Work

We presented a technique for the automatic parallelization of lazy functional programs, which uses a strictness analyser, based on the technique of abstract interpretation, for the detection of implicit parallelism, and an oracle function to restrict the parallelization to expressions, for which a parallel execution seems to be profitable. In order to keep locality, we enable the activation of parallel subprocesses only immediately before the evaluation of the expression, that consumes the result of the subprocess, is initiated. The most natural and, with respect to our runtime experiments, best parallelization could be achieved by the oracle, that only allows the parallel evaluation of combinator applications.

A natural generalization of our parallelization algorithm will be to consider not only the direct subexpressions of an expression for the generation of the *letpar*-construct, but the maximal subexpressions for which the oracle allows a parallel evaluation. Then, the *comb* oracle will e.g. lift the recursive calls of the quicksort combinator to the same level, which is the parallelization of this algorithm, one usually has in mind.

A disadvantage of our parallelizing compiler is its time complexity, where most of the time is needed to compute the abstract interpretation of combinators. Therefore, it will be important to investigate whether alternative, more efficient analysis methods, as they have e.g. been proposed in [Hughes 90], [Nöcker 90], [Hartel et al. 91], can be incorporated in our parallelizing compiler.

Acknowledgements

The authors are grateful to the anonymous referees for their valuable comments.

References

[Abramsky 85] S.Abramsky: *Strictness Analysis and Polymorphic Invariance*, Workshop on Programs as Data Objects, LNCS 217, Springer Verlag 1985.

[Abramsky, Hankin 87] S.Abramsky, C.Hankin (eds.): *Abstract Interpretation of Declarative Languages*, Ellis Horwood Limited 1987.

[Burn et al. 86] G.Burn, C.L.Hankin, S.Abramsky: *Strictness Analysis for Higher-Order Functions*, Science of Computer Programming, Vol.7, November 1986.

[Burn 87a] G.Burn: *Evaluation Transformers — A Model for the Parallel Evaluation of Functional Languages*, Conf. on Functional Progr. Lang. and Computer Architecture, LNCS 274, Springer Verlag 1987.

[Burn 87b] G.Burn: *Abstract Interpretation and the Parallel Evaluation of Functional Languages*, Ph.D. Thesis, Imperial College, London 1987.

[Burn 88] G.Burn: *A shared memory parallel G-machine based on the evaluation transformer model of computation*, Workshop on the Impl. of Lazy Functional Languages, Report 53, Programming Methodology Group, Chalmers University of Technology, Göteborg 1988.

[Clack, Peyton-Jones 85] C.Clack, S.Peyton-Jones: *Strictness Analysis — A Practical Approach*, Conf. on Functional Progr. Languages and Computer Architecture, LNCS 201, Springer Verlag 1985.

[van Eekelen et al. 88] M.C.J.D.van Eekelen, M.J.Plasmeijer, J.E.W.Smeetsers: *Parallel Graph Rewriting on Loosely Coupled Machine Architectures*, Technical Report 88-9, University of Nijmegen 1988.

[Hammond, Peyton Jones 90] K.Hammond, S.Peyton-Jones: *Some Early Experiments on the GRIP Parallel Reducer*, Workshop on the Impl. of Functional Languages on Parallel Architectures, Technical Report no. 90–16, University of Nijmegen 1990.

[Hartel et al. 91] P.Hartel, H.Glaser, J.Wild: *On the Benefits of Different Analyses in the Compilation of Lazy Functional Languages*, Workshop on the Parallel Impl. of Functional Languages, Technical Report CSTR 91-7, University of Southampton 1991.

[Hogen 91] G.Hogen: *Integration of the Evaluator Technique in the Parallel Abstract Machine PAM*, Diploma Thesis, RWTH Aachen 1991 (in german).

[Hudak 86] P.Hudak: *Para-functional programming, a paradigm for programming multiprocessor systems*, ACM Symp. on Principles of Progr. Languages 1986.

[Hudak, Goldberg 85a] P.Hudak, B.Goldberg: *Serial Combinators: Optimal Grains of Parallelism*, Conf. on Functional Progr. Languages and Computer Architecture, LNCS 201, Springer Verlag 1985.

[Hudak, Goldberg 85b] P.Hudak, B.Goldberg: *Efficient Distributed Evaluation of Functional Programs Using Serial Combinators*, IEEE Transactions on Computers, Vol. C-34, No. 10, October 85.

[Hudak, Young 86] P.Hudak, J.Young: *Higher Order Strictness Analysis in Untyped Lambda Calculus*, ACM Symp. on Principles of Progr. Languages, POPL 1986.

[Hughes 90] J.Hughes: *Compile-time analysis of functional programs*, in Turner (ed.): Research Topics in Functional Programming, Addison-Wesley 1990.

[Johnsson 85] Th.Johnsson: *Lambda Lifting*, Conf. on Functional Progr. Languages and Computer Architectures 1985, LNCS 201, Springer Verlag 1985.

[Kindler 91] A.Kindler: *Automatic Parallelization of Functional Programs*, Diploma Thesis, RWTH Aachen 1991 (in german).

[Kuchen, Wagener 90] H.Kuchen, A.Wagener: *Comparison of Dynamic Load Balancing Strategies*, Workshop on Distributed and Parallel Processing, Sofia 1990, Elsevier Publishers 1990.

[Lester, Burn 89] D.Lester, G.Burn: *An Executable Specification of the HDG-Machine*, Technical Report, GEC Research Centre, East Lane, Wembley, Middlesex HA9 7PP, United Kingdom.

[Loogen et al. 89] R.Loogen, H.Kuchen, K.Indermark, W.Damm: *Distributed Implementation of Programmed Graph Reduction*, Conf. on Parallel Architectures and Languages Europe 1989, LNCS 365, Springer Verlag 1989.

[Martin, Hankin 87] C.Martin, C.Hankin: *Finding Fixed Points in Finite Lattices*, Conf. on Functional Progr. Languages and Computer Architecture, LNCS 274, Springer Verlag 1987.

[Maurer 85] D.Maurer: *Strictness Computations Using Special λ-expressions*, Workshop on Programs as Data Objects, LNCS 217, Springer Verlag 1985.

[McBurney, Sleep 90] D.McBurney, R.Sleep: *Concurrent Clean on ZAPP*, Workshop on the Impl. of Functional Lang. on Parallel Architectures, Technical Report no. 90–16, University of Nijmegen 1990.

[Mycroft 81] A.Mycroft: *Abstract Interpretation and Optimizing Transformations for Applicative Programs*, Ph.D. Thesis, University of Edinburgh, 1981.

[Nöcker 90] E.Nöcker: *Strictness Analysis Using Abstract Reduction*, Workshop on the Impl. of Functional Languages on Parallel Architectures, Technical Report no. 90–16, University of Nijmegen 1990.

[Raber et al. 88] M.Raber, Th.Remmel, E.Hoffmann, D.Maurer, F.Müller, H.-G.Oberhauser, R.Wilhelm: *Compiled Graph Reduction on a Processor Network*, GI/ITG Tagung, Paderborn, Informatik Fachberichte, Springer Verlag 1988.

[Vrancken 90] J.Vrancken: *Reflections on Parallel Functional Languages*, Workshop on the Impl. of Functional Lang. on Parallel Architectures, Technical Report no. 90–16, University of Nijmegen 1990.

[Wadler 87] P.Wadler: *Strictness analysis on non-flat domains (by Abstract interpretation over finite domains)*, in: [Abramsky, Hankin 87].

[Wadler, Hughes 87] P.Wadler, J.Hughes: *Projections for Strictness Analysis*, Conf. on Functional Progr. Languages and Computer Architecture, LNCS 274, Springer Verlag 1987.

[Young, Hudak 86] J.Young, P.Hudak: *Finding Fixpoints on Function Spaces*, Research Report YALEU/DCS/RR-505, Yale University, December 1986.

Reversing Abstract Interpretations

John Hughes and John Launchbury*
Department of Computing Science,
University of Glasgow,
{rjmh, jl}@dcs.glasgow.ac.uk

1 Introduction

Many semantic analyses of functional languages have been developed using the
Cousots' *abstract interpretation* framework [CC77]. Some, such as Mycroft's pio-
neering strictness analysis [Myc81] and Burn, Hankin and Abramsky's extension of
it to higher-order [BHA86], operate on *abstract values* representing the past history
of the computation, and are therefore called *forwards analyses*. Others, such as
Wadler and Hughes' projection-based strictness analysis [WH87], or Hall's analysis
of strictness patterns [Hal87] propagate *abstract contexts* representing the future of
the computation, and are called *backwards analyses*. However, although the type
of abstract information may suggest a "natural" direction, it is in fact possible to
perform any analysis in either direction. The goal of this paper is to show how to
reverse any given analysis.

Why might one prefer one direction of analysis over another? We shall draw
an analogy with solving a differential equation on an interval. Solutions may be
found by iterating from one end of the interval to the other, with the two possible
directions corresponding to backwards and forwards analysis. But the purpose of
an analysis is to answer a question, and such questions correspond to giving the
boundary conditions at one end of the interval and asking for the function's value
at the other. In such a case it's clearly preferable to start solving the equation at
the end where the boundary conditions are known. Note that it's not impossible
to work in the other direction—one can always use trial and error to find boundary
conditions at the beginning that produce the right values at the end—but in general
working in the "wrong" direction will require many solutions to be calculated where
one would suffice in the other direction. We will see exactly this effect arising in the
case of strictness analysis.

Every analysis associates with each function in the source program a corresponding abstract function. To reverse an analysis we have to "invert" these abstract
functions. We begin by considering the conditions under which one function can be
said to safely approximate the inverse of another. We show that there is a best re-

---

*Work supported by ESPRIT BRA 3124 - Semantique

versal of each abstract function; and how best reversals interact with the combining forms of a programming language.

Sometimes the best reversal of an abstract function carries less information than the original. This raises the question "How much less?" One way to compare abstract functions with their reversals is to reverse the reversal again, but this may lose still more information. However, there is a class of functions whose reversal carries exactly the same information, and which may therefore be reversed any number of times with no loss. These turn out to be *Galois connections*. There is a best approximating Galois connection to each abstract function, which provides an upper bound on the information lost by reversal.

The application we consider in this paper is the reversal of Burn, Hankin and Abramsky's strictness analysis. The analysis of the conditional proves hard to reverse; we therefore derive a rule for backwards analysis directly from the concrete semantics. The power of this backwards rule is incomparable with that of the forwards rule, disproving the old chestnut that conditionals are better analysed forwards. The analysis derived is a previously known backwards analysis, but it's relation to BHA and the corresponding proof of correctness were previously unknown.

We go on to consider Wadler's 4-point abstract domain for lists [Wad87]. The reversal of his analysis turns out to be simpler than the original. In fact, Wadler's forwards analysis of **case** expressions contains a complication which can be seen as necessary to obtain a good reversal of a backwards form!

Finally, we derive a backwards analysis of higher-order programs from the BHA forwards analysis. Perhaps not surprisingly, we fail to obtain a particularly accurate analysis.

2 Background

2.1 The Object Language

We will discuss analyses in the context of a simple typed functional language based on categorical notation. Types are base types (such as Int), and types built from them using $\times$, List (in section 5) and $\rightarrow$ (in section 6). Terms denote continuous functions, and are built from an unspecified collection of primitive functions using combining forms. The basic term syntax is

$$term \quad ::= \quad ide \mid term \circ term \mid \; < term, term > \; \mid \mu ide. \; term$$

Here $\circ$ denotes composition, $< f, g >$ denotes the function $< f, g > \; x = (f \; x, g \; x)$ and $\mu f.H(f)$ is the recursive function satisfying $\mu f.H(f) = H(\mu f.H(f))$. The primitives include at least the projection functions π_1, π_2, and the constant functions $K_c \; x = c$. Although our language is monomorphic, for notational convenience we will allow polymorphic *primitives* such as $\sqcup : \forall X. \; X \times X \rightarrow X$. Occurrences of such primitives should be read as the appropriate member of a family of monomorphic functions.

We will consider extensions of the language with other combining forms such as the conditional $(p \rightarrow f; g)$ (see section 3.4). In particular, we can extend this first-order language to a higher-order one by adding the combining form Λ (curry) and the polymorphic primitive ap, where $(\Lambda f) \; x = \lambda y.f(x, y)$ and ap $(f, x) = f \; x$.

2.2 Abstract Interpretation

We'll use the same language to express *abstract functions*, which we distinguish notationally using italics. We restrict the types over which abstract functions are defined to be *finite lattices*. This is consistent with [BHA86] and [WH87] for example, where the restriction is used to guarantee termination of analysis[1]. Finiteness is important here for a different reason: it means continuity reduces to monotonicity in the proofs which follow, and indeed some of the functions we construct need not be continuous in the infinite case.

Abstract functions come with a notion of *safe approximation*: we say it is safe to approximate *upwards* if an abstract function f can be replaced by any $f' \sqsupseteq f$ without compromising the correctness of conclusions drawn from the analysis. Less commonly, it may be safe to approximate downwards. When an analyser cannot predict which of two abstract functions f or g applies (for example, in the analysis of a conditional) it may safely approximate by $f \sqcup g$ if the direction of safe approximation is upwards, or by $f \sqcap g$ if it is downwards.

To define an analysis we associate each type A with a corresponding abstract type $A^\sharp$, and give a safety condition relating concrete functions $f : A \to B$ to abstract functions $f : A^\sharp \to B^\sharp$ for a forwards analysis, or $f : B^\sharp \to A^\sharp$ for a backwards one. The safety condition tells us when an abstract function faithfully reflects the behaviour of the concrete one, and must be consistent with the notion of safe approximation for abstract functions. Since this condition relates the *semantics* of a concrete function to an abstract function it is not immediately useful in a compiler, but we can compute safe abstract functions for any term given abstract functions for the primitives and ways of deriving abstract functions for compound terms from those for their subterms. This process is called abstract interpretation.

2.3 The Burn, Hankin and Abramsky Framework

In the BHA approach, concrete and abstract types are related by a family of *abstraction functions* $abs_A : A \to A^\sharp$ and the safety condition relating $f : A \to B$ to $f : A^\sharp \to B^\sharp$ is $abs_B \circ f \sqsubseteq f \circ abs_A$.

Abstract values are associated with Scott-closed[2] sets of concrete values via *concretisation* functions, $conc_A\ a = \{x \mid abs_A\ x \sqsubseteq a\}$. The safety condition can be reformulated as $\forall x, a\ .\ x \in conc\ a \Rightarrow f\ x \in conc(f\ a)$.

There is a best abstract function for each concrete function $f : A \to B$ given by $\sqcup \circ \wp_H(abs_B \circ f) \circ conc_A$ where $(\wp_H f)\ X = \{f\ x \mid x \in X\}^*$ and X^* denotes the Scott-closure of X. Products are abstracted as products, so $(A \times B)^\sharp = A^\sharp \times B^\sharp$ and $abs_{A \times B}\ (x, y) = (abs_A\ x, abs_B\ y)$.

The following theorems justify a very simple abstract interpretation of terms:

Theorem 1
If f and g are safe for f and g respectively, then
(i) $f \circ g$ is safe for $f \circ g$
(ii) $< f, g >$ is safe for $< f, g >$

---

[1] Although finiteness is commonly required there are other ways of ensuring termination — see [CC77].
[2] A set S is Scott-closed if it is downwards closed, and whenever all the elements of a chain lie in S, so does the limit.

Theorem 2
Let H and H be functionals such that whenever f is safe for f, then H f is safe for H f. Then $\mu f.H$ f is safe for μf.H f.

Similar theorems must be proved for each proposed analysis. This approach extends very naturally to the higher-order case. We define $(A \rightarrow B)^{\natural} = A^{\natural} \rightarrow B^{\natural}$ and $abs_{A \rightarrow B}$ f $= \sqcup \circ \wp_H(abs_B \circ f) \circ conc_A$, with abstract interpretation justified by:

Theorem 3
If f is safe for f, then (i) Λf is safe for Λf, and (ii) ap is safe for ap.

Strictness analysis is cast in this framework by abstracting base types as the 2-point domain $2 = \{0 \sqsubseteq 1\}$, with abstraction defined by

$$abs_{Base} \; x \;\; = \;\; \left\{ \begin{array}{ll} 0 & \text{if } x = \bot \\ 1 & \text{otherwise} \end{array} \right.$$

It follows that all abstraction functions are strict and $\bot$-reflecting: in other words $abs \; x = \bot \Leftrightarrow x = \bot$. From this and the safety condition $abs \circ$ f $\sqsubseteq$ $f \circ abs$ we see that if f is strict, f must be too. We can test for strictness of f by testing whether $f \; 0 \; = \; 0$.

2.4 Galois Connections

Definition
A *Galois connection* between lattices A and B is a pair of monotonic functions $f : A \rightarrow B$ and $g : B \rightarrow A$ such that $f \circ g \sqsupseteq id$ and $g \circ f \sqsubseteq id$, or equivalently $\forall x, y. \; g \; y \sqsubseteq x \Leftrightarrow y \sqsubseteq f \; x$. f is called the *upper component* and g is called the *lower component*. □

Theorem 4
Let (f, g) be a Galois connection. Then (i) $f \; \top = \top$ and $g \; \bot = \bot$, (ii) f distributes over $\sqcap$, g distributes over $\sqcup$, and (iii) $g \; y$ is the least x such that $y \sqsubseteq f \; x$ and $f \; x$ is the greatest y such that $g \; y \sqsubseteq x$.

Corollary 5
Each component of a Galois connection uniquely determines the other.

In view of the Corollary we will sometimes be sloppy and say "the Galois connection f" instead of "the upper-component of a Galois connection f".

Galois connections were used by the Cousots to relate abstraction and concretisation, and consequently often appear in papers on abstract interpretation. The use we are making of them is quite different: we use Galois connections as *abstract* functions, the Cousots used them as *abstraction* functions.

3 Reversing an Analysis

3.1 Safe Reversals

Suppose we're given an abstract function $f : A \rightarrow B$ to reverse. In general, f will not have an exact inverse and we will need to approximate. We therefore need to know in which direction approximation is safe: suppose the safe direction is upwards so that any $f' \sqsupseteq f$ may safely be used instead of f. Furthermore, suppose the questions we want to answer are of the form

$$\text{Does } y \sqsubseteq f \ x \ ?$$

Since it's safe to approximate f upwards, such questions can safely be answered 'yes' when the correct answer is 'no', but must never be answered 'no' when the correct answer is 'yes'. Thus, 'no' means 'no', whereas 'yes' means 'maybe'.

When can a reversed function $f^r : B \to A$ be used to answer such questions? Since f^r is a kind of inverse, we'll ask instead

$$\text{Does } f^r \ y \sqsubseteq x \ ?$$

We can use the answer to this question as an answer to the previous one provided $y \sqsubseteq f \ x \Rightarrow f^r \ y \sqsubseteq x$, since then we can never answer 'no' by mistake (negate both sides to obtain the more intuitive implication).

Definition
f^r is a *safe reversal* of f if $\forall x, y \ . \ y \sqsubseteq f \ x \Rightarrow f^r \ y \sqsubseteq x$, or equivalently, if $f^r \circ f \sqsubseteq id$
$\square$

Note that safe reversals are always strict, and that any $f^{r'} \sqsubseteq f^r$ is also a safe reversal of f. In other words, safe reversals can be safely approximated in the opposite direction from abstract functions.

3.1.1 Example

In the case of BHA strictness analysis the test for strictness is usually phrased slightly differently. For example, if f is an integer-valued function of three integer parameters and f is its abstract function, then strictness is tested in each argument separately by asking the questions

$$\text{Does } f \ (0, 1; 1) = 0 \ ?$$
$$\text{Does } f \ (1, 0, 1) = 0 \ ?$$
$$\text{Does } f \ (1, 1, 0) = 0 \ ?$$

Of course, we can instead ask

$$\text{Does } 1 \sqsubseteq f \ (0, 1, 1) \ ?$$
$$\text{Does } 1 \sqsubseteq f \ (1, 0, 1) \ ?$$
$$\text{Does } 1 \sqsubseteq f \ (1, 1, 0) \ ?$$

whose answers are the negations of those above. But suppose f^r is a safe reversal of f, and $f^r 1 = (1, 1, 0)$. Now we can answer the three questions by answering

$$\text{Does } f^r 1 \sqsubseteq (0, 1, 1) \ ?$$
$$\text{Does } f^r 1 \sqsubseteq (1, 0, 1) \ ?$$
$$\text{Does } f^r 1 \sqsubseteq (1, 1, 0) \ ?$$

So with a *single* call of f^r, we discover that f is strict in its first and second arguments, but not necessarily in its third.

Forwards analysis may require many abstract evaluations to find all the strictness of a function, especially if its arguments are of complex types. The reversed analysis finds all the strictness in one abstract evaluation. Recalling our discussion of differential equations, this suggests that the boundary conditions for strictness analysis make it "naturally" a backwards analysis.

3.1.2 Computing Safe Reversals

Safe reversals of abstract functions can be computed efficiently if we know safe reversals for the primitives, and if we can derive safe reversals of compound terms from safe reversals of their subterms. We'll discuss primitives in the next subsection; the following theorem helps us do the latter.

Theorem 6

If f^r and g^r are safe reversals of f and g respectively, then (i) $g^r \circ f^r$ is a safe reversal of $f \circ g$, and (ii) $f^r \circ \pi_1 \sqcup g^r \circ \pi_2$ is a safe reversal of $< f, g >$.

Proof

$$(i) \ (g^r \circ f^r) \circ (f \circ g) = g^r \circ f^r \circ f \circ g \sqsubseteq g^r \circ g \sqsubseteq id$$
$$(ii) \ (f^r \circ \pi_1 \sqcup g^r \circ \pi_2) \circ < f, g > \ = f^r \circ f \sqcup g^r \circ g \sqsubseteq id \qquad \qquad \Box$$

To find a safe reversal of recursive functions we need a safe reversal of $K_\perp$, the constant undefined function. One such is

$$K_\perp^r \ y \ = \ \begin{cases} \perp & \text{if } y = \perp \\ \top & \text{otherwise} \end{cases}$$

Now we can reverse recursive functions using the following theorem.

Theorem 7

Let H and H^r be functionals such that for all f, H^r maps safe reversals of f to safe reversals of $H(f)$. Then $\bigsqcap_{n=0}^{\infty} (H^r)^n (K_\perp^r)$ is a safe reversal of $\mu f. H(f)$.

Proof

Since $K_\perp^r \circ K_\perp \sqsubseteq id$, we can show by induction that $\forall n \ . \ (H^r)^n (K_\perp^r) \circ H^n(K_\perp) \sqsubseteq id$. But since we are working in finite lattices all ascending and descending chains are eventually stationary[3], so there is an N such that

$$\bigsqcap_{n=0}^{\infty} (H^r)^n (K_\perp^r) \ \circ \ \bigsqcup_{n=0}^{\infty} H^n(K_\perp) = (H^r)^N (K_\perp^r) \ \circ \ H^N(K_\perp) \sqsubseteq id$$

$\Box$

In applications the functional H will be built up using composition, tupling, and so on, and a suitable H^r will be constructed using the rules above.

---

[3]This theorem could be proved for infinite lattices using continuity, but its dual cannot.

3.2 Best Reversals

Since safe reversals can safely be approximated downwards, it's natural to ask whether there are best, or greatest safe reversals. The following definition and theorem assure us that there are.

Definition
Given any function f, we define $f^- \, y = \bigsqcap \{x \mid y \sqsubseteq f \, x\}$ □

Theorem 8
f^- is the greatest safe reversal of f.

Proof
It is clear from the definition that $y \sqsubseteq f \, x \Rightarrow f^- \, y \sqsubseteq x$, so f^- is a safe reversal of f. Moreover, it is the greatest safe reversal, for if f^r is any other safe reversal of f, then $y \sqsubseteq f \, x \Rightarrow f^r \, y \sqsubseteq x$, and so $f^r \, y \sqsubseteq \bigsqcap \{x \mid y \sqsubseteq f \, x\} = f^- \, y$ □

As a corollary to this theorem, we can now show that any function f^r is a safe reversal of f merely by showing that $f^r \sqsubseteq f^-$.

Best reversals of primitives are now easily calculated. For example,

$$K_\perp^- \, y = \begin{cases} \perp & \text{if } y = \perp \\ \top & \text{otherwise} \end{cases}$$
$$id^- \, y = y$$
$$\pi_1^- \, y = (y, \perp)$$
$$\pi_2^- \, y = (\perp, y)$$
$$\sqcap^- \, y = (y, y)$$
$$\sqcup^- \, y = (\perp, \perp)$$

Clearly the last of these loses all information; abstract functions involving $\sqcup$ are therefore hard to reverse accurately.

One may ask whether the methods above for reversing compound terms produce best reversals from best reversals. Unfortunately they do not. For example, $\sqcup \circ <f, f> \; = f$ and so $(\sqcup \circ <f, f>)^- = f^-$ but applying the methods developed yields

$$
\begin{aligned}
(\sqcup \circ <f, f>)^- &\sqsupseteq \; <f, f>^- \circ \sqcup^- \\
&\sqsupseteq \; (f^- \circ \pi_1 \sqcup f^- \circ \pi_2) \circ \sqcup^- \\
&= \; f^- \circ K_\perp \\
&= \; K_\perp \qquad \text{[since all reversals are strict]}
\end{aligned}
$$

so all information is lost. It can therefore be worthwhile deriving special reversal rules for constructs defined as combinations of the primitives.

3.3 Reversible Analyses are Galois Connections

Suppose we are given a safe reversal f^r of f. Can we reconstruct (a safe approximation to) f from it? Reversals are just like abstract functions, except that it's safe to approximate them downwards rather than upwards. Clearly we can construct a dual theory by inverting the ordering: f^{rr} will be a safe reversal of f^r if

$$\forall x, y \,.\, f^r \, y \sqsubseteq x \;\Rightarrow\; y \sqsubseteq f^{rr} \, x$$

or equivalently, $f^{rr} \circ f^r \sqsupseteq id$. We'll write the best reversal of f^r in this dual theory as $(f^r)^+$, and where there's no risk of confusion we'll be sloppy and write $(f^-)^+$ also as f^+.

It's easy to show that if f is an abstract function, then $f \sqsubseteq f^+$. In other words, the safe reversal of a safe reversal safely approximates the original abstract function. But what if f^+ is actually equal to f? In that case the two safety conditions can be combined to give

$$\forall x, y \,.\, f^- \, y \sqsubseteq x \;\Leftrightarrow\; y \sqsubseteq f^+ \, x$$

This tells us that the two directions of analysis have exactly the same power. Any question of the form $y \sqsubseteq f^+ \, x$ can be exactly answered by a question of the form $f^- \, y \sqsubseteq x$, and vice versa. Interestingly, it is also the condition under which f^+ and f^- form a Galois connection. Hence the slogan: *reversible analyses are Galois connections*. We can now strengthen Theorem 6 in a pleasing way.

Theorem 9
If f and g are (the upper components of) Galois connections, then

  (i) $f \circ g$ is a Galois connection

  (ii) $< f, g >$ is a Galois connection

Proof
The lower components of these Galois connections are given in Theorem 6, and the proof is very similar to the proof given there. □

Of the primitives discussed so far, id, π_1, π_2 and $\sqcap$ are all (the upper components of) Galois connections, and so can be analysed equally well in either direction. However, $K_\perp$ and $\sqcup$ are not. Their double reversals are

$$K_\perp^+ \, x \;=\; \begin{cases} \top & \text{if } x = \top \\ \bot & \text{otherwise} \end{cases}$$
$$\sqcup^+ \, x \;=\; \top$$

It turns out that the triple reversals of these primitives are the same as their single reversals, so that $K_\perp^+$ and $\sqcup^+$ *are* Galois connections. Such cases are very important because it means that the double reversal of an abstract function is of exactly the same power as the single reversal. Thus the power of the single reversal may be directly compared with the original. In the case just above, for example, we can see that a backwards analysis using $\sqcup^-$ will have the same power as a forwards analysis that approximates $x \sqcup y$ by $\top$. It is clear that this is a very poor approximation.

We can extend the same idea to show that every abstract function has a best approximating Galois connection.

Theorem 10
For every abstract function f, there is a least $g \sqsupseteq f$ such that g is the upper component of a Galois connection.

Proof

We construct g as follows. We know that the double reversal of f satisfies $f \sqsubseteq f^+$, and therefore $f \sqsubseteq f^+ \sqsubseteq (f^+)^+ \sqsubseteq \ldots$ Because we are working in finite lattices, this increasing chain must eventually be stationary: call the limit g. Clearly $f \sqsubseteq g$. Moreover, since $g^+ = g$, g is a Galois connection.

It remains to show that if h is a Galois connection with $f \sqsubseteq h$, then $g \sqsubseteq h$ also. But, we know that best reversal is anti-monotonic, and so double reversal is monotonic. From $f \sqsubseteq h$ we may therefore conclude $f^+ \sqsubseteq h^+ = h$. By induction $f^{+^n} \sqsubseteq h$ for all n, and so $g \sqsubseteq h$. □

The only combining form we have not yet discussed is recursion. Since $K_\perp$ is not a Galois connection, it's hardly surprising that recursive functions are not necessarily Galois connections either. However, we can prove an analogue of Theorem 7.

Theorem 11

Let H be a functional which maps Galois connections to Galois connections. Then $\bigsqcup_{n=0}^{\infty} H^n(K_\perp^+)$ is a Galois connection, with lower component $\bigsqcap_{n=0}^{\infty} (H^-)^n(K_\perp^-)$ where
$$H^-(g^-) = (H(g^+))^-$$

Proof

Similar to Theorem 7. □

Thus backwards analysis of a recursive function has the same power as forwards analysis using a variant of recursion which starts from $K_\perp^+$ rather than $K_\perp$. By inspection, $K_\perp^+$ is the hyper-strict function, and so at least for the purpose of strictness analysis it seems that little useful information will be lost.

3.4   Example: Reversing Conditionals

In this section we apply the theory developed so far to the analysis of conditionals. The conditional construct we analyse works at the function level:

$$(p \rightarrow f; g) \ x = \begin{cases} f \ x & \text{if } p \ x = \text{true} \\ g \ x & \text{if } p \ x = \text{false} \\ \perp & \text{otherwise} \end{cases}$$

To give the BHA abstract interpretation we need a new operator:

$$x \triangleright y = \begin{cases} \perp & \text{if } x = 0 \\ y & \text{otherwise} \end{cases}$$

Promoting $\triangleright$ to operate on functions, we can write the abstract interpretation of a conditional as $p \triangleright (f \sqcup g)$.

How can we reverse this abstract function? It turns out that $\triangleright$ is a Galois connection with lower component

$$\triangleright^- y = \begin{cases} (0, \perp) & \text{if } y = \perp \\ (1, y) & \text{otherwise} \end{cases}$$

from which we can infer

$$(p \, \triangleright \, h)^- \, y \;\sqsupseteq\; \begin{cases} \bot & \text{if } y = \bot \\ p^- \, 1 \,\sqcup\, h^- \, y & \text{otherwise} \end{cases}$$

Intuitively, for the result of a conditional to be defined, the condition must be defined and the branches must be sufficiently defined.

We still need to reverse $(f \,\sqcup\, g)$, which we can do as follows:

$$\begin{aligned} (f \,\sqcup\, g)^- \;&=\; (\sqcup \circ <f, g>)^- \\ &\sqsupseteq\; <f, g>^- \circ \sqcup^- \\ &=\; <f, g>^- \circ K_\bot \\ &=\; K_\bot \end{aligned}$$

Using this reversal we find

$$\begin{aligned} (p \, \triangleright \, (f \,\sqcup\, g))^- \;&\sqsupseteq\; <p, f \,\sqcup\, g>^- \circ \triangleright^- \\ &\sqsupseteq\; (p^- \circ \pi_1 \,\sqcup\, (f \,\sqcup\, g)^- \circ \pi_2) \circ \triangleright^- \\ &=\; p^- \circ \pi_1 \circ \triangleright^- \end{aligned}$$

That is,

$$(p \, \triangleright \, (f \,\sqcup\, g))^- \, y \;\sqsupseteq\; \begin{cases} \bot & \text{if } y = \bot \\ p^- \, 1 & \text{otherwise} \end{cases}$$

If p is a Galois connection, then this is the lower component of a Galois connection whose upper component is $p \, \triangleright \, \top$. Thus backwards analysis of a conditional is equivalent to forwards analysis where we ignore the branches and simply use the strictness in the condition.

In some cases this is the best we can do. For example, consider the function cond defined by $\text{cond} = \pi_1 \to \pi_2 ; \pi_3$. The best reversal of $\pi_2 \,\sqcup\, \pi_3$ really is $K_\bot$, and so all we can say about cond is that it is strict in its first argument. However, if f and g have some strictness in common then we may be able to find a much better reversal of $f \,\sqcup\, g$:

$$\begin{aligned} (f \,\sqcup\, g)^- \, y \;&=\; \sqcap\{x \mid y \sqsubseteq f \, x \,\sqcup\, g \, x\} \\ &=\; \sqcap\{x \mid y \sqsubseteq y_1 \,\sqcup\, y_2 \,\wedge\, y_1 \sqsubseteq f \, x \,\wedge\, y_2 \sqsubseteq g \, x\} \\ &\sqsupseteq\; \sqcap\{x \mid y \sqsubseteq y_1 \,\sqcup\, y_2 \,\wedge\, f^- \, y_1 \sqsubseteq x \,\wedge\, g^- \, y_2 \sqsubseteq x\} \\ &=\; \sqcap\{f^- \, y_1 \,\sqcup\, g^- \, y_2 \mid y \sqsubseteq y_1 \,\sqcup\, y_2\} \end{aligned}$$

Although we've now expressed a safe reversal of $f \,\sqcup\, g$ in terms of f^- and g^- the need to consider all $\sqcup$-factorisations of y makes this formula unsuitable for use in practice: in general there are too many of them. In the particular case when y is an element of the two-point domain, however, it can be simplified to

$$(f \,\sqcup\, g)^- \, y \;\sqsupseteq\; f^- \, y \sqcap g^- \, y$$

In the next section we'll show that, in fact, this form can always be used.

4 Relating Backwards Analysis to the Concrete Semantics

So far we have studied reversal of *abstract functions*, using only the notion of safe approximation of one abstract function by another and, except for examples, have made no reference to the concrete semantics. The theory is therefore applicable to any analysis, including those such as Wadler and Hughes' projection analysis which do not fit the BHA framework. Now we restrict ourselves to this framework: not surprisingly, we can derive better results in this special case.

BHA abstract functions satisfy the following safety condition: an abstract function f is *safe* for a concrete function f if $abs \circ f \sqsubseteq f \circ abs$. If f^r is a safe reversal of f, then we have $f^r \circ abs \circ f \sqsubseteq f^r \circ f \circ abs \sqsubseteq abs$. We can take this relationship between f^r and f as a *definition* of safety for backwards abstract functions.

Definition
An abstract function f^r is *safe backwards* for a concrete function f if $f^r \circ abs \circ f \sqsubseteq abs$, or equivalently $\forall x, a . a \sqsubseteq abs (f\ x) \Rightarrow f^r\ a \sqsubseteq abs\ x$. □

That is, if f's result is at least as defined as a, then f's argument must be at least as defined as $f^r\ a$. Clearly, this safety condition justifies the test for strictness developed in section 3.1.

We can now construct a theory of backwards abstract interpretation dual to BHA. We associate abstract values with Scott-open sets[4] via a concretisation function $conc\ a = \{x \mid a \sqsubseteq abs\ x\}$. The safety condition can then be re-expressed as

$$\forall x, a . f\ x \in conc\ a \Rightarrow x \in conc\ (f^r\ a)$$

Scott-open sets form a complete lattice ordered by superset (isomorphic to the Hoare power domain including $\{\}$); $conc$ and $\sqcap$ are monotonic.

There is a best backwards abstract function for each concrete function f given by

$$f^{\sharp} = \sqcap \cdot \circ \ \wp_0 abs \ \circ \ f^{-1} \circ conc$$

where $(\wp_0\ f)\ X = \{f\ x \mid x \in X\}^{\circ}$ and $f^{-1}\ Y = \{x \mid f\ x \in Y\}$. Here X° denotes the *interior* of the upward closure of X.

The following theorems, analogous to Theorems 6 and 7, enable us to compute backwards abstract functions by abstract interpretation.

Theorem 12
If f^r and g^r are safe backwards for f and g respectively, then

(i) $g^r \circ f^r$ is safe backwards for $f \circ g$

(ii) $f^r \circ \pi_1 \sqcup g^r \circ \pi_2$ is safe backwards for $< f, g >$.

Proof
omitted for space reasons. □

---

[4]A set S is *Scott-open* if it is upwards-closed, and whenever the limit of a chain $\bigsqcup_i x_i \in S$, there is some n such that $x_n \in S$. Equivalently, a set is Scott-open if its complement is Scott-closed.

Theorem 13

Let H and H^r be functionals such that whenever f^r is safe backwards for f then H^r f^r is safe backwards for H f. Then $\bigsqcap_{n=0}^{\infty} (H^r)^n(K_{\bot}^-)$ is safe backwards for μf.H f.

Proof

$(\mu f.H\ f)\ x\ \in\ conc\ a$

$\Rightarrow\ \bigsqcup_{n=0}^{\infty}\ H^n(K_{\bot})\ x\ \in\ conc\ a$

$\Rightarrow\ \exists n.\ H^n(K_{\bot})\ x\ \in\ conc\ a$ [since $conc\ a$ is Scott-open]

$\Rightarrow\ \exists n.\ x\ \in\ conc((H^r)^n(K_{\bot}^-)\ a)$ [by safety of H^r]

$\Rightarrow\ x\ \in\ conc(\bigsqcap_{n=0}^{\infty}\ (H^r)^n(K_{\bot}^-)\ a)$

$\square$

Clearly a safe reversal of a safe forwards abstract function is safe backwards, but our interest is in safe backwards abstract functions which are *not* safe reversals of forwards ones. In particular consider the conditional $(p \to f; g)$. The best safe backwards abstract function is $(p \to f; g)^{\sharp} = \bigsqcap \circ \wp_0 abs \circ (p \to f; g)^{-1} \circ conc$. But

$$(p \to f; g)^{-1}\ S = \begin{cases} \{\bot\}^{\uparrow} & \text{if } \bot \in S \\ (p^{-1}\{\text{true}\} \cap f^{-1}\ S)\ \cup & \\ \quad (p^{-1}\{\text{false}\} \cap g^{-1}\ S) & \text{otherwise} \end{cases}$$

where $\{\bot\}^{\uparrow}$ is the upwards closure of $\{\bot\}$. Using this, and the fact that *abs* (and therefore *conc*) are strict and $\bot$-reflecting we obtain,

$$(p \to f; g)^{\sharp}\ y \sqsupseteq \begin{cases} \bot & \text{if } y = \bot \\ p^{\sharp}\ 1 \sqcup (f^{\sharp}\ y \sqcap g^{\sharp}\ y) & \text{otherwise} \end{cases}$$

and so $(p \to f; g)^{\sharp} \sqsupseteq \sqcup \circ (p^{\sharp} \times (f^{\sharp} \sqcap g^{\sharp})) \circ \triangleright^-$.

There are functions that can be shown strict using this rule that cannot be shown strict by the forwards analysis. An example is $+ \circ (\pi_1 \to\ < K_1, \pi_2 >;\ < \pi_2, K_1 >)$. Backwards analysis shows

$(+ \circ (\pi_1 \to\ < K_1, \pi_2 >;\ < \pi_2, K_1 >))^{\sharp}\ 1$

$=\ (\pi_1 \to\ < K_1, \pi_2 >;\ < \pi_2, K_1 >)^{\sharp}\ (1, 1)$

$=\ \pi_1^{\sharp}\ 1 \sqcup (< K_1, \pi_2 >^{\sharp}\ (1, 1) \sqcap\ < \pi_2, K_1 >^{\sharp}\ (1, 1))$

$=\ (1, 0) \sqcup ((K_1^{\sharp}\ 1 \sqcup \pi_2^{\sharp}\ 1) \sqcap (\pi_2^{\sharp}\ 1 \sqcup K_1^{\sharp}\ 1))$

$=\ (1, 0) \sqcup (((0, 0) \sqcup (0, 1)) \sqcap ((0, 1) \sqcup (0, 0)))$

$=\ (1, 0) \sqcup ((0, 1) \sqcap (0, 1))$

$=\ (1, 1)$

and so the function is strict in both arguments. Forwards analysis cannot discover strictness in the second argument, because when it has abstract value 0 then the values of the two branches of the conditional are $(1, 0)$ and $(0, 1)$, and taking the least upper bound loses the information that the argument was 0. This example has also been noticed by Hunt [Hun91].

It is not true, therefore, that conditionals are "good" forwards and "bad" backwards. They are bad in both directions, but in different ways! An analyser which repeatedly worked backwards and forwards, using the results of each stage to improve the next, could discover more information than an analyser working in either direction alone.

The backwards analysis we have derived in this section is essentially the same as Johnsson's [Joh81] or the simplest strictness analysis discussed in [Hug88]. It can also be thought of as an abstraction of Dybjer's inverse image analysis [Dyb91], which also used inverse images of Scott-open sets.

5   Wadler's 4-point Domain

In this section we consider the abstraction of lists of atomic values by elements of Wadler's 4-point domain [Wad87]. The abstract domain is

$$
\begin{array}{c}
1\in \\
| \\
0\in \\
| \\
\infty \\
| \\
\bot
\end{array}
$$

$\bot$ abstracts just the undefined list; ∞ abstracts lists whose last tail is $\bot$ and their limits, infinite lists; $0\in$ abstracts lists ending in nil and containing an undefined element; $1\in$ abstracts lists ending in nil all of whose elements are defined. For example,

$$
\begin{aligned}
abs \ (\text{cons 1 (cons 2 } \bot)) \ &= \ \infty \\
abs \ [1,2,\bot] \ &= \ 0\in \\
abs \ [1,2] \ &= \ 1\in
\end{aligned}
$$

If f's abstract function maps ∞ to $\bot$ we may conclude that f is tail-strict; if it maps $0\in$ to $\bot$ we may conclude that f is head-and-tail-strict.

Lists are built using cons and nil and taken apart by pattern matching. Wadler gives a special rule for analysing **case** expressions, but we will instead simulate pattern-matching with the functions null and uncons:

$$
\text{uncons } xs \ = \ \begin{cases} (x, xs') & \text{if } xs = \text{cons } x \ xs' \\ \bot & \text{otherwise} \end{cases}
$$

The abstract value of nil is $1\in$, and the abstraction of cons is given below.

cons	$\bot$	∞	$0\in$	$1\in$
0	∞	∞	$0\in$	$0\in$
1	∞	∞	$0\in$	$1\in$

For our analysis of conditionals of the form (null $\rightarrow$ f; g) to match Wadler's rule for **case** in accuracy, we have to abstract null's boolean result by an element of the four-point domain $\{\bot, \textit{true}, \textit{false}, \top\}$. With this abstraction of booleans better forwards and backwards analyses of conditionals can be derived: the new backwards rule is

$$(p \to f;g)^\sharp \; y \; \sqsupseteq \; \begin{cases} \bot & \text{if } y = \bot \\ (p^\sharp \; true \; \sqcup \; f^\sharp \; y) \; \sqcap \\ \quad (p^\sharp \; false \; \sqcup \; g^\sharp \; y) & \text{otherwise} \end{cases}$$

The abstractions of null and uncons are now:

$null$			$uncons$	
$\bot$	$\bot$		$\bot$	$(0, \bot)$
∞	$false$		∞	$(1, \infty)$
$0\in$	$false$		$0\in$	$(1, 1\in)$
$1\in$	$\top$		$1\in$	$(1, 1\in)$

But there is a problem — *uncons* does not distinguish $0\in$ from $1\in$! The reason is that $0\in = cons \; 1 \; 0\in = cons \; 0 \; 1\in$, and *uncons* must approximate both possibilities by their least upper bound. The resulting analysis has very little power, which is why Wadler gave a special rule for entire **case** expressions.

But now consider a backwards analysis. K_{nil}, *cons*, and *null* are all Galois connections and so may be reversed at once. Reversing *uncons* is pointless—it would produce an equally uninformative backwards abstract function—but we can instead determine the best backwards abstract function for uncons. It is:

$uncons^r$	$\bot$	∞	$0\in$	$1\in$
0	$\bot$	∞	$0\in$	$0\in$
1	∞	∞	$0\in$	$1\in$

(To interpret this table intuitively, think of the first argument as the demand for the head of a cons-cell, and the second argument as the demand for the tail. The result is then the demand for the whole cons-cell. $1\in$ should be interpreted as a head-and-tail-strict demand, and $0\in$ as a tail-strict demand.)

Now all four values of the second argument are properly distinguished, and indeed an accurate backwards analysis can be based on these functions[5]. It corresponds to projection-based strictness analysis with the projections for head-strictness discarded [WH87, Bur90]. But *uncons*^{r} is not the lower component of a Galois connection since there is no greatest argument mapped to $0\in$, and hence no equally powerful forwards function exists.

We can compare this to the example in section 4 of a function where backwards analysis is more accurate than forwards: the need for forwards analysis to approximate $(0, 1)$ and $(1, 0)$ by $(1, 1)$ in that example is analogous to the need to approximate *cons* $0 \; 1\in$ and *cons* $1 \; 0\in$ by *cons* $1 \; 1\in$ here.

What if we reverse this backwards analysis to derive a more accurate forwards one? We model **case** constructs by $case(n, f) = null \to K_n$; $f \circ uncons$. The interesting term here is $f \circ uncons$. Given a forwards abstract function f for f, a safe backwards abstract function for this term is $uncons^r \circ f^-$. So a safe forwards abstract function for the composition is

$$(uncons^r \circ f^-)^+ \; x \; = \; \sqcup\{y \mid (uncons^r \circ f^-) \; y \sqsubseteq x\}$$

---

[5]Choosing hd and tl as primitives instead of uncons does *not* lead to a good analysis. The best backwards abstract function for tl is $tl^r \; y = uncons^r \; (0, y)$ corresponding to the first row of the table, which again fails to distinguish $0\in$ from $1\in$.

Taking x to be $0\in$ for example, the right hand side is

$$
\begin{aligned}
&\bigsqcup\{y \mid uncons^r \ (f^- \ y) \sqsubseteq 0\in \} \\
&= \bigsqcup\{y \mid f^- \ y \sqsubseteq (0, 1\in) \ \lor \ f^- \ y \sqsubseteq (1, 0\in)\} \\
&= \bigsqcup\{y \mid f^- \ y \sqsubseteq (0, 1\in)\} \ \sqcup \ \bigsqcup\{y \mid f^- \ y \sqsubseteq (1, 0\in)\} \\
&= f^+ \ (0, 1\in) \ \sqcup \ f^+ \ (1, 0\in)
\end{aligned}
$$

The other cases are similar, but simpler since there is a unique largest value mapped below x by $uncons^r$. Using this abstract function and interpreting the other parts of $case(n,f)$ in the standard way leads us to

$$
case(n,f) \ = \ \begin{cases}
\bot & \text{if } x = \bot \\
f^+ \ (1,\infty) & \text{if } x = \infty \\
f^+ \ (1, 0\in) \ \sqcup \ f^+ \ (0, 1\in) & \text{if } x = 0\in \\
n \ \sqcup \ f^+ \ (1, 1\in) & \text{otherwise}
\end{cases}
$$

which is almost exactly Wadler's rule. The difference is that Wadler omitted the double reversal of f that appears here. Of course the double reversal is unnecessary, but to derive this via reversal we need theory developed in [HL91].

6 Higher-order Functions

Since one of the strengths of BHA analysis is its ability to handle higher-order functions, it's natural to ask what happens when we reverse the corresponding abstract functions. Unfortunately, the reversals are not very informative. This is not surprising since backwards analyses in general have difficulty with higher-order functions.

Consider first ap, with type $(X \rightarrow Y) \times X \rightarrow Y$. Its best reversal is

$$
\begin{aligned}
ap^- \ y \ &= \ \bigsqcap\{(f,x) \mid y \sqsubseteq f \ x\} \\
&= \ \bigsqcap\{([x \mapsto y], x) \mid x \in X\} \\
&= \ (\bigsqcap\{[x \mapsto y] \mid x \in X\}, \bigsqcap\{x \mid x \in X\}) \\
&= \ ([\top \mapsto y], \bot)
\end{aligned}
$$

where $[x \mapsto y]$ is the step function that maps any $x' \sqsupseteq x$ to y and all other arguments to $\bot$. This is the lower component of a Galois connection whose upper component is $ap^+ \ (f,x) = f \ \top$. Thus all of the information about strictness in the argument is lost: backwards analysis can only discover strictness in the *function*.

In the case of currying,

$$
\begin{aligned}
(\Lambda f)^- \ g \ &= \ \bigsqcap \ \{a \mid g \sqsubseteq (\Lambda f) \ a\} \\
&= \ \bigsqcap \ \{a \mid \forall x \ . \ g \ x \sqsubseteq f(a,x)\} \\
&\sqsupseteq \ \bigsqcap \ \{a \mid \forall x \ . \ f^r(g \ x) \sqsubseteq (a,x)\} \\
&= \ \bigsqcap \ \{a \mid \forall x \ . \ \pi_1(f^r(g \ x)) \sqsubseteq a \ \land \ \forall x \ . \ \pi_2(f^r(g \ x)) \sqsubseteq x\} \\
&= \ \bigsqcap \ \{a \mid \pi_1(f^r(g \ \top)) \sqsubseteq a \ \land \ \pi_2 \circ f^r \circ g \sqsubseteq id\} \\
&= \ \begin{cases} \pi_1(f^r(g \ \top)) & \text{if } \pi_2 \circ f^r \circ g \sqsubseteq id \\ \top & \text{otherwise} \end{cases}
\end{aligned}
$$

where f^r is a safe reversal of f. If f is a Galois connection then this is the lower component of a Galois connection with upper component

$$
(\Lambda f)^+ \ a = \begin{cases} \top & \text{if } a = \top \\ (\Lambda f) \ a & \text{otherwise} \end{cases}
$$

from which we see that backwards analysis cannot discover strictness in the second argument of a curried function, since this is equivalent to testing whether $(\Lambda f)^{+} \top \bot = \bot$.

7 Relational Reversal

As we've seen, the reversal of an analysis is usually less accurate than the original. However, by working with *sets* of abstract values it's possible to derive an analysis in the opposite direction with *equal* power. Such an analysis is called *relational*.

The basic idea is to promote each abstract function f to $\wp_O\, f$, operating on upwards-closed sets of abstract values. Whatever f is, it turns out that $\wp_O\, f$ is the upper component of a Galois connection, with lower component f^{-1}. So backwards abstract functions of the form f^{-1} carry just as much information as the original functions f. Unfortunately, relational analyses seem to be far too costly to use in practice.

One compromise is to combine a locally relational analysis with either backwards or forwards non-relational analyses; the idea being to use the rather expensive relational analysis just for small parts of a program that would be analysed badly by a non-relational method. Within those parts we can mix backwards and forwards abstract functions. For instance, Wadler's rather tricky analysis of **case** expressions can be derived as a locally relational combination of the accurate backwards abstract function for **uncons** with the forwards abstract functions used in BHA strictness analysis.

These results are beyond the scope of this article. They appear in a companion paper [HL91], where we provide generalised backwards and forwards safety conditions relating relational abstract functions to the concrete semantics, and show that a relational analysis may be used as part of a non-relational analysis in the same direction.

8 Related Work and Conclusions

Strictness analysis has given rise to a rich variety of analyses, both forwards and backwards, and the relationship between these has not always been clear. Not only are the directions of analysis often different, but commonly so are the abstract values and their interpretations. Working towards a unified understanding, Burn showed the relationship between BHA strictness analysis and Wadler and Hughes' projection-based strictness analysis through the use of so-called "smash projections" [Bur90]. This allowed the results of each analysis to be related to the results of the other.

Soon afterwards, Hunt presented a forwards strictness analysis based on partial equivalence relations (PERs) [Hun90]. These were particularly interesting as most of the PERs used at the ground types corresponded exactly with projections. In particular, the ever elusive property of head-strictness was captured. However in order for the analysis to be able to derive head-strictness information a double analysis within the **case** construct was required. Again, this may be viewed as an instance of obtaining the best reversal of a backwards analysis by considering the case construct as a whole.

Meanwhile, spurred by the discovery of a "naturally forwards" projection-based analysis[6] [Lau89, Lau91], Hughes and Launchbury studied a direction-independent formulation of projection analysis [HL90], in order to assess when a view of the analysis from one direction may equal or be superior to a view from the other. The concept of Galois connections arose here as a means of demonstrating equality. Following this lead, Hunt reformulated much of [HL90] in terms Scott-closed sets, so divesting it of its dependence on projections [Hun91].

The present paper develops the use of Galois connections as abstract functions (i.e. *within* an analysis), and shows that such abstract functions may safely be reversed with no loss of accuracy. Furthermore, *any* abstract function may be safely reversed, though possibly losing information in the process. In the particular case where the reversal is itself a Galois connection, its reduced power may be compared against the original by reversing once more to obtain an abstract function in the original direction having the same power as the reversal.

These ideas and methods were then applied to BHA style abstract interpretation, and provided a link between this and a previously unconnected backwards analysis. In an effort to improve the reversal of the conditional we showed that the best backwards abstraction of the conditional is *incomparable* with the best forwards abstraction. Consequently, neither forwards nor backwards analysis of the conditional may be said to be superior to the other.

Wadler's 4-point abstract domain requires a special interpretation of the case construct to achieve good results. With the experience of reversals, we were able to see exactly where a naive abstract interpretation would lose information: uncons has a good backwards abstraction, but a poor forwards abstraction. Unfortunately the non-relational techniques of this paper are insufficiently powerful to derive Wadler's rule for case directly, but they were able to produce a very similar version.

Finally we applied the techniques to higher order constructs, in order to obtain a backwards analysis of higher order functions. We obtained a simple reversal which may be of some use in practice, but one whose power is significantly less than the forwards version.

Recent work by the Nielsons on complexity measures in abstract interpretation has an interesting connection with the work here [NN92]. They show that finding fixed points over lattices of *completely additive* functions may require at most a quadratic number of unfoldings, whereas general fixpoint finding is exponential. As completely additive functions are lower components of Galois connections, our result that every abstract function has a best approximating Galois connection (obtained by repeated reversal) may be seen as a generic method for deriving cheap approximating analyses.

Although the development of this paper has been with an eye on strictness analysis, many of the results are further reaching: strictness analysis is used mainly as a pedagogic tool, and the techniques may be applied to other analyses.

---

[6]namely binding-time analysis, as used in partial evaluation

References

[AH87] S.Abramsky and C.L.Hankin eds., *Abstract Interpretation of Declarative Languages*. Ellis Horwood, Chichester, England, 1987.

[BHA86] G.L.Burn, C.L.Hankin and S.Abramsky, *Strictness analysis for higher order functions*, In *Science of Computer Programming*, 7, 249-278, 1986.

[Bur90] G.L.Burn, *A relationship between abstract interpretation and projection analysis*, POPL, 1990.

[CC77] P.Cousot and R.Cousot, *Abstract Interpretation: A unified lattice model for static analyses of programs by construction of approximation of fixpoints*, POPL, 1977.

[Dyb91] P.Dybjer, *Inverse Image Analysis Generalises Strictness Analysis*, Information and Computation 90, 2, 1991, pp 194-216.

[Hal87] C.V.Hall, *Strictness Analysis Applied to Programs with Lazy List Constructors*, Ph.D. thesis, Indiana University, 1987.

[HL90] R.J.M.Hughes and J.Launchbury, *Towards Relating Forwards and Backwards Analyses*, Glasgow Functional Programming, Ullapool, In *Workshops in Computing*, S-V, 1991.

[HL91] R.J.M.Hughes and J.Launchbury, *Locally Relational Abstract Interpretation*, in preparation, Glasgow University, 1991.

[Hug88] R.J.M.Hughes, *Backwards Analysis of Functional Programs*, In D. Bjørner, A. Ershov and N.D. Jones eds. *Partial Evaluation and Mixed Computation*, Proc. IFIP TC2 Workshop, Denmark, Oct 1987; North-Holland, 1988.

[Hun90] S.Hunt, *PERs generalise projections for strictness analysis*, Glasgow Functional Programming, Ullapool, In *Workshops in Computing*, S-V, 1991.

[Hun91] S.Hunt, *Forwards and Backwards Strictness Analysis: Continuing the Comparison*, unpublished draft, Imperial College, 1991.

[Joh81] T.Johnsson, *Detecting when Call-by-Value can be used instead of Call-by-Need*, Programming Methodology Group, PMG-14, Chalmers, Gothenburg, 1981.

[Lau89] J.Launchbury. *Projection Factorisations in Partial Evaluation*. Ph.D. Thesis, Glasgow University, 1989; *Distinguished Dissertations in Computer Science*, Vol 1, C.U.P. 1991.

[Lau91] J.Launchbury. *Strictness and Binding-Time Analyses: Two for the Price of One*, SIGPLAN PLDI, Toronto, 1991.

[Myc81] A.Mycroft, *Abstract interpretation and optimising transformations for applicative languages*, Ph.D. thesis, University of Edinburgh, 1981.

[NN92] H.R.Nielson and F.Nielson, *Bounded Fixed Point Iteration*, POPL 92.

[WH87] P.Wadler and R.J.M.Hughes, *Projections for Strictness Analysis*, FPCA 87.

[Wad87] P.Wadler, *Strictness analysis on non-flat domains*, In [AH87], 1987.

A theory of qualified types

Mark P. Jones
Programming Research Group
Oxford University Computing Laboratory
8–11 Keble Road
Oxford OX1 3QD
(email: mpj@prg.ox.ac.uk)

Introduction

In a language with a polymorphic type system, a term of type $\forall t.f(t)$ can be treated (possibly after suitable instantiation) as having any of the types in the set:

$$\{ f(t) \mid t \text{ is a type} \}.$$

It is natural to consider a more restricted form of polymorphism in which the value taken by t may be constrained to a particular subset of types. In this situation, we write $\forall t.\pi(t) \Rightarrow f(t)$, where $\pi(t)$ is a predicate on types, for the type of an object which can be treated (after suitable instantiation) as having any of the types in the set:

$$\{ f(t) \mid t \text{ is a type such that } \pi(t) \text{ holds} \}.$$

A term with a restricted polymorphic type of this kind is often said to be *overloaded*, having different interpretations for different argument types.

This paper presents a general theory of overloading based on the use of *qualified types*, which are types of the form $\pi \Rightarrow \sigma$ denoting those instances of type σ which satisfy the predicate π. The main benefits of using qualified types are:

- A general approach which includes a range of familiar type systems as special cases. Results and tools developed for the general system are immediately applicable to each particular application.

- A precise treatment of the relationship between implicit and explicit overloading. This is particularly useful for describing the implementation of systems supporting qualified types.

- The ability to include local constraints as part of the type of an object. This enables the definition and use of polymorphic overloaded values within a program.

Outline of paper

Each of the type systems considered in this paper is parameterised by the choice of a system of predicates on type expressions, whose basic properties are described in Section 1. A number of examples are included to illustrate the use of this framework to describe a range of type systems including Haskell type classes, extensible records and subtyping. Section 2 describes the use of qualified types in the context of polymorphic λ-calculus with explicit typing. This is extended in Section 3 using a general notion of *evidence* to explore the relationship between implicit and explicit overloading. An alternative approach, suitable for use in an implicitly typed language, is introduced in Section 4 using an extension of the ML type system [Mil78] to support qualified types. Although substantially less powerful than polymorphic λ-calculus, we show that the resulting system is suitable for use in a language based on type inference, which allows the type of a term to be determined without explicit type annotations.

1 Predicates

Each of the type systems considered in this paper is parameterised by the choice of a language of *predicates* π together with an entailment relation $\Vdash$ between (finite) sets of predicates. Individual predicates may be written using expressions of the form $\pi = p \; \tau_1 \; \ldots \; \tau_n$ where p is a predicate symbol corresponding to an n-place relation between types; the predicate π represents the assertion that the types $\tau_1, \ldots, \tau_n$ are in this relation. The definition of $\Vdash$ varies from one application to another. The only properties that we will assume are:

- **monotonicity.** $P \Vdash P'$ whenever $P \supseteq P'$.

- **transitivity.** if $P \Vdash Q$ and $Q \Vdash R$ then $P \Vdash R$.

- **closure property.** if $P \Vdash Q$ then $SP \Vdash SQ$ for any substitution S mapping type variables (and hence type expressions) to type expressions.

If P is a set of predicates and π is a predicate then we write $P \Vdash \pi$ and P, π as abbreviations for $P \Vdash \{\pi\}$ and $P \cup \{\pi\}$ respectively.

The following subsections illustrate the languages of predicates used in three applications of qualified types. Only the basic ideas are sketched here; further details may be found in [Jon91a].

1.1 Example: type classes

Introduced in [WB89] and adopted as part of the standard for the programming language Haskell [HPJW91], type classes are particularly useful for describing the implementation of standard polymorphic operators such as computable equality. Much of the original motivation for qualified types came from the study of type classes.

Broadly speaking, a *type class* is a family of types (the *instances* of the class) on which a number of values (the *member functions*) are defined. In this case, each predicate symbol corresponds to a user-defined class and a predicate of the form $C \; \tau$ represents the assertion that the type τ is an instance of the class named C. The class Eq is a standard example whose instances are those types whose elements can be tested for equality using the operator $(==) :: \forall a.Eq \; a \Rightarrow a \to a \to Bool$.

Differences in the basic approach to type classes are reflected in the properties of the $\Vdash$ relation. In a standard Haskell system we have axioms such as $\emptyset \Vdash Eq \; Int$ and $Eq \; a \Vdash Eq \; [a]$. The same framework can also be used to describe the use of Haskell *superclasses*, and to support the extension to classes with multiple parameters as used in Gofer [Jon92].

Type classes are best suited to systems with a type inference algorithm such as that described in Section 6 where the appropriate instances of each overloaded operator can be determined automatically as part of the type inference process.

1.2 Example: extensible records

A record is a set of values labelled by the elements l of a specified set of *labels*. There has been considerable interest in the use of record types to model inheritance in object oriented programming languages and a number of different approaches have been considered. Using the type system to be described in Section 2 we can construct a system of extensible records, strongly reminiscent of [HP90] using predicates of the form:

> r has $l : t$ indicating that a record of type r has a field labelled l of type t.
>
> r lacks l indicating that a record of type r does not have a field labelled l.

This also requires an extension of the language of type expressions to allow types of the form $\langle\rangle$ (the empty record, which lacks any fields), $r \setminus l$ (the type of a record obtained by removing a field labelled l from a record of type r) and $(r \mid l : t)$ (the type of a record obtained by extending a record of type r with a new field of type t labelled l). The definition of the entailment relation includes axioms such as $\emptyset \Vdash (\langle\rangle$ lacks $l)$ and $\{r$ lacks $l\} \Vdash ((r \mid l : t)$ has $l : t)$.

The primitive operations of record *restriction*, *extension* and *selection* can then be represented by families of functions (indexed by labels) of type:

$$
\begin{aligned}
(\_\setminus l) \quad &:: \quad \forall r.\forall t.(r \text{ has } l : t) \Rightarrow r \to r \setminus l \\
(\_\mid l = \_) \quad &:: \quad \forall r.\forall t.(r \text{ lacks } l) \Rightarrow r \to t \to (r \mid l : t) \\
(\_.l) \quad &:: \quad \forall r.\forall t.(r \text{ has } l : t) \Rightarrow r \to t
\end{aligned}
$$

Details of the relationship between this approach and those of [Rem89, CM90] are given in [HP90].

1.3 Example: subtyping

Type systems with various forms of subtyping can be described using predicates of the form $\sigma \subseteq \sigma'$, representing the assertion that σ is a subtype of σ'. Many such systems, including those of [Mit84, FM89], allow the use of implicit coercion from one type to another. The extensions required to support this are discussed in Section 7.3.

2 Polymorphic λ-calculus with qualified types

2.1 Basic definitions

In this section, we work with a variant of polymorphic λ-calculus which includes qualified types using type expressions of the form:

$$\sigma ::= t \mid \sigma \to \sigma \mid \forall t.\sigma \mid \pi \Rightarrow \sigma$$

where t ranges over a given set of type variables. The $\to$ and $\Rightarrow$ symbols are treated as right associative infix binary operators with $\to$ binding more tightly than $\Rightarrow$. Additional type constructors such as those for integers, lists and record types will be used as required. The set of type variables appearing (free) in an expression X is denoted $TV(X)$.

To begin with we use an unmodified form of the (unchecked) terms of polymorphic λ-calculus, given by expressions of the form:

$$M ::= x \mid MN \mid \lambda x : \sigma.M \mid M\sigma \mid \lambda t.M$$

where x ranges over a given set of term variables. The set of free (term) variables appearing in a term M will be denoted $FV(M)$. Note that we do not provide constructs for the introduction of new overloadings such as **inst** and **over** in [WB89]. If none of the free variables for a given term have qualified (i.e. overloaded) types then no overloading will be used in the expression.

2.2 Typing rules

A *type assignment* is a (finite) set of *typing statements* of the form $x : \sigma$ in which no term variable x appears more than once. If A is a type assignment, then we write $dom\ A = \{\, x \mid (x : \sigma) \in A \,\}$, and if x is a term variable with $x \notin dom\ A$ then we write $A, x : \sigma$ as an abbreviation for the type assignment $A \cup \{x : \sigma\}$. The type assignment obtained from A by removing any typing statement for the variable x is denoted A_x. A type assignment A can be interpreted as a function mapping each element of $dom\ A$ to a type scheme. In particular, if $(x : \sigma) \in A$ then we write $A(x) = \sigma$.

An expression of the form $P \mid A \vdash M : \sigma$ represents the assertion that the term M has type σ when the predicates in P are satisfied and the types of free variables in M are as specified in the type assignment A. The typing rules for this system are given in Figure 1. Most of these are similar to the rules for explicit typing of polymorphic λ-calculus and do not involve the predicate set.

Standard rules:	*(var)*	$P \mid A \vdash x : \sigma$	$(x : \sigma) \in A$
	$(\to E)$	$\dfrac{P \mid A \vdash M : \sigma' \to \sigma \quad P \mid A \vdash N : \sigma'}{P \mid A \vdash MN : \sigma}$	
	$(\to I)$	$\dfrac{P \mid A, x : \sigma' \vdash M : \sigma}{P \mid A \vdash \lambda x : \sigma'.M : \sigma' \to \sigma}$	
Qualified types:	$(\Rightarrow E)$	$\dfrac{P \mid A \vdash M : \pi \Rightarrow \sigma \quad P \Vdash \pi}{P \mid A \vdash M : \sigma}$	
	$(\Rightarrow I)$	$\dfrac{P, \pi \mid A \vdash M : \sigma}{P \mid A \vdash M : \pi \Rightarrow \sigma}$	
Polymorphism:	$(\forall E)$	$\dfrac{P \mid A \vdash M : \forall t.\sigma}{P \mid A \vdash M\tau : [\tau/t]\sigma}$	
	$(\forall I)$	$\dfrac{P \mid A \vdash M : \sigma}{P \mid A \vdash \lambda t.M : \forall t.\sigma}$	$t \notin TV(A) \cup TV(P)$

Figure 1: Typing rules for polymorphic λ-calculus with qualified types

By an abuse of notation, we will also use $P \mid A \vdash M : \sigma$ as a proposition asserting the existence of a derivation of $P \mid A \vdash M : \sigma$.

3 Evidence

Although the system of qualified types described in the previous sections is suitable for reasoning about the types of overloaded terms, it cannot be used to describe their evaluation. For example, the knowledge that *Int* is an instance of the class *Eq* is not sufficient to determine the value of the expression $2 == 3$; we must also be provided with the value of the equality operator which makes *Int* an instance of *Eq*. In general, we can only use a term of type $\pi \Rightarrow \sigma$ if we are also supplied with suitable *evidence* that the predicate π does indeed hold.

This leads us to consider an extension of the term language which makes the role of evidence explicit, using:

- **Evidence expressions:** A language of *evidence expressions* e denoting evidence values, including a set of *evidence variables* v.

- **Evidence construction:** An *evidence assignment* is a set of elements of the form $(v : \pi)$ in which no evidence variable appears more than once. The $\Vdash$ relation is extended to a three place relation $P \Vdash e : \pi$, indicating that it is possible to construct evidence e for the predicate π in any environment binding the variables in the evidence assignment P to appropriate evidence values. Thus predicates play a similar role for evidence expressions as types for simple λ-calculus terms.

- **Evidence abstraction:** A term M of type $\pi \Rightarrow \rho$ is implemented by a term of the form $\lambda v : \pi.M'$ where v is an evidence variable and M' is a term of type ρ corresponding to M using v in each place where evidence for π is needed.

- **Evidence application:** Each use of an overloaded expression N of type $\pi \Rightarrow \rho$ is replaced by a term of the form $N'e$ where N' is a term corresponding to N and e is an evidence expression for π.

- **Evidence reduction:** The standard rules of computation are augmented by a variant of β-reduction for evidence abstraction and application:

$$(\lambda v.M)e \vartriangleright_{\beta e} [e/v]M.$$

Most of the typing rules given in Figure 1 can be used with the extended system without modification. The only exceptions are the rules for dealing with qualified types; suitably modified versions of these are given in Figure 2.

Notice that extending the term language to make the use of evidence explicit gives unicity of type; each well-typed term has a uniquely determined type. This approach is very similar to the technique used to make polymorphism explicit in the translation from implicit to explicit typed λ-calculus using abstraction and application over types [Mit90]. As in that situation, there is a simple correspondence

$$
(\Rightarrow E) \quad \frac{P, v : \pi \mid A \vdash M : \sigma}{P \mid A \vdash \lambda v : \pi.M : \pi \Rightarrow \sigma}
$$

$$
(\Rightarrow I) \quad \frac{P \mid A \vdash M : \pi \Rightarrow \sigma \quad P \Vdash e : \pi}{P \mid A \vdash Me : \sigma}
$$

Figure 2: Modified rules for qualified types with evidence

between derivations in the two systems, described by means of a function *Erase* mapping explicitly overloaded terms to their implicitly overloaded counterparts:

$$
\begin{aligned}
Erase(x) \quad &= \quad x \\
Erase(MN) \quad &= \quad (Erase(M))(Erase(N)) \\
&\vdots \\
Erase(\lambda v : \pi.M) \quad &= \quad Erase(M) \\
Erase(Me) \quad &= \quad Erase(M)
\end{aligned}
$$

The correspondence between the two systems can now be described by:

Theorem 1 $P \mid A \vdash M : \sigma$ *using the original typing rules if and only if* $P' \mid A \vdash M' : \sigma$ *by a derivation of the same structure in the extended system such that* $P = \{\pi \mid (v : \pi) \in P'\}$ *and* $Erase(M') = M$.

Given a term M in the original system, each corresponding term using explicit overloading is called a *translation* (or *implementation*) of M and can be used to give a semantics for the term. We use the notation $P' \mid A \vdash M \rightsquigarrow M' : \sigma$ to refer to the translation of a term in a specific context. Note that the translation of a given term may not be uniquely defined (with distinct translations corresponding to distinct derivations of $P \mid A \vdash M : \sigma$). This problem is discussed in more detail in Section 7.1.

The form of evidence required will vary from one application to another. Suitable choices for each of the examples described in Section 1 are as follows:

- **Type classes:** The evidence for a type class predicate of the form $C\ \tau$ is a *dictionary* (i.e. a tuple or record) containing the values of the members of C at the instance τ.

- **Extensible records:** The evidence for a predicate of the form $(r\ \textbf{lacks}\ l)$ is the function:

$$
(\_ \mid l = \_) \quad :: \quad \forall t . r \rightarrow t \rightarrow (r \mid l : t)
$$

The evidence for a predicate of the form $(r\ \textbf{has}\ l : t)$ is the pair of functions:

$$
\begin{aligned}
(\_ \backslash l) \quad &:: \quad r \rightarrow r \backslash l \\
(\_ . l) \quad &:: \quad r \rightarrow t
\end{aligned}
$$

In practice, a concrete implementation of extensible records is likely to use offsets into a table of values used to store a record as evidence, passing these values to generic functions for updating or selecting from a record where necessary.

- **Subtypes:** The evidence for a predicate $\sigma \subseteq \sigma'$ is a coercion function which maps values of type σ to values of type σ'.

4   An extension of ML using qualified types

Polymorphic λ-calculus is not a suitable language to describe an implicitly typed language in which the need for explicit type annotations is replaced by the existence of a type inference algorithm. In practice, the benefits of type inference are often considered to outweigh the disadvantages of a less powerful type system. The ML type system [Mil78, DM82] is a well-known example in which the price of type inference is the inability to define functions with polymorphic arguments. Nevertheless, the ML type system has proved to be very useful in practice and has been adopted by a number of later languages.

Detailed proofs of the results presented in this and following sections may be found in [Jon91b]; they are not included here for reasons of space.

4.1   Basic definitions

Following the definition of types and type schemes in ML we consider a structured language of types, with the principal restriction being the inability to support functions with either polymorphic or overloaded arguments:

$$
\begin{aligned}
\tau &::= t \mid \tau \rightarrow \tau && \text{types} \\
\rho &::= P \Rightarrow \tau && \text{qualified types} \\
\sigma &::= \forall T.\rho && \text{type schemes}
\end{aligned}
$$

(P and T range over finite sets of predicates and finite sets of type variables respectively).

It is convenient to introduce some abbreviations for qualified type and type scheme expressions. In particular, if $\rho = (P \Rightarrow \tau)$ and $\sigma = \forall T.\rho$ then we write:

Abbreviation	Qualified type	Abbreviation	Type scheme
τ	$\emptyset \Rightarrow \tau$	ρ	$\forall \emptyset.\rho$
$\pi \Rightarrow \rho$	$P, \pi \Rightarrow \tau$	$\forall t.\sigma$	$\forall(T \cup \{t\}).\rho$
$P' \Rightarrow \rho$	$P \cup P' \Rightarrow \tau$	$\forall T'.\sigma$	$\forall(T \cup T').\rho$

In addition, if $\{\alpha_i\}$ is an indexed set of variables, we write $\forall \alpha_i.\rho$ as an abbreviation for $\forall \{\alpha_i\}.\rho$. As usual, type schemes are regarded as equal if they are equivalent upto renaming of bound variables.

Using this notation, any type scheme can be written in the form $\forall \alpha_i.P \Rightarrow \tau$, representing the set of qualified types:

$$\{ [\tau_i/\alpha_i]P \Rightarrow [\tau_i/\alpha_i]\tau \mid \tau_i \in \textit{Type} \}$$

where $[\tau_i/\alpha_i]$ is the substitution mapping each of the variables α_i to the corresponding type τ_i and *Type* is the set of all simple type expressions.

As in [Mil78, DM82, CDK86], we use a term language based on simple untyped λ-calculus with the addition of a *let* construct to enable the definition and use of polymorphic (and in this case, overloaded) terms.

$$M ::= x \mid MN \mid \lambda x.M \mid \text{let } x = M \text{ in } N$$

A suitable set of typing rules for this system is given in Figure 3. Note the use of the symbols τ, ρ and σ to restrict the application of certain rules to specific sets of type expressions.

Standard rules:	(var)	$P \mid A \vdash x : \sigma$	$(x : \sigma) \in A$

$$(\rightarrow E) \quad \frac{P \mid A \vdash M : \tau' \rightarrow \tau \quad P \mid A \vdash N : \tau'}{P \mid A \vdash MN : \tau}$$

$$(\rightarrow I) \quad \frac{P \mid A_x, x : \tau' \vdash M : \tau}{P \mid A \vdash \lambda x.M : \tau' \rightarrow \tau}$$

Qualified types:

$$(\Rightarrow E) \quad \frac{P \mid A \vdash M : \pi \Rightarrow \rho \quad P \Vdash \pi}{P \mid A \vdash M : \rho}$$

$$(\Rightarrow I) \quad \frac{P, \pi \mid A \vdash M : \rho}{P \mid A \vdash M : \pi \Rightarrow \rho}$$

Polymorphism:

$$(\forall E) \quad \frac{P \mid A \vdash M : \forall t.\sigma}{P \mid A \vdash M : [\tau/t]\sigma}$$

$$(\forall I) \quad \frac{P \mid A \vdash M : \sigma}{P \mid A \vdash M : \forall t.\sigma} \qquad t \notin TV(A) \cup TV(P)$$

Local Definition:

$$(let) \quad \frac{P \mid A \vdash M : \sigma \quad Q \mid A_x, x : \sigma \vdash N : \tau}{P \cup Q \mid A \vdash (\text{let } x = M \text{ in } N) : \tau}$$

Figure 3: ML-like typing rules for qualified types

4.2 Constrained type schemes

A typing judgement $P \mid A \vdash M : \sigma$ assigns a type scheme σ to a term M, but also constrains uses of this typing to environments satisfying the predicates in P. It is therefore convenient to introduce a notation for a type scheme coupled with a set of predicates specifying constraints on the environment in which the type scheme may be used.

Definition 1 A constrained type scheme *is an expression of the form* $(P \mid \sigma)$ *where* P *is a set of predicates and* σ *is a type scheme.*

Note that a type scheme σ may be treated as an abbreviation for the constrained type scheme $(\emptyset \mid \sigma)$ (and in fact, every constrained type scheme can be represented by a simple type scheme using a renaming of bound variables).

Definition 2 A qualified type $R \Rightarrow \mu$ is said to be a generic instance *of the constrained type scheme* $(P \mid \forall \alpha_i.Q \Rightarrow \tau)$ *if there are types* τ_i *such that:*

$$R \Vdash P \cup [\tau_i/\alpha_i]Q \quad and \quad \mu = [\tau_i/\alpha_i]\tau.$$

The generic instance relation can be used to define a general ordering $(\leq)$ on constrained type schemes. The principal motivation for the definition of this relation is that a statement of the form $\sigma' \leq \sigma$ should mean that it is possible to use an object of type σ wherever an object of type σ' is required.

Definition 3 The constrained type scheme $(Q \mid \eta)$ is said to be more general *than a constrained type scheme* $(P \mid \sigma)$, *written* $(P \mid \sigma) \leq (Q \mid \eta)$, *if* ρ *is a generic instance of* $(P \mid \sigma)$ *whenever it is a generic instance of* $(Q \mid \eta)$.

It is straightforward to show that this defines a preorder on the set of constrained type schemes, such that a qualified type ρ is a generic instance of the type scheme σ if and only if $\rho \leq \sigma$. Although ($\leq$) is far from anti-symmetric, we will usually treat it as such by regarding type schemes as equal if they are equivalent under ($\leq$). The following properties are easily established:

- If ρ is a qualified type and P is a set of predicates, then $(P \mid \rho) = P \Rightarrow \rho$.

- If σ is a type scheme and P is a set of predicates then $(P \mid \sigma) \leq \sigma$.

- If $\sigma' \leq \sigma$ and $P' \Vdash P$ then $(P' \mid \sigma') \leq (P \mid \sigma)$.

- If none of the variables α_i appear in P, then the constrained type scheme $(P \mid \forall \alpha_i.\rho)$ is equivalent to the type scheme $\forall \alpha_i.P \Rightarrow \rho$.

The application of a substitution S to a constrained type scheme $(P \mid \sigma)$ is defined by $S(P \mid \sigma) = (SP \mid S\sigma)$. The next proposition describes an important property of the ordering on constrained type schemes.

Proposition 1 *For any substitution S and constrained type schemes $(P \mid \sigma)$ and $(Q \mid \eta)$:*

$$(P \mid \sigma) \leq (Q \mid \eta) \quad \Rightarrow \quad S(P \mid \sigma) \leq S(Q \mid \eta).$$

4.3 Ordering of type assignments

The definition of constrained type schemes and the ordering ($\leq$) extends naturally to an ordering on (constrained) type assignments.

Definition 4 *If A and A' are type assignments and P, P' are sets of predicates, then we say that $(P \mid A)$ is* more general than *$(P' \mid A')$, written $(P' \mid A') \leq (P \mid A)$, if $\mathrm{dom}\, A = \mathrm{dom}\, A'$ and $(P' \mid A'(x)) \leq (P \mid A(x))$ for each $x \in \mathrm{dom}\, A$.*

The results of the previous section can be used to prove that this ordering on type assignments is reflexive, transitive and preserved by substitutions. In this paper, we will only use the special case where $P = \emptyset$ in which case we write $(P' \mid A') \leq A$. This can be interpreted as indicating that each of the types assigned to a variable in A is more general than the type assigned in A' in any environment which satisfies the predicates in P'.

4.4 Generalisation

Given a derivation $P \mid A \vdash M : \tau$, it is useful to have a notation for the most general type scheme that can be obtained for M from this derivation using the rules ($\Rightarrow I$) and ($\forall I$) given in Figure 3.

Definition 5 *The* generalisation *of a qualified type ρ with respect to a type assignment A is written $Gen(A, \rho)$ and defined by:*

$$Gen(A, \rho) \;=\; \forall (TV(\rho) \setminus TV(A)).\rho.$$

In other words, if $\{\alpha_i\} = TV(\rho) \setminus TV(A)$, then $Gen(A, \rho) = \forall \alpha_i.\rho$. The following propositions describe the interaction of generalisation with predicate entailment and substitution.

Proposition 2 *Suppose that A is a type assignment, P and P' are sets of predicates and τ is a type. Then $Gen(A, P' \Rightarrow \tau) \leq Gen(A, P \Rightarrow \tau)$ whenever $P' \Vdash P$.*

Proposition 3 *If A is a type assignment, ρ is a qualified type and S is a substitution then:*

$$Gen(SA, S\rho) \leq S(Gen(A, \rho)).$$

Furthermore, there is a substitution R such that:

$$RA = SA \quad and \quad SGen(A, \rho) = Gen(RA, R\rho).$$

5 A syntax-directed approach

The typing rules in Figure 3 provide clear descriptions of the treatment of each of the syntactic constructs of the term and type languages. Unfortunately, they are not suitable for use in a type inference algorithm where it should be possible to determine an appropriate order in which to apply the typing rules by a simple analysis of the syntactic structure of the term whose type is required.

In this section, we introduce an alternative set of typing rules with a single rule for each syntactic construct in the term language. We refer to this as the *syntax-directed* system because it has the following important property:

> All typing derivations for a given term M (if there are any) have the same structure, uniquely determined by the syntactic structure of M.

We regard the syntax-directed system as a tool for exploring the type system of Section 4 and we establish a congruence between the two systems so that results about one can be translated into results about the other. The advantages of working with the syntax-directed system are:

- The rules are better suited to use in a type inference algorithm; having found types for each of the subterms of a given term M, there is at most one rule which can be used to obtain a type for the term M itself.

- Only type expressions are involved in the matching process. Type schemes and qualified types can only appear in type assignments.

- There are fewer rules and hence fewer cases to be considered in formal proofs.

A similar approach is described in [CDK86] which gives a deterministic set of typing rules for ML and outlines their equivalence to the rules in [DM82].

5.1 Syntax-directed typing rules

The typing rules for the syntax-directed system are given in Figure 4. Typings in this system are written in form $P \mid A \overset{s}{\vdash} M : \tau$, where τ ranges over the set of type expressions rather than the set of type schemes as in the typing judgements of Section 4. Other than this, the principal differences between the two systems are in the rules $(var)^s$ and $(let)^s$ which use the operations of instantiation and generalisation introduced in Sections 4.2 and 4.4.

$$
(var)^s \quad \frac{(x : \sigma) \in A}{P \mid A \overset{s}{\vdash} x : \tau} \qquad (P \Rightarrow \tau) \leq \sigma
$$

$$
(\rightarrow E)^s \quad \frac{P \mid A \overset{s}{\vdash} M : \tau' \rightarrow \tau \quad P \mid A \overset{s}{\vdash} N : \tau'}{P \mid A \overset{s}{\vdash} MN : \tau}
$$

$$
(\rightarrow I)^s \quad \frac{P \mid A_x, x : \tau' \overset{s}{\vdash} M : \tau}{P \mid A \overset{s}{\vdash} \lambda x.M : \tau' \rightarrow \tau}
$$

$$
(let)^s \quad \frac{P \mid A \overset{s}{\vdash} M : \tau \quad P' \mid A_x, x : \sigma \overset{s}{\vdash} N : \tau'}{P' \mid A \overset{s}{\vdash} (\text{let } x = M \text{ in } N) : \tau'} \qquad \sigma = Gen(A, P \Rightarrow \tau)
$$

Figure 4: Syntax-directed inference system

5.2 Properties of the syntax-directed system

The following proposition illustrates the parametric polymorphism present in the syntax-directed system; instantiating the free type variables in a derivable typing with arbitrary types produces another derivable typing.

Proposition 4 *If $P \mid A \overset{s}{\vdash} M : \tau$ and S is a substitution then $SP \mid SA \overset{s}{\vdash} M : S\tau$.*

A similar result is established in [Dam85] where it is shown that for any derivation $A \vdash M : \tau$ in the usual (non-deterministic) ML type system and any substitution S, there is a derivation $SA \vdash M : S\tau$ which can be chosen in such a way that the height of the latter is bounded by the height of the former. This additional condition is needed to ensure the validity of proofs by induction on the size of a derivation. This complication is avoided by the syntax-directed system; the derivations in proposition 4 are guaranteed to have the same structure because the term M is common to both.

Proposition 5 *If $P \mid A \overset{s}{\vdash} M : \tau$ and $Q \Vdash P$ then $Q \mid A \overset{s}{\vdash} M : \tau$.*

This result describes a form of polymorphism over the sets of environments in which a particular typing can be used. This seemingly obvious property does not hold in the original type system; it is possible for Q to contain variables not mentioned in P and hence to prohibit the use of $(\forall I)$ where it might have otherwise been applicable.

Proposition 6 *If $P \mid A' \overset{s}{\vdash} M : \tau$ and $(P \mid A') \leq A$ then $P \mid A \overset{s}{\vdash} M : \tau$.*

The hypothesis $(P \mid A') \leq A$ means that the types assigned to variables in A are more general than those given by A' in any environment which satisfies the predicates in P. For example:

$$
(Eq \; Int \mid \{(==) : Int \rightarrow Int \rightarrow Bool\}) \quad \leq \quad \{(==) : \forall a.Eq \; a \Rightarrow a \rightarrow a \rightarrow Bool\}
$$

and hence, by the proposition above, it is possible to replace an integer equality function with a generic equality function of type $\forall a.Eq \; a \Rightarrow a \rightarrow a \rightarrow Bool$ in any environment which satisfies $Eq \; Int$.

5.3 Relationship with original type system

In order to use the syntax-directed system as a tool for reasoning about the type system described in Section 4, we need to investigate the way in which the existence of a derivation in one system determines the existence of derivations in the other.

Our first result establishes the soundness of the syntax-directed system with respect to the original typing rules, showing that any derivable typing in the former system is also derivable in the latter.

Theorem 2 *If* $P \mid A \overset{s}{\vdash} M : \tau$ *then* $P \mid A \vdash M : \tau$.

The translation of derivations in the original type system to those of the syntax-directed system is less obvious. For example, if $P \mid A \vdash M : \sigma$ then it will not in general be possible to derive the same typing in the syntax-directed system because σ is a type scheme, not a simple type. However, for any derivation $P' \mid A \overset{s}{\vdash} M : \tau$, theorem 2 guarantees the existence of a derivation $P' \mid A \vdash M : \tau$ and hence $\emptyset \mid A \vdash M : Gen(A, P' \Rightarrow \tau')$ by definition 5. The following theorem shows that it is always possible to find a derivation in this way such that the inferred type scheme $Gen(A, P' \Rightarrow \tau')$ is more general than the constrained type scheme $(P \mid \sigma)$ determined by the original derivation.

Theorem 3 *If* $P \mid A \vdash M : \sigma$ *then there is a set of predicates* P' *and a type* τ *such that* $P' \mid A \overset{s}{\vdash} M : \tau$ *and* $(P \mid \sigma) \leq Gen(A, P' \Rightarrow \tau)$.

6   A type inference algorithm

In this section, we give an algorithm for calculating a typing for a given term, using an extension of Milners algorithm W [Mil78] to support qualified types. We show that the typings produced by this algorithm are derivable in the syntax-directed system and that they are, in a certain sense, the most general typings possible. Combining this with the results of the previous section, the algorithm can be used to reason about the type system in Section 4.

6.1   Unification

This section describes the unification algorithm which is a central component of the type inference algorithm. A substitution S is called a *unifier* for the type expressions τ and τ' if $S\tau = S\tau'$. The following theorem is due to [Rob65].

Theorem 4 (Unification algorithm) *There is an algorithm whose input is a pair of type expressions* τ *and* τ' *such that either:*

> *the algorithm succeeds with a substitution* U *as its result and the unifiers of* τ *and* τ' *are precisely those substitutions of the form* RU *for any substitution* R. *The substitution* U *is called a* most general unifier *for* τ *and* τ', *and is denoted* $mgu(\tau, \tau')$.

> *or the algorithm fails and there are no unifiers for* τ *and* τ'.

In the following, we write $\tau \overset{U}{\sim} \tau'$ for the assertion that the unification algorithm succeeds by finding a most general unifier U for τ and τ'.

6.2 Type inference algorithm W

Following the presentation of [Rem89], we describe the type inference algorithm using the inference rules in Figure 5. These rules use typings of the form $P \mid TA \stackrel{w}{\vdash} M : \tau$ where P is a set of predicates, T is a substitution, A is a type assignment, M is a term and τ is a simple type expression. The typing rules can be interpreted as an attribute grammar in which A are M inherited attributes, while P, T and τ are synthesised.

$$(var)^w \quad \frac{(x : \forall \alpha_i.P \Rightarrow \tau) \in A}{[\beta_i/\alpha_i]P \mid A \stackrel{w}{\vdash} x : [\beta_i/\alpha_i]\tau} \quad \beta_i \text{ new}$$

$$(\rightarrow E)^w \quad \frac{P \mid TA \stackrel{w}{\vdash} M : \tau \quad Q \mid T'TA \stackrel{w}{\vdash} N : \tau' \quad T'\tau \stackrel{U}{\sim} \tau' \rightarrow \alpha}{U(T'P \cup Q) \mid UT'TA \stackrel{w}{\vdash} MN : U\alpha} \quad \alpha \text{ new}$$

$$(\rightarrow I)^w \quad \frac{P \mid T(A_x, x : \alpha) \stackrel{w}{\vdash} M : \tau}{P \mid TA \stackrel{w}{\vdash} \lambda x.M : T\alpha \rightarrow \tau} \quad \alpha \text{ new}$$

$$(let)^w \quad \frac{P \mid TA \stackrel{w}{\vdash} M : \tau \quad P' \mid T'(TA_x, x : \sigma) \stackrel{w}{\vdash} N : \tau'}{P' \mid T'TA \stackrel{w}{\vdash} (\text{let } x = M \text{ in } N) : \tau'} \quad \sigma = Gen(TA, P \Rightarrow \tau)$$

Figure 5: Type inference algorithm W

The algorithm may also be described in a more conventional style by defining a function W such that $P \mid TA \stackrel{w}{\vdash} M : \tau$ if and only if $W(A, M)$ succeeds with result (P, T, ν). One of the advantages of our choice of notation is that it highlights the the relationship between W and the syntax-directed type system, as illustrated by the following theorem.

Theorem 5 *If* $P \mid TA \stackrel{w}{\vdash} M : \tau$ *then* $P \mid TA \stackrel{s}{\vdash} M : \tau$.

Combining this with the result of theorem 2 gives the following important corollary.

Corollary 1 (Soundness of W) *If* $P \mid TA \stackrel{w}{\vdash} M : \tau$ *then* $P \mid TA \vdash M : \tau$.

With the exception of $(let)^w$, each of the rules in Figure 5 introduces 'new' variables; i.e. variables which do not appear in the hypotheses of the rule nor in any other distinct branches of the complete derivation. Note that it is always possible to choose type variables in this way because the set of type variables is assumed to be countably infinite. In the presence of new variables, it is convenient to work with a weaker form of equality on substitutions, writing $S \approx R$ to indicate that $St = Rt$ for all but a finite number of new variables t. In most cases, we can treat $S \approx R$ as $S = R$, since the only differences between the substitutions occur at variables which are not used elsewhere in the algorithm.

This notation enables us to give an accurate statement of the following result which shows that the typings obtained by W are, in a precise sense, the most general derivable typings for a given term.

Theorem 6 *Suppose that* $P \mid SA \stackrel{s}{\vdash} M : \tau$. *Then* $Q \mid TA \stackrel{w}{\vdash} M : \nu$ *and there is a substitution R such that* $S \approx RT$, $\tau = R\nu$ *and* $P \Vdash RQ$.

Combining the result of theorem 6 with that of theorem 3 we obtain a similar completeness result for W with respect to the type system of Section 4.

Corollary 2 *Suppose that $P \mid SA \vdash M : \sigma$. Then $Q \mid TA \overset{w}{\vdash} M : \nu$ and there is a substitution R such that $S \approx RT$ and $(P \mid \sigma) \leq RGen(TA, Q \Rightarrow \nu)$.*

6.3 Principal type schemes

The *principal type scheme* of a term corresponds to the most general derivable typing with respect to the ordering on type schemes under a given type assignment.

Definition 6 *A* principal type scheme *for a term M under a type assignment A is a constrained type scheme $(P \mid \sigma)$ such that $P \mid A \vdash M : \sigma$, and $(P' \mid \sigma') \leq (P \mid \sigma)$ whenever $P' \mid A \vdash M : \sigma'$.*

The following result gives a sufficient condition for the existence of principal type schemes, by showing how they can be constructed from typings produced by W.

Corollary 3 *Suppose that M is a term, A is a type assignment and $Q \mid TA \overset{w}{\vdash} M : \nu$ for some Q, T and ν. Then $Gen(TA, Q \Rightarrow \nu)$ is a principal type scheme for M under TA.*

Combining this with corollary 2 gives a necessary condition for the existence of principal type schemes: a term is well-typed if and only if it has a principal type scheme which can be calculated using the type inference algorithm.

7 Topics for further research

7.1 The coherence problem

At this point, it is important to point out that the type systems described by the rules in the previous sections are not *coherent* (in the sense of [BCGS89]). In other words, it is possible to construct translations $P \mid A \vdash M \rightsquigarrow M_1' : \sigma$ and $P \mid A \vdash M \rightsquigarrow M_2' : \sigma$ in which the terms M_1' and M_2' are not equivalent, and hence the semantics of M are not well-defined.

For an example in which the coherence problem arises, consider the term *out* (*in x*) under the evidence assignment $P = \{u : C\ Int, v : C\ Bool\}$ and the type assignment:

$$A = \{x : Int, \ in : \forall a.C\ a \Rightarrow Int \rightarrow a, \ out : \forall a.C\ a \Rightarrow a \rightarrow Int\}$$

for some unary predicate symbol C. Instantiating the quantified type variable in the type of *in* (and hence also in that of *out*) with the types *Int* and *Bool* leads to distinct derivations $P \mid A \vdash$ *out* (*in x*) : *Int* in which the corresponding translations, *out u* (*in u x*) and *out v* (*in v x*) are clearly not equal.

Note that the principal type scheme of *out* (*in x*) in this example is $\forall a.C\ a \Rightarrow Int$ and that the type variable a (the source of the lack of coherence in the derivations above) appears only in the predicate qualifying the type of the term, not in the type itself. Motivated by the functional programming language Haskell [HPJW91], we say that a type of the form $\forall \alpha_i.P \Rightarrow \tau$ is *unambiguous* if $TV(P) \subseteq TV(\tau)$. It is believed that the coherence problem described above can be avoided by prohibiting the use of terms with ambiguous principal type schemes and restricting type assignments to types containing only unambiguous type schemes. A similar result has been established in [Blo90] for the special case of [WB89]. We expect this result to generalise to the framework used in this paper.

7.2 Eliminating evidence parameters

Using translations as described in Section 3, a term M of type $\forall \alpha_i.P \Rightarrow \tau$ will be implemented by a term of the form $\lambda v_1. \ldots . \lambda v_n.M'$, where $P = \{\pi_1, \ldots, \pi_n\}$ and each v_i is an evidence variable for the corresponding predicate π_i. In the following sections we describe a number of situations in which the number of evidence parameters required can be reduced using a more sophisticated variant of the type inference algorithm.

7.2.1 Minimisation/simplification

The translation of a term whose type is qualified by a set of predicates P requires one evidence abstraction for each element of P. Thus the number of evidence parameters that are required can be reduced by finding a smaller set of predicates Q, equivalent to P in the sense that $P \Vdash Q$ and $Q \Vdash P$ (and hence the type of the new term is equivalent to that of the original term). In this situation, we have a compromise between:

- Reducing the number of evidence parameters required.

- The cost of constructing evidence for P from the evidence supplied for Q. The fact that this is possible is guaranteed by the assertion $Q \Vdash P$.

In general, the task of finding an optimal set of predicates with which to replace P is likely to be intractable. One potentially useful approach would be to determine a minimal subset $Q \subseteq P$ such that $Q \Vdash P$. To see that this is likely to be a good choice, note that:

- $P \Vdash Q$, by monotonicity of $\Vdash$ and hence Q is equivalent to P as required.

- Since $Q \subseteq P$, the number of evidence abstractions required using Q is less than or equal to the number required when using P.

- The construction of evidence for a predicate in P using evidence for Q is trivial for each predicate which is already in Q.

7.2.2 Evidence parameters considered harmful

The principal motivation for including the let construct in the term language was to enable the definition and use of polymorphic and overloaded values. In practice, the same construct is also used for a number of other purposes:

- To avoid repeated evaluation of a value which is used at a number of points in an expression.

- To create *cyclic data structures* using recursive bindings [BW89].

- To enable the use of identifiers as abbreviations for the subexpressions of a large expression.

Note however that the addition of evidence parameters to the value defined in a **let** expression may mean that the evaluation of an overloaded term will not behave as intended. For example, if M is a term of type $\forall a.C\ a \Rightarrow a \rightarrow Int$ then we have:

$$\text{let } x = M\ 1 \text{ in } x + x \quad \leadsto \quad \lambda e\,.\,\text{let } x = (\lambda v.M'\ v\ 1) \text{ in } (x\ e + x\ e)$$

and the evaluation of $x\ e$ in the translation is no longer shared. There are a number of potential solutions to this problem. In the example above, one method would be to transform the translated term to:

$$\lambda e\,.\,\text{let } x = (\lambda v.M'\ v\ 1) \text{ in } (\text{let } y = x\ e \text{ in } y + y).$$

Another possibility would be the use of a *monomorphism restriction* such as that proposed for Haskell [HPJW91] which restricts the amount of overloading which can be used in particular syntactic forms of binding. In this case, the corresponding translation is likely to be:

$$\lambda e\,.\,\text{let } x = M'\ e\ 1 \text{ in } x + x.$$

7.2.3 Constant and locally-constant overloading

Consider the typing of local definitions in the type system of Section 4 using the rule:

$$\frac{P\,|\,A \vdash M : \sigma \quad Q\,|\,A_x, x : \sigma \vdash N : \tau}{P \cup Q\,|\,A \vdash (\text{let } x = M \text{ in } N) : \tau}$$

Notice that this allows some of the predicates constraining the typing of M (i.e. those in P) to be retained as a constraint on the environment in the conclusion of the rule rather than being included in the type scheme σ. However, in the corresponding rule $(let)^s$ for the syntax-directed system, all of the predicates constraining the typing of M are included in the type $Gen(A, P \Rightarrow \tau)$ that is inferred for M:

$$\frac{P\,|\,A \overset{s}{\vdash} M : \tau \quad P'\,|\,A_x, x : Gen(A, P \Rightarrow \tau) \overset{s}{\vdash} N : \tau'}{P'\,|\,A \overset{s}{\vdash} (\text{let } x = M \text{ in } N) : \tau'}$$

As a consequence, evidence parameters are needed for all of the predicates in P, even if the evidence values used for some of these parameters are the same for each occurrence of x in N. In particular, this includes *constant* evidence (corresponding to predicates with no free type variables) and *locally-constant* evidence (corresponding to predicates, each of whose free variables also appears free in A).

From the relationship between the type inference algorithm W and the syntax-directed system, it follows that W has the same behaviour; indeed, this is essential to ensure that W calculates principal types: If $x \notin FV(N)$ then none of the environment constraints described by P need be reflected by the constraints on the complete expression in P'.

However, if $x \in FV(N)$, it is possible to find a set $F \subseteq P$ such that $P' \Vdash F$ and hence the type scheme assigned to x can be replaced by $Gen(A, (P \setminus F) \Rightarrow \tau)$, potentially decreasing the number of evidence parameters required by x. To see this, suppose that $Gen(A, P \Rightarrow \tau) = (\forall \alpha_i . P \Rightarrow \tau)$. A straightforward induction, based on the hypothesis that $x \in FV(N)$, shows that $P' \Vdash [\tau_i / \alpha_i]P$ for some types τ_i. If we now define:

$$FP(A, P) = \{ (v : \pi) \in P \mid TV(\pi) \subseteq TV(A) \}$$

then $F = FP(A, P)$ is the largest subset of P which is guaranteed to be unchanged by the substitution $[\tau_i / \alpha_i]$. These observations suggest that $(let)^s$ could be replaced by the two rules:

- In the case where $x \notin FV(N)$:

$$\frac{P \mid A \overset{s}{\vdash} M : \tau \quad P' \mid A \overset{s}{\vdash} N : \tau'}{P' \mid A \overset{s}{\vdash} (\text{let } x = M \text{ in } N) : \tau'} \; (let)_f{}^s$$

The typing judgement involving M serves only to preserve to property that all subterms of a well-typed term are also well-typed.

- In the case where $x \in FV(N)$:

$$\frac{P \mid A \overset{s}{\vdash} M : \tau \quad P' \mid A_x, x : Gen(A, P \setminus F \Rightarrow \tau) \overset{s}{\vdash} N : \tau' \quad P' \Vdash F}{P' \mid A \overset{s}{\vdash} (\text{let } x = M \text{ in } N) : \tau'} \; (let)_b{}^s$$

where $F = FP(A, P)$.

Whilst these rules retain the syntax-directed character necessary for use in a type inference algorithm, they are not suitable for typing top-level definitions (such as those in Haskell or ML) which are treated as let expressions in which the scope of the defined variable is not fully determined at compile-time. A more realistic approach would be to use just $(let)_b{}^s$ in place of $(let)^s$, with the understanding that type schemes inferred by W are only guaranteed to be principal in the case where $x \in FV(N)$ for all subterms of the form let $x = M$ in N in the term whose type is being inferred. Justification for this approach is as follows:

- For a top-level declaration of the identifier x, we can take the scope of the declaration to be the set of all terms which might reasonably be evaluated in the scope of such a declaration, which of course includes the term x.

- For let expressions in which the scope of the defined variable is known, the local definition in an expression of the form let $x = M$ in N is redundant, and the expression is semantically equivalent to N. However, expressions of this form are sometimes used in implicitly typed languages to force a less general type than might otherwise be obtained by the type inference mechanism. For example, if $(==)$ is an integer equality function and 0 is an integer constant, then $\lambda x.\text{let } y = (x == 0) \text{ in } x$ has principal type scheme $Int \to Int$, whereas the principal type scheme for $\lambda x.x$ is $\forall a.a \to a$. Such ad-hoc 'coding-tricks' become unnecessary if the term language is extended to allow explicit type declarations.

In a practical implementation, it would be useful to arrange for suitable diagnostic messages to be generated whenever an expression of the form let $x = M$ in N with $x \notin FV(N)$ is encountered; this would serve as a warning to the programmer that the principal type property may be lost (in addition to catching other potential program errors).

7.3 The use of subsumption

The typing rules in Figure 1 are only suitable for reasoning about systems with explicit coercions. For example, if $Int \subseteq Real$, then we can use an addition function:

$$add :: \forall a. a \subseteq Real \Rightarrow a \rightarrow a \rightarrow Real$$

to add two integers together, obtaining a real number as the result. More sophisticated systems, such as those in [Mit84, FM89], cannot be described without adding a form of the rule of subsumption:

$$\frac{P \mid A \vdash M : \tau' \quad P \Vdash \tau' \subseteq \tau}{P \mid A \vdash M : \tau}$$

Each use of this rule corresponds to an implicit coercion; the addition of two integers to obtain a real result can be described without explicit overloading using a function:

$$add :: Real \rightarrow Real \rightarrow Real$$

with two implicit coercions from Int to $Real$. As a further example, in the framework of Section 2, the polymorphic identity function $\lambda t.\lambda x : t.x$ can be treated as having type $\forall a.\forall b. a \subseteq b \Rightarrow a \rightarrow b$ and hence acts as a generic coercion function.

No attempt has been made to deal with systems including the rule of subsumption in the development of the type inference algorithm in Section 6, which is therefore only suitable for languages using explicit coercions. The results of [FM89] and [Smi91] are likely to be particularly useful in extending the present system to support the use of implicit coercions.

7.4 Other issues

In addition to the problems already mentioned, we list the following topics as areas for further work.

- **Semantic issues.** The correspondence between typing derivations and translations provides a simple semantic interpretation for overloaded terms in a language without built-in support for overloading. By demonstrating that any translation of a well-typed term is itself well-typed, we can extend Milner's result for the ML type system that "well-typed programs do not go wrong" to the system described in Section 4.

- **Decidability and satisfiability.** It has recently been shown [VS91] that, using a definition of well-typing that takes account of the satisfiability of predicate sets, the task of determining whether a given expression is well-typed in an unrestricted version of [WB89] is undecidable. Clearly this is unacceptable for any practical application of such type systems. In the framework used in this paper, decidability of type checking is completely determined by the properties of $\Vdash$ and it remains an interesting problem to investigate what restrictions on the definition of $\Vdash$ are needed to guarantee decidability.

Further refinements are likely to be suggested by the development, currently in progress, of an implementation of qualified types, based on the ideas described in this paper [Jon92].

Acknowledgements

I am very grateful for conversations with members of the Department of Computing Science, Glasgow whose suggestions prompted me to investigate the ideas presented in this paper, and in particular to Phil Wadler for his comments on several earlier versions of this paper.

A number of features of this paper were motivated by the functional programming language Haskell [HPJW91]. The notation $\pi \Rightarrow \sigma$ for qualified types is modelled on the syntax of Haskell *predicated types* and the concept of evidence is a generalisation of Haskell dictionaries. The static semantics described in [PJW90] uses similar methods to those presented here, introducing explicit dictionary abstraction and application to make overloading explicit.

The Science and Engineering Council of Great Britain provided financial support for this work.

References

[BCGS89] V. Breazu-Tannen, T. Coquand, C. A. Gunter and A. Scedrov. Inheritance and coercion. Proceedings of the fourth annual symposium on logic in computer science, 1989.

[Blo90]   Stephen Blott. An approach to overloading with polymorphism. Ph.D. thesis, Department of computing science, University of Glasgow, 1990 (in preparation).

[BW89]   Richard Bird and Philip Wadler. Introduction to functional programming. Prentice Hall International, 1989.

[CDK86]   Dominique Clément, Joëlle Despeyroux, Thierry Despeyroux and Gilles Kahn. A simple applicative language: Mini-ML. ACM symposium on LISP and functional programming, 1986.

[CM90]   Luca Cardelli and John Mitchell. Operations on records. Proceedings of the Fifth International Conference on Mathematical Foundations of Programming Language Semantics. Lecture notes in computer science 442, Springer Verlag, 1990.

[Dam85]   Luis Damas. Type assignment in programming languages. PhD thesis, University of Edinburgh, CST-33-85, 1985.

[DM82]   Luis Damas and Robin Milner. Principal type schemes for functional programs. Proceedings of the 8th annual ACM symposium on Principles of Programming languages, Albuquerque, New Mexico, January 1982.

[FM89]   You-Chin Fuh and Prateek Mishra. Polymorphic subtype inference: Closing the theory-practice gap. Lecture notes in computer science 352, Springer Verlag, 1990.

[HP90]   Robert W. Harper and Benjamin C. Pierce. Extensible records without subsumption. Technical report CMU-CS-90-102, Carnegie Mellon University, School of computer science, February 1990.

[HPJW91] Paul Hudak, Simon Peyton Jones and Philip Wadler (editors). Report on the programming language Haskell, a non-strict purely functional language (Version 1.1). Technical Report YALEU/DCS/RR777, Yale University, Department of Computer Science, August 1991.

[Jon91a] Mark P. Jones. Towards a theory of qualified types. Technical report PRG-TR-6-91, Programming Research Group, Oxford University Computing Laboratory, April 1991.

[Jon91b] Mark P. Jones. Type inference for qualified types. Technical report PRG-TR-10-91, Programming Research Group, Oxford University Computing Laboratory, June 1991.

[Jon92] Mark P. Jones Practical issues in the implementation of qualified types. Forthcoming technical report, Oxford University Computing Laboratory, 1992.

[Mil78] Robin Milner. A theory of type polymorphism in programming. Journal of Computer and System Sciences, 17, 3, 1978.

[Mit84] John C. Mitchell. Coercion and type inference (summary). Proceedings of the 11th annual ACM symposium on Principles of Programming Languages, 1984.

[Mit90] John C. Mitchell A type-inference approach to reduction properties and semantics of polymorphic expressions. Logical Foundations of Functional Programming, Gérard Huet (ed.), Addison Wesley, 1990.

[PJW90] Simon L. Peyton Jones and Philip Wadler A static semantics for haskell (draft). Department of Computing Science, University of Glasgow, August 1990.

[Rem89] Didier Rémy. Typechecking records and variants in a natural extension of ML. Proceedings of the 16th annual ACM symposium on Principles of Programming Languages, Austin, Texas, January 1989.

[Rob65] J. A. Robinson. A machine-oriented logic based on the resolution principle. Journal of the Association for Computing Machinery, 12, 1965.

[Smi91] Geoffrey Smith. Polymorphic type inference for languages with overloading and subtyping. Ph.D. thesis, Department of Computer Science, Cornell University, August 1991.

[VS91] Dennis Volpano and Geoffrey Smith. On the complexity of ML typability with overloading. Proceedings of the 5th ACM conference on Functional Programming Languages and Computer Architecture. Lecture notes in computer science 523, Springer Verlag, 1991.

[WB89] Philip Wadler and Stephen Blott. How to make *ad-hoc* polymorphism less *ad-hoc*. Proceedings of the 16th annual ACM symposium on Principles of Programming Languages, Austin, Texas, January 1989.

A Semantics for Multiprocessor Systems

by
Padmanabhan Krishnan
Department of Computer Science
University of Canterbury
Christchurch 1, New Zealand
E-mail: paddy@cosc.canterbury.ac.nz

Abstract

In this paper we present a multiprocessor semantics for CCS [Mil80]. An operational semantics for processes under a finite number of processors is developed. The effect of adding or removing processors from the system is studied. A notion of strong bisimulation induced by the new semantics is defined. Issues related to a complete axiomatization of this congruence are examined and a complete equational system for a subset of CCS is presented.

1   Introduction

The idea of using observations or labeled transition systems as the basis for describing behaviors for concurrent systems is well known. However, most of the initial work for concurrent systems resulted in an 'interleaving semantics'. That is, parallelism was not distinguishable from non-determinism. Work by [DDM88] uses the notion of causality to present a non-interleaving semantics for CCS. [CH89] develop a theory based on the spatial distribution of processes. [KHCB91] uses the notion of location to develop a theory which accounts for the parallel nature of processes. While these theories differentiate parallelism and non-determinism, they do so only at the logical level. They do not study the behavior by 'actually executing' the process on a physical system. In other words, the architectural implications on behavior have not been addressed.

Given that there are many different types of architecture, it is only natural that a theory characterizing one system will not characterize another. The logical characterization can be thought of as the least common denominator; if processes identified by the theory will exhibit similar behavior on all systems which satisfy the assumptions of the theory. For example, if one considers only uniprocessor systems, parallelism will indeed be reduced to non-determinism. If one had an unbounded number of processors, behaviors consistent with pomset semantics [Pra86] could be exhibited. In real systems, it is not always possible to realize the architecture assumed by the theory. Resource limitations will induce restrictions on the possible behavior. Therefore it is necessary to index the behavior by the available resources.

In this paper we study the behavior of concurrent processes for a specific architecture, viz. shared memory systems. A shared memory system has a number of processors

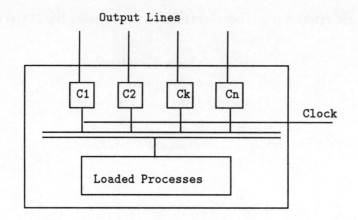

Figure 1: Machine Model

and a single memory unit which is accessed by the processor using a bus [JS80] (see figure 1).

This machine model is similar to the Chemical Abstract Machine [BB89]. The Chemical Abstract Machine models processes as being suspended in a solution with the ability to interact with one another. Our machine model can be considered to be a Chemical Abstract Machine with a bounded number of catalysts (processing elements) which are essential for any evolution.

The machine and language described in [BCM88] forms the basis for the semantics described here. We assume that the processors are homogeneous and memory is uniformly accessible to all processors. This allows 'logical migration', i.e., any process can use any processor. Scalability (the ability to add more processors) and fault-tolerance (the ability to function inspite of losing a processor) are important properties of a multiprocessor system. We consider the effect of adding/removing processors from a system on processes.

A theory for distributed memory systems has been studied in [Kri91] and is orthogonal to the work presented here. There the approach was to consider loosely coupled systems. The idea was to use a concept of location (introduced in [KHCB91]) to represent a virtual node. Processes were anchored to a particular location. Processes at different locations could evolve independently. Communication between locations was indicated by special asynchronous (i.e., had no complement in the CCS sense) message passing actions.

2 Multiprocessor Semantics

The language for which we develop a multiprocessor semantics is CCS [Mil80]. We first present an operational semantics based on labeled transitions systems for it. The semantics is indexed by a finite number of processors. Based on the operational semantics we develop a notion of bisimulation and relate the behaviors of processors with different numbers of processing elements. We also discuss the issues related to a complete axiomatization of the bisimulation equivalence.

As in CCS, we assume a set of actions Λ. As usual we assume $\bar{}$, to be a bijection on Λ such that $\bar{\bar{a}} = a$. Typical elements of Λ are denoted by $a, b \ldots$. A special action τ not in Λ is used for synchronization.

The syntax of the language is as follows.

$$P = nil \mid a;P \mid P+P \mid (P \mid P) \mid (P \setminus a)$$

nil is a process which can exhibit no action, ';' denotes action or τ prefix, '+' non-determinism, '$\mid$' parallel composition and '$\setminus$' action restricting.

A structural operational semantics [Plo81] is defined as a generalization of the rules for CCS. We assume that the following black-box is a model of a multi-processor system which runs a process given n processing elements. There is a 'clock' line which when toggled advances each processing element by one step. The observer first toggles the 'clock' and then notes the behavior on the n-lines (which may appear at different times with respect to some real clock) and the process continues. This is shown in figure 1. The semantics developed here is similar to the step semantics developed in [vGV87] but the number of actions in a step is bounded. However as will be seen later, we do not assume a synchronous model. Therefore, our semantics is different from SCCS [Mil83].

Not all processors in the system may be required by a process at all the steps. For example, if a system has 2 processors to execute $a;P$ only one of them can execute the action 'a'. The other will necessarily be idle. (P may or may not be able to use both the processors.) Let δ represent idling (of a processor) and let $Act = \Lambda \cup \{\delta, \tau\}$

For the observations (the labels in the transition relation) we use n-tuples as opposed to multisets. This facilitates the requirement that synchronization of processes occur on the same processor. It would be unrealistic to assume synchronization across different processing elements. This captures the intuition that synchronization occurs at a location; the processor representing the location. Using the Chemical Abstract Machine analogy, synchronization can occur only by moving the processes physically close to each another. Architecturally, synchronization across processors would require the bus to support a particular protocol. It would be unrealistic to demand such a protocol for multiprocessor systems.

Definition: 1 *Let $\mathcal{O}_n$ denote the function space from n to Act (or n-tuples) and for any $S \in \mathcal{O}_n$, Actions(S) = codomain(S).*

The intuition in using $\mathcal{O}_n$ is that if one is given n processing elements one can observe n actions at every step.

Prefix	$\forall\, 0 \leq i \leq$ (n-1) $a;P \xrightarrow[n]{<\delta\ (i\ times)\ a\ \delta\ (n-1-i)\ times>} P$
Non-Determinism	$\dfrac{P \xrightarrow{S}_n P'}{P+Q \xrightarrow{S}_n P',\ Q+P \xrightarrow{S}_n P'}$
Parallelism	$\dfrac{P \xrightarrow{S1}_n P',\ Q \xrightarrow{S2}_n Q',\ S = S1 +_n S2}{P\mid Q \xrightarrow{S}_n P'\mid Q'}$
Interleaving	$\dfrac{P \xrightarrow{S}_n P'}{P\mid Q \xrightarrow{S}_n P'\mid Q,\ Q\mid P \xrightarrow{S}_n Q\mid P'}$
Hiding	$\dfrac{P \xrightarrow{S}_n P',\ a, \bar{a} \notin \text{Actions}(S)}{P\setminus a \xrightarrow{S}_n P'\setminus a}$

Figure 2: Operational Semantics

Legal combinations of observations are defined as follows.

Definition: 2 *Define a partial function $+_n$ on $\mathcal{O}_n \times \mathcal{O}_n \to \mathcal{O}_n$ as follows: $O1 +_n O2$ = O where*

$$O(x) = \begin{cases} O1(x) & if\ O2(x) = \delta \\ O2(x) & if\ O1(x) = \delta \\ \tau & if\ O1(x) = \overline{O2(x)} \end{cases}$$

As processes can compete for the processors, one has to define consistency of processor allocation. We assume that only one action can be exhibited by a processor at any time. As mentioned earlier, if two processes are attempting to synchronize, they are required to be on the same processor.

An element of $\mathcal{O}_n$ can be thought of as observing n actions simultaneously. Thus $+_n$ defines combining observations in a truly parallel fashion. The definition requires a processor to be idle with respect to one process if the other is to be able to use it except in the case of synchronization. If both processes do not use a processor, it is idle in their combination. If both processes use the processor to exhibit unsynchronizable actions,, their parallel combination is undefined.

Definition: 3 *Let $\longrightarrow_n \subseteq Processes \times \mathcal{O}_n \times Processes$, be the smallest relation satisfying the axioms in figure 2. It describes the behavior of processes when n processing elements are available.*

A brief and informal explanation of the operational semantics is as follows. The elementary action can be executed on any of the processors and due to sequentiality all but one will be idle. We do not require a process to be fixed to a processor. If the machine architecture is to be exploited, the migration of processes to different processors has to be permitted. An atomic action can be considered to be the basic unit of scheduling. The process is preempted after executing a single action and returned to the pool of processes competing for the limited resources.

Non-deterministic choice also has the usual definition; i.e., if a process can exhibit an action (or set of actions) so can its non-deterministic combination with other processes. The rules that determine the behavior under parallel composition are as follows. The first requires the assignment of processes P and Q to be compatible for the parallel composition to be successful. The second interleaves the execution. The rule for hiding is as usual; i.e., $P \setminus a$ cannot exhibit a behavior in which the action a or $\bar{a}$ is involved.

It is possible to impose a step optimal parallelism requirement (under a limited number of processors) by requiring that all possible processor assignments fail before applying the interleaving law. This would be the adaptation of the maximal parallelism model [SM82] to suit limited resources. For example, one could require that the only acceptable behavior of (a|b) given 2 processors is executing them on different processors; interleaving is disallowed (i.e, "no unnecessary waiting" is modeled.) Interleaving would have to be permitted for a|b|c given 2 processors. However, this results in the parallel operator being not associative as shown in the example below.

Example 1 *A possible behavior for the process (a | b) | c is the a and b followed by c. However a | (b | c) cannot exhibit this as (b | c) can only exhibit b and c.*

As this goes against the intuition of the parallel operator, the step optimal semantics is not adopted.

3   Strong Bisimulation

Park in [Par81] defines strong bisimulation, an equivalence relation on processes. That is, processes which have 'identical' operational behavior are equivalent. We define a generalization of strong bisimulation for defining equivalences between processes.

Definition: 4 $P \lesssim_n Q$ iff $P \xrightarrow{S1}_n P'$ implies $\exists Q': Q \xrightarrow{S1}_n Q'$ and $P' \lesssim_n Q'$.

In other words, $P \lesssim_n Q$ if Q can exhibit all behaviors of P. We write $\sim_n$ for the equivalence induced by $\lesssim_n$.

The properties of $\sim_n$ are similar to the CCS case.

Proposition 1
$\sim_n$ *is a congruence* $P+Q \sim_n Q+P$
$(P+Q)+R \sim_n P+(Q+R)$ $P+P \sim_n P$
$P \mid Q \sim_n Q \mid P$ $(P \mid Q) \mid R \sim_n P \mid (Q \mid R)$
$P \mid nil \sim_n P$

As only the parallel operator introduces multiple observations, it is natural that if a process P exhibits k non-idling actions, P must be composed of at least k parallel processes.

Proposition 2 *If* $P \xrightarrow{S}_n P'$ *and the number of non-idling actions of S (i.e, cardinality of Actions(S)) is greater than 1, then there exists: 1) Processes P1, P2 and P3, 2) Observations S1 and S2 and 3) A subset of* Λ *(possibly empty) H, such that:*
1) $P1 \xrightarrow{S1}_n P1'$, *2)* $P2 \xrightarrow{S2}_n P2'$, *3)* $S1+S2=S$ *and*
4) Either $(P1' \mid P2' \mid P3) \sim_n P'$ *(H is the empty set) or* $((P1' \mid P2' \mid P3) \backslash H) \sim_n P'$

Proof Outline: By induction on the structure of the process. Let P be (R1 | R2). In this case H will be the empty set. If both R1 and R2 contribute to form S then P1 is R1, P2 is R2, and P3 is *nil* . If only one evolved say R1, then by the induction hypothesis, there are R_{11}, R_{12} and R_{13}, such that $R_{11} \xrightarrow{S1}_n R'_{11}$ and $R_{12} \xrightarrow{S2}_n R'_{12}$ and $R'_{11} \mid R'_{12} \mid R_{13} \sim_n R1'$. Now $P' \sim_n$ (R1' | R2). Then letting P1 be R_{11}, P2 being R_{12} and P3 being (R_{13} | R2) satisfies the condition.

If P is of the form (R1 | R2)\\H_1, the above argument is valid but with H equal to H_1.
$\Box$

Note that in the above result we do not derive the structure for P, as P could have made various choices and one has to introduce choices at every point where an action prefix occurs. For example,

$(\ (((a;P1 + P1') \mid (c;Q1 + Q1')) + R1') \mid (((b;P2 + P2') \mid (d;Q2 + Q2')) +$
$R2') \mid P3) + P4'$

under 4 processors and the observation $< a, b, c, d >$ requires the introduction of P1', Q1' etc. (which may be nil). While this can be done in principle it is not very illuminating.

It is also easy to see that if a set of actions is exhibited by a process, any non-idling subset of it can also be exhibited.

Definition: 5 *Let R and* $S \in \mathcal{O}_n$. *Define* $R \leq S$, *iff there is a 1-1 map F, on* $\{1 \ .. \ n\}$ *such that* $\forall \ i,\ R(i) \neq \delta$ *implies* $R(i) = S(F(i))$. *i.e., S observes more actions but with possibly different processor usage.*

Proposition 3 *If* $P \xrightarrow{S}_n P'$ *and* $R \leq S$, *and* $\exists \ i,\ R(i) \neq \delta$, *then* $\exists \ P''$ *such that* $P \xrightarrow{R}_n P''$

Proof By structural induction. □

CCS has an expansion theorem (i.e., reduction of parallelism to non-determinism). For example, (a | b) $\sim_{CCS}$ (a;b+b;a), and one would expect a similar law for the n-processor case. The expansion theorem could be expected to be a reduction of a process which can exhibit $n + 1$ actions, but is given only n processors, to a process which can exhibit only n actions. But unfortunately that is not the case.

Example 2 *Consider P= (a | b | c) given 2 processors. If it is bisimilar to a term T then T can exhibit all the 3 actions in one step given 3 processes. The argument is as follows. Assume T cannot exhibit the 3 actions in one step. As P can exhibit a and evolve to the process (b | c), T could involve terms such as (a;b) | c or a;(b | c). The first type is disallowed as it can exhibit c and evolve to (a;b). But no c evolution of P is bisimilar to (a;b). The second type term is not sufficient as P can exhibit action a and b in one step.*

The lack of an expansion theorem for P can formally be stated as follows.

Proposition 4 *Let P = (a | b | c). If P $\sim_2$ Q+R, then either P $\sim_2$ Q or P $\sim_2$ R.*

The intuition behind this result is that the | combinator does not force both its branches to evolve. As the transition rule for parallel composition permits interleaving, it is impossible to force a process to exhibit multiple actions at a particular step. This problem also prevents the axiomatization of the n processor bisimulation. In section 4 we describe how this drawback can be overcome.

Our semantics is a generalization of the standard CCS semantics by explicitly considering the number of processors in the system. Clearly, if there is only one processor in the system, the standard behavior must be exhibited. This is indeed the case.

Proposition 5 $\sim_1 = \sim_{CCS}$.

Proof: It is easy to verify that $\longrightarrow_1$ is identical to the $\longrightarrow$ rules for CCS. □

As we have n processing elements, we develop a theory relating processes and processors. It is easy to see that if two processes are similar under n+1 processors, they will be related under n processors.

Proposition 6 $P \lesssim_{n+1} Q$ implies $P \lesssim_n Q$.

Proof: From proposition 3.

Clearly P $\lesssim_n$ Q then P $\lesssim_{n+1}$ Q, does not hold as by adding more resources one can expose 'true concurrency'. For example, (a | b) $\lesssim_1$ (a;b + b;a), but (a | b) $\not\lesssim_2$ (a;b + b;a). However, if the process on the right is the 'more parallel one', the result holds.

Proposition 7 *If Q is a process not involving +, $P \mathrel{\underset{\sim}{\scriptstyle\subseteq}}_n Q$ implies $P \mathrel{\underset{\sim}{\scriptstyle\subseteq}}_{n+1} Q$.*

Proof Outline: Let Q have no +, $P \mathrel{\underset{\sim}{\scriptstyle\subseteq}}_n Q$ but $P \mathrel{\underset{\not\sim}{\scriptstyle\subseteq}}_{n+1} Q$. As $P \mathrel{\underset{\not\sim}{\scriptstyle\subseteq}}_{n+1} Q$, either there is a transition $P \xrightarrow{S}_n P'$ and Q has no transition labeled by S or $Q \xrightarrow{S}_n Q'$ and $P' \mathrel{\underset{\not\sim}{\scriptstyle\subseteq}}_{n+1} Q'$. Consider the first case. It is clear that the cardinality of S is n+1 (if less than n it violates $P \mathrel{\underset{\sim}{\scriptstyle\subseteq}}_n Q$). Thus, by proposition 2 S is composed of S1 and S2 such that $P \xrightarrow{S1}_n$ and $P \xrightarrow{S2}_n$. As the cardinality of S1 and S2 is less than n+1, $Q \xrightarrow{S1}_n$ and $Q \xrightarrow{S2}_n$. If Q cannot exhibit S, then either 1) S1+S2 is not defined which is not the case or 2) there is a choice between S1 and S2 in which case Q has a +. $\qquad\square$

4 Axiomatization

In this section we discuss the issues related to the axiomatization of finite processes of the bisimulation equivalence for n processors. For the moment consider the language without hiding. Consider the set of equations in figure 3.

$$
\begin{array}{ll}
P + P = P & P + nil = P \\
P + Q = Q + P & P \mid Q = Q \mid P \\
(P + Q) + R = P + (Q + R) & (P \mid Q) \mid R = P \mid (Q \mid R) \\
(P \mid nil) = P &
\end{array}
$$

Figure 3: Tentative Equations

The parallel axioms are necessary as (a | b) $\sim_2$ (b | a), but cannot be decomposed into various components. However, this set of axioms is not complete. For example, (a | b) $\sim_2$ (a | b) + a;b cannot be proved. Furthermore, the lack of an expansion theorem (as explained via an example) is not satisfactory. That is, (a | b | c) under two processors will exhibit some interleaving and is in 'normal form'.

The principal problem is that | is too 'powerful'. It permits any non-empty subset of the actions that can be exhibited in one step. Therefore, it is essential to have a construct which forces multiple actions to be performed in one step. For this we alter a single action prefix to a multiset prefix. A multiset captures multiple actions that occur in one step. Interleaving of the actions within a multiset is *not* permitted. That is, if the cardinality of the multiset is greater than the number of available processors no evolution is possible.

This can be used to model parallelism. For example, (a | b) can be considered to be an abbreviation for a;b + b;a + {a,b}. If there is only one processor {a,b} cannot contribute to the behavior and (a | b) is equivalent to a;b+b;a. Similarly, (a | b | c) can be thought of as a;(b | c)+ b;(a | c)+ c;(a | b)+ {a,b};c + {a,c};b + {b,c};a + {a,b,c} and if there are only 2 processors, {a,b,c} will not contribute to the behavior.

Thus a multiset prefix represents 'forced' parallelism. Therefore, for a complete axiomatization of the bisimulation equivalence the appropriate generalization of CCS for the multiprocessor case is: 1) Observing multiple actions and 2) Replacing the single action prefix by a multiset prefix.

In the rest of this section we show that if the language permits a multiset prefix, the resulting bisimulation equivalence for finite processes can be completely axiomatized. We also assume that the number of processors is fixed ($n \geq 1$).

Definition: 6 *Define a multiset m as a function, m: Act $\to \mathcal{N}$*

Define the cardinality of a multiset m, $| m |$, as $\sum\limits_{a \in Act} m(a)$ where $\sum$ indicates integer addition.

The following is the syntax for a multiprocessor language whose bisimulation semantics is axiomatized.

$$P = nil \mid ms;P \mid (P \mid P) \mid (P + P) \mid (P \setminus a)$$

The only difference from the initial language is that action prefix (a) is replaced by a multiset prefix (ms). The semantics of an atomic action permitted the use of any of the available processors. Similarly the semantics of a multiset of actions permits any possible assignment of processors to the actions. The multiset prefix introduces another level of scheduling. Given a multiset an allocation of actions to processors is required. This is defined by the function *Assign*, which behaves as follows. Given an empty set, all the processors in the system are idle and that is the only possible assignment. Given an assignment of k actions, the k+1st action can be scheduled on any of the idle processors. Complementary actions within a multiset prefix cannot synchronize with one another. For example, if m is a multiset such that $\underset{\cdot}{m}(a)=1$ and $m(\bar{a})=1$, *Assign* will require at least two processors to execute it.

Definition: 7 *Assume a fixed n. Assign is the smallest set satisfying the following*

- *Assign $\emptyset = \{ < \delta , \ ... \ ,\delta > \}$*

- *If $(Y \in Assign\ m)$ and $Y(i) = \delta$ and*
  $$X(j) = \begin{cases} a & if\ j = i \\ Y(j) & otherwise \end{cases} \quad and$$
  $$m'(\mu) = \begin{cases} m(\mu)+1 & if\ \mu = a \\ m(\mu) & otherwise \end{cases}$$
  then $X \in Assign\ m'$.

Given an observation, the multiset that gave rise to it can be obtained by the function $Assign^{-1}$ defined as follows.

Definition: 8 $Assign^{-1}(S) = m$ such that $m(a) = cardinality(\{i$ such that $S(i) = a\})$

As *Assign* permits all possible allocations of actions to processors, the following hold.

Proposition 8 *If $S \in Assign(m)$ and S' is a permutation of S then $S' \in Assign(m)$.*

Proposition 9 *If $S \in Assign(m)$ then $Assign^{-1}(S) = m$.*

Example 3 *Consider a 2 processor system. If $m(a)=1, m(b)=1$ then Assign $m = \{ < a, b > , < b, a > \}$. $Assign^{-1}(< a, b >) = \{a,b\}$.*

The semantics of multiset prefix (ms;P) is given in figure 4. The transition rules for the other constructs are as before.

$$\text{Multi-set Prefix} \quad \frac{S \in Assign(ms)}{ms;P \xrightarrow{S}_n P}$$

Figure 4: Operational Semantics for Multiset Prefix

Define strong bisimulation equivalence for the language as before. The principal aim of considering a language with multi-set prefixes is to be able to have an axiomatization of bisimulation. To do this we need a generalization of the expansion theorem. The CCS version needs to be generalized not only to handle multiset prefixes but also to combine multiset prefixes from two processes to form another prefix.

Towards that aim we define the functions *Combine* and *Choice*. *Combine* m1 m2 as the set of all possible behaviors that can result by exhibiting the multisets m1 and m2 in one step. *Choice* is used by *Combine* to synchronize two elements to exhibit τ.

Definition: 9 *Combine of two multisets is the smallest set satisfying the following conditions.*

- *Combine $\emptyset$ m1 = Combine m1 $\emptyset$ = $\{$ m1 $\}$*

- *If $m1(a) \neq 0$ and $m2(\bar{a}) = 0$ then*
    Combine m1 m2 = $\{$ $S \cup \{ < a, m1(a) > \}$ $\}$ for $S \in$ Combine m1' m2 where
    $m1' = m1(\lceil (dom(m1)-\{a\}) \}$

- *If $m1(a) = k1$ and $m2(\bar{a}) = k2$ then*
    Combine m1 m2 = $\{$ $S \cup D$ where $S \in$ Combine m1' m2',
    $m1' = m1(\lceil (dom(m1)-\{a\}, m2' = m2 (\lceil (dom(m2)-\{\bar{a}\})$ and
    $D \in$ Choice m1(a) m2(a) a $\}$

$P + P = P$	$P + nil = P$
$(P + Q) + R = P + (Q + R)$	$(m;P) \setminus a = nil$ if $m(a)$ or $m(\overline{a}) \neq 0$
$(m;P) \setminus a = m;(P \setminus a)$ if $m(a)$ and $m(\overline{a}) = 0$	$(P + Q) \setminus a = (P \setminus a) + (Q \setminus a)$
$(m;P) = nil$ if $\mid m \mid > n$.	$nil \setminus a = nil$

Figure 5: Equations

- *Choice k1 k2 a* = { { $< \tau, i >$, $< a, k1-i >$, $< \overline{a}, k2-i >$ } *where* $0 \leq i \leq min(k1, k2)$
  }

Two multisets can be combined to yield all possible synchronizations (including none). For example, $\{a,b\}$ $\{\overline{a},\overline{b}\}$ can result in { $a,b,\overline{a},\overline{b}$ } or { $a, \tau,\overline{a}$ } or { $b, \tau,\overline{b}$ } or { τ, τ}. The first being no synchronization, the second the synchronization of b, the third the synchronization of a and the fourth, both a and b are synchronized. Not all combinations may contribute to legal behavior. In the above example if there are only 2 processors, only the last combination can be observed. Note that in the CCS case, actions can only be combined to yield a set of cardinality 1, viz., only τ is legal.

We should remark that the multiset prefix could have been replaced by a tuple-prefix without affecting the completeness results. For example, $\{ab\};P$ (which is multiset prefix) can be represented as $(\langle ab \rangle;P + \langle ba \rangle;P)$ in the tuple-prefix. The tuple-prefix representation does not require the auxiliary definitions *Assign*, *Combine* and *Choice*. However, the representation is more concrete than the multiset form. Given the usefulness of multisets for multiprocessor systems [BCM88], we use the multiset prefix.

4.1 Completeness

Having defined the auxiliary functions, we can now present a set of axioms which completely axiomatize bisimulation equivalence for multiset prefix CCS. As the operational semantics was defined for a fixed n, the set of axioms also assumes a fixed n. The proof technique for CCS is adequate. That is, we define a normal form, show that all finite process can be reduced to normal form and via an absorption lemma we show that the set of axioms is complete.

Consider the equations defined in figure 5 (the usual axioms) and 6 (the expansion theorem).

Proposition 10 *The set of axioms is sound; that is $P = Q$ implies that $P \sim_n Q$.*

Proof Standard.

The proof of completeness involves the definition of a normal form, then showing that all process can be proved to have a normal form and if two processes are bisimilar, they

$$\boxed{\begin{array}{c} \text{If } P = \sum_i m_i; P_i \text{ and } Q = \sum_j m_j; Q_j \text{ and } C_{i,j} = \text{Combine } m_i \ m_j \text{ then} \\ (P \mid Q) = \sum_i m_i; (P_i \mid Q) + \sum_j m_j; (P \mid Q_j) + \sum_i \sum_j \sum_{m \in C_{i,j}} m; (P_i \mid Q_j) \end{array}}$$

Figure 6: Expansion Theorem

can be proved to have identical normal forms. The proofs are only outlined as the proof techniques are well known.

Definition: 10 *Define a process to be in normal form if it is of the form* $\sum_i m_i; P_i$ *and each P_i is in normal form. and for all i, $\mid m_i \mid \ \leq n$*

Proposition 11 *All process can be reduced to normal form using the equational rules.*

Proof: By induction on the size of the process. □

Proposition 12 *(Absorption Lemma) Let P be in normal form. If $P \xrightarrow{S}_n P'$ and $P' = Q$ then $P + m1; Q = P$ where $m1 = Assign^{-1}(S)$*

Proof: Let $P = \sum_i m_i; P_i$ If $P \xrightarrow{S}_n P'$ then $\exists i, S \in Assign(m_i)$ and P' identical to P_i. Hence, $P + m_i; Q = P$. □

Proposition 13 *The set of axioms is complete; i.e., $P \sim_n Q$ implies $P = Q$.*

Proof: It is sufficient to consider only normal forms as all processes can be reduced to normal form. We prove by induction on the length of the normal forms. Let $P = \sum_{i \in I} m_i; P_i$ and $Q = \sum_{j \in J} m'_j; Q_j$ such that $P \sim_n Q$. We show that this implies $P = P + Q = Q$. To prove $P + Q = P$, it is sufficient to show $\forall j, P + m'_j; Q_j = P$. As $P \sim_n Q$, there is a m_i equal to m'_j and $P_i \sim_n Q_j$. Furthermore, $P_i = Q_j$. Therefore, from the absorption lemma $P + m'_j; Q_j = P$. □

5 Conclusion

We have presented a semantics for multiprocessor CCS. The axiomatization of the bisimulation equivalence required the introduction of multi-set prefixes. The analogy between the expansion theorem for CCS and multiprocessor CCS is that in CCS | was translated to choice with action prefix, while in multiset CCS | was translated to choice with multiset prefix. From a programming view point, the user can use CCS, a compiler for a multiprocessor system will convert it to CCS with multiset prefix and a scheduler (for a particular machine) will ignore certain multisets (due to cardinality) and make the processor assignments.

As mentioned in the introduction, there are a number of non-interleaving semantics for concurrency [DDM88, BB89, BC87]. Current work is on in trying to prove a "limiting" theorem, i.e., given sufficient number of processors, the semantics in this paper coincides with the other semantics.

Acknowledgment

The author thanks Uffe Engberg, Jens Palsberg, Peter Mosses and Rod Harries for their comments and encouragement. Many thanks to the anonymous referees for several useful suggestions.

References

[BB89]   G. Berry and G. Boudol. The Chemical Abstract Machine. Technical Report 1133, INRIA-Sophia Antipolis, December 1989.

[BC87]   G. Boudol and I. Castellani. On Semantics of Concurrency: Partial Orders and Transition Systems. In *Proceedings of the Internation Joint Conference on TAPSOFT: LNCS 249*. Springer Verlag, 1987.

[BCM88]   J. P. Banatre, A. Coutant, and D. Metayer. A Parallel Machine for Multiset Transformation and its Programming Style. *Future Generation Computer Systems*, 4:133–144, 1988.

[CH89]   I. Castellani and M. Hennessy. Distributed Bisimulations. *Journal of the Association for Computing Machinery*, 36(4):887–911, October 1989.

[DDM88]   P. Degano, R. DeNicola, and U. Montanari. A Distributed Operational Semantics for CCS Based on Condition/Event Systems. *Acta Informatica*, 26:59–91, 1988.

[JS80]   A. Jones and P. Schwarz. Experience using multiprocessor systems — A status report. *ACM Computing Surveys*, 12(2), 1980.

[KHCB91] A. Kiehn, M. Hennessy, I. Castellani, and G. Boudol. Observing localities. In *Mathematical Foundations of Computer Science(MFCS)*, 1991.

[Kri91]   P. Krishnan. Distributed CCS. In *Theories of Concurrency: Unification and Extension: CONCUR-91, LNCS:527*, August 1991.

[Mil80]   R. Milner. *A Calculus of Communicating Systems*. Lecture Notes on Computer Science Vol. 92. Springer Verlag, 1980.

[Mil83]   R. Milner. Calculus for Synchrony and Asynchrony. *Theoretical Computer Science*, 25:267–310, 1983.

[Par81]   D. Park. Concurrency and Automata on Infinite Sequences. In *Proceedings of the 5th GI Conference, LNCS-104*. Springer Verlag, 1981.

[Plo81]   G. D. Plotkin. A Structural Approach to Operational Semantics. Technical Report DAIMI FN-19, Computer Science Department, Aarhus University, 1981.

[Pra86]   V. Pratt. Modelling Concurrency with Partial Orders. *International Journal of Parallel Programming*, 15(1), 1986.

[SM82]   A. Salwicki and T. Muldner. On the Algorithmic Properties of Concurrent Programs. In *LNCS-125*. Springer Verlag, 1982.

[vGV87]   R. J. van Glabbeek and F. W. Vaandrager. Petri Net Models for Algebraic Theories of Concurrency. In J. W. deBakker, A. J. Nijman, and P. C. Treleaven, editors, *PARLE-II , LNCS 259*. Springer Verlag, 1987.

Interprocedural type propagation
for object-oriented languages

J.M. Larchevêque
INRIA*
BP 105, 78153 Le Chesnay Cedex. France
e-mail: jml@minos.inria.fr

Abstract

This paper presents a flow-sensitive interprocedural method for type propagation in an object-oriented language. The primary goal of this method is to obtain a precise call graph in the presence of late binding for function names. Thus, it can be viewed as a preliminary step for interprocedural constant propagation and/or procedure integration in an object-oriented language. It uses a new efficient form of symbolic interpretation in order to limit the amount of *intra*procedural analysis required to a single pre-pass over each function. The cost of both this pre-pass and the interprocedural propagation itself is linear in the program size. Furthermore, the output of symbolic interpretation lends itself to efficient incremental computation and can be reused for other tasks, such as constant propagation or code motion.

1 Introduction

1.1 Motivation

Late binding of function names is a crucial feature of object-oriented languages. It consists in binding a function name to an implementation at call time based on the type of a distinguished argument called the *receiver*. The set of functions whose name is thus overloaded is called a *method*. An ordering over types is specified by the programmer, and the type specified for a variable in the program text (its *static type*) is an upper bound on its actual (or *dynamic*) type. When only the static type t of the receiver is known at a call site for a method m, any implementation of m attached to t or one of its subtypes must be considered callable. Therefore, unless dynamic types are somehow inferred before building the call graph of a program, late binding will induce imprecision in interprocedural analysis and unduly inhibit procedure integration (i.e. in-lining). Furthermore, when the dynamic type of a receiver can be determined statically, a method call can be replaced by an ordinary function call, which can be considerably more efficient.

---

*Part of the research presented here was carried out in the Altair consortium. A preliminary version appeared as Altair report 64–90–V1 [Lar91].

This paper proposes an efficient method for interprocedural object-oriented type propagation which supports recursion, side-effects and aliasing. It is based on the solution of standard bit-vector data flow problems and a novel form of symbolic interpretation.

While this method was designed with optimization in mind, it can be used, with a minor variation (Section 6.2.1), for type-checking a language with optional variable declarations.

The class of languages amenable to the method described is fairly large. However, it is important to note that it requires the types of method implementations to be declared. Consequently, languages with no mandatory declarations at all, like standard Smalltalk, cannot easily be handled by our algorithm. Thus, mandatory function declarations appear as the price to pay for efficient type inference. Note that, without such declarations, object-oriented type-checking in the presence of recursion is an undecidable problem, as shown in [AKW90].

1.2 Example

To illustrate motivations and desirable characteristics for object-oriented type propagation, consider the fragment of a type hierarchy and the two functions in C-like code in Figure 1.1.

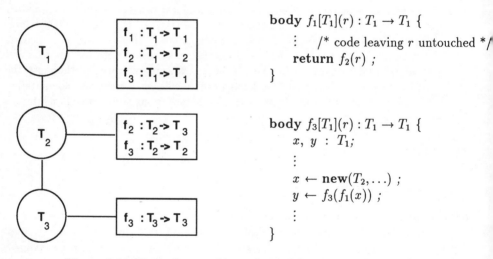

Figure 1.1 Example type hierarchy and function bodies.

The diagram in Figure 1.1 represents for each type the functions attached to it and their declared types. For example, there is a method named f_3 which has 3 implementations, attached respectively to T_1, T_2 and T_3. This means that when the single argument passed in a call to f_3 —which is the receiver— has dynamic type T_2 for example, then the implementation attached to T_2 will be executed. We will note $f[T]$ the implementation of method f attached to type T. Method f_1, on the contrary, has one implementation, which is *inherited* by T_2 and T_3, meaning that $f_1[T_1]$ is called when the receiver is of type T_2 or T_3[1].

---

[1]An equivalent way of putting it is to say that $f_1[T_1] = f_1[T_2] = f_1[T_3]$

Now consider in Figure 1.1 the implementation of f_3 that is attached to T_1, i.e. the function $f_3[T_1]$, and suppose we want to determine possible dynamic types for y. The primitive **new** creates and initializes an object of the type passed as its first argument. So, after the assignment to x, the dynamic type of x can be inferred to be T_2, from which it follows (somewhat trivially) that the implementation of f_1 called at the next instruction is $f_1[T_1]$ (through inheritance). Then, considering the type declared for $f_1[T_1]$, namely $T_1 \rightarrow T_1$, we can infer that an upper bound on the set of possible types for $f_3(f_1(x))$, and therefore for y after the assignment, is T_1, because the type of $f_3[T_1]$ is $T_1 \rightarrow T_1$. However, this could be improved upon if, while analyzing $f_3[T_1]$, we could use information on the bodies of the functions that are called, and in particular on the body of $f_1[T_1]$. Thus, integration (in-lining) of $f_1[T_1]$ would reveal that an upper bound for the type of $f_1(x)$ is T_3 rather than T_1. Indeed, after in-lining the body of $f_1[T_1]$, the expression $f_3(f_1(x))$ becomes $f_3(f_2(x))$, with $f_2[T_2]$ of type $T_2 \rightarrow T_3$ and $f_3[T_3]$ of type $T_3 \rightarrow T_3$.

In fact, the method proposed in this paper does not rely on procedure integration, but on a form of symbolic analysis that provides more precise information on the effects of method calls while keeping the analysis of individual functions mostly separate and avoiding any commitment to particular program transformations during the analysis phase. In this particular case, our method will discover that the type of y is T_3, but it is also capable of synthesizing information about several possible calls at sites where procedure integration is not possible.

The example just given illustrates typical opportunities for gaining precision over user-declared types through type propagation. On the one hand, the declaration of $f_1[T_1]$ announces an upper bound of T_1 on the return type, although the actual bound is T_2. Such discrepancies do make sense in so far as declared types are self-documentary features which reflect intended, but not necessary minimal, bounds. On the other hand, there is no specific declaration for $f_1[T_2]$, whose implementation and type declaration are inherited from T_1; thus, only type propagation can determine that passing a receiver of type T_2 to f_1 will produce a result of type T_3.

1.3   Algorithm outline

The algorithm to be described involves propagating upper bounds to the dynamic types of variables[2]. This algorithm consists of the following steps[3]:

Step 1 Build for each function an expression for the value returned in terms of argument values and constant values irrespective of the execution path taken inside the function (i.e. compute a *symbolic expression*).

For example, the symbolic expression for the value returned by $f_1[T_1]$ (Figure 1.1), noted $\dot{f}_1[T_1](\alpha)$, where α is the receiver's value, equals $\dot{f}_2(\alpha)$. The notation $\dot{f}$ refers to the mapping over symbolic values associated with a function f. In the context of type propagation, the symbolic values we are interested in are types. Thus, $\dot{f}_1[T_1] = \lambda\,\alpha.\dot{f}_2(\alpha)$, which we will call a *type function*, maps an input type to the result type of $f_1[T_1]$.

---

[2]As explained in Section 5, this need not involve any significant precision loss compared with the propagation of type sets.

[3]For an explanation of data flow analysis concepts, refer to the Appendix.

Note that $\dot{f}_2$ is the symbolic mapping associated with *method* f_2 rather than any particular implementation of it. This means that the graph of $\dot{f}_2$ (i.e. the set of pairs $\langle argument, result \rangle$ for $\dot{f}_2$) is a disjoint union of function graphs, namely $graph(\dot{f}_2[T_1]) \cup graph(\dot{f}_2[T_2])$. We will call $\dot{f}_2$ a *type method*, so as to distinguish it from its constituent *type functions* $\dot{f}_2[T_1]$ and $\dot{f}_2[T_2]$.

Step 2 Compute the graph of each type method by solving fixed-point equations.

In the example given, the type function $\dot{f}_1[T_1]$ can be defined as $\lambda \ \alpha.\dot{f}_2(\alpha)$, i.e. in terms of a type method, which itself is necessarily defined in terms of type functions (its graph being a union of type function graphs). Because of this circular dependency, it is desirable to build for a type function a representation which does not involve type methods. Now, the graph of a type function is such a representation and, since an object-oriented program will involve a finite, and comparatively small, set of types, such graphs can be computed at reasonable space and time cost.

Graphs for type methods are initialized using function declarations, and iteratively refined using a worklist algorithm (Section 4). The point of using fixed point iteration is its capacity to handle recursion.

Step 3 Compute symbolic expressions for receivers at call sites and use the function graphs built in step 2 to evaluate these expressions. Then infer sets of possible function calls so as to obtain a precise call graph.

Part of the output of step 1 can be used to build the symbolic expressions needed. These expressions are used in lieu of more conventional intraprocedural propagation techniques.

The next section defines a property of instances of the *intra*procedural type-propagation framework which we call *cyclic k-boundedness*. This property is necessary for the analysis of the *inter*procedural propagation algorithm, which is carried out respectively in Section 3, on symbolic interpretation, Section 4, on fixed-point computation of graphs for symbolic functions, and Section 5, on the computation of receiver types at call sites. The last two sections give concluding remarks and compare the results with related works.

2 Data flow framework for type propagation

This section defines type propagation as a strictly intraprocedural problem, in which all that is known about called functions is their declared types. It is shown that the framework for solving this problem has a property which we call *cyclic k-boundedness* and that this property is preserved after step 2 of the algorithm has replaced declared function types by inferred types.

This section describes a standard form of intraprocedural type propagation. The algorithm which was outlined in the previous section dispenses with this exhaustive propagation and uses instead a form of symbolic interpretation. However, the symbolic interpretation proposed (Section 3) is tailored to the cyclic bound of a particular problem, hence the necessity of considering the problem in its standard form in order to determine this cyclic bound[4].

2.1 General description of the intraprocedural framework

The framework for intraprocedural type determination is a tuple $\langle L, \mathcal{F}, \vee \rangle$, where L is a join semilattice with ordering $\leq$ such that $T \leq T'$ if and only if T is a subtype of T', $\vee$ is the lattice join, which maps two elements of L to their closest common supertype, and $\mathcal{F}$ is a set of monotone transfer functions. Note that, under the subtype ordering, smaller means more informative, which is why we use a *join* semilattice, contrary to the convention prevailing in data flow analysis.

Considering that data flow analysis is carried out on intermediate language statements, what follows is valid for most object-oriented languages. Relevant events are assignments[5]. Expressions are built using variables, constants, object creations and method calls. Initially, declared variables are assigned their declaration types and undeclared variables the type *Object* (the lattice $\top$). At each assignment, the type of the right-hand side is computed using function declarations and current type assignments, and assigned to the left-hand side, much as was done in Section 1.2.

It can be shown that the transfer functions thus defined are monotone. Informally, this is due to the fact that the return type and the receiver's type are covariant in the declarations of function types. In other words, if $T_2 \leq T_1$ and the return type declared for $f[T_1]$ is T_i, then the return type declared for $f[T_2]$ is necessarily less or equal to T_i. Therefore, the transfer function for an assignment of the form $x \leftarrow E(y, z)$ (where $E(y, z)$ is an arbitrary expression with input variables y and z) assigns a new type to x monotonically in terms of the types of y and z.

2.2 Boundedness of the function space

2.2.1 k-boundedness

The concept of k-boundedness was introduced in [Tar81] to express a bound on the length of useful execution paths in the presence of loops.

Let F be a monotone function in a join semilattice[6] and $F^{[i]}$ be defined as follows:

$$F^{[i]} = \bigvee_{j=0}^{i} F^j$$

Intuitively, if transfer functions are associated not only with edges, but also with paths, and the ascending chain $\{F^{[i]}\}$ has an upper bound $F^* = \bigvee_{j=0}^{\infty} F^j$, this upper bound is

---

[4]The framework-dependent character of the symbolic expressions found by our method sets it off from previous approaches and allows to replace problems which —in their full generality— are undecidable by restricted problems solvable in linear time (Section 7).

[5]Where necessary, dummy assignments can be introduced, for example after branching tests or before method calls (see Section 6.2.1).

[6]The original definition supposed a meet semilattice; but switching between the two perspectives might be confusing.

the optimal transfer function for a loop whose body has transfer function F. This is the motivation for the concept of k-boundedness, which can be defined as follows:

Definition 2.1 *A function space $\mathcal{F}$ is k-bounded if and only if, for any F in $\mathcal{F}$, the ascending chain $\{F^{[i]}\}$ admits an upper bound $F^{[k-1]}$.*

It can be proved [Mar89] that, F being monotone, $F^{[k-1]}$ is an upper bound on $\{F^{[i]}\}$ if an only if

$$F^k \leq F^{[k-1]} \tag{2.1}$$

Equation (2.1) is actually the definition given by Tarjan for k-boundedness [Tar81].

2.2.2 Cyclic k-boundedness

For the purpose of building symbolic expressions tailored to the properties of the type-propagation framework, we are interested in a weaker property, which we will call *cyclic k-boundedness*. This concept does not apply to functions in general, but specifically to the transfer functions of data flow frameworks.

We define an *instance* of a framework $\langle L, \mathcal{F}, \vee \rangle$ as a tuple $\langle L_G, \mathcal{F}_G, \vee \rangle$ in which the semilattice L_G and the function space $\mathcal{F}_G$ are contained respectively in L and $\mathcal{F}$ and include only the elements necessary to analyze the control flow graph G [7].

In order to define cyclic k-boundedness for a framework instance, we consider statements of the form $x \leftarrow E(x)$, in which $E(x)$ is an expression involving arbitrary functions and operators occurring in the flow graph to analyze. Let C_G be the set of such assignments for a flow graph G; let $\mathcal{F}_{C_G}$ be the set of transfer functions for single-statement blocks containing such assignments; cyclic k-boundedness can be defined as follows:

Definition 2.2 *A framework instance for flow graph G is cyclically k-bounded if and only if, for any transfer function F_C in $\mathcal{F}_{C_G}$, $F_C{}^k \leq F_C{}^{[k-1]}$.*

Note that the height of the lattice in a framework instance is always a cyclic bound on the function space (owing to monotonicity), but it is not necessarily a standard bound. For example, constant propagation is $2 \times |V| + 1$-bounded, where $|V|$ is the number of variables in the program to analyze, but cyclically 3-bounded. Indeed, each variable can change its value twice in the constant-propagation lattice; and, as each function in $\mathcal{F}_{C_G}$ involves a single variable, $\mathcal{F}_{C_G}$ is 3-bounded, i.e. $2 \times |V| + 1$-bounded with $|V| = 1$.

2.2.3 Cyclic bound of the type propagation framework

Definition 2.2 indicates that, in order to find a cyclic bound for a framework instance, it is enough to find the maximal number of useful iterations for propagating information through a loop of the form

$$\textbf{while cond do}$$
$$x \leftarrow E(x) ;$$
$$\textbf{od} ;$$

---

[7]Precise rules for building the lattice and function space of a framework instance can be found for example in [GW76].

Let $\dot{E}$ be the type mapping associated with E in $E(x)$. We note that possible subexpressions of $E(x)$ are pre-loop values, constants, object creations, method calls, and x itself. Only information contributed by the last two items, viz. method calls and x, are sensitive to input information and so can possibly require more than one application of $\dot{E}$ in order to reach a fixed point solution. Therefore, we can restrict our attention to expressions $E(x)$ involving "interesting method calls", i.e. method calls whose receiver is either x or the result of an interesting method call.

We can further restrict the class of expressions to consider if we are content to prove a sufficient condition for cyclic k-boundedness, which can be expressed as

$$\forall F_C \in \mathcal{F}_{C_G} : \ F_C{}^k \leq F_C{}^{k-1} \tag{2.2}$$

One can observe that any bound found using (2.2) for a single method is also valid for a composition of methods, for monotonicity implies the following:

$$\forall f,g \ : \ f^k \leq f^{k-1} \text{ and } g^k \leq g^{k-1} \Rightarrow (f \circ g)^k \leq (f \circ g)^{k-1}$$

Therefore, equation (2.2) translates into the following theorem:

Theorem 2.1 *If for any method f occurring in a flow graph G, $\dot{f}^k \leq \dot{f}^{k-1}$, then the instance $\langle L_G, \mathcal{F}_G, \vee \rangle$ of the type propagation framework is cyclically k-bounded.*

In the intraprocedural problem being considered, $\dot{f}$ is directly derived from the type declarations for f. Therefore, if in a framework instance all declared function types $t_i \rightarrow t_j$ are such that $t_j \leq t_i$, all type methods $\dot{f}$ are descending, meaning that the framework instance is cyclically 1-bounded ($\dot{f} \leq \iota$). If some function declarations are not descending, then the framework instance is cyclically $k+1$-bounded, where k is the maximal length of a chain of non-descending function types $\langle\langle T_1 \rightarrow T_2\rangle, \langle T_2 \rightarrow T_3\rangle, \ldots, \langle T_{k-1} \rightarrow T_k\rangle\rangle$. For example, with the type declarations represented in Figure 2.2, $\dot{f}^2 = \dot{f}^3$, which implies

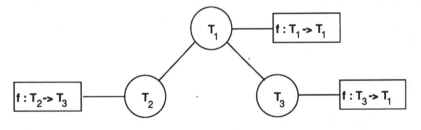

Figure 2.2

that the framework instance is 3-bounded. And indeed, the length of the chain of non-descending function declarations $\langle f[T_2] : T_2 \rightarrow T_3, f[T_3] : T_3 \rightarrow T_1 \rangle$ equals 2. This gives rise to the following theorem:

Theorem 2.2 *If the chains of non-descending function declarations associated with a flow graph G have maximal length $k-1$, then the instance $\langle L_G, \mathcal{F}_G, \vee \rangle$ of the type propagation framework is cyclically k-bounded.*

In fact, since nontrivial chains of non-descending function declarations are likely to be extremely rare *in practice, most instances of the type-propagation framework will be cyclically bounded to 2.*

Now, to show that cyclic k-boundedness is preserved when fixed-point graphs of symbolic functions are used instead of function declarations, consider that the fixed-point algorithm described in Section 4 finds return types less or equal to the return types declared. Therefore, all descending functions will remain so and the actual cyclic bound is necessarily less or equal to the cyclic bound inferred from function declarations.

3 Symbolic interpretation

3.1 General principle

The general idea consists in (i) building a set of use-definition edges (or ud-edges for short) for each function, (ii) considering each ud-edge as a reduction rule that replaces a variable occurrence by the join of its reaching definitions, and (iii) transforming ("normalizing") the resulting reduction system using cyclic k-boundedness in order to give it the property of termination, so that a symbolic expression for any variable occurrence can be obtained by deriving a normal form in a finite number of steps.

Many advantages accrue from this approach

1. Other problems, like constant propagation, can reuse ud-edges [Ken81]. In addition, for the purposes of our algorithm, ud-edges can indifferently be replaced by SSA edges, which are necessary for propagating constants efficiently and accurately [WZ91]. Furthermore, some steps involved in the process of putting a program into SSA form can be reused by our algorithm for normalizing reduction systems (footnote to page 10).

2. Use-definition edges can be built by solving the Reaching Definition problem which, being partitionable, is amenable to a form of incremental analysis particularly well suited to the requirements of a Language-Based Editor [Zad84].

3. No exhaustive intraprocedural type analysis is needed at all, for reduction systems enable one to solve the intraprocedural problem for selected statements. So intraprocedural analysis and flow-sensitive interprocedural analysis can be combined without any redundant computations.

Note that special measures must be taken in order to accommodate side-effects and aliasing (Section 3.5).

3.2 Representing ud-edges as reduction rules

To illustrate the process, we will consider the control flow graph in Figure 3.3.

We construct a set of rules in which x_s represents the symbolic value assigned to the use of x at site s. When several definitions reach a given use, as at site s in the example, the representation merges the corresponding expressions through the confluence operator ($\vee$ in our framework)[8]. So, the ud-edges for the example will be represented as:

---

[8]If SSA edges are used, then explicit conditions rather than joins can be used in reductions.

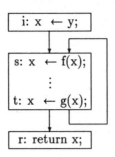

Figure 3.3   Cyclical use-definition dependences

$$x_r \quad \to \quad \dot{g}(x_t) \tag{3.3}$$

$$x_t \quad \to \quad \dot{f}(x_s) \tag{3.4}$$

$$x_s \quad \to \quad \dot{g}(x_t) \vee y_i \tag{3.5}$$

3.3   Identifying self-embedding occurrences

The system is self-embedding, meaning that it produces derivations like $x_t \Rightarrow \dot{f}(\dot{g}(x_t) \vee y_i)$ or $x_s \Rightarrow \dot{g}(\dot{f}(x_s)) \vee y_i$. It is important to note that such circularity is necessarily due to the presence of a loop in the Control Flow Graph. Supposing the framework instance to be cyclically k-bounded, we can handle it easily if the flow graph is reducible[9].

To this end, we draw up the *Inverse Dependency Graph* of the reduction system, defined as $\langle N, E \rangle$ where N is the set of variable occurrences appearing in the reduction system and E the set of all pairs $\langle a_i, b_j \rangle$ such that there is a rule defining b_j in terms of an expression involving a_i. In the example, the IDG is

---

[9]Intraprocedural flow graphs (as opposed to call graphs) for structured languages are almost invariably reducible.

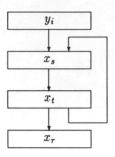

Intuitively, an arrow in the diagram can be read as "defines". It can be shown that the IDG can be derived from the flow graph by reducibility-preserving transformations; therefore it is possible to assume the IDG reducible whenever the flow graph is. Consequently, cycles in the IDG are regions. The header of a strongly connected region will be termed a *self-embedding occurrence*. In our example, x_s can be seen to be a self-embedding occurrence.

3.4 Eliminating self-embedding occurrences

A self-embedding occurrence is a variable occurrence whose defining rule in the reduction system contains loop-induced definitions and definitions occurring prior to the loop. In the example, the rule $x_s \rightarrow \dot{g}(x_t) \lor y_i$ assigns to the self-embedding occurrence x_s the loop-induced definition $\dot{g}(x_t)$ and the pre-loop definition y_i[10].

Therefore, cyclic k-boundedness can be used as follows: A *k-bounded normal form* for x_s is computed by deriving x_s exhaustively using the original rule for x_s only $k-1$ times and thereafter replacing it by a rule incorporating only pre-loop definitions, namely $x_s \rightarrow y_i$.

Supposing the example to be a cyclically 2-bounded problem, this method yields the 2-bounded normal form $\dot{g}(\dot{f}(y_i)) \lor y_i$ for x_s. Then, the rule for x_s can be modified using this form, which yields the following 2-bounded reduction system.

$$x_r \;\rightarrow\; \dot{g}(x_t) \tag{1'}$$
$$x_t \;\rightarrow\; \dot{f}(x_s) \tag{2'}$$
$$x_s \;\rightarrow\; \dot{g}(\dot{f}(y_i))) \lor y_i \tag{3'}$$

---

[10]If no pre-loop definition appears, a used-before-defined error can be diagnosed and a fake assignment of a typed *error* value inserted in a preheader to the function. Here, if x had not been assigned any value prior to the loop, a fake assignment would have been added at the beginning of the function, conferring to x its declaration type and the value *error*.

Also note that the algorithm described in [RWZ88] for computing SSA forms involves identifying pre-loop values ("landing-pad definitions") in a reducible graph, which offers opportunities for reuse if our algorithm is made to work with SSA edges.

Note that self-embedded occurrences must be processed in reverse order of nesting level in the IDG. This ensures that, whenever a self-embedded occurrence is processed, it is the header of an inner loop of the IDG associated with the current reduction system.

3.5 Dealing with side-effects and aliasing

A strong point of the algorithm presented here is that the only intraprocedural problem that has to be solved is a bit-vector problem (typically Reaching Definitions), in order to build *ud*-edges. If some form of flow-sensitive alias analysis was factored into the construction of *ud*-edges, this feature would be lost, and the interprocedural problem might become intractable [Mye81].

On the other hand, there exist a number of algorithms for collecting the side-effects of procedures in a flow-insensitive way (for example [CK89]). Therefore, a simple idea consists in using the *MOD* information obtained through such an algorithm to determine if reduction rules for a variable v occurring in a function f are to be built using *ud*-edges or a pessimistic estimate, namely the declared type. More precisely, given *MOD* information for each function, i.e. a set $MOD(f)$ of global variables and reference parameters which may be modified by a function f, we compute in a flow-insensitive way for each function f the set $SMOD(f)$ of all variables —both local and global— which may be modified by side-effect at call sites in f. Then, a reduction rule of the form

$$x_s \rightarrow E$$

will take the form $x_s \rightarrow$ *if* $x \in SMOD$ *then* $decl(x)$ *else* E, where $decl(x)$ is the type declared for x and $SMOD$ is the $SMOD$ information for the function being analyzed.

This means that a normal form will contain conditionals, and so does not need to be updated when the $SMOD$ information changes. A similar solution is described in [CCKT86] for a representation of "jump functions" supporting incremental changes (see Section 7).

The form of aliasing taken into account by algorithms computing MOD information for procedures is aliasing through reference parameters. Another form of aliasing is aliasing through pointers. An elegant treatment of their incidence on interprocedural analysis can be found in [Wei80]. It is based on closures, inversions, and compositions of copy and alias relations throughout a program. Applied to the problem at hand, it could be used to compute a set $ALIAS$ of aliasing relations induced by pointers (and taking reference passing into account). Such a set being computed for the whole program rather than a particular function, its use will lead to more pessimistic assumptions than the use of MOD information. Improvements are certainly possible but lie outside the scope of this paper[11]. A simple, but pessimistic, approach consists in assigning its declaration type to any variable participating in the $ALIAS$ relation using the same mechanism as for the $SMOD$ sets.

Solutions yielding more accurate (partly flow-sensitive) analysis of side-effects and aliasing are considered in Sections 6.3 and 6.4. These solutions involve the whole interprocedural algorithm rather than just symbolic interpretation.

---

[11]Possible improvements to Weihl's approach in the context of an object-oriented language are described in [Lar92, Sec. 9.2.6]

4 Fixed-point graphs for symbolic methods

Once a reduction system has been built for each function, chaotic fixed point iteration can be used to compute graphs of type methods as shown in Algorithm 4.1.

> initialize the graphs of symbolic functions and methods
> to the types declared;
> place all symbolic functions in the work list ;
> **until** the work list is empty **do**
>   remove an arbitrary symbolic function $\dot{f}[T]$ from the work list ;
>   compute $graph(\dot{f}[T])$ using the symbolic expression
>   for $\dot{f}[T]$ and the types found so far ;
>   **if** this value has changed **then**
>   update the corresponding method graph $graph(\dot{f})$;
>   insert all symbolic functions
>   whose definition involves $\dot{f}$ into the work list ;
>   **fi** ;
> **od** ;

Algorithm 4.1 Fixed-point iteration for graphs of type methods

The step summed up as "update the corresponding method graph $graph(\dot{f})$" involves ensuring that 2 conditions are met by constituent function graphs $graph(\dot{f}[T])$: *(i)* the result type for $\dot{f}[T]$ is the join of the result types of all $\dot{f}[T']$, $T' \leq T$, and *(ii)* the graph for $\dot{f}[T]$ is extended to types inheriting an implementation of f from T.

Dependence relations between symbolic functions are determined using a "raw" call graph, in which all possible calls implied by declared types are considered.

Chaotic (i.e. worklist-based) iteration is preferable to regular iteration because the visit order is given straightforwardly by the call graph, whereas regular iteration would additionally require finding a topological order of the call graph so as to keep down the number of iterations [ASU86, HU73]. Section 6.1 shows that the time bound for this step is on the average proportional to the number of functions in a program.

5 Computing receiver types

Once a reduction system has been obtained for each function and the graphs of type methods are available, computing the type of the receiver at a call site is immediate. A symbolic expression is derived from the reduction system, and the effect of method calls in this expression is interpreted using the type method graphs[12]. For example, if we consider the statement $y \leftarrow f_3(f_1(x))$ in function $f_3[T_1]$ (Figure 1.1), the symbolic expression for the receiver of f_3 is $f_1(T_2)$, which —using the graph of symbolic method f_1— will be found to equal T_3, which shows $f_3[T_3]$ to be the only implementation of f_3 that can be called at this site.

---

[12]The solutions thus found are acceptable in the sense of [GW76], as proved in [Lar92, Sec. 8.3.5].

In [Lar92, Sec. 8.5], we show that added precision can be obtained by introducing one-element type sets to represent *(i)* the type of an object-creation expression and *(ii)* the initial type of the first formal parameter (receiver) of a function. This does not change the construction and use of reduction systems in any essential way and can be made transparent to the interprocedural step. In addition, the resulting precision is practically comparable to the precision obtained by propagating type sets throughout.

6 Concluding remarks

6.1 Cost

6.1.1 Fixed-point computation of graphs for symbolic methods

In the iterative determination of type method graphs, the number of visits for a given type function is 1 plus the number of times a predecessor in the call graph changes. Therefore, if F is the dependence factor, i.e. the average number of predecessors in the dependence graph for each type function, and H is the height of the subtype semilattice, the cost is $O(F \times N \times (H-1))$. If we assume that F in practice does not depend on the size of a program, we can write this cost $O(N \times (H-1))$. If on the other hand, H can be expected to grow very slowly with the size of a program and be asymptotically constant, we find a cost essentially proportional to the number of functions, which in turn can be estimated proportional to the size of a program for a given language.

6.1.2 Symbolic interpretation

If we assume the derivation of a normal form is cheap and performed in constant time on the average, the significant part in the cost of symbolic interpretation is attributable to the construction of a k-bounded reduction system.

This cost breaks down into the following items:

1. Computation of *ud*-edges or SSA edges: Almost linear algorithms exist for both. In addition, the output of this computation is eminently reusable.

2. Determination of a cyclic bound k: This requires exploring sequentially each function declaration in subtype order, and can be performed in time linear in the number of functions.

3. Detection of self-embedding occurrences, sorted by order of nesting level in the Inverse Dependency Graph: most of this operation consists in building a spanning tree for the IDG, which can be achieved in time linearly related to the number of nodes, i.e. of variable occurrences.

4. Derivation of a k-bounded form for each self-embedding occurrence, in reverse order of nesting level. The cost of this operation is absorbed in the cost of detecting self-embedding occurrences.

If the average number of variable occurrences in a function and the number of functions are considered proportional to program size, then the cost of symbolic interpretation, like that of interprocedural propagation, turns out to be linearly related to program size.

6.2 Other applications

6.2.1 Type-checking

If the algorithm just described was used for type-checking a language with no variable declarations, then —in order to obtain enough precision— it would be necessary to insert after each method call a statement whose effect is to assign to the receiver the closest common *sub*type between its current type assignment and the maximal type for a receiver of the given method. It does not seem that this would affect the essential properties of the type propagation framework, apart from the fact that we would need to introduce a lattice $\perp$, so that a closest common subtype can always be computed.

6.2.2 Constant propagation

In order to compute autonomous representations of symbolic functions, we use method graphs, exploiting the finiteness of the type propagation semilattice. In the constant propagation framework, this solution is obviously not available. One way in which symbolic functions could be used, however, is by performing β-reductions, i.e. expanding calls to symbolic methods for those parts of the call graph which are not recursive. Note that the expansion of a *method* may be the join of several expressions. The symbolic representations obtained after the expansion process can be used to determine if the value returned by a function being passed constant parameters is constant. Wegman and Zadeck [WZ91] note that the passing of constant parameters occurs very frequently, so the profitability of such an approach could be fairly high.

6.3 Accurate side-effect analysis

If a function returns values not only through its result, but also through side-effects to global variables and value-return parameters, this is readily amenable to the kind of symbolic analysis performed for function results, provided there is no aliasing. Note by the way that value-return as well as reference passing do not fare well with object-oriented languages, as these can only be performed in a semantically safe way if the static types of actual and formal parameters match exactly, which runs counter to the philosophy of subtype polymorphism. This is one of the reasons why we will consider here only global variables, the other reason being that they illustrate all the problems which may arise in dealing with alias-free side-effects.

The idea consists in replacing a method call $x \leftarrow f(\ldots)$ by a series of assignments of the form

$$v_1 \leftarrow f_{v_1}(\ldots) ;$$
$$v_2 \leftarrow f_{v_2}(\ldots) ;$$
$$\vdots$$
$$v_n \leftarrow f_{v_n}(\ldots) ;$$
$$x \leftarrow f_\rho(\ldots) ;$$

The v_i's denote the variables global to the program portion under analysis. Note that the assignment to x must come last, because x might be a global variable. The function noted f_{v_i} is a function which makes no side-effect (a "pure" function) and returns the value of v_i as updated by f. The function f_ρ is a pure version of the original function. Of course, these functions do not have to be built, and the substitution is performed only for the sake of symbolic interpretation. The symbolic function associated with each of the functions f_{v_i} is derived by adding a dummy use of v_i to the exit block of f before ud-edges are built, and then computing a normal form for this occurrence.

Note that by adding one assignment per global variable v_i and equating if needed f_{v_i} to the identity function, we avoid having to modify all call sites when a variable becomes affected or unaffected by a given function.

6.4 Feedback possibilities

The algorithm described in this paper could fit into a scheme like the following:

1. Carry out flow-insensitive alias and side-effect analysis.

2. Put the program into SSA form and build SSA edges.

3. Build k-bounded reduction systems for functions, where k is the cyclic bound for the type propagation problem at hand. Reduction rules should contain conditionals rather than join operations (footnote to page 8).

4. Build graphs for type methods and compute receiver types so as to improve the call graph.

5. Perform conditional constant propagation, as in [WZ91]. Improve the call graph as dead code is eliminated.

6. Use constant propagation interprocedurally, as described in [WZ91], to provide flow-sensitive feed-back to alias analysis.

7. If the call graph has been improved, iterate, skipping redundant computations.

Considerable precision could be derived from such a scheme, but opportunities for incremental processing are diminished if feed-back is used between the different steps. Note that the bound on the maximum number of iterations can be made arbitrarily constant and all the operations involved can be performed in almost linear time, so that this scheme is practically linear in the program size.

7 Comparison with related works

Interprocedural type propagation is performed in the Self optimizer [CU90], where type analysis relies on procedure integration and code duplication. The method described here, on the contrary, allows to keep the analysis phase separate from the transformation phase, which results in more flexibility, more modularity, and therefore more potential for incrementality.

Suzuki [Suz81] describes a very powerful method for interprocedural type propagation which combines intraprocedural data flow analysis and inequality propagation through transitive closure and unification. The emphasis of this approach is on type-checking, so the scheme described is not intended to fit in the global context of an optimizer. A main drawback of the algorithm described is that intraprocedural analysis has to be carried out exhaustively each time a function is visited during interprocedural propagation.

Borning and Ingalls [BI82] describe a very practical scheme for flow-insensitive type determination inside a procedure for a version of Smalltalk with function declarations and optional variable declarations. It does not include any interprocedural type propagation.

[CCKT86] contains the description of a scheme for interprocedural constant propagation. It involves symbolic interpretation to compute "jump functions" (symbolic expressions for actual parameters) and "return jump functions" ("symbolic functions" in our terminology). Most of the paper, however, is devoted to the use of jump functions, and the properties of return jump functions —which seem much more interesting— are only given cursory, if insightful, consideration.

Wegman and Zadeck [WZ91] describe an algorithm for constant propagation which shares many objectives with the present paper: this algorithm propagates constants to branching conditionals, so as to eliminate superfluous flow graph edges, just as the present scheme propagates types to eliminate superfluous call graph edges; it uses sparse representations (SSA edges) for the sake of efficiency (which is an improvement over [Weg75]), just as we use such representations to avoid redundant computations (which is an improvement over [Suz81]).

Reif and Lewis [RL86] describe a linear-time algorithm for symbolic interpretation. It is not equivalent in effect to the method used here, however. The symbolic value of an expression is expressed in terms of functions and particular variable occurrences. A set of symbolic values for all variable occurrences is called a *cover* of the program. A *minimal cover* relates the value of each occurrence to its earliest definition points in the program. Reif and Lewis show that finding a minimal cover is generally undecidable, and accordingly propose an algorithm to find the best possible cover in linear time. However, expressing, as we do, the type of a returned expression in terms of values on entry to the function involves computing a *minimal cover* for the function. Thus, at the cost of restricting the validity of the cover found to cyclically k-bounded problems, our approach makes it possible to compute a minimal cover in linear time. In other words, the originality of the approach presented in this paper consists in trading off generality for expressive power.

Acknowledgements

I wish to thank all the people who helped me with their suggestions and encouragements while I worked on this paper. In particular, I owe special thanks to Thomas Marlowe for his detailed review of an earlier version of the paper, and to Martin Jourdan and Bernard Lang for their advice and moral support. I am also indebted for insightful and stimulating remarks to Ken Zadeck, François Rouaix, François Thomasset, Véronique Benzaken, Françoise Gire and Claude Delobel.

References

[AKW90] S. Abiteboul, P. Kanellakis, and E. Waller. Method schemas. In *Proceedings of the Ninth ACM Symposium on Principles of Database Systems (Nashville, TN)*, pages 16–27, April 1990.

[ASU86] A. Aho, R. Sethi, and J. Ullman. *Compilers : principles, techniques and tools.* Addison-Wesley, 1986.

[BI82] Alan H. Borning and Daniel H. H. Ingalls. A type declaration and inference system for Smalltalk. In *Conference record of the Ninth Annual ACM Symposium on the Principles of Programming Languages, Albuquerque (NM)*, pages 133–141, January 1982.

[Cal88] David Callahan. The program summary graph and flow-sensitive interprocedural data flow analysis. In *Proceedings of the SIGPLAN '88 Conference on Programming Language Design and Implementation, Atlanta, Georgia*, pages 47–56. ACM, June 1988.

[CCKT86] David Callahan, Keith D. Cooper, Ken Kennedy, and Linda Torczon. Interprocedural constant propagation. In *Proceedings of the SIGPLAN '86 Symposium on Compiler Construction, June 86*, pages 152–161, June 1986.

[CK89] Keith D. Cooper and Ken Kennedy. Fast interprocedural alias analysis. In *Conference Record of the Annual ACM Symposium on Principles of Programming Languages, Austin (TX)*, pages 49–59, January 1989.

[CU90] C. Chambers and D. Ungar. Iterative type analysis and extended message splitting. In *Proceedings of the ACM SIGPLAN '90 Conf. on Programming Language Design and Implementation, White Plains, NY*, pages 150–164, June 1990. published as SIGPLAN Notices, Vol. 25, Num. 6.

[GW76] Susan L. Graham and Mark Wegman. A fast and usually linear algorithm for global flow analysis. *Journal of the ACM*, 23(1):172–202, January 1976.

[HU73] Matthew S. Hecht and Jeffrey D. Ullman. Analysis of a simple algorithm for global data flow problems. In *Conference Record of the ACM Symposium on the Principles of Programming Languages*, pages 207–217, September 1973.

[Ken81] Ken Kennedy. A survey of data flow analysis techniques. In S. Muchnick and N. Jones, editors, *Program Flow Analysis, Theory and Applications*, chapter 1, pages 5–54. Prentice-Hall, 1981.

[Klo87] Jan Willem Klop. Term rewriting systems: a tutorial. *Bulletin of the EATCS*, 32:143–182, 1987.

[KU77] J.B. Kam and J.D. Ullman. Monotone data flow analysis frameworks. *Acta Informatica*, 7(3):305–318, 1977. Originally published as Research Report TR-169, Computer Sciences Laboratory, Princeton University.

[Lar91] J.-M. Larchevêque. Interprocedural type propagation for object-oriented languages. Rapport Technique 64–90–V1, GIP Altaïr, Rocquencourt, France, September 1991.

[Lar92] J.-M. Larchevêque. *Compilation techniques for incremental development in a persistent object-oriented environment*. PhD thesis, LRI, Université de Paris-Sud, January 1992.

[Mar89] T.J. Marlowe. *Data Flow Analysis and Incremental Iteration*. PhD thesis, Rutgers University, New Brunswick, New Jersey 08903, October 1989. Report DCS-TR-25.

[Mye81] Eugene W. Myers. A precise inter-procedural data flow algorithm. In *Conference record of the Eighth Annual ACM Symposium on the Principles of Programming Languages*, pages 219–230, January 1981.

[RL77] John H. Reif and Harry R. Lewis. Symbolic evaluation and the global value graph. In *Conference record of the Fourth Annual ACM Symposium on the Principles of Programming Languages, Los Angeles (CA)*, pages 104–118, January 1977.

[RL86] John H. Reif and Harry R. Lewis. Efficient symbolic analysis of programs. *Journal of Computer and System Sciences*, 32:280–314, June 1986.

[Rou90] François Rouaix. Safe run-time overloading. In *Conference Record of the Annual ACM Symposium on Principles of Programming Languages, San Francisco (CA)*, pages 355–366, January 1990.

[RWZ88] Barry K. Rosen, Mark N. Wegman, and F. Kenneth Zadeck. Global value numbers and redundant computations. In *Proceedings of the Fifteenth Annual ACM SIGACT-SIGPLAN Symposium on Principles of Programming Languages, San Diego (CA)*, pages 12–27, January 1988.

[Suz81] Norihisa Suzuki. Inferring types in Smalltalk. In *Conference record of the Eighth Annual ACM Symposium on the Principles of Programming Languages*, pages 187–198, January 1981.

[Tar81] R. Endre Tarjan. A unified approach to path problems. *Journal of the ACM*, 28(3):576–593, 1981.

[Weg75] Ben Wegbreit. Property extraction in well-founded property sets. *IEEE Trans. Software Eng.*, SE-1(3):270–285, September 1975.

[Wei80] William E. Weihl. Interprocedural data flow analysis in the presence of pointers, procedure variables, and label variables. In *Conference record of the Seventh Annual ACM Symposium on the Principles of Programming Languages*, pages 83–94, June 1980.

[WZ91] Mark N. Wegman and F. Kenneth Zadeck. Constant propagation with conditional branches. *ACM Transactions on Programming Languages and Systems*, 13(2):181–210, April 1991.

[Zad84] F. K. Zadeck. Incremental data flow analysis in a structured program editor. *SIGPLAN Notices*, 19(6):132–143, June 1984. Proceedings of the SIGPLAN Symposium on Compiler Construction (Montreal, Canada).

Appendix

Data-flow theoretical definitions

I Framework

Solving a global (or intraprocedural) data flow analysis problem consists in decorating nodes of a control flow graph, which is essentially a flow chart, with information on a program's behavior. Nodes in the flow graph are basic blocks, i.e. single-entry single-exit sequences of statements. The information associated with a basic block represents assertions which hold on entry to the block. This information is modeled as a semilattice, usually a meet semilattice, but this paper uses a join semilattice for conformity with the subtype ordering. If a join semilattice is used, information on entry to a block B located at the confluence of several paths is the result of applying the join operator $\vee$ among information items coming from each path. Information on entry to a block B is mapped to information on entry to each successor S of B by a *transfer function*, which can be associated either with block B or with each edge $\langle B, S \rangle$. A *monotone framework* $\langle L, \vee, \mathcal{F} \rangle$ is made up of a join semilattice L with join operator $\vee$, and a set $\mathcal{F}$ of monotone transfer functions. Monotonicity is important to prove the termination of most data flow analysis algorithms. Beside monotonicity, a useful property of $\mathcal{F}$ is closure under join and composition, which makes it possible to extend the definition of transfer functions from edges to paths in the natural way.

II Use-definition edges, SSA edges

A use-definition edge, or *ud*-edge for short, for variable occurrence x_s is a pair $\langle x_s, t \rangle$, where t is a possible definition site for x_s.

SSA edges are essentially information edges (use-definition or definition-use edges) for a program in SSA form. A program is in SSA form if variables are renamed so that there is only one assignment to each variable in the program text. At a join point, a statement of the form $v_i \leftarrow \phi(v_j, v_k)$ is inserted for each variable v with different renamings in the branches that are joined. The ϕ function returns the value of v_j or v_k according as control comes from the branch where v_j or v_k is defined. One advantage of using SSA edges is that the effect of two confluent SSA edges like $\langle v_i, v_j \rangle$ and $\langle v_i, v_k \rangle$ can be predicated on the value of a branching condition (as part of the static evaluation of $v_i \leftarrow \phi(v_j, v_k)$). On the contrary, when several ud-edges exist for a variable occurrence, the corresponding definitions can only be related through the confluence operator of the framework, which may lead to more pessimistic results.

III   Symbolic interpretation

Symbolic interpretation consists in assigning values to variables at each point in a program irrespective of the possible execution paths leading to this point. To solve the problems induced by joins and circular definitions, the domains of program operations are replaced by sets of symbols with adequate properties. For example, in the type propagation problem described in the paper, the domain of program operations (methods) is replaced by sets of upper bounds on types and a join operation is defined on them.

Using the Centaur system for data-parallel SIMD programming: a case study

Jean-Luc Levaire

LIP, ENS Lyon,

46 Allée d'Italie,

F-69364 Lyon Cedex 07, France

Email: jllevair@lip.ens-lyon.fr

Abstract

We discuss the application of Centaur to designing data-parallel SIMD languages. We first present the main functionalities of this system. We describe a simple language, called $\mathcal{L}$, which embodies the basic concepts of real SIMD languages like C*, MPL or POMPC. We give an operational semantics to this language and we discuss in detail its implementation under Centaur. Finally, we present a SIMD programming environment created with Centaur for the $\mathcal{L}$ language.

Introduction

The Centaur system [17] is a software toolbox to design and develop programming languages. It provides a variety of tools to study their syntactic and semantic aspects, and enables to create specific editors, interpreters or debuggers. Centaur is based on the manipulation of abstract trees, which are the internal representation of programs in the specified language.

The syntactic aspect of a language is given by the correspondence between the representation of a program as a linear text and as an abstract tree. For the semantic aspect, Centaur uses the notion of natural semantics. Evaluating a program amounts to prove a particular proposition using a set of inference rules and axioms. This set constitutes in fact the semantic specification of the language. Finally, a windowing system is also provided to develop specialized multiwindow programming environments.

Centaur has already been used to study the semantics of sequential languages such as Pascal [6], functional languages such as ML [8] and parallel languages such as ADA. Until now, those parallel languages were *control-parallel* languages, aimed at MIMD (Multiple Instruction, Multiple Data) architectures [7]. Parallelism is there expressed with new parallel control structures. But *data-parallel* languages, such as those designed for SIMD (Single Instruction, Multiple Data) architectures are of interest too. In these languages, control is centralized and data are distributed: the processors execute all the same instruction, but on their own data.

Unlike MIMD languages, few theoretical studies of SIMD languages have been made, even though many such languages are commercially available. A number of SIMD languages are derived from the C language: C* [5] for the Connection Machine [9], MPL [11] for the Maspar MP-1 [1] and POMPC [14] for the data-parallel POMP machine [10]. Recently, Bougé and Garda have proposed in [2] and [3] a simple language called $\mathcal{L}$, which embodies the basic concepts of those languages. In particular, they show that $\mathcal{L}$ is minimal and expressive in a certain sense.

We discuss here the implementation of the $\mathcal{L}$ language using Centaur. We choose this language because of its simplicity and its expressiveness. This ensures that any SIMD algorithm can be written in the $\mathcal{L}$ language. We also describe the basic functionalities of a programming environment for SIMD languages. Centaur is well suited to design, study and improve such an environment.

First, we describe the Centaur system and its main components. Then, we present the $\mathcal{L}$ language and give its operational semantics. Based on this precise semantic definition, we describe its implementation under Centaur. Finally, we present the resulting programming environment through an example of program.

1 Centaur

Centaur is a software toolbox to assist users in designing programming languages and developing programming environments. It mainly consists in a kernel which manipulates internal objects, a number of specification languages to define the syntactic and semantic aspects of a language, and an interface which handles communication between Centaur and the user.

1.1 The kernel

The kernel is divided into two parts. The first part is concerned with the syntactic aspect of a language. The fundamental object manipulated by the kernel is the abstract syntax tree. It corresponds to the arborescent representation of program terms. The nodes of these trees are called *operators*. Two types of operators are distinguished.

▷ The atomic operators correspond to the leaves of the trees. One specifies the type of their values using the following classes: INTEGER, IDENTIFIER, CHAR, STRING, SINGLETON (operator without value). An additional class, called TREE, is used when the value of the operator is a tree from an another language. This mechanism allows to stratify the specification of languages, and to use common parts in different languages.

▷ The non-atomic operators correspond to the internal nodes. One specifies their arity (fixed arity, list, non-empty list) and the type of their descendents. Such a type consists for each possible son in a set of valid operators. This set is called a *phylum*.

The Virtual Tree Processor (VTP), a collection of Lisp [4] primitives, enables the user to create, modify or examine these trees.

The second part of the kernel is a semantic machine which evaluates programs written in the language under study. The semantics of a language is specified with a collection of rules concerning its terms. This machine is a logical engine, written in Mu-Prolog [13], which constructs proofs corresponding to a given term using this set of rules. Such a proof corresponds in fact to a computation of the program. Finally, communication primitives between the VTP and Mu-Prolog enable the conversion of abstract trees into Prolog terms and conversely. They are called before and after each evaluation.

1.2 Using Centaur

Implementing a language with Centaur consists in the following steps.

▷ The user specifies the concrete syntax (text) of his language, its abstract syntax (VTP tree) and the translation from the first syntax to the second one. He describes in fact a parser which is used when loading a program to detect syntax errors, and to construct the corresponding abstract syntax tree. The specification language used to define such a translation is called Metal (Meta-Language).

▷ Then, he has to describe the inverse process: translation from an abstract tree to text. This is done with PPML (Pretty Printer Meta Language). At this point, the user has generated a language-oriented editor for programs in his language.

▷ The semantic aspect is specified with the Typol language. This Typol specification is compiled into a set of Prolog clauses used by the logical engine to evaluate a program.

▷ Finally, the user builds a specific programming environment in the Lisp language, using window managing primitives. He can manipulate the abstract trees with the VTP, and call the semantic engine from his environment.

1.3 The Typol semantic specification language

A Typol program consists in a set of rules, which are either axioms, or inference rules. Inference rules look like

$$\frac{premises}{conclusion}$$

This means that the conclusion is proved as soon as premises are. A premise is either a condition, or a sequent. A sequent is a proposition (the consequent) associated with the hypotheses required to prove it. It is denoted

$$hypotheses \vdash consequent$$

A conclusion is always a sequent. Finally, different infix symbols (->, =>, :) can be used in the propositions, in order to separate various semantic aspects of terms in a language (instructions and expressions for instance). Intuitively, the expression at the left of the proposition symbol in a consequent corresponds to an abstract tree of the language. The right part represents its semantics. Typol uses pattern matching to find the inference rule or the axiom corresponding to the given program.

Let us consider the following rule

```
sigma |- EXP : v  & sigma |- X, v => sigma'
----------------
sigma |- assign(X, EXP) -> sigma';
```

It means

Executing instruction assign(X,EXP) from environment sigma produces an environment sigma', so that sigma' is deduced from sigma by substituing the value of X with v, where v is the evaluation of expression EXP in sigma.

The abstract tree of the consequent is the instruction assign(X, EXP). Its evaluation (symbol ->) yields an environment (a function which binds a variable to its value). In the same way, the evaluation (symbol :) of an expression yields a value, an integer for instance.

2 The $\mathcal{L}$ language and its semantics

The $\mathcal{L}$ language has been proposed by Bougé and Garda as a simple programming model. This model covers most recent SIMD machines, such as the Connection Machine CM-2 or the Maspar MP-1. We consider a set of Processing Elements (PEs), each managing a private memory. The PEs are controlled by a unique external sequencer, which broadcasts the common instruction to be executed. Thus, all PEs do the same instruction, but on their own data. Furthermore, an inhibition mechanism, called the *context*, is associated to each processor. A PE modifies its local memory only if its context is in an *active* state. A PE which is not active is said to be idle. This possibility is essential to implement parallel conditioning branch. Finally, a global bus links the set of PEs to the sequencer, and computes the global *or* of the elements of a boolean vector, of which each component is local to a PE. This feature enables the sequencer to detect the termination of loops.

The $\mathcal{L}$ language includes five constructions: assignation, communication, sequencing, iteration and conditioning. We give here a Structured Operational Semantics (SOS) [15] for $\mathcal{L}$. This kind of semantics defines a transition system, given by a set of rules and axioms. It works by induction on a program P. The states of the semantics consist in the program remaining to be executed, the environment σ, and a stack ct of contexts, which are boolean vectors. A stack is necessary to implement nested conditional structures.

We adopt the following notations. Identifiers with an initial uppercase letter denote parallel variables, which we also called vectors (possibly multidimensionnal). Processor locations will be denoted u, v etc. $X|_u$ denotes the element of X located on the processor whose address is u. The states of the semantics will be denoted $\langle P, \sigma, ct \rangle$ and $\bullet$ denotes the empty program. $[E](\sigma)$ is the evaluation of the expression E in the environment σ. ϵ is the empty stack. By convention $Pop(\epsilon) = \epsilon$ and $Top(\epsilon) = Tt$, the boolean vector whose all elements have the *true* value. Finally, we define the *active* predicate as follows

$$\text{active}(u) \equiv (Top(ct)|_u = tt).$$

Assignment The instruction $X := E$ stores into variable X the value of expression E. An idle processor remains idle, and leaves its local memory unchanged.

$$\langle X := E, \sigma, ct \rangle \longrightarrow \langle \bullet, \sigma', ct \rangle$$

with

▷ $\sigma'(X)|_u = [E](\sigma)|_u$ if active(u);

▷ $\sigma'(T)|_u = \sigma(T)|_u$ if $T \neq X$ or $\neg$ active(u).

In $\mathcal{L}$, all expressions are required to be elementwise: the value of an expression at a PE depends on the value of variables at this PE only.

Communication For simplicity, we consider only regular communication patterns here. The instruction shift X along d shifts the vector X along the constant common direction d. Again, an idle processor leaves its local memory unchanged. For a PE located at u, $\bar{d}(u)$ is the address of the PE located in the direction opposite to d.

$$\langle \text{shift } X \text{ along } d, \sigma, ct \rangle \longrightarrow \langle \bullet, \sigma', ct \rangle$$

with

▷ $\sigma'(X)|_u = \sigma(X)|_{\bar{d}(u)}$ if $active(u)$;

▷ $\sigma'(T)|_u = \sigma(T)|_u$ si $T \neq X$ or $\neg\,active(u)$.

Sequencing The construct $P; Q$ executes P then Q.

$$\frac{\langle P, \sigma, ct\rangle \longrightarrow \langle P', \sigma', ct'\rangle \quad P' \neq \bullet}{\langle P; Q, \sigma, ct\rangle \longrightarrow \langle P'; Q, \sigma', ct'\rangle} \qquad \frac{\langle P, \sigma, ct\rangle \longrightarrow \langle \bullet, \sigma', ct'\rangle}{\langle P; Q, \sigma, ct\rangle \longrightarrow \langle Q, \sigma', ct'\rangle}$$

Iteration The construct while B do P end iterates program P upto a point where the *element-wise* boolean expression B evaluates to false at each *active* PE. Notice that this construct does not modify the context stack.

$$\frac{(\exists u\,(\llbracket B \rrbracket(\sigma)|_u \wedge active(u))) = tt}{\langle \text{while } B \text{ do } P \text{ end}, \sigma, ct\rangle \longrightarrow \langle P; \text{while } B \text{ do } P \text{ end}, \sigma, ct\rangle}$$

$$\frac{(\exists u\,(\llbracket B \rrbracket(\sigma)|_u \wedge active(u))) = f\!f}{\langle \text{while } B \text{ do } P \text{ end}, \sigma, ct\rangle \longrightarrow \langle \bullet, \sigma, ct\rangle}$$

Conditioning The construct where B do P end inhibits, during the execution of program P, those PEs whose *elementwise* boolean expression B evaluates locally to false. The new activity corresponds to the boolean vector $Top(ct) \wedge \llbracket B \rrbracket(\sigma)$, and is pushed on the context stack. To keep track of conditional blocks, we introduce the new syntactic construction begin P end.

$$\langle \text{where } B \text{ do } P \text{ end}, \sigma, ct\rangle \longrightarrow \langle \text{begin } P \text{ end}, \sigma, ct'\rangle$$

with $ct' = Push(Top(ct) \wedge \llbracket B \rrbracket(\sigma), ct)$. The following rules express that P is executed up to its termination, and, at that time, the former activity is restored by popping the context stack.

$$\frac{\langle P, \sigma, ct\rangle \longrightarrow \langle P', \sigma', ct'\rangle}{\langle \text{begin } P \text{ end}, \sigma, ct\rangle \longrightarrow \langle \text{begin } P' \text{ end}, \sigma', ct'\rangle}$$

$$\langle \text{begin } \bullet \text{ end}, \sigma, ct\rangle \longrightarrow \langle \bullet, \sigma, Pop(ct)\rangle$$

3 Implementing $\mathcal{L}$ under Centaur

The first step of this implementation is to define a grammar for $\mathcal{L}$, particularly for the boolean and arithmetic expressions. We use the syntax of the C language, except incrementation and decrementation operators which have side effects. Thus, writing the Metal and PPML specifications presents no specific difficulties. The only technical point is to set correctly the priorities on the operators of the language. Vectors are implemented by list operators, so that we can choose the size and the geometry of them. Moreover, they have no concrete syntax, because $\mathcal{L}$ provides no way to define vectors extensively.

In the following Typol rules, **sigma** represents the environment. It is implemented as a list of assignment operators. These operators bind a variable name to its vectorial value. A variable named POSITION is defined in the initial environment. It associates to each processor a unique identifier, starting at 0. The context is denoted ct in the Typol rules. It is a list of vectors, and represents the stack ct previously defined. Two alternative approaches are possible to write the Typol specification of $\mathcal{L}$.

3.1 The direct method

This is the more natural and simple approach. It is used for the implementation of classical sequential languages. The method corresponds to a *Big-Step* operational semantics in that sense that a program evaluation consists in only one big derivation. The program is not modified by its evaluation, but only the environment. The definition of such a semantics amounts to describing the modifications of the environment made by the statements and the constructs of the language. This method could also be applied to SIMD languages, like $\mathcal{L}$. The only difference with the sequential case comes from the context, which is also modified during the evaluation. Thus, this semantics of $\mathcal{L}$ would be specified as a function with two variables. Let us consider the rules for iteration. The Prolog predicates `for_all_actif_not(ct,v)` and `exist_actif(ct,v)` respectively test whether the value of the vector v is false on all *active* PEs, and whether there exists at least one active PE such that this value is true.

```
sigma |- EXP : v & for_all_actif_not(ct,v)
-----------------
sigma, ct |- while(EXP, P) -> sigma, ct ;

sigma |- EXP : v & exist_actif(ct,v) &
sigma, ct |- P -> sigma', ct' &
sigma', ct' |- while(EXP, P) -> sigma'', ct''
-----------------
sigma, ct |- while(EXP, P) -> sigma'', ct'' ;
```

The first rule expresses the termination of the loop, in which case environment and context remain unchanged. The second one contains a recursive call to itself, after the derivation of one iteration. Notice here that the environment and context resulting from this iteration, **sigma'** and **ct'**, become the initial environment and context of the following iteration. This corresponds to function composition.

When using this type of semantics, the evaluation of a whole program consists in evaluating exactly one Prolog term. Indeed, this evaluation is recursively made on the structure of the program. The main advantage of this method is that Centaur provides directly a debugger during the evaluation of a term, the Typol debugger. It traces the Typol rules successively applied, and the user can set breakpoints in his program, or examine variables which appear in the rule. An interesting feature is that he can also make a rule to fail, which forces Prolog to backtrack. The program is then executed upside down. Figure 1 shows, in the left window, the environment with the rule to be applied, and, in the right window, the current value of **sigma**. It is assumed here that the architecture is a 4 × 4 square grid of PEs.

The main drawback of this method is that the whole evaluation of a program is made under Prolog: since it keeps track of its whole proof, environment and context are stored between each application of rules. The memory space is then rapidly exhausted especially if vectors of large size (say, more than 16 elements) are manipulated.

3.2 The transformational method

This approach is more complex than the previous one. It has already been used with Centaur for languages with explicit control parallelism, such as MIMD languages. It is based on a *Small-Step* operational semantics where a step modifies the program under evaluation. An entire program

```
┌─┬──────────────────────────────────────────┬─┬─┬────────────────────┬─┐
│□│ Display  Edit  Delete  Set-name: eval_prog│▲│□│ Display   Edit     │▲│
├─┼──────────────────────────────────────────┤ ├─┴────────────────────┤ │
│ TRY │sigma |- EXP : v  &  EXIST_ACTIF(ct, v)  & │ │N= 0,1,2,3          │ │
├─────┤sigma, ct |- P -> sigma', ct'  &           │ │   1,2,3,4          │ │
│Step │sigma', ct' |- while(EXP, P) -> sigma'', ct│ │   2,3,4,5          │ │
│Skip │-------------                              │ │   3,4,5,6          │ │
│Fail │sigma, ct |- while(EXP, P) -> sigma'', ct''│ │I= 1,2,3,3          │ │
├─────┤                                           │ │   2,3,3,3          │ │
│Abort│                                           │ │   3,3,3,3          │ │
├─────┤                                           │ │   3,3,3,3          │ │
│Break│                                           │ │F= 1,1,2,2          │ │
├─────┤                                           │ │   1,2,2,2          │ │
│ Go  │                                           │ │   2,2,2,2          │ │
├─────┤                                           │▼│   2,2,2,2          │▼│
│Examine│◄│░░░░░░░░░░░░░░░░░░░░░░░░░░░░░░░░│►│◄│░░░░░░░░░░░░░░│►│
└─────┴────────────────────────────────────────┴─┴──────────────────────┴─┘
```

Figure 1: The Typol debugger.

evaluation consists then in many steps. This semantics transforms a program associated with an environment and a context into a new program, environment and context. It corresponds exactly to the operational semantics given in the previous section. The implementation is easier than for the MIMD case: the $\mathcal{L}$ language is deterministic, and communications are synchronous. We deduce Typol rules directly from the SOS rules. For instance, the rule for conditioning is

```
evaluate(EXP, sigma, V) &
push_and(ct, V, ct')
-----------------
|- where(EXP, P), sigma, ct |-> begin(P), sigma, ct' ;
```

where `evaluate` and `push_and` are Prolog predicates which respectively evaluate the expression EXP and modify the context stack accordingly.

We can now see that the evaluation of a program consists in a sequence of term evaluation, each term being derived from the previous one by application of a semantic rule. Each call to Prolog corresponds to one transition in our semantics. Observe that it may involve many Typol inferences, as Typol rules are recursive in general. The result is a new state made of the new program, environment and context. Computing an entire program requires then as many calls to Prolog as transitions in the SOS semantics. The evaluation of a program stops when the returned program is • and no more rule applies.

The interesting point of this method is that the memory space required by Prolog for the evaluation of an entire program corresponds to that required for computing one transition. It amounts to the space used to represent the environment and the context, and to evaluate an expression. Hence, this method avoids the memory overflow if the complexity of expressions remains beyond reasonable limits.

On the other hand, we have to design a specific debugger. The Typol debugger is only available during the computation of a transition, that is during a call to Prolog. Between each Prolog computation, the control returns to the Lisp top-level. The debugger has to combine both Centaur and Lisp graphic primitives. It uses the communication primitives between the VTP and Prolog in order to exchange program, environment and context at each step. The skeleton of the debugger is a simple loop which iterates calls to Prolog and displays the new program at each iteration. In practice, this implementation works fine with bidimensionnal vectors of size 16×16. However, this size can be interactively modified by the user before the execution of a program.

3.3 The programming environment

Centaur and Lisp provide various graphic and interface functions to develop a specific programming environment. In our case, we have implemented the functionalities of the Maspar MP-1 programming environment MPPE (Maspar Programming Environment [12]) with several extensions.

Regarding the execution control, the user can choose between two modes: a step-by-step mode, with or without a call to the Typol debugger (Step and Step(db)), and a continuous mode (Go). In the second case, the evaluation can be stopped by clicking on a button (Break). The direct definition of breakpoints is difficult because the program is modified during its evaluation. It would require to add new structures to keep track of the localization of the breakpoints.

The more natural way to display vectors is to use grids. But rather than displaying the value of their elements, we show the value of a predicate concerning the selected variable, $X = 0$ for instance. To obtain the value of an element, the user simply clicks on it and a window will present the coordinates of the chosen element and its value. The context is displayed with a grid too, so the user can inspect at any time the current activity. Our implementation provides also the capability to trace predicates. These predicates can depend on both variable values and activity. For instance, the set of active processors so that the condition $A = (B + 1)$ holds is represented by the predicate ACTIF && (A == (B + 1)). This is an important improvement on MPPE, which resticts predicates to the comparison between one variable and a constant.

The following figures present these functionalities using a program which computes the connected component of a point in the image IMAGE. The point coordinates are $(10, 3)$, so it is located in the bottom left square of the image. The connected component C is build by dilating a wave from the initial point. The final component is found when the wave does not extend in the current iteration.

The left window of Figure 2 is the main window, containing the program and the execution control button. The window on the right displays the environment with a button (Examine) to display a selected variable, and a button (Predicate) to trace a predicate. The two left windows of Figure 3 show two variables, with the value of one element. The right window displays a predicate with a dialog box used to modify it.

Conclusion

This work presents the first implementation of a SIMD data-parallel language under Centaur. The $\mathcal{L}$ language is fairly primitive. It can be extended to include the complex data-parallel flow control structures of MPL, such as the plural while with the associated plural break and continue. We actually implemented under Centaur an extension of $\mathcal{L}$ containing such control rupture statements.

We can observe a hierarchy of languages in terms of adequacy to Centaur. Classical sequential languages are the most easier to implement because of the simplicity of their control and data structures. Conversely, implementing MIMD languages is very difficult due to non-determinism, asynchronous communication and parallel execution. Finally, SIMD languages lie between these extreme cases. They are closer to sequential languages in terms of control. The main difficulty comes from the large size of data.

Centaur appears as an interesting semantic design tool. Implementing a language under Centaur helps the designer to study various alternatives for its semantics and to explore their

```
□  File  Display  Edit  Selections
 Step        C := IMAGE && C;
             while (CPRIME != C) do
 Step (db)     CPRIME := C;
 Go            AUX := C;
               grid_shift AUX along north fill 0;
 Break         C := C || AUX;
               AUX := C;
               grid_shift AUX along east fill 0;
               C := C || AUX;
               AUX := C;
               grid_shift AUX along south fill 0;
               C := C || AUX;
               AUX := C;
               grid_shift AUX along west fill 0;
 Restore       C := C || AUX;
               C := IMAGE && C
```

```
□  Environnement  Examine  Predicate
POSITION
POSX
POSY
IMAGE
A
C
CPRIME
AUX
```

Figure 2: Connected component of a point in an image. Windows presenting the program and the environment.

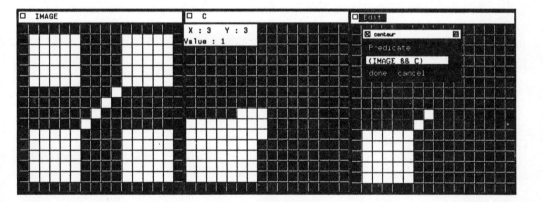

Figure 3: Windows presenting the variables IMAGE and C. The point is located in the bottom left square of the image IMAGE and variable C is the current component. The right window shows the predicate (IMAGE && C) with its dialog box.

impact. The existing SIMD languages present some differences as a consequence of the choices made during their design. For instance, in MPL the body of a conditional block is not executed if all the processors become inactive. This is not the case in C* and POMPC. Those differences may generate expressiveness problems between SIMD languages.

We can also use this implementation to refine SIMD programming environment and to develop software engineering tools. The existing software tools for sequential languages may be adapted to SIMD languages. These adaptations can be performed by the use of this application.

Finally, various extensions are possible. We can extend the language to include more generalized communication commands. We can also improve it by adding notion of shape as in C* or POMPC. Moreover the Centaur system can be used to provide intelligent syntax-directed editors to commercial languages. Our research group is currently developing a proof system based on Hoare's logic [16]. A future work will consist in integrating it in this environment.

References

[1] Blank T. The MasPar MP-1 Architecture. Proc. of the 35th IEEE Computer Society Int. Conf. (Spring Compcon 90), San Fransisco, 1990, pp. 20–24.

[2] Bougé L. On the semantics of languages for massively parallel SIMD architectures. Proc. Parallel Arch. and Lang. Europe Conf. (PARLE), Eindhoven, Lect. Notes in Comp. Science 506, Springer Verlag, 1991, pp. 166–183.

[3] Bougé L., Garda P. Towards a Semantic Approach to SIMD Architectures and their Languages. Semantics of Systems of Concurrent Processes, Proc. LITP Spring School on Theor. Comp. Science, La Roche Posay, France, 1990, Lect. Notes in Comp. Science 469, Springer Verlag, pp. 142–175.

[4] Chailloux J., et al. LeLisp v15.2: Le manuel de référence. INRIA, 1986.

[5] C* Programming Guide. Thinking Machine Corporation, 1990.

[6] Van Deursen A. An algebraic specification for the static semantics of Pascal. Report CS-R91, Centrum voor Wiskunde en Informatica (CWI), Amsterdam, 1991.

[7] Flynn M.J. Some Computer Organizations and Their Effectiveness. IEEE Trans. on Computers C-21, 9, 1972, pp 948–960.

[8] Hendriks P.R.H. Typechecking Mini-ML. ACM Press Frontier Series. The ACM Press in co-operation with Addison-Wesley, 1989, pp 299–337.

[9] Hillis W.D. The Connection Machine. MIT Press, 1985.

[10] Hoogvorst P., Keryell R., Matherat P., Paris N. POMP or how to design a massively parallel machine with small developments. Proc. Parallel Arch. and Arch. Europe Conf. (PARLE), Eindhoven, Lect. Notes in Comp. Science 505, Springer Verlag, 1991, pp. 83–100.

[11] MasPar Parallel Application Language Reference Manual. MasPar Computer Corporation, 1990.

[12] MasPar Programming Environment Reference Manual. MasPar Computer Corporation, 1991.

[13] Naish L. Mu-Prolog 3.2 Reference Manual. Tech. Rept. 85, University of Melbourne, 1987.

[14] Paris N. Définition de POMPC (version 1.9). Draft Version, LIENS, Paris, 1991.

[15] Plotkin G. An operational semantics for CSP. D. Bjorner (Ed.), Formal description of programming concepts, IFIP TC-2 Working Conference, Garmish-Partenkirchen, RFA, 1982.

[16] Utard G.E. Un système axiomatique pour les languages massivement parallèles SIMD. Master's Thesis, LIP, ENS Lyon, 1991.

[17] Centaur Reference Manual. Sema Group, 1990.

The Tensor Product in Wadler's Analysis of Lists

Flemming Nielson & Hanne Riis Nielson,
Dept. of Comp. Science, Aarhus University,
DK-8000 Aarhus C, Denmark.

E-mail: fnielson@daimi.aau.dk

We consider abstract interpretation (in particular strictness analysis) for pairs and lists. We begin by reviewing the well-known fact that the best known description of a pair of elements is obtained using the tensor product rather than the cartesian product. We next present a generalisation of Wadler's strictness analysis for lists using the notion of open set. Finally, we illustrate the intimate connection between the case analysis implicit in Wadler's strictness analysis and the precision that the tensor product allows for modelling the inverse cons operation.

1 Introduction

Let us begin with pairs. It is common belief that to describe a pair one must use a pair of descriptions. As an example consider a pair (true,false) and an analysis for detecting constants (see the figure). It is immediate that T is the best description of 'true' and F is the best description of 'false' so that it is natural to use (T,F) as the description of (true,false).

It is well-known (but perhaps to too few!) that in general this approach does not give the best description possible. As an example consider the pair $(\mathbf{x},\mathbf{x})$ where $\mathbf{x}$ is either 'true' or 'false' and thus is described by 1. Here the above strategy would call for using $(1,1)$. A similar description would arise for the pair $(\mathbf{x},\neg\mathbf{x})$ and if the use of the pair was to test for equality of the two booleans we will obviously not obtain precise information: it would appear that the result of the test is $(1=1)$ which clearly is 1.

The solution is immediate: we will describe $(\mathbf{x},\mathbf{x})$ by (T,T) *or* (F,F) and $(\mathbf{x},\neg\mathbf{x})$ by (T,F) *or* (F,T) — assuming of course that $\mathbf{x}$ is described by 1. Then the test will always yield T in case of $(\mathbf{x},\mathbf{x})$ and always F in case of $(\mathbf{x},\neg\mathbf{x})$.

This observation is by no means novel. It dates back (at least) to [9] that distinguished between independent attribute analyses (the first kind) and relational analyses (the second kind). The first systematic treatment was given in [11] and the highlights are also presented in [12, 13, 14]. It amounted to the following identifications:

$$\text{independent attribute method} \equiv \text{cartesian product}$$
$$\text{relational method} \equiv \text{tensor product}$$

The notion of tensor product is a very general notion from category theory [10]. One has to be specific about the category (complete lattices) and the property (additivity or distributivity) in order to home in on the concept. An early reference to tensor products of complete lattices is [2] and [11] gave a direct construction that was closer to motivating **why** the tensor product would be useful for the relational method; the construction we give in Section 2 is a cut-down version that applies to finite complete lattices only. (Hence the reader can happily forget about compact elements, consistently complete cpo's, algebraicity, ideal completions etc. for the duration of this paper.)

Let us now turn to lists. Here the difficulty is not to find a general description of lists but to find one that is useful for the analysis of lazy languages. The first remarkable success in this area was Wadler's strictness analysis for lists [17]. For lists of base types, like **Int list**, it used a four-point domain:

$$
4 = \quad
\begin{array}{ll}
\bullet\ 1\varepsilon & \text{describing all lists} \\[1em]
\bullet\ 0\varepsilon & \text{describing all lists that contain a } \bot\text{-element if finite} \\[1em]
\bullet\ 1 & \text{describing all non-finite lists} \\[1em]
\bullet\ 0 & \text{describing only the } \bot\text{-list}
\end{array}
$$

Here a list is finite if it is of the form $v_1{:}...{:}v_n{:}\text{NIL}$, and is non-finite if it is either infinite, i.e. $v_1{:}v_2{:}...$, or else partial, i.e. $v_1{:}...{:}v_n{:}\bot$.

Much work has been directed at generalizing Wadler's construction to other recursive data structures (e.g. [5]). In a sense this is not hard; however, it would seem that no one has been able to obtain a generalisation that is equally natural. (Almost all generalisations contain far too many descriptive elements and more or less ad-hoc ways have to be found to throw some of them out again.) Here we consider the more mundane task of generalising Wadler's analysis from lists of base types to arbitrary lists. One easy approach (discovered by many) is to note that Wadler's construction amounts to the double lifting of the two-point domain

$$
2 = \quad
\begin{array}{ll}
\bullet\ 1 & \text{describing all elements} \\[1em]
\bullet\ 0 & \text{describing only the } \bot\text{-element}
\end{array}
$$

used to describe the strictness properties of base types. However, this does not give the desired descriptive power when the elements of the lists have more structure. This was also observed in [5] and in Section 3 we shall see how to do better — without first introducing many more descriptive elements and next making sure that only the interesting ones **are** retained.

The success of Wadler's analysis is not only due to the use of a four-point domain but rests at least as much on the (implicit) use of case analysis when analysing function definitions. In Section 4 we then show that case analysis amounts to nothing but the use of an inverse cons operation — provided that the range of the inverse cons operation is modelled using tensor product. This amounts to a formalisation of Wadler's remark that the case analysis is performed by using the abstraction of cons "in a backward manner".

2 Tensor products for pairs

Let us consider a small *lazy* functional language with types given by[1]

$$t ::= \text{Int} \mid \text{Bool} \mid t \times t \mid t \rightarrow t \mid t \otimes t \mid t \text{ list}$$

The first step in describing an analysis by means of abstract interpretation is to describe the complete lattice $\mathbf{A}(t)$ associated with each type t. For strictness analysis it is common to model the base types using the two-point lattice $\mathbf{2}$ described above. However, to illustrate how lists of structured types are handled we shall be a bit more ambitious in some of our choices:

$$\mathbf{A}(\text{Int}) = \mathbf{2}$$
$$\mathbf{A}(\text{Bool}) = \mathbf{2}^2$$

Thus our modelling of Int is a proper strictness analysis whereas our modelling of Bool amounts to an analysis for detecting constants; however, *if only the 0 and 1 elements are retained we have a proper strictness analysis* corresponding to the use of $\mathbf{A}(\text{Bool}) = \mathbf{2}$.

For composite types our starting point will be the following definitions:

$$\mathbf{A}(t_1 \times t_2) = (\mathbf{A}(t_1) \times \mathbf{A}(t_2))_\perp$$
$$\mathbf{A}(t_1 \rightarrow t_2) = (\mathbf{A}(t_1) \rightarrow \mathbf{A}(t_2))_\perp$$

The basic idea is that a property of a pair of elements is a pair of properties (one for each component) and that a property of a function is a function that maps properties of arguments to properties of results. There is the additional twist that we use an outer lifting. This is in order to distinguish between the undefined element of a product or function space and the least "defined" element (a pair of $\perp$-properties or the function mapping any property to the $\perp$-property). The choice corresponds to the choice made in the standard semantics (see the Appendix) and is invaluable in order to model the behaviour of a lazy functional language.

Example 1 Consider the function eq : Bool $\times$ Bool $\rightarrow$ Bool that tests for equality of its two arguments. In the analysis $\mathbf{A}$ it will be natural to set

$$\mathbf{A}(\text{eq}) = up(eq \circ dn)$$

---

[1] In a realistic language one would have only one of $\times$ and $\otimes$, say $\times$. Some occurrences of $\times$ will then be interpreted as we interpret $\times$ and others as we interpret $\otimes$. The actual choice will depend on the precision wanted and the context of the occurrence.

where $eq : \mathbf{2}^2 \times \mathbf{2}^2 \to \mathbf{2}^2$ is given by

$$eq(T,T) = T, \; eq(F,F) = T, \; eq(T,F) = F, \; eq(F,T) = F, \; eq(1,1) = 1, \; \cdots$$

and where up and dn are the standard "polymorphic operators" that transform between domains D and $D_\perp$, i.e.

$$up : D \to D_\perp$$
$$dn : D_\perp \to D$$

with $dn(\perp) = \perp$ as well as $dn(up(\perp)) = \perp$; thus $dn \circ up$ is the identity, id, but $up \circ dn$ is greater than the identity because it sends $\perp$ to $up(\perp)$. $\qquad\qquad\qquad \Box$

Returning to the example of the Introduction let us consider the behaviour of a function

```
f(x) = eq(x,x)
```

upon an element $\mathbf{x}$ that can be either 'true' or 'false'. Here 1 describes $\mathbf{x}$ and using $\mathbf{A}(eq)$ as specified in Example 1 we obtain 1 as the result, even though **we** know that the result must be 'true' so that one would have hoped for T as the result of the analysis.

The crux of the problem is that

$$up((T,T)) \sqcup up((F,F)) = up((T,F)) \sqcup up((F,T))$$

and that we are therefore not able to describe the difference between the pairs $(\mathbf{x},\mathbf{x})$ and $(\mathbf{x},\neg\mathbf{x})$ where $\mathbf{x}$ is described by 1. The solution we propose is to use lifted *tensor product* rather than lifted cartesian product. This will enable us to achieve

$$up(cross(T,T)) \sqcup up(cross(F,F)) \neq up(cross(T,F)) \sqcup up(cross(F,T))$$

for a suitable function *cross*. However, to be able to compare the possibilities we shall keep the interpretation of $\mathbf{A}(t_1 \times t_2)$ and instead interpret $\mathbf{A}(t_1 \otimes t_2)$ as stated.

To conduct this development we need a few auxiliary notions. A function $f:L \to M$ is (binary) *additive* if $f(l_1 \sqcup l_2) = f(l_1) \sqcup f(l_2)$ holds for all l_1 and l_2 in L. A function $f:L \times L' \to E$ is *separately* (binary) *additive* if

$$f(l_1 \sqcup l_2, l') = f(l_1, l') \sqcup f(l_2, l'), \text{ and } f(l, l'_1 \sqcup l'_2) = f(l, l'_1) \sqcup f(l, l'_2)$$

for all choices of l_1, l_2, l, l'_1, l'_2 and l'. It is easy to show that if $f:L \times L' \to M$ is additive then it is also separately additive but the converse does not hold. The tensor product may then be regarded as a way of turning separately additive functions into additive ones. To be more precise consider complete lattices L and L'.

Definition 2 A pair $(L \otimes L', cross)$ is a tensor product of L and L' (with respect to additivity) provided that

- $L \otimes L'$ is a complete lattice,

- *cross*: $L \times L' \to L \otimes L'$ is a continuous function that is separately additive,

- for all complete lattices M and for all continuous functions $f: L \times L' \to M$ that are separately additive the following universal property holds: there exists precisely one continuous function $f^\otimes$: $L \otimes L' \to M$ that is additive and satisfies the equation $f^\otimes \circ cross = f$. □

This may all be illustrated by the following diagram:

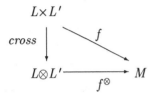

More precisely we have "defined" the tensor product (with respect to additivity) within the category **CL** of complete lattices (as objects) and continuous functions (as morphisms). We have as yet no guarantee that the tensor product always exists in **CL** or in subcategories. However, it follows from general categorical reasoning that the tensor product — if it exists — is unique up to isomorphism; this means that if $(M_1, cross_1)$ and $(M_2, cross_2)$ are both tensor products of L and L' there is an isomorphism θ from M_1 to M_2 such that $\theta \circ cross_1 = cross_2$. (Here an isomorphism θ is a bijection such that it and its inverse are both morphisms of the category in question.)

Example 3 The lower powerdomain $\mathcal{P}(D)$ of an algebraic cpo D is

$$\mathcal{P}(D) = (\{Y \subseteq B_D | Y \neq \emptyset \wedge Y = LC(Y)\}, \subseteq)$$

where B_D is the set of compact elements of D and

$$LC(Y) = \{d | \exists y \in Y : d \sqsubseteq y\}$$

is the left-closure of a subset Y. (If D is finite one has $B_D = D$.) Then

$$(\mathcal{P}(D \times D'), \lambda(Y, Y').\{(y, y') | y \in Y \wedge y' \in Y'\})$$

is a tensor product of $\mathcal{P}(D)$ and $\mathcal{P}(D')$. □

The above example shows that the tensor product always exists in the category of distributive and finite lattices and monotonic (hence continuouos) functions; this follows from [6, Section 7] that in effect shows that L is a finite and distributive lattice if and only if $L = \mathcal{P}(D)$ for a finite cpo D. A much more general result may be found in [2] but note that the notion of tensor product studied there is slightly different[2]. Here we shall be content with demonstrating the existence of the tensor product within the category **FCL** of finite complete lattices and monotonic (hence continuous) functions.

The elements of $L \otimes L'$ will be be certain subsets Y of $L \times L'$. To this end we shall say that a set Y is *left-closed* when $Y = LC(Y)$ and where $LC(Y)$ is as above. We shall say that a set Y is *closed in both components* when $Y = CC_1(Y)$ and $Y = CC_2(Y)$ and where

---

[2]It is the tensor product with respect to complete additivity. Which tensor product is the more adequate depends on the setting at hand. We believe that the tensor product studied in this paper is well suited for lazy languages whereas that of [2] is well suited for eager languages.

$$CC_1(Y) = \{(l_1 \sqcup l_2, l') \mid (l_1,l'),(l_2,l') \in Y \}$$
$$CC_2(Y) = \{(l, l_1' \sqcup l_2') \mid (l, l_1'),(l, l_2') \in Y \}$$

denote the closure in the first and second components, respectively.

Fact 4 For each subset $Y \subseteq L \times L'$ the set

$$TC(Y) = \cap \{Y' \subseteq L \times L' \mid Y \subseteq Y' \wedge Y' = LC(Y') \wedge$$
$$Y' = CC_1(Y') \wedge Y' = CC_2(Y') \}$$

is the least left-closed set that contains Y and that is closed in both components. □

Proposition 5 The following data

$$L \otimes L' = (\{Y \subseteq L \times L' \mid Y \neq \emptyset \wedge Y = LC(Y) = CC_1(Y) = CC_2(Y)\}, \subseteq)$$
$$cross = \lambda(l,l').~LC(\{(l,l')\})$$
$$f^\otimes = \lambda Y.~\sqcup\{f(l,l') \mid (l,l') \in Y\}$$

constructs a tensor product (with respect to additivity) in the category **FCL** of finite complete lattices and monotonic (hence continuous) functions. □

Proof: See [15, Chapter 7] or possibly [11] or [14]. □

We can now return to the definition of the analysis **A** where we have already hinted at the desire to use

$$\mathbf{A}(t_1 \otimes t_2) = (\mathbf{A}(t_1) \otimes \mathbf{A}(t_2))_\perp$$

Example 6 In Example 1 we considered the analysis of the function **eq**. Now consider the similar function **eq'** : Bool $\otimes$ Bool $\to$ Bool. For this it is natural to set

$$\mathbf{A}(\mathbf{eq'}) = up(\lambda a.~\sqcup\{eq(l,l') \mid (l,l') \in dn(a)\})$$

In this way $\mathbf{A}(\mathbf{eq'})$ will give F when applied to $up(cross(T, F)) \sqcup up(cross(F, T))$ and will give T when applied to $up(cross(T,T)) \sqcup up(cross(F,F))$. Thus the required precision has been obtained. □

3 Wadler-like analysis of general lists

To prepare for our analysis of lists we need some terminology. Given a partially ordered set D and a subset $Y \subseteq D$ we define the right-closure of Y, or upwards closure of Y, as

$$RC(Y) = \{ d \in D \mid \exists y \in Y: y \sqsubseteq d \}$$

(In the literature this is sometimes written $\uparrow Y$.) A subset $Y \subseteq D$ is Scott-open, or open in the Scott-topology, if and only if

- Y is right-closed, and

- for all chains $(d_n)_n$: if $\sqcup_n d_n \in Y$ then $d_n \in Y$ for some n.

Given our restriction to finite lattices the second condition is trivial and Scott-open just means right-closed throughout this paper. It is immediate that $\mathrm{RC}(Y)$ is the least right-closed set that contains Y. We now define

$$\mathcal{O}(D) = (\{\,Y \subseteq D \mid Y = \mathrm{RC}(Y) \wedge Y \neq \emptyset\,\}, \supseteq)$$

as the partially ordered set of non-empty right-closed sets.

Fact 7 If D is a finite complete lattice then $\mathcal{O}(D)$ is a finite complete lattice with least element D, greatest element $\{\top_D\}$ where $\top_D$ is the greatest element of D, and least upper bounds and greatest lower bounds given by $\cap$ and $\cup$, respectively. □

Example 8 $\mathcal{O}(\mathbf{A}(\texttt{Int}))$ has elements $\{0,1\}$ and $\{1\}$ with $\{0,1\} \sqsubseteq \{1\}$; thus $\mathcal{O}(\mathbf{A}(\texttt{Int}))$ is isomorphic to **2**.

$\mathcal{O}(\mathbf{A}(\texttt{Bool}))$ has elements $\{1\}$, $\{F,1\}$, $\{T,1\}$, $\{T,F,1\}$, and $\{0,T,F,1\}$. The partial order may be depicted as follows

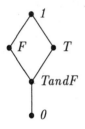

where *1* denotes $\{1\}$, *T* denotes $\{T,1\}$, *TandF* denotes $\{T,F,1\}$ etc. (Clearly it is isomorphic to $(\mathbf{2^2})_\perp$.)

Since $\mathbf{A}(\texttt{Int} \times \texttt{Int})$ is isomorphic to $\mathbf{A}(\texttt{Bool})_\perp$ it follows that $\mathcal{O}(\mathbf{A}(\texttt{Int} \times \texttt{Int}))$ is as above but with an additional least element. □

For our analysis of lists we shall then use the following generalisation of Wadler's construction:

$$\mathbf{A}(t\ \texttt{list}) = (\mathcal{O}(\mathbf{A}(t))_\perp)_\perp$$

To overcome the growing notational complexity it is helpful to write

    0   for $\perp$,
    1   for $up(\perp)$,
    $Y\varepsilon$ for $up(up(Y))$,
    $y\varepsilon$ for $\mathrm{RC}(\{y\})\varepsilon$, that is $up(up(\mathrm{RC}(\{y\})))$.

The intended meaning of these elements is as follows:

    0   describes the $\perp$-list,
    1   additionally describes all infinite lists and all partial lists,
    $\top\varepsilon$ describes all lists.

Finally, let $Y\varepsilon \in \mathbf{A}(t\ \texttt{list})$ satisfy $Y \neq \mathrm{RC}(\{\top\})$. We may write $Y = \{a_1, \cdots, a_k\}$ and we know that k>0. Then

$Y\varepsilon$ describes all infinite lists and all partial lists and some finite lists; a finite list $[v_1,\cdots,v_n] = v_1:\cdots:v_n:\text{NIL}$ is described if there are k values $j_1,\cdots,j_k$ such that the property a_i describes the element v_{j_i}.

A more precise definition of the relationship between properties of lists and concrete lists may be found in the Appendix.

Example 9 For the strictness analysis we get $\mathbf{A}(\texttt{Int list}) = 4$ as in Wadler's approach because $\mathcal{O}(\mathbf{A}(\texttt{Int}))$ is isomorphic to $\mathbf{A}(\texttt{Int})$ (cf. Example 8). A similar remark applies to lists of lists of base types etc.

The difference between Wadler's approach and ours arises when the elements have more structure as for lists of booleans. Here we get:

$\mathbf{A}(\texttt{Bool list}) =$

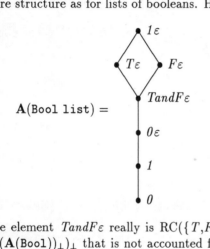

The element $TandF\varepsilon$ really is $\text{RC}(\{T,F\})\varepsilon = \{1,T,F\}\varepsilon$ and it is the only element of $(\mathcal{O}(\mathbf{A}(\texttt{Bool}))_\perp)_\perp$ that is not accounted for in $(\mathbf{A}(\texttt{Bool})_\perp)_\perp$. Thus we are able to give a more precise description of a list like [true,false] than Wadler is, because we can record that both 'true' and 'false' are present in the list.

As follows from Example 8 the analysis of $\mathbf{A}((\texttt{Int}\times\texttt{Int})\ \texttt{list})$ would be very similar except that there would be an additional element between 1 and 0ε. The list [true,false] now corresponds to the list $[up((1,\perp)),up((\perp,2))]$ which does not have an adequate description in Wadler's approach (cf. the discussion of [5] where the inadequacy of a generalisation of Wadler's approach is described). The Appendix contains a slightly more detailed discussion of these matters. □

Example 10 Returning to Example 9 the concrete lists described by these properties may be described as follows:

0 describes $\perp$,

1 additionally describes all infinite lists and all partial lists (e.g. true:false:$\perp$),

0ε additionally describes all finite lists with at least one $\perp$-element (e.g. [$\perp$]),

TandFε	additionally describes all finite lists with at least one 'true'-element and at least one 'false'-element (e.g. [true,false]),
Tε	additionally describes all finite lists with at least one 'true'-element (e.g. [true]),
Fε	additionally describes (wrt. *TandFε*) all finite lists with at least one 'false'-element (e.g. [false]),
1ε	additionally describes [].

To illustrate the benefit of using $(\mathcal{O}(\mathbf{A}(\mathtt{Bool}))_\perp)_\perp$ rather than $(\mathbf{A}(\mathtt{Bool})_\perp)_\perp$ consider the (Miranda-like) function

```
g l = isnil (filter (=true) l) ∨ isnil(filter (=false) l)
```

Here `isnil` tests for a list being `nil` and `filter (=x) l` denotes the list consisting of those elements of `l` that equal `x`. Thus

g([true,false]) = false

g([true,⊥]) = ⊥

g(false:⊥) = ⊥

g([true]) = true

g([false]) = true

If we let *g* denote the optimal analysis of g it follows that

$g(0\varepsilon) = 0$

$g(TandF\varepsilon) = F$

$g(T\varepsilon) = g(F\varepsilon) = 1$

Now consider the list [true,false]. It is described by all of *Tε*, *Fε* and *TandFε* but not by *0ε*; hence *TandFε* is the optimal description of [true,false]. Thus the inclusion of *TandFε* allows the analysis of g([true,false]) to give a better result than if *TandFε* had not been included.

An analogous example can be constructed for the type (Int×Int) list. □

4   Tensor products and case analysis for lists

So far we have not shown how to interpret the functions associated with the tensor product, nor the notion of case analysis implicit in Wadler's analysis. This is all rectified in this section where the connection is also demonstrated. When doing so we shall introduce the required language primitives as the need arises; we do not have the space to give a full interpretation, nor do we have the space to explain the intricacies of the fixed point operator.

Example 11 Turning to operations on lists of integers we recall the strictness properties *0*, *1*, *0ε* and *1ε* and consider the functions hd that takes the head of a list, length that computes the lenght of a list and sum that adds a list of integers. The *optimal analysis* of these functions are $up(hd)$, $up(length)$ and $up(sum)$ where hd, $length$ and sum are given by

	0	1	0ε	1ε
hd	0	1	1	1
$length$	0	0	1	1
sum	0	0	0	1

We shall regard hd as a primitive of the functional language whereas length and sum will be programs; as we shall see it will cost some effort to obtain a compositional and optimal analysis **A** of length and sum. □

To account for Wadler's notion of case-analysis we shall assume that there is a case construct. Informally, the meaning of $case(e_1,e_2)$ should be "equivalent" to[3] cond(isnil, e_1, e_2∘tuple(hd,tl)) where cond is the familiar conditional, isnil is the test for whether a list is empty or not, hd and tl are the selection functions for lists and $tuple(e_1,e_2)$ is intended to map v to $(e_1(v),e_2(v))$. By incorporating case as a language primitive we will be able to specify the strictness properties of case freely.

Example 12 Using the case construct we may define the following version of the length and sum programs:

```
length₁ : Int list → Int
length₁ = fix(λf. case(zero, add∘tuple(one, f∘snd)))

sum₁ : Int list → Int
sum₁ = fix(λf. case(zero, add∘tuple(fst, f∘snd)))
```

We shall return to their analysis, when we have defined the analysis **A**. □

Most of the definitions needed are rather straightforward:

$\mathbf{A}(\text{zero}) = up(\lambda a.\ 1)$

$\mathbf{A}(\text{one}) = up(\lambda a.\ 1)$

$\mathbf{A}(\text{add}) = up(\lambda a.\ a_1 \sqcap a_2$ where $(a_1,a_2)=dn(a))$

$\mathbf{A}(\text{tuple}) = strict(\lambda h_1.\ strict(\lambda h_2.\ up(\lambda a.$
$\qquad up((dn(h_1)(a),dn(h_2)(a))))))$

$\mathbf{A}(\text{fst}) = up(\lambda a.\ a_1$ where $(a_1,a_2) = dn(a))$

$\mathbf{A}(\text{snd}) = up(\lambda a.\ a_2$ where $(a_1,a_2) = dn(a))$

$\mathbf{A}(\text{cons}) = strict(\lambda h_1.\ strict(\lambda h_2.\ up(\lambda a.$
$\qquad \begin{cases} 1 & \text{if } dn(h_2)(a)\sqsubseteq 1 \\ Y\varepsilon \sqcap (dn(h_1)(a))\varepsilon & \text{if } dn(h_2)(a)=Y\varepsilon \end{cases})))$

$\mathbf{A}(\text{nil}) = up(\lambda a.\ \top\varepsilon)$

---

[3]They will be equivalent in the semantics **S** of the Appendix but the whole point is that they will not be equivalent in the analysis **A**.

$$\mathbf{A(hd)} = up(\lambda a. \begin{cases} \bot & \text{if } a=0 \\ \top & \text{if } a \sqsupseteq 1 \end{cases})$$

$$\mathbf{A(tl)} = up(\lambda a. \begin{cases} 0 & \text{if } a=0 \\ 1 & \text{if } a=1 \\ \top \epsilon & \text{if } a=Y\epsilon \end{cases})$$

$$\mathbf{A(isnil)} = up(\lambda a. \begin{cases} 0 & \text{if } a=0 \\ F & \text{if } a \neq 0 \wedge a \neq \top \epsilon \\ 1 & \text{if } a=\top \epsilon \end{cases})$$

$$\mathbf{A(fix)} = \mathrm{FIX}' \text{ where } \mathrm{FIX}' = \lambda H. \bigsqcup_{n \geq 1} H^n(up(\bot))$$

Here we have used the notation

$$strict(H) = \lambda h. \begin{cases} H\,h & \text{if } h \neq \bot \\ \bot & \text{otherwise} \end{cases}$$

Note that if $\mathbf{A(Bool)} = \mathbf{2}$ was used instead of $\mathbf{A(Bool)} = \mathbf{2^2}$ then we would have to let $\mathbf{A(isnil)}$ return 1 rather than F and thus loose precision. The more interesting construct is case:

$$\mathbf{A(case)} = strict(\lambda h_1.\ strict(\lambda h_2.\ up(\lambda a.$$
$$\begin{cases} \bot_{A(t_1)} & \text{if } a=0 \\ dn(h_2)(up((\top_{A(t_0)},1))) & \text{if } a=1 \\ \bigsqcup \{ dn(h_2)(up((\sqcap Y', (Y \ominus Y')\epsilon))) \mid Y' \subseteq Y \} & \text{if } a=Y\epsilon \neq \top \epsilon \\ dn(h_2)(up((\top_{A(t_0)}, \top \epsilon))) \sqcup dn(h_1)(\top \epsilon) & \text{if } a=\top \epsilon \end{cases})))$$

where we have used the notation

$$Y \ominus Y' = \mathrm{RC}(Y \backslash \mathrm{RC}(Y')) \cup \{\top\}$$

The two first and the last clause should be fairly straightforward. In the third clause Y' is the set of possible descriptions of the first element of the list and then $Y \ominus Y'$ will be the corresponding description of the tail of the list. All choices of $Y' \subseteq Y$ are possible so we join the results. The correctness of this definition is demonstrated in the Appendix.

Example 13 In the case of lists of base types the above definition of $\mathbf{A(case)}$ amounts to the following:

$$\mathbf{A(case)} = strict(\lambda h_1.\ strict(\lambda h_2.\ up(\lambda a.$$
$$\begin{cases} 0 & \text{if } a=0 \\ dn(h_2)(up((1,1))) & \text{if } a=1 \\ dn(h_2)(up((1,0\epsilon))) \sqcup dn(h_2)(up((0,1\epsilon))) & \text{if } a=0\epsilon \\ dn(h_2)(up((1,1\epsilon))) \sqcup dn(h_1)(1\epsilon) & \text{if } a=1\epsilon \end{cases})))$$

We shall explain the definition in the case where $a=0\epsilon$. Here we use that $a=0\epsilon$ really stands for $a=Y\epsilon$ with $Y=\{0,1\}$. The subsets Y' of Y are $\emptyset$, $\{0\}$, $\{1\}$ and $\{0,1\}$ but we only need to consider $\{1\}$ and $\{0,1\}$. Since

$$\sqcap \{0,1\} = 0 \text{ and } \{0,1\} \ominus \{0,1\} = \{1\}$$
$$\sqcap \{1\} = 1 \text{ and } \{0,1\} \ominus \{1\} = \{0,1\}$$

this gives the contribution

$$dn(h_2)(up((1,0\varepsilon))) \sqcup dn(h_2)(up((0,1\varepsilon)))$$

as stated. Thus our general definition of **A**(case) specializes to Wadler's notion of case analysis for lists of base types. □

Example 14 As we have already said hd is a primitive and thus there is no need to analyse it here. We may now perform the following analysis of length:

$$[\![length_1]\!](\mathbf{A}) = up(\lambda a.\text{case } a \text{ of}$$
$$\quad 0: 0$$
$$\quad 1: 0$$
$$\quad 0\varepsilon: 1$$
$$\quad 1\varepsilon: 1)$$

Thus $dn([\![length_1]\!](\mathbf{A}))$ equals the optimal result of Example 11. Turning to sum we may perform the following analysis:

$$[\![sum_1]\!](\mathbf{A}) = up(\lambda a.\text{case } a \text{ of}$$
$$\quad 0: 0$$
$$\quad 1: 0$$
$$\quad 0\varepsilon: 0$$
$$\quad 1\varepsilon: 1)$$

Thus also $dn([\![sum_1]\!](\mathbf{A}))$ equals the optimal result of Example 11. □

We shall now see how to obtain a similar effect by using the tensor product and then dispensing with the **case** construct. We begin by considering the operators tuple′, fst′ and snd′ associated with (tensor) products:

$$\mathbf{A}(\text{tuple}') \in \mathbf{A}(t_0 \rightarrow t_1) \rightarrow \mathbf{A}(t_0 \rightarrow t_2) \rightarrow \mathbf{A}(t_0 \rightarrow t_1 \otimes t_2)$$
$$\mathbf{A}(\text{tuple}') = strict(\lambda h_1. \ strict(\lambda h_2. \ up(\lambda a.$$
$$\quad up(cross(dn(h_1)(a), \ dn(h_2)(a))))))$$
$$\mathbf{A}(\text{fst}') \in \mathbf{A}(t_1 \otimes t_2 \rightarrow t_1)$$
$$\mathbf{A}(\text{fst}') = up(\lambda a. \ \bigsqcup\{l|(l,l') \in dn(a)\})$$
$$\mathbf{A}(\text{snd}') \in \mathbf{A}(t_1 \otimes t_2 \rightarrow t_2)$$
$$\mathbf{A}(\text{snd}') = up(\lambda a. \ \bigsqcup\{l'|(l,l') \in dn(a)\})$$

Furthermore,

$$\mathbf{A}(\text{add}') \in \mathbf{A}(\text{Int} \otimes \text{Int} \rightarrow \text{Int})$$
$$\mathbf{A}(\text{add}') = up(\lambda a. \ \bigsqcup\{ a_1 \sqcap a_2 \mid (a_1, a_2) \in dn(a) \})$$

However, the weak point is that tuple′ is the only operator that constructs an element of the tensor product and that this element is of the form $cross(\cdots, \cdots)$ and so does not exploit the additional precision of the tensor product. This can be rectified by letting the interpretation of tuple′ consider the atoms or the irreducible elements of the argument a (or $dn(a)$); references to approaches following these ideas may be found in the

Conclusion. Here we shall take a shortcut and introduce special operators for exploiting the tensor product. One is split which is the inverse cons operation and it is supposed to be "equivalent" to tuple'(hd,tl). The other is pair(e_1, e_2) that is supposed to be "equivalent" to tuple'(e_1∘fst', e_2∘snd'). For the analysis we then have

$A(\texttt{split}) \in A(t \; \texttt{list} \rightarrow t \otimes (t \; \texttt{list}))$
$A(\texttt{split}) = up(\lambda a. \; up($
$$\begin{cases} cross(\bot,0) & \text{if } a{=}0 \\ cross(\top,1) & \text{if } a{=}1 \\ \bigsqcup\{cross(\sqcap Y', (Y \ominus Y')\varepsilon) \mid Y' \subseteq Y\} & \text{if } a{=}Y\varepsilon \neq \top\varepsilon \\ cross(\top,\top\varepsilon) & \text{if } a{=}\top\varepsilon \end{cases}))$$

$A(\texttt{pair}) \in A(t_1 \rightarrow t_3) \rightarrow A(t_2 \rightarrow t_4) \rightarrow A(t_1 \otimes t_2 \rightarrow t_3 \otimes t_4)$
$A(\texttt{pair}) = strict(\lambda h_1. \; strict(\lambda h_2. \; up(\lambda a.$
$$up(\bigsqcup\{cross(dn(h_1)(l), \; dn(h_2)(l')) \mid (l,l') \in dn(a)\}))))$$

Note the similarities between the definition of $A(\texttt{split})$ and that of $A(\texttt{case})$.

Example 15 In the case of lists of base types the above definition of $A'(\texttt{split})$ amounts to the following:

$$A'(\texttt{split}) = up(\lambda a. up(\begin{cases} cross(0,0) & \text{if } a{=}0 \\ cross(1,1) & \text{if } a{=}1 \\ cross(0,1\varepsilon) \sqcup cross(1,0\varepsilon) & \text{if } a{=}0\varepsilon \\ cross(1,1\varepsilon) & \text{if } a{=}1\varepsilon \end{cases}))$$

Naturally this has many similarities to the simplification of $A(\texttt{case})$ obtained in Example 13. □

We also need

$A(\texttt{cond}) \in A(t_0 \rightarrow \texttt{Bool}) \rightarrow A(t_0 \rightarrow t_1) \rightarrow A(t_0 \rightarrow t_1) \rightarrow A(t_0 \rightarrow t_1)$
$A(\texttt{cond}) = strict(\lambda h_1. \; strict(\lambda h_2. \; strict(\lambda h_3. \; up(\lambda a.$
$$\begin{cases} \bot & \text{if } dn(h_1)(a){=}0 \\ dn(h_2)(a) & \text{if } dn(h_1)(a){=}\top \\ dn(h_3)(a) & \text{if } dn(h_1)(a){=}F \\ dn(h_2)(a) \sqcup dn(h_3)(a) & \text{if } dn(h_1)(a){=}1 \end{cases})))) $$

Example 16 Using split and sum we may now consider the following definitions of length and sum:

```
length₂ : Int list → Int
length₂ = fix(λf. cond(isnil, zero, add'∘pair(one,f)∘split))

sum₂ : Int list → Int
sum₂ = fix(λf. cond(isnil, zero, add'∘pair(id,f)∘split))
```

Again there is no need to redefine hd and thus no need to analyse it. We may then perform the following analysis of length:

$$[\![\texttt{length}_2]\!](\mathbf{A}) = up(\lambda a.\text{case } a \text{ of}$$
$$\quad 0:\ 0$$
$$\quad 1:\ 0$$
$$\quad 0\varepsilon:\ 1$$
$$\quad 1\varepsilon:\ 1\,)$$

Thus $dn([\![\texttt{length}_2]\!](\mathbf{A}))$ equals the optimal result of Example 11. This is not due to the use of tensor product but more to the use of $\mathbf{A}(\texttt{Bool}) = \mathbf{2}^2$ instead of $\mathbf{A}(\texttt{Bool}) = \mathbf{2}$ (cf. the definition of $\mathbf{A}(\texttt{isnil})$ given earlier).

Turning to $\textsf{sum}$ we may perform the following analysis:

$$[\![\texttt{sum}_2]\!](\mathbf{A}) = up(\lambda a.\text{case } a \text{ of}$$
$$\quad 0:\ 0$$
$$\quad 1:\ 0$$
$$\quad 0\varepsilon:\ 0$$
$$\quad 1\varepsilon:\ 1\,)$$

Thus also $dn([\![\texttt{sum}_2]\!](\mathbf{A}))$ equals the optimal result of Example 11. This is in contrast to what would happen if cartesian product was used instead of tensor product. $\square$

5 Conclusion

Judging from the development of the previous section we can obtain optimal results for key functions using either $\textsf{case}$-analysis or the tensor product. Admittedly our treatment had a few special operators but these may be dispensed with at the price of a more complex theory: [11] contains formulations for a general $\textsf{tuple}'$-construct where the *join-irreducible elements* are used for case analysis. A similar development but using *atoms* is contained in [12]. This all relates to the study of so-called *expected forms* [11, 14].

One should take care, however, to note that there is a certain "duality" in the sets considered. For lists we are using right-closed sets whereas for tensor products we are using left-closed sets (that are additionally closed in each component). The use of left-closed sets is rather natural for abstract interpretation as is evidenced by the central role the lower powerdomain plays in many formulations of abstract interpretation. The use of right-closed sets for lists seems to be necessary to capture the essence of Wadler's insight: the ability to describe long finite lists that may have arbitrary elements except that one of these has to be $\bot$. In the terminology of [1] one might say that the Wadler-like analysis of lists necessitates a formulation of liveness aspects in addition to the safety aspects.

We should like to investigate the relationship between our use of open sets and the use of least Moore families in [4] for extending abstraction lattices with additional elements. It is important to note that (unlike [5]) our construction specialises to that of [17] in the case where the abstraction lattice for the element type is a chain. One may view our use of $\mathbf{A}(t\ \texttt{list}) = ((\mathcal{O}(\mathbf{A}(t)))_\bot)_\bot$ as opposed to $\mathbf{A}(t\ \texttt{list}) = ((\mathbf{A}(t))_\bot)_\bot$ as a way of introducing the required 'meets'.

A final note concerns the exclusion of the empty set in the definition of $\mathcal{O}(\cdots)$. We believe that a more "uniform" development would result if the empty set was admitted; in particular the correctness predicate *val* of the Appendix could then be defined in a more "natural" way on the top-element. However, for lists of base types we would then get a five-point domain rather than Wadler's four-point domain.

Acknowledgement

The Semantique meeting at Barra gave the impetus for writing this paper. The present research is part of The DART-Project which is funded by The Danish Research Councils.

References

[1] S.Abramsky: Abstract Interpretation, Logical Relations and Kan Extensions, *Journal of Logic and Computation* **1** *1* (1990), 5–40.

[2] H.-J.Bandelt: The tensorproduct of continuous lattices, *Mathematische Zeitschrift* **172** (1980) 89–96.

[3] G.L.Burn, C.Hankin, S.Abramsky: Strictness analysis for higher-order functions, *Science of Computer Programming* **7** (1986) 249–278.

[4] P.Cousot, R.Cousot: Systematic Design of Program Analysis Frameworks, *Procedings POPL 1979.*

[5] A.B.Ferguson, R.J.M.Hughes: An Iterative Powerdomain Construction, *Functional Programming, Glasgow 1989*, K.Davis and J.Hughes (eds.), Springer-Verlag (1989) 41–55.

[6] G.Grätzer: *Lattice Theory: First concepts and distributive lattices*, W.H.Freeman and Company (1971).

[7] J.Hughes: Strictness detection in non-flat domains, *Proc. Programs as Data Objects*, Springer Lecture Notes in Computer Science **217** (1986) 112–135.

[8] J.Hughes: Backwards Analysis of Functional Programs, *Partial Evaluation and Mixed Computation*, D.Bjørner, A.P.Ershov and N.D.Jones (eds.), North-Holland (1988) 187–208.

[9] N.D.Jones, S.S.Muchnick: Complexity of flow analysis, inductive assertion synthesis and a language due to Dijkstra, *Program Flow Analysis: Theory and Applications*, S.S.Muchnick and N.D.Jones (eds.), Prentice-Hall (1981).

[10] S. Mac Lane: *Categories for the Working Mathematician*, Springer-Verlag (1971).

[11] F.Nielson: Abstract Interpretation using Domain Theory, *Ph.D.-thesis CST-31-84, University of Edinburgh, Scotland* (1984).

[12] F.Nielson: Tensor Products Generalize the Relational Data Flow Analysis Method, *Proceedings of the 4'th Hungarian Computer Science Conference* (1985) 211–225.

[13] F.Nielson: Towards a Denotational Theory of Abstract Intepretation, *Abstract Interpretation of Declarative Languages*, S.Abramsky and C.Hankin (eds.), Ellis Horwood (1987) 219–245.

[14] F.Nielson: Two-Level Semantics and Abstract Interpretation, *Theoretical Computer Science — Fundamental Studies* **69** *2* (1989) 117–242.

[15] F.Nielson, H.R.Nielson: *Two-Level Functional Languages*, Cambridge University Press (to appear 1992).

[16] G.D.Plotkin: Lambda definability in the full type hierarchy, *To H.B.Curry: Essays on Combinatorial Logic, Lambda Calculus and Formalism*, Academic Press (1980).

[17] P.Wadler: Strictness analysis on non-flat domains (by abstract interpretation over finite domains), *Abstract Interpretation of Declarative Languages*, S.Abramsky and C.Hankin (eds.), Ellis Horwood (1987) 266–275.

[18] P.Wadler, R.J.M.Hughes: Projections for Strictness Analysis, *Proceedings Functional Programming Languages and Computer Architecture*, Springer Lecture Notes in Computer Science **274** (1987), 385–407.

Appendix: Correctness

So far we have only given informal explanations of the intended meaning of the (strictness) properties in $\mathbf{A}(t)$. Since the definition of the analysis presupposes a clear understanding of these meanings we shall begin by explaining some facets of the semantics, $\mathbf{S}$, and then define a safety predicate val_t.

The semantics of types, $\mathbf{S}(t)$, is given by the following definitions where $\mathbf{T}$ is the flat cpo of truth values ('true', 'false' and $\bot$) and $\mathbf{Z}$ is the flat cpo of integers $(\cdots,-1,0,1,\cdots$ and $\bot)$:

$$\mathbf{S}(\texttt{Int}) = \mathbf{Z},\ \mathbf{S}(\texttt{Bool}) = \mathbf{T},\ \mathbf{S}(t_1{\times}t_2) = (\mathbf{S}(t_1){\times}\mathbf{S}(t_2))_\bot,$$

$$\mathbf{S}(t_1{\to}t_2) = (\mathbf{S}(t_1){\to}\mathbf{S}(t_2))_\bot,\ \mathbf{S}(t_1{\otimes}t_2) = \mathbf{S}(t_1{\times}t_2),\ \mathbf{S}(t_0\ \texttt{list}) = \mathbf{S}(t_0)^\infty$$

Here we note that the lifting used for product allows to distinguish between the completely undefined value $(\bot)$ of a product type and the value being a pair of undefined values $(up((\bot,\bot)))$. Similarly for functions we distinguish between the undefined function $(\bot)$ and the function $(up(\lambda v.\bot))$ that always yields an undefined result when applied.

To explain the semantics of lists consider a partially ordered set $(D,\sqsubseteq)$ and how to define the partially ordered set $(D^\infty,\sqsubseteq)$ of *potentially infinite lists*. Let us say that a set of positive integers is *convex* if it equals $\{1,2,\cdots\}$ or if it equals $\{1,2,\cdots,n\}$ for some $n{\geq}0$; we shall say that the set has supremum n exactly when it equals $\{1,2,\cdots,n\}$. Assuming that $\star$ is an element not in D we define

$$D^\infty = \{\ l{:}K{\to}D{\cup}\{\star\}\ |\ (K \text{ is a } \textit{convex} \text{ set of positive integers})\ \wedge$$
$$(\forall n{\in}K{:}\ l(n){=}\star \Rightarrow n \text{ is the supremum of } K)\ \}$$

We shall feel free to write $\text{dom}(l) = K$ when $l{:}K{\to}D{\cup}\{\star\}$ and we define $\text{dom}^\star(l) = \{i{\in}\text{dom}(l)|l(i) \neq \star\}$. Next define

$$l{\sqsubseteq}l' \text{ if and only if } (\ (\text{dom}(l){\subseteq}\text{dom}(l')) \wedge (\forall n{\in}\text{dom}(l){:}\ l(n){\sqsubseteq}l'(n))\ )$$

where $l(n) \sqsubseteq l'(n)$ implies that if one of $l(n)$ or $l'(n)$ is $\star$ then so is the other. — To allow for a more convenient notation for the elements of D^∞ we shall write the least element of D^∞ as $\bot$ and allow the usual notation involving ':', i.e. infix `cons`, for constructing elements.

Turning now to the issue of correctness we shall define a safety relation

$$val_t : \mathbf{S}(t) \times \mathbf{A}(t) \to \{\text{true,false}\}$$

by structural induction over types t. This technique is commonly called *logical relations* [16] although the use of tensor product gives a twist:

$$val_{\text{Int}}(v,a) \equiv (a{=}0 \Rightarrow v{=}\bot)$$

$$val_{\text{Bool}}(v,a) \equiv (a{=}0 \Rightarrow v{=}\bot) \wedge (a{=}T \Rightarrow v \sqsubseteq \text{true}) \wedge (a{=}F \Rightarrow v \sqsubseteq \text{false})$$

$$\begin{aligned} val_{t_1 \times t_2}(v,a) \equiv\ & (a{=}\bot \Rightarrow v{=}\bot) \wedge \\ & val_{t_1}(v_1,a_1) \wedge val_{t_2}(v_2,a_2) \\ & \text{where } (v_1,v_2) = dn(v) \\ & \text{and } (a_1,a_2) = dn(a) \end{aligned}$$

$$\begin{aligned} val_{t_1 \to t_2}(f,h) \equiv\ & (h{=}\bot \Rightarrow f{=}\bot) \wedge \\ & \forall v{\in}\mathbf{S}(t_1)\colon \forall a{\in}\mathbf{A}(t_1)\colon \\ & \quad val_{t_1}(v,a) \Rightarrow val_{t_2}(dn(f)(v),dn(h)(a)) \end{aligned}$$

$$\begin{aligned} val_{t_1 \otimes t_2}(v,a) \equiv\ & (a{=}\bot \Rightarrow v{=}\bot) \wedge \\ & (\exists (a_1,a_2){\in}dn(a)\colon val_{t_1}(v_1,a_1) \wedge val_{t_2}(v_2,a_2) \\ & \text{where } (v_1,v_2) = dn(v)) \end{aligned}$$

$$\begin{aligned} val_{t\ \text{list}}(vl,al) \equiv\ & (al{=}0 \Rightarrow vl{=}\bot) \wedge \\ & (al{=}1 \Rightarrow \forall i{\in}\text{dom}(vl)\colon vl(i){\neq}\star) \wedge \\ & (al{\notin}\{0,1,T\varepsilon\} \wedge (\exists i{\in}\text{dom}(vl)\colon vl(i){=}\star) \\ & \Rightarrow \forall a{\in}dn(dn(al))\colon \exists i{\in}\text{dom}^*(vl)\colon val_t(vl(i),a)) \end{aligned}$$

The cases of base types, product types and function types should be rather straightforward. In the case of tensor product we use an existential quantifier to reflect that an element of the tensor product is a set of possible properties where only one of them needs to hold. The clause for lists formalises the meaning of properties of the form $al{=}Y\varepsilon$. It is here important to realise that for each property a of Y there must be some element of the concrete lists that enjoys that property. In the case where the type t of the elements has $\mathbf{A}(t)$ to be a chain (as for t one of `Int`, `Int list` etc.) this is equivalent to Wadler's requirement that the 'meet' of all the elements in the concrete list must be described by a. As was also observed in [5] this does not make sense in general, hence our use of a universal quantifier.

The safety predicate val_t enjoys a number of properties that are indicative of what one would expect to hold for an arbitrary analysis. (Just think of $val_t(v,a)$ as a shorthand for $\beta_t(v) \sqsubseteq a$ for a sufficiently well-behaved function β_t, i.e. one that is strict and continuous and maps compact elements to compact elements[4].)

---

[4]**Note on terminology:** Our β_t corresponds to *abs* of [3]; in an analogous way the α and γ of [11, 14] correspond to *Abs* and *Conc*, respectively, of [3]. (The use of α and γ is motivated by the notation in the original papers on abstract interpretation, e.g. [4].)

Lemma 17 The above clauses define an admissible (or inductive) predicate

$$val_t : S(t) \times A(t) \to \{true, false\}$$

that enjoys the following properties:

$\forall a \in A(t)$: $val_t(\perp_{S(t)}, a)$

$\forall v \in S(t)$: $val_t(v, \top_{A(t)})$

$\forall v \in S(t)$: $\forall a_1, a_2 \in A(t)$: $val_t(v, a_1) \wedge a_1 \sqsubseteq a_2 \Rightarrow val_t(v, a_2)$

$\forall v \in S(t)$: $\forall a_1, a_2 \in A(t)$: $val_t(v, a_1) \wedge val_t(v, a_2) \Rightarrow val_t(v, a_1 \sqcap a_2)$

$\forall v_1, v_2 \in S(t)$: $\forall a \in A(t)$: $v_1 \sqsubseteq v_2 \wedge val_t(v_2, a) \Rightarrow val_t(v_1, a)$ $\qquad \square$

The safety predicate val_t also enjoys another property that only holds because we were careful to use lifting when interpreting $\times$ and $\to$. It is a key result for the analysis **A** to be useful for optimizations based on strictness analysis. (In terms of the function β_t mentioned above just suppose that it reflects $\perp$, i.e. $\beta_t(v) = \perp \Rightarrow v = \perp$.)

Lemma 18 $\forall v \in S(t)$: $val_t(v, \perp_{A(t)}) \Rightarrow v = \perp$ $\qquad \square$

The correctness of the analysis **A** with respect to the standard semantics **S**, in the sense of the *val* predicate, is demonstrated in [15, Chapter 7]. One of the more interesting ingredients in this proof is the correctness of **A**(case).

Lemma 19 (Correctness of **A**(case)) Whenever

$$val_{t_0 list \to t_1}(f_1, h_1)$$

$$val_{(t_0 \times (t_0 list)) \to t_1}(f_2, h_2)$$

we also have

$$val_{(t_0 list) \to t_1}(S(\text{case}) \, f_1 \, f_2, \, A(\text{case}) \, h_1 \, h_2)$$

(for an 'obvious' definition of **S**(case)). $\qquad \square$

Proof: For the proof we shall assume that

$$val_{t_0 list \to t_1}(f_1, h_1)$$

$$val_{(t_0 \times (t_0 list)) \to t_1}(f_2, h_2)$$

$$val_{t_0 list}(v, a)$$

and that none of f_1, f_2, h_1 or h_2 equals $\perp$. The definition of **A**(case)$(h_1)(h_2)$ applied to a then amounts to a case analysis upon the strictness property a.

If $a = 0$ we know that the list v is $\perp$ so that $S(\text{case})(f_1)(f_2)$ applied to v gives $\perp_{S(t_1)}$. It is therefore natural to use the strictness property $\perp_{A(t_1)}$.

If $a = 1$ we know that the list v is infinite or partial. Hence any element v' of $S(t_0)$ may be the head of v (unless v is $\perp$) and the tail v'' of v will still be infinite or partial. Hence $\top_{A(t_0)}$ aptly describes v' and 1 aptly describes v'' so that

$$dn(h_2)(up((\top_{A(t_0)}, 1)))$$

aptly describes $dn(f_2)(up((v',v'')))$ as well as $\perp_{S(t_1)}$ (in case v is $\perp$).

If $a=\top\varepsilon$ we know nothing about the list v; it may be the empty list $[\,]$, its head v' may be any element of $\mathbf{S}(t_0)$ and its tail v'' may be any list of $\mathbf{S}(t_0 \text{ list})$. Thus

$$dn(h_1)(\top\varepsilon)$$

aptly describes $dn(f_1)([\,])$ and

$$dn(h_2)(up((\top,\top\varepsilon)))$$

aptly describes $dn(f_2)(up((v',v'')))$ as well as $\perp_{S(t_1)}$. By using the least upper bound we obtain a strictness property that aptly describes both possibilities.

Finally consider the case where $a=Y\varepsilon$ and $Y\varepsilon \neq \top\varepsilon$; we then know that the list v cannot be $[\,]$. It therefore might be natural to use the strictness property

$$dn(h_2)(up((\top,\top\varepsilon)))$$

since indeed the head v' of the list v may be any element of $\mathbf{S}(t_0)$. However, the snag is that the tail v'' cannot necessarily be any list of $\mathbf{S}(t_0 \text{ list})$ because there are certain constraints from Y that may still have to be satisfied. Thus while $dn(h_2)(up((\top,\top\varepsilon)))$ would not be incorrect we shall be able to do better.

Consider the situation where v is a finite list; since v is not $\perp$ it will be of the form $v=v':v''$. We then have a mapping

$$\jmath : Y \rightarrow \text{dom}^*(v)$$

such that $val_{t_0}(v(\jmath(a)),a)$ holds for all $a\in Y$. We now have a number of possibilities concerning

$$Y' = \{a\in Y\,|\,\jmath(a)=1\}$$

For each of these we shall argue that

$$\forall a\in Y': \; val_{t_0}(v',a)$$
$$val_{t_0\text{list}}(v'',(Y\ominus Y')\varepsilon)$$

The first of these is immediate and gives

$$val_{t_0}(v',\sqcap Y')$$

using Lemma 17 where we set $\sqcap\emptyset=\top$. The second of these is immediate if $Y\ominus Y' = \{\top\}$; so assume that $Y\ominus Y'\neq\{\top\}$ and note that $\text{RC}(Y')$ then is a proper subset of Y. For each $a\in Y\backslash\text{RC}(Y')$ we have $a\notin Y'$ and hence $\jmath(a)\neq 1$. Thus

$$\jmath'(a) = \jmath(a)\text{-}1$$

defines a mapping

$$\jmath' : (Y\backslash\text{RC}(Y')) \rightarrow \text{dom}^*(v'')$$

such that $val_{t_0}(v''(\jmath'(a)),a)$ holds for all $a\in Y\backslash\text{RC}(Y')$. This mapping may be extended (in at least one way) to a mapping

$$j'' : \ Y \ominus Y' \rightarrow \text{dom}^*(v'')$$

such that $val_{t_0}(v''(j''(a)),a)$ holds for all $a \in Y \ominus Y'$.

Returning to each choice of $Y' \subseteq Y$ we now have a contribution

$$dn(h_2)(up((\sqcap Y',(Y \ominus Y')\varepsilon)))$$

and by taking the least upper bound of all of these we aptly describe all possibilities. Actually we may assume that Y' is nonempty, or $Y' \ni \top$, as $\sqcap \emptyset = \sqcap \{\top\}$ and $Y \ominus \emptyset = Y \ominus \{\top\}$, and therefore no contributions will be missed. Furthermore one may assume that Y' is right-closed as $\sqcap Y' = \sqcap RC(Y')$ and $Y \ominus Y' = Y \ominus RC(Y')$, and therefore no contributions will be missed. In summary we only need to consider those $Y' \in \mathcal{O}(\mathbf{A}(t_0))$ such that $Y' \subseteq Y$. $\qquad\qquad$ □

Basic Superposition is Complete

Robert Nieuwenhuis and Albert Rubio

Universidad Politécnica de Cataluña
Dept. Lenguajes y Sistemas Informáticos
Pau Gargallo 5, E-08028 Barcelona, Spain
E-mail: roberto@lsi.upc.es rubio@lsi.upc.es

Abstract: We define *equality constrained* equations and clauses and use them to prove the completeness of what we have called *basic* superposition: a restricted form of superposition in which only the subterms *not* created in previous inferences is superposed upon. We first apply our results to the equational case and define an unfailing Knuth-Bendix completion procedure that uses basic superposition as inference rule. Second, we extend the techniques to completion of full first-order clauses with equality. Moreover, we prove the refutational completeness of a new simple inference system.

1. Introduction

Reasoning about equality has many applications in computer science, including automated theorem proving, logic and equational programming, symbolic algebraic computation, and program specification and verification. Knuth-Bendix-like completion techniques [KB 70, Rus 87, HR 89, BDP 89, BG 91, NO 91] are one of the most successful approaches for dealing with equality. Completion procedures can be seen as refutationally complete processes that moreover transform sets of axioms in such a way that, by using the final *complete* set, efficient *normal form* proof strategies become complete (e.g. *rewrite* proofs or *linear* proofs). Completion is normally based on a form of paramodulation with strong ordering restrictions, called *superposition*.

In this paper we develop a notion of *equality constraints* and use it to prove the completeness of *basic* superposition. This result has important consequences for Knuth-Bendix completion of equations and other first-order clauses with equality, and has been searched for since the completeness of *basic narrowing* was proved in [Hul 80]. Roughly speaking, the inference rule of basic superposition is the restriction of normal superposition in which the only inferences that have to be computed are the ones at subterms that have *not* been created in previous inference steps. Consider for example the inference by (equational) superposition

$$\frac{f(g(a)) \simeq a \qquad h(f(x)) \simeq h(x)}{h(a) \simeq h(g(a))}$$

obtained by unifying in $h(f(x))$ the subterm $f(x)$ with $f(g(a))$. Its conclusion is an instance with the unifier $\{x \mapsto g(a)\}$ of the equation $h(a) \simeq h(x)$. Therefore, no further *basic* superposition steps have to be applied to subterms of $g(a)$ in this conclusion, whereas in normal superposition *all* subterms of $h(g(a))$ must be considered.

In this paper we will describe such situations by means of *equations with equality constraints*. In the example above the conclusion would be $h(a) \simeq h(x) [\![x = g(a)]\!]$, i.e. the instantiations caused by inference steps are kept in the constraints. Normal superposition can then be used for the non-variable subterms of the equation part (in the example, $h(a) \simeq h(x)$). The inference rule of (here for simplicity equational) basic superposition can then be expressed as

$$\frac{s \simeq s' [\![T']\!] \qquad t \simeq t' [\![T]\!]}{t[s']_u \simeq t' [\![T \wedge T' \wedge t|_u = s]\!]} \quad \text{where } t|_u \notin \mathcal{V}ars(t)$$

if moreover the usual ordering restrictions for superposition are fulfilled. As we can see, equality constraints provide a simple and elegant representation for this inference rule. Information from the meta-level, in this case the accumulated unifiers, is kept in the constraints and used later on. Of course, other notations and practical implementations for basic superposition are possible, such as pairs clause-substitution or clauses in which "forbidden" subterms are marked somehow.

Obviously, basic superposition is a considerable improvement over normal super-position as defined in e.g. [BG 91], allowing to importantly reduce the search space, and to obtain complete systems in more cases. One of the reasons is that by normal superposition many superfluous consequences are generated. Sometimes one can try to eliminate these consequences (e.g. in the equational case some –but not all– redundant critical pairs are *joinable*), but this is not always possible (almost never in the non-equational cases), and very expensive in general. By basic superposition, many of these superfluous consequences are simply not created.

This paper is structured as follows. After the basic definitions of section 2, in the third section we apply our techniques to the particular case of equational logic and define a new unfailing Knuth-Bendix completion procedure that uses basic superposition as inference rule. In section 4 we extend the results to the case of Horn-clauses with equality and further to full first-order clauses with equality. Our style of proof is based on the model construction techniques and redundancy notions defined by Bachmair and Ganzinger in [BG 91]. We prove the refutational completeness of a basic superposition-based inference system, which moreover uses a simple new factoring rule. Section 5 is on further work.

Related work (simultaneously and independently developed) on similar "basic" re-strictions, but for paramodulation, has recently been presented by W. Snyder and C. Lynch at the *UNIF-91* workshop in Barbizon, France. Their method is less useful for Knuth-Bendix completion, since it needs paramodulation on right hand sides, and gives no simplification and deletion mechanisms for redundant equations and clauses. Their proof methods are completely different from ours and more complex. We have also learned that L. Bachmair, H. Ganzinger, C. Lynch and W. Snyder have very recently further developed the previous method obtaining basic superposition calculi more sim-ilar to ours.

2. Basic notions and terminology

We adopt the standard notations and definitions for term rewriting given in [DJ 90, 91].

Furthermore, by *equality constraints* we mean conjunctions of equalities of terms $t = t'$, where $=$ denotes syntactic equality of the terms t and t'. An equality constraint T of the form $t_1 = t_1' \wedge \ldots \wedge t_n = t_n'$ is satisfiable iff there exists a (most general) unifier σ of T, i.e. σ simultaneously unifies every t_i with t_i' for $i = 1 \ldots n$. Every unifier θ of T is called a *solution* of T, and then we say that $T\theta$ is (equivalent to) true, denoted $T\theta \equiv true$.

By an *equation* we mean a multiset $\{s, t\}$, denoted by $s \simeq t$ (or equivalently by $t \simeq s$), where s and t are terms in $\mathcal{T}(\mathcal{F}, \mathcal{X})$. A first-order clause $\Gamma \to \Delta$ is a pair of (finite) multisets of equations Γ and Δ, called respectively the *antecedent* and the *succedent* of the clause.

An *equality constrained clause* is a pair (C, T), denoted $C \llbracket T \rrbracket$, where C is a clause and T is an equality constraint. Such a pair can be seen as a shorthand for the set of *ground instances* of $C \llbracket T \rrbracket$: those ground clauses $C\sigma$ such that $T\sigma$ is true. We will suppose distinct equality constrained clauses not to share variables.

Like in [BG 91], here we consider interpretations that are congruences on ground terms. An interpretation I satisfies a ground clause $\Gamma \to \Delta$, denoted by $I \models \Gamma \to \Delta$, if $I \not\supseteq \Gamma$ or else $I \cap \Delta \neq \emptyset$. An interpretation I satisfies (is a model of) $C \llbracket T \rrbracket$, denoted $I \models C \llbracket T \rrbracket$, if it satisfies every ground instance of $C \llbracket T \rrbracket$, i.e. clauses with unsatisfiable constraints are tautologies. The empty clause (with a satisfiable constraint!) is satisfied by no interpretation. I satisfies a set of clauses S, denoted by $I \models S$, if it satisfies every clause in S. A clause C *can be deduced* from a set of clauses S (denoted $S \models C$), if C is satisfied by every model of S.

For dealing with non-equality predicates, we express atoms A by equations $A \simeq true$ where *true* is a special symbol, i.e. we treat atoms as terms. Here $\succ$ denotes a total simplification ordering on ground terms, where the special symbol *true* is the smallest symbol. We use $\succ_{mul}$ ($\succ_{mul^n}$) to denote its (n-fold) multiset extension.

We use the definitions of [DJ 91] for rewriting-related notions like *normal form*, *confluence, convergence, reducibility,* etc. We denote *ground rewrite rules* (ground equations $t \simeq t'$ with $t \succ t'$) by $t \Rightarrow t'$. The congruence generated by a set of ground rewrite rules R (which is an interpretation) will be denoted by R^*.

3. Basic superposition in the equational case

In this section we deal with clauses of the form $\to s \simeq t$, denoted here by $s \simeq t$.

Definition 1: The inference rule of *equational basic superposition* is defined as follows:

$$\frac{s \simeq s'\,[\![T']\!] \qquad t \simeq t'\,[\![T]\!]}{t[s']_u \simeq t'\,[\![T \wedge T' \wedge t|_u = s]\!]} \qquad \text{where } t|_u \notin \mathcal{V}ars(t)$$

if, for some ground substitution σ, $[\![T \wedge T' \wedge t|_u = s]\!]\sigma$ is true, $s\sigma \succ s'\sigma$ and $t\sigma \succ t'\sigma$.

As said, constraint solving for equality constraints is just unification (in practice, every satisfiable constraint T can be kept in a simplest form, which is its most general unifier, and non-relevant variables can be eliminated, although here we will not go into these details).

The difficulty with basic superposition (and with all forms of deduction with constrained formulae) is that lifting lemmas like the critical pair lemma [KB 70] do not hold:

Example 2: No inference by basic superposition can be made between the two equations $a \simeq b$ and $f(x) \simeq b\,[\![x = a]\!]$, where $a \succ b$. Now the term $f(a)$ rewrites into $f(b)$ by the first equation, and into b by the second one, but there is no term t such that $f(b)$ and b are both reducible to t, i.e. the critical pair lemma does not hold when considering only critical pairs by basic superposition.

Another conclusion that we can draw from this example is that basic superposition is *not* complete as inference rule for equational Knuth-Bendix completion when starting from an *arbitrary* set of equations with equality constraints: there is no rewrite proof at all for the consequence $f(b) \simeq b$, although the set of equations is closed under basic superposition.

Therefore, here we will suppose that the *initial* set of axioms contains only clauses without constraints*, i.e. clauses of the form $C\,[\![T]\!]$ where T is an empty (or trivially true) constraint, sometimes written $C\,[\![true]\!]$.

For simplicity, we will first study basic superposition without simplification. It is proved that the closure under basic superposition of an initial set of equations without constraints is ground confluent. We do this by first defining a (canonical) set of ground rewrite rules R_E *generated* from a set E of equations, by selecting ground instances of equations in E that fulfil certain properties (this is similar to [BG 91], but adapted to equations with equality constraints). Then we show that $R_E^* \models E$ if E is closed under basic superposition, and we prove that this implies that E is ground confluent.

To overcome the problems of the non-existence of a critical pair lemma, we will sometimes consider only ground instances of equations with *irreducible* substitutions, defined as follows:

---

* In fact, this restriction can be slightly weakened

Definition 3: A ground substitution σ is *irreducible* wrt. a set of ground rewrite rules R if $x\sigma$ is irreducible wrt. R, for every variable x in the domain of σ. A *normal form* of σ wrt. R is a substitution σ' with the same domain as σ, and such that $x\sigma'$ is a normal form wrt. R of $x\sigma$, for every variable x in the domain.

Definition 4: Let $s\sigma \simeq t\sigma$ be a ground instance with $s\sigma \succ t\sigma$ of an equation $s \simeq t\,[\![T]\!]$ in a set of equations E. Then $s\sigma \simeq t\sigma$ *generates* the rule $s\sigma \Rightarrow t\sigma$ if $s\sigma$ and σ are irreducible wrt. the rules generated by ground instances $e\theta$ of equations in E with $s\sigma \simeq t\sigma \succ_{mul} e\theta$.

The set of rules generated by all ground instances of equations in E is denoted by R_E.

Definition 5: Let E be a set of constrained equations, and let R be a set of ground rewrite rules. The set of ground instances of equations in E with substitutions that are irreducible wrt. R is denoted by $irred_R(E)$, i.e.

$$irred_R(E) = \{\ e\sigma \ \mid \ e\,[\![T]\!] \in E, \ T\sigma \equiv true, \ \sigma \ ground, \ \sigma \ irreducible \ wrt. \ R\ \}$$

Lemma 6: Let $s \simeq s'\,[\![T]\!]$ be an equation in E such that $s\theta \simeq s'\theta$ generates the rule $s\theta \Rightarrow s'\theta$ for some ground substitution θ. Then $x\theta$ is irreducible wrt. R_E for every x in $\mathcal{V}ars(s')$.

Proof. If $s\theta \Rightarrow s'\theta$ is generated as a rule, then $x\theta$ is irreducible wrt. the rules generated by ground instances smaller wrt. $\succ_{mul}$ than $s\theta \simeq s'\theta$, and also $s\theta \succ s'\theta$. All rules generated by instances greater or equal than $s\theta \simeq s'\theta$ have left hand sides that are strictly greater than $s'\theta$. Therefore, none of these rules can reduce a subterm of $s'\theta$. ∎

Lemma 7: Let E be a set of equations with equality constraints that is closed under basic superposition. Then $R_E^* \models irred_{R_E}(E)$.

Proof. We will derive a contradiction from the existence of a minimal (wrt. $\succ_{mul}$) element $t\sigma \simeq t'\sigma$ in $irred_{R_E}(E)$ such that $R_E^* \not\models t\sigma \simeq t'\sigma$.

Let $t\sigma \simeq t'\sigma$ be a ground instance of an equation $t \simeq t'\,[\![T]\!]$ in E. We can suppose w.l.o.g. that $t\sigma \succ t'\sigma$. Since $R_E^* \not\models t\sigma \simeq t'\sigma$, the equation does not generate any rule in R_E. Therefore $t\sigma$ must be reducible by R_E, e.g. with a rule $s\theta \Rightarrow s'\theta$ generated by an equation $s\theta \simeq s'\theta$ smaller (wrt. $\succ_{mul}$) than $t\sigma \simeq t'\sigma$, where $s\theta \simeq s'\theta$ is a ground instance of an equation $s \simeq s'\,[\![T']\!]$ in E. Now we have $t\sigma|_u = s\theta$, where $t|_u$ cannot be a variable, since σ is irreducible wrt. R_E, and therefore the following inference can be made:

$$\frac{s \simeq s'\,[\![T']\!] \qquad t \simeq t'\,[\![T]\!]}{t[s']_u \simeq t'\,[\![T \wedge T' \wedge t|_u = s]\!]}$$

Since E is closed under basic superposition, its conclusion is in E. It has a ground instance d of the form $t\sigma[s'\theta]_u \simeq t'\sigma$ such that $R_E^* \not\models d$ (otherwise $R_E^* \models t\sigma \simeq t'\sigma$). Moreover, by the previous lemma and since σ is irreducible by R_E, the instance d is an instance of this conclusion with a ground substitution that is irreducible by R_E. Furthermore, we have $t\sigma \simeq t'\sigma \succ_{mul} d$, which altogether contradicts the minimality of $t\sigma \simeq t'\sigma$. ∎

Lemma 8: Let E_0 be a set of equations without constraints, and let E be the closure of E_0 under basic superposition. Then $R_E^* \models E$.

Proof. First note that $E_0 \models E$, by soundness of basic superposition. Therefore, it suffices to show that $R_E^* \models E_0$, i.e. $R_E^* \models e\sigma$ for every ground instance $e\sigma$ of an equation $e \llbracket true \rrbracket$ in E_0. Now let σ' be a normal form of σ wrt. R_E. Since $E_0 \subseteq E$, by the previous lemma it holds that $R_E^* \models e\sigma'$, because σ' is irreducible wrt. R_E, and $e\sigma'$ is an existing instance of $e \llbracket true \rrbracket$. From $R_E \cup \{e\sigma'\} \models e\sigma$ and $R_E^* \models e\sigma'$ it follows that $R_E^* \models e\sigma$. ∎

Lemma 9: Let E be a set of constrained equations such that $R_E^* \models E$. Then E is ground confluent.

Proof. Let s, s' and t be ground terms such that s and s' are normal forms of t wrt. E. We prove that s and s' must be syntactically equal. We have $E \models s \simeq s'$, and $R_E^* \models E$, which implies $R_E^* \models s \simeq s'$ and $R_E \models s \simeq s'$. If s and s' are normal forms wrt. E, then they are also normal forms wrt. R_E, because R_E is a set of instances of equations of E. Moreover, by its construction, R_E is a canonical set of ground rewrite rules because there are no overlappings between left hand sides. This implies that s and s' are equal. ∎

Theorem 10: Let E_0 be a set of equations without constraints, and let E be the closure of E_0 under basic superposition. Then E is ground confluent.

3.1. Completion by basic superposition: the equational case

Now we know that if E is the closure under basic superposition of a set of equations without constraints, then E is ground confluent. In this section we show that basic superposition is also the appropriate inference rule for unfailing Knuth-Bendix completion, i.e. for computing ground confluent sets in practice, even when applying the existing powerful simplification and deletion methods that can be used in normal superposition-based completion. However, at first sight there seems to be a problem with simplification:

Example 11: Consider the ordering $f \succ g \succ a \succ b$ and three initial equations:

   1) $\quad a \simeq b$

   2) $\quad f(g(x)) \simeq g(x)$

   3) $\quad f(g(a)) \simeq b$

Now a completion process including simplification could generate:

   4) $\quad g(x) \simeq b \llbracket x = a \rrbracket$ (by basic superposition of 2 and 3)

   5) $\quad f(b) \simeq b$ (simplifying 3 by 4)

   6) $\quad f(b) \simeq g(x) \llbracket x = a \rrbracket$ (by basic superposition of 2 and 4)

Now the set $\{1, 2, 4, 5, 6\}$ is closed under basic superposition, i.e. this set would be the final set generated by the completion process. However, there is no rewrite proof for $g(b) \simeq b$ using instances of this set. The conclusion of this example is that, even when starting with equations without constraints, it is incorrect to apply simplification steps like the one made above, where the equation $f(g(a)) \simeq b$ is simplified into $f(b) \simeq b$ using the instance $g(a) \simeq b$ of $g(x) \simeq b \, [\![x = a]\!]$, which would be a quite natural simplification method.

However, as we will see, this problem appears only in (quite special) concrete situations, and can be solved in such a way that all intuitive simplification and deletion techniques can be allowed if sometimes certain equality constraints are slightly *weakened*.

Our notions of completion and redundancy are based on the ones defined in [BG 91], where an axiom is redundant if all its ground instances can be deduced from smaller instances of other axioms. Analogously, an *inference* is redundant if, for all its instances, the conclusion can be deduced from instances smaller than the maximal premise. These redundancy notions include, as far as we know, all correct methods that make completion procedures more efficient and terminate in more cases. Here we adapt these notions by considering only instances with substitutions that are, in some sense, irreducible.

Now we first give some definitions, which we do not pretend to be constructive. For instance, the definition of *completion derivations* below does not provide (yet) a way to compute them (at least not if the redundancy notions are exploited). This point will be made clear below.

Definition 12: Let $E_0, E_1, \ldots$ be a sequence of sets of constrained equations.

a) The set E_∞ of *persistent* equations in $E_0, E_1, \ldots$ is defined as $\cup_j (\cap_{k \geq j} E_k)$.

b) An equation $e \, [\![T]\!]$ is *redundant* in E_j if for every ground instance $e\sigma$ of it with σ irreducible wrt. R_{E_∞}, there exist instances d_i in $irred_{R_{E_\infty}}(E_j)$, for $i = 1 \ldots m$, such that $e\sigma \succ_{mul} d_i$ and $R_{E_\infty} \cup \{d_1, \ldots, d_m\} \models e\sigma$.

Definition 13: A *completion derivation* is a sequence of sets of constrained equations $E_0, E_1, \ldots$ such that T_0 is *true* for every equation $e_0 \, [\![T_0]\!]$ in E_0 and

$$E_i = E_{i-1} \cup \{e \, [\![T]\!]\} \quad \text{where } E_{i-1} \models e \, [\![T]\!], \text{ or}$$
$$E_i = E_{i-1} \setminus \{e \, [\![T]\!]\} \quad \text{if } e \, [\![T]\!] \text{ is redundant in } E_{i-1}.$$

Definition 14: Let $E_0, E_1, \ldots$ be a completion derivation, and let π be a basic superposition inference with premises $e_1 \, [\![T_1]\!]$ and $e_2 \, [\![T_2]\!]$, and with conclusion $e \, [\![T]\!]$. Then every inference by basic superposition with premises $e_1\sigma$ and $e_2\sigma$, and conclusion $e\sigma$ with $T\sigma \equiv true$, for some ground substitution σ, is a *ground instance* $\pi\sigma$ of π. The inference π is *redundant* in E_j if for every ground instance $\pi\sigma$ of π with σ irreducible wrt. R_{E_∞}, there exist instances d_i in $irred_{R_{E_\infty}}(E_j)$, for $i = 1 \ldots m$, such that $max(e_1\sigma, e_2\sigma) \succ_{mul} d_i$ and $R_{E_\infty} \cup \{d_1 \ldots d_m\} \models e\sigma$, where max denotes maximality wrt. $\succ_{mul}$.

Definition 15: A completion derivation $E_0, E_1, \ldots$ is *fair* if every inference by basic superposition with premises in E_∞ is redundant in some E_j.

As we can see, in completion derivations we consider instances with substitutions irreducible wrt. R_{E_∞}. For example, an *equation* is redundant if all its instances that are irreducible in that sense can be deduced from other smaller irreducible instances.

However, in practice, during the computation of a fair derivation, one cannot prove the redundancy of equations or inferences in a set E_j, since at that point R_{E_∞} is unknown. Therefore, sufficient conditions for redundancy have to be used. We will define them in detail at the end of this section, and we suppose for the moment that we can indeed compute fair completion derivations.

Definition 16: Let $E_0, E_1, \ldots$ be a completion derivation. Then E_∞ is *complete* if every inference by basic superposition with premises in E_∞ is redundant in E_∞.

Lemma 17: Let $E_0, E_1, \ldots$ be a completion derivation. Then for every set E_j and instance $e\sigma$ in $irred_{R_{E_\infty}}(E_j)$, there are instances d_i for $i = 1 \ldots m$ in $irred_{R_{E_\infty}}(E_\infty)$, such that $R_{E_\infty} \cup \{d_1, \ldots, d_m\} \models e\sigma$ and $e\sigma \succeq_{mul} d_i$.

Proof. We derive a contradiction from the existence of an instance $e\sigma$ that is minimal (w.r.t. $\succ_{mul}$) in all sets $irred_{R_{E_\infty}}(E_j)$ such that there are no such instances d_i in $irred_{R_{E_\infty}}(E_\infty)$. The corresponding equation $e\,[\![T]\!]$ in E_j is not persistent, because otherwise $e\sigma$ is in $irred_{R_{E_\infty}}(E_\infty)$. This means that $e\,[\![T]\!]$ is redundant in some E_k, with $k \geq j$, i.e. there exist instances d_q' with $q = 1 \ldots n$, in $irred_{R_{E_\infty}}(E_k)$ such that $R_{E_\infty} \cup \{d_1', \ldots, d_n'\} \models e\sigma$, with $e\sigma \succ_{mul} d_q'$. However, if the result holds for the instances $d_1', \ldots, d_n'$ (which must be the case, because $e\sigma$ is minimal), then it also holds for $e\sigma$. ∎

Lemma 18: Let $E_0, E_1, \ldots$ be a completion derivation. If an inference by basic superposition is redundant in some E_j, then it also is in E_∞.

Proof. Let π be an inference with premises $e_1\,[\![T_1]\!]$ and $e_2\,[\![T_2]\!]$, and with conclusion $e\,[\![T]\!]$, such that π is redundant in E_j. Then, by definition of redundant inference, for every ground instance $\pi\sigma$ of π with σ irreducible wrt. R_{E_∞}, there exist instances d_i in $irred_{R_{E_\infty}}(E_j)$, for $i = 1 \ldots m$, such that $max(e_1\sigma, e_2\sigma) \succ_{mul} d_i$ and $R_{E_\infty} \cup \{d_1, \ldots, d_m\} \models e\sigma$. By the previous lemma, each of the instances d_i can be deduced from R_{E_∞} and other instances $\{d_1', \ldots, d_n'\}$ in $irred_{R_{E_\infty}}(E_\infty)$ such that $d_i \succeq_{mul} d_j'$. This implies that π is also redundant in E_∞. ∎

Lemma 19: If $E_0, E_1, \ldots$ is a fair completion derivation, then E_∞ is complete.

Proof. By fairness, every inference π with premises in E_∞ is redundant in some E_j. By the previous lemma, then π is also redundant in E_∞, that is, E_∞ is complete. ∎

We now apply the same method as above to prove that E_∞ is ground confluent. The following lemma states that in fair completion derivations $R_{E_\infty}^* \models irred_{R_{E_\infty}}(E_\infty)$. After this, in lemma 21, we show that $R_{E_\infty}^* \models E_\infty$, which, as we know by lemma 9, implies that E_∞ is ground confluent.

Lemma 20: If $E_0, E_1, \ldots$ is a fair completion derivation then $R_{E_\infty}^* \models irred_{R_{E_\infty}}(E_\infty)$.

Proof. This proof is an easy extension of that of lemma 7, where the same result is proved for sets E that are *closed* under basic superposition, instead of what we need here: proving it for E_∞ which we only know to be *complete*, i.e. closed *up to redundant inferences*.

Let $t\sigma \simeq t'\sigma$ be a minimal (wrt. $\succ_{mul}$) instance in $irred_{R_{E_\infty}}(E_\infty)$ such that $R_{E_\infty}^* \not\models t\sigma \simeq t'\sigma$. We will derive a contradiction from the existence of such an equation. We can suppose w.l.o.g. that $t\sigma \succ t'\sigma$. Since $R_{E_\infty}^* \not\models t\sigma \simeq t'\sigma$, the equation has not generated any rule in R_{E_∞}. Therefore $t\sigma$ must be reducible by R_{E_∞}, e.g. with a rule $s\theta \Rightarrow s'\theta$ generated by an equation $s\theta \simeq s'\theta$ smaller than $t\sigma \simeq t'\sigma$. Now we have $t\sigma|_u = s\theta$, where $t|_u$ cannot be a variable, since σ is irreducible, and therefore the following inference can be made:

$$\frac{s \simeq s' \; [\![T']\!] \qquad t \simeq t' \; [\![T]\!]}{t[s']_u \simeq t' \; [\![T \wedge T' \wedge t|_u = s]\!]}$$

Its conclusion has a ground instance d of the form $t\sigma[s'\theta]_u \simeq t'\sigma$ such that $R_{E_\infty}^* \not\models d$ (otherwise $R_{E_\infty}^* \models t\sigma \simeq t'\sigma$). Moreover, d is an instance of this conclusion with a ground substitution that is irreducible by R_{E_∞} (as in lemma 7).

Since E_∞ is complete, the inference must be *redundant* in E_∞, i.e. there exist instances d_i in $irred_{R_{E_\infty}}(E_\infty)$, for $i = 1 \ldots m$, such that $t\sigma \simeq t'\sigma \succ_{mul} d_i$ and $R_{E_\infty} \cup \{d_1, \ldots, d_m\} \models d$. But if $R_{E_\infty}^* \not\models d$ then also $R_{E_\infty}^* \not\models d_i$ for some d_i, contradicting the minimality of $t\sigma \simeq t'\sigma$. ∎

Lemma 21: If $E_0, E_1, \ldots$ is a fair completion derivation then $R_{E_\infty}^* \models E_\infty$.

Proof. We have $R_{E_\infty}^* \models irred_{R_{E_\infty}}(E_\infty)$ by the previous lemma. Moreover, $R_{E_\infty} \cup irred_{R_{E_\infty}}(E_\infty) \models irred_{R_{E_\infty}}(E_0)$ is a direct consequence of lemma 17. Now, since $R_{E_\infty} \cup irred_{R_{E_\infty}}(E_0) \models E_0$ holds as in lemma 8 (equations in E_0 have no constraints), and $E_0 \models E_\infty$ holds since $E_i \models E_{i+1}$ for all i, together we have $R_{E_\infty}^* \models E_\infty$. ∎

Theorem 22: If $E_0, E_1, \ldots$ is a fair completion derivation then E_∞ is ground confluent.

3.2. Redundancy notions for basic superposition

In this section we study in which concrete situations the usual notions of redundancy are incorrect when dealing with basic superposition. It is shown that these situations can be avoided by sometimes slightly *weakening* constraints, in such a way that basic superposition only in the very worst case may degenerate into normal superposition.

Roughly speaking, the notions of redundant axioms and inferences for normal superposition of [BG 91] state that a clause is redundant if all its ground instances can be deduced from smaller instances of other clauses, and an *inference* is redundant if, for all its instances, the conclusion can be deduced from instances smaller than the maximal premise. These notions include most simplification techniques and *critical pair criteria* for proving the redundancy of superpositions. For example, the simplification of an equation e into e' can be modelled in a completion derivation by first adding e', and then deleting e, which has become redundant.

Below we prove that these notions of redundancy can also be used in basic superposition. However, our notion of redundant equation (defin. 12) requires every instance *with an irreducible substitution* to be deducible from other smaller instances *with irreducible substitutions*, and also R_{E_∞} may be used in redundancy proofs:

Example 23: In example 11, the equation $f(g(a)) \simeq b$ is simplified into $f(b) \simeq b$ using $g(x) \simeq b \llbracket x = a \rrbracket$ with the substitution σ, which is $\{x \mapsto a\}$.

However, $f(g(a)) \simeq b$ does *not* become redundant by adding $f(b) \simeq b$, because we need $g(x) \simeq b \llbracket x = a \rrbracket$ instantiated with σ, but σ is *not* irreducible, since R_{E_∞} contains the equation $a \simeq b$, with $a \succ b$.

Before giving other sufficient conditions for redundancy in our framework, let us remark that by our notion of definition 12 we obtain an interesting result: a constrained equation $e \llbracket T \rrbracket$ is redundant (i.e. it can be deleted) if σ is the most general unifier of T and, for some variable x in e, $x\sigma$ is reducible by an equation e' in some E_j. This is true because if $x\sigma$ is reducible by e' then it is also reducible by some rule in R_{E_∞}, and therefore $e \llbracket T \rrbracket$ has no irreducible ground instances at all.

Definition 24: Let $e \llbracket T \rrbracket$ be an equation, and let θ be the most general unifier of the equality constraint T. Then T *binds* each variable x in $\mathcal{V}ars(e)$ with $x\theta \neq x$ to $x\theta$.

Lemma 25: Let $E_0, E_1, \ldots$ be a completion derivation. The equation $e \llbracket T \rrbracket$ is redundant in a set E_j if

(i) for every ground instance $e\sigma$ there are ground instances $d_i\sigma_i$ for $i = 1 \ldots m$ of equations $d_i \llbracket T_i \rrbracket$ in E_j such that $\{d_1\sigma_1, \ldots, d_m\sigma_m\} \models e\sigma$ and $e\sigma \succ_{mul} d_i\sigma_i$, and

(ii) for every i in $1 \ldots m$, and for every x in $\mathcal{V}ars(d_i)$, T_i does not bind x, or else $x\sigma_i = y\sigma$, for some variable y in e.

Proof. We have to prove that the conditions imply that for every $e\sigma$ where σ is ground and irreducible wrt. R_{E_∞}, there exist instances d'_k in $irred_{R_{E_\infty}}(E_j)$, for $k = 1 \ldots n$, such that $e\sigma \succ_{mul} d'_k$ and $R_{E_\infty} \cup \{d'_1, \ldots, d'_k\} \models e\sigma$.

If every substitution σ_i is irreducible wrt. R_{E_∞}, then the result holds. This is certainly the case if for every variable x in every d_i we have $x\sigma_i = y\sigma$, for some variable y in e, since σ is irreducible.

Otherwise, if $x\sigma_i$ is reducible by R_{E_∞}, we can replace $d_i\sigma_i$ by $d_i\theta_i$, where θ_i is the ground substitution such that $x\theta_i$ is a normal form wrt. R_{E_∞} of $x\sigma_i$, and $z\theta_i = z\sigma_i$ for every other variable z in d_i. Now $d_i\theta_i$ is an existing instance of d_i, since x is not bound by the corresponding constraint T_i. Moreover, we have $R_{E_\infty} \cup \{d_i\theta_i\} \models d_i\sigma_i$. By doing so for all such variables x, we obtain the instances d'_k in $irred_{R_{E_\infty}}(E_j)$, for $k = 1 \ldots n$, such that $e\sigma \succ_{mul} d'_k$ and $R_{E_\infty} \cup \{d'_1, \ldots, d'_k\} \models e\sigma$. ∎

The lemma above means for instance that, roughly speaking, one can apply an equation $e \llbracket T \rrbracket$ in a redundancy proof if, for every variable x in $Vars(e)$, x is not bound by T, or else the "corresponding" position in the equation proved is also a variable:

Example 26: The equation $h(f(y)) \simeq y \llbracket y = a \rrbracket$ can be simplified* by the equation $f(x) \simeq b \llbracket x = a \rrbracket$ into $h(b) \simeq y \llbracket y = a \rrbracket$, because, although the variable x is bound, its corresponding position in $h(f(y))$ is the variable y.

A lemma equivalent to lemma 25 for proving the redundancy of *inferences* also holds: it is obtained by using the instance of the maximal premise as upper bound for the instances $d_1, \ldots, d_m$, instead of $e\sigma$.

Might all the conditions of the previous lemma fail, for some variable x, then we can always *weaken T* for x:

Lemma 27: Let $e \llbracket T \rrbracket$ be an equation, and let θ be the most general unifier of T, with θ of the form $\{x_1 \mapsto t_1, \ldots, x_n \mapsto t_n\}$. Now let σ be $\{x_1 \mapsto t_1\}$. Then the equation $e\sigma \llbracket x_2 = t_2 \wedge \ldots \wedge x_n = t_n \rrbracket$, obtained by *weakening $e \llbracket T \rrbracket$* for x_1, is logically equivalent to $e \llbracket T \rrbracket$.

Weakening the constraint of an equation is equivalent to turning basic superposition into normal superposition for the given subterm in the equation (t_1 in the previous lemma), since it becomes again necessary to apply superposition on it, while it was not before weakening.

In fact, one can also apply *partial* weakening steps, i.e. instantiating the variable x_1 only with the outermost symbol of the term t_1 (or doing this several times) if this is enough for fulfilling the conditions of lemma 25. For example, if t_1 is of the form $f(s_1 \ldots s_m)$ the constraint becomes $\llbracket T \wedge T' \wedge y_1 = s_1 \wedge \ldots \wedge y_m = s_m \rrbracket$ and the substitution $\sigma = \{x_1 \mapsto f(y_1 \ldots y_m)\}$ is applied to the equation, where $y_1 \ldots y_m$ are new variables.

For simplicity, we have not considered here redundancy of equations by *subsumption*, which can be proved by combining $\succ_{mul}$ with the subsumption ordering (but note that, in order to fulfil the conditions of lemma 25, the subsuming constrained equation has to be weakened until its equation part is, in some sense, as instantiated as the subsumed equation).

Practical implementations, such as the one we are working on based on the TRIP system [NOR 90], will show whether it pays off to weaken constraints for simplification steps, or whether it is always more efficient to use basic superposition in its full power. For the moment, it seems to us that some mixed strategy has to be used.

---

* If we use a notion of simplification where matching has to be compatible with the equality constraints. Here we will not define concrete simplification methods for equality constrained equations. As far as we know, the previous lemma covers all intuitive extensions of known methods to the equality constraint case.

4. Completion of first-order clauses by basic superposition

In this section we extend the techniques defined above to the case of full first-order clauses with equality. As done by Bachmair and Ganzinger in [BG 91], we obtain an unfailing completion procedure for first-order clauses with equality, including powerful notions of redundancy for clauses and inferences. This procedure is refutationally complete and, moreover, very efficient complete strategies can be used for refutational theorem proving with *complete* sets of clauses.

The main new result given here is that our completion procedure, while conserving these properties, uses an inference system that has as main inference rule the one of strict *basic* superposition, instead of normal strict superposition, with the corresponding advantages of a more reduced search space and higher termination probabilities.

Moreover, apart from using basic superposition, the new inference system we define below (first proved complete in [Nie 91]) is also interesting because there is only one inference rule for equality factoring, instead of including, apart from "normal" factoring, inference rules for *merging paramodulation* or *equality factoring left* and *equality factoring right* [BG 91]. The fact that we use here this specific inference system does not mean that our methods depend on it: our lifting techniques can be easily adapted to each one of these other systems. Our results can also be extended to calculi which consider only one arbitrary *marked* negative literal for superposition, as done in [NN 91] for Horn clauses with equality, and in [BG 91] as *selection functions* on negative literals of full first-order clauses.

In the following ordering $\succ_C$ on ground clauses, the terms appearing in antecedents of clauses are slightly more complex than the ones in succedents:

Definition 28: The *multiset expression* of an equation $t \simeq t'$ in a clause $\Gamma \to \Delta$ is

(i) $\{\{t,t\},\{t',t'\}\}$ if $t \simeq t'$ belongs to Γ
(ii) $\{\{t\},\{t'\}\}$ if $t \simeq t'$ belongs to Δ

The ordering $\succ_e$ on ground equations is defined as the ordering $\succ_{mul^2}$ on their multiset expressions.
The ordering $\succ_C$ on ground clauses is defined as the ordering $\succ_{mul^3}$ on the multisets containing the multiset expressions of their equations.

Definition 29: A ground equation e is called *maximal* (resp. *strictly maximal*) in a ground clause C if $e \succeq_e e'$ (resp. $e \succ_e e'$), for every other equation e' in C.

In the following inference system $\mathcal{B}$ (here $\mathcal{B}$ stands for "Basic superposition") inferences take place only in equations of succedents that are strictly maximal and in equations of antecedents that are maximal, for some ground instance. Moreover, only the maximal terms in each equation are used. These conditions imply that, for each ground inference, the conclusion is strictly smaller (wrt. $\succ_C$) than the maximal premise.

Definition 30: The inference rules of $\mathcal{B}$ are the following (we always consider maximality of equations in clauses wrt. $\succ_e$):

1) *strict basic superposition right:*

$$\frac{\Gamma' \to \Delta', s \simeq s' \; [\![T']\!] \qquad \Gamma \to \Delta, t \simeq t' \; [\![T]\!]}{\Gamma', \Gamma \to \Delta', \Delta, t[s']_u \simeq t' \; [\![T \wedge T' \wedge t|_u = s]\!]} \qquad \text{where } t|_u \notin \mathit{Vars}(t)$$

if $[\![T \wedge T' \wedge t|_u = s]\!]\sigma$ is true for some ground substitution σ such that

    a) $t\sigma \succ t'\sigma$, $s\sigma \succ s'\sigma$, and $t\sigma \simeq t'\sigma \succ_e s\sigma \simeq s'\sigma$
    b) $s\sigma \simeq s'\sigma$ is strictly maximal in $\Gamma'\sigma \to \Delta'\sigma, s\sigma \simeq s'\sigma$
    c) $t\sigma \simeq t'\sigma$ is strictly maximal in $\Gamma\sigma \to \Delta\sigma, t\sigma \simeq t'\sigma$.

2) *strict basic superposition left:*

$$\frac{\Gamma' \to \Delta', s \simeq s' \; [\![T']\!] \qquad \Gamma, t \simeq t' \to \Delta \; [\![T]\!]}{\Gamma', \Gamma, t[s']_u \simeq t' \to \Delta', \Delta \; [\![T \wedge T' \wedge t|_u = s]\!]} \qquad \text{where } t|_u \notin \mathit{Vars}(t)$$

if $[\![T \wedge T' \wedge t|_u = s]\!]\sigma$ is true for some ground substitution σ such that

    a) $t\sigma \succ t'\sigma$ and $s\sigma \succ s'\sigma$
    b) $s\sigma \simeq s'\sigma$ is strictly maximal in $\Gamma'\sigma \to \Delta'\sigma, s\sigma \simeq s'\sigma$
    c) $t\sigma \simeq t'\sigma$ is maximal in $\Gamma\sigma, t\sigma \simeq t'\sigma \to \Delta\sigma$.

3) *equality resolution:*

$$\frac{\Gamma, t \simeq t' \to \Delta \; [\![T]\!]}{\Gamma \to \Delta \; [\![T \wedge t = t']\!]}$$

if $[\![T \wedge t = t']\!]\sigma$ is true for some ground substitution σ such that

    a) $t\sigma \simeq t'\sigma$ is maximal in $\Gamma\sigma, t\sigma \simeq t'\sigma \to \Delta\sigma$.

4) *factoring:*

$$\frac{\Gamma \to \Delta, t \simeq s, t' \simeq s' \; [\![T]\!]}{\Gamma, s \simeq s' \to \Delta, t \simeq s \; [\![T \wedge t = t']\!]}$$

if $[\![T \wedge t = t']\!]\sigma$ is true for some ground substitution σ such that

    a) $t\sigma \succ s\sigma$ and $t'\sigma \succ s'\sigma$
    b) $t\sigma \simeq s\sigma$ is maximal in $\Gamma\sigma \to \Delta\sigma, t\sigma \simeq s\sigma, t'\sigma \simeq s'\sigma$.

Note that our inference rule for factoring is a generalization to the equality case of "normal" factoring. For instance, if t and t' are atoms, then both s and s' are the symbol *true* and the equation *true* $\simeq$ *true* can be omitted in the antecedent.

In order to prove the correctness of completion procedures based on this inference system $\mathcal{B}$, we will proceed in a similar way as done in the previous section for the equational case. In fact, we will extend almost all the definitions and results to the case of first-order clauses with equality, of which equations are a proper subset. For instance, definitions 31 - 36 are extensions of the equivalent ones in the previous section, and the same thing happens with the lemmas 37 - 39 and 41, whose proofs are omitted here.

Now first we associate to a set of constrained clauses S a canonical set of ground rewrite rules R_S, in a similar way as it was done for the equational case. After this, it will be shown that, in a fair completion derivation for first-order clauses $S_0, S_1, \ldots$, if the empty clause* is not in S_∞, then $R^*_{S_\infty} \models S_\infty$, i.e. S_∞ has a model. So we obtain the result (just as $R^*_{E_\infty} \models E_\infty$ implied the confluence of E_∞) that the completion procedure is refutationally complete.

Definition 31:   Let C be a ground instance $\Gamma \to \Delta, t \simeq s$ of a clause $D\,[\![T]\!]$ in a set S, i.e. C is $D\sigma$ for some ground substitution σ such that $T\sigma \equiv true$.

Then C *generates* a rule $t \Rightarrow s$ if the following conditions hold:

(1) $R^*_C \not\models C$

(2) $t \simeq s$ is maximal (wrt. $\succ_e$) in C with $t \succ s$

(3) $R^*_C \not\models s \simeq s'$, for every $t \simeq s'$ in Δ

(4) t is irreducible by R_C

(5) σ is irreducible by R_C

where R_C is the set of rules generated by ground instances smaller than C (wrt. $\succ_C$) of clauses in S.

The set of rules generated by all ground instances of clauses in S is denoted by R_S.

Definition 32:   Let $S_0, S_1, \ldots$ be a sequence of sets of constrained clauses.

a) The set S_∞ of *persistent* clauses in $S_0, S_1, \ldots$ is defined as $\cup_j (\cap_{k \geq j} S_k)$.

b) A clause $C\,[\![T]\!]$ is *redundant* in S_j if for every ground instance $C\sigma$ of it with σ irreducible wrt. R_{S_∞}, there exist instances D_i in $irred_{R_{S_\infty}}(S_j)$, for $i = 1 \ldots m$, such that $C\sigma \succ_C D_i$ and $R_{S_\infty} \cup \{D_1, \ldots, D_m\} \models C\sigma$.

Definition 33:   A *theorem proving derivation* is a sequence of sets of constrained clauses $S_0, S_1, \ldots$ such that T_0 is *true* for every clause $C_0\,[\![T_0]\!]$ in S_0 and

$$S_i = S_{i-1} \cup \{C\,[\![T]\!]\} \quad \text{where } S_{i-1} \models C\,[\![T]\!], \text{ or}$$

$$S_i = S_{i-1} \setminus \{C\,[\![T]\!]\} \quad \text{if } C\,[\![T]\!] \text{ is redundant in } S_{i-1}.$$

---

* The empty clause with a satisfiable constraint. Clauses with unsatisfiable constraints are tautologies.

Definition 34: Let $S_0, S_1, \ldots$ be a theorem proving derivation, and let π be an inference of $\mathcal{B}$ with premises $C_1 \llbracket T_1 \rrbracket, \ldots, C_n \llbracket T_n \rrbracket$, and with conclusion $C \llbracket T \rrbracket$.

Then every existing inference of $\mathcal{B}$ with premises $C_1 \sigma, \ldots, C_n \sigma$, and conclusion $C\sigma$ with $T\sigma \equiv true$, for some ground substitution σ, is a *ground instance* $\pi\sigma$ of π.

The inference π is *redundant* in S_j if for every ground instance $\pi\sigma$ of π with σ irreducible wrt. R_{S_∞}, there exist instances D_i in $irred_{R_{S_\infty}}(S_j)$, for $i = 1 \ldots m$, such that $max(C_1\sigma, \ldots, C_n\sigma) \succ_C D_i$ and $R_{S_\infty} \cup \{D_1, \ldots, D_m\} \models C\sigma$, where max denotes maximality wrt. $\succ_C$.

Definition 35: A theorem proving derivation $S_0, S_1, \ldots$ is *fair* if every inference of the inference system $\mathcal{B}$ with premises in S_∞ is redundant in some S_j.

Definition 36: Let $S_0, S_1, \ldots$ be a theorem proving derivation. Then S_∞ is *complete* if every inference of the inference system $\mathcal{B}$ with premises in S_∞ is redundant in S_∞.

Lemma 37: Let $S_0, S_1, \ldots$ be a theorem proving derivation. Then for every set S_j and instance C in $irred_{R_{S_\infty}}(S_j)$, there are instances D_i for $i = 1 \ldots m$ in $irred_{R_{S_\infty}}(S_\infty)$, such that $R_{S_\infty} \cup \{D_1, \ldots, D_m\} \models C$ and $C \succeq_C D_i$.

Lemma 38: Let $S_0, S_1, \ldots$ be a theorem proving derivation. If an inference is redundant in some S_j, then it also is in S_∞.

Lemma 39: If $S_0, S_1, \ldots$ is a fair theorem proving derivation, then S_∞ is complete.

For technical reasons which we explain in the lemma below, we apply a minimal weakening step to consequences of inferences with non-horn clauses where the left premise is of the form $\Gamma \rightarrow \Delta, x \simeq s, x \simeq s' \llbracket T \rrbracket$ and where $x \simeq s$ is the equation superposed on the right premise using x as left hand side. In fact, this weakening is not really needed*, but without doing it all proof techniques become quite more complicated and a lot of power wrt. redundancy (e.g. lemma 43) is then lost, which we think does not pay off. Note that this quite special case only applies to non-Horn clauses, since there are at least two equations in the succedent, and only if x does not appear in Γ (otherwise $x\sigma \simeq s\sigma$ cannot be maximal for any ground substitution σ). Now after an inference step by e.g. basic superposition left

$$\frac{\Gamma \rightarrow \Delta, x \simeq s, x \simeq s' \llbracket T \rrbracket \qquad \Gamma', t \simeq t' \rightarrow \Delta' \llbracket T' \rrbracket}{\Gamma, \Gamma', t[s]_u \simeq t' \rightarrow \Delta, \Delta', x \simeq s' \llbracket T \wedge T' \wedge t|_u = x \rrbracket} \qquad \text{where } t|_u \notin \mathcal{V}ars(t)$$

the conclusion is minimally weakened for the variable x (as done in section 3.2), i.e. the variable x in the clause is instantiated with the outermost symbol of the term $t|_u$ it is superposed upon.

More precisely, if $t|_u$ is of the form $f(t_1 \ldots t_n)$ the constraint of the conclusion becomes $\llbracket T \wedge T' \wedge x_1 = t_1 \wedge \ldots \wedge x_n = t_n \rrbracket$ and the substitution $\sigma = \{x \mapsto f(x_1 \ldots x_n)\}$ is applied to the whole constrained clause. From now on we suppose that this weakening is done after all such inferences by strict superposition left and right.

---

* This has been recently pointed out to us by H. Ganzinger.

The only lemma of this section that is significantly different to the equational case is the following one. The reason is that it depends on the inference system used.

Lemma 40: Let $S_0, S_1, \ldots$ be a fair theorem proving derivation, such that S_∞ does not contain the empty clause. Then $R^*_{S_\infty} \models irred_{RS_\infty}(S_\infty)$.

Proof. Let $C\sigma$ be a minimal (wrt. $\succ_C$) instance $irred_{RS_\infty}(S_\infty)$ of a clause $C \llbracket T \rrbracket$ in S_∞, such that $R^*_{S_\infty} \not\models C\sigma$. We will derive a contradiction from the existence of such a clause. There are several cases to be analyzed, depending on which one is the maximal equation in $C\sigma$:

a) Let $C\sigma$ be a clause $\Gamma\sigma \to \Delta\sigma, t\sigma \simeq t'\sigma$, with a maximal equation $t\sigma \simeq t'\sigma$, and $t\sigma \succ t'\sigma$. Since $R^*_{S_\infty} \not\models C\sigma$, the clause $C\sigma$ has not generated the rule $t\sigma \Rightarrow t'\sigma$. This must be because one of the conditions 3) or 4) of definition 31 do not hold.

a1) If condition 3) does not hold, then $\Delta\sigma$ must be of the form $\Delta'\sigma, s\sigma \simeq s'\sigma$, where $t\sigma$ is $s\sigma$ and $R^*_{C\sigma} \models t'\sigma \simeq s'\sigma$. In this case, consider the following inference π by factoring

$$\frac{\Gamma \to \Delta', t \simeq t', s \simeq s' \llbracket T \rrbracket}{\Gamma, t' \simeq s' \to \Delta', t \simeq t' \llbracket T \wedge t = s \rrbracket}$$

Its conclusion has a ground instance D of the form $\Gamma\sigma, t'\sigma \simeq s'\sigma \to \Delta'\sigma, t\sigma \simeq t'\sigma$ such that $R^*_{S_\infty} \not\models D$. Moreover, D is an instance of this conclusion with a ground substitution that is irreducible by R_{S_∞}.

Since S_∞ is complete, π must be redundant in S_∞. But then there exist instances $D_1, \ldots, D_m$ in $irred_{RS_\infty}(S_\infty)$ such that $R_{S_\infty} \cup \{D_1, \ldots, D_m\} \models D$ and $C\sigma \succ_C D_i$. Now $R^*_{S_\infty} \not\models D$ implies that $R^*_{S_\infty} \not\models D_i$ for at least one D_i, which contradicts the minimality of $C\sigma$.

a2) If condition 4) does not hold, then $t\sigma$ is reducible by $R_{C\sigma}$, e.g. with a rule $s\theta \Rightarrow s'\theta$ generated by a clause $C'\theta$ smaller than $C\sigma$. Let C' be a clause $\Gamma' \to \Delta', s \simeq s'$ in S_∞ and $t\sigma|_u = s\theta$. Now consider the inference π by strict superposition right

$$\frac{\Gamma' \to \Delta', s \simeq s' \llbracket T' \rrbracket \qquad \Gamma \to \Delta, t \simeq t' \llbracket T \rrbracket}{\Gamma', \Gamma \to \Delta', \Delta, t[s']_u \simeq t' \llbracket T \wedge T' \wedge t|_u = s \rrbracket}$$

Its conclusion has a ground instance D of the form $\Gamma'\theta, \Gamma\sigma \to \Delta'\theta, \Delta\sigma, t\sigma[s'\theta]_u \simeq t'\sigma$, such that $R^*_{S_\infty} \not\models D$. Moreover, D is an instance of this conclusion with a ground substitution that is irreducible by R_{S_∞}. This is true since σ is irreducible wrt. R_{S_∞}, θ is irreducible wrt. $R_{C'\theta}$, and since we apply weakening steps for certain non-Horn clauses, as defined above. Since S_∞ is complete, π must again be redundant in S_∞, which, as above, leads to a contradiction with the minimality of $C\sigma$.

b) If $C\sigma$ is a clause $\Gamma\sigma, t\sigma \simeq t'\sigma \to \Delta\sigma$, where $t\sigma \simeq t'\sigma$ is maximal in $C\sigma$, and $t\sigma$ is $t'\sigma$, then consider the following equality resolution inference:

$$\frac{\Gamma, t \simeq t' \to \Delta \llbracket T \rrbracket}{\Gamma \to \Delta \llbracket T \wedge t = t' \rrbracket}$$

The conclusion of this inference has a ground instance D of the form $\Gamma\sigma \to \Delta\sigma$, such that $R^*_{S_\infty} \not\models D$. Since the inference is redundant, as above, a contradiction is obtained.

c) The only remaining case is that $C\sigma$ is a clause $\Gamma\sigma, t\sigma \simeq t'\sigma \to \Delta\sigma$, where $t\sigma \simeq t'\sigma$ is maximal in $C\sigma$ and $t\sigma \succ t'\sigma$. In this case $R^*_{S_\infty} \models t\sigma \simeq t'\sigma$, because $R^*_{S_\infty} \not\models C\sigma$. Then $t\sigma$ must be reducible by a rule $s\theta \Rightarrow s'\theta$ in R_{S_∞} generated by a clause in S_∞ of the form $\Gamma' \to \Delta', s \simeq s'\,[\![T']\!]$, where $t\sigma|_u = s\theta$. The following inference π by strict basic superposition left can then be made:

$$\frac{\Gamma' \to \Delta', s \simeq s'\,[\![T']\!] \qquad \Gamma, t \simeq t' \to \Delta\,[\![T]\!]}{\Gamma', \Gamma, t[s']_u \simeq t' \to \Delta', \Delta\,[\![T \wedge T' \wedge t|_u = s]\!]}$$

For the corresponding ground instance, $C\sigma$ is the maximal premise, and, as in case a2), for its conclusion D we have $R^*_{S_\infty} \not\models D$. This implies as before that, since π is redundant, a contradiction is obtained. ∎

Lemma 41: Let $S_0, S_1, \ldots$ be a fair theorem proving derivation. Then $R^*_{S_\infty} \models S_\infty$.

Theorem 42: Let $S_0, S_1, \ldots$ be a fair theorem proving derivation. Then S_0 is inconsistent if, and only if, the empty clause belongs to some S_j.

Proof. If the empty clause belongs to some S_j, then, since S_i is logically equivalent to S_{i+1} for all i, S_0 is inconsistent. For the reverse implication, suppose the empty clause belongs to no S_j. Then it is not in S_∞, and by the previous lemma, $R^*_{S_\infty} \models S_\infty$. But then S_0 must be consistent, since it also has the model $R^*_{S_\infty}$. ∎

With respect to the redundancy notions, again the same discussion as in the previous section applies. All known redundancy notions can be applied, although sometimes weakening is needed. Therefore completion based on the inference rule of basic superposition strictly improves normal superposition-based completion. The following lemma, equivalent to lemma 25, tells us when constraint weakening has to be applied in redundancy proofs for first-order clauses:

Lemma 43: Let $S_0, S_1, \ldots$ be a theorem proving derivation. The clause $C\,[\![T]\!]$ is redundant in a set S_j if
(i)   for every ground instance $C\sigma$, there are ground instances $D_i\sigma_i$ for $i = 1\ldots m$ of clauses $D_i\,[\![T_i]\!]$ in S_j such that $\{D_1\sigma_1,\ldots, D_m\sigma_m\} \models C\sigma$ and $C\sigma \succ_C D_i\sigma_i$, and moreover
(ii)   for every i in $1\ldots m$, and for every x in $Vars(D_i)$, T_i does not bind x, or else $x\sigma_i = y\sigma$, for some variable y in C.

The interest of applying basic superposition to completion of first-order clauses with equality lies not only in the gain of efficiency as a consequence of the more reduced search space, but also in the higher probability of obtaining *complete* systems. By using such complete systems S, i.e. sets of clauses in which no more non-redundant inferences can be computed, very efficient complete strategies can be applied for refutational theorem proving, since no new inferences between clauses in S have to be computed.

5. Further work

Some of the techniques of this paper can be applied to other kinds of constraints. Here we briefly outline some results of our follow-up paper [NR 91] on the combination of basic superposition modelled by the use of equality constraints, and the notion of *ordering constraints*. The interest of similar ordering constraints has been pointed out earlier, e.g. in [KKR 90], but, as far as we know, no completeness proofs had been found up to now.

The basic idea is very simple. In ordered inference rules like superposition the search space is reduced by selecting only the maximal terms in the maximal literals to paramodulate upon. Therefore, if a clause is obtained in an inference, we are in fact only interested in those ground instances of it for which the literal (and term) selected is really the biggest one. This information can be kept in its constraint. Future choices of maximal literals that are incompatible with this constraint can then be shown to be unnecessary by proving the unsatisfiability of constraints (the satisfiability of ordering constraints is shown to be decidable in [Com 90]).

For example, if we denote by $t \simeq t' \; [\![T]\!]$ the ground instances of an equation $t \simeq t'$ satisfying the combined ordering and equality constraint T, then the inference rule of basic superposition with ordering constraints for the equational case is:

$$\frac{s \simeq s' \; [\![T']\!] \qquad t \simeq t' \; [\![T]\!]}{t[s']_u \simeq t' \; [\![T' \wedge T \wedge s \succ s' \wedge t \succ t' \wedge t|_u = s]\!]} \quad \text{where } t|_u \notin \mathcal{V}ars(t)$$

which, as we can see, is a very powerful and also elegant representation for ordered inference rules, since information from the meta-level, such as the ordering restrictions and accumulated unifiers generated in ancestors, is included into the formulae and used later on.

Especially in the case of full first-order clauses, but also in the equational case, the ordering constraints become quickly very restrictive, which cuts down the search space drastically. We have reasons to believe that complete systems can be obtained in many more cases, including full first-order specifications. In [NR 91] we define a completion procedure for full first-order clauses with ordering constraints where, as above, redundant inferences can be ignored and redundant clauses can be deleted without loosing completeness. This improves the techniques for ordering constrained completion for the equational case given in [Pet 90], since we can deal with full first-order clauses, we do not need to compute additional kinds of inferences, we allow initial axioms with constraints, and we can combine our methods with basic superposition. In [NR 91] we also report two new results needed for efficiently dealing with ordering constraints.

Acknowledgements: We wish to thank Marianne Haberstrau, Fernando Orejas, Pilar Nivela, Harald Ganzinger and Leo Bachmair and all those who commented our preliminary manuscript introducing this kind of techniques during the RTA '91 conference.

6. References

[BDP 89]   L. Bachmair, N. Dershowitz, D. Plaisted: Completion without failure. In H. Ait-Kaci and M. Nivat, editors, Resolution of equations in algebraic structures, vol 2: Rewriting Techniques, pp 1-30, Academic Press, (1989).

[BG 91]   L. Bachmair, H. Ganzinger: Completion of first-order clauses with equality. (final version) 2nd Intl. Workshop on Conditional and Typed Term Rewriting, Montreal, LNCS 516, pp. 162-181, (1991).

[Com 90]   H. Comon: Solving Symbolic Ordering Constraints. In proc. 5th IEEE Symp. Logic in Comp. Sc. Philadelphia. (June 1990).

[DJ 90]   N. Dershowitz, J-P. Jouannaud: Rewrite systems, in Handbook of Theoretical Computer Science, vol. B: Formal Methods and Semantics. (J. van Leeuwen, ed.), North Hollad, Amsterdam, 1990.

[DJ 91]   N. Dershowitz, J-P. Jouannaud: Notations for Rewriting. in Bulletin of the EATCS, no. 43, Feb 1991.

[HR 89]   J. Hsiang, M. Rusinowitch: Proving refutational completeness of theorem proving strategies: The transfinite semantic tree method. Submitted for publication (1989).

[Hul 80]   J.M. Hullot: Compilation de Formes Canoniques dans les Teories Equationnelles, These de 3eme Cycle, Universite de Paris Sud, 1980.

[KB 70]   D.E. Knuth, P.B. Bendix: Simple word problems in universal algebras. J. Leech, editor, Computational Problems in Abstract Algebra, 263-297, Pergamon Press, Oxford, 1970.

[KKR 90]   C. and H. Kirchner, M. Rusinowitch: Deduction with Symbolic Constraints. Revue Francaise d'Intelligence Artificielle. Vol 4. No. 3. pp. 9-52. Special issue on automatic deduction. (1990).

[Nie 91]   R. Nieuwenhuis: First-order completion techniques. Research report UPC-LSI, 1991.

[NN 91]   R. Nieuwenhuis, P. Nivela: Efficient deduction in equality Horn logic by Horn-completion, Information Processing Letters, no. 39, pp. 1-6, July 1991.

[NO 91]   R. Nieuwenhuis, F. Orejas: Clausal Rewriting. 2nd Intl. Workshop on Conditional and Typed Term Rewriting, Montreal, LNCS 516, pp. 246-261, (1991).

[NOR 90]   R. Nieuwenhuis, F. Orejas, A. Rubio: TRIP: an implementation of clausal rewriting. In Proc. 10th Int. Conf. on Automated Deduction. Kaiserslautern, 1990. LNCS, pp 667-668.

[NR 91]   R. Nieuwenhuis, A. Rubio: Theorem Proving with Ordering Constrained Clauses. Research report UPC-LSI, 1991. (submitted).

[Pet 90]   G.E. Peterson: Complete Sets of Reductions with Constraints. In Proc. 10th Int. Conf. on Automated Deduction. Kaiserslautern, 1990. LNCS, pp 381-395.

[Rus 87]   M. Rusinowitch: Theorem-proving with resolution and superposition: an extension of Knuth and Bendix procedure as a complete set of inference rules. Report 87-R-128, CRIN, Nancy, 1987.

Observers for Linear Types

Martin Odersky*

Yale University, Department of Computer Science,
Box 2158 Yale Station, New Haven, CT 06520

odersky@cs.yale.edu

Abstract

Linear types provide the framework for a safe embedding of mutable state in functional languages by enforcing the principle that variables of linear type must be used exactly once. A potential disadvantage of this approach is that it places read accesses to such variables under the same restriction as write accesses, and thus prevents reads to proceed in parallel. We present here an extension of linear types which augments the usual distinction between linear and non-linear by a third state, *observers* of linear variables. Since, unlike linear variables, observers can be duplicated, multiple concurrent reads are made possible. On the other hand, observers must be short-lived enough to never overlap with mutations. The resulting type system is in many aspects similar to the one of ML: It is polymorphic, has principal types, and admits a type reconstruction algorithm.

1 Introduction

We are investigating a type system that addresses the update problem in functional languages: How can we implement updates efficiently, but still retain a declarative semantics? Methods to solve this problem — of which there are many — usually come under the name of effect analysis. Effect analysis looks for opportunities to replace costly non-destructive operations on aggregates such as arrays or hash tables by cheaper destructive ones. This can take place at run-time, using reference counting [GSH88] or reverse difference lists [Coh84]. It can also be performed at compile-time, using one of the optimization techniques of [Hud87, NPD87, Blo89, Deu90, DP90], for instance. A third alternative is to let the programmer perform effect analysis, and reduce the task of the computer to *effect checking*; the computer simply verifies that the transition from non-destructive to destructive operations is semantics preserving. In this setting it is natural to regard effect information to be a kind of type information and effect checking to be an extension of type checking.

The main advantage of this programmer-directed approach is that the choice between copying and in-place updates is made visible. Hence, the programmer can avoid the

---

*work was done in part while at IBM T.J. Watson Research Center.

potentially drastic efficiency loss which could otherwise result from missed optimization opportunities. This is most important in the presence of separate compilation and software component libraries. Users of such libraries have to know how they can access the exported components without risking performance degradation. As the standard way of communicating such legal use-patterns is a type system, it seems to be a good idea to augment types with effect information. However, effect checking type systems face the double challenge of avoiding being either too restrictive or too complex. After all, unlike automatic optimizers, programmers are willing to digest only a limited amount of effect information.

We present here an approach towards an effect checking type system which meets these challenges. Observable linear types are loosely based on Wadler's "steadfast, standard" version of linear types and extend it by adding "read-only" (in our terms: observer) accesses to linear variables. In [Wad91] this extension was acknowledged to be an open research problem.

Linear type systems [Laf88, Abr90, Wad91] are related by the Curry-Howard isomorphism to Girard's linear logic [Gir87]. They are based on the principle that a variable of linear type must be used exactly once. If linear types are steadfast, that is, not convertible with non-linear types, this principle allows updates to linear variables to be performed destructively and also obviates the need for garbage collecting them. In the terminology of [Wad90b], linear variables make up the "world", which can be neither duplicated nor discarded.

The "no-duplication" restriction on linear variables makes them a bit awkward to use in programming. Observation of the world is placed under precisely the same restrictions as changes to it, although it is clearly much less intrusive. To address this shortcoming, Wadler suggested in [Wad90b] a construct which exceeds linear logic by allowing the world to be observed in a local context. This is written

$$\text{let! } (a)\ x = e'\text{ in } e. \tag{1}$$

Here, the linear variable a, used once in the outer expression e, may also be read arbitrarily often in the local expression e'. To make this construct safe, Wadler proposed the following measures: First, a hyperstrict evaluation rule which specifies that e' be reduced to normal form before evaluation of e is begun. Second, a static restriction that all components of a and x have mutually distinct types. Finally, a static restriction that x may not be of function type. The static restrictions prevent the normal form of x from sharing the value of the linear variable a. Together with the hyperstrict evaluation rule this ensures safety, but at quite drastic cost: In particular the "mutually distinct types" requirement is an overly conservative approximation to the actual aliasing in a let! construct. The approximation becomes even worse if the type system is polymorphic (the one in [Wad90b] isn't). In that case, the notion of equality between types has to be replaced by unifiability. As a consequence, virtually every let! construct is unsafe in which the type of either the linear or the bound variable is polymorphic. Hence, we see that linear types have so far been better at changing the world than at observing it.

In this paper, we look at a more thorough solution to the observer problem. We will be concerned only with the "no-duplication" property of linear types, not with the "no-discarding" property which allows static garbage collection. The principal idea is to extend the distinction between linear and nonlinear variables by a third state, which denotes observers of linear variables. In the *let!* construct (1), all occurrences of the linear variable a in e' would now have type "observer". Unlike linear types themselves, observers can be duplicated freely (this implies that updates to observers are forbidden). However, observers have to be short-lived, they may not be exported out of the scope of a let! binding. This enforces observation and updating of linear variables to occur in a strictly alternating fashion, where no observer lives long enough to observe an update.

Linear, non-linear and observer constitute the three basic aliasing states of a variable. These states are attributes of the types in our system. The type system has the following useful properties:

- It is polymorphic in types and alias states. Type polymorphism means that a type variable ranges over all types, linear, non-linear and observers. Aliasing polymorphism means that the aliasing attribute of a type may be a variable.

- It has the principal type property. That is, given a closed initial type assignment A, every well-typed expression has a most general type-scheme σ.

- It admits a type reconstruction algorithm which assigns an expression its principal type-scheme. Type reconstruction can work without type declarations for bound variables.

- With a few straightforward abbreviations, function signatures can be written in a concise form, of comparative complexity to the use of *in* and *out* specifiers in Ada. This observation might seem somewhat surprising, since our type system is definitely more complex than the standard Hindley/Milner system, say. A partial explanation might be that much of our machinery has to do with observer types which occur only in a local context, and by definition do not show up in the type signatures of defined variables.

Other Related Work

Schmidt [Sch85] suggested a simple type system which gives conditions for safety of in-place updates. Other early work was done in the FX project [LG88, JG91] and the area has been an active research subject in the last few years. Observable linear types build on several previous approaches. Besides the strong connection to linear types, there is also a connection to Baker's "free" region analysis [Bak90] for type reconstruction. Regions do not enter our system explicitly, but the notion of region in [Bak90] or [TJ91] corresponds exactly to a collection of types with the same alias variable as an attribute.

Another popular approach to the update problem uses abstract data types to encapsulate accesses to mutable data structures. The idea is to have an abstract type of "state transformers", but no type for the transformed data structures itself [Wad90a]. There is a single operation, *block*, which creates a mutable data structure serving as a scratch area, applies a state transformer to it, and returns the (immutable) result of the application while discarding the scratch area. This has the advantage that no extension to traditional type systems is needed, but it requires programming in a continuation passing style. Also, it is currently not clear how the method should be extended to deal with several mutated data structures. The latter problem is addressed in the non-standard type system of [SRI91] which again requires continuation passing style. Continuation passing style is problematic since it fully sequentializes lookups as well as updates. By contrast, observable linear types allow lookups to proceed in parallel and generally impose much less restrictions on programming style. The latter point is important in the situation where a purely functional program is transformed into a program with transparent updates by changing the implementation of some data types. Observable linear types allow such efficiency-improving transformations to be performed incrementally, without requiring a complete rewrite.

Compared to analyses based on liabilities and function effects [GH90, Ode91], linear types augmented with observers are less precise in some cases and more precise in others. Liabilities give information about which variables are possible aliases of each other, whereas alias states only record the fact that a variable might be aliased. Hence, using liabilities we can verify some expressions to be safe which cannot be handled by all other approaches. On the other hand, current liability-based approaches are less accurate for non-flat mutable structures. Moreover, when extended to higher-order functions, they do not admit "nice" principal types (i.e. they need disjunctive constraints, see [Ode91] for an example). We believe that approaches based on linear types will turn out to be more practical than liability-based approaches because they tend to be more concise and generalize naturally to the higher-order case.

The rest of this paper is organized as follows: Section 2 defines the syntax of types in a small example language. Section 3 discusses their use in several program examples. Section 4 presents typing rules. Section 5 discusses a type reconstruction algorithm. Section 6 concludes.

2 Observable Linear Types

Language

We use essentially the language of [Wad90b], with the exception of let! constructs, where in our case observers of linear variables need not be quoted. Quoting these variables explicitly is undesirable since it restricts polymorphism, and our type reconstruction algorithm can work without it.

Expressions	e	::=	x	identifiers
		|	$e\ e'$	application
		|	$\lambda x.e$	abstraction
		|	$\lambda_1 x.e$	linear abstraction
		|	let $x = e'$ in e	definition
		|	let! $x = e'$ in e	sequential definition
		|	if e_1 then e_2 else e_3	conditional

Monomorphic Types

We start with a type system which is monomorphic in its aliasing aspects (but polymorphic in its structural aspects). A type in this system (called a *monotype* in the following) consists of two parts $\alpha \cdot v$ which describe outside aliasing and internal structure, respectively. The components are separated by an infix dot (.).

Monomorphic types	τ	$=$	κ	basic type
		$\mid$	$list\ \tau$	list type
		$\mid$	$\tau_1 \rightarrow \tau_2$	function type
		$\mid$	$\alpha \cdot \tau$	alias state · type
		$\mid$	t	type variable
Alias states	α	$=$	$0 \mid 1 \mid 2$	observer, linear, non-linear

In our example language, we will use only a few different forms of types τ, namely (immutable) basic types, mutable lists, and function types. We will see in Section 3 how other mutable data structures such as arrays or matrices can be constructed from mutable lists. Hence, there is no need for modeling these structures in the type system (although an implementation should certainly treat them as special cases).

The aliasing part α of a monotype is one of the three constants 0, 1, and 2. Variables of a 1-type may be accessed only once, and we have the invariant that at most one reference can exist to values of these types. 1-types correspond to linear types, and, in a slight misuse of language, we will also call them linear. The correspondence is not exact, since we are concerned only with the "no-duplication" property of 1-types, and allow discarding a value of 1-type, whereas this is forbidden in pure linear type systems. Variables of 2-type (or: non-linear type) may be accessed arbitrarily often and may share references with other non-linear variables. The third category of types are the observer-, or 0-types. Observer types allow linear variables to be used more than once. They don't "add to" linear uses (that's why they are given denotation 0). When used locally in a let! construct, all occurrences of a variable which is linear at the outside are given observer type inside. There may be several such occurrences, but no observer variable may form part of the value which is locally defined in that expression. Put in other words, all components of the type of a variable defined by a let! must have 1- or 2-type. Assuming that the evaluation of let! definitions is hyperstrict, we can hence ensure that observation and updating of linear variables occur in a strictly alternating fashion.

Composite list types have an aliasing attribute for the whole type and an attribute for the element type at each level. Not every combination of alias attributes is permissible, we require that a list type is well-formed:

Definition. The monotype $\alpha \cdot list\ (\beta \cdot v)$ is *well-formed* iff

$$\alpha \in \{0, 2\} \quad \Rightarrow \quad \beta \in \{0, 2\}$$

The well-formedness condition is needed to ensure that a linear element is not shared (or observed) indirectly by sharing (or observing) its parent.

Monomorphic observable linear types give rise to a type system which extends the steadfast types of [Wad91] with observers. As an example of its use, consider a function which copies an array element to another index position. Assume for the time being that arrays are implemented as lists, with operations (!) for indexing and (*update*) for in-place updates.

$$assign \quad = \quad \lambda i. \, \lambda j. \, \lambda a. \, \text{let!} \, x = a!i \, \text{in} \, update \, j \, x \, a$$

Our type system will assign type $0 \cdot list \, (2 \cdot v)$ to the first, local occurrence of the array a. The type of the locally defined variable x is $(2 \cdot v)$ and thus satisfies the restriction that local definitions in a *let!* cannot be of observer type. The last occurrence of a has type $1 \cdot list \, 2 \cdot v$, reflecting the fact that variable a is modified. The type of the whole function is:

$$assign \quad : \quad int \rightarrow int \rightarrow 1 \cdot list \, (2 \cdot v) \rightarrow 1 \cdot list \, (2 \cdot v).$$

This expresses that the array argument is modified (and therefore has to be linear), whereas one of its elements is duplicated (and therefore must be non-linear). The observer state was used only locally; it allowed us to use the linear variable a twice.

The monomorphic type system is still quite inflexible. For instance, it is not possible to formulate a function *head* which works equally on linear and non-linear lists, since the alias state of function arguments is fixed. The obvious way to lift this restriction is to introduce variables which range over alias states, and we will do so in the next sub-section.

Polymorphic Types

A polymorphic observable linear type (called *polytype* in the following) has a variable in its alias component. The variable usually ranges over the three alias states, but its range can be constrained by predicates. Following [Jon91a], we express this using the syntax of *qualified types*:

Alias Parts	α	$= \quad 0 \mid 1 \mid 2 \mid t \mid O \, \alpha$
Qualified Types	ρ	$= \quad \pi \Rightarrow \rho \mid \tau$
Predicates	π	$= \quad \alpha \leq \overline{0} \mid \alpha \leq \overline{1} \mid \alpha \leq \overline{2} \mid \alpha \supseteq \tau$
Type Schemes	σ	$= \quad \forall t.\sigma \mid \rho$

Observer tags O are the polymorphic equivalent of the mapping from (monomorphic) linear to observer status in the monomorphic system. If a bound variable x has type $a \cdot v$ outside of a *let!*-construct, it is given type $O \, a \cdot v$ inside. This serves as a "reminder" that any value assumed by variable a at the outside has to be translated to observer status inside.

Type variables can be constrained by predicates. There are two forms of such predicates. The first form, $\alpha \leq \overline{n}$, constrains the range of α to a a subset of all three alias-sets. The three two-element alias-sets are characterized as complements of a singleton set. $\overline{0}$ (non-observer, or original) encompasses 1 and 2. Variables defined in a let! are required to be originals. $\overline{1}$ (aliased) encompasses 0 and 2. If a function uses an argument several times outside of a let! construct, the argument's type falls in this set. Finally, $\overline{2}$ encompasses 0 and 1.

Note that by combining any two of these constraints, we get a monotypej. For instance, $\forall a. a \leq \overline{0} \Rightarrow a \leq \overline{1} \Rightarrow a \cdot \tau$ is equivalent to $2 \cdot \tau$. If a variable is simultaneously bounded by all three constraints, the constraint set is unsatisfiable and the corresponding type is empty.

The second form of constraint makes the well-formedness criterion for list types explicit. The predicate $\alpha \supseteq \tau$ is equivalent to the constraint set

$$\alpha \leq \overline{1} \quad \Rightarrow \quad \beta \leq \overline{1}$$

where β ranges over all the alias parts of τ and its component types. The typing rules are such that every occurrence of $\alpha \cdot (list\ \tau)$ in a principal type is constrained by a predicate $\alpha \supseteq (list\ \tau)$.

Example 2.1 The type of function map would be expressed as follows:

$$map \quad : \quad \forall s \forall t \forall a \forall b. (a \supseteq list\ s) \Rightarrow (b \supseteq list\ t) \Rightarrow 2 \cdot (s \to t) \to a \cdot list\ s \to b \cdot list\ t,$$

For conciseness, we will in the following drop $(\alpha \supseteq \tau)$ constraints on a type if they are implied by the structure of the type itself, i.e. if the type contains a subtype of the form $\alpha \cdot \tau$. We will also drop the alias part of a type altogether if it is trivial, i.e. equal to an unconstrained, unshared type variable. Finally, we allow multiple predicates to be grouped together, i.e. $(\pi_1 \Rightarrow \pi_2 \Rightarrow \rho) = (\pi_1, \pi_2 \Rightarrow \rho)$.

Example 2.2 Using these shorthands, the type of map would be written:

$$map \quad : \quad \forall s \forall t. 2 \cdot (s \to t) \to list\ s \to list\ t.$$

Predefined Identifiers

As predefined we assume the fixpoint operator fix, and a set of operators on lists. Besides the conventional operators $nil, cons, hd$ and tl, we also have a destructive update operation on lists. $rplac$ takes as arguments two functions f and g which map list heads to list heads and list tails to list tails. Its third argument is a list xs of linear type. The value of

$$rplac\ f\ g\ xs \quad is \quad cons\ (f\ (hd\ xs))\ (g\ (tl\ xs)),$$

and as a side-effect the first $cons$-node of xs is replaced by this value. The types of the predefined identifiers are:

$$
\begin{array}{lll}
nil & : & \forall a \forall t.\ a \cdot list\ t \\
cons & : & \forall a \forall t.\ t \to a \cdot list\ t \to a \cdot list\ t \\
hd & : & \forall a \forall t.\ a \cdot list\ t \to t \\
tl & : & \forall a \forall t.\ a \cdot list\ t \to a \cdot list\ t
\end{array}
$$

$$rplac \quad : \quad \forall a \forall b \forall t.\ 2 \cdot (t \to t) \to 2 \cdot (a \cdot list\ t \to b \cdot list\ t) \to 1 \cdot list\ t \to b \cdot list\ t$$
$$fix \quad : \quad \forall v.\ 2 \cdot (2 \cdot v \to 2 \cdot v) \to 2 \cdot v\ .$$

The type of *rplac* merits further consideration. One might think that since the tail-replacing function in the second argument is passed a linear list, its type should really be $(1 \cdot list\ t \to b \cdot list\ t)$. This would lead to some needless loss of polymorphism, however. After all, just because an argument is linear (i.e. unshared), a function applied to it should not be required to exploit the linearity by overwriting the argument. The correct interpretation is that arguments which are known to be linear can safely be used in any way whatsoever. The most general type of the tail-replacing function is therefore $(a \cdot list\ t \to b \cdot list\ t)$.

The type of the fixpoint operator also needs some explanation. *fix* is defined only on transformations between non-linear values and its result is again a non-linear value. To see why taking the fixpoint of a transformation between linear values is problematic, consider the expression

$$mkcirc \quad : \quad 1 \cdot list\ Int \to 1 \cdot list\ Int$$
$$mkcirc \quad = \quad \lambda xs.\ cons\ 1\ (rplac\ (-1)\ id\ xs)\ ,$$

where (-1) is the predecessor function on integers. If *fix* were defined for transformations between linear values, *fix mkcirc* would be legal, of type $1 \cdot\ list\ Int$. But what is the value of this expression? If we disregard side-effects and look at the definition of *rplac*'s result above, it should be the list $[1, 0, 0, ...]$. If we take side-effects into account, however, and assume that the list is evaluated in a head-strict order, we get the list $[0, 0, 0, ...]$. This violates the requirement that all side-effects of well-typed expressions should be transparent.

3 Examples

This section tries to give a "feel" of our type system by means of small example programs. We hope to convey the impression that the type signatures of most functions occurring in practice are quite reasonable in size and complexity and also closely correspond to the programmer's intuition. First, here is a side-effecting version of the *append* function:

$$append \quad = \quad fix\ \lambda append.\ \lambda xs.\ \lambda_1 ys.$$
$$\text{if } xs = nil \text{ then } ys$$
$$\text{else } rplac\ id\ (\lambda tl.\ append\ tl\ ys)\ xs$$

The typing rules presented in the next section give *append* the type:

$$append \quad : \quad \forall a \forall t.\ 1 \cdot list\ t \to 1 \cdot (a \cdot list\ t \to a \cdot list\ t)$$

Since the first list argument to *append* gets updated, it must be linear, of type $1 \cdot list\ t$. The type of a curried application like *append xs* must also be linear, because *append xs* contains a reference to a linear variable. Otherwise, we could duplicate accesses to xs in an expression such as

$$(\lambda f. (f\ ys, f\ zs))\ (append\ xs).$$

The language has a special form of λ-abstraction, denoted λ_1, to define linear functions which have "global" side-effects (i.e. which modify variables other than their arguments). Having two forms of λ-abstraction does cause some loss of polymorphism in that we have to declare statically whether a function is going to have a global side-effect or not. This can be difficult to predict for higher-order functions. It appears that our type system could be extended to deal with just one kind of λ abstraction for linear and non-linear functions using a technique similar to the one in [Wad91]. This would add constraints to type signatures, however, something we wanted to avoid because of the syntactic overhead associated with it. A good alternative, which also avoids the use of λ_1, is to have the modified argument come last:

$$
\begin{aligned}
append' &\quad:\quad \forall a \forall t.\ a \cdot list\ t \rightarrow 1 \cdot list\ t \rightarrow a \cdot list\ t \\
append'\ xs\ ys &\quad=\quad append\ ys\ xs
\end{aligned}
$$

To simplify presentation, we will from now on allow functions to be written in the equational style. The translation to λ-abstractions and fixpoint operators should be obvious.

The $append$ function uses the rather "heavyweight" operation $rplac$. We can simplify this by using specialized versions of $rplac$ which replace only heads or only tails:

$$
\begin{aligned}
rplhd &\quad:\quad \forall t.\ 2 \cdot (t \rightarrow t) \rightarrow 1 \cdot list\ t \rightarrow list\ t \\
rpltl &\quad:\quad \forall a \forall t.\ 2 \cdot (list\ t \rightarrow a \cdot list\ t) \rightarrow 1 \cdot list\ t \rightarrow a \cdot list\ t \\[4pt]
rplhd\ f &\quad=\quad rplac\ f\ id \\
rpltl\ f &\quad=\quad rplac\ id\ f
\end{aligned}
$$

Remember that $list\ t$, the result type of $rplhd$, is an abbreviation for $a \cdot list\ t$, where a is a fresh type variable. That is, the alias part of $rplhd$'s result type is unconstrained.

Here are linear equivalents of the higher order functions map and $foldl$:

$$
\begin{aligned}
maplin &\quad:\quad \forall t.\ 2 \cdot (t \rightarrow t) \rightarrow 1 \cdot list\ t \rightarrow list\ t \\
maplin\ f &\quad=\quad rplac\ f\ (maplin\ f) \\[4pt]
foldlin &\quad:\quad \forall s. \forall t.\ 2 \cdot (t \rightarrow s \rightarrow s) \rightarrow list\ t \rightarrow s \rightarrow s. \\
foldlin\ f\ xs\ acc &\quad=\quad \textbf{if}\ xs = nil\ \textbf{then}\ acc \\
&\qquad\quad\ \textbf{else}\ foldlin\ f\ (tl\ xs)\ (f\ (hd\ xs)\ acc)
\end{aligned}
$$

$maplin$ maps a function on a linear list, replacing every node of that list by its corresponding node in the result list. $foldlin$ does not restrict any argument to be linear, in fact it is just Haskell's $foldl$ with the second and third argument swapped. $foldlin\ f$ is side-effecting if f is, and is pure otherwise.

Here are some other functions on lists:

$$
\begin{aligned}
upd \quad &: \quad \forall t.\ int \to 2{\cdot}(t \to t) \to 1{\cdot}list\ t \to list\ t \\
upd\ i\ f \quad &= \quad \textbf{if}\ i = 0\ \textbf{then}\ rplhd\ f\ \textbf{else}\ upd\ (i-1)\ f \circ tl \\[4pt]
swap \quad &: \quad \forall t.\ int \to int \to 1{\cdot}list\ t \to list\ t \\
swap\ i\ j\ xs \quad &= \quad \textbf{let!}\ x\ =\ xs!i\ \textbf{in} \\
&\qquad \textbf{let!}\ y\ =\ xs!j \\
&\qquad \textbf{in}\ \ (upd\ i\ (K\ y)\ \circ upd\ j\ (K\ x))\ xs
\end{aligned}
$$

Function *upd* updates a selected element of a list, and *swap* exchanges two list elements. Using lookups (!) and updates (*upd*), we can express mutable vectors in terms of lists. Higher-dimensional mutable arrays can be defined, too. For instance, the update operation for a matrix, represented as a list of lists, is:

$$
\begin{aligned}
\textbf{type}\ a{\cdot}mat\ t \quad &= \quad a{\cdot}list\ (a{\cdot}list\ t) \\[4pt]
upd2 \quad &: \quad int \to int \to 2{\cdot}(t \to t) \to 1{\cdot}mat\ t \to mat\ t \\
upd2\ i\ j\ f \quad &= \quad upd\ i\ (upd\ j\ f)
\end{aligned}
$$

For a larger example, we now turn to topological sorting. We want to find a total order for the nodes of a graph in which every node precedes its successors. To make our task of designing an efficient algorithm easier, we assume that the graph is in a convenient representation, given by:

- the list *sources* : *list node* of all sources in the graph,

- a list *succs* : *list (list node)* which contains for every node in the graph the list of all its successors.

- a linear list *npreds* : $1 \cdot list\ int$ which contains for every node in the graph the number of its predecessors. This list serves as a "scratch area".

We also assume that *node* = *int* such that we can index lists with nodes. Given this graph representation, we can formulate the topological sorting function as follows:

$$
tsort\ :\ 2{\cdot}list\ node \to list\ (list\ node) \to 1{\cdot}list\ int \to list\ node
$$

$$
\begin{aligned}
&tsort\ sources\ succs\ npreds\ = \\
&\quad \textbf{if}\ sources = nil\ \textbf{then} \\
&\qquad\qquad nil \\
&\quad \textbf{else} \\
&\qquad\qquad \textbf{let}\ \ src\ \ \ \ \ \ =\ hd\ sources\ \textbf{in} \\
&\qquad\qquad \textbf{let}\ \ decnth\ =\ \lambda n.\ upd\ n\ (-1)\ \textbf{in} \\
&\qquad\qquad \textbf{let!}\ npreds'\ =\ foldlin\ decnth\ (succs!src)\ npreds\ \textbf{in} \\
&\qquad\qquad \textbf{let!}\ sources'\ =\ filter\ (\lambda x.\ npreds'!x = 0)\ (succs!src)\ \mathbin{+\!\!+}\ tl\ sources \\
&\qquad\qquad \textbf{in}\ \ cons\ src\ (tsort\ sources'\ succs\ npreds')
\end{aligned}
$$

If we assume that mutable lists are implemented as vectors, such that lookups and updates have both constant cost, then the complexity of *topsort* is $O(|nodes| + |edges|)$,

$$var \quad A, P \vdash x : \sigma \quad (x : \sigma \in A)$$

$$\forall I \quad \frac{A, P \vdash e : \sigma}{A, P \vdash e : \forall t.\sigma} \quad (t \notin tv\ A \cup tv\ P)$$

$$\forall E \quad \frac{A, P \vdash e : \forall t.\sigma}{A, P \vdash e : [\tau =: t]\ \sigma}$$

$$\Rightarrow I \quad \frac{A, P.\pi \vdash e : \rho}{A, P \vdash e : \pi \Rightarrow \rho}$$

$$\Rightarrow E \quad \frac{A, P \vdash e : \pi \Rightarrow \rho}{A, P \vdash e : \rho} \quad (P \Vdash \pi)$$

Figure 1: Structural Rules for OLT

$$taut \quad P \Vdash \pi \quad (\pi \in P)$$

$$lit \quad
\begin{array}{ll}
P \Vdash 1 \leq \overline{0} & \quad P \Vdash 2 \leq \overline{0} \\
P \Vdash 0 \leq \overline{1} & \quad P \Vdash 2 \leq \overline{1} \\
P \Vdash 0 \leq \overline{2} & \quad P \Vdash 1 \leq \overline{2}
\end{array}$$

$$obs \quad P \Vdash O\alpha \leq \overline{1} \qquad \frac{P \Vdash \alpha \leq \overline{2}}{P \Vdash O\alpha \leq \overline{2}}$$

$$wf \quad \frac{P \Vdash \alpha \supseteq list\ (\beta \cdot \tau)}{P \Vdash \alpha \supseteq \tau} \qquad \frac{P \Vdash \alpha \supseteq list\ (\beta \cdot \tau) \quad P \Vdash \alpha \leq \overline{1}}{P \Vdash \beta \leq \overline{1}}$$

Figure 2: Entailment Rules for $\Vdash$

which matches the best known imperative algorithms. This remains true even if we use a more standard graph representation consisting of a node list and an edge list, since these lists can be converted in $O(|nodes| + |edges|)$ time into the representation we have assumed.

4 Typing Rules

We formulate the system OLT of observable linear types as a a system of qualified types [Jon91a]. Sequents are of the form $A, P \vdash e : \sigma$, where the type assignment A is a set of assumptions $x : \sigma'$, and the context P is a set of predicates π. We use $tv\ \sigma$ or $tv\ A$ to denote the free type variables in a type scheme or type assignment. We use $fv\ e$ to denote the free program variables in an expression. We use letters P, Q, R to denote

$$\to I \quad \frac{A.x\!:\!\tau',P \;\vdash\; e:\tau}{A,P \;\vdash\; \lambda x.e:\alpha\cdot(\tau'\to\tau)} \quad (P \Vdash NL\ A)$$

$$\to_1 I \quad \frac{A.x\!:\!\tau',P \;\vdash\; e:\tau}{A,P \;\vdash\; \lambda_1 x.e:1\cdot(\tau'\to\tau)}$$

$$\to E \quad \frac{A,P \;\vdash\; e:\alpha\cdot(\tau'\to\tau) \qquad A,P \;\vdash\; e':\tau'}{A,P \;\vdash\; e\ e':\tau} \quad (P \Vdash \{\alpha\le\overline{0},\}\cup NL\ A|_{fv\ e'\cap fv\ e})$$

$$let \quad \frac{A,P \;\vdash\; e':\sigma \qquad A.x\!:\!sigma,P \;\vdash\; e:\tau}{A,P \;\vdash\; \textbf{let}\ x=e'\ \textbf{in}\ e:\tau} \quad (P \Vdash NL\ A|_{fv\ e'\cap fv\ e})$$

$$let! \quad \frac{A',P \;\vdash\; e':\sigma \qquad A.x\!:\!\sigma,P \;\vdash\; e:\tau}{A,P \;\vdash\; \textbf{let!}\ x=e'\ \textbf{in}\ e:\tau} \quad (obs(A',A,fv\ e),\ orig\ (P\Rightarrow\sigma))$$

$$if \quad \frac{A',P \;\vdash\; e_1:bool \quad A,P \;\vdash\; e_2:\tau \quad A,P \;\vdash\; e_3:\tau}{A,P \;\vdash\; \textbf{if}\ e_1\ \textbf{then}\ e_2\ \textbf{else}\ e_3:\tau} \quad (obs(A',A,fve_1\cup fv\ e_2))$$

Figure 3: Logical Rules for OLT

sets of predicates π. Type schemes σ will often be written $\forall\alpha_i.P\Rightarrow\tau$, where α_i denotes the bound variables and P denotes the predicates in σ. Analogous to qualified types, we will also use *qualified type schemes* of the form $P\Rightarrow\sigma$, where the predicate P constrains the free variables in σ.

Structural rules for OLT are given in Figure 1. Rule $(\Rightarrow E)$ is based on an entailment relation $\Vdash$ between predicate sets and predicates, which is defined in Figure 2. Here, rules (lit) define the relationship between monomorphic alias sets $0,1,2$ and alias sets $\overline{0},\overline{1},\overline{2}$, as explained Section 2. Rules (obs) determine the predicates that hold for tagged alias parts $O\alpha$: they are never linear, and are of 2-type iff the untagged alias part is of 2-type. Finally, rules (wf) correspond to the well-formedness criterion on list types.

Relation $\Vdash$ is extended to a relation between predicate sets by defining $Q \Vdash P$ iff $Q \Vdash \pi$ for all $\pi\in P$. It has the following useful properties:

Theorem 4.1 (a) $\Vdash$ is monotonic, $\pi\in P$ implies $P \Vdash \pi$.
(b) $\Vdash$ is transitive, $P \Vdash Q$ and $Q \Vdash R$ imply $P \Vdash R$.
(c) $\Vdash$ is closed under substitution, $P \Vdash Q$ implies $SP \Vdash SQ$ for every substitution S.

Proof: (a) follows from rule $(taut)$, (b) and (c) follow from the fact that $\Vdash$ is defined by a sequent calculus.

Definition. Let F denote the constraint set $\{\alpha\le\overline{n}\mid n\in\{0,1,2\}\}$, for an arbitrary alias part α. A constraint set P is *satisfiable* iff $P \not\Vdash F$. A qualified type scheme $P\Rightarrow(\forall\alpha_i.Q\Rightarrow\rho)$ is *empty* if $P\cup Q$ is unsatisfiable.

Theorem 4.2 (a) For every constraint set P and substitution S, If P is unsatisfiable, then so is SP.
(b) For every constraint set P, it is decidable whether P is satisfiable or not.

Proof: (*a*) is a direct consequence of Theorem 4.1(*c*). We now prove (*b*). Let P be a set of predicates and let P^* be the $\Vdash$ closure of P. Then, $P \Vdash F$ iff $P^* \supseteq F$. We show that it suffices to look at the subset P' of P^* which consist of all predicates in P^* whose alias-parts also appear in P. A predicate on an alias part that is in P^* but not in P can only be generated by application of rule (*obs*), with conclusion $O\alpha \leq \overline{n}$, say. But then there is no way to deduce $O\ \alpha \leq \overline{0}$, since there is no rule with a conclusion of this form. Hence, $P \Vdash F \Leftrightarrow P^* \supseteq F \Leftrightarrow P' \supseteq F$. Since P' is finite, (*b*) follows. ∎

Logical rules are given in Figure 3. There are two rules for the introduction of functions. Rule $(\rightarrow_1 I)$ introduces linear functions which can have global side-effects. Rule $(\rightarrow I)$ introduces functions without such effects. Absence of global side-effects is enforced in $(\rightarrow I)$ by the condition that no identifier in the type assignment A can have linear type.

Rules $(\lambda I), (\rightarrow E)$ and (*let*) impose a nonlinearity constraint on (part of a) type assignment. *NL A* yields a set of constraints which together imply that A contains no linear types. It is defined by:

$$NL\ A\ =\ \{\alpha \leq \overline{1} \mid x : \alpha \cdot \tau \in A\}$$

The conditions in rule (*let!*) replace the "distinct types" condition of [Wad90b]. First, the local environment A' and the global environment A are related by a constraint $obs(A', A, fv\ e)$, in words: A' observes A on the free variables of e. We define relation *obs* between type assignments, type schemes and types, and alias parts by a set of Horn clauses as follows:

$$
\begin{aligned}
\forall x \in fvs.obs(A'x, Ax) &\Rightarrow obs(A', A, fvs) \\
obs(\sigma', \sigma) &\Rightarrow obs(\forall\alpha.\sigma', \forall\alpha.\sigma) \\
obs(\rho', \rho) &\Rightarrow obs(\pi \Rightarrow \rho', \pi \Rightarrow \rho) \\
obs(\tau', \tau) &\Rightarrow obs(O\,t\cdot\tau', t\cdot\tau) \\
obs(\tau', \tau) &\Rightarrow obs(2\cdot\tau', 2\cdot\tau) \\
obs(\tau', \tau) &\Rightarrow obs(0\cdot\tau', 1\cdot\tau) \\
obs(\tau', \tau) &\Rightarrow obs(list\ \tau', list\ \tau) \\
obs(\tau'_1, \tau_1),\ obs(\tau'_2, \tau_2) &\Rightarrow obs(\tau'_1 \rightarrow \tau'_2, \tau_1 \rightarrow \tau_2) \\
&\qquad obs(\kappa, \kappa)
\end{aligned}
$$

This expresses that the local environment is isomorphic to the global environment, but with every part in $A|_{fvs}$ mapped to observer status. This mapping to observer state, together with the requirement that the type τ of the locally defined value may not contain observers, make the **let!** construct safe. The latter requirement is expressed by *orig* $(P \Rightarrow \sigma)$, defined as follows:

$$orig\ (P \Rightarrow \forall\alpha_i.Q \Rightarrow \tau)\ =\ P \cup Q \Vdash \{\alpha \leq \overline{0} \mid \alpha \text{ is an alias part in } \tau\}$$

The interpretation of these rules has to take into account that constraint sets may be unsatisfiable and that types may be empty. Since the primary motivation for type checking is to detect empty types, we adopt the following definition:

$$var \quad A, P \vdash x : \tau \quad (x : \sigma \in A, \; \sigma \succeq (P \Rightarrow \tau))$$

$$\rightarrow I \quad \frac{A.x : \tau', P \vdash e : \tau}{A, P \vdash \lambda x.e : \alpha \cdot (\tau' \rightarrow \tau)} \quad (P \Vdash NL\, A)$$

$$\rightarrow_1 I \quad \frac{A.x : \tau', P \vdash e : \tau}{A, P \vdash \lambda_1 x.e : \mathbf{1} \cdot (\tau' \rightarrow \tau)}$$

$$\rightarrow E \quad \frac{A, P \vdash e : \alpha \cdot (\tau' \rightarrow \tau) \qquad A, P \vdash e' : \tau'}{A, P \vdash e\, e' : \tau} \quad (P \Vdash \{\alpha \leq \overline{0}\} \cup NL\, A|_{fv\, e' \cap fv\, e})$$

$$let \quad \frac{A, P' \vdash e' : \tau' \qquad A.x : gen(A, P' \Rightarrow \tau'), P \vdash e : \tau}{A, P \vdash \mathbf{let}\, x = e'\, \mathbf{in}\, e : \tau} \quad (P \Vdash NL\, A|_{fv\, e' \cap fv\, e})$$

$$let! \quad \frac{\begin{array}{c} A', P' \vdash e' : \tau' \\ A.x : gen(A', P' \Rightarrow \tau'), P \vdash e : \tau \end{array}}{A, P \vdash \mathbf{let!}\, x = e'\, \mathbf{in}\, e : \tau} \quad (obs(A', A, fv\, e)),\; orig\, (P' \Rightarrow \tau'))$$

$$if \quad \frac{A', P' \vdash e_1 : bool \quad A, P \vdash e_2 : \tau \quad A, P \vdash e_3 : \tau}{A, P \vdash \mathbf{if}\, e_1\, \mathbf{then}\, e_2\, \mathbf{else}\, e_3 : \tau} \quad (obs(A', A, fv\, e_1 \cup fv\, e_2))$$

Figure 4: Deterministic Typing Rules for DOLT

Definition. An expression e has a type scheme σ under type assignment A and constraints P, written $A, P \supset e : \sigma$, if there is a proof in OLT of $A, P \vdash e : \sigma$ such that every proof step has a conclusion $A', P' \vdash e' : \sigma'$ with $P' \Rightarrow \sigma'$ satisfiable.

5 Principal Typings and Type Reconstruction

This section states and proves the principal type property for observable linear types and gives a sketch of a type reconstruction algorithm. To simplify our task, we first define in Figure 4 another type system, DOLT, and prove its equivalence to OLT. Unlike OLT, DOLT is deterministic and syntax-directed; the structure of all proof trees for a given typing are isomorphic, and every proof step is determined uniquely by the form of the expression e. The typing rules of DOLT translate directly into a Prolog or Typol [CDD+85] program for type reconstruction.

The following definitions, theorems, and proofs lean heavily on the theory of qualified types developed in [Jon91a, Jon91b]. We will concentrate here on aspects which are specific to observable linear types, while referring to Jones' work for all aspects that apply to systems of qualified types in general. This is possible since the entailment relation $\Vdash$ satisfies the requirements set out in [Jon91a], as stated in Theorem 4.1.

Definition. A qualified type scheme $P \Rightarrow (\forall \alpha_i.Q \Rightarrow \tau)$ has a *generic instance* $R \Rightarrow \mu$, written $P \Rightarrow (\forall \alpha_i.Q \Rightarrow \tau) \succeq R \Rightarrow \mu$, iff there are types τ_i such that

$$\mu = [\alpha_i \mapsto \tau_i]\, \tau \quad and \quad R \Vdash P \cup [\alpha_i \mapsto \tau_i]\, Q.$$

Definition. A qualified type scheme $P \Rightarrow \sigma$ is *more general* than a qualified type scheme $P' \Rightarrow \sigma'$, written $P \Rightarrow \sigma \succeq P' \Rightarrow \sigma'$, iff $(P' \Rightarrow \sigma') \succeq \rho \Rightarrow (P \Rightarrow \sigma') \succeq \rho$. for all qualified types ρ. Clearly, $\succeq$ is a preorder.

Definition. A qualified type scheme $P \Rightarrow \sigma$ is *principal* for an expression e and a type assignment A, iff $A, P \supset e : \sigma$, and, if $A, P' \supset e : \sigma'$ then $P \Rightarrow \sigma \succeq P' \Rightarrow \sigma'$.

In the following, we will use $\vdash'$ for deduction in DOLT, and continue to use $\vdash$ for deduction in OLT.

Theorem 5.1 (Soundness of DOLT) If $A, P \vdash' e : \tau$ then $A, P \vdash e : \tau$.

Proof: A straightforward induction on the structure of the proof of $A, P \vdash' e : \tau$.

The next four lemmata have equivalents in [Jon91b] and are proved in essentially the same way as done there.

Lemma 5.2 (Substitution lemma) If $A, P \vdash' e : \tau$ then $SA, SP \vdash' e : S\tau$, for every substitution S.

Lemma 5.3 If $A, P \vdash' e : \tau$ and $Q \Vdash P$ then $A, Q \vdash' e : \tau$.

Lemma 5.4 If $P \Vdash P'$ then $gen(A, P' \Rightarrow \tau) \succeq gen(A, P \Rightarrow \tau)$.

Lemma 5.5 If $A.x : \sigma, P \vdash' e : \tau$ and $\sigma' \succeq P \Rightarrow \sigma$ then $A.x : \sigma', P \vdash' e : \tau$.

Theorem 5.6 (Completeness of DOLT) If $A, P \vdash e : \tau$ then there is a set of predicates P' and a type τ such that $A, P' \vdash e : \tau$ and $gen(A, P' \Rightarrow \tau) \succeq P \Rightarrow \sigma$.

Proof: By induction on the structure of the proof of $A, P \vdash e : \tau$. The structural rules are treated exactly as in the proof of Theorem 2, [Jon91b]. The cases for the logical rules are as follows:

Case($\to I$) : We have a derivation of the form

$$\frac{A.x : \tau', P \vdash e : \tau}{A, P \vdash \lambda x.e : \alpha \cdot (\tau' \to \tau)} \quad (P \Vdash NL\ A).$$

By induction, $A.x : \tau', P' \vdash' e : v$ for some P', v with $gen(A.x : \tau', P' \Rightarrow v) \succeq P \Rightarrow \tau$. By the definition of gen, there is a substitution S on the free type variables α_i of $P' \Rightarrow v$, such that $P \Vdash SP'$ and $\tau = Sv$. By Lemma 5.2, and the fact that none of the α_i appear in $A.x : \tau'$, $A.x : \tau', SP' \vdash' e : \tau$. Define $R = SP' \cup NL\ A$. Then $P \Vdash R \Vdash SP'$. We can thus construct the derivation:

$$\frac{\dfrac{A.x : \tau', SP' \vdash' e : \tau}{A.x : \tau', R \vdash' e : \tau} \quad (Lemma\ 5.3)}{A, R \vdash' \lambda x.e : \alpha \cdot (\tau' \to \tau)} \quad (\to I)$$

Furthermore, by Lemma 5.4, $gen(A, R \Rightarrow \alpha \cdot (\tau' \to \tau)) \succeq gen(A, P \Rightarrow \alpha \cdot (\tau' \to \tau)) \succeq P \Rightarrow \alpha \cdot (\tau' \to \tau)$.

Case $(\to E)$: We have a derivation of the form:

$$\frac{A, P \vdash e : \alpha \cdot (\tau' \to \tau) \qquad A, P \vdash e' : \tau'}{A, P \vdash e\, e' : \tau} \quad (P \Vdash \alpha \le \overline{0}, P \Vdash NL\, A|_{fv\, e' \cap fv\, e})$$

By induction, $A, P' \vdash' e : v$ with $gen(A, P' \Rightarrow v) \succeq P \Rightarrow \alpha \cdot (\tau' \to \tau)$. By the definition of gen, there is a substitution S on the free type variables α_i of $P' \Rightarrow v$, such that $P \Vdash SP'$ and $\alpha \cdot (\tau' \to \tau) = Sv$. By Lemma 5.2, and the fact that none of the α_i appear in A, $A, SP' \vdash' e : \alpha \cdot (\tau' \to \tau)$. Using the induction hypothesis on the second premise of $(\to E)$, we can show by a similar argument that $A, S'Q' \vdash' e' : \tau'$ for some predicate set Q' and substitution S' such that $P \Vdash S'Q'$. Define $R = SP \cup S'P' \cup \{\alpha \le \overline{0}\} \cup NL\, A|_{fv\, e' \cap fv\, e}$. Then $P \Vdash R$. We can thus construct the following derivation:

$$\frac{\dfrac{A, SP' \vdash' e : \alpha \cdot (\tau' \to \tau)}{A, R \vdash' e : \alpha \cdot (\tau' \to \tau)}(Lemma\ 5.3) \qquad \dfrac{A, S'Q' \vdash' e' : \tau'}{A, R \vdash' e' : \tau'}(Lemma\ 5.3)}{A, R \vdash' e\, e' : \tau} \quad (\to E)$$

Also, by construction, $R \Vdash \{\alpha \le \overline{0}\} \cup NL\, A|_{fv\, e' \cap fv\, e}$. Furthermore, using Lemma 5.4, $gen(A, R \Rightarrow \tau) \succeq gen(A, P \Rightarrow \tau) \succeq P \Rightarrow \tau$.

Case $(let!)$: We have a derivation of the form:

$$\frac{A', P \vdash e' : \sigma \qquad A.x : \sigma, P \vdash e : \tau}{A, P \vdash let!\, x = e' \text{ in } e : \tau} \quad (obs(A', A, fv\, e), orig(P \Rightarrow \sigma))$$

By induction, we have

$$A', P' \vdash' e : v, \qquad \sigma' = gen(A', P' \Rightarrow v) \succeq P \Rightarrow \sigma,$$
$$A.x : \sigma, Q' \vdash' e' : \tau', \qquad gen(A.x : \sigma, Q' \Rightarrow \tau') \succeq P \Rightarrow \tau.$$

Without loss of generality, we can assume (A): $tv\, P \cap tv\, (Q' \Rightarrow \tau') \subseteq tv\, (A.x : \sigma)$. This can always be achieved by a suitable renaming of the free variables in $Q' \Rightarrow \tau'$. We can construct the derivation

$$\frac{A', P' \vdash' e : v \qquad \dfrac{\dfrac{A.x : \sigma, Q' \vdash' e' : \tau'}{A.x : \sigma, P \cup Q' \vdash' e' : \tau'}(Lemma\ 5.3)}{A.x : \sigma', P \cup Q' \vdash' e' : \tau'}(Lemma\ 5.5)}{A, P \cup Q' \vdash' let!\, x = e' \text{ in } e : \tau'} \quad (let!)$$

with conditions $obs(A', A, fv\, e)$, $orig(P \cup Q' \Rightarrow \sigma)$ satisfied. Furthermore, using the induction hypothesis and (A):

$$\begin{aligned} gen(A, P \cup Q' \Rightarrow \tau') &\succeq gen(A.x : \sigma, P \cup Q' \Rightarrow \tau') \\ &\succeq P \Rightarrow gen(A.x : \sigma, Q' \Rightarrow \tau') \\ &\succeq P \Rightarrow P \Rightarrow \tau \\ &= P \Rightarrow \tau \end{aligned}$$

Cases (*let*) and (*if*) are similar to cases (*let!*) and ($\rightarrow$ *E*). ∎

The rules in OLT translate directly into a Prolog program where every application of a clause is determined uniquely by the outermost constructor of an expression. This program can be used to find a candidate σ for a principal type scheme of an exprssion e, together with its proof tree. Given this proof tree, we can check with Theorem 4.2 (*b*) that the type schemes in the conclusions of all proof steps are nonempty. If they are, σ is a principal type scheme for e. If one of the types is empty, we can show with Theorem 4.2 (*a*) that e has no type. It therefore follows:

Theorem 5.7 (*a*) If an expression e has a type scheme then it has a principal type scheme. (*b*) There is a decision procedure *tp* which returns the principal type scheme of an expression if it has one, and returns failure otherwise.

6 Conclusion

We have presented a type system which augments linear types with observers. We claim that the extension makes linear types practical, since it is polymorphic, accommodates a familiar programming style, and allows observer accesses to proceed in parallel. Although the typing rules are more complex than those of the classical Hindley/Milner system, typical type signatures occurring in practice are quite moderate in size and complexity. Furthermore, programmers need not write down types since principal types can be reconstructed. We see the type system as a possible candidate for future programming languages which add state to a functional core.

On the theoretical side, more research is needed to explore connections between observer types and linear logic.

References

[Abr90] S. Abramsky. Computational interpretations of linear logic. Preprint, Imperial College, London, 1990.

[Bak90] H.G. Baker. Unify and conquer (garbage, updating, aliasing, ...) in functional languages. In *Proc. ACM Conf. on LISP and Functional Programming*, pages 218–226, June 1990.

[Blo89] A. Bloss. Update analysis and the efficient implementation of functional aggregates. In *Proc. ACM Conf. on Functional Programming Languages and Computer Architecture*, August 1989.

[CDD+85] D. Clement, J. Despeyroux, T. Despeyroux, L. Hascoet, and G. Kahn. Natural semantics on the computer. Technical Report RR 416, INRIA, June 1985.

[Coh84] S. Cohen. Multi-version structures in prolog. In *Proc. Conf. on Fifth Generation Computer Systems*, pages 265–274, 1984.

[Deu90] A. Deutsch. On determining lifetime and aliasing of dynamically allocated data in higher-order functional specifications. In *Proc. 17th ACM Symposium on Principles of Programming Languages*, Jan. 1990.

[DP90]   M. Draghicescu and S. Puroshothaman. A compositional analysis of evaluation order and its application. In *Proc. ACM Conf. on Lisp and Functional Programming*, June 1990.

[GH90]   J.C. Guzmán and P. Hudak. Single-threaded polymorphic lambda calculus. In *Proc. 5th IEEE Symp. on Logic in Computer Science*, June 1990.

[Gir87]   J.-Y. Girard. Linear logic. *Theoretical Computer Science*, 50:1–102, 1987.

[GSH88]   K. Gharachorloo, V. Sarkar, and J.L. Hennessy. A simple and efficient approach for single assignment languages. In *Proc. ACM Conf. on Lisp and Functional Programming*, 1988.

[Hud87]   P. Hudak. A semantic model of reference counting and its abstraction. In S. Abramsky and C. Hankin, editors, *Abstract interpretation of declarative languages*. Ellis Horwood Ltd., 1987.

[JG91]   P. Jouvelot and D.K. Gifford. Algebraic reconstruction of types and effects. In *Proc. 18th ACM Symp. on Principles of Programming Languages*, pages 303–310, Jan. 1991.

[Jon91a]   Mark P. Jones. Towards a theory of qualified types. Technical Report PRG-TR-6-91, Oxford University Computing Laboratory, Oxford, UK, 1991.

[Jon91b]   Mark P. Jones. Type inference for qualified types. Technical Report PRG-TR-10-91, Oxford University Computing Laboratory, Oxford, UK, 1991.

[Laf88]   Y. Lafont. The linear abstract machine. *Theoretical Computer Science*, 59:157–180, 1988.

[LG88]   J. Lucassen and D.K. Gifford. Polymorphic effect systems. In *Proc. 15th ACM Symp. on Principles of Programming Languages*, pages 47–57, Jan. 1988.

[NPD87]   A. Neirynk, P. Panangaden, and A. Demers. Computation of aliases and support sets. In *Proc. 14th ACM Symp. on Principles of Programming Languages*, pages 274–283, Jan. 1987.

[Ode91]   M. Odersky. How to make destructive updates less destructive. In *Proc. 18th ACM Symp. on Principles of Programming Languages*, pages 25–36, Jan. 1991.

[Sch85]   D.A. Schmidt. Detecting global variables in denotational specifications. *ACM Transactions on Programming Languages and Systems*, 5(2):299–310, 1985.

[SRI91]   V. Swarup, U.S. Reddy, and E. Ireland. Assignments for applictive languages. In *Proc. ACM Conf. on Functional Programming Languages and Computer Architecture*, August 1991.

[TJ91]   J.-P. Talpin and P. Jouvelot. Type, effect and region reconstruction in polymorphic functional languages. In *Workshop on Static Analysis of Equational, Functional, and Logic Programs*, Bordeaux, Oct. 1991.

[Wad90a]   P. Wadler. Comprehending monads. In *Proc. ACM Conf. on LISP and Functional Programming*, pages 61–78, June 1990.

[Wad90b]   Phil Wadler. Linear types can change the world! In *Proc. IFIP TC2 Working Conference on Programming Concepts and Methods*, pages 547–566, April 1990.

[Wad91]   P. Wadler. Is there a use for linear logic? In *Proc. ACM Symp. on Partial Evaluation and Semantic-Based Program Manipulation*, pages 255–273, June 1991.

Type Inference for Partial Types is Decidable

Patrick M. O'Keefe

ICAD, Inc.
201 Broadway
Cambridge, MA 02139
pmo@icad.com

Mitchell Wand*

College of Computer Science
Northeastern University
360 Huntington Avenue, 161CN
Boston, MA 02115, USA
wand@corwin.ccs.northeastern.edu

Abstract

The type inference problem for partial types, introduced by Thatte [15], is the problem of deducing types under a subtype relation with a largest element Ω and closed under the usual antimonotonic rule for function types. We show that this problem is decidable by reducing it to a satisfiability problem for type expressions over this partial order and giving an algorithm for the satisfiability problem. The satisfiability problem is harder than the one conventionally given because comparable types may have radically different shapes.

1 Introduction

Statically-typed languages are desirable for many reasons, but they are often more restrictive than dynamically-typed languages. In particular, it is desirable to allow strongly-typed languages to have "holes" in the type structure, so that portions of the program that are not fully understood may be written using dynamic typing. There have been several proposals for creating such holes, such as [5, 15, 17]. Typically, one gives the result of such an untyped computation a special type, untyped. Such a value can be passed as an ordinary value, but is not manipulable except by a polymorphic procedure, such as print [17]. Thatte [15] called this *partial* type inference.

The addition of a type untyped allows several different kinds of flexibility. It allows portions of a program to escape the scrutiny of the type-checker [17]; it allows for heterogeneous lists and persistent data [15]; and it can also be used to facilitate binding-time analysis or analysis of type errors [5]. It also serves as a basis for dealing with the "don't care" types for records in [14].

Here we consider the problem of type inference for a language with a type untyped. In [15], Thatte proposed a type system for dealing with this problem. His idea was to treat this as a subtyping problem, with the inequalities between types generated by

---

*Work supported by the National Science Foundation and DARPA under grants CCR-9002253 and CCR-9014603.

$t \leq \Omega$ for all types t; we follow Thatte by using Ω to denote the type **untyped**. By well-known reductions [18, 16], the type inference problem for untyped lambda-terms reduces to determining the satisfiability of inequalities over this system. Thatte presented the system and showed how to determine the satisfiability of single inequalities. Here we show how to solve general sets of inequalities, thus solving the partial type inference problem.

2 The Formal System

2.1 Types

The set of types is defined by the following grammar:

$$\langle \text{type} \rangle ::= \Omega \mid \langle \text{type} \rangle \rightarrow \langle \text{type} \rangle$$

Note that types have no variables. It is easy to extend these results to allow additional base types [16].

The inclusions between types are defined by the rules:

$$t \leq \Omega$$

$$\frac{s' \leq s \quad t \leq t'}{s \rightarrow t \leq s' \rightarrow t'}$$

where s, t, etc., range over types. We will refer to the second rule as the *congruence* rule for arrow types.

Thus, typical inclusions are $\Omega \rightarrow \Omega \leq \Omega$, $\Omega \rightarrow \Omega \leq (\Omega \rightarrow \Omega) \rightarrow \Omega$, etc.

While our coercions are not atomic in the sense of [13], they have the property that for any t and u there is at most one proof of $t \leq u$, and this proof follows the structure of u. This makes it easier to reason about these inequalities. For example, we do not include the reflexive or transitive rules, because these are admissible:

Theorem 1 *The relation $\leq$ is a partial order.*

Proof: It is easy to show that for all types t, $t \leq t$ is provable from these rules. The base case is $\Omega \leq \Omega$, and the rest follows by induction on the size of t.

For the transitive property, assume $t \leq t'$ and $t' \leq t''$ are provable. We need to show that $t \leq t''$ is provable as well. We proceed by induction on the structure of t''. If $t'' = \Omega$, then $t \leq t''$. If $t' = \Omega$, then $t'' = \Omega$, so $t \leq t''$. Otherwise all of t, t', and t'' are arrow types, and both proofs must have the congruence rule as their last step. Then the result follows by induction on the components.

For the asymmetry property, assume that $t \leq t'$ and $t' \leq t$. If either t or t' is Ω, then the other must be Ω also. If neither is Ω, then both proofs must have the congruence rule as their last step, and the result follows by induction. $\square$

2.2 Programs

Programs are ordinary untyped lambda-terms with typed constants. Polymorphic **let** can be treated by using the equivalence let $x = M$ in N as $N[M/x]$. We use the usual typing rules plus the subsumption rule

$$\frac{A \vdash M : t \quad t \leq t'}{A \vdash M : t'}$$

The details are routine.

This system types terms which are not typable in the simply-typed lambda-calculus without coercions. For example, consider $\lambda f.(fK(fI))$, where K and I are the usual combinators. This is not typable in the ordinary calculus, since K and I have different types, but it is typable under partial typing: assign f the type $\Omega \to \Omega \to \Omega$. both the K and I can be coerced to type Ω, and the result (fI), of type $\Omega \to \Omega$, can be coerced to Ω to form the second argument of the first f. Therefore the entire term has type $(\Omega \to \Omega \to \Omega) \to \Omega$.

Similarly, some self-application is possible: $(\lambda x.xx)$ has type $(\Omega \to t) \to t$ for all t, since the final x can be coerced to Ω.

However, not all terms are typable in this system. For example:

Proposition 1 $(\lambda x.xx)(\lambda x.xx)$ *is not typable in this system.*

Proof: The types of $(\lambda x.xx)$ are those types which are bounded below by a type of the form $(t_1 \to t_2) \to t_2$ where $t_1 \to t_2 \leq t_1$. In order to type $(\lambda x.xx)(\lambda x.xx)$, we need to find two such types, one for each occurrence of $(\lambda x.xx)$, such that the type of the second coerces to the argument type of the first. By a standard argument, we need consider only the case in which the types are actually of the lower-bound types; all the coercion can be incorporated into the coercion of the argument. That is, we need to find two types of the form $(t_1 \to t_2) \to t_2$ and $(u_1 \to u_2) \to u_2$, where $(u_1 \to u_2) \to u_2 \leq (t_1 \to t_2)$. After splitting the last equation, we are left with four inequalities to solve:

$$t_1 \to t_2 \leq t_1$$
$$u_1 \to u_2 \leq u_1$$
$$t_1 \leq u_1 \to u_2$$
$$u_2 \leq t_2$$

From these a short deduction leads to $u_1 \to u_2 \leq u_1 \leq u_1 \to u_2$. Since $\leq$ is a partial order, we have $u_1 = u_1 \to u_2$, which has no solution in our system. $\square$

We will use this as a running example in the paper. It can be shown that every term typable in this system is strongly normalizing; we hope to present this result elsewhere.

2.3 Semantics

We can give semantics for these rules in the fashion of [9]: the rules are obviously sound for either the simple or the F-semantics, interpreting Ω as the entire set. A more interesting semantics is given via PERs: Let D be a model of the untyped lambda calculus, and define a type to be any partial equivalence relation (that is, a symmetric, transitive, but not necessarily reflexive relation) on D, with type inclusion given by set-theoretic inclusion between the PERs. Let Ω denote the PER $D \times D$. Then the rules for inclusion and type inference are sound. This model has the property that elements of type Ω are indistinguishable; this nicely mimics the idea that elements of type Ω are not manipulable by any ordinary functions. The completeness of these rules (in the sense of [9]) is considered in [13].

3 The Problem

We begin by introducing type expressions, which are defined by

$$\langle \text{type exp} \rangle ::= \langle \text{type variable} \rangle \mid \Omega \mid \langle \text{type exp} \rangle \rightarrow \langle \text{type exp} \rangle$$

A *constraint* is a judgement of the form $s \leq t$, where s and t are type expressions. We say that a set E of constraints is *satisfiable* iff there is some substitution σ, mapping type variables to types, such that for each constraint $s \leq t$ in the set, $s\sigma \leq t\sigma$ is provable. We write σ_v for the value of σ on the variable v, and we write $E\sigma$ for the effect of applying σ to some composite object (type, constraint, set of constraints) E.

It is well-known that the type inference problem reduces to the problem of satisfying a set of constraints between type expressions. For type inference without subtyping, this reduction is folkloric (e.g. [3, 2, 18]), and is implicit in [8, 11]. For the case of subtyping, the reduction is given in detail in [13].

The solution of the satisfiability problem depends on the details of the definition of the ordering $\leq$. In the case where the ordering is generated by the congruence rule alone, a solution can be obtained by observing that comparable types must have the same shape [12, 13]; see also [4].

The satisfiability problem for the system considered here is harder, because it no longer has the same-shape property. Indeed, in constrast to ordinary unification, one may have satisfiable constraints $v \leq t$ where v occurs in t. For example, $v \leq v \rightarrow \Omega$ is satisfiable, since $\Omega \rightarrow \Omega \leq (\Omega \rightarrow \Omega) \rightarrow \Omega$. However, there appears to be no simple rule characterizing which such occurrences are solvable.

4 The Algorithm

The algorithm has three main steps. The first step puts the constraints in a standard form, by introducing a new variable for every interior node of a tree in the original constraints. The second step calculates lower and upper bounds for each variable. The third step generates a satisfying assignment while propagating necessary information and doing a check for circularity. The steps are divided into substeps.

Step 1: Convert every constraint $t \leq t'$ to constraints of the form $v_1 \rightarrow v_2 \leq w$ or $w \leq v_1 \rightarrow v_2$ or $\Omega \leq v$ or $v \leq w$, where the v and w's are type variables. To do this we proceed as follows:

Step 1a: First, if any constraint has one side that is a term $t_1 \rightarrow t_2$ where either t_1 or t_2 is not a variable, replace each non-variable t_i by a variable v_i and add two new constraints $v_i \leq t_i$ and $t_i \leq v_i$. This transformation preserves satisfiability and always decreases the number of interior nodes in the set of constraints.

Step 1b: When this step is done, we are left with constraints where each side is either a variable v, the constant Ω, or a type expression $v_1 \rightarrow v_2$. These can be cleaned up as follows:

- Replace $v \rightarrow w \le v' \rightarrow w'$ by $v' \le v$ and $w \le w'$.

- Replace $t \le \Omega$ by nothing. Such a constraint is always provable.

- If any constraint is of the form $\Omega \le v_1 \rightarrow v_2$, then terminate and report failure, as this constraint is not satisfiable.

Note that there is no substitution during this phase of the algorithm; there is an implicit substitution in step 1a, but these substitutions are bounded by the size of the problem.

Step 2: Let A denote the set of arrows $v \rightarrow w$ in the set of constraints at the end of the Step 1. For each variable appearing in the constraints, we will keep track of the those arrows in A which are lower and upper bounds for that variable. We will also do this for Ω. More precisely, let v be a variable or Ω. Define L_v and U_v to be the smallest subsets of A such that:

1. If $v \le v_1 \rightarrow v_2$ is among the constraints, then $(v_1 \rightarrow v_2) \in U_v$.

2. If $v_1 \rightarrow v_2 \le v$ is among the constraints, then $(v_1 \rightarrow v_2) \in L_v$.

3. If $v \le w$ is among the constraints, then $U_w \subseteq U_v$ and $L_v \subseteq L_w$.

4. If $v_1 \rightarrow v_2 \in L_w$ and $w_1 \rightarrow w_2 \in U_w$, then

$$U_{v_1} \subseteq U_{w_1}$$
$$L_{w_1} \subseteq L_{v_1}$$
$$U_{w_2} \subseteq U_{v_2}$$
$$L_{v_2} \subseteq L_{w_2}$$

These sets can be built by a simple closure operation. Since each L_v and U_v is a subset of the finite set A, this closure process must terminate in finite time. Furthermore, it is clear that for any satisfying assignment σ, $(L_v)\sigma$ and $(U_v)\sigma$ will be sets of lower and upper bounds for v. Therefore, if at the end of this step U_Ω is non-empty, then terminate and report failure, since Ω is not less than or equal to any arrow type.

From now on, we discard the constraints and work entirely with the the bound sets L_v and U_v.

For our example of $(\lambda x.xx)(\lambda x.xx)$, Step 1 is trivial, since the constraints are already of the desired form. For Step 2, the first two closure conditions give:

	L	U
t_1	$t_1 \rightarrow t_2$	$u_1 \rightarrow u_2$
u_1	$u_1 \rightarrow u_2$	

All the other sets are empty. Iterating condition 4 twice gives:

	L	U
t_1	$t_1 \to t_2$	$u_1 \to u_2$
	$u_2 \to u_2$	
u_1	$u_1 \to u_2$	$u_1 \to u_2$

which satisfies all the closure conditions.

Step 3: In this section of the algorithm, we develop the satisfying assignment σ. As we do this, we will generate a new variable for each interior node of the assignment, and for each such variable v we will generate sets of bounds L_v and U_v; these bounds will also be subsets of A.

Step 3a: Choose a variable v. If there are no more variables to process, return the substitution σ. If U_v is empty, then set $\sigma_v = \Omega$ and go to step 3a.

Step 3b: (Occurs Check). Consider the set $\{ w \mid v$ occurs in $\sigma_w \}$. This is the set of variables above v in the tree described by σ. If, for any such w, $L_w = L_v$ and $U_w = U_v$, then terminate and report failure.

Step 3c: If v passes the occurs check, proceed as follows: Since v is bounded above by an arrow, it must also be an arrow. Generate two new variables v_1 and v_2, and set $\sigma = \sigma[v := v_1 \to v_2]$.

We must next define the bound sets for v_1 and v_2. We do this by looking at the bound sets for v. For example, if $(a \to b) \in U_v$, then we must have $\sigma_a \le \sigma_{v_1}$ for any satisfying assignment σ. Therefore $L_a \subseteq L_{v_1}$ for each $(a \to b) \in U_v$. Therefore we set $L_{v_1} = \bigcup \{ L_a \mid (a \to b) \in U_v \}$. We proceed similarly for each of the four sets:

$$L_{v_1} = \bigcup \{ L_a \mid (a \to b) \in U_v \}$$
$$U_{v_1} = \bigcup \{ U_a \mid (a \to b) \in L_v \}$$
$$L_{v_2} = \bigcup \{ L_b \mid (a \to b) \in L_v \}$$
$$U_{v_2} = \bigcup \{ U_b \mid (a \to b) \in U_v \}$$

Then go to step 3a.

This completes the description of the algorithm.

For our example, we can assign Ω to any variable except t_1 or u_1. If we select u_1, then we assign $\sigma(u_1) = u_{11} \to u_{12}$. Calculating the bound sets for u_{11} and u_{12} gives

	L	U
t_1	$t_1 \to t_2$	$u_1 \to u_2$
	$u_2 \to u_2$	
u_1	$u_1 \to u_2$	$u_1 \to u_2$
u_{11}	$u_1 \to u_2$	$u_1 \to u_2$
u_{12}	$\emptyset$	$\emptyset$

When we select u_{11} for expansion, we discover that its bounds sets are the same as those of u_1, so the occurs check fails and the algorithm reports that the term is untypable, as desired.

5   Proof of the Main Theorem

We must show two things: if the algorithm reports failure, then there is no satisfying solution; and if the algorithm reports success, then all the original constraints are satisfied.

Lemma 1 *For any satisfying assignment σ, $L_v\sigma$ and $U_v\sigma$ will be sets of lower and upper bounds for v.*

Proof: Easy. □

Lemma 2 *If the algorithm reports failure, then there is no satisfying solution.*

Proof: The algorithm can report failure in two ways: either by noting that U_Ω is nonempty, or by failure of the occurs check. If U_Ω is nonempty, then the constraints imply that Ω is less than some arrow type, which is impossible. So the constraints are unsatisfiable.

Next, consider the occurs check. Let w be a variable such that v occurs in σ_w. For every variable z along the path from w to v, $U_z \neq \emptyset$, since otherwise the path would terminate at z.

The path from w to v is determined entirely by L_w and U_w, since each bounds pair (L_z, U_z) along the path is determined by the preceding bounds pair. Since $L_v = L_w$ and $U_v = U_w$, if the occurs check were omitted, then the algorithm would loop by duplicating this path indefinitely. Every node between w and v must be an arrow node, and this path would be replicated infinitely.

Now, recall that if a type has an upper bound which is an arrow type, then it must be an arrow type itself. In the algorithm, a variable is assigned an arrow type only if it has an arrow upper bound. Hence, if the algorithm assigns an arrow type to a variable, that variable must be an arrow type in any satisfying assignment. Therefore, if there is a path from w to v in the generated assignment σ, there must be a path from w to v in any satisfying assignment.

If the upper and lower bounds for v are the same as those for w, then the algorithm is guaranteed (in the absence of the occurs check) to loop by duplicating this path infinitely. But since every satisfying assignment must have an arrow type at every node along this path, we conclude that every satisfying assignment must have an infinite repetition of this path. Hence there is no (finite) satisfying assignment. □

We need the following lemma:

Lemma 3 *If $L_v \subseteq L_w$ and $U_w \subseteq U_v$, then $\sigma_v \leq \sigma_w$.*

Proof: Define a relation $\sqsubseteq$ on variables by $v \sqsubseteq w$ iff $L_v \subseteq L_w$ and $U_w \subseteq U_v$. Then the lemma can be rephrased as $v \sqsubseteq w \Rightarrow \sigma_v \leq \sigma_w$. We proceed by induction on the size of σ_v and σ_w.

If $\sigma_w = \Omega$, then the conclusion holds trivially. If $\sigma_v = \Omega$, then we must have had $U_v = \emptyset$. But $v \sqsubseteq w$ implies $U_w \subseteq U_v$, so $U_w = \emptyset$ and $\sigma_v = \Omega$ as well.

The remaining case is that both σ_v and σ_w are compound, that is,

$$\sigma_v = \sigma_{v_1} \to \sigma_{v_2}$$
$$\sigma_w = \sigma_{w_1} \to \sigma_{w_2}$$

However, in this case, if we check the set-theoretic arithmetic in Step 3c, we discover that $v \sqsubseteq w$ implies that $w_1 \sqsubseteq v_1$ and $v_2 \sqsubseteq w_2$. For example, since $v \sqsubseteq w$, we have $L_v \subseteq L_w$, so

$$U_{v_1} = \bigcup \{ U_c \mid (c \to d) \in L_v \} \subseteq \bigcup \{ U_c \mid (c \to d) \in L_w \} = U_{w_1}$$

The other inclusions follow similarly.

Hence, by induction, $\sigma_{w_1} \leq \sigma_{v_1}$ and $\sigma_{v_2} \leq \sigma_{w_2}$. Therefore $\sigma_v \leq \sigma_w$. $\square$

Theorem 2 *Given a set of constraints E, the algorithm always terminates, and it returns a substitution σ iff E is satisfiable.*

Proof: The algorithm always terminates, since the occurs check prevents any branch of the solution from being longer than $2^{|A|+1}$. We have already shown that if the algorithm reports failure, then the constraints are unsatisfiable. We can now complete the proof of the theorem by showing that σ satisfies each of the constraints at the end of step 3.

If the constraint is of the form $v \leq w$, Step 2 guarantees that $L_v \subseteq L_w$ and $U_w \subseteq U_v$. Hence σ satisfies the constraint.

If the constraint is of the form $\Omega \leq v$, then U_v is empty (otherwise we would have failed), and the algorithm assigns $\sigma_v = \Omega$, which satisfies the constraint.

If the constraint is of the form $v_1 \to v_2 \leq w$, then there are two cases: either U_w is empty or not. If U_w is empty, then $\sigma_w = \Omega$, and the constraint is satisfied. If U_w is nonempty, then we have $\sigma_w = \sigma_{w_1} \to \sigma_{w_2}$. We claim that $L_{w_1} \subseteq L_{v_1}$, $U_{v_1} \subseteq U_{w_1}$, $L_{v_2} \subseteq L_{w_2}$, and $U_{w_2} \subseteq U_{v_2}$.

Let us do the lower-bound cases of the claim. To show $L_{w_1} \subseteq L_{v_1}$, we recall that $L_{w_1} = \bigcup \{ L_a \mid (a \to b) \in U_w \}$. So choose $(a \to b) \in U_w$. We have $(v_1 \to v_2) \in L_w$ and $(a \to b) \in U_w$, so by closure condition 4 in Step 2, $L_a \subseteq L_{v_1}$. So L_{v_1} is an upper bound for all the L_a. L_{w_1} is their least upper bound, so $L_{w_1} \subseteq L_{v_1}$. To show $L_{v_2} \subseteq L_{w_2}$, we observe that $v_1 \to v_2 \in L_w$, and $L_{w_2} = \bigcup \{ L_b \mid (a \to b) \in L_w \}$. The upper-bound cases follow symmetrically.

We can now apply lemma 3 to deduce that $\sigma_{w_1} \leq \sigma_{v_1}$, $\sigma_{v_2} \leq \sigma_{w_2}$, and therefore the constraint is satisfied.

If the constraint is of the form $w \leq v_1 \to v_2$, then U_w is nonempty, so we have $\sigma_w = \sigma_{w_1} \to \sigma_{w_2}$. The result then follows by an argument like the preceding one. $\square$

The algorithm runs in exponential space, since it has a number of states bounded by the number of (L, U) pairs, which is $2^{|A|+1}$. If one builds a cache of these states, then the algorithm requires only exponential time.

6 Related Work

In addition to the applications cited in the introduction, there are a number of related topics. Gomard [5] used a variant of this system to do binding-type analysis, in which untyped represented an untyped run-time value. Henglein [6] gives an almost-linear-time algorithm for doing this analysis. We do not currently understand the gap between Henglein's algorithm and our exponential algorithm, but there appear to be some essential differences [7].

This work is somewhat related to the work on dynamics in ML [10]. Dynamic types are oriented towards persistent objects, which have some type that is part of its representation; the hard part about such a system is reading the object back into the system within something close to the ML type system. This is rather different from our approach.

Amadio and Cardelli have solved a related but different problem. They consider a type system with both a bottom and top element, so that $\perp \leq t \leq \top$ for all types, and with recursive types. In [1] they solve the problem of *validity* (truth under all substitutions) for recursive type expressions in this system. It would be interesting to see if this result could be extended to satisfiability, as this is the natural problem arising from type inference.

7 Conclusions and Future Work

We have shown the decidability of the satisfiability problem, and therefore the type inference problem, for Thatte's system of partial types. We have formulated the problem in the simplest way possible in order to facilitate theoretical study; the next step is to extend the system with enough features to make it practical. It should be easy to extend it to allow a bottom element, as in [1], or additional base types under an arbitrary partial order, as in [16]. Product types should also pose no difficulties. Polymorphic let can be included by translating let $x = M$ in N as $N[M/x]$, but a more efficient method would be preferable. We conjecture that this system can also be used to solve the system of flags in [14]. A more difficult problem is to extend it to handle recursive types, as in [1]. Also it would be desirable to have some lower bounds on the complexity of these problems.

Acknowledgements

Thanks to Jonathan Young for numerous conversations on types and coercions. Thanks also to Fritz Henglein who enthusiastically predicted the outcome.

References

[1] Amadio, R.M., and Cardelli, L. "Subtyping Recursive Types," *Conf. Rec. 1991 ACM Symp. on Principles of Programming Languages*, 104–118.

[2] Clément, D., Despeyroux, J., Despeyroux, T., and Kahn, G. "A Simple Applicative Language: Mini-ML" *Proc. 1986 ACM Symp. on Lisp and Functional Programming*, 13–27.

[3] Cardelli, L. "Basic Polymorphic Typechecking," *Polymorphism Newsletter 2*,1 (Jan, 1985). Also appeared as Computing Science Tech. Rep. 119, AT&T Bell Laboratories, Murray Hill, NJ.

417

[4] Fuh, Y.-C., and Mishra, P. "Type Inference with Subtypes," *Proc. European Symposium on Programming* (1988), 94–114.

[5] Gomard, C.K. "Partial Type Inference for Untyped Functional Programs," *Proc. 1990 ACM Conf. on Lisp and Functional Programming*, 282–287.

[6] Henglein, F. "Efficient Type Inference for Higher-Order Binding-Time Analysis," *Functional Programming Languages and Computer Architecture, 5th ACM Conference* (J. Hughes, ed.), Springer Lecture Notes in Computer Science, Vol. 523, 1991, pp. 448–472.

[7] Henglein, F. personal communication, 1991.

[8] Hindley, R. "The Principal Type-Scheme of an Object in Combinatory Logic," *Trans. Am. Math. Soc. 146* (1969) 29–60.

[9] Hindley, R. "The Completeness Theorem for Typing λ-Terms" *Theoret. Comp. Sci. 22* (1983) 1–17. See also Hindley, R. "Curry's Type-rules are Complete with Respect to the F-Semantics Too" *Theoret. Comp. Sci. 22* (1983) 127–133.

[10] LeRoy X., and Mauny, M. "Dynamics in ML," *Functional Programming Languages and Computer Architecture, 5th ACM Conference* (J. Hughes, ed.), Springer Lecture Notes in Computer Science, Vol. 523, 1991, pp. 406–426.

[11] Milner, R. "A Theory of Type Polymorphism in Programming," *J. Comp. & Sys. Sci. 17* (1978), 348–375.

[12] Mitchell, J.C. "Coercion and Type Inference (summary)," *Conf. Rec. 11th Ann. ACM Symp. on Principles of Programming Languages* (1984), 175–185.

[13] Mitchell, J.C. "Type Inference with Simple Subtypes," *J. of Functional Programming 1* (1991), 245–285.

[14] Rémy, D. "Typechecking records and variants in a natural extension of ML," *Conf. Rec. 16th Ann. ACM Symp. on Principles of Programming Languages* (1989), 77–88.

[15] Thatte, S. "Type Inference with Partial Types," *Proc. ICALP '88* (1988), 615–629.

[16] Wand, M., and O'Keefe, P. "On the Complexity of Type Inference with Coercion," *Conf. on Functional Programming Languages and Computer Architecture* (London, September, 1989).

[17] Wand, M. "A Semantic Prototyping System," *Proc. ACM SIGPLAN '84 Compiler Construction Conference* (1984) 213–221.

[18] Wand, M. "A Simple Algorithm and Proof for Type Inference" *Fundamenta Informaticae 10* (1987), 115–122.

A Provably Correct Compiler Generator

Jens Palsberg

palsberg@daimi.aau.dk

Computer Science Department, Aarhus University
Ny Munkegade, DK–8000 Aarhus C, Denmark

Abstract

We have designed, implemented, and proved the correctness of a compiler generator that accepts action semantic descriptions of imperative programming languages. The generated compilers emit absolute code for an abstract RISC machine language that currently is assembled into code for the SPARC and the HP Precision Architecture. Our machine language needs no run-time type-checking and is thus more realistic than those considered in previous compiler proofs. We use solely algebraic specifications; proofs are given in the initial model.

1   Introduction

The previous approaches to proving correctness of compilers for non-trivial languages all use target code with run-time type-checking. The following semantic rule is typical for these target languages:

$$(FIRST : C, \langle v_1, v_2 \rangle : S) \rightarrow (C, v_1 : S)$$

The rule describes the semantics of an instruction that extracts the first component of the top-element of the stack, *provided* that the top-element is a pair. If not, then it is implicit that the executor of the target language halts the execution. Hence, the executor has to do run-time type-checking.

Run-time type-checking imposes an unwelcome penalty on execution time because more work has to be done by the executor of the target language. It may be argued, though, that the executor can rely on the source language being statically type-checked, and thus avoid the run-time type-checks. This implies an unwelcome *coupling* of the source and target languages, however, which prevents

the target language from being an independent product, for general use.

This paper addresses the use of independent, realistic target languages without type information in the semantics. The paper also concerns the possibility of proving correctness of a compiler *generator*, thus making correctness proof a once-and-for-all effort.

We have overcome these problems. We have designed, implemented, and proved the correctness of a compiler generator, called Cantor, that accepts action semantic descriptions of programming languages. The generated compilers emit absolute code for an abstract RISC [57] machine language without run-time type-checking. The considered subset of action notation, see appendix A, is suitable for describing imperative programming languages featuring:

- Complicated control flow;

- Block structure;

- Non-recursive abstractions, such as procedures and functions; and

- Static typing.

For an example of a language description that has been processed by Cantor, see appendix B. The abstract RISC machine language can easily be expanded into code for existing RISC processors. Currently, implementations exist for the SPARC [25] and the HP Precision Architecture [42].

The technique needed for managing without run-time type-checking in the target language is the following:

- Define the relationships between semantic values in the source and target languages with respect to *both* a type and a machine state.

Thus, we define an operation which given a target value V, a machine state M, and a type T will yield the *sort* of source values which have type T and are represented by V and M. Here, "sort" can be thought of as "set". For example, an integer can represent a value of type truth-value-list by pointing to a heap where the list components are represented. In this case, our operation will yield a sort containing precisely that truth-value-list, when given the integer, the type "truth-value-list", and the heap.

In contrast, for example Nielson and Nielson [40] does *not* involve the machine state when relating semantic values. Instead, they require target values to be "self-contained". Hence, they need to have several types of target values and a target machine that does run-time type checking. With our approach we can make do with just *one* type of target values, namely integer, thus avoiding run-time type-checking and getting close to the 32-bit words used in the SPARC. Note that we do *not* insert type tags in the run-time representations of source values; *no* type information is present at run-time.

The relationship between semantic values allows the proof of a lemma expressing "code well-behavedness" which is essential when reasoning about executions of compiled code. The required type information is useful during compilation, too; it is collected by the compiler in a separate pass before the code generation. This pass also collects the information needed for generating absolute, rather than relative, code.

The development of Cantor was guided by the following principles:

- Correctness is more important than efficiency; and

- Specification and proof must be completed before implementation begins.

As a result, on the positive side, the Cantor implementation was quickly produced, and only a handful of minor errors (that had been overlooked in the proof!) had to be corrected before the system worked. On the negative side, the generated compilers emit code that run at least two orders of magnitude slower than corresponding target programs produced by handwritten compilers.

The specification and proof of correctness of the Cantor system is an experiment in using the framework of unified algebras, developed by Mosses [35, 33, 34]. Unified algebras allows the algebraic specification of both abstract data types and operational semantics in a way such that initial models are guaranteed to exist, except when axioms contradict constraints, in which case *no* models of the specification exist. We have demonstrated that also a non-trivial compiler can be elegantly specified using unified algebras. In comparison with structural operational semantics and natural semantics, we replace inference rules by Horn clauses. The notational difference is minor, and only superficial differences appear in the proofs of theorems about unified specifications. Where Despeyroux [10] could prove lemmas by induction in the length of inference, we instead adopt an axiomatization of Horn logic and prove lemmas by induction in the number of occurrences of "modus ponens" in the proof in the initial model.

This paper gives an overview of the author's forthcoming PhD thesis [44]. Most definitions and proofs are omitted. For an overview of our experiments with generating a compiler for a subset of Ada, see [43].

In the following section we examine the major previous approaches to compiler generation and compiler correctness proofs. In section 3 we outline the structure of the Cantor system, including the abstract RISC machine language and the action compiler, and we give some performance measures. In section 4 we state the correctness theorem, and finally in section 5 we survey our approach to proving correctness in the absence of run-time type-checking in the target language. We also discuss why we do not treat recursion.

The reader is assumed to be familiar with algebraic specification [12], compilation of block structured languages [64], and the notion of a RISC architecture [57].

2 Previous Work

2.1 Compiler Generation

The problem of compiler generation is usually approached by choosing a particular definition of a specific target language [46]. The task is then to write and prove the correctness of a compiler for a notation for defining source languages. Such a compiler can then be composed with a language definition to yield a correct compiler for the language, see figure 1. Compiler generators that

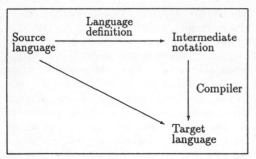

Figure 1: Semantics-directed compiler generation.

operate in this way are often called *semantics-directed* compiler generators. The Cantor system described in this paper is an example of a semantics-directed compiler generator. It accepts language definitions written in action notation, and it outputs compilers that emit code in an abstract RISC machine language.

The traditional approach to compiler generation is based on *denotational semantics* [53]. Examples of existing compiler generators based on this idea include Mosses' Semantics Implementation System (SIS) [29], Paulson's Semantics Processor (PSP) [45, 46], and Wand's Semantic Prototyping System (SPS) [62]. In SIS, the lambda expressions are executed by a direct implementation of beta-reduction; in PSP and SPS they are compiled into SECD and Scheme code, respectively. There are no considerations of the possible correctness of either the implementation of beta-reduction, the translations to SECD or Scheme code, or the implementation of SECD or Scheme. The target programs produced by these systems have been reported to run at least three orders of magnitude slower than corresponding target programs produced by handwritten compilers [22].

After these systems were built, several translations of lambda notation into other abstract machines have been proved correct. Notable instances are the categorical abstract machine [8] and the abstract machines that can be derived systematically from an operational semantics of lambda notation, using Hannan's method [16, 14, 15]. It remains to be demonstrated, however, if a compiler which incorporates one of them will be more efficient than the classical systems. Also, the correctness of implementations of these abstract machines has not been considered.

It appears that the poor performance characteristics of the classical compiler generators do not simply stem from inefficient implementations of lambda notation. Mosses observed that denotational semantics intertwine model details with the semantic description, thus blurring the underlying conceptual analysis [31]. Pleban and Lee further observed that not only a human reader but also an automatic compiler generator will have difficulty in recovering the underlying analysis [48]. Attempts to recover useful information from lambda expressions include Schmidt's work on detecting so-called single-threaded store arguments and stack single-threaded environment arguments [52, 54], and the binding-time analysis of Nielson and Nielson [41]. Despite that, it seems unlikely that the performance characteristics of compiler generators based on denotational semantics soon will be improved beyond that of existing such systems.

A number of compiler generators have been built that produce compilers of a quality that compare well with commercially available compilers. Major examples are the CAT system of Schmidt and Völler [55, 56], the compiler generator of Kelsey and Hudak [21], and the Mess system of Pleban and Lee [47, 23, 49, 22]. These approaches are based on rather ad hoc notations for defining languages, and they lack correctness proofs, like the classical systems. They indicate, however, that better performance of the produced compiler is obtained when:

- Some model details are omitted from a language definition; and

- The notation for defining languages is biased towards "compilable languages".

A radically different approach to compiler generation is taken by Dam and Jensen [9]. They consider the use of natural semantics [20] (which they call "relational semantics") as the basis of a compiler generator. They devise an algorithm for transforming a natural semantic definition into a compiling specification. The algorithm requires a language definition to satisfy some conditions; it is sufficiently general to apply to a language of while-programs, but has not been implemented. The generated compilers emit code for a stack machine; the correctness of these compilers has been sketched, whereas the implementation of the stack machine is not considered.

Finally, compiler generation can be obtained by self-application of a partial evaluator. The Ceres system of Tofte [60] is an early example of this, demonstrating that even compiler generators can be automatically generated. Ceres uses a language of flowcharts with an implicit state as the notation for defining source languages. Another notable partial evaluator is the Similix of Bondorf and Danvy [5, 6] which treats a subset of Scheme. Gomard and Jones implemented a self-applicable partial evaluator, called mix, for an untyped lambda notation [13]. It has been used to generate a compiler for a language of while-programs. The generated compiler emits programs in lambda notation. The correctness of this compiler generator has been proved; it remains to be seen, however, if the partial evaluation approach will lead to the generation of compilers for conventional machine architectures.

The lack of correctness proofs for the realistic compiler generators limits the confidence we can have in a generated compiler. Let us therefore examine the major previous approaches to compiler correctness proofs.

2.2 Compiler Correctness Proofs

The traditional approach to proving compiler correctness is based on denotational semantics [24, 26, 58, 51, 39] or algebraic variations hereof [7, 28, 59, 3, 30]. The correctness statement can be pictured as a commuting diagram, see figure 2.

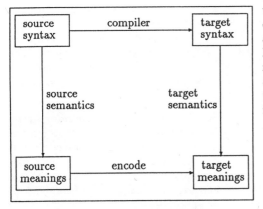

Figure 2: Compiler correctness.

It has been demonstrated that complete proofs of compiler correctness can be automatically checked. Two significant instances are Young's

[65] work, using the Boyer-Moore theorem prover, and Joyce's [19, 18] work using the HOL system. In both cases, the target code of the translation is a non-idealized machine-level architecture whose implementation has been verified with respect to a low level of the computer, see for example [17, 27]. The verification of both architectures has even been automatically checked. These examples of systems verification [4] are important: they minimize the amount of distrust one need have to such a verified system. Of course, one can still suspect errors in the implementation of the gate-level of the computer, or in the implementation of the theorem prover, but many other sources of errors have been eliminated.

The use of denotational semantics renders difficult the specification of languages with nondeterminism and parallelism. Such features can be specified easily, however, by adopting the framework of structural operational semantics [50]. For a survey of recent work on proving the correctness of compilers for such languages, see the paper by Gammelgaard and Nielson [11], which also contains a detailed account of the approach taken in the ProCoS project, where the source language considered is Occam2.

In a special form of structural operational semantics, called natural semantics [20], one considers only steps from configurations to *final* states. When both the source and target languages have a natural semantics, then there is hope for proving the correctness of a compiler using the proof technique of Despeyroux [10]. As with the proof techniques used when dealing with denotational semantics, Despeyroux's technique amounts to giving a proof by induction on the length of a computation. The correctness statement is different, though. Instead of proving that a diagram commutes, she proves the validity of two properties, which informally can be stated as follows:

- **Completeness:** if the source program terminates, then so does the target program, and with the same result; and

- **Soundness:** if the target program terminates, then so does the source program, and with the same result.

Despeyroux proves the correctness statement by induction in the length of the proofs of the assumptions of these properties. A central lemma states that the code for an expression behaves in a disciplined way. We call this property "code well-behavedness". We will use a variation of Despeyroux's technique, adapted to the framework of unified algebras, see later.

A major deficiency of all the previous approaches to compiler correctness, except that of Joyce [19, 18], is their using a target language that performs *run-time* type-checking, as explained above. Joyce considers only a language of while-programs, and it is not clear how to generalize his approach.

Our concern can be sloganized as follows:

- If "well-typed programs don't go wrong", then it should be possible to generate correct code for an independent, realistic machine language that does not perform runtime type-checking.

The Cantor system is based on the use of such a machine language.

3   The Cantor System

Our compiler generator accepts action semantic descriptions. Action semantics is a framework for formal semantics of programming languages, developed by Mosses [31, 32, 33, 37, 36] and Watt [38, 63]. It is intended to allow useful semantic descriptions of realistic programming languages, and it is *compositional*, like denotational semantics. It differs from denotational semantics, however, in using semantic entities called *actions*, rather than higher-order functions.

We have designed a subset of action notation which is amenable to compilation and which we have given a natural semantics, by a systematic transformation of its structural operational semantics [36]. The syntax of this subset is given in appendix A together with a brief overview of the principles behind action semantics. Appendix B presents a complete description of a toy programming language. (Readers who are unfamiliar with action semantics are *not* expected to understand the details in appendix B, despite the suggestiveness of the symbols used. See [36] for a full presentation of action semantics.)

The central part of the Cantor system is a compiler from action notation to an abstract RISC machine language. This section presents both the machine language and the compiler, and it states

some performance measurements of the Cantor system.

All specifications in this paper, including those of syntax, are given in Mosses' meta-notation for unified algebras [36].

3.1   An Abstract RISC Machine Language

The machine language is patterned after the SPARC architecture; it is called Pseudo SPARC. It contains 14 instructions that operate on the following machine state:

sparc-state =
    (program, program-counter, was-zero,
    was-negative, globals, windows, memory) .

'program' is a mapping from linenumbers to instructions. 'program-counter' is a linenumber, and 'was-zero' and 'was-negative' are status-bits (truth-values). 'globals' models the global registers, and 'windows' models a non-overlapping version of the SPARC register-windows. Finally, 'memory' models six separate "pages" of the main memory, as a mapping from page-identifications to pages. A page is a mapping from addresses (natural numbers) to integers. For example, one of the pages is used as a stack, another as a heap.

The only data manipulated by this language are integers. This means that it is impossible to see from a given data value if it should be thought of as a pointer to an instruction in the program, as an address in the memory, or as modeling a truth-value, an integer, etc.

The uniformity of the data values makes the Pseudo SPARC language more realistic than those considered in previous compiler proofs. It contains two major idealizations, however, as follows:

- **Unbounded word and memory size:** The data values are *unbounded* integers and this requires unbounded word size. We also assume that the program and memory sizes, the number of of registers in a register window, and the number of register windows are unbounded.

- **Read-only code:** The program is placed separately, not in 'memory'. This implies that code will not be overwritten, and that data will not be "executed".

These idealizations simplify the correctness proof considerably, without removing any of the difficulties that we address.

Pseudo SPARC	Real SPARC
skip	sub %g0, %g0, %g0
jump Z	jmpl Z, %g0
branchequal Z	be Z
branchlessthan Z	bneg Z
call	jmpl global, %r8
return	jmpl %r8+8, %g0
store $R1$ in $R2$ Z P	st $R1$, $R2+Z+P$
load $R1$ Z P into $R2$	ld $R1+Z+P$, $R2$
storeregisters	save
loadregisters	restore
move RI to R	or %g0, RI, R
move sum R RI to R'	add R, RI, R'
move difference R RI to R'	sub R, RI, R'
compare R with RI	subcc R, RI, %g0

Figure 3: The Pseudo SPARC machine language.

Figure 3 shows the 14 Pseudo SPARC instructions and how they (approximately) can be expanded to real SPARC instructions. In practice, the expansion has to take care of fitting instructions using large integers into several real SPARC instructions. It also has to insert additional "nop" instructions into so-called "delay slots". Pseudo SPARC instructions can also be expanded to instructions for the HP Precision Architecture, though with a little more difficulty.

The function that models one step of computation is defined as follows:

step _ :: sparc-state → sparc-state (*total*) .

step m = next
((program of m) at
(program-counter of m) default skip) m .

'step _' models the loading of the current instruction, followed by its execution. The operation 'next _ _ ' is defined in the following style (we give only a single example):

next _ _ ::
instruction, sparc-state → sparc-state (*total*) .

next call (p, pc, cz, cn, g, w, q) =
$(p, g$ at global default 0, cz, cn, g,
update w (map of return-address to pc), q) .

Here, 'global' is one of the global registers, and 'return-address' is a user-inaccessible register in the register-window. The use of 'default' models that all registers and memory addresses are initialized to 0 before execution starts. Likewise, the program area contains 'skip' instructions everywhere before the program is loaded.

Note that 'step _' and 'next _ _' are total functions. This emphasizes that computation continues infinitely, once started. For example, the 'call' instruction will be executed even though the global register contained a value that we thought of as a truth-value! It also means that we have avoided alignment problems, etc., so that a typical run-time error such as "bus error" will not occur. This is accomplished by having a word-rather than byte-oriented definition of the Pseudo SPARC machine.

3.2 Compiling Action Notation

The compiler from action notation to Pseudo SPARC machine code proceeds in two passes:

1. Type analysis and calculation of code size; and

2. Code generation.

For each pass there is a function defined for every syntactic category. Those defined for 'Act' have the following signatures (we cheat a little bit here, compared to [44], to improve the readability):

a-count _ _ _ :: Act, data-type, symbol-table →
(natural, truth-value, data-type,
truth-value, data-type, block) .

perform _ _ _ _ _ _ _ _ _ _ _ _ ::
Act, data-type, general-register,
frozen, symbol-table,
cleanup, cleanup, cleanup,
linenumber, linenumber-complete,
linenumber-escape, linenumber-fail →
(program, general-register, general-register) .

Since action notation contains unusual constructs, e.g., 'complete', 'escape', 'fail', the definition of the type analysis and code generation employ unusual techniques, though not very difficult. For example, the definition of 'perform' requires as argument both the desired start-address ('linenumber') of the code to be generated, but also addresses of where to jump to,

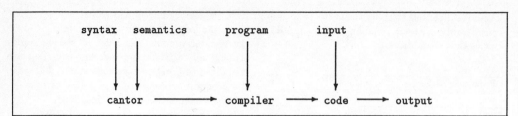

Figure 4: The Cantor system.

should the performance complete ('linenumber-complete'), escape ('linenumber-escape'), or fail ('linenumber-fail'). These addresses are calculated using 'a-count' which, in addition to type analysis, calculates the size of the code to be generated.

The function 'a-count' is defined as a forwards abstract interpretation, computing with types of tuples of data ('data-type'), types of bindings ('symbol-table'), and code sizes ('natural'). The first 'truth-value' component tells if the action being analyzed has a chance of completing. If it does, then the following 'data-type' component tells the type of the tuple of data that will produced. The next two components give similar information about escaping.

The function 'perform' takes as arguments the 'data-type' and 'symbol-table' that are also supplied to 'a-count'. In addition, it takes a 'general-register' which at run-time will contain a pointer to a representation of the tuples of data that will be received when executing then code. The set 'frozen' contains those registers that the code to be produced must not modify, and the three 'cleanup' values are natural numbers that indicate how much to pop from the stack, should the performance complete, escape, or fail.

The calculation of whether an action can complete or not, and whether it can escape or not, are examples of the compile time analyses that are built into the compiler. They are used to generate better code, and they are fully integrated in the proof of correctness, see later.

3.3   Performance Evaluation

The Cantor system has the structure shown in figure 4. In practice, a session with Cantor looks as follows on the screen:

```
cantor syntax semantics compiler
compiler program code
code input output
```

The compiler generator cantor is written in Perl [61], and the generated compilers are written in Scheme [1]. Examples of a syntax and a semantics are given in appendix B; it is the LaTeX source of the appendix that is processed by cantor. The generated compiler contains a syntax checker, a program-to-action transformer, the action compiler described above, and finally a Pseudo SPARC assembler that currently can emit code for the SPARC and the HP Precision Architecture. The input file is a sequence of integers, as is the output file.

The HypoPL language, defined in appendix B, is taken from Lee's book on realistic compiler generation [22], with the difference that we treat nesting of procedures in its full generality but do not allow recursion. (For a discussion of why recursion is problematic, see later.)

- Generating a compiler for HypoPL takes 3 seconds.

We have used this compiler to translate Lee's bubblesort program (50 lines).

- Compile time: 486 seconds;

- Object code size: 114688 bytes; and

- Object code execution time (for sorting 10 integers): 0.1 seconds.

These figures indicate that the system is rather tedious to work with in practice. Additional experiments, see [43], have shown that the code runs at least two orders of magnitude slower than a corresponding target program produced by the C compiler (without optimization). This is somewhat disappointing but still an improvement compared to the classical systems of Mosses, Paulson, and Wand where a slow-down of three orders of magnitude has been reported [22]. Inspection of the code emitted by Cantor-generated compilers reveals that the inefficiency mainly stems from three sources:

- Lack of compile time constant propagation;

- Poor register allocation; and

- Naive representation of bindings, closures, and lists.

Improving the action compiler to avoid this inefficiency would significantly complicate the correctness theorem, which we consider next.

4 The Correctness Theorem

To give an overview of the correctness theorem, we will introduce a bit of notation, as follows (we cheat a little bit again, compared to [44], to improve the readability):

run _ _ :: Act, [integer] list → state .

sparc-run _ _ ::
    program, natural, page → sparc-state .

compile _ :: Act →
    (program, truth-value, data-type,
    truth-value, data-type,
    general-register, general-register) .

abstract _ _ _ _ _ _ _ ::
    sparc-state, truth-value, data-type,
    truth-value, data-type,
    general-register, general-register → state .

i-abs _ _ :: natural, page → [integer] list .

(1) a-count A () (list of empty-list) =
     (n, z_n, h_n, z_e, h_e, empty-list) ;

(2) perform A () (reg 0) empty-set
     (list of empty-list) 0 0 0 0 n n n =
     (p, a_n, a_e)

⇒ compile A = (p, z_n, h_n, z_e, h_e, a_n, a_e) .

We have only given the definition of 'compile _', in terms of 'a-count' and 'perform'. The operations have the following informal meaning:

1. The operation 'run A il' specifies the performance of an action A which is given the empty tuple of data, no bindings, an empty-storage, an empty output-file, and the input-file il (an integer-list). If the performance terminates, then that will result in a final state ('state') which can be either completed, escaped, or failed.

2. The operation 'sparc-run p n se' specifies loading the program p into the program area, and then taking n steps starting in line 0. It also records if the execution at any point "jumps outside the code". The memory, registers, status bits, and output file are initialized appropriately, the input file is initialized to se. 'sparc-run' is defined in terms of 'step', described above.

3. The operation 'compile A' translates the action A into a machine language program p and it also gives type information about what will be produced when performing A. The program p will start in line 0.

4. The operation 'abstract m_p z_n h_n z_e h_e a_n a_e' will give a *sort* of all those states (from the action-level) that are represented by the sparc-state m_p, and that have the type expressed by the following four arguments. The last two arguments are those registers which will contain pointers to the representations of the data produced, should the action complete or escape.

5. The operation 'i-abs n se' will give the input-file ('[integer] list') which is represented by the natural number n and the page se.

The use of both type information and a machine-state in the definition of 'abstract' makes it possible to make do without type information in the semantics of Pseudo SPARC.

None of the above five operations are total. The performance of an action may diverge; the execution of a machine program may "jump outside the code"; the compilation of an action may find a type error; the machine state may represent no state at all from the action-level; and the page for input-files may contain something without the right format.

The meta-notation for unified algebras makes it particularly easy to specify such partial operations. This is because it supports a *unified* treatment of sorts and individuals: an individual is treated as a special case of a sort. Thus operations can be applied to sorts as well as individuals. A vacuous sort represents the lack of an individual, in particular the 'undefined' result of a partial operation. For example, if the performance of the action A with input-file il terminates, then 'run A il' will be an individual, otherwise it will be a vacuous sort. We need not specify that such sorts are vacuous; if it does not follow from the specification that they contain an individual, then they will automatically be vacuous.

The operations 'run', 'sparc-run', 'compile', and 'i-abs' will all yield either an individual or a vacuous sort. In contrast, 'abstract' may yield a sort containing *several* individuals, and it may also yield a vacuous sort. The possibility of yielding a sort containing several individuals is needed when abstracting with respect to a closure type. This is because if two actions differs only in the naming of tokens (they are equal with respect to "alpha-conversion"), then the compiled code for them will be identical.

We can now state the correctness theorem. Note that 't :- s' is another syntax for 's : t'. The meaning is that s is an individual contained in t.

Theorem:

(1) compile A:Act =
$\quad$ (p:program z_n:truth-value h_n:data-type
$\quad$ z_e:truth-value h_e:data-type
$\quad$ a_n:general-register a_e:general-register) ;

(2) i-abs (se at 0) $se = il$:[integer] list

$\Rightarrow$ (1) run A $il = m_a$:state $\Rightarrow$
$\quad$ ($\exists$ m_p:sparc-state $\exists$ n:natural .
$\quad$ sparc-run p n $se = m_p$;
$\quad$ abstract m_p z_n h_n z_e h_e a_n a_e :- m_a) ;

$\quad$ (2) sparc-run p n $se = m_p$:sparc-state $\Rightarrow$
$\quad$ ($\exists$ m_a:state .
$\quad$ run A $il = m_a$;
$\quad$ abstract m_p z_n h_n z_e h_e a_n a_e :- m_a) .

The structure of the theorem resembles the correctness statement of Despeyroux. Informally:

If the action A is compiled into a machine language program p (and some additional type information, etc., is produced), and the input-file il is represented properly in the machine as se, then two properties hold:

1. **Completeness:** If the performance of the action A (with input-file il) terminates in state m_a, then there exists a sparc-state m_p and a number n such that an n-step execution of p will reach m_p, and m_p represents m_a (and the program-counter points to the last line of p).

2. **Soundness:** If an n-step execution of p (with input se) reaches m_p (and the program-counter points to the last line of p), then there exists a state m_a, represented by m_p, such that a performance of A (with input il) will terminate in m_a.

Notice that it is built into the definition of 'sparc-run', and hence the correctness theorem, that the execution of the machine language program never "jumps outside the code".

5 The Proof Technique

A number of lemmas are needed to prove the theorem; here is an overview:

- **Compiler consistency:** These lemmas state that the calculation of code size is correct. They also state that the code is placed consecutively, starting in the desired line.

- **Correctness of analysis:** These lemmas state that the type analysis asserts correct typings, relative to the semantics of actions.

- **Code well-behavedness:** These lemmas state that if the execution of some compiled code at some point reaches "the end of the code", then it used the memory and registers in a disciplined fashion, and, in addition, the machine state will represent an abstract state (with the type given by the compiler).

It is also necessary to prove strengthened versions of completeness and soundness.

Let us now consider how to adopt Despeyroux's proof technique to the framework of unified algebras.

Despeyroux expresses natural semantics in the Gentzen's system style, with axioms and inference rules. In such a system one can make natural deduction, and can then prove lemmas about the system by induction in the length of such deductions. In contrast, the framework of unified algebras provide Horn clauses, and there are no build-in deduction rules. We have replaced inference rules by Horn clauses, so to be able to do deduction, we adopt a standard axiomatization of Horn logic, as follows.

All specifications in the meta-notation for unified algebras can be transformed into a core notation which is outlined in the following. Let Ω

$$\frac{}{(\Omega, \Gamma) \vdash t = t} \qquad \text{(Reflexivity)}$$

$$\frac{(\Omega, \Gamma) \vdash s = t \qquad (\Omega, \Gamma) \vdash t = u}{(\Omega, \Gamma) \vdash s = u} \qquad \text{(Transitivity)}$$

$$\frac{\{(\Omega, \Gamma) \vdash s_i = t_i\}_{i=1}^{n}}{(\Omega, \Gamma) \vdash f(s_1, \ldots, s_n) = f(t_1, \ldots, t_n)} \text{ if } f \in \Sigma \qquad \text{(Functional Congruence)}$$

$$\frac{\{(\Omega, \Gamma) \vdash s_i = t_i\}_{i=1}^{2} \qquad (\Omega, \Gamma) \vdash p(s_1, s_2)}{(\Omega, \Gamma) \vdash p(t_1, t_2)} \text{ if } p \in \{\_ \leq \_, \_ : \_\} \quad \text{(Predicative Congruence)}$$

$$\frac{\{(\Omega, \Gamma) \vdash F_i\}_{i=1}^{n}}{(\Omega, \Gamma) \vdash F} \text{ if } (F_1; \ldots; F_n \Rightarrow F) \in \Gamma \qquad \text{(Modus Ponens)}$$

Figure 5: Axiomatization of Horn clause logic.

be a so-called homogeneous first-order signature, that is, a pair $\langle \Sigma, \Pi \rangle$ where Σ is a set of operation symbols and Π is a set of predicate symbols. In the setting of unified algebras, it is required that

$$\Sigma \supseteq \{\text{nothing}, \_ \mid \_, \_ \& \_\}$$

and

$$\Pi = \{\_ = \_, \_ \leq \_, \_ : \_\}$$

The value of the constant 'nothing' is a vacuous sort, included in all other sorts. The operation '$\_ \mid \_$' is sort union, and '$\_ \& \_$' is sort intersection. The predicate '$\_ = \_$' asserts equality, '$\_ \leq \_$' asserts sort inclusion, and '$T_1 : T_2$' asserts that the value of the term T_1 is an individual included in the (sort) value of the term T_2.

Further, let Γ be a set of Horn clauses built up from Ω. Any specification Γ of such Horn clauses will be augmented with some basic Horn clauses, stating for example the reflexivity of '$\_ \leq \_$', see [34]. Finally, let F be a formula built up from Ω. We will then write

$$(\Omega, \Gamma) \vdash F$$

(read F is (Ω, Γ)-deducible) if $(\Omega, \Gamma) \vdash F$ can be obtained by finitely many applications of the deduction rules shown in figure 5. A deduction rule consists of a *conclusion* (given beneath the line), none, one, or several *premises* (given above the line), and possibly a *condition* (given at the right-hand side of the line). A deduction rule stands for the statement:

- If all premises are deducible, the condition is satisfied, and F is a formula built up from Ω, then the conclusion $(\Omega, \Gamma) \vdash F$ is deducible.

With these deduction rules, we can do proof by induction in the number of occurrences of "modus ponens" in deductions. Note that a single application of modus ponens corresponds closely to a natural deduction step. This makes our proof strategy close to Despeyroux's. All lemmas proved by induction in the length of deduction are satisfied by the *initial* model of the specification. The key property of an initial model needed here is that it only contain entities that are values of ground terms (it contains "no junk").

We will end this section by explaining why we do not treat recursion, in contrast to Despeyroux. The reason for this is rather subtle; it hinges on the expressiveness of the unified meta-notation.

Full action notation offers self-referential bindings as the means for describing for example recursive procedures. A self-referential binding is a cyclic structure; the run-time representation will obviously also be cyclic. In Despeyroux's paper, such cyclic structures are represented as graphs with self-loops—both in the source and target languages. This allows her to uniquely determine the run-time representation of a self-referential environment.

Compared to Despeyroux, we use a much more low-level target language where values can be placed in more than one place in the memory. This means that not only can one target value represent more than one source value, as in Despeyroux's paper, it is also possible for one source value to be represented by different parts of the memory. In other words, there is no *functional* connection between source and target values; there is only a *relation* stating which source values are represented by a given part of the memory.

In the case of cyclic structures, the relation between semantic values seems to be impossible to define in the unified meta-notation. This is because the meta-notation only allows the expression of Horn clauses. Evidence for this is found in Amadio and Cardelli's paper on subtyping recursive types [2]. They axiomatize several relationships between cyclic structures, and it seems that a rule of the following non-Horn kind cannot be avoided:

$$(x \ R \ y \Rightarrow \alpha \ R \ \beta) \Rightarrow \mu x. \alpha \ R \ \mu y. \beta$$

Since we want to apply the unified meta-notation exclusively in all specifications, we avoid self-referential bindings. Thus we cannot treat recursion.

6   Conclusion

Our compiler generator is specified and proved correct solely in an algebraic framework. To our knowledge, it is the first time that this has been accomplished.

The generated compilers emit realistic, albeit poor, machine code. Future work includes building in more analyses, for the benefit of the code generator.

The use of action semantics makes the processable specifications easy to read and pleasant to work with. We believe that the Cantor system is a promising first step towards user-friendly and automatic generation of realistic and *correct* compilers.

Acknowledgements. This work has been supported in part by the Danish Research Council under the DART Project (5.21.08.03). The author thanks Peter Mosses, Michael Schwartzbach, and the referees for helpful comments on a draft of the paper. The author also thanks Peter Ør- bæk for implementing the Cantor system.

Appendix A: Action Notation

grammar:

```
Act   = "complete" | "escape" | "fail" |
        "commit" | "diverge" | "regive" |
        [ "give" Dep ] | [ "check" Dep ] |
        [ "bind" token "to" Dep ] |
        [ "store" Dep "in" Dep ] |
        [ "allocate" "truth-value" "cell" ] |
        [ "allocate" "integer" "cell" ] |
        [ "batch-send" Dep ] |
        [ "batch-receive" "an" "integer" ] |
        [ "enact" "application" Dep
        "to" Tuple ] |
        [ "indivisibly" Act ] |
        [ "unfolding" Unf ] |
        [ Act Infix Act ] |
        [ [ "furthermore" Act ] "hence" Act ] |
        [ [ "furthermore" Act ] "thence" Act ] .

Unf   = [ Act Infix Unf ] | [ Unf "or" Act ] |
        "unfold" .

Tuple = "()" | Dep | [ Tuple "," Tuple ] |
        "them" .

Dep   = "true" | "false" | natural |
        [ "empty-list" "&" "[" Type "]" "list" ] |
        [ "closure" "abstraction" "of" Act "&"
        "[" "perhaps" "using" Data "]" "act" ] |
        [ Unary Dep ] |
        [ Binary "(" Dep "," Dep ")" ] |
        [ Dep "is" Dep ] |
        [ Dep [ "is" "less" "than" ] Dep ] |
        [ "component#" Dep "items" Dep ] |
        "it" |
        [ "the" "given" Datum "#" natural ] |
        [ "the" Datum "bound" "to" token ] |
        [ "the" Datum "stored" "in" Dep ] |
        [ "(" Dep ")" ] .

Infix = [ "and" "then" ] | "then" | "before" |
        "trap" | "or" .

Unary = "not" | "negation" | [ "list" "of" ] |
        "head" | "tail" .

Binary = "both" | "either" | "sum" |
         "difference" | "concatenation" .

Datum = "datum" | "cell" | "abstraction" |
        "list" | [ Datum "|" Datum ] | Type .

Data  = "()" | Type | [ Data "," Data ] .
```

```
Type  =  "truth-value"  |  "integer"  |
          [[ "truth-value" "cell" ]]  |
          [[ "integer" "cell" ]]  |
          [[ "[" Type "]" "list" ]] .
```

A.1   Action Principles

Action notation is designed to allow comprehensible and accessible descriptions of programming languages. Action semantic descriptions scale up smoothly from small example languages to realistic languages, and they can make widespread reuse of action semantic descriptions of related languages.

Actions reflect the gradual, stepwise nature of computatiqn. A performance of an action, which may be part of an enclosing action, either

- *completes*, corresponding to normal termination (the performance of the enclosing action proceeds normally); or

- *escapes*, corresponding to exceptional termination (the enclosing action is skipped until the escape is trapped); or

- *fails*, corresponding to abandoning the performance of an action (the enclosing action performs an alternative action, if there is one, otherwise it fails too); or

- *diverges*, corresponding to nontermination (the enclosing action also diverges).

The information processed by action performance may be classified according to how far it tends to be propagated, as follows:

- *transient*: tuples of data, corresponding to intermediate results;

- *scoped*: bindings of tokens to data, corresponding to symbol tables;

- *stable*: data stored in cells, corresponding to the values assigned to variables;

- *permanent*: data communicated between distributed actions.

Transient information is made available to an action for immediate use. Scoped information, in contrast, may generally be referred to throughout an entire action, although it may also be hidden temporarily. Stable information can be changed, but not hidden, in the action, and it persists until explicitly destroyed. Permanent information cannot even be changed, merely augmented.

When an action is performed, transient information is given only on completion or escape, and scoped information is produced only on completion. In contrast, changes to stable information and extensions to permanent information are made *during* action performance, and are unaffected by subsequent divergence or failure.

Our subset of action notation omits all notation for communication. Instead, the ad hoc constructs 'batch-send' and 'batch-receive' allow a primitive form of communication with batch-files, as in standard Pascal.

The information processed by actions consist of items of *data*, organized in structures that give access to the individual items. Data can include various familiar mathematical entities, such as truth-values, integers, and lists. Actions themselves are not data, but they can be incorporated in so-called abstractions, which are data, and subsequently 'enacted' back into actions.

Dependent data are entities that can be *evaluated* to yield data during action performance. The data yielded may depend on the current information, i.e., the given transients, the received bindings, and the current state of the storage and batch-files. Evaluation cannot affect the current information. Data is a special case of dependent data, and it always yields itself when evaluated.

Appendix B: HypoPL Action Semantics

B.1   Abstract Syntax

grammar:

Program   =   ⟦ "program" Identifier Block ⟧ .

Declaration =   ⟦ "int" Identifier ⟧ |
⟦ "bool" Identifier ⟧ |
⟦ "const" Identifier "=" Integer ⟧ |
⟦ "array" Identifier "[" Integer "]" ⟧ |
⟦ "procedure" Identifier
"(" Identifier ")" Block ⟧ |
⟦ Declaration ";" Declaration ⟧ .

Block   =   ⟦ Declaration
"begin" Statement "end" ⟧ |
⟦ "begin" Statement "end" ⟧ .

Statement =   ⟦ Expression ":=" Expression ⟧ |
⟦ "write" Expression ⟧ |
⟦ "read" Expression ⟧ |
⟦ "if" Expression "then" Statement
"else" Statement "endif" ⟧ |
⟦ "while" Expression "do"
Statement "endwhile" ⟧ |
⟦ Identifier "(" Expression ")" ⟧ |
⟦ Statement ";" Statement ⟧ | "skip" .

Expression =   "true" | "false" | Integer |
Identifier |
⟦ Identifier "[" Expression "]" ⟧ |
⟦ Expression Operation Expression ⟧ |
⟦ "not" Expression ⟧ .

Operation =   "+" | "−" | "<" | "=" | "and" .

Integer   =   natural | ⟦ "−" natural ⟧ .

Identifier =   token .

B.2   Semantic Entities

B.2.1   Items

introduces: item .

item = truth-value | integer .

B.2.2   Coercion

introduces: coercively _ .

• coercively _ :: act → act .

coercively A:act =
| A
then
| give the given item #1 or
| give the item stored in the given cell #1 .

B.3   Semantic Functions

introduces:
run _ , establish _ , activate _ , execute _ ,
evaluate _ , operation-result _ ,
integer-value _ , id _ .

B.3.1   Programs

• run _ :: Program → act .

run ⟦ "program" I:Identifier B:block ⟧ = activate B .

B.3.2   Declarations

• establish _ :: Declaration → act .

establish ⟦ "int" I:Identifier ⟧ =
allocate integer cell then bind id I to it .

establish ⟦ "bool" I:Identifier ⟧ =
allocate truth-value cell then bind id I to it .

establish ⟦ "const" I:Identifier "=" j:integer ⟧ =
bind id I to integer-value j .

establish ⟦ "array" I:Identifier "[" j:integer "]" ⟧ =
give empty-list & [integer cell] list and then
give sum(integer-value j, 1)
then
| unfolding
| | check the given integer #2 is 0 and then
| | give the given list #1
| or
| | regive and then allocate integer cell
| then
| | give concatenation(
| | list of the given integer cell #3,
| | the given list #1)
| and then
| | give difference(
| | the given integer #2, 1)
| then
| | unfold
then
| bind id I to the given list #1 .

establish ⟦ "procedure" I_1:Identifier
  "(" I_2:Identifier ")" B:Block ⟧ =
bind id I_1 to
closure abstraction of
  | | furthermore
  | | | give the given integer #1 and then
  | | | allocate integer cell
  | | then
  | | | store the given integer #1
  | | | in the given cell #2
  | | and then
  | | | bind id I_2 to the given cell #2
  | thence activate B
  & [perhaps using integer] act .

establish ⟦ D_1:Declaration ";" D_2:Declaration ⟧ =
  establish D_1 before establish D_2 .

B.3.3 Blocks

• activate _ :: Block → act .

activate ⟦ D:Declaration
  "begin" S:Statement "end" ⟧ =
  | furthermore establish D
  hence execute S .

activate ⟦ "begin" S:Statement "end" ⟧ = execute S .

B.3.4 Statements

• execute _ :: Statement → act .

execute ⟦ E_1:Expression ":=" E_2:Expression ⟧ =
  | evaluate E_1 and then
  | coercively evaluate E_2
  then
  | store the given item #2
  | in the given cell #1 .

execute ⟦ "write" E:Expression ⟧ =
  coercively evaluate E then batch-send it .

execute ⟦ "read" E:Expression ⟧ =
  | batch-receive an integer and then evaluate E
  then
  | store the given integer #1
  | in the given integer cell #2 .

execute ⟦ "if" E:Expression "then" S_1:Statement
  "else" S_2:Statement "endif" ⟧ =
  | coercively evaluate E
  then
  | | check it then execute S_1
  | or
  | | check not it then execute S_2 .

execute ⟦ "while" E:Expression "do" S:Statement
  "endwhile" ⟧ =
unfolding
  | | coercively evaluate E
  | then
  | | check it then execute S then unfold
  | | or check not it .

execute ⟦ I:Identifier "(" E:Expression ")" ⟧ =
  | give the abstraction bound to id I and then
  | coercively evaluate E
  then
  | enact application the given abstraction #1
  | to the given integer #2 .

execute ⟦ S_1:Statement ";" S_2:Statement ⟧ =
  execute S_1 and then execute S_2 .

execute "skip" = complete .

B.3.5 Expressions

• evaluate _ :: Expression → act .

evaluate "true" = give true .

evaluate "false" = give false .

evaluate i:Integer = give integer-value i .

evaluate I:Identifier = give the datum bound to id I .

evaluate ⟦ I:Identifier "[" E:Expression "]" ⟧ =
  | | give the list bound to id I and then
  | | coercively evaluate E then give sum(it, 1)
  | then
  | give component# (the given integer #2)
  | items (the given list #1) .

evaluate
  ⟦ E_1:Expression O:Operation E_2:Expression ⟧ =
  | coercively evaluate E_1 and then
  | coercively evaluate E_2
  then give operation-result O .

evaluate ⟦ "not" E:Expression ⟧ =
  coercively evaluate E then
  give not it .

B.3.6 Operations

• operation-result _ ::
  Operation → dependent datum .

operation-result "+" =
  sum(the given integer #1,
      the given integer #2) .

```
operation-result "-" =
    difference(the given integer #1,
              the given integer #2) .
```

```
operation-result "<" =
    (the given integer #1) is less than
    (the given integer #2) .
```

```
operation-result "=" =
    (the given item | cell #1) is
    (the given item | cell #2) .
```

```
operation-result "and" =
    both(the given truth-value #1,
         the given truth-value #2) .
```

B.3.7 Integers

• integer-value _ :: Integer → integer .

integer-value n:natural = n .

integer-value ⟦ "-" n:natural ⟧ = negation n .

B.3.8 Identifiers

• id _ :: Identifier → token .

id k:token = k .

References

[1] Harald Abelson, Gerald Jay Sussman, and Julie Sussman. *Structure and Interpretation of Computer Programs*. MIT Press, 1985.

[2] Roberto M. Amadio and Luca Cardelli. Subtyping recursive types. In *Eightteenth Symposium on Principles of Programming Languages*. ACM Press, January 1991.

[3] Rudolf Berghammer, Herbert Ehler, and Hans Zierer. Towards an algebraic specification of code generation. *Science of Computer Programming*, 11:45–63, 1988.

[4] William R. Bevier, Warren A. Hunt, J. Strother Moore, and William D. Young. An approach to systems verification. *Journal of Automated Reasoning*, 5:411–428, 1989.

[5] Anders Bondorf. Automatic autoprojection of higher order recursive equations. In *Proc. ESOP'90, European Symposium on Programming*. Springer-Verlag (*LNCS* 432), 1990.

[6] Anders Bondorf and Olivier Danvy. Automatic autoprojection of recursive equations with global variables and abstract data types. *Science of Computer Programming*, 16:151–195, 1991.

[7] Rod M. Burstall and Peter J. Landin. Programs and their proofs: an algebraic approach. In B. Meltzer and D. Mitchie, editors, *Machine Intelligence, Vol. 4*, pages 17–43. Edinburgh University Press, 1969.

[8] G. Cousineau, P.-L. Curien, and M. Mauny. The categorical abstract machine. *Science of Computer Programming*, 8:173–202, 1987.

[9] Mads Dam and Frank Jensen. Compiler generation from relational semantics. In *Proc. ESOP'86, European Symposium on Programming*. Springer-Verlag (*LNCS* 213), 1986.

[10] Joëlle Despeyroux. Proof of translation in natural semantics. In *LICS'86, First Symposium on Logic in Computer Science*, June 1986.

[11] Anders Gammelgaard and Flemming Nielson. Verification of the level 0 compiling specification. Technical report, Department of Computer Science, Aarhus University, July 1990.

[12] Joseph A. Goguen, James W. Thatcher, and Eric G. Wagner. An initial algebra approach to the specification, correctness, and implementation of abstract data types. In Raymond T. Yeh, editor, *Current Trends in Programming Methodology, Volume IV*. Prentice-Hall, 1978.

[13] Carsten K. Gomard and Neil D. Jones. A partial evaluator for the untyped lambda-calculus. *Journal of Functional Programming*, 1(1):21–69, 1991.

[14] John Hannan. Making abstract machines less abstract. In *Proc. Conference on Functional Programming Languages and Computer Architecture*. Springer-Verlag *LNCS*, 1991.

[15] John Hannan. Staging transformations for abstract machines. In *Proc. ACM SIGPLAN Symposium on Partial Evaluation and Semantics Based Program Manipulation*. Sigplan Notices, 1991.

[16] John Hannan and Dale Miller. From operational semantics to abtract machines. *Journal of Mathmatical Structures in Computer Science*, To appear, 1991.

[17] Warren A. Hunt. Microprocessor design verification. *Journal of Automated Reasoning*, 5:429–460, 1989.

[18] Jeffrey J. Joyce. Totally verified systems: Linking verified software to verified hardware. In *Proc. Hardware Specification, Verification and Synthesis: Mathmatical Aspects*, July 1989.

[19] Jeffrey J. Joyce. A verified compiler for a verified microprocessor. Technical report, University of Cambridge, Computer Laboratory, England, March 1989.

[20] Gilles Kahn. Natural semantics. In *Proc. STACS'87*. Springer-Verlag (*LNCS* 247), 1987.

[21] Richard Kelsey and Paul Hudak. Realistic compilation by program transformation. In *Sixteenth Symposium on Principles of Programming Languages*. ACM Press, January 1989.

[22] Peter Lee. *Realistic Compiler Generation*. MIT Press, 1989.

[23] Peter Lee and Uwe F. Pleban. A realistic compiler generator based on high-level semantics. In *Fourteenth Symposium on Principles of Programming Languages*, pages 284–295. ACM Press, January 1987.

[24] John McCarthy and James Painter. Correctness of a compiler for arithmetic expressions. In *Proc. Symposium in Applied Mathematics of the American Mathmatical Society*, April 1966.

[25] Sun Microsystems. A RISC tutorial. Technical Report 800-1795-10, revision A, May 1988.

[26] Robert E. Milne and Christopher Strachey. *A Theory of Programming Language Semantics*. Chapman and Hall, 1976.

[27] J. Strother Moore. A mechanically verified language implementation. *Journal of Automated Reasoning*, 5:461–492, 1989.

[28] Francis Lockwood Morris. Advice on structuring compilers and proving them correct. In *Symposium on Principles of Programming Languages*, pages 144–152. ACM Press, October 1973.

[29] Peter D. Mosses. SIS—semantics implementation system. Technical Report Daimi MD–30, Computer Science Department, Aarhus University, 1979.

[30] Peter D. Mosses. A constructive approach to compiler correctness. In *Proc. Seventh Colloquium of Automata, Languages, and Programming*, July 1980.

[31] Peter D. Mosses. Abstract semantic algebras! In *Proc. IFIP TC2 Working Conference on Formal Description of Programming Concepts II (Garmisch-Partenkirchen, 1982)*. North-Holland, 1983.

[32] Peter D. Mosses. A basic abstract semantic algebra. In *Proc. Int. Symp. on Semantics of Data Types (Sophia-Antipolis)*. Springer-Verlag (*LNCS* 173), 1984.

[33] Peter D. Mosses. Unified algebras and action semantics. In *Proc. STACS'89*. Springer-Verlag, 1989.

[34] Peter D. Mosses. Unified algebras and institutions. In *LICS'89, Fourth Annual Symposium on Logic in Computer Science*, 1989.

[35] Peter D. Mosses. Unified algebras and modules. In *Sixteenth Symposium on Principles of Programming Languages*. ACM Press, January 1989.

[36] Peter D. Mosses. Action semantics. Lecture Notes, Version 9 (a revised version is to be published by Cambridge University Press in the Series *Tracts in Theoretical Computer Science*), 1991.

[37] Peter D. Mosses. An introduction to action semantics. Technical Report DAIMI IR–102, Computer Science Department, Aarhus University, July 1991. Lecture Notes for the Marktoberdorf'91 Summer School.

[38] Peter D. Mosses and David A. Watt. The use of action semantics. In *Proc. IFIP TC2 Working Conference on Formal Description of Programming Concepts III (Gl. Avernæs, 1986)*. North-Holland, 1987.

[39] Flemming Nielson and Hanne Riis Nielson. Two-level semantics and code generation. *Theoretical Computer Science*, 56, 1988.

[40] Flemming Nielson and Hanne Riis Nielson. Two-level functional languages. Draft book. To be published by Cambridge University Press, 1991.

[41] Hanne R. Nielson and Flemming Nielson. Automatic binding time analysis for a typed λ-calculus. *Science of Computer Programming*, 10:139–176, 1988.

[42] Hewlett Packard. Precision architecture and instruction. Technical Report 09740–90014, June 1987.

[43] Jens Palsberg. An automatically generated and provably correct compiler for a subset of Ada. In *Proc. ICCL'92, Fourth IEEE International Conference on Computer Languages*, 1992.

[44] Jens Palsberg. *Provably Correct Compiler Generation*. PhD thesis, Computer Science Department, Aarhus University, 1992. Forthcoming.

[45] Lawrence Paulson. A semantics-directed compiler generator. In *Ninth Symposium on Principles of Programming Languages*, pages 224–233. ACM Press, January 1982.

[46] Uwe F. Pleban. Compiler prototyping using formal semantics. In *Proc. ACM SIGPLAN'84 Symposium on Compiler Construction*, pages 94–105. Sigplan Notices, 1984.

[47] Uwe F. Pleban and Peter Lee. On the use of LISP in implementing denotational semantics. In *Proc. ACM Conference on LISP and Functional Programming*, August 1986.

[48] Uwe F. Pleban and Peter Lee. High-level semantics, an integrated approach to programming language semantics and the specification of implementations. In *Proc. Mathmatical Foundations of Programming Language Semantics*, April 1987.

[49] Uwe F. Pleban and Peter Lee. An automatically generated, realistic compiler for an imperative programming language. In *Proc. SIGPLAN'88 Conference on Programming Language Design and Implementation*, June 1988.

[50] Gordon D. Plotkin. A structural approach to operational semantics. Technical Report DAIMI FN–19, Computer Science Department, Aarhus University, September 1981.

[51] Wolfgang Polak. *Compiler Specification and Verification*. Springer-Verlag (*LNCS* 213), 1981.

[52] David A. Schmidt. Detecting global variables in denotational specifications. *ACM Transactions on Programming Languages and Systems*, 7(2):299–310, 1985.

[53] David A. Schmidt. *Denotational Semantics*. Allyn and Bacon, 1986.

[54] David A. Schmidt. Detecting stack-based environments in denotational semantics. *Science of Computer Programming*, 11:107–131, 1988.

[55] Uwe Schmidt and Reinhard Völler. A multilanguage compiler system with automatically generated codegenerators. In *Proc. ACM SIGPLAN'84 Symposium on Compiler Construction*. Sigplan Notices, 1984.

[56] Uwe Schmidt and Reinhard Völler. Experience with VDM in Norsk Data. In *VDM'87. VDM—A Formal Method at Work*. Springer-Verlag (*LNCS* 252), March 1987.

[57] William Stallings. *Reduced Instruction Set Computers*. IEEE Computer Society Press, 1986.

[58] Joseph E. Stoy. *Denotational Semantics: The Scott-Strachey Approach to Programming Language Theory*. MIT Press, 1977.

[59] James W. Thatcher, Eric G. Wagner, and Jesse B. Wright. More on advice on structuring compilers and proving them correct. *Theoretical Computer Science*, 15:223–249, 1981.

[60] Mads Tofte. *Compiler Generators*. Springer-Verlag, 1990.

[61] Larry Wall and Randal L. Schwartz. *Programming Perl*. O'Reilly, 1991.

[62] Mitchell Wand. A semantic prototyping system. In *Proc. ACM SIGPLAN'84 Symposium on Compiler Construction*, pages 213–221. Sigplan Notices, 1984.

[63] David Watt. *Programming Language Syntax and Semantics*. Prentice-Hall, 1991.

[64] Niklaus Wirth. *Algorithms + Data Structures = Programs*. Prentice-Hall, 1976.

[65] William D. Young. A mechanically verified code generator. *Journal of Automated Reasoning*, 5:493–518, 1989.

An Adequate Operational Semantics of Sharing in Lazy Evaluation *

S. Purushothaman and Jill Seaman
Dept of Computer Science
The Pennsylvania State University
University Park, PA 16802
e-mail: purush@cs.psu.edu and jseaman@cs.psu.edu

Abstract

We present LAZY-PCF+SHAR, an extension of **PCF**, that deals with lazy evaluation and explicit substitutions to model the sharing engendered by the lazy evaluation strategy. We present a natural operational semantics for LAZY-PCF+SHAR and show that it is equivalent to the standard fixed-point semantics. Sharing is modeled by explicit substitutions, which require a great deal of careful attention in the proof.

1 Introduction

In this paper we develop an operational semantics for an extension of PCF, called LAZY-PCF+SHAR, that provides a formalism for dealing with the sharing involved in lazy evaluation. The language is different from PCF in that explicit substitutions are made part of the language. The central part of the paper is a soundness theorem and an adequacy theorem which show that the operational semantics developed is equivalent to standard fixed-point semantics, as found in the literature.

The work presented here is aimed at providing the basis (and the tools necessary) for developing analyses of sharing in lazy functional languages. Compile-time analysis of sharing is fundamental to a number of other compile-time analyses such as garbage collection and order of evaluation (and its use in parallelization) [3,6,4]. Hence there is a need for a study of sharing.

In [4] we showed how a *compositional* compile-time analysis for evaluation order and aggregate update of a first-order lazy language can be developed from an operational semantics. The technique is to define predicates based on the operational semantics and to extend these predicates to the denotational semantics based on the equivalence of the

---

*Supported in part by NSF grants CDA-89-14587 and CCR-90-04121

two semantics. Then compositional analysis can be done using abstract interpretation with the denotational semantics. The advantage was that we were able to avoid development of complicated continuation based semantics and the development of abstract interpretation to deal with such continuations. Of course, the entire development hinged on the equivalence theorem between the operational and the fixed-point semantics. The work reported here was started as the basis for extending the ideas of [4] to higher-order lazy evaluation. The equivalence shown here should also be of independent interest in the study of lazy evaluation and in the study of establishing equivalence between semantic definitions.

The characteristics of lazy evaluation have typically been identified from the theoretical perspective as the use of weak-head normal forms in λ-calculus, and from the implementation perspective as an evaluation strategy that improves on the space-and-time requirements of call-by-name evaluation mechanism by explicit sharing of actual parameters in function calls.

Abramsky has formalized lazy evaluation in an untyped λ-calculus as the reduction of the outermost function to weak-head normal form before applying to an unevaluated argument [2]. Howard and Mitchell have similarly considered a lazy version of PCF with algebraic datatypes in [7]. The languages (and their semantics) considered in both of these papers do not deal explicitly with the sharing engendered in lazy evaluation.

Recently, there has been lot of research activity on explicit substitutions [1,5,8]. In the first two papers the reduction system $\lambda\sigma$ is considered, while in [8] a calculus, weak-$\lambda\sigma$, with weak-head normal forms has been considered. Our work is more closely related to the work of [8] in that we consider weak-head normal forms as the normal form for λ-abstractions and use explicit substitutions. But each of these papers studies the reduction system with emphasis on optimality of reduction strategies, while we fix the reduction strategy by the operational semantics and are more interested in the relation between the operational (i.e., the reduction system) and the fixed-point approach to semantics. As compared to all of these papers our semantics is defined over a typed language.

In the next section we introduce the language LAZY-PCF+SHAR which includes explicit substitutions as components of expressions. In Section 3 we present the soundness theorem and in Section 4 we prove the adequacy theorem. Both of these theorems, especially the adequacy theorem, are complicated, compared to Plotkin's original proof of equivalence between operational and fixed-point semantics of PCF [10]. The main difficulty in extending Plotkin's proof are due to (a) the presence of explicit substitutions, and (b) the assumption of a fixed evaluation strategy, i.e., lazy evaluation strategy. For example, the soundness theorem, whose proof is very simple in Plotkin's paper, depends on properties of a relationship between the environments that arise in the operational semantics and those of the fixed-point semantics. The adequacy proof, though similar to Plotkin's proof, is complicated because of the presence of the explicit substitutions, as opposed to syntactic substitutions. The proof sketches for all the important theorems have been presented. A more thorough presentation of the proofs is contained in [11].

Types:	

Types:
$$t = \textbf{nat} \mid \textbf{bool} \mid t_1 \rightarrow t_2$$
Expressions:
$$e = 0 \mid true \mid false \mid$$
$$\lambda x\!:\!t.e \mid e_1\, e_2$$
$$\mid if(e_1, e_2, e_3) \mid x \mid$$
$$succ(e) \mid pred(e) \mid$$
$$iszero(e) \mid \mu x\!:\!t.e \mid$$
$$\langle e, [x\!:\!t \mapsto e_1]\rangle$$

$$FV(x) = \{x\}$$
$$FV(0) = FV(true) = FV(false) = \{\,\}$$
$$FV(succ(e)) = FV(pred(e)) = FV(e)$$
$$FV(iszero(e)) = FV(e)$$
$$FV(\lambda x\!:\!t.e) = FV(\mu x\!:\!t.e) = FV(e) - \{x\}$$
$$FV(e_1\, e_2) = FV(e_1) \cup FV(e_2)$$
$$FV(\langle e, [x\!:\!t \mapsto e_1]\rangle) = FV((\lambda x\!:\!t.e)\, e_1)$$
$$FV(if(e_1, e_2, e_3)) = FV(e_1) \cup FV(e_2) \cup FV(e_3)$$

Figure 1: Syntax of LAZY-PCF+SHAR

2 The Language and its Semantics

The language that we use, LAZY-PCF+SHAR, is a lazy version of **PCF** extended to include explicit substitutions in order to capture the sharing involved in parameter passing. The syntax, along with the rules for free variables, is as given in Figure 1. As usual, an expression e such that $FV(e) = \emptyset$ is called closed. The only syntactic difference between PCF and our language is the explicit use of the substitution $[x\!:\!t \mapsto e_1]$ in the closure $\langle e, [x\!:\!t \mapsto e_1]\rangle$. In such a closure, the substitution is a binding for the free variable x in e. The purpose of these closures is to model function application according to the rules of lazy evaluation, which require that the argument is not evaluated until needed, and then evaluated only once (it is not reevaluated if it is needed more than once). The substitution in a closure provides storage for the initially unevaluated argument which can be updated if and when it is evaluated. This explains why $FV(\langle e, [x\!:\!t \mapsto e_1]\rangle)$ is defined in terms of application. Closures could also be used to model the *let* expression, as in $\langle e, [x\!:\!t \mapsto e_1]\rangle$ for "let $x\!:\!t = e_1$ in e".

Every valid expression has a unique type. The type t of an expression e is constructed with respect to a type environment, which maps the free variables of e to types. Type environments are denoted as a list $H = [x_1 : t_1, \ldots, x_n : t_n]$, where the variables x_i are unique. As is customary we will use the notation $H[s/x]$ to denote a perturbed environment which respects H on all variables other than x, and binds x to type s. The type judgement rules are provided in Figure 2. An expression e has type t in type environment H if $H \vdash e : t$ can be justified by an inference built up from the type rules. We refer to the types **nat** and **bool** as *basic* types.

2.1 The Operational Semantics

The main task of the operational semantics is to model function application according to the lazy evaluation rules. As described above, closures provide the means to model the storing of the argument, but the semantics will be responsible for modeling the evaluation and updating of the arguments appropriately. Furthermore, since a given expression

$$\text{C0:} \quad \vdash 0 : \mathbf{nat}$$

$$\text{CS:} \quad \frac{H \vdash e : \mathbf{nat}}{H \vdash succ(e) : \mathbf{nat}}$$

$$\text{CT:} \quad \vdash true : \mathbf{bool}$$

$$\text{CP:} \quad \frac{H \vdash e : \mathbf{nat}}{H \vdash pred(e) : \mathbf{nat}}$$

$$\text{CF:} \quad \vdash false : \mathbf{bool}$$

$$\text{CZ:} \quad \frac{H \vdash e : \mathbf{nat}}{H \vdash iszero(e) : \mathbf{bool}}$$

$$\text{Var:} \quad H[t/x] \vdash x : t$$

$$\text{Abs:} \quad \frac{H[s/x] \vdash e : t}{H \vdash \lambda x : s.e : s \rightarrow t} \qquad \text{App:} \quad \frac{H \vdash e : s \rightarrow t \quad H \vdash e_1 : s}{H \vdash e\, e_1 : t}$$

$$\text{Cond:} \quad \frac{H \vdash e_1 : \mathbf{bool} \quad H \vdash e_2 : t \quad H \vdash e_3 : t}{H \vdash if(e_1, e_2, e_3) : t}$$

$$\text{Rec:} \quad \frac{H[t/x] \vdash e : t}{H \vdash \mu x : t.e : t} \qquad \text{CL:} \quad \frac{H \vdash e_1 : s \quad H[s/x] \vdash e : t}{H \vdash \langle e, [x : s \mapsto e_1] \rangle : t}$$

Figure 2: Type Rules

may have several levels or nestings of closures, binding each of the free variables of that expression, the operational semantics must be able to maintain several bindings at once. In order to evaluate an expression, the semantics collects these bindings into a list, called the *environment* of the expression. An environment will be listed as follows:

$$[x_1 : t_1 \mapsto e_1, \ldots, x_n : t_n \mapsto e_n]$$

and must have the special properties that each x_i is unique and for each expression e_i, $FV(e_i) \in \{x_{i+1}, \ldots, x_n\}$. An expression is paired with an environment in a *configuration*, as in the following: $\ll e, [x_1 : t_1 \mapsto e_1, \ldots, x_n : t_n \mapsto e_n] \gg$ with the property that $FV(e) \in \{x_1, \ldots, x_n\}$. Note that configurations are more general than closures, since their second element is a *list* of bindings.

The operational semantics defines a relation between configurations which models the evaluation of an expression within an environment. They are actually described as a *natural* semantics, which is a style of describing semantics where one expression (or configuration, in this case) "reduces" to another if an inference or proof tree can be demonstrated using the rules and axioms of the semantics to justify the reduction. In fact this is the only way one expression reduces to another—there is no notion of transitive closure or many-step reductions in natural semantics. Therefore, an expression reduces directly to its normal form, and the intermediate steps of the evaluation can be found in each level of the inference. Consequently, in a natural semantics a normal form is an expression that evaluates to itself. Since there are no many-step reductions, this does not cause the problem of infinite reductions as is found in the traditional rewriting systems.

The operational semantics for LAZY-PCF+SHAR are shown in Figure 3. In this description, note that $A_1 \cdot A_2$ is used to denote concatenation of environments, where the binding $[x:t \mapsto e]$ of a closure is considered a one-element environment.

The first four rules, C0, CT, CF, and L show that $0, true, false$, and expressions of the type $\lambda x:t.e$ are normal forms (they reduce to themselves in any environment). The first three are as expected, but λ-abstractions are also normal forms. This prevents the body of a function from being evaluated until it is applied, which is part of the evaluation strategy dictated by lazy evaluation. The next five rules simply carry out the evaluation of the primary functions $pred, succ$, and $iszero$.

The rules Var1 and Var2 manipulate the environment whenever the evaluation calls for a variable access. The rule Var1 does two things. First it evaluates the expression bound to the variable, and then it updates the environment to bind that variable to the new normal form. The rule Var2 is used when the variable being looked up in the environment is not the leftmost binding in the environment. It searches for the binding of that variable in the tail of the environment.

The rule Appl carries out application of a function to an argument by first evaluating the function, e_1, to a functional normal form, N. Then the function Ap, also defined in Figure 3, is used to create the appropriate closure of the body of N with the argument e_2. The new closure created by the Ap function is evaluated in the updated environment A' to find the normal form of the original application.

As an example of how the Ap function works, consider the evaluations of the expressions f_1 and f_2 defined as follows: $f \equiv \lambda x:s.\lambda y:t.p\,x\,y$, $f_1 \equiv (f\ 4)$ and $f_2 \equiv (f_1\ 5)$ in an environment P that contains a binding for the function p. From the Appl rule, we can infer that $\ll f_1, P \gg \rightarrow \ll \langle \lambda y:t.p\,n\,y, [n:s \mapsto 4] \rangle, P \gg$ (since f evaluates to itself in P by rule L and $Ap(f, 4) \equiv \langle \lambda y:t.p\,n\,y, [n:s \mapsto 4] \rangle$, which also evaluates to itself in P by rules CL and L). In the evaluation of f_2 in P, the closure $\langle \lambda y:t.p\,n\,y, [n:s \mapsto 4] \rangle$ will be constructed and then applied to 5. Clearly, the operational semantics should be able to deal with the application of a closure to an argument, which the function Ap is defined to do. It recursively searches inside the closure for a λ-expression to discover the variable to which the argument is to be bound. Ap also renames the variable found in the body of the λ-expression and binds the argument to this new variable at the outermost level. The new variable is used in order to maintain the property that all environments will always contain unique variable names. This simulates the creation of a new location in storage. In this example $Ap(\langle \lambda y:t.p\,n\,y, [n:s \mapsto 4] \rangle, 5)$ yields $\langle \langle p\,n\,m, [n:s \mapsto 4] \rangle, [m:t \mapsto 5] \rangle$, which is then evaluated in P to get the final result.

IfTrue and IfFalse operate symmetrically. First the boolean expression e_1 is evaluated to $true$ or $false$, and then either e_2 or e_3 is evaluated in the updated environment to find the appropriate result. The rule Rec evaluates the recursive operator μ by creating a closure with the body of the μ expression and a binding of the bound variable to the entire μ expression. Actually, a new variable is used in the binding (and appropriately substituted into the body) as described in the Appl rule. The binding of the body of the μ-expression with the μ-expression itself is in effect one unfolding of the recursive expression. Whenever the bound variable is encountered in the body, this unfolding will occur again.

C0: $\ll 0, A \gg \;\to\; \ll 0, A \gg$

$$\text{P0:}\quad \frac{\ll e, A \gg \;\to\; \ll 0, A' \gg}{\ll pred(e), A \gg \;\to\; \ll 0, A' \gg}$$

CT: $\ll true, A \gg \;\to\; \ll true, A \gg$

$$\text{P:}\quad \frac{\ll e, A \gg \;\to\; \ll succ(e_1), A' \gg}{\ll pred(e), A \gg \;\to\; \ll e_1, A' \gg}$$

CF: $\ll false, A \gg \;\to\; \ll false, A \gg$

$$\text{ZT:}\quad \frac{\ll e, A \gg \;\to\; \ll 0, A' \gg}{\ll iszero(e), A \gg \;\to\; \ll true, A' \gg}$$

L: $\ll \lambda x{:}t.e, A \gg \;\to\; \ll \lambda x{:}t.e, A \gg$

$$\text{ZF:}\quad \frac{\ll e, A \gg \;\to\; \ll succ(e_1), A' \gg}{\ll iszero(e), A \gg \;\to\; \ll false, A' \gg}$$

$$\text{S:}\quad \frac{\ll e, A \gg \;\to\; \ll e_1, A' \gg}{\ll succ(e), A \gg \;\to\; \ll succ(e_1), A' \gg}$$

$$\text{Var1:}\quad \frac{\ll e, A \gg \;\to\; \ll N, A' \gg}{\ll x, [x{:}t \mapsto e]\cdot A \gg \;\to\; \ll N, [x{:}t \mapsto N]\cdot A' \gg}$$

$$\text{Var2:}\quad \frac{\ll y, A \gg \;\to\; \ll N, A' \gg}{\ll y, [x{:}t \mapsto e]\cdot A \gg \;\to\; \ll N, [x{:}t \mapsto e]\cdot A' \gg} \quad y \not\equiv x$$

$$\text{Appl:}\quad \frac{\ll e_1, A \gg \;\to\; \ll N, A' \gg \qquad \ll Ap(N, e_2), A' \gg \;\to\; \ll N', A'' \gg}{\ll e_1\,e_2, A \gg \;\to\; \ll N', A'' \gg}$$

$$\text{IfTrue:}\quad \frac{\ll e_1, A \gg \;\to\; \ll true, A' \gg \qquad \ll e_2, A' \gg \;\to\; \ll N, A'' \gg}{\ll if(e_1, e_2, e_3), A \gg \;\to\; \ll N, A'' \gg}$$

$$\text{IfFalse:}\quad \frac{\ll e_1, A \gg \;\to\; \ll false, A' \gg \qquad \ll e_3, A' \gg \;\to\; \ll N, A'' \gg}{\ll if(e_1, e_2, e_3), A \gg \;\to\; \ll N, A'' \gg}$$

$$\text{Rec:}\quad \frac{\ll (e[nx/x], [nx{:}s \mapsto \mu x{:}t.e]), A \gg \;\to\; \ll N, A' \gg}{\ll \mu x{:}t.e, A \gg \;\to\; \ll N, A' \gg}$$

$$\text{CL:}\quad \frac{\ll e, [x{:}t \mapsto e_1]\cdot B \gg \;\to\; \ll N, [x{:}t \mapsto e_1']\cdot B' \gg,\ N \text{ is NOT basic}}{\ll \langle e, [x{:}t \mapsto e_1]\rangle, B \gg \;\to\; \ll \langle N, [x{:}t \mapsto e_1']\rangle, B' \gg}$$

$$\text{CL':}\quad \frac{\ll e, [x{:}t \mapsto e_1]\cdot B \gg \;\to\; \ll c, [x{:}t \mapsto e_1']\cdot B' \gg,\ c \text{ is basic type}}{\ll \langle e, [x{:}t \mapsto e_1]\rangle, B \gg \;\to\; \ll c, B' \gg}$$

$$\begin{aligned}
Ap(\lambda x{:}t.e_0, e) &= \langle e_0[nx/x], [nx{:}t \mapsto e]\rangle \\
Ap(\langle N, [x{:}t \mapsto e_1]\rangle, e) &= \langle \langle K, [x{:}t \mapsto e_1]\rangle, [n{:}s \mapsto e]\rangle \\
&\quad\text{where } Ap(N, e) = \langle K, [n{:}s \mapsto e]\rangle
\end{aligned}$$

Note: nx denotes a new variable.

Figure 3: The Operational Semantics of LAZY-PCF+SHAR

The rules CL and CL′ evaluate closures. They do so by evaluating the expression inside the closure in an environment formed by concatenating its original closure binding with the enclosing environment. Their difference is in whether or not the resulting normal form is a closure or not. If the expression evaluates to a normal form of basic type (**nat** or **bool**) then CL′ is used and the binding is no longer included in the normal form. In this way, every constant of basic type has only one normal form so that a constant contained in a closure with a binding is not a normal form. On the other hand, if the resulting normal form is not basic type, then it is a function type and we must include the bindings in the normal form because the function body may contain a free occurrence of that variable.

There are some special properties of the operational semantics that should be noted. Recall that all of the variables bound by an environment must be unique. A special property of the semantic rules is that if all of the variables in an initial configuration that are bound either in a closure or in the environment are distinct from each other (we call such a configuration *strict*), then every environment in the inference for the reduction of that configuration will also define unique variables. This property, is captured in the following lemma:

Lemma 2.1 *Let* $\ll e, A \gg \rightarrow \ll N, A' \gg$ *be a reduction. Then if* $\ll e, A \gg$ *is strict then all environments that arise in the proof tree of* $\ll e, A \gg \rightarrow \ll N, A' \gg$ *will not contain more than one binding of a given variable.*

In working with the operational semantics, it will be beneficial to know what the structure of the normal forms is. We will consider an expression e to be a normal form if it reduces to itself in any environment ($\ll e, A \gg \rightarrow \ll e, A \gg$). The normal forms are the set NF, described as follows:

$$
\begin{aligned}
NF &= 0 \mid true \mid false \mid succ^n(0) \mid F \\
F &= \lambda x : t.e \mid \langle F, [x : t \mapsto e_1] \rangle
\end{aligned}
$$

It is easy to see that 0, *true*, *false*, and $\lambda x : t.e$ are normal forms. $succ^n(0)$ denotes n applications of *succ* to 0, and represents the natural number n. It is easy to show that $succ^n(0)$ is a normal form by induction on n using the rule for *succ*. The subset F of NF describes lambda expressions nested in zero or more closures. Those nested in closures are lambda expressions having free variables which are bound in the closures. These expressions can be shown to be normal forms by structural induction on the set F using the rules L and CL. All other well-typed expressions that reduce to some expression according to the operational semantic rules will reduce to an expression in NF. This can be shown by induction on the height of the inference tree justifying the reduction, and can be seen easily by examining the operational semantics rules.

2.2 The Fixed-Point Semantics

In this section we provide the standard fixed-point semantics for LAZY-PCF+SHAR. The biggest difference between the operational semantics and the fixed-point semantics is the

$$E[\![0]\!]\sigma = 0$$

$$E[\![pred(e)]\!]\sigma \;=\; \begin{cases} 0 & \text{if } E[\![e]\!]\sigma = 0 \\ \perp & \text{if } E[\![e]\!]\sigma = \perp \\ E[\![e]\!]\sigma - 1 & \text{otherwise} \end{cases}$$

$$E[\![true]\!]\sigma = true$$

$$E[\![succ(e)]\!]\sigma \;=\; \begin{cases} E[\![e]\!]\sigma + 1 & \text{if } E[\![e]\!]\sigma \neq \perp \\ \perp & \text{otherwise} \end{cases}$$

$$E[\![false]\!]\sigma = false$$

$$E[\![x]\!]\sigma = \sigma(x)$$

$$E[\![iszero(e)]\!]\sigma \;=\; \begin{cases} true & \text{if } E[\![e]\!]\sigma = 0 \\ \perp & \text{if } E[\![e]\!]\sigma = \perp \\ false & \text{otherwise} \end{cases}$$

$$E[\![\lambda x : t.e]\!]\sigma = \lambda v. E[\![e]\!]\sigma[v/x] \qquad E[\![e_1\, e_2]\!]\sigma = (E[\![e_1]\!]\sigma)\,(E[\![e_2]\!]\sigma)$$

$$E[\![\mu x : t.e]\!]\sigma = fix(\lambda d. E[\![e]\!]\sigma[d/x]) \qquad E[\![\langle e, [x:t \mapsto e_1]\rangle]\!]\sigma = E[\![(\lambda x : t.e)\, e_1]\!]\sigma$$

$$E[\![if(e_1, e_2, e_3)]\!]\sigma = \begin{cases} E[\![e_2]\!]\sigma & \text{if } E[\![e_1]\!]\sigma = true \\ E[\![e_3]\!]\sigma & \text{if } E[\![e_1]\!]\sigma = false \\ \perp & \text{if } E[\![e_1]\!]\sigma = \perp \end{cases}$$

Figure 4: Fixed-point semantics of LAZY-PCF+SHAR

type of environments used. While the environment A used in a configuration $\ll e, A \gg$ binds arbitrary expressions to variables, the environments used here bind variables to denotable values of natural numbers, booleans, and functions over them. More concretely, we have:

$$\begin{aligned} D &= N_\perp + B_\perp + (D \to D) \\ FEnv &= Var \to D \end{aligned}$$

where N denotes the set of natural numbers and B the set of Boolean values.

The fixed-point semantics provided by the function $E : exp \to FEnv \to D$ is presented in Figure 4. What is notable in this semantics is the absolute lack of details regarding sharing and memory management. Note how the semantics of closures is defined in terms of λ-expressions and applications. This corresponds to the observation that the difference between call-by-name and lazy evaluation is sharing of arguments.

2.3 Properties of Ap

In the fixed-point semantics, application is carried out by evaluating the function body in an environment that contains the fixed-point value of the argument. In the operational semantics, the function Ap creates a closure containing the argument so that it is not evaluated until it is needed. It is essential that this function be consistent with the fixed-point semantics, as the following lemma states.

Lemma 2.2 *Let M be an expression of non-basic type (i.e., function type) in normal form.*

$$\forall\sigma\forall a E[\![Ap(M,a)]\!]\sigma = E[\![Ma]\!]\sigma$$

Proof By induction on the structure of M. ∎

The next lemma characterizes the normal forms of a string of applications as being either a normal form of basic type or a nesting of closures containing a binding corresponding to each of the arguments. This characterization will be useful in later proofs.

Lemma 2.3 $\ll e\,e_1 \ldots e_n, A\gg \to \ll M, A'\gg$ *where either M is of basic type or $M \equiv \langle\langle N, [x_1 \mapsto e'_1]\rangle, \ldots [x_n \mapsto e'_n]\rangle$ for some normal form N.*

Proof The proof is by induction on n and uses the Appl, CL, and CL' rules. ∎

3 The Soundness Theorem

The two parts of the equivalence theorem are the soundness and adequacy theorems. In this section we will deal with the soundness theorem which shows that the fixed-point semantics respects the operational semantics. More formally,

Theorem 3.1 (Soundness) *If e is a closed expression such that $\ll e, [\,]\gg \to \ll N, [\,]\gg$ then $E[\![e]\!]\bot = E[\![N]\!]\bot$.*

Here and throughout the rest of the paper we will use $\bot$ to signify the fixed-point environment that maps all variables to $\bot$. We will also use the term *inference induction* to denote induction on the height of the proof tree engendered by the operational semantics rules.

In showing that expressions yield equal values we will want to use inference induction on the reduction $\ll e, [\,]\gg \to \ll N, [\,]\gg$, but in doing so, environments will inevitably arise in the proof trees. Thus we will need a more general statement of the theorem that includes environments, and we will need a way of relating operational environments to fixed-point environments. We will do the latter through the definition of the function ρ. This function maps an operational environment A to a corresponding fixed-point environment $\rho(A)$. More specifically, $\rho(A)$ is a fixed-point environment which binds each variable x of A to the fixed-point value of the expression e, where x is bound to e in A. Formally, we have the following definition:

Definition 3.1 $\rho(A)$:

$$
\begin{aligned}
\rho([\,]) &= \bot \\
\rho([x:s\mapsto e_1]\cdot A_1) &= \rho(A_1)[E[\![e_1]\!]\rho(A_1)/x]
\end{aligned}
$$

∎

A consequence of such a definition is the following lemma. It shows that the fixed-point semantics can simulate the closure rules of the operational semantics and is necessary in the closure case of the inference induction proof.

Lemma 3.1 $E[\![\langle e, [x\!:\!s \mapsto e_1]\rangle]\!]\rho(A) = E[\![e]\!]\rho([x\!:\!s \mapsto e_1]\cdot A)$.

Proof The proof simply uses the rules of the fixed-point semantics and the definition of $\rho([x\!:\!s \mapsto e_1]\cdot A)$. ∎

With this definition and lemma, we are now ready to state and prove the more general statement of the Soundness Theorem (Theorem 3.1). The proof depends upon the fact that reduction preserves the fixed-point interpretation of environments (part (a)). The Soundness Theorem is a direct corollary of this theorem (the case where $A = [\,]$).

Theorem 3.2 (Generalized Soundness Theorem)

$$\ll e, A\gg \to \ll N, A'\gg \Rightarrow \quad (a)\rho(A) = \rho(A') \text{ and}$$
$$(b)E[\![e]\!]\rho(A) = E[\![N]\!]\rho(A')$$

Proof *Sketch:* The proof is by inference induction. The harder cases are Var1, Var2, Appl, and CL, of which three are shown below (Var2 is similar to Var1). The type annotations are left out for readability. Let $A = [x \mapsto e']\cdot A_1$ for Var1 and Var2.

1. Var1: $\ll x, [x \mapsto e']\cdot A_1\gg \to \ll N, [x \mapsto N]\cdot A_1'\gg$ because $\ll e', A_1\gg \to \ll N, A_1'\gg$.
   $\rho(A) = \rho(A_1)[E[\![e']\!]\rho(A_1)/x]$ by definition. By induction, $\rho(A_1) = \rho(A_1')$ and $E[\![e']\!]\rho(A_1) = E[\![N]\!]\rho(A_1')$ so $\rho(A) = \rho(A_1')[E[\![N]\!]\rho(A_1')/x]$ which is $\rho(A')$ by definition.

   For part (b), $E[\![x]\!]\rho(A) = \rho(A)(x) = E[\![e']\!]\rho(A_1)$ by definition of $\rho(A)$. But this equals $E[\![N]\!]\rho(A_1')$ by induction. Now since $x \notin FV(N)$, this is equal to $E[\![N]\!]\rho(A')$.

2. Appl: $\ll e_1\,e_2, A\gg \to \ll N, A''\gg$ because $(I)\ll e_1, A\gg \to \ll M, A'\gg$ and $(II)\ll Ap(M, e_2), A'\gg \to \ll N, A''\gg$.
   For (a), $\rho(A) = \rho(A')$ and $\rho(A') = \rho(A'')$ by induction. Thus $\rho(A) = \rho(A'')$.
   For part(b), by induction $E[\![e_1]\!]\rho(A) = E[\![M]\!]\rho(A')$ and $E[\![Ap(M, e_2)]\!]\rho(A') = E[\![N]\!]\rho(A'')$. By lemma 2.2, this is equivalent to $E[\![M\,e_2]\!]\rho(A') = E[\![N]\!]\rho(A'')$. Using the fixed-point rules and induction on (I), this equals $E[\![e_1]\!]\rho(A)\,E[\![e_2]\!]\rho(A')$. Since $\rho(A) = \rho(A')$ (also by induction), the environments of both terms are the same, so they can be combined to get $E[\![e_1\,e_2]\!]\rho(A)$.

3. CL: $\ll\langle e, [x \mapsto e_a]\rangle, A\gg \to \ll\langle N, [x \mapsto e_a']\rangle, A'\gg$ because $\ll e, [x \mapsto e_a]\cdot A\gg \to \ll e, [x \mapsto e_a']\cdot A'\gg$.
   For part (a), $\rho([x \mapsto e_a]\cdot A) = \rho([x \mapsto e_a']\cdot A')$ by induction. It is easy to see that this implies that $\rho(A) = \rho(A')$.
   For part(b), $E[\![\langle e, [x \mapsto e_a]\rangle]\!]\rho(A) = E[\![e]\!]\rho([x \mapsto a]\cdot A)$ by lemma 3.1. This equals $E[\![N]\!]\rho([x \mapsto e_a']\cdot A')$, which, by lemma 3.1, equals $E[\![\langle N, [x \mapsto e_a']\rangle]\!]\rho(A')$. ∎

4 Adequacy Theorem

The adequacy theorem establishes that the operational semantics respects the fixed-point semantics. We will treat values of the base type (**bool** and **nat**) as the "observables" in the following.

Theorem 4.1 (Adequacy) *If e is a closed expression of basic type and c is an expression of basic type in normal form then $E[\![e]\!]\bot = E[\![c]\!]\bot$ implies $\ll e, [\,]\gg \to \ll c, [\,]\gg$.*

The proof of this theorem will be by structural induction on e, and thus will require induction on expressions that are not of basic type. Therefore we (again) must prove something stronger than Theorem 4.1 that is able to deal with functional types and non-closed expressions. Specifically, we will prove that all expressions are *computable*, a characterization that extends the notion of adequacy to treat higher types and environments. Our definition of computability is based on the definition used by Plotkin [10], but is revised to suit our semantics better. It differs from Plotkin's in that it does not treat closed expressions separately from those with free variables and it uses environments in the place of syntactic substitutions to close expressions.

Definition 4.1   Computability of Expressions
If $x_1 : s_1, \ldots, x_n : s_n \vdash e : s$, and $A = [x_1 : s_1 \mapsto e_1, \ldots, x_n : s_n \mapsto e_n]$ for any computable e_i satisfying $x_{i+1} : s_{i+1}, \ldots, x_n : s_n \vdash e_i : s_i$ then e is computable if one of the following is met:

1. s is a basic type and $E[\![e]\!]\rho(A) = E[\![c]\!]\rho(A) \Rightarrow \ll e, A\gg \to \ll c, A'\gg$,

2. $s \equiv t_1 \to t_2$ and $e\,e'$ is computable for all computable e' satisfying $x_1 : s_1, \ldots, x_n : s_n \vdash e' : t_1$

∎

If closed terms of basic type are computable, then for any environment A that meets the criteria listed above we know $E[\![e]\!]\rho(A) = E[\![c]\!]\rho(A) \Rightarrow \ll e, A\gg \to \ll c, A'\gg$. Since the environment $[\,]$ meets the criteria when e is closed, the implication is also true when $A = [\,]$, which is precisely the adequacy theorem.

Plotkin's definition uses what we will refer to as syntactic substitutions to close expressions and then determine their computability. These syntactic substitutions are the common, syntactically defined substitutions mapping variables to expressions as are used in lambda calculus, usually denoted as $e[e_1/x]$ or $e[x := e_1]$. This definition works well in Plotkin's proof that all terms are computable because his operational (as well as fixed-point) semantics defines application in terms of syntactic substitutions. Our semantics, on the other hand, defines application in terms of closures, which become part of the environment in the process of evaluation. Thus we define computability using environments to close expressions.

Plotkin's proof that all terms are computable is by structural induction on expressions, and depends on inherent properties of syntactic substitutions, such as the fact that they distribute over application $((e_1\ e_2)[a/x] = e_1[a/x]\ e_2[a/x])$. Thus, a significant part of our proof amounts to showing that semantically environments have these same properties that syntactic substitutions have. We begin with several lemmas that establish these properties. The first states that the order of certain bindings may be changed under the right conditions. It imitates the following property of syntactic substitutions: $e_0[e/x][a/y] = e_0[a/y][e/x]$ if $y \notin FV(e)$.

In the statements and proofs of the following lemmas and theorems, the type annotations will be left out to make the expressions more readable.

Lemma 4.1 *If $y \notin FV(e)$ then*

$$\ll e_0, B \cdot [x \mapsto e] \cdot [y \mapsto a] \cdot A \gg \ \to\ \ll N, B' \cdot [x \mapsto e'] \cdot [y \mapsto a'] \cdot A' \gg$$
$$\Rightarrow\ \ll e_0, B \cdot [y \mapsto a] \cdot [x \mapsto e] \cdot A \gg \ \to\ \ll N, B' \cdot [y \mapsto a'] \cdot [x \mapsto e'] \cdot A' \gg$$

Proof The proof of this lemma is fairly simple by inference induction. The only interesting cases are Var1 and Var2 when $B = [\ ]$. ∎

The next lemma shows that a binding may be moved into an arbitrary level of nestings of closures. It is an extension of the previous lemma.

Lemma 4.2 *If $x \notin \cup_i FV(e_i)$ then*

$$\ll \langle\langle e, [x_1 \mapsto e_1]\rangle, \ldots [x_n \mapsto e_n]\rangle, [x \mapsto a] \cdot A \gg \ \to\ \ll M, [x \mapsto a'] \cdot A' \gg$$
$$\Rightarrow\ \ll \langle\langle\langle e, [x \mapsto a]\rangle, [x_1 \mapsto e_1]\rangle, \ldots [x_n \mapsto e_n]\rangle, A \gg \ \to\ \ll M', A' \gg$$

where

1. $M \equiv M'$, *if M is of basic type OR*

2. $M \equiv \langle\langle N, [x_1 \mapsto e_1']\rangle, \ldots [x_n \mapsto e_n']\rangle$ *and*
   $M' \equiv \langle\langle\langle N, [x \mapsto a']\rangle, [x_1 \mapsto e_1']\rangle, \ldots [x_n \mapsto e_n']\rangle$
   if M is NOT of basic type for some normal form N.

Proof The proof is by induction on n, using CL, CL', and lemma 4.1. ∎

The next lemma shows that bindings in environments can be distributed to the subexpressions of an application. It is restricted to bindings of variables that are not free in arguments of the application, and thus the substitution is not applied to the arguments. This lemma imitates the syntactic substitution rule $(e\,e_1)[a/x] = e[a/x]\,e_1$ if $x \notin FV(e_1)$. An additional property characterized by this lemma is that the closure $\langle e, [x \mapsto a]\rangle$ can be replaced by the corresponding lambda expression and application $(\lambda x.e)\,a$ with the same results.

Lemma 4.3 *If* $x \notin \cup_i FV(e_i)$ *then*

    I. $\ll e\, e_1\, \ldots\, e_n, [x \mapsto a] \cdot A \gg\, \rightarrow\, \ll M, [x \mapsto a'] \cdot A' \gg\, \Rightarrow$
                $\ll \langle e, [x \mapsto a] \rangle\, e_1\, \ldots\, e_n, A \gg\, \rightarrow\, \ll M', A' \gg$ *and*

    II. $\ll e\, e_1\, \ldots\, e_n, [x \mapsto a] \cdot A \gg\, \rightarrow\, \ll M, [x \mapsto a'] \cdot A' \gg\, \Rightarrow$
                $\ll (\lambda x.e)\, a\, e_1\, \ldots\, e_n, A \gg\, \rightarrow\, \ll M', A' \gg.$

where

    1. $M \equiv M'$, *if* M *is of basic type OR*

    2. $M \equiv \langle\langle N, [x_1 \mapsto e'_1]\rangle, \ldots [x_n \mapsto e'_n]\rangle$ *and*
         $M' \equiv \langle\langle\langle N, [x \mapsto a']\rangle, [x_1 \mapsto e'_1]\rangle, \ldots [x_n \mapsto e'_n]\rangle$
         if M *is NOT of basic type.*

Proof By induction on n, using CL, CL$'$, Appl, and lemmas 2.3 and 4.2.   ■

Theorem 4.2 *All expressions are computable.*

The proof is similar to Plotkin's original proof, and is carried out by structural induction on e. As in Plotkin's proof, the hardest case is $\mu x.e$, which relies on a notion of syntactic approximation and unwindings of the μ-expression. For this proof, the unwindings $\mu^n x.e$ are defined as follows:

$$\mu^0 x.e \quad \equiv \quad \Omega_s \equiv \mu x.x$$
$$\mu^{n+1} x.e \quad \equiv \quad \langle e[nx/x], [nx \mapsto \mu^n x.e]\rangle$$

In order for the proof to work correctly, these syntactic approximations must satisfy the following lemma:

Lemma 4.4 $E[\![\mu x.e]\!]\bot = \sqcup_i E[\![\mu^i x.e]\!]\bot$

Proof From the fixed-point rules, $E[\![\mu x.e]\!]\bot = fix(\lambda d.E[\![e]\!]\bot[d/x])$. From fixed-point theory, we know that this is equal to $\sqcup_i d_i$ where $d_0 = \bot$ and $d_{n+1} = E[\![e]\!]\bot[d_n/x]$. To complete the proof we need only show that $d_n = E[\![\mu^n x.e]\!]\bot$ which is easy using induction on n and the fixed-point rules.   ■

The syntactic approximation relation $\leq$, given in Figure 5, allows one to relate the syntactic notion of unwindings of μ expressions to the semantic use of Kleene sequences in providing the semantics of μ-expressions. The significant intermediate step in completing the adequacy proof for the case of μ is the following theorem which establishes that the operational semantics (i.e., $\rightarrow$) is monotonic with respect to the relation $\leq$. It will allow us to relate $\mu x.e$ to $\mu^k x.e$ in the operational semantics.

$$H \vdash 0 \leq 0 : \mathbf{nat}$$

$$H \vdash true \leq true : \mathbf{bool}$$

$$H \vdash false \leq false : \mathbf{bool}$$

$$H[s/x] \vdash x \leq x : s$$

$$\frac{H \vdash e \leq e' : \mathbf{nat}}{H \vdash succ(e) \leq succ(e') : \mathbf{nat}}$$

$$\frac{H \vdash e \leq e' : \mathbf{nat}}{H \vdash pred(e) \leq pred(e') : \mathbf{nat}}$$

$$\frac{H \vdash e \leq e' : \mathbf{nat}}{H \vdash iszero(e) \leq iszero(e') : \mathbf{bool}}$$

$$\frac{H, x:s \vdash e \leq e' : t}{H \vdash \lambda x:s.e \leq \lambda x:s.e' : s \rightarrow t} \qquad \frac{H \vdash e_1 \leq e_1' : s \rightarrow t \quad H \vdash e_2 \leq e_2' : s}{H \vdash e_1\, e_2 \leq e_1'\, e_2' : t}$$

$$\frac{H \vdash e_1 \leq e_1' : \mathbf{bool} \quad H \vdash e_2 \leq e_2' : t \quad H \vdash e_3 \leq e_3' : t}{H \vdash if(e_1, e_2, e_3) \leq if(e_1', e_2', e_3') : t}$$

$$\frac{H \vdash e_a \leq e_a' : s \quad H[s/x] \vdash e \leq e' : t}{H \vdash \langle e, [x:s \mapsto e_a] \rangle \leq \langle e', [x:s \mapsto e_a'] \rangle : t} \qquad \frac{H[t/x] \vdash e \leq e' : t}{H \vdash \mu x:t.e \leq \mu x:t.e' : t}$$

$$H \vdash \Omega_s \leq e : s \qquad \frac{H[s/x] \vdash e \leq e' : s}{H \vdash \mu^n x:s.e \leq \mu x:s.e'}$$

Figure 5: Ordering Rules

Theorem 4.3 *If $H \vdash e \leq e' : s$ then*

$$\ll e, A \gg \rightarrow \ll N, A' \gg \Rightarrow \ll e', A \gg \rightarrow \ll N', A'' \gg$$

where $H \vdash N \leq N' : s$

Though Plotkin's proof uses a similar theorem, our proof of this theorem differs significantly from Plotkin's proof as we again have to deal with explicit substitutions. In order to prove this inductively, a relation on environments must be established, and a more general statement of the theorem must be made, in a manner similar to the soundness theorem. The relation on environments is simply an extension of $\leq$ (defined on expressions) to environments.

Definition 4.2 $\leq$ extended to environments is as follows: $H \vdash A \leq B$ if either:

1. $A = B = [\,]$.
2. $A = [x:s \mapsto e_a] \cdot A_1$, $B = [x:s \mapsto e_b] \cdot B_1$ and
   (a) $H \vdash A_1 \leq B_1$, and
   (b) $H \vdash e_a \leq e_b : s$

Now we can state the generalized version of theorem 4.3 (theorem 4.3 is the case where $S = A$).

Theorem 4.4 *If $H \vdash e \leq e' : s, H \vdash A \leq S$ then*

$$\ll e, A \gg \,\to\, \ll N, A' \gg \,\Rightarrow\, \ll e', S \gg \,\to\, \ll N', S' \gg$$

where $H \vdash N \leq N' : s$ and $H \vdash A' \leq S'$

Proof The proof of this theorem is by inference induction on the operational semantic rules, but the proof proceeds on a case by case consideration for $H \vdash e \leq e' : s$. Most of the cases are simple induction, but the more interesting cases are $H \vdash e_1 \, e_2 \leq e_1' \, e_2' : s$ and $H \vdash \mu^n x.e \leq \mu x.e' : s$. The application case is basic once it is shown that $H \vdash Ap(M, e_2) \leq Ap(M', e_2')$ where $\ll e_1, A \gg \,\to\, \ll M, A' \gg$. The recursive case is done by induction on n and depends on the rules CL, CL', and Rec. ∎

Now we are ready to prove theorem 4.2, that all terms are computable.

Proof The proof is by structural induction on the term e. Some representative cases will be shown here.

$e \equiv x$ Then $H[s/x] \vdash x : s$ and $A = A_1 \cdot [x \mapsto e_x] \cdot A_2$. Only the case where s is basic is considered here. Then $E[\![x]\!]\rho(A) = \rho(A)(x) = E[\![e_x]\!]\rho(A_2)$. Since e_x is computable and of type s, by definition $E[\![e_x]\!]\rho(A_2) = E[\![c]\!]\rho(A_2) \Rightarrow \ll e_x, A_2 \gg \,\to\, \ll c, A_2' \gg$. By Var1, we get from this $\ll x, [x \mapsto e_x] \cdot A_2 \gg \,\to\, \ll c, [x \mapsto c] \cdot A_2' \gg$. Now we can get the final result by induction on the structure of A_1. If it is empty, we already have the result. If $A_1 = [y \mapsto e_y] \cdot A_1'$ then by induction on A_1' we get $\ll x, A_1' \cdot [x \mapsto e_x] \cdot A_2 \gg \,\to\, \ll c, A_1' \cdot [x \mapsto c] \cdot A_2' \gg$. Then from this by Var2 we get $\ll x, [y \mapsto e_y] \cdot A_1' \cdot [x \mapsto e_x] \cdot A_2 \gg \,\to\, \ll c, [y \mapsto e_y] \cdot A_1' \cdot [x \mapsto c] \cdot A_2' \gg$.

$e \equiv \lambda x.a$ Then $H \vdash \lambda x : s.a : s \to t$. For this expression, we need consider only the non basic case, so we start with $E[\![(\lambda x.a) \, e_1 \, \ldots \, e_n]\!]\rho(A) = E[\![c]\!]\rho(A)$. Using the fixed point rules, we can show $E[\![(\lambda x.a) \, e_1]\!]\rho(A) = E[\![a]\!]\rho(A)[E[\![e_1]\!]\rho(A)/x]$. We can then rename x so that it does not interfere with any x occurring free in any other e_i, and then we have the following: $E[\![a[nx/x]e_2 \ldots e_n]\!]\rho(A)[E[\![e_1]\!]\rho(A)/nx] = E[\![c]\!]\rho(A)$. By induction, a is computable, so we can claim the following reduction: $\ll a[nx/x] \, e_2 \ldots e_n, [nx \mapsto e_1] \cdot A \gg \,\to\, \ll c, [nx \mapsto e_1'] \cdot A' \gg$. But according to lemma 4.3 this implies $\ll (\lambda x.a) \, e_1 \, \ldots \, e_n, A \gg \,\to\, \ll c, A' \gg$.

$e \equiv \mu x : s.a$ For this case, Plotkin's proof is imitated.

First we show $\mu^k x : s.a$ is computable for all k. For $k = 0$, $E[\![\mu^0 x.a]\!]\rho(A) = \bot$ which implies $E[\![\mu^0 x.a]\!]\rho(A) \neq E[\![c]\!]\rho(A)$ for any basic c. By theorem 3.1, then, $\ll \mu^0 x.a, A \gg \,\not\to\, \ll c, A' \gg$, so the case is vacuous. For $k > 0$, $\mu^k x.a \equiv \langle a, [x \mapsto \mu^{k-1} x.a] \rangle$. By structural induction, a is computable, and by induction on k, $\mu^{k-1} x.a$ is computable, and since closures are computable when their subparts are (from the closure case), $\mu^k x.a$ is computable.

Now for $\mu x.a$: By lemma 4.4, $E[\![\mu x.a]\!]\rho(A) = E[\![\mu^k x.a]\!]\rho(A)$ for some k. Since $\mu^k x.a$ is computable, this implies $\ll\mu^k x.a\, e_1 \ldots e_n, A\gg \to \ll c, A'\gg$. Since $\mu^k x.a \le \mu x.a$, by theorem 4.3 we have $\ll\mu x.a\, e_1 \ldots e_n, A\gg \to \ll c', A''\gg$ where $c \le c'$. Since c and c' are normal forms of basic type, it must be that $c \equiv c'$.

∎

5 Conclusion

In this paper we have proposed a natural operational semantics for lazy evaluation which takes into account the sharing involved in evaluation of actual parameters. We have also shown it equivalent to the standard fixed-point semantics. The proof was fairly complicated due to the presence of semantically defined explicit substitutions. We can now hope to base our compile-time sharing analyses of higher-order lazy languages on operational semantics and show the semantic soundness of such schemes easily.

References

[1] M. Abadi, L. Cardelli, P.-L. Curien, and J.-J. Levy. Explicit Substituition. In *Proc of XVII ACM Symposium on Principles of Programming Languages*, ACM, Jan 1990.

[2] S. Abramsky. *The Lazy Lambda Calculus*, pages 65–116. Addison-Wesley, 1990.

[3] A. Bloss. *Path Analysis and the Optimization of Non-Strict Functional Languages*. PhD thesis, Yale University, 1989.

[4] M. Draghicescu and S. Purushothaman. Compositional Analysis of Evaluation Order and its Application. In *Proc of 1990 ACM Symposium on LISP and Functional Programming*, pages 242–250, 6 1990.

[5] J. Field. On Laziness and Optimality in Lambda Interpreters: Tools for Specification and Analysis. In *Proc of XVII ACM Symposium on Principles of Programming Languages*, ACM, Jan 1990.

[6] J. Guzman and P. Hudak. Single-Threaded Polymorphic Lambda Calculus. In *V Annual IEEE Symposium on Logic in Computer Science*, 1990.

[7] B. Howard and J. Mitchell. Operational and Axiomatic Semantics of PCF. In *Proc of 1990 ACM Symposium on LISP and Functional Programming*, pages 298–306, 6 1990.

[8] L. Maranget. Optimal Derivations in Weak Lambda-Calculi and in Orthogonal Term Rewriting Systems. In *Proc of XVIII ACM Symposium on Principles of Programming Languages*, pages 255–269, ACM, Jan 1991.

[9] S. Peyton-Jones. *The Implementation of Functional Programming Languages*. Prentice-Hall, 1987.

[10] G. Plotkin. LCF considered as a Programming Language. *Theoretical Computer Science*, 5:223–255, 1977.

[11] S. Purushothaman and Jill Seaman. *An Adequate Operational Semantics of Sharing in Lazy Evaluation*. Tech Report PSU-CS-91-18, Penn State Univ., July 1991.

Modules for a model-oriented specification language: A proposal for MetaSoft

Andrzej Tarlecki

Institute of Computer Science
Polish Academy of Sciences
Warsaw, Poland.

This is a preliminary sketch of rather tentative ideas.
I would be grateful for any criticism and/or comment.

1 Introduction

MetaSoft [MSoft 90] is a project intended to provide mathematical foundations, methodological basis and computer support tools for software design, development and validation. One, at present perhaps the most important part of the project is devoted to the development of a formal language to build software specifications. In this paper we propose structuring facilities for this language, necessary to make specifications easier to construct, understand and use.

The MetaSoft specification language is primarily *model-oriented*. The user is intended to construct a *model* of the software system being specified rather than to describe its properties in an axiomatic way. *Axiomatic specifications*, although not banned entirely in MetaSoft, are certainly pushed out to its peripheries. This is much as in VDM [BjJ 78], [BjJ 82], [Jon 86], on which MetaSoft builds in many ways. In MetaSoft, the software model constructed by the user is *denotational*, which for us means simply its *compositionality* [ScS 71]. We refrain from using the full technical machinery of standard denotational semantics with reflexive domains [Sc 76], [Sc 82] and continuations [Gor 79]. The "naive" semantic foundations are provided by [BlT 83]. Most roughly, a model of a software system in MetaSoft consists of an algebra of system denotations, a similar algebra of syntax and a homomorphism from the syntax to the denotations (*denotational semantics*). We propose a methodology where the algebra of denotations is developed in the first place, and an appropriate syntax for it is constructed later [Bl 89], [BlTT 91].

The main task of the MetaSoft specification language mentioned above is to provide convenient means for formal definitions of algebras, such as the algebras of denotations around which software models are built. The core of the language is an applicative, strongly-typed definitional language as presented in [BBP 90a]. Using this language, the user can define one by one semantic domains (or just sets) represented as *symbolic types* and values (constants and functions) of these types. Since an algebra is just an environment of named sets (carriers of the algebra) and functions on these sets (operations of the algebra) this is sufficient to define algebras, and hence model-oriented specifications. A similarly "flat" definitional language forms the core of VDM, currently given a formal semantic definition [Lar 89].

Unfortunately, any application of such a flat definitional language to practical examples results in a long list of definitions, which is usually much too large to be manageable in any way. Therefore, the language must be augmented by some facilities to conveniently structure such lists of definitions. This is, of course, hardly a new idea. Many specification languages, starting with CLEAR [BG 80] and then including for example CIP-L [Bau 85], Larch [GHW 85], COLD-K [FJKR 87], ASL [SW 83], [Wir 86], ACT TWO [EM 90], RAISE [NHWG 88] and many others, have been designed for the very purpose of supporting building formal specifications in a structured manner.

In our view, much work on structuring specifications done in the area of algebraic specification addressed the fundamental issues of manipulating specifications, rather than more down-to-earth, specific issues of a specification language design. One aspect of this is that much of this work is rather abstract and independent of many details of the underlying formalism to build elementary specifications. This has been made explicit, for example, for the specification language ASL [SW 83] redefined in [ST 88] in the framework of an arbitrary institution [GB 84]. In contrast, the purpose of this proposal is to define structuring mechanisms for a particular definitional language. Of course, we freely build on the more fundamental work mentioned above.

However, the main source of inspiration for the exact design of the modularisation mechanisms presented in this paper comes from the area of programming, rather than specification languages. We believe that this is appropriate for a model-oriented specification language, where the main task is to define a certain algebra by providing explicit definitions of all its components. This is much the same as in any programming language, where the task is to define a coherent collection of data types and programs (functions, procedures) to perform required operations. The need for adequate structuring mechanisms has been recognized in this area quite early, and by now many modern programming languages, starting perhaps with Simula [DMN 70] and including Modula [Wirth 88], CLU [Lis 81], Ada [Ada 80] and Standard ML [MTH 90] provide some notion of a program module to allow the programmer to structure the code being written.

The proposal presented in this paper unashamedly follows the modularisation concepts and ideas of the Standard ML programming language [MacQ 86], [MTH 90]. Of course, there are many differences. Some of them follow from the different underlying core definitional language. Some others result from a different design decisions concerning for example the type-visibility rules of the language. Finally, some generalisations are made as well, for example admitting higher-order parameterised modules.

We have already used the modularisation facilities of Standard ML in another project with aims broadly similar to MetaSoft, namely in the design of the Extended ML specification language and methodology [ST 89], [ST 91a]. It should be stressed, though, that the role of modularisation units (called *functors* and *structures* in ML) in Extended ML is quite different from their interpretation in the current proposal. An Extended ML functor is not a piece of a specification; rather, it forms a phase in the development of an independent programming task specified by the functor heading and (perhaps only partially as yet) implemented by its body. Extended ML functors are not used to structure specifications; they are used to structure program development.

The paper is organised as follows. We start by sketching the overall ideas of the modularisation proposal, phrased in rather general terms of many-sorted signatures, algebras and their arbitrary definitions (Section 2). In Section 3 we recall the core definitional language of MetaSoft as presented in [BBP 90a]. Then, in Section 4 we sketch how the general ideas of Section 2 may be realised in the specific framework of this definitional language. Clearly, in the limited space given here it is impossible to present the proposal in full technical detail — we just attempt to sketch the major decisions, and refer the interested reader to [Tar 92] for all the details and a complete technical definition. Finally, in Section 5 we point out some alternatives to two crucial design decisions taken in the proposal presented in this paper, and discuss a number of further developments we view useful or even necessary for the practical applications of the MetaSoft definitional language with modules.

Acknowledgements

I am grateful to the MetaSoft group, and in particular to Andrzej Blikle, for many stimulating discussions — this paper has been written as a contribution to the MetaSoft project. Jacek Leszczyłowski has influenced some particular technical decisions by constantly nodging me to point out a double role of algebra interfaces in the module language proposed here. Much of the work presented follows what I have learnt in a continuing close collaboration with Don Sannella on many issues of software specification and development. The core of the ideas in this paper crystalized during my stays at the Department of Computer Science of the University of Manchester in numerous discussions with Cliff Jones and John Fitzgerald, which I found very stimulating and fruitful.

The research has been partially supported by a grant from the Polish Academy of Sciences and by a grant from the Wolfson Foundation (during my stays in Manchester in May–July 1990 and April–June 1991).

2 Basic ideas — mechanisms to define algebras

The overall aim of the proposal is to introduce a language to define algebras.

An *algebra* is a collection of data classified into different sorts (*carriers* of the algebra) and functions to build and manipulate these data (*operations* of the algebra). The carriers and the operations are *named*. The collection of the names of carriers and operations, the latter equipped with the sorts of arguments and results, forms a *signature* of the algebra.

We will omit here the standard technical definition of many-sorted algebras and their signatures — for example, [EM 85] is a standard reference for a tedious presentation of all the details of one of the essentially equivalent versions of these concepts and some related theory.

2.1 Simple algebra definitions

The formalism we are designing here is a declarative language in the usual sense, where the user gradually builds up an environment of the entities of interest — here, an environment of algebras with explicitly given signatures. The entities are defined using the mechanisms provided by the language, and then stored in the environment by binding them to *identifiers*.

The basic construction available to the user is to define an algebra by listing its components (carriers and operations) defined in turn using an underlying core language.[1]

$$
\begin{array}{ll}
\text{algebra } A : ASig = & \text{where} \quad \text{signature } ASig = \\
\quad zielone = \text{integer} \times \{0\} & \qquad \text{sorts } zielone, czerwone \\
\quad czerwone = \text{integer} \times \{1\} & \qquad \text{opns } z\_zero : zielone \\
\quad z\_zero = \langle 0, 0 \rangle & \qquad\qquad zmien : zielone \rightarrow czerwone \\
\quad zmien.\langle n, 0 \rangle = \langle n, 1 \rangle & \qquad \text{end} \\
\text{end}
\end{array}
$$

Two other examples of algebras over the same signature are:

$$
\begin{array}{ll}
\text{algebra } A' : ASig = & \qquad \text{algebra } A'' : ASig = \\
\quad zielone = \text{integer} \times \{0\} & \qquad\quad zielone = \text{integer} \\
\quad czerwone = \text{integer} \times \{1\} & \qquad\quad czerwone = \text{bool} \\
\quad z\_zero = \langle 0, 0 \rangle & \qquad\quad z\_zero = 0 \\
\quad zmien.\langle n, 0 \rangle = \langle n + 1, 1 \rangle & \qquad\quad zmien.n = is\_even(n) \\
\text{end} & \qquad \text{end}
\end{array}
$$

---

[1] We use some *ad hoc*, though hopefully sufficiently clear notation in the examples below and throughout the rest of the paper. No final syntax for the MetaSoft language exists as yet — according to the methodology we support, the mechanisms and their semantics which form the real essence of the formalism are designed first.

Nondescriptive identifiers are used below to name algebra components. For our purposes, they seem at least as mnemonic as $s1$, t_{39}, c'', f, or *factorial*.

Following the notational convention of MetaSoft, in the above definitions and throughout the rest of the paper we use the dot notation to denote function application.

Once an algebra is introduced into the overall algebra environment, the algebra and its components may be used in further definitions. Algebra components are referred to using the "dot notation". For instance, in the context of the above definition of an algebra A, $A.zielone$ stands for integer $\times \{0\}$, $A.czerwone$ for integer $\times \{1\}$, and $A.zmien$ for the function mapping any $\langle n,0 \rangle \in$ integer $\times \{0\}$ to $\langle n,1 \rangle$. This is consistent with the dot notation used for the function application. In fact, an algebra may be viewed as a "small environment" mapping the names of the components of the algebra (listed in its signature) to their semantic meanings.

For example, in the context of the above definition of A, we can define:

algebra $B : BSig =$ where signature $BSig =$
    $niebieskie = A.zielone$ sorts $niebieskie, czarne, nowy$
    $czarne = A.czerwone$ opns $cz\_zero : czarne$
    $nowy = $ bool $zmien : niebieskie \rightarrow czarne$
    $cz\_zero = (A.zmien).(A.z\_zero)$ end
    $zmien.x = (A.zmien).x$
end

To keep definitions like the one of B above more self-contained, we require the user to indicate explicitly the algebras from the environment that may be referred to in the particular definition. Thus, actually the correct form of the definition of B should be:

algebra $B : BSig =$
  using A
    $niebieskie = A.zielone$
    $czarne = A.czerwone$
    $nowy = $ bool
    $cz\_zero = (A.zmien).(A.z\_zero)$
    $zmien.x = (A.zmien).x$
end

The signature of A may be grabbed from the environment, so it is not repeated explicitly here.

In the MetaSoft definitional language, algebras are intended to play the role of modules — self-contained, encapsulated specification units, with the access to their actual contents limited by an explicitly given interface. The role of such interfaces is played by algebra signatures.

The signature of an algebra determines the names of the algebra components. We "know" that the above algebra A has exactly four components, named $zielone$, $czerwone$, z_zero, and $zmien$. Perhaps even more importantly, the signature determines some information about what the components are and how they can be used. $A.zielone$ and $A.czerwone$ are sorts of data, $A.z\_zero$ is a constant in $A.zielone$, and $A.zmien$ is a function mapping data in $A.zielone$ to data in $A.czerwone$. This information has been used in the definition of B above. The definition of B may be proved well-formed using only the information given in the signature $ASig$ of A.

This is in contrast with the following definitions:

algebra $B1 : BSig =$ algebra $B2 : BSig =$
  using A using A
    $niebieskie = $ integer $\times \{0\}$ $niebieskie = A.zielone$
    $czarne = $ integer $\times \{1\}$ $czarne = A.czerwone$
    $nowy = $ bool $nowy = $ bool
    $cz\_zero = (A.zmien).(A.z\_zero)$ $cz\_zero = \langle 0,1 \rangle$
    $zmien.x = (A.zmien).x$ $zmien.\langle n,0 \rangle = \langle n,1 \rangle$
end   end

In the definition of $B1$ we have defined *niebieskie* as integer $\times$ $\{0\}$ and *czarne* as integer $\times$ $\{1\}$. The information in the signature $ASig$ ensures that $A.zmien$ maps $A.zielone$ to $A.czerwone$, and $A.z\_zero$ is in $A.zielone$ — but nothing more. Consequently, to justify that the definitions of cz_zero and $zmien$ in $B1$ are well-formed, that is, to justify that indeed $B1.cz\_zero$ is in $B1.czarne$ and $B1.zmien$ maps $B1.niebieskie$ into $B1.czarne$, we have to look into the "body" of A and check the exact definitions of *zielone* and *czerwone* there. The situation with the definition of $B2$ is quite similar, although the reason that forces us to look into the definitions of *zielone* and *czerwone* in A seems subtly different here.

We consider only the original definition of B as acceptable, and reject the definitions of $B1$ and $B2$. This is the consequence of the intention to use the interfaces (algebra signatures) to control the information available about the algebras defined and to abstract away from the "internal" details of particular algebra definitions. The well-formedness of the definitions using algebras already defined is justified entirely on the basis of the information in the interfaces. In this way an algebra interface insulates the environment using the algebra from the particular algebra definition. Well-formed references to algebra components remain well-formed even if the components of the algebra are changed (as long as the signature remains the same).

This view may be sometimes rather restrictive. In particular, it is impossible to indicate in algebra signatures that some carriers are identical, and that two algebras "share" some of them. For instance, given the algebras A and B, the following attempt to combine them is not well-formed (for example, the definition of $zero2$ cannot be shown to yield a value in $kolor2$):

signature $ABSig =$	**algebra** $AB : ABSig =$
sorts $kolor1, kolor2, kolor3$	**using** A, B
opns $zero1 : kolor1$	$kolor1 = A.zielone$ $(= B.niebieskie)$
$zero2 : kolor2$	$kolor2 = A.czerwone$ $(= B.czarne)$
$zmien : kolor1 \rightarrow kolor2$	$kolor3 = B.nowy$
end	$zero1 = A.z\_zero$
	$zero2 = B.cz\_zero$
	$zmien = A.zmien$ $(= B.zmien)$
	end

Without relaxing unduly this rather strict view, we will introduce some mechanism to make such definitions possible (by enriching the information in algebra interfaces) in Section 4.

Similar comments apply to the analysis of two algebras over the same signature, like A and A' over the signature $ASig$. Even though the names of the corresponding carriers are the same (the algebras are over the same signature) the carriers themselves may be quite different (compare A and A' with A'' above). Consequently, we cannot allow operations of one algebra to be applicable to data in the carriers of the other. Just as in the argument above, this applies even if the carriers happen to be identical. For example, in the context of the above definitions, $A'.zmien$ cannot be applied to $A.z\_zero$, the expression $(A'.zmien).(A.z\_zero)$ is not well-formed.

No axioms in interfaces

When arguing about properties of algebras being defined, we may want to state formally such properties directly in algebra definitions and interfaces. For example, we may want to make it explicit that $AB.zero2 = (AB.zmien).(AB.zero1)$ in the algebra AB we attempted to define above. To show this, we need to know that $B.cz\_zero = (A.zmien).(A.z\_zero)$, and so, even this very simple fact needs some rather involved argument, where three algebras defined above are referred to.

This may lead one to be tempted to allow such properties to be put explicitly in algebra interfaces. We believe that in a specification language, like the one we are defining here, there is no need for such "axioms" in interfaces. To support this view, let us point out that in a model-oriented specification language algebras are built to be used as specifications, not to be checked against any specifications. This is quite in contrast with the situation in development formalisms, like Extended ML, where the starting point is a (property-oriented) specification, and the task is to build an algebra that would satisfy (or "fit") this specification.

In our language, interfaces control the flow of information used to justify the well-formedness of algebra definitions, not their semantic correctness w.r.t. some given *a priori* requirements specification. We assume (cf. Section 3) that in our core definitional language some static "type" information is sufficient to justify the well-formedness of definition. No further semantic properties of algebras and their components need to be explicitly included in interfaces.

Of course, the decision not to put axioms in algebra interfaces should not prevent the user from proving *a posteriori* some properties of the algebras forming a model-oriented specification. We do not give any explicit tool for this in our proposal. In our view, this can be done at a meta-level, for example by labelling the interfaces of particular algebras with some property-oriented information (e.g. formulae of a suitable logic the algebra is checked to satisfy). This is much as in Hoare's verification logic for iterative programs [Hoa 69] where the properties (of the state of computation) label the control points of the program being verified. Notice that, again as in the verification of iterative programs, different intermittent properties of algebra components may be useful to prove different overall properties of the entire specification. Unlike in formalisms to develop software systems, it seems rather unrealistic to expect that every algebra in its role of a model-oriented specification would come with a fixed list of properties stating all and only relevant information about the algebra.

2.2 Parametric algebra definitions

It is practically important to be able to make some algebra definitions reusable by allowing them to be parameterised by other algebras they depend on. This yields "parametric algebras" that are simply functions mapping algebras to algebras. The domain of such a function is determined by algebra interfaces the parameters are required to fit. Notice that such parametric algebras play here the role of parameterised (model-oriented) specifications. This is only superficially in contrast with the ideas of [SST 92], [ST 91b].

For example, the dependence of the algebra B on A (cf. Section 2.1) may be made functional as follows:

$$\text{algebra } BF(X : ASig) : BSig =$$
$$niebieskie = X.zielone$$
$$czarne = X.czerwone$$
$$nowy = \textbf{bool}$$
$$cz\_zero = (X.zmien).(X.z\_zero)$$
$$zmien.x = (X.zmien).x$$
$$\text{end}$$

Now, the algebra B may be defined by a straightforward application of BF to A, or as we will sometimes say, by *instantiating* the parametric algebra BF with the actual parameter A for the formal parameter X:

$$\text{algebra } B = BF(X \mapsto A)$$

When instantiating a parametric algebra as in the above definition, we require that the actual parameters are explicitly attached to their corresponding formal identifiers used in the parametric algebra definition (consequently, they may be listed in an arbitrary order). This seems well-justified in a formalism to define large entities like algebras or modules (cf. [LB 88] where this point of view is taken, argued for, and pushed even further by treating bindings like $X \mapsto A$ above as usual data the language manipulates).

To check that the above definition is well-formed, it is sufficient to realise that the interface of A, the argument for BF in the algebra expression used, coincides with the required interface of the parameter X of BF indicated in its definition. Notice that we do not need to state again that the signature of $BF(X \mapsto A)$, and hence that of B, is $BSig$ — this can be straightforwardly deduced from the result signature in the declaration of BF.

The parametric algebra BF may be used to define other algebras over the signature $BSig$ by instantiating it with different actual parameters (fitting the required parameter interface). For example (A' and A'' are $ASig$-algebras defined in Section 2.1):

    algebra $B' = BF(X \mapsto A')$
    algebra $B'' = BF(X \mapsto A'')$

Complete information about how a parametric algebra can be used is given by its heading: the list of formal parameters with their interfaces and the result signature. The former gives the required interfaces of the actual parameters the parametric algebra may be instantiated with, and the latter determines the signature of the result of such instantiations. Thus, a parametric-algebra heading, like $(X : ASig) : BSig$ for BF, is a complete parametric algebra interface. Notice that this is a proper generalisation of the concept of a simple algebra interface (an algebra signature — cf. Section 2.1). A simple algebra may be viewed as a parameterless parametric algebra, and its interface (the signature) as the corresponding parameteric algebra interface with the empty parameter list omitted.

Parametric algebras may be defined using other (possibly parametric) algebras defined in the environment. Just as in Section 2.1, we require then a complete list of algebras used to be given explicitly in the algebra definition.

Let us point out the rather obvious fact that parametric algebras are not algebras, they are functions yielding algebras when applied to actual parameters. Consequently, it makes no sense to refer to "parametric-algebra components". For example, nothing like $BF.niebieskie$ or $BF.zmien$ is well-formed — the function BF as such has no component; it is the result of full instantiation of BF by giving all its required parameters that is a well-defined algebra, and hence has components listed in the result signature. For example, $BF(X \mapsto A).niebieskie$ and $BF(X \mapsto A').cz\_zero$ both make sense and are well-formed.

Since we now have a concept of an interface for parametric algebras, it is straightforward to generalise the notion of a parametric algebra so that parameters that in turn are parametric are allowed. In other words, we introduce higher-order parametrisation, believing that this may be useful in practice (see e.g. [SST 92] for closely related examples and some discussion). Since each parameteric algebra interface contains as its part the interfaces of all its parameters, higher-order parametric algebras form a proper hierarchy, and no form of self-application is allowed.

We do not allow any form of recursive algebra definitions either, so that dependences between algebras defined are hierarchical. We believe that this is methodologically well-justified. Any apparent need for mutual recursion in algebra definitions (X uses an operation $Y.f$ of Y, and Y uses an operation $X.g$ of X) intuitively shows some inadequacy in the design of the overall structure of the definition (if some definitions in X and Y are inseparable, they should not be split between different modules). A direct recursion (an algebra defined in terms of itself, whatever formally this would mean) seems unnecessary, as we believe that it can always be sensibly reduced to a recursion within the algebra (in the definitions of its carriers and operations).

No pushout parameterisation

One standard technique of defining parameterisation in the context of monomorphic algebraic specifications, where an algebraic specification is viewed as a definition of a unique (up to isomorphism) algebra, is based on the concept of a pushout of signatures, algebraic specifications, and then the amalgamated union of algebras. This approach has been perhaps first introduced in the specification language CLEAR [BG 80] and then intensively studied in the area, cf. [EM 85].

One characteristic feature is that in the pushout approach the entire parameter is included in the result of the instantiation. This is in contrast with the approach we pursue here, where if some part of the parameter is to be included in the result, it must be placed there explicitly.

The pushout approach seems fully justified in a formalism used to gradually construct a single specification by adding more and more pieces. The idea would be to incorporate in this specification all potentially useful components, as otherwise they may be lost. We find this quite unnecessary in specification languages shaped after the usual declarative languages, such as the formalism we propose, where a specification once introduced into the environment stays there and is always available. Moreover, it is always possible to access each particular component of all the algebras stored in the environment. Thus, after instantiating a parameterised specification there is no danger that some components of the actual parameter are not available anymore. If needed, they can always be grabbed from the environment and used subject only to the constraints of the "type system". This would not be flexible enough under the type system for algebra components as suggested in this section, where outside an algebra definition only "abstract" sort information is available about the operations of the algebra. The "type-visibility" mechanisms of the current proposal are designed sufficiently permissive with this very purpose in mind — cf. Section 4.

3 MetaSoft core definitional language

In this section we recall the most important aspects of the core definitional language of MetaSoft, as presented in [BBP 90a]. Of course, we cannot repeat here the entire design — the interested reader should refer directly to [BBP 90a]. Only the ideas most relevant to and used in the current proposal of the module layer of the language are sketched.

The core definitional language of MetaSoft is a simple declarative language to build an environment of sets of data and objects in these sets. The former are represented as *symbolic types*.

The starting point for the definition and interpretation of the notion of a symbolic type in MetaSoft is a suitably rich universe $\mathcal{D}$ of domains (sets of data) closed under the standard set-theoretic operators used to construct domains: Cartesian product $\times$, disjoint union $\uplus$, partial function space $\rightharpoonup$, and mapping space $\underset{m}{\rightarrow}$. It is also assumed that $\mathcal{D}$ contains the empty set $\emptyset$ and a one-element set $\{*\}$. Thus, we have an *algebra of domains*, in which we can interpret in the obvious way all the closed terms built over the type operators mentioned above. If convenient, we may consider additional constants denoting some specific standard domains, like integer or bool (even though they are definable using the operations already mentioned and recursion).

It turns out technically convenient to represent such terms as trees with nodes labelled by the domain operators (with the number of ordered successors of each node equal to the arity of the operator labelling this node). The next step is to generalise such trees and deal with arbitrary pointed (the point indicating the "root") directed graphs with nodes labelled in the similar manner. Now, such graphs may be unambiguously interpreted in the algebra of domains, with cycles used to indicate the least (w.r.t. the inclusion of domains) fixed points, under the additional assumption that the cycles do not contain nodes labelled by the partial function space operator (cf. [BIT 83] for the "naive domain theory" which underlies and justifies this definition).

Moreover, any such (finite) graph may be expanded by unfolding its cycles to a (possibly infinite) tree, which gives the structure of the domain defined by the original graph. We want to identify graphs expanding to isomorphic trees. It turnes out that the resulting equivalence relation is "easily" decidable [BBP 90b]. Any two graphs equivalent in this sense determine the same domain in the algebra $\mathcal{D}$. Notice, however, that the opposite implication does not hold in general: there are non-equivalent graphs that determine identical domains. This is hardly surprising, as in fact the intention is to identify the graphs with the same structure, not just with the same set-theoretic interpretion.

The symbolic types, $st : SymType$, of the definitional langauge of MetaSoft, are defined as equivalence classes of such graphs. Any symbolic type $st : SymType$ determines a domain (a set) $[\![st]\!]$ of *objects of this type*.

In the core definitional language symbolic types are constructed using the available type operators in the standard manner. They may be bound to identifiers, thus gradually building up an environment of types. Recursive definitions may be used to introduce sets of mutually recursive types (graphs with cycles). This is subject to the restriction that no recursion loop may go through the function-space operator.

For example, the following two recursive type definitions introduce symbolic types represented by the graphs given below.

rec_type
$$N = \{*\} \uplus N$$
end

rec_type
$$N' = \{*\} \uplus (\{*\} \uplus N')$$
end

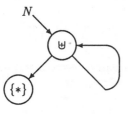

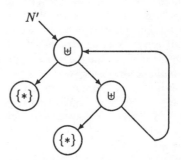

It is quite straightforward to see that the two graphs are equivalent and so the two symbolic types are equal. In fact, they define (a set which may be identifdied with) the set of natural numbers. Then, the type of finite lists of funtions from N to N may be defined as follows:

rec_type
$$LFN = (N \twoheadrightarrow N) \times LFN$$
end

yielding

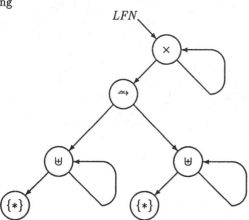

Notice that the above recursive type does involve the function-space operator, but only in a non-essential way: no recursion goes through this operator.

The definitional language of **MetaSoft** is *strongly typed*. That is, the objects constructed in the language are always built and then stored in the environment together with their symbolic types. Hence, the environment being constructed consists in fact of two parts: a "dynamic" environment storing the objects bound to identifiers, and a "static" environment storing symbolic types of these objects. The overall invariant of the entire langauge definition is that any object built is an element in the domain determined by the symbolic type of this object. Somewhat informally in this paper, we will write $x : st$ to denote the fact that the object x is of type st. A consequence of this is that every phrase of the definitional language is first elaborated "statically", to check its well-formedness and compute the types of the objects being defined, and only then evaluated "dynamically" to compute the actual meanings of the entire phrase and of the objects.

The structure of a symbolic type determines the operations that can be used to construct objects of this type and the operations which can be applied to objects of this type. For example, if a type is given as a product of two types, $st = st' \times st''$, then the pairing operation $\langle \_ , \_ \rangle$ may be used to construct objects of this type: for $x' : st'$ and $x'' : st''$, $\langle x', x'' \rangle : st$. Similarly, projection operations may be applied to any object of type st, yielding the first and second, respectively, element of the pair this object is. The operations like pairing, used to build the objects of a given type are often referred to as *constructors* for this type, the operations like projections, which may be applied to objects of a given type to build intuitively simpler objects are referred to as *desctructors* for this type. The usual object constructors and desctructors corresponding to the particular type operators are introduced in **MetaSoft**.

Perhaps function-space types require some further remarks. The only desctructor for function types is the operation of application. Given an object of a function type, say $f : st' \rightsquigarrow st''$, the binary operation of application may be applied to f and an object $x : st'$ to yield an object $f.x : st''$. This says that the function $f : st' \rightsquigarrow st''$ may be "applied" (via the binary application operation) to any object $x : st'$. λ-abstraction is used to construct objects of function-space types. To evaluate a function expression of the form $\lambda x{:}st'.exp$ to obtain an object of a function type $st' \rightsquigarrow st''$, we first "statically" elaborate the body expression exp in the "static" environment enriched by indicating x as an object of type st', check whether the computed symbolic type of exp is st'', and only then define a (partial) function that maps any element $a \in [\![st']\!]$ to the "dynamically" computed value of exp in the environment enriched by mapping x to the value a (in the "dynamic" environment) and to the symbolic type st' (in the "static" environment). Notice that the static elaboration and the dynamic evaluation of the body expression exp cannot be done at the same time here. At the time of evaluation of the λ-expression, when the static analysis must be performed, no value $a \in [\![st']\!]$ can be singled out. The only alternative would be to evaluate this expression for all potential values $a \in [\![st']\!]$ — but the very point of the static analysis is to avoid such a necessity.

Objects of some types may be defined recursively. The interpretation of recursive definitions is given by the least fixed points in the appropriate domains. This is meaningful due to the fact that all the domains definable by symbolic types come equipped with an ordering (non-trivial orderings are introduced for function-space domains and then lifted up through the domain operators in the standard way). It turns out that all the domains form complete partial orders, and all the operations definable in the language are continuous w.r.t. these orderings. Although not all of the domains contain least elements, it is easy to statically identify symbolic types defining domains that do so. Objects of these types may be defined recursively, with the usual least-fixed-point interpretation.

4 Modules for MetaSoft

In this section we present the basic concepts underlying the formal definition of the MetaSoft definitional language with modules in [Tar 92]. The overall design of the language results, in a sense, from recasting the ideas sketched in Section 2 in the specific framework of definitional mechanisms for domains represented by symbolic types and objects in these domains as presented in [BBP 90a] and briefly recalled in Section 3.

Let us list the basic assumptions of the proposal. They will be gradually discussed and explained in more detail throughout the rest of this section.

- A usual declarative language to build an environment of MetaSoft *algebras* is designed.

- A MetaSoft *algebra* is a representation of an algebra in the usual sense. It consists of a set of named symbolic types, which determine the carriers of the algebra, and of a set of named objects, which correspond to the operations of the algebra. MetaSoft algebras are always constructed with their *signatures*.

- A MetaSoft *signature* contains a set of names of the carriers (or symbolic types) and a set of names of the objects of MetaSoft algebras over this signature. As in algebraic signatures, the names of objects are equipped with the types of the objects. Unlike algebraic signatures, MetaSoft signatures may give some extra information about the required structure and mutual relationships of the symbolic types representing algebra carriers.

- MetaSoft algebra definitions may be parametric, which yields the concept of a MetaSoft *module*, a central concept of the current proposal. MetaSoft modules come always equipped with their *interfaces*.

- The MetaSoft module parameterisation may be of higher-order, that is, there are modules parameterised by modules etc.

- A MetaSoft *module interface* gives the list of the names of algebra and module parameters with the required interfaces as well as the result algebra interface. The interfaces in general contain some extra information about the symbolic types involved, stating the required structure and mutual relationships between the types in the parameters, as well as providing some information about the structure and relationship to the given types of the types in the result interface. In particular, the result algebra interface lists the set of types newly defined by the module.

- A MetaSoft module may be *applied to* (or *instantiated with*) a list of actual algebra and module parameters with interfaces fitting the required parameter interfaces. The result is a MetaSoft algebra with the signature calculated out of the result algebra interface given in the module interface. This is done in a "generative" fashion, that is, the types newly introduced by the module are treated as new each time the module is instantiated.

- MetaSoft modules may use other MetaSoft modules and algebras already defined in the environment. Components of MetaSoft algebras listed in their signatures may be accessed by naming the algebra and its particular component (cf. the "dot notation" of Section 2). Only the type information given in the algebra signature is available about algebra components accessed in such a way.

4.1 Abstract types

As discussed in Section 3, the structure of the type of an object determines the operations that may be applied to this object. In the core definitional language there is no way to hide this structure. The type of an object is always fully visible. On the other hand, as suggested by the discussion in Section 2, it seems important to use module interfaces to limit the flow of information about the types of objects. The goal is to achieve abstraction by allowing only *some* operations that in principle may be applied to an object to be actually used outside the encapsulated module in which the object is defined. In this way the particular definitions of the types and objects within a module may be changed without affecting the way they are used outside, provided that the new definitions still fit the module interface.

To provide appropriate technical tools for this, we propose to extend the concept of a symbolic type as recalled in Section 3 so that no structural information about some types (or their subparts) needs to be given. Consider a new set of *token types*, $tt : TType$, which are just arbitrary new tokens (in the usual sense of VDM definitions — unknown entities, distinct from all the others around). Their primary role is to be used as *abstract types* with an entirely hidden internal structure. Now, extend the set of symbolic types by allowing the token types as constant type operators to label the nodes of the graphs used in the construction of the symbolic types. Notice that since the new token type operators are constants, no recursion may go through them.

Since in principle we know nothing about the interpretation of the token types, the symbolic types now do not necessarily denote domains in the domain algebra $\mathcal{D}$ on which the semantics of the langauge is built (cf. Sec. 3). We will refer to the symbolic types which do not actually contain any token types as *real* symbolic types. Of course, each real symbolic type determines a domain in $\mathcal{D}$ as before.

A type given as a token type provides no information about its structure. Hence no built-in constructors may be used to define objects of such a type. Similarly, no built-in destructors may be applied to objects of such type either. This seems to make the abstract token types quite useless — apparently we could neither construct nor use objects of such types.

The trick is to give the abstract token types a real identity throughout the entire definition in the MetaSoft langauge. That is, we will assume that whenever the same abstract token type is used in a certain definition, it hides an unknown but always the same type. For example, given an object $a : tt$ of a token type tt and a function $f : tt \nrightarrow$ bool, we may apply f to a (and obtain an object $f.a :$ bool, if f is defined on a). Similarly, a function $g :$ bool $\nrightarrow tt$ (or even simpler, a constant $c : tt$) may be used to construct objects of type tt.

Notice that any function $sbst : TType \nrightarrow SymType$ (we call such functions *substitutions*) extends in the obvious "structural" way to a function $sbst : SymType \nrightarrow SymType$. The extended function is undefined only on the types containing token types not in the domain of the original substitution. Moreover, substitutions will be implicitly extended to any structure containing symbolic types (e.g., to environments storing symbolic types).

Abstract token types are introduced when a number of type and object definitions are encapsulated to form a module. The structure of real symbolic types may then be partially hidden, by replacing some of them by abstract token types. Throughout a MetaSoft definition a substitution of real symbolic types for the abstract token types that hide them is implicitly built.

4.2 Objects and types

In Section 3 we have used the example of λ-expression defining a function to argue for the need to separate the "static" elaboration from the "dynamic" evaluation of any phrase of the definitional language. This is needed even more in the context of the current module proposal. As we will see in Section 4.4, MetaSoft module definitions are very close to "λ-expressions-in-the-large", and hence force the need for a separate "static" elaboration of all the phrases of the language (since all of them may occur in a module body).

In the core language, for any object, apart from its actual value (the "dynamic" information) its type (the "static" information) is stored as well. The object environment built in the core language consists of two parts: "static", yielding the types of objects, and "dynamic", yielding actual values. These two parts are required to be *consistent* with one another in the sense that the values stored must always be in the domains determined by the symbolic types bound to the corresponding object identifiers.

In the current proposal we extend this idea to all the entities of the language[2]. Perhaps somewhat surprisingly, in particular this includes types defined in MetaSoft. The type environment consists again of a "dynamic" part, storing the real symbolic types denoted by type identifiers, and of a "static" part, storing the symbolic types (possibly containing abstract token types) that represent the currently available information about the actual structure of the type and about its relationship with other types. Of course, these two parts of the type environment must be *consistent* with one another in the sense that the current substitution of real for the abstract token types used maps the "static" to the "dynamic" type environment (that is, the two type environments have the same domains and for every identifier in the domain, the static

---

[2]With one exception: module interfaces are purely "static" entities, hence no separate "dynamic" information about them is given.

type bound to the identifier in the static environment is mapped to the real type bound to the identifier in the dynamic environment).

For example, suppose that we define

> type $luty$ = integer
> function $dodaj$: $luty \leadsto luty$
> $\qquad dodaj.n = n + 5$

and then these definitions are encapsulated (see Section 4.3 below) so that the real interpretation of the type $luty$ is hidden by a new abstract token type att : $TType$ with an implicit substitution $att \mapsto$ integer. Consequently, even though in the dynamic environments we have $luty \mapsto$ integer and $dodaj \mapsto \lambda n$:integer.$n + 5$, in the static environments $luty \mapsto att$ and $dodaj \mapsto att \leadsto att$. Then, in this context we can define

> type maj = $luty \times luty$
> function raz_dodaj : $maj \leadsto maj$
> $\qquad raz\_dodaj.\langle x, y \rangle = \langle dodaj.x, y \rangle$

Now, the new type maj "really" stands for integer $\times$ integer, but in the static environment it denotes $att \times att$. The function raz_dodaj : $(att \times att) \leadsto (att \times att)$ is well-defined — the "static" structure of maj and the "static" type of $dodaj$ provide information sufficient to justify that its definition is well-formed. This is in contrast with the following ill-formed definition:

> function dwa_dodaj : $maj \leadsto maj$
> $\qquad dwa\_dodaj.\langle x, y \rangle = \langle dodaj.x, y + 5 \rangle$

The fact that $luty$ stands for (or rather, that att hides) the real type integer is not statically visible and cannot be used to justify the well-formedness of the subexpression $y + 5$.

4.3 Algebras and their signatures

A MetaSoft *algebra* consists of two environments: a dynamic type environment, storing the real symbolic types that correspond to carriers of the usual algebras, and a dynamic object environment, storing the actual values corresponding to operations of the usual algebras.

A MetaSoft *signature* consists of two environments: a static type environment, storing the symbolic types (possibly containing abstract token types) that provide information about the "carriers", and a static object environment storing the symbolic types (possibly containing abstract token types) of the "operations".

A MetaSoft *algebra is of a* MetaSoft *signature* if the dynamic type environment of the algebra is consistent with the static type environment of the signature and the dynamic object environment of the algebra is consistent with the static object environment of the signature w.r.t. the current substitution of real types for the abstract token types used.

For example (recall the definition of algebra A in Section 2.1) consider an algebra A given as a pair of dynamic environments

$$A = \langle [zielone \mapsto \text{integer} \times \{0\}, czerwone \mapsto \text{integer} \times \{1\}],$$
$$[z\_zero \mapsto \langle 0, 0 \rangle, zmien \mapsto \lambda \langle n, 0 \rangle : \text{integer} \times \{0\}.\langle n, 1 \rangle] \rangle$$

and a signature $ASig$ given as a pair of static environments

$$ASig = \langle [zielone \mapsto att_1, czerwone \mapsto att_2], [z\_zero \mapsto att_1, zmien \mapsto att_1 \leadsto att_2] \rangle$$

Then the algebra A clearly is of the signature $ASig$ (under the obvious substitution of real types for the two abstract token types involved).

We will also need an auxiliary technical concept of a MetaSoft *algebra interface*. Algebra interfaces are much like algebra signatures, except that some of token types occuring in them may be indicated as "flexible", not fixed, and in a sense local to the interface rather than common throughout the entire definition. These indicated token types play the role of "place-holders" for symbolic types to replace them later, and are considered to be *bound*. We consider algebra interfaces up to the obvious α-conversion of the bound token types.

Here is an example of an interface definition. Notice that we do not give explicitly the set of bound token types. We simply list the type identifiers the interface is to contain, and if no further information about them is given, they are assigned new token types, subsequently treated as bound in the interface.

> interface $AInt =$
>   types   *zielone*
>   *czerwone*
>   objects *z_zero* : *zielone*
>   *zmien* : *zielone* $\rightsquigarrow$ *czerwone*
> end

This defines (the bound token types of an algebra interface are placed in parentheses in front of the signature component, much as in [HMT 90]):

$$AInt = (tt_1, tt_2)\langle[zielone \mapsto tt_1, czerwone \mapsto tt_2], [z\_zero \mapsto tt_1, zmien \mapsto tt_1 \rightsquigarrow tt_2]\rangle$$

In the current proposal there will be no way to directly define algebra signatures. They will be always generated out of a corresponding algebra interface. As a part of this process, bound token types will be replaced by newly generated abstract token types, now considered as fixed and visible throughout the rest of the definition.

For example:

> algebra $A : AInt =$
>   *zielone* = integer $\times \{0\}$
>   *czerwone* = integer $\times \{1\}$
>   *z_zero* = $\langle 0, 0 \rangle$
>   *zmien*.$\langle n, 0 \rangle = \langle n, 1 \rangle$
> end

builds the algebra A with the signature $ASig$ as defined above. The signature $ASig$ is generated out of the algebra interface $AInt$ by substituting new abstract token types att_1 and att_2 for the bound token types tt_1 and tt_2, respectively.

We will say that *a* MetaSoft *signature fits an algebra interface* if there exists a substitution modifying only the bound token types of the interface that maps the static type environment of the interface to the static type environment of the signature, and the static object environment of the interface to the static object environment of the signature. MetaSoft algebras will be always evaluated and stored together with their signatures. We will say that an algebra fits an interface if the algebra signature does so. For example, the algebra A and its signature $ASig$ fit the interface $AInt$ defined above.

Here are some further examples, well-formed in the context of the definitions listed above.

> interface $BInt =$
>   types *niebieskie* = $A.zielone$
>   *czarne* = $A.czerwone$
>   *nowy*
>   objects *cz_zero* : *czarne*
>   *zmien* : *niebieskie* $\rightsquigarrow$ *czarne*
> end

This defines an interface

$$BInt = (tt_3)\langle[niebieskie \mapsto att_1, czarne \mapsto att_2, nowy \mapsto tt_3],$$
$$[cz\_zero \mapsto att_1, zmien \mapsto att_1 \rightsquigarrow att_2]\rangle$$

with only one bound token type, named by *nowy*. The other two types (*niebieskie* and *czarne*) are mapped to the abstract types denoted by *A.zielone* and *A.czerwone*, respectively.

> algebra $B : BInt =$
> using A
> > $niebieskie = A.zielone$
> > $czarne = A.czerwone$
> > $nowy =$ bool
> > $cz\_zero = (A.zmien).(A.z\_zero)$
> > $zmien.x = (A.zmien).x$
>
> end

This defines the MetaSoft algebra corresponding to the algebra B of Section 2.1 with the signature where *niebieskie* and *czarne* are mapped to the same abstract types as *zielone* and *czerwone*, respectively, in *ASig* (and *nowy* is bound to a new abstract type). Therefore, we can now combine A and B, as unsuccessfullly attempted in Section 2.1:

> interface $ABInt =$
> > types $kolor1, kolor2, kolor3$
> > objects $zero1 : kolor1$
> > > $zero2 : kolor2$
> > > $zmien : kolor1 \rightsquigarrow kolor2$
> >
> end

> algebra $AB : ABInt =$
> > using A, B
> > > $kolor1 = A.zielone$
> > > $kolor2 = A.czerwone$
> > > $kolor3 = B.nowy$
> > > $zero1 = A.z\_zero$
> > > $zero2 = B.cz\_zero$
> > > $zmien = A.zmien$
> >
> end

We have chosen to define the interface $ABInt$ so that the information that the algebra AB shares the types with A and B is not propagated.

Since the interface $AInt$ for the algebra A does not provide the information that the types *zielone* and *czerwone* are in fact integer $\times \{0\}$ and integer $\times \{1\}$, respectively, the following two definitions are not well-formed, similarly as in Section 2.1:

> algebra $B1 : BInt =$
> > using A
> > > $niebieskie =$ integer $\times \{0\}$
> > > $czarne =$ integer $\times \{1\}$
> > > $nowy =$ bool
> > > $cz\_zero = (A.zmien).(A.z\_zero)$
> > > $zmien.x = (A.zmien).x$
> >
> end

> algebra $B2 : BInt =$
> > using A
> > > $niebieskie = A.zielone$
> > > $czarne = A.czerwone$
> > > $nowy =$ bool
> > > $cz\_zero = \langle 0, 1\rangle$
> > > $zmien.\langle n, 0\rangle = \langle n, 1\rangle$
> >
> end

We have used above the most straightforward way to define an algebra by defining one by one all its components, as suggested in Section 2.1. For technical reasons, this is not formally allowed in the current proposal, where he only way to construct algebras is by module instantiation (cf. Section 4.4). The above examples stretch the actual formalism somewhat. However, the possibility of directly defining an algebra in such a way may be easily introduced as a notational convention to abbreviate a definition of a parameterless module and its immediate instantiation (with the empty list of parameters).

4.4 Modules and their interfaces

A MetaSoft *module interface* consists of the following items:

- *a result algebra interface*;
  Any module with this interface, when instantiated with admissible parameters, produces an algebra fitting the result algebra interface.

- *a parameter interface*;
  The parameters of a module may be either algebras or other modules. Hence, this is split into two parts:

  - *an algebra-parameter interface*, given as an environment of signatures, and

  - *a module-parameter interface*, given as an environment of module interfaces.

The distinction between algebra parameters and module parameters is necessary. Under so-called *generative semantics* of module application (see the description of module instantiation below and some further discussion in Section 5) parameterless modules are quite different from algebras. Two occurrences of an algebra stand for the same algebra, with the same types as carriers; two occurrences of a parameterless module instantiation (no parameters required) may denote different algebras — the new types will be different.

- an indicated set of *flexible token types*;
  These are "flexible" token types of the algebra-parameter interface (all factored out, so that algebra signatures, rather than algebra interfaces form the algebra-parameter interface). The flexible token types will be substituted for in the process of module instantiation in a way determined by the signatures of the actual algebra parameters. The tokens in this set may occur in the interfaces of a number of parameters, thus indicating the requirements that some types are to be shared between actual parameters, and in the result algebra interface, thus indicating the type propagation in any module with this interface.

The flexible tokens types are regarded as local for the module interface, their occurences are bound, and the module interfaces are considered up to the obvious α-conversion.

The role of bound token types hidden in the result algebra interface is quite different from the bound token types of the module interface: the latter are used to express type sharing constraints, the former are "place-holders" for new abstract types to be generated.

Consider the following definition of a module interface (see Section 4.3 for *AInt*).

$$
\begin{aligned}
&\text{interface } BFInt = \\
&\quad \text{params} \quad \text{algs} \quad X : AInt \\
&\quad \text{result} \quad \text{types} \quad niebieskie = X.zielone \\
&\qquad\qquad\qquad\quad\; czarne = X.czerwone \\
&\qquad\qquad\qquad\quad\; nowy \\
&\qquad\qquad \text{objects} \quad cz\_zero : czarne \\
&\qquad\qquad\qquad\qquad\; zmien : niebieskie \rightsquigarrow czarne \\
&\quad \text{end}
\end{aligned}
$$

This introduces a module interface $BFInt$ with the result algebra interface listing types *niebieskie*, *czarne* and *nowy*, and objects *cz_zero* and *zmien* of the indicated types. Among the types in the result interface, the first two are propagated from the parameter X. No further information is given about *nowy*, hence it is understood to be a new type generated by the modules fitting this interface, and so is bound to a token type local to the result algebra interface. There are no module parameters, and only one algebra parameter X. The bound token types of its required interface $AInt$ are factored out as bound token types of the module interface. Formally, $BFInt$ is the following complex tuple (we leave this as an exercise for the reader to carefully interpret all its components):

$$BFInt = (tt_1, tt_2)\langle\langle[X \mapsto XSig], [\,]\rangle, R_{BF}Int\rangle$$

where

$$XSig = \langle[zielone \mapsto tt_1, czerwone \mapsto tt_2], [z\_zero \mapsto tt_1, zmien \mapsto tt_1 \dashrightarrow tt_2]\rangle$$

$$R_{BF}Int = (tt_3)\langle[niebieskie \mapsto tt_1, czarne \mapsto tt_2, nowy \mapsto tt_3],$$
$$[cz\_zero \mapsto tt_1, zmien \mapsto tt_1 \dashrightarrow tt_2]\rangle$$

Another example is an interface of a two-argument module.

interface $ABFInt =$
  params algs $X : AInt$
                  $Y :$ interface   types $niebieskie = X.zielone$
                                        $czarne = X.czerwone$
                                        $nowy$
                        objects $cz\_zero : czarne$
                                $zmien : niebieskie \dashrightarrow czarne$
                end
    result   types $kolor1, kolor2, kolor3$
             objects $zero1 : kolor1$
                     $zero2 : kolor2$
                     $zmien : kolor1 \dashrightarrow kolor2$
  end

Here in turn no types are declared to be propagated from the parameters, but the interface indicated for the algebra parameter Y imposes some sharing requirements on the types in the corresponding parameter. The resulting module interface formally is the following.

$$ABFInt = (tt_1, tt_2, tt_3)\langle\langle[X \mapsto XSig, Y \mapsto YSig], [\,]\rangle, R_{ABF}Int\rangle$$

where

$$XSig = \langle[zielone \mapsto tt_1, czerwone \mapsto tt_2], [z\_zero \mapsto tt_1, zmien \mapsto tt_1 \dashrightarrow tt_2]\rangle$$

$$YSig = \langle[niebieskie \mapsto tt_1, czarne \mapsto tt_2, nowy \mapsto tt_3],$$
$$[cz\_zero \mapsto tt_1, zmien \mapsto tt_1 \dashrightarrow tt_2]\rangle$$

$$R_{ABF}Int = (tt_4, tt_5, tt_6)\langle[kolor1 \mapsto tt_4, kolor2 \mapsto tt_5, kolor3 \mapsto tt_6],$$
$$[zero1 \mapsto tt_4, zero2 \mapsto tt_5, zmien \mapsto tt_4 \dashrightarrow tt_5]\rangle$$

MetaSoft modules are functions which take actual parameters explicitly bound to formal parameter identifiers as arguments and yield algebras (or generate an error). As with other entities of the language, they are always evaluated and stored together with their interfaces. A module fitting an interface takes actual parameters fitting the parameter interfaces and yields an algebra with a signature fitting the result algebra interface (in the non-error case).

The definition of "a module fitting an interface" implicit in the previous paragraph may seem unpleasantly circular (and hence formally incorrect). However, due to the strict use of parameter interfaces, the MetaSoft modules form a hierarchy where no self-application can occur. Therefore, the above definition is a simple inductive definition over the hierarchy of modules implicitly given by their interfaces.

Module definitions

A module definition consists of a module interface, a list of algebras and modules from the environment to be used in the definition, and a *module body*.

The module body is simply a list of type and object definitions in a slightly extended core language. The extension allows the user to select components of algebras either available in the environment or built by module instantiation. This is quite straightforward and does not require any further discussion. Let us just point out that recursive type or object definitions involving in an essential way module instantiations (that is, where recursion actually "goes through" a module instantiation) may yield somewhat unexpected results. As a consequence of the generative semantics of module instantiation mixed with the iterative way to generate the least-fixed-point solutions, some of the objects and types defined by mutual recursion may share fewer abstract types than expected.

To statically elaborate such a module definition, that is, to check whether the definition is well-formed and the module being defined indeed fits the interface, we first have to check whether the current environment actually stores the algebras and modules listed as "to be used" by the module being defined. Then, a "static" algebra and module environment is formed by cutting down the current environment (actually, its static part) to the "to be used" algebra and module identifiers, and adding the formal parameter identifiers with signatures and interfaces indicated in the parameter interface. Some renaming of the flexible token types of the module interface may be necessary to avoid unintended clashes with the abstract types already in use. The next step is to statically elaborate the module body in this environment to obtain the static type and object environments generated by the type and object definitions. Finally, we have to check whether these environments fit the corresponding parts of the result algebra interface.

If all this is successful, then the module defined is a function computed as follows.

Given actual parameters for the module, explicitly bound to the formal parameter identifiers, we first check whether the actual algebra-parameter signatures fit the algebra-parameter interface w.r.t. a substitution for the flexible token types of the module interface. This substitution is then used to replace the flexible token types in the module-parameter interface and in the result algebra interface. The next step is to check that the actual module-parameter interfaces coincide with the formal module-parameter interfaces[3]. If this is successful then an environment is constructed by selecting the "to be used" components of the global environment (they must be there because the static elaboration has been successful) and adding the actual parameters bound to the formal parameter identifiers. The module body is evaluated in this environment (no static error may occur now!). The result consists of a type environment and of an object environment, which fit the result algebra interface.

The result of the module instantiation is the algebra obtained by cutting out the appropriate parts of the dynamic type and object environments computed by the body evaluation. The signature of this result algebra is obtained from the result algebra interface by replacing its local "place-holder" token types by some newly generated ones, which do not clash with any abstract types already in use. These new abstract types are generated anew each time the module is instantiated, even if the same actual parameter list has already been used in some previous instantiation. Notice that the result algebra interface, not the static environments generated by the body elaboration, is used here, so that the signature of the result of module instantiation may be calculated entirely on the basis of the module interface and of the actual parameter signatures and interfaces. Thus, the static elaboration of a module instantiation may be performed without referring to the module body at all, as expected and required.

Here are simple examples of two modules fitting the interfaces given above:

---

[3]This requirement may be somewhat relaxed by allowing the actual parameter interfaces to be "more general" than the formal parameter ones. The idea is quite simple: the actual parameter interface must ensure that the actual parameter may be used as a module with the interface given by the formal parameter interface. For example, we can allow the actual parameter module to require fewer parameters or less sharing than indicated by the corresponding formal parameter interface, or looking at the potential results, the actual parameter module may ensure more components or more sharing in its results than required by the corresponding formal parameter interface.

module $BF : BFInt =$
    $niebieskie = X.zielone$
    $czarne = X.czerwone$
    $nowy = \mathsf{bool}$
    $cz\_zero = (X.zmien).(X.z\_zero)$
    $zmien.x = (X.zmien).x$
end

module $ABF : ABFInt =$
    $kolor1 = X.zielone$
    $kolor2 = X.czerwone$
    $kolor3 = Y.nowy$
    $zero1 = X.z\_zero$
    $zero2 = Y.cz\_zero$
    $zmien = X.zmien$
end

It is easy to check that indeed the bodies of the two modules are well-formed in the environment formed by binding the algebra-parameter signatures to the corresponding formal parameter identifiers, and the results of their elaboration fit the corresponding result algebra interfaces.

The modules may now be instantiated (we use the algebra A introduced in Section 4.3).

algebra $B = BF(X \mapsto A)$

It is again easy to check that the actual parameter indeed fits the parameter signature of the module interface under a uniquely determined substitution of types for the flexible token types ($[tt_1 \mapsto att_1, tt_2 \mapsto att_2]$). As described above, this substitution is then propagated to the result algebra interfaces, so that the signature of the algebra B defined above is the following:

$$BSig = \langle [niebieskie \mapsto att_1, czarne \mapsto att_2, nowy \mapsto att_3],$$
$$[cz\_zero \mapsto att_1, zmien \mapsto att_1 \rightsquigarrow att_2] \rangle$$

where att_3 is a new abstract token type generated during the module instantiation. Further instantiations of BF, even with the same parameter, lead to new **MetaSoft** algebras:

algebra $BB = BF(X \mapsto A)$

BB is an algebra over a new signature:

$$BBSig = \langle [niebieskie \mapsto att_1, czarne \mapsto att_2, nowy \mapsto att_3'],$$
$$[cz\_zero \mapsto att_1, zmien \mapsto att_1 \rightsquigarrow att_2] \rangle$$

where att_3' is a new, distinct abstract token type generated during the module instantiation.

Either of the above algebras fitting the interface $BInt$ may be used as a parameter for the module ABF.

algebra $AB = ABF(X \mapsto A, Y \mapsto B)$ algebra $ABB = ABF(X \mapsto A, Y \mapsto BB)$

Since in the interface of ABF no type propagation has been declared, the signatures of the two algebras thus defined use newly generated, distinct abstract types for $kolor1$, $kolor2$ and $kolor3$.

5 Further extensions and final remarks

Let me point out two major doubts about the presented proposal.

The first doubt concerns the major design decision on the module semantics in the language proposed. Namely, we have adopted here the so-called generative semantics of module instantiation. This means that each application of a module to an argument generates new abstract types, different from the ones generated before, even by the same module for identical arguments (of course, this may be overridden by an explicit sharing declaration in the result algebra interface). The are at least two other options:

- Define modules as functions which yield the same results, including abstract types, when given the same arguments. This would be perhaps conceptually most clear, but not very practical. Namely, this would lead to a type system with full dependent types (dependent on static as well as dynamic objects, including modules as well!). Thus, no reasonable static analysis would be decidable.

- Explore in full the fact that the underlying core type system does not admit dependent types. New types defined in a module may depend only on the static components of the module arguments. Consequently, two module instantiations would yield the same static results provided that their arguments have identical static parts. This should be decidable, and so it seems that such a type discipline may be imposed (although the details are far from clear, and much work would be necessary — cf. [Mog 89] for related theory).

Unfortunately, this may lead to intuitively doubtfull identification of types which are not intended to be identified. For example, given a module that produces a type of stacks of a bounded depth, where the depth is a part of the module parameter, the user would not be prevented from using the stack operations produced by the module when applied to a parameter setting the depth to 100000, to stacks built using the operations produced by the same module applied to the same parameter but with the depth changed to 10.

The second doubt is on the boderline between the technicalities and design of the language. Namely, following the decisions made in [BBP 90] for the core MetaSoft langauge, we háve assumed here that all the objects definable in the language are continuous, and hence any recursive definitions of objects of appropriate types make sense. In our view, there is no reason to adopt such a strong assumption of "continuity of everything" in a *specification* language. For example, there seems to be no reason to prevent the user from testing the identity of objects of any type, including function types (it is not as clear if testing the identity of objects of abstract types should be allowed, though...). Consequently, it may be justified to resign this assumption and work with potentially non-continuous objects and operations. This would require, however, a major change in the semantics of the recursive object definitions.

The proposal presented here should be extended in a number of important directions.

First, one of the original motivations which led us to believe that the "naive domain theory" underlying MetaSoft is sufficient for practical purposes was that it turned out possible to describe standard hierarchies of higher-order objects (such as procedures with procedural parameters in modern programming languages or modules of the current proposal) as long as some type discipline is imposed to prevent any form of self-application (cf. [BlT 83]). However, this requires dealing in the definitional langauge with infinite hierarchies of domains and their unions. A proposal to include such hierarchies of symbolic types in the MetaSoft core language has been recently formulated in [BBP 91]. Although there should be no major problems to incorporate such an extended core language into our module proposal, the details are not entirely clear. The infinite type hierarchies introduce dependent types, albeit in a very limited, statically-checkable form.

Then, one aspect in which our proposal is more restrictive than the modularisation facilities of Standard ML is that we have not allowed MetaSoft algebras with MetaSoft algebras as components. This is just for the simplicity of the first definition — no technical difficulties are envisaged, and in fact we plan to include both algebra and module components in MetaSoft algebras (and module bodies) in the final proposal.

A practical issue which has become apparent even in the extremely simplified examples used in this paper is that writing module interfaces is often a very tedious task. A separate, non-trivial sublanguage for defining interfaces should be carefully chosen as a part of the complete proposal.

We have allowed here no form of axiomatic requirements in module interfaces. It would be useful to follow one of the standard VDM techniques and allow *invariants* to be imposed on types defined in modules (and hence potentially used in module interfaces as well). In the construction of the universe of domains for VDM in [TW 90] we have proposed that type invariants should be imposed on types in a sense *a posteriori*. They would not be taken into account by the type analysis ensuring the well-formedness of the definitions at all, but the appropriate proof obligations would be generated. It seems that in order to meet this proof obligations some "dynamic" properties of the algebras defined would have to be stated and proved, perhaps in the way suggested towards the end of Section 2.1.

Finally, it would be interesting to try to generalise the current proposal to deal with "loose algebras", that is, to use the formalism proposed here to define, store and manipulate property-oriented specifications interpreted as classes of algebras rather than as single algebras.

References

[Ada 80] *The Programming Language Ada: Reference Manual.* LNCS 106, Springer 1980.

[Bau 85] Bauer, F.L. *et al* *The Wide Spectrum Language CIP-L.* LNCS 183, Springer 1985.

[BBP 90a] Bednarczyk, M., Borzyszkowski, A., Pawłowski, W. Towards the semantics of the definitional language of MetaSoft. In: *VDM and Z — Formal Methods in Software Development*, Proc. VDM-Europe Symp. 1990, Kiel, LNCS 428, pp. 477–503, Springer 1990.

[BBP 90b] Bednarczyk, M., Borzyszkowski, A., Pawłowski, W. Recursive definitions revisited. In: *VDM and Z — Formal Methods in Software Development*, Proc. VDM-Europe Symp. 1990, Kiel, LNCS 428, pp. 452–476, Springer 1990.

[BBP 91] Bednarczyk, M., Borzyszkowski, A., Pawłowski, W. Towards the semantics of the definitional language of MetaSoft: Dependent types. Technical report, Institute of Computer Science PAS, Gdańsk, December 1991.

[BjJ 78] Bjørner, D., Jones, C.B. *The Vienna Development Method: The Meta-Language.* Springer LNCS 61, 1978.

[BjJ 82] Bjørner, D., Jones, C.B. *Formal Specification and Software Development.* Prentice Hall 1982.

[Bl 89] Blikle, A. Denotational engineering. *Science of Computer Programming* 12(1989), pp. 207–253.

[BlT 83] Blikle, A., Tarlecki, A. Naive denotational semantics. In: *Information Processing 83*, Proc. IFIP World Congress'83, Paris 1983, R.E.A.Mason, ed., pp. 345–355, North-Holland 1983.

[BlTT 91] Blikle, A., Tarlecki, A., Thorup, M. On conservative extensions of syntax in system development. In: *Images of Programming*, dedicated to the memory of A. P. Ershov, D.Bjørner, V.Kotov, eds., pp. 209–233, North-Holland 1991.

[BG 80] Burstall, R.M., Goguen, J.A. The semantics of CLEAR, a specification language. Proc. *of Advanced Course on Abstract Software Specification*, Copenhagen, LNCS 86, pp. 292–332, Springer 1980.

[DMN 70] Dahl, O.-J., Myrhaug, B., Nygaard, K. *Simula 67 common base language.* Report S-22, Norwegian Computing Center, Oslo, 1970.

[EH 85] Ehrig, H., Mahr, B. *Fundamentals of Algebraic Specification 1: Equations and Initial Semantics.* Springer 1985.

[EM 90] Ehrig, H., Mahr, B. *Fundamentals of Algebraic Specification 2: Module Specifications and Constraints.* Springer 1990.

[FJKR 87] Feijs, L.M.G., Jonkers, H.B.M., Koymans, C.P.J., Renardel de Lavalette, G.R. *Formal definition of the design language COLD-K.* METEOR Report t7/PRLE/7, Philips Research Laboratories, April 1987.

[GB 84] Goguen, J.A., Burstall, R.M. Introducing institutions. Proc. *Logics of Programming Workshop*, Carnegie-Mellon, LNCS 164, pp. 221-256, Springer 1984.

[Gor 79] Gordon, M.J.C. *The denotational description of Programming Languages: An Introduction.* Springer 1979.

[GHW 85] Guttag, J.V., Horning, J.J., Wing, J. *Larch in five easy pieces.* Report 5, DEC Systems Research Center, Palo Alto 1985.

[Hoa 69] Hoare, C.A.R. An axiomatic basis for computer programming. *Communications of the ACM* 12(1969), pp. 576–580, 583.

[Jon 86] Jones, C.B. *Systematic Software Development Using VDM.* Prentice Hall 1986.

[LB 88] Lampson, B., Burstall, R. Pebble, a kernel language for modules and abstract data types. *Information and Computation* 76(1988) pp. 278–346.

[Lar 89] Larsen, P.G. The Dynamic Semantics of the BSI/VDM Specification Language. Technical report, Dept. of Computer Science, Technical University of Denmark, Lyngby, October 1989.

[Lis 81] Liskov, B.H. *et al. CLU Reference Manual*. LNCS 114, Springer 1981.

[MacQ 86] MacQueen, D.B. Modules for Standard ML. In: Harper, R., MacQueen, D.B. and Milner, R. Standard ML. Report ECS-LFCS-86-2, Univ. of Edinburgh 1986.

[MTH 90] Milner, R., Tofte, M., Harper, R. *The Definition of Standard ML*. MIT Press 1990.

[Mog 89] Moggi, E. A category-theoretic account of program modules. Proc. *Category Theory and Computer Science*, D.H.Pitt, D.E.Rydeheard, P.Dybjer, A.M.Pitts, A.Poigné, eds., LNCS 389, 101–117, Springer 1989.

[MSoft 90] *Project MetaSoft*. Project description, Institute of Computer Science, Polish Academy of Sciences, Warsaw, March 1990.

[NHWG 88] Nielsen, M., Havelund, K., Wagner, K.R., George, Ch. The RAISE language, method and tools. In: *VDM — The Way Ahead*, Proc. VDM-Europe Symp. VDM'88, Dublin, R.Bloomfield, L.Marshall, R.Jones, eds., LNCS 328, pp. 376–405, Springer 1988.

[SST 92] Sannella, D., Sokołowski, S., Tarlecki, A. Toward formal development of programs from algebraic specifications: parameterisation revisited. *Acta Informatica*, to appear; also Bericht 6/90, Informatik, Technische Universität Bremen, April 1990.

[ST 88] Sannella, D., Tarlecki, A. Specifications in an arbitrary institution. *Information and Computation* 76(1988), pp. 165–210.

[ST 89] Sannella, D., Tarlecki, A. Toward formal development of ML programs: foundations and methodology. Report ECS-LFCS-89-71, Laboratory for Foundations of Computer Science, Dept. of Computer Science, Univ. of Edinburgh 1989; extended abstract in Proc. Colloq. *Current Issues in Programming Languages*, 3rd Joint Conf. *Theory and Practice of Software Development* TAPSOFT'89, Barcelona, LNCS 352, pp. 375–389, Springer 1989.

[ST 91a] Sannella, D., Tarlecki, A. Extended ML: past, present and future. Proc. 7th Intl. Workshop *Specification of Abstract Data Types*, Wusterhausen/Dosse, LNCS 534, pp. 297–322, Springer 1991.

[ST 91b] Sannella, D., Tarlecki, A. A kernel specification formalism with higher-order parameterisation. Proc. 7th Intl. Workshop *Specification of Abstract Data Types*, Wusterhausen/Dosse, LNCS 534, pp. 274–296, Springer 1991.

[SW 83] Sannella, D., Wirsing, M. A kernel language for algebraic specification and implementation. Proc. Intl. Conf. *Foundations of Computation Theory*, Borgholm, Sweden, LNCS 158, pp. 413–427, Springer 1983.

[Sc 76] Scott, D. Data types as lattices. *SIAM Jour. on Computing* 5(1976), pp. 522–587.

[Sc 82] Scott, D. Domains for denotational semantics. Proc. ICALP'82, LNCS 140, Springer 1982.

[ScS 71] Scott, D., Strachey, Ch. Towards a mathematical semantics for computer languages. Technical report, Oxford University Computing Laboratory 1971.

[Tar 92] Tarlecki, A. Modules for MetaSoft: a technical definition. Technical report, Institute of Computer Science PAS, Warsaw, in preparation.

[TW 90] Tarlecki, A., Wieth, M. A naive domain universe for VDM. In: *VDM and Z — Formal Methods in Software Development*, Proc. VDM-Europe Symp. 1990, Kiel, LNCS 428, pp. 552–579, Springer 1990.

[Wir 86] Wirsing, M. Structured algebraic specifications: a kernel language. *Theoretical Computer Science* 42(1986) pp. 123–249.

[Wirth 88] Wirth, N. *Programming in Modula-2* (third edition). Springer 1988.

Typing References by Effect Inference

Andrew K. Wright*

Department of Computer Science
Rice University
Houston, TX 77251-1892
wright@cs.rice.edu

Abstract

Hindley/Milner-style polymorphism is a simple, natural, and flexible type discipline for functional languages, but incorporating imperative extensions is difficult. We present a new technique for typing references in the presence of polymorphism by inferring a concise summary of each expression's allocation behavior—a *type effect*. A simple technique for proving soundness with respect to a reduction semantics demonstrates that the type system prevents type errors. By establishing that the system corresponds to an alternate system better suited to implementation, we obtain an algorithm to perform type and effect inference.

1   Polymorphism and References

Hindley/Milner-style polymorphism [8, 12] is a simple, natural, and flexible type discipline for functional languages, but incorporating imperative extensions is difficult. While a number of systems for typing reference cells exist [3, 10, 16, 17, 18], we have devised a more direct approach based on inferring a concise summary of each expression's allocation behavior. Our system has several desirable characteristics: the curried version of a function may be used wherever the uncurried version applies; all expressions typable in the functional sublanguage are typable; the system has a direct inference rule formulation; and it can be implemented efficiently. In this paper, we discuss the typing of STANDARD ML's reference cells by our method, give a formal description of a type system for references, and show how it may be implemented. We begin with an illustration of the difficulties involved in typing references in the presence of polymorphism, and outline our solution.

---

*This research was supported in part by the United States Department of Defense under a National Defense Science and Engineering Graduate Fellowship, and by NSF grant CCR 89–17022.

1.1   Hindley/Milner Polymorphism

Hindley/Milner-style type systems express polymorphism with let-expressions. In functional languages, understanding such expressions as abbreviations offers a simple explanation of polymorphism. Semantically, the expression:

$$\text{let } x = e_1 \text{ in } e_2$$

has the same meaning as $e_2[x/e_1]$, the capture-avoiding substitution of e_1 for free x in e_2 (assuming that e_1 does not diverge). However, in typing the substituted expression $e_2[x/e_1]$, each occurrence of the bound expression e_1 may have a different type. For example, if e_1 is $\lambda z.z$, one occurrence could be assigned $int \rightarrow int$, while another occurrence is assigned $bool \rightarrow bool$. Hence to type a let-expression we associate with x the *set* of types of e_1. Each occurrence of x in the body e_2 may have any type in this set. In the expression:

$$\text{let id} = \lambda z.z$$
$$\text{in id 1; id true}$$

id is associated with the infinite set of types $\{\tau \rightarrow \tau \mid \tau \in \textit{Type}\}$.

Type schemes represent the sets of types that are associated with identifiers bound by let-expressions. A type scheme $\forall \alpha_1 \ldots \alpha_n . \tau$ consists of a body (τ), which is a type that may contain *type variables* (α_i), and a set of *bound variables* ($\alpha_1 \ldots \alpha_n$). The set of types described by a type scheme consists of those types that may be obtained by substituting types for the bound variables in the body of the type scheme. The type scheme $\forall \alpha . \alpha \rightarrow \alpha$ describes the set of all function types whose input and output types are the same, *i.e.*, $\{\tau \rightarrow \tau \mid \tau \in \textit{Type}\}$.

To determine the type scheme for x in the expression let $x = e_1$ in e_2, we first find a most general type for e_1 by using type variables wherever possible. For example, a most general type for compose $= \lambda f.\lambda g.\lambda z.f\,(g\,z)$ is:

$$(\beta \rightarrow \gamma) \rightarrow (\alpha \rightarrow \beta) \rightarrow \alpha \rightarrow \gamma.$$

The type scheme for x is obtained by binding or *generalizing* type variables in the type of e_1 (that are not used in typing expressions outside the let-expression in question [13: p. 40]). In the expression:

$$\text{let compose} = \lambda f.\lambda g.\lambda z.f\,(g\,z) \text{ in } \ldots$$

α, β, and γ are generalized to yield type scheme $\forall \alpha \beta \gamma.(\beta \rightarrow \gamma) \rightarrow (\alpha \rightarrow \beta) \rightarrow \alpha \rightarrow \gamma$ for compose.

1.2   References

The operators ref, !, and := provide reference cells as first-class values. When applied to a value, the ref operator creates a reference cell containing that value; applying ! to a reference cell extracts the contents of the cell; and := changes the contents of a cell.

To type reference cells, we introduce the type τ *ref* for reference cells containing values of type τ. Since the ref operator takes a value of any type and returns a cell containing that value, one might naïvely expect ref to have type scheme $\forall \alpha . \alpha \rightarrow \alpha$ *ref*,

! to have type scheme $\forall \alpha.\, \alpha\, ref \to \alpha$, and := to have type scheme $\forall \alpha.\, \alpha\, ref \to \alpha \to \alpha$ (:= returns the value assigned). However, this naïve typing for references is unsound, as the following expression illustrates:

$$\text{let } x = \text{ref } (\lambda z.z) \text{ in } x := (\lambda n.\ n + 1);\ (!\ x)\ \text{true}$$

The most general type for ref $(\lambda z.z)$ is $(\alpha \to \alpha)\, ref$, and generalizing α yields type scheme $\forall \alpha.\, ((\alpha \to \alpha)\, ref)$ for x. This type scheme can be instantiated to $(int \to int)\, ref$ to type the assignment, and to $(bool \to bool)\, ref$ to type the dereference, but when evaluated, this expression causes a type error by attempting to add 1 to true.

Reference cells invalidate the explanation of let-expressions as abbreviations, due to the sharing implied by references: the expression let $x = e_1$ in e_2 no longer has the same meaning as $e_2[x/e_1]$. Just as references change the semantics of let-expressions, they also necessitate a change in how let-expressions are typed.

1.3 The Problem is Generalization

The solution our system and all existing systems use is to require that reference cells have only one type. This is achieved by restricting generalization at let-expressions. In the previous example, if α is not generalized, then it is *free* in the resulting type scheme $\forall.\, ((\alpha \to \alpha)\, ref)$. A free type variable may later be replaced with a specific type; in the above example, typing the assignment replaces α with int. The subsequent dereference can no longer be typed, as x now has type scheme $\forall.\, ((int \to int)\, ref)$.

The type variables that must not be generalized are those that appear in the types of reference cells allocated by the bound expression [18]. However, this set cannot be precisely determined, since the set of cells allocated by an expression cannot be statically determined. Hence any static type system that attempts to integrate reference cells in this way must use a conservative approximation. Our system uses a more direct method than existing systems to approximate the set of type variables that appear in the types of allocated reference cells.

1.4 Controlling Generalization with Effects

The essential idea behind our system is to associate with every expression a conservative approximation to the set of reference cells that the expression allocates, the expression's *allocation effect*.[1] Since our type system needs only the type variables in the types of these reference cells, we infer for each expression a *type effect*—the set of type variables that appear in the expression's allocation effect. In typing a let-expression, the type effect of the bound expression provides the information we need to determine which type variables must not be generalized.

The type effect of an application $(e_1\ e_2)$ is a combination of the effects of evaluating the function and argument subexpressions e_1 and e_2, and of the effect caused by applying the function to which e_1 evaluates. Hence, we record the type effect that the function causes when applied above the arrow in the type of a function. For example, the function:

$$\lambda x.\, (\text{ref } 1;\ \text{ref true};\ \text{ref x};\ \text{false})$$

---

[1] We borrow the term *effect* from FX [11]. Jouvelot and Gifford [9] describe a system that infers types and effects for expressions. While this system records effect information with function types in a manner similar to ours, the information is not used to control generalization of let-expressions.

allocates cells of type *int*, *bool*, and α when applied (where x has type α). The type effect of the set $\{int, bool, \alpha\}$ is α, since α is the only type variable in the set, hence the type of the above function is $\alpha \xrightarrow{\alpha} bool$. The λ-expression itself has the empty type effect, written $\emptyset$, because its evaluation to a closure allocates no cells.

To handle higher-order functions, we introduce *effect variables*, denoted ς. Effect variables are analogous to type variables; for example, the function:

$$\mathsf{apply} = \lambda f.\lambda x.f\ x$$

has type $(\alpha \xrightarrow{\varsigma} \beta) \xrightarrow{\emptyset} \alpha \xrightarrow{\varsigma} \beta$ for any types α and β and type effect ς. Application of apply to a single argument yields a result of type $\alpha \xrightarrow{\varsigma} \beta$, causing no effect. The type effect ς occurs only when apply is given a second argument, as indicated by the empty type effect on its outermost function constructor. As another example, the function:

$$\mathsf{compose} = \lambda f.\lambda g.\lambda x.f\ (g\ x)$$

has type $(\alpha \xrightarrow{\varsigma_1} \beta) \xrightarrow{\emptyset} (\gamma \xrightarrow{\varsigma_2} \alpha) \xrightarrow{\emptyset} \gamma \xrightarrow{\varsigma_1\varsigma_2} \beta$. When applied to three arguments, it causes the combined effects of both f and g.

As in the functional case, the type scheme for x in the expression let $x = e_1$ in e_2 is determined by generalizing variables in the type of the bound expression e_1. To prevent generalizing variables that appear in the types of cells allocated by e_1, we simply restrict generalization to those variables not in the effect of e_1. For example, in the expression:

$$\mathsf{let}\ x = \mathsf{ref}\ (\lambda y.y)\ \mathsf{in}\ \ x := (\lambda n.\ n + 1);\ \ (!\ x)\ \mathsf{true}$$

the bound expression ref $(\lambda y.y)$ has type $(\alpha \xrightarrow{\emptyset} \alpha)$ *ref* and effect $\{\alpha\}$. Since α appears in the effect, it cannot be generalized, and the expression is not typable.

As a further example, consider the following imperative version of map [10]:

$$\begin{aligned}
\mathsf{let}\ \mathsf{imap} = \lambda f.\lambda x.\ &\mathsf{let}\ a = \mathsf{ref}\ x\ \mathsf{and}\ \ b = \mathsf{ref}\ \mathsf{nil}\\
&\mathsf{in}\ \ \mathsf{while}\ \mathsf{not}\ (\mathsf{null}\ !a)\ \mathsf{do}\\
&\qquad\qquad b := (f\ (\mathsf{hd}\ !a)) :: !b;\\
&\qquad\qquad a := \mathsf{tl}\ !a\\
&\quad\ \ \mathsf{reverse}\ !b\\
\mathsf{in} \ldots &
\end{aligned}$$

If f has type $\alpha \xrightarrow{\varsigma} \beta$ and x has type α *list* (τ *list* is the type of lists containing elements of type τ), then the body of the function allocates reference cells of type α *list ref* and β *list ref*. While α and β must not be generalized by the inner let in the type schemes for a and b, they can be generalized by the outer let in the type scheme for imap: $\forall \alpha\beta\varsigma_1\varsigma_2\varsigma_3.(\alpha \xrightarrow{\varsigma_1} \beta) \xrightarrow{\varsigma_2} \alpha$ *list* $\xrightarrow{\varsigma_1\varsigma_3\alpha\beta} \beta$ *list*.

1.5 Outline

In the next section, we present the syntax and semantics of a simple language with references. Section 3 defines our type system for this language in detail, and sketches a proof of soundness. In Section 4 we obtain a corresponding type inference algorithm by reformulating the system in a manner better suited to implementation. We conclude with a comparison to other systems for typing references in the presence of polymorphism.

2   A Polymorphic Language with References

We study our type system in the context of a simple language with references. It is easy to extend this language and its type system to a realistic language including pattern matching, exceptions, and modules, such as STANDARD ML [13, 14].

2.1   Abstract Syntax

Our language has expressions, *Exp*, and values, *Val*, of the form:

(*Exp*)	$e ::= v \mid e_1\ e_2 \mid \text{let } x = e_1 \text{ in } e_2$
(*Val*)	$v ::= x \mid c \mid \lambda x.e \mid \text{setref } v$

$$x \in Id \qquad c, \text{ref}, !, \text{setref} \in Const$$

The set *Id* is a countably infinite set of identifiers (whenever we refer to *variables*, we mean entities of the type system, not identifiers). The set of constants, *Const*, consists of data, of primitive operations, and of the distinguished constants ref, !, and setref.

Juxtaposition denotes application and is left associative; λ constructs call-by-value procedural abstractions. Semantically a let-expression behaves like $((\lambda x.e_2)\ e_1)$; however, the type system allows x to be polymorphic. The constants ref, !, and setref provide the usual operations on references. We use the curried binary assignment operator setref rather than the customary infix := to simplify the language. The application of setref to one value *is* a value—it may be thought of as a *capability* to assign to a cell. Therefore, the application of setref to a value is included in the syntactic class of values.

Free and bound identifiers are defined as usual. Following Barendregt [1], we assume that bound identifiers are always distinct from free identifiers in distinct metavariables ranging over expressions, and we identify expressions that differ by only a consistent renaming of the bound identifiers.

2.2   Semantics

Rather than using (a variant of) structural operational semantics [13, 14] to give a formal semantics for our language, we define the semantics with a term rewriting system, using the technique of *reduction semantics* [5, 6, 7]. This formulation allows a compact and elegant presentation of the semantics and a simple proof of type soundness [19].

Evaluation proceeds as a sequence of rewriting steps, or *reductions*, from one intermediate *state* of evaluation to another. Each state has a syntactic representation:

(*State*)	$s ::= \rho\theta.e$
(*Store*)	$\theta ::= \{\ \langle x, v\rangle\ \}^*$

The sequence θ represents the contents of the store. The first component of a pair $\langle x, v\rangle$ is a location name; the second component is the value stored there. The phrase $\rho\langle x_1, v_1\rangle \ldots \langle x_n, v_n\rangle.e$ binds $x_1, \ldots, x_n$ in $v_1, \ldots, v_n, e$; hence, ρ-phrases permit recursive bindings. While θ is syntactically a sequence of pairs, we treat θ as a finite function, *i.e.*, we disregard the order of pairs and require that the first components be unique.

(δ)	$\rho\theta.E[c\ c'] \longmapsto \rho\theta.E[\delta(c,c')]$	if $\delta(c,c')$ is defined
(β_v)	$\rho\theta.E[(\lambda x.e)\ v] \longmapsto \rho\theta.E[e[x/v]]$	
(let_v)	$\rho\theta.E[\text{let } x = v \text{ in } e] \longmapsto \rho\theta.E[e[x/v]]$	
(ref)	$\rho\theta.E[\text{ref } v] \longmapsto \rho\theta\langle x,v\rangle.E[x]$	
$(!)$	$\rho\theta\langle x,v\rangle.E[!\ x] \longmapsto \rho\theta\langle x,v\rangle.E[v]$	
$(setref)$	$\rho\theta\langle x,v'\rangle.E[\text{setref } x\ v] \longmapsto \rho\theta\langle x,v\rangle.E[v]$	

$$E ::= [] \mid E\ e \mid v\ E \mid \text{let } x = E \text{ in } e$$

Figure 1: The reduction relation $\longmapsto$

As with expressions, we identify states that differ by a consistent renaming of bound identifiers.

Figure 1 specifies the reduction relation $\longmapsto: State \times State$. The notation $e[x/v]$ means the capture-avoiding substitution of v for free x in e. The partial function $\delta : Const \times Const \rightharpoonup Const$ interprets the application of constants other than ref, !, and setref; the type system places some additional constraints on δ to achieve soundness. The renaming conventions ensure that the identifiers bound by ρ-phrases in the ref, !, and *setref* reductions are renamed appropriately to avoid capture, as in β_v.

The definition of the reduction relation relies on *evaluation contexts*, E. An evaluation context is an expression with one subexpression replaced by a hole, denoted $[]$. An expression may be placed in the hole of an evaluation context, yielding an expression; we write $E[e]$. The definition of evaluation contexts forces evaluation to proceed from left to right. As a result, the relation $\longmapsto$ is a function.

The evaluation function *eval* maps *programs* to *answers*:

$$eval(e) = a \text{ if and only if } \rho.e \longmapsto\!\!\!\!\!\rightarrow a$$

where $\longmapsto\!\!\!\!\!\rightarrow$ is the transitive and reflexive closure of the reduction relation $\longmapsto$. Programs are simply closed expressions; answers (a) are states of the form $\rho\theta.v$.

The evaluation function is partial and may be undefined for two reasons: evaluation may *diverge*, or it may become *stuck*. An expression diverges, written $e \Uparrow$, if it has an infinite reduction sequence, *i.e.*, if $e \longmapsto e'$ for some e', and for all e' such that $e \longmapsto\!\!\!\!\!\rightarrow e'$, there exists e'' such that $e' \longmapsto e''$. Evaluation is stuck if it reaches a state that is not an answer, but from which no further reduction is possible. Stuck states represent the application of a primitive function to an argument for which it is not defined, or the application of a non-function; examples are $\rho.(\text{succ true})$ and $\rho.(1\ 2)$. When a program reaches a stuck state, it is said to have caused a *type error*. The intent of a static type system is to filter out programs that may cause type errors.

3 Typing References

The following subsections present a type system for our language. The system requires a syntactic description of types and type inference rules for assigning types to programs. A type soundness theorem establishes that the system filters out all type errors.

3.1 Types and Effects

The sets of types, effects, and type schemes are defined inductively as follows:

(*Type*)	$\tau ::= \iota \mid \alpha \mid \tau \xrightarrow{\Delta} \tau \mid \tau \; ref$
(*Effect*)	$\Delta ::= \nu^{*}$
(*TypeScheme*)	$\sigma ::= \forall \nu^{*}.\tau$
(*Var*)	$\nu ::= \alpha \mid \varsigma$

$$\alpha \in \mathit{TypeVar} \quad \varsigma \in \mathit{EffectVar} \quad \iota \in \mathit{TypeConst}$$

The set *TypeConst* is a finite set of ground types, like *int* and *bool*. The sets *TypeVar* and *EffectVar* are countably infinite and disjoint. An effect is syntactically a sequence of type and effect variables, but we treat effects as finite sets, identifying effects that have the same elements. We write $\emptyset$ for the empty effect. We also identify $\forall.\tau$ with τ; hence, the set of types is a proper subset of the set of type schemes.

A type scheme $\forall \nu_1 \ldots \nu_n. \tau$ binds ν_1 through ν_n in τ, giving rise to free and bound variables for types and type schemes; $FV(\sigma)$ is the set of free variables of σ. A type scheme $\forall \nu_1 \ldots \nu_n.\tau$ denotes the set of types that may be obtained by substituting for its bound variables:

$$\{\tau' \mid \tau' = \mu\tau \text{ for some substitution } \mu \text{ with domain } \{\nu_1, \ldots, \nu_n\}\}.$$

Substitutions are finite maps from type variables to types and effect variables to effects; juxtaposition denotes application. Substitutions are applied to types as usual, but the application of a substitution μ to an effect Δ yields the set of variables appearing in the pointwise application of μ to each member of Δ:

$$\mu\Delta = \bigcup_{\nu \in \Delta} FV(\mu\nu).$$

For example, with $\mu = \{\alpha \mapsto (\beta \xrightarrow{\gamma} \beta)\}$ and $\Delta = \alpha\varsigma$,

$$\mu\Delta = FV(\mu\alpha) \cup FV(\mu\varsigma) = FV(\beta \xrightarrow{\gamma} \beta) \cup FV(\varsigma) = \beta\gamma\varsigma.$$

So far, our definitions admit several different type schemes that denote the same set of types. As usual, we identify type schemes that differ by only a consistent renaming of bound variables. However, this does not identify all type schemes that denote the same set of types; witness $\forall\alpha\varsigma. (\alpha \xrightarrow{\varsigma} \alpha) \xrightarrow{\varsigma} \alpha$ and $\forall\beta\varsigma_1\varsigma_2. (\beta \xrightarrow{\varsigma_1\varsigma_2} \beta) \xrightarrow{\varsigma_1\varsigma_2} \beta$. To identify these type schemes, we extend the renaming process to allow the consistent replacement of an effect variable by one or more effect variables. Under this extended process of renaming, all type schemes that denote the same set of types are equivalent.

3.2 Type and Effect Assignment

The type system in Figure 2 is a deductive proof system that assigns a type and an effect to an expression. A type judgement $\Gamma \vdash e : \tau, \Delta$ states that expression e has type τ and effect Δ in type environment Γ. A type environment is a finite map from identifiers to type schemes; type environments give types to the free identifiers of an

$$TypeOf(\text{ref}) = \forall \alpha \varsigma.\, \alpha \xrightarrow{\alpha \varsigma} \alpha\ ref$$
$$TypeOf(!) = \forall \alpha \varsigma.\, \alpha\ ref \xrightarrow{\varsigma} \alpha$$
$$TypeOf(\text{setref}) = \forall \alpha \varsigma_1 \varsigma_2.\, \alpha\ ref \xrightarrow{\varsigma_1} \alpha \xrightarrow{\varsigma_2} \alpha$$

(id)
$$\Gamma \vdash x : \tau, \emptyset \ \text{ if } \ \tau \in \Gamma(x)$$

$(const)$
$$\Gamma \vdash c : \tau, \emptyset \ \text{ if } \ \tau \in TypeOf(c)$$

(abs)
$$\frac{\Gamma[x/\tau_1] \vdash e : \tau_2, \Delta}{\Gamma \vdash \lambda x.e : \tau_1 \xrightarrow{\Delta} \tau_2, \emptyset}$$

(app)
$$\frac{\Gamma \vdash e_1 : \tau_1 \xrightarrow{\Delta_3} \tau_2, \Delta_1 \quad \Gamma \vdash e_2 : \tau_1, \Delta_2}{\Gamma \vdash e_1\ e_2 : \tau_2, \Delta_1 \cup \Delta_2 \cup \Delta_3}$$

(let)
$$\frac{\Gamma \vdash e_1 : \tau_1, \Delta_1 \quad \Gamma[x/Close(\tau_1, \Gamma, \Delta_1)] \vdash e_2 : \tau_2, \Delta_2}{\Gamma \vdash \text{let } x = e_1 \text{ in } e_2 : \tau_2, \Delta_1 \cup \Delta_2}$$

(sub)
$$\frac{\Gamma \vdash e : \tau, \Delta_1 \quad \Delta_1 \subseteq \Delta_2}{\Gamma \vdash e : \tau, \Delta_2}$$

$$Close(\tau, \Gamma, \Delta) = \forall \nu_1 \ldots \nu_n.\, \tau \ \text{ where } \{\nu_1, \ldots, \nu_n\} = FV(\tau) \setminus (FV(\Gamma) \cup FV(\Delta))$$

Figure 2: Type and effect assignment

expression. The notation $\Gamma[x/\sigma]$ means the functional extension or update of Γ at x to σ. An expression e is *well-typed* if there exists a derivation that assigns a type τ and an effect Δ to e in the empty environment; we write $\vdash e : \tau, \Delta$.

The rules for typing variables and constants depend on a notion of *generalization*. A type scheme $\sigma = \forall \nu_1 \ldots \nu_n.\, \tau'$ generalizes a type τ, written $\tau \in \sigma$, if there exists a substitution μ with domain $\{\nu_1, \ldots, \nu_n\}$ such that $\mu \tau' = \tau$, *i.e.*, if τ is in the set of types denoted by σ. Alternatively, we say that τ is an instance of σ. For example,

$$int \xrightarrow{\emptyset} int \in \forall \alpha \varsigma.\, \alpha \xrightarrow{\varsigma} \alpha$$
$$(\beta \xrightarrow{\gamma} \beta) \xrightarrow{\beta \gamma} (\beta \xrightarrow{\gamma} \beta)\ ref \in \forall \alpha \varsigma.\, \alpha \xrightarrow{\alpha \varsigma} \alpha\ ref$$

In the last example, note that when the substitution $\{\alpha \mapsto (\beta \xrightarrow{\gamma} \beta);\ \varsigma \mapsto \emptyset\}$ is applied to the effect $\alpha \varsigma$ on the function arrow, the result is the "flattened" effect $\beta \gamma$.

As rule (id) indicates, an identifier may have any type that is an instance of its type scheme in the type environment. As an identifier has a binding in the type environment only if it is bound by a surrounding let- or λ-expression, well-typed programs are closed. An identifier has the empty effect since its evaluation allocates no reference cells.

Rule $(const)$ uses the function $TypeOf : Const \rightarrow TypeScheme$ to assign type schemes to constants. For type soundness to make sense for an unspecified set of constants, we impose a *typability* condition on the interpretation of constants:

$(\delta\text{-typability})$
$$\tau' \xrightarrow{\Delta} \tau \in TypeOf(c_1) \text{ and } \tau' \in TypeOf(c_2)$$
implies
$$\delta(c_1, c_2) \text{ is defined and } \tau \in TypeOf(\delta(c_1, c_2)).$$

This condition requires δ to be defined for all constants of functional type and arguments of matching type, and restricts the range of values that it may produce.[2]

The type of an abstraction $\lambda x.e$ is determined from the type and effect of its body, as (abs) indicates. Assuming that the argument x has type τ_1, if the body e has type τ_2 and effect Δ, then the abstraction is a function of type $\tau_1 \xrightarrow{\Delta} \tau_2$. Since the evaluation of an abstraction itself creates no reference cells, the effect of an abstraction is empty.

To determine the type of an application, the argument's type is required to match the function's type as usual. The effect of an application is the union of the effects of its subexpressions and of the effect the function causes.

The type of a let-expression is determined from the type of the body, in a type environment extended with a generalization of the most general type of the bound expression. The function $Close$ generalizes free type and effect variables of the bound expression's type that are not also free in the type environment or in the bound expression's effect (the function FV is extended pointwise to type environments).

The subsumption rule (sub) allows any expression to be treated as having more effects than it actually does. By applying subsumption to the body of an abstraction, the abstraction may be treated as causing more effects when applied than it actually does; for example, $\lambda x.x$ may be typed as $\alpha \xrightarrow{\Delta} \alpha$ for any effect Δ. Hence the type scheme for a function includes an effect variable in its type. For example, the type scheme for the identity function $\lambda x.x$ is $\forall \alpha \varsigma. \alpha \xrightarrow{\varsigma} \alpha$; likewise, the type scheme for ref is $\forall \alpha \varsigma. \alpha \xrightarrow{\alpha \varsigma} \alpha$ ref. Without subsumption, a value of type $int \xrightarrow{\emptyset} int$ and a value of type $int \xrightarrow{int} int$ could not both be passed as arguments to the same (non-polymorphic) function, because the function and argument types would have to match exactly.

3.3 Type Soundness

To prove that this type system is sound, we use our extension of subject reduction to imperative languages [19]. By expressing the semantics of the language as a term rewriting system, we can use the type system to check that each intermediate state of evaluation is well-typed, and thus show that evaluation preserves typing. Since no stuck state is typable, it follows that evaluation cannot reach a stuck state and cause a type error. The soundness theorem states that all well-typed programs either diverge or produce an answer of the expected type.

Theorem 3.1 (Type Soundness) *If* $\vdash s : \tau, \Delta$ *then* $s \Uparrow$ *or* $s \longmapsto a$ *and* $\vdash a : \tau, \Delta$.

Proof Sketch. In order to show that evaluation preserves typing, it must be possible to type all intermediate states of evaluation. Therefore, we augment the type system with a typing rule for states:

$$(state) \quad \frac{\emptyset[x_1/\tau_1 \ ref] \dots [x_n/\tau_n \ ref] \vdash e : \tau, \Delta \qquad \emptyset[x_1/\tau_1 \ ref] \dots [x_n/\tau_n \ ref] \vdash v_i : \tau_i, \emptyset \quad 1 \leq i \leq n}{\vdash \rho \langle x_1, v_1 \rangle \dots \langle x_n, v_n \rangle . e : \tau, \Delta}$$

---

[2] This condition precludes partial constant functions that are not defined on all values of their input type, such as $\div : int \times int \rightarrow int$. Such functions may be extended to total functions by raising *exceptions*. Typing exceptions requires similar restrictions on polymorphism as typing references; type soundness for exceptions is treated in [19].

In the augmented system, reductions preserve the type and effect of a state:

$$if \vdash s_1 : \tau, \Delta \ and \ s_1 \longmapsto s_2 \ then \ \vdash s_2 : \tau, \Delta.$$

This lemma (subject reduction) is proved by case analysis according to the reduction. Stuck states have the form:

$$\rho\theta.E[c \ v] \ where \ \delta(c, v) \ is \ undefined \ and \ c \neq \mathsf{ref}, !, \mathsf{setref};$$
$$\rho\theta.E[! \ v] \ where \ v \notin Id;$$
$$\rho\theta.E[\mathsf{setref} \ v_1 \ v_2] \ where \ v_1 \notin Id; \ or$$
$$\rho\theta\langle x, v_1 \rangle.E[x \ v_2].$$

By examining each case in the definition of stuck states, we can show that no stuck state is typable.

Finally, we know that either $s \Uparrow$, $s \longmapsto a$, or $s \longmapsto s'$ and s' is stuck. Since $\vdash s : \tau, \Delta$, type and effect preservation implies $\vdash a : \tau, \Delta$ and $\vdash s' : \tau, \Delta$. Suppose $s \longmapsto s'$ and s' is stuck. Since stuck states are untypable, $\vdash s' : \tau, \Delta$ is a contradiction, therefore this case cannot occur. Hence either $s \Uparrow$ or $s \longmapsto a$ and $\vdash a : \tau, \Delta$. ∎

4 Implementing the Type System

The type system of the preceding section may be used to verify that a typing is valid, but we would like an *algorithm* that infers a typing if one exists. The algorithms for functional languages rely on ordinary unification to achieve efficient implementation. However, our function types include effect sets, hence unifying two function types apparently requires unifying two sets. Fortunately, we can obtain an *indirect* reformulation of the type system that has a corresponding algorithm using ordinary unification.

Subsumption is the key to avoiding set unification. To type the application $(e_1 \ e_2)$ where e_1 and e_2 have types:

$$e_1 : (\tau \xrightarrow{\Delta_1} \tau') \to \tau'' \quad and \quad e_2 : \tau \xrightarrow{\Delta_2} \tau'$$

we must unify $\tau \xrightarrow{\Delta_1} \tau'$ and $\tau \xrightarrow{\Delta_2} \tau'$. But subsumption permits embedded effects to be unbounded, hence we can retype e_1 and e_2 as:

$$e_1 : (\tau \xrightarrow{\Delta_1 \cup \Delta_2} \tau') \to \tau'' \quad and \quad e_2 : \tau \xrightarrow{\Delta_1 \cup \Delta_2} \tau'.$$

The function and argument types now match appropriately.

To permit the use of ordinary unification, we replace the effect sets on function arrows with labels and record the effect information separately in a *constraint*. The constraint is simply a list of label–effect pairs; the effect information corresponding to a given label is determined by pairs in the constraint with that label. To unite two effects embedded in types, we simply unify their labels in both the types and the constraint. Effect variables provide a convenient source of labels.

In the following subsections we present the indirect system, sketch a proof of its correspondence to the direct system, and give the type inference algorithm.

4.1 The Indirect System

In the indirect system, functions are labeled with only a single effect variable. *Constraints* record the effect information separately:

(*Type*)	$\tau ::= \iota \mid \alpha \mid \tau \xrightarrow{\varsigma} \tau \mid \tau \; ref$
(*Constraint*)	$\kappa ::= \{ \langle \varsigma, \nu \rangle \}^*$
(*TypeScheme*)	$\sigma ::= \forall \nu^*. \tau \; \text{with} \; \kappa$

A constraint is treated as a set of pairs of an effect variable and either a type variable or an effect variable. The effect information associated with an effect variable ς under constraint κ is the least set $\mathcal{E}$ of type and effect variables such that $\varsigma \in \mathcal{E}$, and if $\varsigma' \in \mathcal{E}$ and $\langle \varsigma', \nu \rangle \in \kappa$ then $\nu \in \mathcal{E}$. For example, the effect information corresponding to ς_1 in the constraint $\langle \varsigma_1, \alpha_1 \rangle \langle \varsigma_1, \alpha_2 \rangle \langle \varsigma_1, \varsigma_2 \rangle \langle \varsigma_2, \alpha_3 \rangle \langle \varsigma_3, \alpha_4 \rangle$ is $\{\alpha_1, \alpha_2, \alpha_3, \varsigma_1, \varsigma_2\}$.

Generalization for the indirect system is defined as:

$$(\tau, \kappa) \in \forall \nu_1 \ldots \nu_n . \tau' \; \text{with} \; \kappa'$$
$$\text{iff}$$
$$\text{Dom}(S) = \{\nu_1, \ldots, \nu_n\} \; \text{and} \; S\tau' = \tau \; \text{and} \; S\kappa' \subseteq \kappa$$

where S is a substitution from type variables to types and from effect variables *to effect variables*. Application of substitutions to types is defined as usual; substitution on constraints is defined as follows:

$$S\kappa = \bigcup_{\langle \varsigma, \nu \rangle \in \kappa} \{\langle S\varsigma, \nu' \rangle \mid \nu' \; \text{occurs in} \; S\nu\}.$$

The indirect system derives judgements of the form $\Gamma \rhd e : \tau, \varsigma, \kappa$, meaning that expression e has type τ and effect ς in type environment Γ under constraint κ. Figure 3 presents the typing rules for the indirect formulation; Figure 4 defines the function IFV to compute free type and effect variables for the indirect formulation.

4.2 Correspondence of the Direct and Indirect Systems

To prove that an expression has a type in the indirect system if and only if it has a type in the direct system, we must account for two differences between the direct and indirect systems. First, the indirect system represents effect information by constraints. Second, the indirect system does not have an explicit subsumption rule, but instead folds subsumption into the other rules. We prove each direction separately by constructing translations from a type derivation in one system into a derivation in the other system.

For the translation from the indirect system to the direct system, Figure 5 defines the translation $\mathcal{D}$ from indirect types to direct types. The two systems must agree on the types of constants, hence we require that all constants be of closed type, and that:

$$\text{TypeOf}(c) = \mathcal{D}[\![\text{Ind TypeOf}(c)]\!]\kappa \; \text{for all} \; \kappa.$$

If e has a derivation in the indirect system, then e has a corresponding derivation in the direct system.

$$IndTypeOf(\text{ref}) = \forall \alpha \varsigma.\, \alpha \xrightarrow{\varsigma} \alpha\ ref \text{ with } \langle \varsigma, \alpha \rangle$$
$$IndTypeOf(!) = \forall \alpha \varsigma.\, \alpha\ ref \xrightarrow{\varsigma} \alpha \text{ with } \emptyset$$
$$IndTypeOf(\text{setref}) = \forall \alpha \varsigma_1 \varsigma_2.\, \alpha\ ref \xrightarrow{\varsigma_1} \alpha \xrightarrow{\varsigma_2} \alpha \text{ with } \emptyset$$

(id)
$$\Gamma \triangleright x : \tau, \varsigma, \kappa \text{ if } (\tau, \kappa) \in \Gamma(x)$$

$(const)$
$$\Gamma \triangleright c : \tau, \varsigma, \kappa \text{ if } (\tau, \kappa) \in IndTypeOf(c)$$

(abs)
$$\frac{\Gamma[x/\tau_1] \triangleright e : \tau_2, \varsigma, \kappa}{\Gamma \triangleright \lambda x.e : \tau_1 \xrightarrow{\varsigma} \tau_2, \varsigma', \kappa}$$

(app)
$$\frac{\Gamma \triangleright e_1 : \tau_1 \xrightarrow{\varsigma'} \tau_2, \varsigma, \kappa \quad \Gamma \triangleright e_2 : \tau_1, \varsigma, \kappa}{\Gamma \triangleright e_1\, e_2 : \tau_2, \varsigma, \kappa \cup \{\langle \varsigma, \varsigma' \rangle\}}$$

(let)
$$\frac{\Gamma \triangleright e_1 : \tau_1, \varsigma, \kappa_1 \quad (\sigma, \kappa_2) = Close(\tau_1, \Gamma, \varsigma, \kappa_1) \quad \Gamma[x/\sigma] \triangleright e_2 : \tau_2, \varsigma, \kappa_2}{\Gamma \triangleright \text{let } x = e_1 \text{ in } e_2 : \tau_2, \varsigma, \kappa_2}$$

$$Close(\tau, \Gamma, \varsigma, \kappa) = (\forall \alpha_1 \ldots \alpha_m \varsigma_1 \ldots \varsigma_n.\, \tau \text{ with } \kappa', \kappa \setminus \kappa')$$
$$\text{where } \{\alpha_1, \ldots, \alpha_m, \varsigma_1, \ldots, \varsigma_n\} = IFV(\tau, \kappa) \setminus (IFV(\Gamma, \kappa) \cup IFV(\varsigma, \kappa))$$
$$\kappa' = \{\langle \varsigma, \nu \rangle \mid \langle \varsigma, \nu \rangle \in \kappa, \varsigma \in \{\varsigma_1, \ldots, \varsigma_n\}\}$$

Figure 3: Indirect type assignment

$$IFV(\iota, \kappa) = \emptyset$$
$$IFV(\alpha, \kappa) = \{\alpha\}$$
$$IFV(\tau\ ref, \kappa) = IFV(\tau, \kappa)$$
$$IFV(\tau_1 \xrightarrow{\varsigma} \tau_2, \kappa) = IFV(\tau_1, \kappa) \cup IFV(\tau_2, \kappa) \cup IFV(\varsigma, \kappa)$$
$$IFV(\varsigma, \kappa) = \{\varsigma\} \cup \bigcup_{\langle \varsigma, \nu \rangle \in \kappa} IFV(\nu, \{\langle \varsigma', \nu' \rangle \mid \langle \varsigma', \nu' \rangle \in \kappa, \varsigma' \neq \varsigma\})$$
$$IFV(\forall \nu_1 \ldots \nu_n.\, \tau \text{ with } \kappa', \kappa) = IFV(\tau, \kappa' \cup \kappa) \setminus \{\nu_1, \ldots, \nu_n\}$$
$$IFV(\Gamma, \kappa) = \bigcup_{x \in Dom(\Gamma)} IFV(\Gamma(x), \kappa).$$

Figure 4: Free variables for the indirect system

Theorem 4.1 (Indirect to Direct) *If* $\Gamma \triangleright e : \tau, \varsigma, \kappa$ *then* $\mathcal{D}[\![\Gamma]\!]\kappa \vdash e : \mathcal{D}[\![\tau]\!]\kappa, \mathcal{D}[\![\varsigma]\!]\kappa$.

The proof of this theorem proceeds by induction on the derivation of $\Gamma \triangleright e : \tau, \varsigma, \kappa$. For this induction, it is critical that the translation $\mathcal{D}$ preserve free type and effect variables:

$$IFV(\tau, \kappa) = FV(\mathcal{D}[\![\tau]\!]\kappa); \quad IFV(\sigma, \kappa) = FV(\mathcal{D}[\![\sigma]\!]\kappa);$$
$$IFV(\varsigma, \kappa) = FV(\mathcal{D}[\![\varsigma]\!]\kappa); \quad IFV(\Gamma, \kappa) = FV(\mathcal{D}[\![\Gamma]\!]\kappa).$$

For the translation from the direct system to the indirect system, Figure 6 defines the translation $\mathcal{I}$ from direct types to indirect types. The function $\mathcal{F}$ is any one-to-one function from effects to effect variables such that its range is fresh (no element appears in any derivation). Σ represents sets of effect variables. Let $\sqsubseteq$ be the relation between constraints such that $\kappa_1 \sqsubseteq \kappa_2$ iff:

$$Dom(\kappa_1) \subseteq Dom(\kappa_2) \text{ and } IFV(\varsigma, \kappa_1) = IFV(\varsigma, \kappa_2) \text{ for all } \varsigma \in Dom(\kappa_1).$$

$$
\begin{aligned}
\mathcal{D}[\![\iota]\!]\kappa &= \iota \\
\mathcal{D}[\![\alpha]\!]\kappa &= \alpha \\
\mathcal{D}[\![\tau\ ref]\!]\kappa &= (\mathcal{D}[\![\tau]\!]\kappa)\ ref \\
\mathcal{D}[\![\tau_1 \xrightarrow{\varsigma} \tau_2]\!]\kappa &= \text{let } \Delta = \mathcal{D}[\![\varsigma]\!]\kappa,\ \tau_1' = \mathcal{D}[\![\tau_1]\!]\kappa,\ \tau_2' = \mathcal{D}[\![\tau_2]\!]\kappa \ \text{ in } \tau_1' \xrightarrow{\Delta} \tau_2' \\
\mathcal{D}[\![\varsigma]\!]\kappa &= IFV(\varsigma, \kappa) \\
\mathcal{D}[\![\forall \nu_1 \ldots \nu_n.\ \tau \text{ with } \kappa']\!]\kappa &= \forall \nu_1 \ldots \nu_n.\ \mathcal{D}[\![\tau]\!](\kappa \cup \kappa') \qquad (\nu_1, \ldots, \nu_n \notin \kappa) \\
\mathcal{D}[\![\Gamma]\!]\kappa &= \{x \mapsto \mathcal{D}[\![\Gamma(x)]\!]\kappa \mid x \in \mathrm{Dom}(\Gamma)\}
\end{aligned}
$$

Figure 5: Translation from indirect types to direct types

$$
\begin{aligned}
\mathcal{I}[\![\iota]\!] &= (\iota, \emptyset, \emptyset) \\
\mathcal{I}[\![\alpha]\!] &= (\alpha, \emptyset, \emptyset) \\
\mathcal{I}[\![\tau\ ref]\!] &= \text{let } (\tau', \kappa, \Sigma) = \mathcal{I}[\![\tau]\!] \text{ in } (\tau'\ ref, \kappa, \Sigma) \\
\mathcal{I}[\![\tau_1 \xrightarrow{\Delta} \tau_2]\!] &= \text{let } (\tau_1', \kappa_1, \Sigma_1) = \mathcal{I}[\![\tau_1]\!],\ (\tau_2', \kappa_2, \Sigma_2) = \mathcal{I}[\![\tau_2]\!],\ (\varsigma, \kappa_3) = \mathcal{I}[\![\Delta]\!] \\
&\quad\ \text{in } (\tau_1' \xrightarrow{\varsigma} \tau_2', \kappa_1 \cup \kappa_2 \cup \kappa_3, \Sigma_1 \cup \Sigma_2 \cup \{\varsigma\}) \\
\mathcal{I}[\![\Delta]\!] &= \text{let } \varsigma = \mathcal{F}(\Delta) \text{ in } (\varsigma, \{\langle \varsigma, \nu \rangle \mid \nu \in \Delta\} \cup \{\langle \varsigma, \varsigma \rangle\}) \\
\mathcal{I}[\![\forall \nu_1 \ldots \nu_n.\ \tau]\!] &= \text{let } (\tau', \kappa, \Sigma) = \mathcal{I}[\![\tau]\!],\ \kappa' = \{\langle \varsigma_i, \tau_i \rangle \in \kappa \mid \varsigma_i \in \{\nu_1, \ldots, \nu_n\} \cup \Sigma\} \\
&\quad\ \text{in } (\forall \nu_1 \ldots \nu_n \Sigma.\ \tau' \text{ with } \kappa', \kappa \setminus \kappa') \\
\mathcal{I}[\![\Gamma]\!] &= \text{let } (\sigma_i, \kappa_i) = \mathcal{I}[\![\Gamma(x_i)]\!] \text{ for } x_i \in \mathrm{Dom}(\Gamma) \\
&\quad\ \text{in } (\{x_i \mapsto \sigma_i\}, \bigcup_i \kappa_i)
\end{aligned}
$$

Figure 6: Translation from direct types to indirect types

If e has a derivation in the direct system, then e has a derivation in the indirect system.

Theorem 4.2 (Direct to Indirect) *If* $\Gamma \vdash e : \tau, \Delta$ *and* $(\overline{\tau}, \kappa_\tau, \Sigma) = \mathcal{I}[\![\tau]\!]$ *and* $(\overline{\varsigma}, \kappa_\Delta) = \mathcal{I}[\![\Delta]\!]$ *and* $(\overline{\Gamma}, \kappa_\Gamma) = \mathcal{I}[\![\Gamma]\!]$ *then* $\overline{\Gamma} \rhd e : \overline{\tau}, \overline{\varsigma}, \kappa$ *where* $\kappa_\Gamma, \kappa_\tau, \kappa_\Delta \sqsubseteq \kappa$.

Again, the proof relies on the translation $\mathcal{I}$ preserving free type and effect variables:

$$
\begin{aligned}
&\text{if } \mathcal{I}[\![\tau]\!] = (\overline{\tau}, \kappa, \Sigma) \quad \text{then } IFV(\overline{\tau}, \kappa) = FV(\tau) \cup \Sigma; \\
&\text{if } \mathcal{I}[\![\Delta]\!] = (\overline{\varsigma}, \kappa) \quad\ \text{then } IFV(\overline{\varsigma}, \kappa) = FV(\Delta) \cup \{\overline{\varsigma}\}; \\
&\text{if } \mathcal{I}[\![\sigma]\!] = (\overline{\sigma}, \kappa) \quad\ \text{then } IFV(\overline{\sigma}, \kappa) = FV(\sigma); \\
&\text{if } \mathcal{I}[\![\Gamma]\!] = (\overline{\Gamma}, \kappa) \quad\ \text{then } IFV(\overline{\Gamma}, \kappa) = FV(\Gamma).
\end{aligned}
$$

4.3 Algorithm

Obtaining an algorithm from the indirect system is straightforward [10]. Given an expression, a type environment, and a constraint, algorithm W in Figure 7 computes a type, a substitution to be applied to the type environment, an effect variable, and a new constraint. The function *unify* performs ordinary unification, returning a substitution that unifies its arguments; I is the identity substitution. Soundness and completeness theorems may be demonstrated to establish the correspondence of the algorithm to the indirect system as usual [2, 17].

$$W(x, \Gamma, \kappa) \quad = \text{if } x \notin \text{Dom}(\Gamma) \text{ then } \mathbf{fail} \text{ (expression is not closed)}$$
$$\text{let } \varsigma, \alpha'_1, \ldots, \alpha'_m, \varsigma'_1, \ldots, \varsigma'_n \text{ be fresh}$$
$$\forall \alpha_1 \ldots \alpha_m \varsigma_1 \ldots \varsigma_n . \tau \text{ with } \kappa' = \Gamma(x)$$
$$S = \{\alpha_i \mapsto \alpha'_i, \varsigma_j \mapsto \varsigma'_j\}$$
$$\text{in } (S\tau, I, \varsigma, \kappa \cup S\kappa')$$

$$W(c, \Gamma, \kappa) \quad = \text{let } \varsigma, \alpha'_1, \ldots, \alpha'_m, \varsigma'_1, \ldots, \varsigma'_n \text{ be fresh}$$
$$\forall \alpha_1 \ldots \alpha_m \varsigma_1 \ldots \varsigma_n . \tau \text{ with } \kappa' = IndTypeOf(c)$$
$$S = \{\alpha_i \mapsto \alpha'_i, \varsigma_j \mapsto \varsigma'_j\}$$
$$\text{in } (S\tau, I, \varsigma, \kappa \cup S\kappa')$$

$$W(\lambda x.e, \Gamma, \kappa) \quad = \text{let } \alpha, \varsigma \text{ be fresh}$$
$$(\tau, S, \varsigma', \kappa') = W(e, \Gamma[x/\alpha], \kappa)$$
$$\text{in } (S\alpha \xrightarrow{\varsigma} \tau, S, \varsigma, \kappa')$$

$$W((e_1 \ e_2), \Gamma, \kappa) \quad = \text{let } \alpha, \varsigma \text{ be fresh}$$
$$(\tau_1, S_1, \varsigma_1, \kappa_1) = W(e_1, \Gamma, \kappa)$$
$$(\tau_2, S_2, \varsigma_2, \kappa_2) = W(e_2, S_1\Gamma, \kappa_1)$$
$$S_3 = unify(S_2\tau_1, \tau_2 \xrightarrow{\varsigma} \alpha) \quad (\text{may } \mathbf{fail})$$
$$S_4 = unify(S_3 S_2 \varsigma_1, S_3 \varsigma_2) \quad (\text{will not } \mathbf{fail})$$
$$\text{in } (S_4 S_3 \alpha, \ S_4 \circ S_3 \circ S_2 \circ S_1, \ S_4 S_3 \varsigma_2, \ S_4 S_3 (\kappa_2 \cup \{\langle \varsigma, \varsigma_2 \rangle\}))$$

$$W(\text{let } x = e_1 \text{ in } e_2, \Gamma, \kappa) = \text{let } (\tau_1, S_1, \varsigma_1, \kappa_1) = W(e_1, \Gamma, \kappa))$$
$$(\sigma, \kappa_2) = Close(\tau_1, S_1\Gamma, \varsigma_1, \kappa_1)$$
$$(\tau_2, S_2, \varsigma_2, \kappa_3) = W(e_2, (S_1\Gamma)[x/\sigma], \kappa_2)$$
$$S_3 = unify(S_2\varsigma_1, \varsigma_2) \quad (\text{will not } \mathbf{fail})$$
$$\text{in } (S_3\tau_2, \ S_3 \circ S_2 \circ S_1, \ S_3\varsigma_2, \ S_3\kappa_3)$$

Figure 7: Type Inference Algorithm

Our algorithm is similar to Milner's algorithm $\mathcal{W}$ [12] for a functional language. In our algorithm, the case for applications contains an additional invocation of *unify*, but this second invocation always unifies two effect variables, and is very cheap. The main difference is that our algorithm must maintain a set of constraints that grows linearly with the number of applications and that must be searched in typing a let-expression. The practical performance of our algorithm depends on the efficiency of constraint handling; the techniques for manipulating constraints discussed by Leroy and Weis [10] should be applicable to our algorithm.

5   Comparison with Other Systems

There are several other systems for typing references in the presence of polymorphism; O'Toole [15] presents detailed comparisons between four of them. Ideally, we would like a simple, intuitive system that is at least as powerful as any of the others, but unfortunately, there are no systems that meet this goal. While we believe our system is relatively simple and natural, it is incomparable to the other systems: there are expressions typable in one system but not the other, and vice versa. Hence comparisons between systems must be pragmatic.

Tofte [18]   A system proposed by Tofte and adopted for STANDARD ML [13, 14] has two kinds of type variables: *imperative* variables and *applicative* variables. Types are classified accordingly: imperative types may only contain imperative type variables; applicative types may contain either. The ref operator may only be applied to values of imperative type. In typing the expression let $x = e_1$ in e_2, imperative variables in the type of e_1 can be generalized only if e_1 is *non-expansive*, that is, if e_1 has a certain syntactic shape which guarantees that its evaluation does not allocate any references (in STANDARD ML, e_1 must be a variable, constant, or λ-expression). We may think of ref as contaminating all type variables in the type of its argument. Generalizing contaminated (imperative) type variables may result in generalizing the type of a value in a reference cell; hence, generalization of contaminated types must be restricted. For example, the expression $\lambda x. !\,(\text{ref } x)$ has type $\alpha^* \to \alpha^*$, where the superscript * indicates that α^* is an imperative type variable. However, α^* can be generalized in the expression:

$$\text{let i} = \lambda x. !\,(\text{ref } x) \text{ in } \ldots$$

as $\lambda x. !\,(\text{ref } x)$ is non-expansive, and hence does not allocate any references.

A drawback to this system is that partial applications of imperative functions cannot be polymorphic. For example, the function imap (from Section 1.4) has type scheme:

$$\forall \alpha^* \beta^*. (\alpha^* \to \beta^*) \to \alpha^* \text{ list} \to \beta^* \text{ list}.$$

When only partially applied, as in:

$$\text{let i} = \text{imap } (\lambda x.x) \text{ in } \ldots$$

i cannot be used polymorphically. The expression imap $(\lambda x.x)$ has type $\alpha^* \text{ list} \to \alpha^* \text{ list}$ and is expansive, hence α^* cannot be generalized. However, in the expression:

$$\text{let i} = \lambda z. \text{ imap } (\lambda x.x) \text{ z in } \ldots$$

α^* can be generalized since the bound expression is non-expansive.

MacQueen [16]   A system proposed by MacQueen and implemented by STANDARD ML OF NEW JERSEY attempts to address the curried application problem described above by recognizing how many arguments a function must be applied to before it creates any references. In this system, imap has type scheme $(\alpha^2 \to \beta^2) \to \alpha^2 \text{ list} \to \beta^2 \text{ list}$. The result of the application imap $(\lambda x.x)$ has type $\alpha^1 \text{ list} \to \beta^1 \text{ list}$ and can be used polymorphically. The superscript indicates the number of times the function must be applied before a cell is allocated whose type involves that type variable; applications decrease the superscript. Variables with superscript 0 may not be generalized.

Although the system addresses common uses of currying, such as the partial application of imap above, there are cases in which it fails. The system assigns a polymorphic type to f in only the second of the following two expressions:

$$\text{let f} = \text{map ref in } \ldots$$
$$\text{let f} = \lambda z. \text{ map ref z in } \ldots$$

The system is unable to recognize that map ref does not allocate any references until it is further applied, since the type scheme for the non-imperative function map : $\forall \alpha \beta. (\alpha \to$

$\beta) \rightarrow \alpha$ *list* $\rightarrow \beta$ *list* does not indicate that the functional argument to map is invoked only after a second argument is provided. Furthermore, the only formal description of the system is the NEW JERSEY compiler's source code; no inference rule formulation exists. The system is believed to be strictly stronger than Tofte's system, *i.e.*, any expression typable by Tofte's system is typable by MacQueen's system [18].

In contrast to the above two systems, our system handles partial applications properly. For example, our system assigns a polymorphic type to f in both of the following expressions:

$$\text{let } f = \text{imap } \lambda x.x \text{ in } \dots$$
$$\text{let } f = \text{map ref in } \dots$$

Our system recognizes when allocations occur with greater precision by recording type effects above function type arrows.

Damas [3] Damas proposed one of the earliest systems for typing references. This system appears to lie between Tofte's and MacQueen's systems in power [18], and although the system has little advantage over Tofte's system, it did inspire our work. The system infers information similar to type effects, but records information on only the outermost arrow of a function type; hence, the determination of when allocation occurs is fairly imprecise. Damas was apparently aware of this problem, as he states that "the inclusion [of effects among function types], which would be the natural thing to do ... would preclude the extension of the type assignment algorithm ... to this extended type inference system" [3: p. 90]. Our insight was to include effects in function types and use the constraint manipulation ideas of Leroy and Weis's system to construct an inference system with a corresponding algorithm.

Leroy & Weis [10] Leroy and Weis propose a closure typing system based on the observation that it is only necessary to prohibit generalization of type variables appearing in the types of cells reachable after the bound expression has been evaluated (*i.e.*, cells that would not be reclaimed by a garbage collection at this point). As cells may be reachable through the free identifiers of closures, the system records the types of the free identifiers of a function in the function's type. This system has the advantage that it can assign a fully polymorphic type to some functions that make purely local use of a reference cell, such as imap: the system is able to recognize when effects can be *masked*. However, it fails to type some purely functional expressions that are typable in the functional sublanguage, such as the following:

$$\lambda z. \text{ let } id = \lambda x. \ ((\text{if true then } z \text{ else } \lambda y.(x; y)); x)$$
$$\text{in } id \ 1; \ id \text{ true}$$

The problem is that by introducing the types of free variables into function types, additional type variables may be introduced into the type environment. In the above example, the if-expression forces z and $\lambda y.(x; y)$ to have the same type. Suppose that x has type α and y has type β. Since x is free in $\lambda y.(x; y)$, this expression has type $\beta \xrightarrow{\alpha} \beta$, hence z has type $\beta \xrightarrow{\alpha} \beta$. As α appears in the type of z, α is free in the type environment of the let-expression, and cannot be generalized. In the ordinary Hindley/Milner system, $\lambda y.(x; y)$ and z have type $\beta \rightarrow \beta$, and α is not free in the type environment. All of the other systems, including ours, will assign types to such functional expressions.

Talpin & Jouvelot [17] Talpin and Jouvelot present an ambitious system that infers types, effects, and regions for expressions in a manner similar to our indirect system.[3] A reference cell containing a value of type τ has type $ref_\rho\tau$; two reference cells share the same region ρ if they may alias. Regions provide finer grained information about allocation behavior than our type effects, and the information about potential aliasing is used to mask local effects. The system includes subsumption on effects, and infers not only allocation effects but also read and write effects that may be useful for compiler optimizations. We conjecture that Talpin and Jouvelot's system is strictly more powerful than our system.

5.1 Effect Masking

A shortcoming of our system is its inability to recognize when a reference is only used locally and to mask the allocation. When local effects are masked, the function imap has the same type as its functional counterpart map. However, just as precisely determining when allocations occur is impossible, so too is precise effect masking. The following expression is rejected by both Leroy and Weis's system and Talpin and Jouvelot's system,[4] although these systems incorporate effect masking:

$$\lambda z.\ \text{let id} = \lambda x.\ ((\text{if true then z else } \lambda y.\ (\underline{\text{ref x}};\ y));\ x)$$
$$\text{in id 1};\ \text{id true}$$

This example is also rejected by our system, but Tofte's, Damas's, and MacQueen's systems accept it.

Abstractly, adding effect masking to our system is easy:

$$(mask) \qquad \frac{\Gamma \vdash e : \tau, \Delta_1 \quad \Delta_2 \text{ is maskable in } e}{\Gamma \vdash e : \tau, \Delta_1 \setminus \Delta_2}$$

Selecting criteria to determine which effects are maskable is more difficult. Data flow analysis and compile time garbage collection techniques [4] might be used to discover references that are not reachable after the bound expression has been evaluated. Even the simplest local flow analysis algorithms would address examples such as the one above.

Effect masking raises the issue of just how far to push static type systems for references. The more powerful the type system is, the more complex its description becomes. If flow analysis is used to mask effects, then a precise description of the flow analysis algorithm is an essential part of the description of the type system. Without a precise description of the type system, the set of well-typed programs is unspecified, and the programmer is left at the mercy of the implementor.

Acknowledgements

I am indebted to Jean-Pierre Talpin and Pierre Jouvelot for many helpful discussions on direct and indirect formulations of effect inference, and to Matthias Felleisen for comments on drafts of this paper.

---

[3] It should be possible to reformulate this system in a direct fashion.

[4] Talpin and Jouvelot now have a refined system that can type this example [personal communication, November '91].

References

[1] BARENDREGT, H. P. *The Lambda Calculus: Its Syntax and Semantics*, revised ed., vol. 103 of *Studies in Logic and the Foundations of Mathematics*. North-Holland, Amsterdam, 1984.

[2] DAMAS, L., AND MILNER, R. Principal type schemes for functional programs. *Proceedings of the 9th Annual Symposium on Principles of Programming Languages* (January 1982), 207–212.

[3] DAMAS, L. M. M. *Type Assignment in Programming Languages*. PhD thesis, University of Edinburgh, 1985.

[4] DEUTSCH, A. On determining lifetime and aliasing of dynamically allocated data in higher-order functional specifications. *Proceedings of the 17th Annual Symposium on Principles of Programming Languages* (January 1990), 157–168.

[5] FELLEISEN, M., AND FRIEDMAN, D. P. A syntactic theory of sequential state. *Theoretical Computer Science 69*, 3 (1989), 243–287. Preliminary version in: *Proceedings of the 14th Annual Symposium on Principles of Programming Languages*, 1987, 314-325.

[6] FELLEISEN, M., FRIEDMAN, D. P., KOHLBECKER, E. E., AND DUBA, B. A syntactic theory of sequential control. *Theoretical Computer Science 52*, 3 (1987), 205–237. Preliminary version in: *Proceedings of the Symposium on Logic in Computer Science*, 1986, 131–141.

[7] FELLEISEN, M., AND HIEB, R. The revised report on the syntactic theories of sequential control and state. Tech. Rep. TR-100, Rice University, June 1989. To appear in: *Theoretical Computer Science*.

[8] HINDLEY, R. The principal type-scheme of an object in combinatory logic. *Transactions of the American Mathematical Society 146* (December 1969), 29–60.

[9] JOUVELOT, P., AND GIFFORD, D. K. Algebraic reconstruction of types and effects. *Proceedings of the 18th Annual Symposium on Principles of Programming Languages* (January 1991), 303–310.

[10] LEROY, X., AND WEIS, P. Polymorphic type inference and assignment. *Proceedings of the 18th Annual Symposium on Principles of Programming Languages* (January 1991), 291–302.

[11] LUCASSEN, J. M., AND GIFFORD, D. K. Polymorphic effect systems. *Proceedings of the 15th Annual Symposium on Principles of Programming Languages* (January 1988), 47–57.

[12] MILNER, R. A theory of type polymorphism in programming. *Journal of Computer and System Sciences 17* (1978), 348–375.

[13] MILNER, R., AND TOFTE, M. *Commentary on Standard ML*. MIT Press, Cambridge, Massachusetts, 1991.

[14] MILNER, R., TOFTE, M., AND HARPER, R. *The Definition of Standard ML.* MIT Press, Cambridge, Massachusetts, 1990.

[15] O'TOOLE JR., J. W. Type abstraction rules for references: A comparison of four which have achieved notoriety. Unpublished, 1990.

[16] Standard ML of New Jersey release notes (version 0.75). AT&T Bell Laboratories, November 1991.

[17] TALPIN, J.-P., AND JOUVELOT, P. The type and effect discipline. Tech. Rep. EMP-CRI A/206, Ecole des Mines de Paris, July 1991.

[18] TOFTE, M. Type inference for polymorphic references. *Information and Computation 89*, 1 (November 1990), 1–34.

[19] WRIGHT, A. K., AND FELLEISEN, M. A syntactic approach to type soundness. Tech. Rep. 91-160, Rice University, April 1991. To appear in: *Information and Computation.*

Lecture Notes in Computer Science

For information about Vols. 1–491
please contact your bookseller or Springer-Verlag

Vol. 492: D. Sriram, R. Logcher, S. Fukuda (Eds.), Computer-Aided Cooperative Product Development. Proceedings, 1989 VII, 630 pages. 1991.

Vol. 493: S. Abramsky, T. S. E. Maibaum (Eds.), TAPSOFT '91. Volume 1. Proceedings, 1991. VIII, 455 pages. 1991.

Vol. 494: S. Abramsky, T. S. E. Maibaum (Eds.), TAPSOFT '91. Volume 2. Proceedings, 1991. VIII, 482 pages. 1991.

Vol. 495: 9. Thalheim, J. Demetrovics, H.-D. Gerhardt (Eds.), MFDBS '91. Proceedings, 1991. VI, 395 pages. 1991.

Vol. 496: H.-P. Schwefel, R. Männer (Eds.), Parallel Problem Solving from Nature. Proceedings, 1990. XI, 485 pages. 1991.

Vol. 497: F. Dehne, F. Fiala. W.W. Koczkodaj (Eds.), Advances in Computing and Information - ICCI '91. Proceedings, 1991. VIII, 745 pages. 1991.

Vol. 498: R. Andersen, J. A. Bubenko jr., A. Sølvberg (Eds.), Advanced Information Systems Engineering. Proceedings, 1991. VI, 579 pages. 1991.

Vol. 499: D. Christodoulakis (Ed.), Ada: The Choice for '92. Proceedings, 1991. VI, 411 pages. 1991.

Vol. 500: M. Held, On the Computational Geometry of Pocket Machining. XII, 179 pages. 1991.

Vol. 501: M. Bidoit, H.-J. Kreowski, P. Lescanne, F. Orejas, D. Sannella (Eds.), Algebraic System Specification and Development. VIII, 98 pages. 1991.

Vol. 502: J. Bārzdiņž, D. Bjørner (Eds.), Baltic Computer Science. X, 619 pages. 1991.

Vol. 503: P. America (Ed.), Parallel Database Systems. Proceedings, 1990. VIII, 433 pages. 1991.

Vol. 504: J. W. Schmidt, A. A. Stogny (Eds.), Next Generation Information System Technology. Proceedings, 1990. IX, 450 pages. 1991.

Vol. 505: E. H. L. Aarts, J. van Leeuwen, M. Rem (Eds.), PARLE '91. Parallel Architectures and Languages Europe, Volume I. Proceedings, 1991. XV, 423 pages. 1991.

Vol. 506: E. H. L. Aarts, J. van Leeuwen, M. Rem (Eds.), PARLE '91. Parallel Architectures and Languages Europe, Volume II. Proceedings, 1991. XV, 489 pages. 1991.

Vol. 507: N. A. Sherwani, E. de Doncker, J. A. Kapenga (Eds.), Computing in the 90's. Proceedings, 1989. XIII, 441 pages. 1991.

Vol. 508: S. Sakata (Ed.), Applied Algebra, Algebraic Algorithms and Error-Correcting Codes. Proceedings, 1990. IX, 390 pages. 1991.

Vol. 509: A. Endres, H. Weber (Eds.), Software Development Environments and CASE Technology. Proceedings, 1991. VIII, 286 pages. 1991.

Vol. 510: J. Leach Albert, B. Monien, M. Rodríguez (Eds.), Automata, Languages and Programming. Proceedings, 1991. XII, 763 pages. 1991.

Vol. 511: A. C. F. Colchester, D.J. Hawkes (Eds.), Information Processing in Medical Imaging. Proceedings, 1991. XI, 512 pages. 1991.

Vol. 512: P. America (Ed.), ECOOP '91. European Conference on Object-Oriented Programming. Proceedings, 1991. X, 396 pages. 1991.

Vol. 513: N. M. Mattos, An Approach to Knowledge Base Management. IX, 247 pages. 1991. (Subseries LNAI).

Vol. 514: G. Cohen, P. Charpin (Eds.), EUROCODE '90. Proceedings, 1990. XI, 392 pages. 1991.

Vol. 515: J. P. Martins, M. Reinfrank (Eds.), Truth Maintenance Systems. Proceedings, 1990. VII, 177 pages. 1991. (Subseries LNAI).

Vol. 516: S. Kaplan, M. Okada (Eds.), Conditional and Typed Rewriting Systems. Proceedings, 1990. IX, 461 pages. 1991.

Vol. 517: K. Nökel, Temporally Distributed Symptoms in Technical Diagnosis. IX, 164 pages. 1991. (Subseries LNAI).

Vol. 518: J. G. Williams, Instantiation Theory. VIII, 133 pages. 1991. (Subseries LNAI).

Vol. 519: F. Dehne, J.-R. Sack, N. Santoro (Eds.), Algorithms and Data Structures. Proceedings, 1991. X, 496 pages. 1991.

Vol. 520: A. Tarlecki (Ed.), Mathematical Foundations of Computer Science 1991. Proceedings, 1991. XI, 435 pages. 1991.

Vol. 521: B. Bouchon-Meunier, R. R. Yager, L. A. Zadek (Eds.), Uncertainty in Knowledge-Bases. Proceedings, 1990. X, 609 pages. 1991.

Vol. 522: J. Hertzberg (Ed.), European Workshop on Planning. Proceedings, 1991. VII, 121 pages. 1991. (Subseries LNAI).

Vol. 523: J. Hughes (Ed.), Functional Programming Languages and Computer Architecture. Proceedings, 1991. VIII, 666 pages. 1991.

Vol. 524: G. Rozenberg (Ed.), Advances in Petri Nets 1991. VIII, 572 pages. 1991.

Vol. 525: O. Günther, H.-J. Schek (Eds.), Advances in Spatial Databases. Proceedings, 1991. XI, 471 pages. 1991.

Vol. 526: T. Ito, A. R. Meyer (Eds.), Theoretical Aspects of Computer Software. Proceedings, 1991. X, 772 pages. 1991.

Vol. 527: J.C.M. Baeten, J. F. Groote (Eds.), CONCUR '91. Proceedings, 1991. VIII, 541 pages. 1991.

Vol. 528: J. Maluszynski, M. Wirsing (Eds.), Programming Language Implementation and Logic Programming. Proceedings, 1991. XI, 433 pages. 1991.

Vol. 529: L. Budach (Ed.), Fundamentals of Computation Theory. Proceedings, 1991. XII, 426 pages. 1991.

Vol. 530: D. H. Pitt, P.-L. Curien, S. Abramsky, A. M. Pitts, A. Poigné, D. E. Rydeheard (Eds.), Category Theory and Computer Science. Proceedings, 1991. VII, 301 pages. 1991.

Vol. 531: E. M. Clarke, R. P. Kurshan (Eds.), Computer-Aided Verification. Proceedings, 1990. XIII, 372 pages. 1991.

Vol. 532: H. Ehrig, H.-J. Kreowski, G. Rozenberg (Eds.), Graph Grammars and Their Application to Computer Science. Proceedings, 1990. X, 703 pages. 1991.

Vol. 533: E. Börger, H. Kleine Büning, M. M. Richter, W. Schönfeld (Eds.), Computer Science Logic. Proceedings, 1990. VIII, 399 pages. 1991.

Vol. 534: H. Ehrig, K. P. Jantke, F. Orejas, H. Reichel (Eds.), Recent Trends in Data Type Specification. Proceedings, 1990. VIII, 379 pages. 1991.

Vol. 535: P. Jorrand, J. Kelemen (Eds.), Fundamentals of Artificial Intelligence Research. Proceedings, 1991. VIII, 255 pages. 1991. (Subseries LNAI).

Vol. 536: J. E. Tomayko, Software Engineering Education. Proceedings, 1991. VIII, 296 pages. 1991.

Vol. 537: A. J. Menezes, S. A. Vanstone (Eds.), Advances in Cryptology – CRYPTO '90. Proceedings. XIII, 644 pages. 1991.

Vol. 538: M. Kojima, N. Megiddo, T. Noma, A. Yoshise, A Unified Approach to Interior Point Algorithms for Linear Complementarity Problems. VIII, 108 pages. 1991.

Vol. 539: H. F. Mattson, T. Mora, T. R. N. Rao (Eds.), Applied Algebra, Algebraic Algorithms and Error-Correcting Codes. Proceedings, 1991. XI, 489 pages. 1991.

Vol. 540: A. Prieto (Ed.), Artificial Neural Networks. Proceedings, 1991. XIII, 476 pages. 1991.

Vol. 541: P. Barahona, L. Moniz Pereira, A. Porto (Eds.), EPIA '91. Proceedings, 1991. VIII, 292 pages. 1991. (Subseries LNAI).

Vol. 543: J. Dix, K. P. Jantke, P. H. Schmitt (Eds.), Nonmonotonic and Inductive Logic. Proceedings, 1990. X, 243 pages. 1991. (Subseries LNAI).

Vol. 544: M. Broy, M. Wirsing (Eds.), Methods of Programming. XII, 268 pages. 1991.

Vol. 545: H. Alblas, B. Melichar (Eds.), Attribute Grammars, Applications and Systems. Proceedings, 1991. IX, 513 pages. 1991.

Vol. 547: D. W. Davies (Ed.), Advances in Cryptology – EUROCRYPT '91. Proceedings, 1991. XII, 556 pages. 1991.

Vol. 548: R. Kruse, P. Siegel (Eds.), Symbolic and Quantitative Approaches to Uncertainty. Proceedings, 1991. XI, 362 pages. 1991.

Vol. 550: A. van Lamsweerde, A. Fugetta (Eds.), ESEC '91. Proceedings, 1991. XII, 515 pages. 1991.

Vol. 551: S. Prehn, W. J. Toetenel (Eds.), VDM '91. Formal Software Development Methods. Volume 1. Proceedings, 1991. XIII, 699 pages. 1991.

Vol. 552: S. Prehn, W. J. Toetenel (Eds.), VDM '91. Formal Software Development Methods. Volume 2. Proceedings, 1991. XIV, 430 pages. 1991.

Vol. 553: H. Bieri, H. Noltemeier (Eds.), Computational Geometry - Methods, Algorithms and Applications '91. Proceedings, 1991. VIII, 320 pages. 1991.

Vol. 554: G. Grahne, The Problem of Incomplete Information in Relational Databases. VIII, 156 pages. 1991.

Vol. 555: H. Maurer (Ed.), New Results and New Trends in Computer Science. Proceedings, 1991. VIII, 403 pages. 1991.

Vol. 556: J.-M. Jacquet, Conclog: A Methodological Approach to Concurrent Logic Programming. XII, 781 pages. 1991.

Vol. 557: W. L. Hsu, R. C. T. Lee (Eds.), ISA '91 Algorithms. Proceedings, 1991. X, 396 pages. 1991.

Vol. 558: J. Hooman, Specification and Compositional Verification of Real-Time Systems. VIII, 235 pages. 1991.

Vol. 559: G. Butler, Fundamental Algorithms for Permutation Groups. XII, 238 pages. 1991.

Vol. 560: S. Biswas, K. V. Nori (Eds.), Foundations of Software Technology and Theoretical Computer Science. Proceedings, 1991. X, 420 pages. 1991.

Vol. 561: C. Ding, G. Xiao, W. Shan, The Stability Theory of Stream Ciphers. IX, 187 pages. 1991.

Vol. 562: R. Breu, Algebraic Specification Techniques in Object Oriented Programming Environments. XI, 228 pages. 1991.

Vol. 563: A. Karshmer, J. Nehmer (Eds.), Operating Systems of the 90s and Beyond. Proceedings, 1991. X, 285 pages. 1991.

Vol. 564: I. Herman, The Use of Projective Geometry in Computer Graphics. VIII, 146 pages. 1992.

Vol. 565: J. D. Becker, I. Eisele, F. W. Mündemann (Eds.), Parallelism, Learning, Evolution. Proceedings, 1989. VIII, 525 pages. 1991. (Subseries LNAI).

Vol. 566: C. Delobel, M. Kifer, Y. Masunaga (Eds.), Deductive and Object-Oriented Databases. Proceedings, 1991. XV, 581 pages. 1991.

Vol. 567: H. Boley, M. M. Richter (Eds.), Processing Declarative Kowledge. Proceedings, 1991. XII, 427 pages. 1991. (Subseries LNAI).

Vol. 568: H.-J. Bürckert, A Resolution Principle for a Logic with Restricted Quantifiers. X, 116 pages. 1991. (Subseries LNAI).

Vol. 569: A. Beaumont, G. Gupta (Eds.), Parallel Execution of Logic Programs. Proceedings, 1991. VII, 195 pages. 1991.

Vol. 570: R. Berghammer, G. Schmidt (Eds.), Graph-Theoretic Concepts in Computer Science. Proceedings, 1991. VIII, 253 pages. 1992.

Vol. 571: J. Vytopil (Ed.), Formal Techniques in Real-Time and Fault-Tolerant Systems. Proceedings, 1992. IX, 620 pages. 1991.

Vol. 572: K. U. Schulz (Ed.), Word Equations and Related Topics. Proceedings, 1990. VII, 256 pages. 1992.

Vol. 573: G. Cohen, S. N. Litsyn, A. Lobstein, G. Zémor (Eds.), Algebraic Coding. Proceedings, 1991. X, 158 pages. 1992.

Vol. 574: J. P. Banâtre, D. Le Métayer (Eds.), Research Directions in High-Level Parallel Programming Languages. Proceedings, 1991. VIII, 387 pages. 1992.

Vol. 575: K. G. Larsen, A. Skou (Eds.), Computer Aided Verification. Proceedings, 1991. X, 487 pages. 1992.

Vol. 576: J. Feigenbaum (Ed.), Advances in Cryptology - CRYPTO '91. Proceedings. X, 485 pages. 1992.

Vol. 577: A. Finkel, M. Jantzen (Eds.), STACS 92. Proceedings, 1992. XIV, 621 pages. 1992.

Vol. 578: Th. Beth, M. Frisch, G. J. Simmons (Eds.), Public-Key Cryptography: State of the Art and Future Directions. XI, 97 pages. 1992.

Vol. 579: S. Toueg, P. G. Spirakis, L. Kirousis (Eds.), Distributed Algorithms. Proceedings, 1991. X, 319 pages. 1992.

Vol. 581: J.-C. Raoult (Ed.), CAAP '92. Proceedings. VIII, 361 pages. 1992.

Vol. 582: B. Krieg-Brückner (Ed.), ESOP '92. Proceedings. VIII, 491 pages. 1992.